European Union and European Community:

A Handbook and Commentary on the post-Maastricht Treaties

CHURCH, CLIVE H. 337.142

European Union And European Community: A
Handbook And Commentary On The
Post-maastricht Treaties

London: Harvester 0745014712
Wheatsheaf, 1994

European Union and European Community:

A Handbook and Commentary on the post-Maastricht Treaties

compiled for the University of Kent by
Clive H. Church and David Phinnemore

 HARVESTER
WHEATSHEAF

New York   London   Toronto   Sydney   Tokyo   Singapore

First published 1994 by
Harvester Wheatsheaf,
Campus 400, Maylands Avenue,
Hemel Hempstead,
Hertfordshire, HP2 7EZ
A division of
Simon & Schuster International Group

Typeset in Garamond and Times
by MHL Typesetting Ltd, Coventry

Printed and bound in Great Britain by
Redwood Books, Trowbridge, Wiltshire

British Library Cataloguing in Publication Data

A catalogue record for this book is available from
the British Library

ISBN 0-7450-1471-2 (pbk)

1   2   3   4   5   98   97   96   95   94

For my wife, Margaret Church

For my parents, Jeffrey and Pauline Phinnemore

Contents

Figures

Boxes

Synoptic Table of Articles, Comments and Readings

Preface

The European Community is amongst the most important international institutions to which Britain belongs. As such it is one of the most controversial and most studied of institutions, and never more so than during the period dominated first by the negotiations leading up to Maastricht Summit and then by the highly fraught process of ratification. Yet the Treaties which constitute it are relatively little known to students and the general public. Despite the acute confrontation caused by Maastricht in Britain it was a standing joke that hardly any copies of the Treaty on European Union had been sold, and those that had been were not always read, even by Cabinet Ministers. This *Handbook* has some of its origins in a desire to remedy this situation.

Equally, the British public has not yet come to terms either with how the Treaty on European Union fits together with the Treaty of Rome, or, indeed, with the differences between the EEC, the EC and the Union. Knowing about this is extremely important in view of the likelihood of further changes to the Union's structure in 1996. The *Handbook* therefore seeks to make both things clearer. By so doing, it also hopes to facilitate the British contribution to the debate about the future of the Union which is now starting. For, whatever happens to the Maastricht settlement in the short run, the arrangements agreed in December 1991 will remain a starting point for future consideration of both Community and Union.

The *Handbook* was, in fact, compiled during the ratification crisis and no doubt bears its marks. It was completed at the end of August 1993 when only the verdict of the German Constitutional Court stood between the Treaty and its ratification. Our assumption is that the Treaty will be ratified and come into effect during the winter of 1993–4. Even if this is not so, we believe that what follows will still be essential for an understanding of the next stages in Community development.

Finally, the *Handbook* also owes a great deal to the Community's 'Jean Monnet Action Programme' which in 1990 awarded the University of Kent a grant to help develop its courses on European Integration. This was used to produce a booklet for students on a variety of courses which provided the text of the Treaty of Rome, information on Community policies and member states, and an introduction to sources on the Community available in Canterbury. A second edition of this was produced in July 1992. We are very grateful to the Community both for its initial help and for its encouragement of the idea of a published version, not to mention for its willingness to allow free reproduction of the texts of the various treaties. Equally we are happy to acknowledge the support of the University of Kent, both as an institution and as a gathering of helpful colleagues.

We also owe a great debt to Mark Allin, then of Harvester Wheatsheaf, who saw the potential of the booklet, encouraged us to develop it for a wider audience and, with Pradeep Jethi and Louise Wilson, introduced us to new forms of reader friendly presentation. The aim is to produce something which will help support both teaching on, and general understanding of, the Community by making available the text of the treaties together with basic commentaries, relevant contextual matter and reference material. For the sake of simplicity the *Handbook* has accepted the structure of the Treaty of European Union, including its amendments of the Treaty establishing the European Economic Community, as its spine. Hence terms used to denote subdivisions of the Treaties have been eschewed in describing the elements of the *Handbook* in order to avoid confusion.

Clive Church is primarily responsible for subdivisions I, II (save ii), V and VII and David Phinnemore for II(ii), III, IV, VI, and the Annexes and Index. However, all of the text has been jointly read, added to, corrected and agreed by both of us. We would like to thank Esperanza Davis-Guzmán and Susan Ratchford of the Liverpool Institute of Higher Education for their assistance with copy-typing. We are also very grateful to Bill Nicoll and other colleagues who commented on the draft text. We hope that they, and the students with whom we have discussed it, will find the finished product of use. Needless to say, we shall be only too happy to receive suggestions about any future editions.

Thanington Without, Canterbury   Wavertree, Liverpool

Abbreviations

ACP	African, Caribbean and Pacific Countries in the Lomé Convention
AIDS	Auto-Immune Deficiency Syndrome
ASEAN	Association of South East Asian Nations
BABEL	Broadcasting Across the Barriers of European Language
BAP	Biotechnology Action Programme
BCCI	Bank of Credit and Commerce International
BRAIN	Basic Research in Adaptive Intelligence and Neurocomputing
BRIDGE	Biotechnology Research for Innovation, Development and Growth in Europe
BRITE	Basic Research in Industrial Technologies for Europe
CAP	Common Agricultural Policy
CCP	Common Commercial Policy
CCT	Common Customs Tariff
CDA	Dutch Christian Democratic Appeal Party
CDU/CSU	German Christian Democratic/Christian Social Union
CE	Council of Europe
CEDEFOP	European Centre for the Development of Vocational Training
CELAD	Coordination Group on Drugs
CET (CCT)	Common External (Commercial) Tariff
CFI	Court of First Instance
CFP	Common Fisheries Policy
CFSP	Common Foreign and Security Policy
CH	Switzerland
CIS	Confederation of Independent States
CITES	Convention on Trade in Endangered Species
CJHA	Common action on Justice and Home Affairs
COA	Court of Auditors
COMETT	Community in Education and Training for Technology
CoR	The Committee of the Regions
COREPER	Committee of Permanent Representatives

COREU	Telex Network amongst EPC 'Correspondents Européens' (European Correspondents)
CSCE	Conference on Security and Cooperation in Europe
CTP	Common Transport Policy
CUBE	Concertation Unit for Biotechnology in Europe
DC	Italian Christian Democratic Party
DG	Directorate-General
DVU	German People's Union
EAEC/T	European Atomic Energy Community/Treaty (= Euratom)
EAGGF	European Agricultural Guidance and Guarantee Fund (often known as FEOGA after its French acronym)
EBRD	European Bank for Reconstruction and Development (often known by its French acronym of BERD)
EC	European Community
ECB	European Central Bank
ECHR	European Court (or Convention) on Human Rights
ECJ	European Court of Justice
ECOFIN	Council of Economic and Finance Ministers
EcoSoc	Economic and Social Committee
ECSC	European Coal and Steel Community
ECU	European Currency Unit
EDC	European Defence Community
EDF	European Development Fund
EEA	European Economic Area
EEA	European Environment Agency
EEC	European Economic Community
EFTA (AELE)	European Free Trade Association
EIB	European Investment Bank
EMAS	Eco-Management and Audit Scheme
EMCF	European Monetary Cooperation Fund
EMI	European Monetary Institute
EMS	European Monetary System
EMU	Economic and Monetary Union
EP	European Parliament
EPC (POCO)	European Political Cooperation
EPU	European Political Union
ERASMUS	European Action Scheme for the Mobility of University Students
ERDF	European Regional Development Fund
ERM	Exchange Rate Mechanism
ERTA	European Road Transport Association
ESCB	European System of Central Banks
ESF	European Social Fund
ESPRIT	European Strategic Programme for Research and Development in Information Technology
ETUC	European Confederation of Trade Unions

Euratom	European Atomic Energy Community
EUREKA	European Research Coordination Agency
EUROFORM	Programme to promote new employment opportunities
EUROSTAT	EC Statistical Office and Its Publications
EUT	EP Draft European Union Treaty
FAST	Forecasting and Assessment in the field of Science and Technology
FDP	German Free Democratic Party
FIFG	Financial Instrument for Fisheries Guidance
FORCE	EC Vocational Training Programme
FPÖ	Austrian Freedom Party
FRG	Federal Republic of Germany
GAM '92	Cooperation to Combat Illegal Trade
GATT	General Agreement on Tariffs and Trade
GDP	Gross Domestic Product
GDR	Former German Democratic Republic
GNP	Gross National Product
GSP	General System of Preferences
HDTV	High Definition Television
HMG	Her Majesty's Government
HORIZON	Community initiative concerning handicapped persons and other disadvantaged groups
IGC	Intergovernmental Conference
IMF	International Monetary fund
IMP	Integrated Mediterranean Programme
IRA	Irish Republican Army
ITER	International Thermonuclear Reactor
JESSI	Joint European Submicron Silicon Initiative
JET	Joint European Torus Programme
JHA	(Cooperation) on Justice and Home Affairs
LINGUA	Action Programme to Promote Foreign Language Competence in the Community
MCA	Monetary Compensatory Amounts
MEP	Member of the European Parliament
MFA	Multi-Fiber Agreement
NATO	North Atlantic Treaty Organization
NOW	New Opportunities for Women
OCT	Overseas Countries and Territories
OECD	Organization for Economic Cooperation and Development
OEEC	Organization for European Economic Cooperation
OJ	Official Journal of the European Communities
OJC	Official Journal of the European Communities (Information and Notices)
OJL	Official Journal of the European Communities (Legislation)
OJS	Official Journal of the European Communities (Supplement)
OOPEC	Office for Official Publications of the EC

PASOK	Greek Socialist Party
PCF	French Communist Party
PD	Irish Progressive Democrat Party
PETRA	Community Action Programme on the Vocational Training of Young People and their Preparation for Adult and Working Life
PHARE	Assistance for the Economic Reconstruction of Central and Eastern Europe
PR	Proportional Representation
PS	French Socialist Party (*Parti Socialiste*)
PSI	Italian Socialist Party
PSOE	Spanish Socialist Workers Party
QR	Quantitative Restriction
RACE	Research and Development in Advanced Communications Technologies for Europe
R&D	Research and Development
RECHAR	*Reconversion des bassins charbonniers* (Coal Areas Reconversion Programme)
RESIDER	*Reconversion de zones sidérurgiques* (Steel Areas Reconversion Programme)
RPR	French Rally for the Republic (*Rassemblement pour la République*)
SCENT	Cooperation Against Fraud
SEA	Single European Act
SIS	Schengen Information System
SME	Small- and Medium-Sized Enterprise
SPD	German Social Democratic Party
SPP	Danish Socialist People's Party
SPRINT	Strategic programme for the Transnational Promotion of Innovation and Technology transfer
STABEX	System of Stabilization of Export Earnings
SYSMIN	System for Safeguarding and Developing Mineral Production
TAC	Total Allowable Catches
TACIS	Technical Assistance to the Commonwealth of Independent States and Georgia
TEMPUS	Trans-European Mobility Scheme for University Students
TEU	Treaty on European Union
TREVI	*Terrorisme, Radicalisme, Extrémisme, Violence Internationale*
UDF	Union for French Democracy (*Union pour la démocratie française*)
UK	United Kingdom
UN	United Nations
UNCTAD	United Nations Conference on Trade and Development
UNECE	United Nations Economic Committee for Europe

UNESCO	United Nations Educational, Scientific, and Cultural Organization
UNICE	*Union des Industries de la Communauté européenne* (EC equivalent of CBI)
UNIDO	United Nations Industrial Development Organization
VER	Voluntary Export Restraint
VP	Vice President of the Commission
VSTF	Very Short-Term Financing Facility
VVD	Dutch Liberal Party
WEU	Western European Union
WFP	World Food Programme
WG	Working Group
YES	Youth for Europe Scheme

Introduction

In the mid-1990s relations with the European Community are again one of the most divisive issues in British politics. Very often the issue has been symbolized by attitudes to the Treaty on European Union (TEU), sometimes known as 'the Maastricht Treaty'. John Major called it 'very good for Britain and good for Europe' but Lady Thatcher attacked it as an idea from yesterday, and one diametrically opposed to British national interests. Yet despite the passion which the Treaty has caused, relatively few people have actually read it. Whereas hundreds of thousands of copies were made available in other Community countries, only a few thousand were sold in Britain, and this in spite of claims that the Treaty creates a European citizenship and has encouraged a new awareness of the need to involve the whole population in European integration and not just elites.

Even though David Pollard of the British Anti-Federalists had earlier produced a cheap printed edition and made the text available electronically, it was not until October 1992 that *The Sunday Times* and other newspapers made the text generally available and others began to produce commentaries. By then the government was still considering producing the booklet on the Treaty which finally appeared in late November, whereas the German authorities published the full text on 12 February 1992. Thereafter Maastricht rose to the heights of its own video and tape versions. Yet neither the government nor the press made available the Treaty of Rome, as amended by the Single European Act (SEA), to which the Maastricht document continually refers and on which Lady Thatcher placed so much stress, when Prime Minister, with her calls for 'the Treaty, the whole Treaty and nothing but the Treaty'.

The problems of the Maastricht Treaty

As the Speaker's Counsel remarked, mass publication is not a panacea because the text presupposes knowledge of other treaties and because it raises unsolved questions. And, while there are general assessments, often of a polemical nature, such publications do not really offer a detailed, line by line explanation either of the Treaty of Maastricht or even of the Treaty of Rome comparable to that provided by Francis Jacobs and others for the European Parliament's Union Treaty. Moreover, British press opinion often rests on a few broad ideas and not on detailed reading of the Treaties. When John Major made two specific references to the text in his speech during the November 1992 paving debate in the Commons, this was described by a radio commentator, as 'virtually a line by line analysis'. There has also been more attention given to the economic than to the political aspects of the treaties. So both the Treaty of Rome and the TEU deserve the nickname of 'Unseen' Treaties as the British anti-Europeans called the latter. This does not facilitate understanding of what the 'European Union' really involves.

All this is especially unfortunate given that the Treaty on European Union, as it is correctly known, is technically very complex and hard to follow. This is especially so for the British who are the least well informed about Europe and who are not used to dealing with written constitutions. Indeed, British legal, parliamentary, and semantic conventions often point in a very different direction. Hence Americans, for all that they are not European, often find it easier to cope with Community affairs than the British, because they are used both to a written document and to a federal-type system. Yet, ironically, even the most virulent of Europhobes can often be found using classic federalist arguments against what they see as Euro-Federalism.

In any case, as we might expect from a document which finally emerged from frantic late-night compromises amongst heads of government in a relatively obscure Dutch provincial town, the text of the TEU is opaque and complicated. It is written in the language of treaties and parliamentary bills with which most people are not familiar. Indeed, most people in Britain have never even read an Act of Parliament. In the case of the TEU some of the drafters have been said to have admitted that if they had realized that it would be read by the public, they would have produced a different document altogether. There have also been complaints that there are variations between the various English versions of the Treaty emanating from Brussels, not to mention the inevitable subtle differences between the official versions in the nine Community languages.

The structure of the document is complicated as well as highly technical. Thus it involves not just new proposals but a host of amendments and changes to existing treaty provisions. Furthermore, as well as the Treaty itself the package includes many protocols and declarations by various member states. The fact that it contains both broad principles and very detailed provisions on aspects of monetary union means it is not an easy document to follow.

Given all this the text as such has been very harshly criticized in Britain and beyond. One former Commission official said it had 'all the readability of a railway timetable', a French member of the European Parliament (MEP), that the Vatican would have drafted it better, and a member of the House of Lords castigated it as a 'shambles with which no lawyer or accountant would wish to be associated'. A former editor of *The Times* went so far as to call it the worst treaty since Versailles, presumably in form and in substance. However, such views often conceal antipathy to the ideas of the Treaty as well as to the way they are expressed.

The British and constitutions

However, the fact that the British have found it hard to come to terms with the TEU is not due simply to prejudice or to the technical difficulties of the text. It is a reflection of different political cultures. Because there has not been a single written constitutional document since the English 'Agreement of the People' of the late 1650s, the British are not very well versed in reading them. British political practice has shied away from dealing with the questions of principle central to constitutions. Both Conservatives and Labour have tended to regard constitutional change as a distraction from the socio-economic issues which are seen as fundamental to modern British politics. The way attention switched from Maastricht to the proposed closure of the majority of British coal mines during the October 1992 Birmingham Summit showed this very clearly. Indeed, it was often said that just because it was a 'constitutional' matter the TEU was irrelevant at a time of economic crisis in Europe.

Moreover, British politicians are used to the very precise and detailed legislative acts produced by British parliamentary draftsmen which seek to cover all contingencies and leave little scope for interpretation.[1] They assume therefore that the TEU is a totally rigid construction. In fact continental drafting is more a matter of principle and purpose. The Treaties are essentially frameworks, indicating general objectives and ways of achieving them, but not laying down detailed provisions.

The way they are applied is thus affected by circumstance and by judicial interpretation. This also makes British critics unhappy because this flexibility opens the way for the very different type of broad-brush interpretation of the spirit of the Treaties practised by the Court of Justice. British tradition, for instance, until the case of *Pepper* v. *Hart* in late 1992, forbad judges even to consult reports of relevant parliamentary debates in Hansard when interpreting statutes. They were expected to work from the text alone. Hence the slightly contradictory complaints about generalities, ambiguities and lack of precise definitions.

One answer to such criticisms is simply to ignore the detail of the Treaties. However, the latter are too important for this. For, although they are in the form of treaties agreed between the governments of the member states, the complex of Treaties signed at Rome, Luxembourg and Maastricht make up what is really the constitution of the Community and the Union. Technically there is some argument about this because, despite superficial similarities, the Treaties actually differ in legal and other ways from ordinary constitutions. Some authorities would thus deny them constitutional status on the legal grounds that they are really bundles of contractual obligations and do not constitute a state. It can also be argued that the Treaties proceed on a case-by-case basis rather than using the

---

1. British legislation, of which there can be over 13,000 pages per year (compared to 1,000 pages before the war), can be immensely detailed and yet can miss out vital points of principle. Matthew d'Ancona pointed out in *The Times* of 7 April 1993 that the 1988 Education Act forgot to require teachers to teach the new national curriculum. Very often the difficulties experienced by Britons in applying EC rules comes not from the rules themselves but from the poor quality of the British implementing legislation.

Box 1.
Functions of
constitutions

1. Set out framework of the State, its institutions and their respective powers
2. Lay down rules of the political game, ensuring fair competition
3. Reflect balance of power inside country
4. Guarantee civic and other rights
5. Provide moral and philosophical justification for regime
6. Enshrine national traditions
7. Provide superior reference points and modes for judging new laws including constitutional amendment

general principles favoured by nation state constitutions. Certainly the result is much more policy flavoured than some other European constitutions. The European Parliament also feels the Treaties are too imperfect and incomplete to be a real constitution, hence their attempts to draft a real one.

However, they are clearly purposive constructions which go far beyond ordinary Treaties and even authorities who dispute their 'constitutional status' often tend to treat them as if they were constitutions. Moreover, they are self-executing and serve as the *fons et origio* of Community law which has emerged as a new legal order. Indeed, some authorities believe that the European Court of Justice (ECJ) has actually turned the Treaties into a constitution by its jurisprudence. So it is both justified and helpful to regard the Treaties in this way. This is the approach adopted here.

Constitutions do, as Box 1 shows, a number of things. Essentially they set out the framework of government and the basic institutions needed to run a state, together with their respective powers and relations. This is particularly necessary, of course, when dealing with a quasi-supranational body like the Community. When touchy nation states are involved there has to be both agreement and a formal compact about common action. Federal-type systems, in other words, need constitutional structures. They cannot function in the way the British system does.

Constitutions thus are also there to lay down the rules by which the political game should be played and suggest what the political process should be. The nature of the rules is, of course, a reflection of the political map and balance at the time a constitution is drafted, often consecrating changes in regime. Normally they also provide guarantees for the citizenry's political and other rights. In other words, they enshrine the compact between the people and the government. By setting out structures, rules and rights, constitutions also provide a moral and philosophical justification for the regime, often setting out the aims which it is meant to achieve. Equally constitutions enshrine the values and traditions which give the entity in question its identity. Finally, they can also provide reference points for judging the acceptability of political change, by laying down basic principles against which other legislation must be judged and preventing too easy change in essential values by giving a special status to constitutional and other basic laws. This includes providing special rules for amending the constitution to ensure that this cannot be done light-heartedly or surreptitiously.

Although constitutions are essentially a European invention, all this stands in contrast to the British organic constitutional tradition. In this there is no conception of basic laws because of the doctrine of the sovereignty of Parliament. All laws have equal status. Hence change comes incessantly and without either coordination or consideration of basic principles. It is also worth noting that the case for a written constitution has recently been advanced by the Charter 88 group and in a Private Members Bill tabled in 1992. And, as already noted, a recent decision in the House of Lords has also opened the way to the use of Hansard in interpreting statutes.

Despite this, United Kingdom antagonism to the TEU rests on a certain bewilderment at the process and not just on objections to the contents and nature of Maastricht. This is ironic because the TEU is, in the last resort, precisely the kind of interstate agreement which many 'Eurosceptics' claim to prefer. Like the 1986 Single European Act (SEA) it is a classic example of the bargaining and reconciling national interests which has always marked integration in Europe. The problem is that it impacts on domestic political arrangements which thus become a matter of wider political interest, which many find uncomfortable, not to say unacceptable.

Moreover, because the Twelve member states have no single ethnic or cultural basis, the Treaties have to provide a foundation for the Community and Union. They are thus controversial because they give identity to the latter. And, if it is true that the Community presently has 'the political dimension of federalism without its constitutional dimension' it is also true that such Treaties can, as history shows, develop into true constitutions.

The Treaties as constitutions

This *Handbook* therefore proceeds, as already suggested, from the belief that the Treaties are the constitution of the Community and the Union, and are best understood in this light. And, as such, they are therefore an integral, if different, part of the British constitution. Hence they do not merely need to be known but also to be explained. The best way to do this, although one not so far used in British studies of the Community, is through the kind of commentary which is found in many continental countries, as well as in the British legal and theological traditions. However, the approach adopted here is a common-sense political one and not a technical legalistic one. It is hoped that this will make the Treaties more accessible and more comprehensible than has so far been the case.

In fact, the complexity of the Treaties that are contained here, is but a pale reflection of the complicated nature of the British constitution as it has evolved over the last four hundred years and more. As with the British constitution, that of the Union has also developed over time, albeit in a somewhat more structured way. More powers have been given to Community institutions as a result of clear inter-state agreements, producing the kind of complex inter-relations shown in Figure 1.

The constitutional development of the Union started with the European Coal and Steel Community (ECSC) Treaty of 1951. Some of the institutions and ideas this contained were then taken up in the 1957 Treaties creating the European

q.v. ECSC Treaty pp. 359–63.

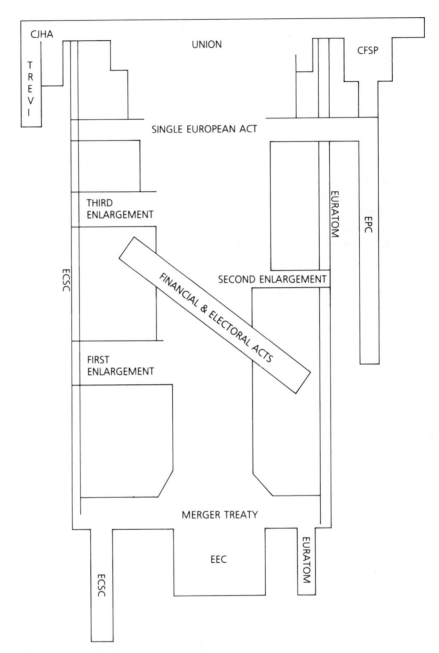

Figure 1. The genealogy of the Community Treaties

Economic Community (EEC) and the European Atomic Energy Community (Euratom). The three Communities were then knitted together by the 1965 Merger Treaty which meant that, from 1967, there was, in practice, if not in law, only one Community with a shared set of institutions. However, the Treaties remained separate even though they were amended to provide consistency.

Further changes were made to the Treaties in three formal ways. To begin with changes were made by the Accession Treaties signed by the six states who joined the Communities in later years. Secondly, a number of changes were made by Council and through Treaty to the budgetary provisions of the Treaties, on the number of Commissioners, and miscellaneous matters including direct elections to the European Parliament. On two occasions changes in financing led to new Treaties. Thirdly, minor changes were made in the process of signing association agreements with former colonies and other states in the African-Caribbean-Pacific (ACP) group. In addition to this a number of informal precedents have become part of the constitutional luggage of the Community. Notable among these is the 1966 Luxembourg Compromise which was interpreted in such a way that the Community would not enforce majority decisions against the clear national interest of member states.

q.v. Luxembourg Compromise pp. 531–2.

In 1986 the Community proceeded to a partial remodelling of the Treaty of Rome by adopting the SEA. This was a new Treaty in its own right which consisted largely of clauses amending the Treaty of Rome and the other Treaties. These were then incorporated into the three main Treaties. However the SEA also consolidated and legitimized the system of European Political Cooperation (EPC) although it did not make this fully a part of the Community structures. Finally there were some provisions common to the Treaties and EPC. Like the ECSC and Euratom Treaties the SEA has almost maintained a life of its own.

The Treaty of European Union, agreed at Maastricht in December 1991 and signed there in February 1992, partially repeats the structure of the SEA. It thus consists of seven Titles (or sections) divided into nineteen Articles, numbered alphabetically. (See Box 3, p. 40) Of these, three amend the existing treaties, notably Title II which is one long amendment to the post-SEA Treaty of Rome. Two are rather like the provisions for EPC in the SEA, in that they create semi-detached procedures for common foreign and security policy activity on the one hand, and judicial and home affairs on the other. The Protocols also include provisions for social action to be taken by the Community without British participation. The other two Titles are common and final provisions relating to the TEU, the separate pillars and the existing Treaties.

Thus the TEU subsumes the Treaty of Rome — which will be amended by the incorporation of the amendments in Article G of the TEU — as it does the ECSC and Euratom Treaties. It is partly superior to the revised Rome Treaty while, at the same time, it will have a legal status of its own, because not all its provisions will be included in the amended Treaty of Rome. Moreover, it creates a somewhat different kind of entity in a Union and not just a Community, the former having the two new pillars as well as the European Community (EC) one.

All this is complicated and is best understood by looking at the actual text. However, it is important to remember that constitutional texts do not rule out change. General de Gaulle once defined a constitution as consisting of 'a conception, institutions and their application'. Application depends on the nature of the rules and the way they are interpreted. In the case of the TEU and the associated Treaties the rules are more flexible than sometimes imagined and the European Court of Justice also plays a large part in interpreting. Such interpretation and application also depends on circumstances prevailing when this is done. In other words, such constitutional documents are 'read' in a way which fits the times. In the case of the TEU this fact is vital because the political storms of ratification clearly suggest that the Treaty will be read in a much less centralist way than appeared likely in December 1991. Further changes of this kind are also possible. This point needs to be borne in mind throughout in assessing the text and the commentaries.

The aims of the Handbook

This *Handbook* is, therefore, neither a structured interpretation of the Community, nor a reader setting out other people's views of it. These things are valuable and very necessary for students. However, they are already catered for in a whole range of valuable texts and courses. The *Handbook* does not seek to replace either these or to offer a workbook for student use in class. Nor does it seek to rival the many detailed reference books now available on the Community.

This says what the *Handbook* is not. What are its positive aims? The *Handbook* has several, closely related to the way it is structured and presented, and set out in Box 2. And, as will be seen, these aims and presentation also have implications for the way students might use the *Handbook*.

Essentially the *Handbook* seeks to support student learning on the Community and Union by making the text of the Treaties, more easily available. As well as providing availability, it also aims at making them more accessible and comprehensible. So, it seeks to make it possible to understand the meaning and interconnections of the Treaties, particularly by relating them to the policies pursued by the Union. In so doing it brings together material which is often hard to find in one place, and subjects it to detailed analysis, using the approaches more often used by lawyers and literary critics than by political commentators. This is in line with the kinds of textual analysis with which students are becoming familiar after having progressed through parts of the National Curriculum. By thus assisting with analysis, the *Handbook* hopes to make complicated and crucial matters more comprehensible.

In so doing it inevitably raises issues about which students need to think and to which attention needs, generally, to be drawn. However, the intention of the *Handbook* is not to present assessments already set in stone, but to approach the Treaties objectively. The aim is to try and empower the student (and the

Box 2. Aims and objectives	**The aims of the *Handbook* are to provide:**
	1. *Availability* of treaty documentation
	2. *Accessibility* for very difficult texts
	3. An *Approach* which is reasonably objective
	4. *Analysis* of their meaning and policy linkages
	5. *Aid* in understanding contexts, dynamics and effects together with making one's own judgements

citizen). Hence, by making the Treaties available in clear and accessible format, both groups can now draw their own conclusions. So, even if it is true that the polemical nature of the subject makes it hard to be taken as objective and that by 'understanding everything one forgives everything' the *Handbook* seeks as detached a presentation as possible.

As is suggested in the second subdivision of the *Handbook* there are a whole range of conflicting approaches to Maastricht. These in turn reflect the way that bargaining amongst actors who differed greatly in their aims and who were pressed by time, produced a messy and unclear compromise. As Peter Luff has said, the TEU is a 'sock into which useful but very different objects have been crammed'. The text itself already allows for varying readings. Changing circumstances will mean that further readings will emerge. Hence, just as the game was not 'all on' at Maastricht so it was not 'all up afterwards', as Helen Wallace has said.

In other words, the essential aim of the *Handbook* is to aid people to cope with the problems of a difficult text, polemical interpretations and all too rapidly changing circumstances. One aspect of the last is the way that public opinion has got bored with the subject. The *Handbook* therefore seeks, by facilitating their understanding of the nature and scope of the embryo polity of which we are now an integral part, to make it easier for people to make up their own minds and come to their own considered judgements. Equally, it seeks to enable them to follow the development of the Union as it unfolds. This has to be done in a structured context since the TEU emerged at a specific moment in time and thanks to actors with distinct aims and objectives.

Structure

These aims have helped to shape the structure of the European Union. As a result the *Handbook* falls into seven subdivisions. These are numbered but not called Parts or Sections because, as already noted, this could cause confusion with the use of terms such as Part, Title, Chapter and Section in the Treaties themselves. The initial subdivision places the Treaties in their historical context, that of economic and political development in general, and of European integration in particular.

The main body of the *Handbook* is then given over to the Union Treaty and those Treaties related to it: the general elements; EC commercial and monetary policies; EC social and general policies; EC institutions; and other treaties and pillars. In each of these cases the *Handbook* seeks to show how the constitution of the Community and the Union is structured, how they can be understood and how policies flow legally and logically from them. While final evaluations are left to readers, some of the detail is explained graphically through figures and boxes.

Where the Treaties in particular are concerned, the *Handbook* normally offers a general comment, followed by the text itself and an analysis of the policies deriving from the text. The Treaty text is picked out in a different, smaller typeface and printed in **bold** or *italic* to show new material. Bold type denotes wholly new material and italic material which, while present in the Treaty of Rome, has been subjected to some change as a result of the TEU. This can involve omissions, altered position or other minor changes such as renumbering.

The commentaries are illustrated and cross-referenced in the margins. There is also a brief list of further reading, normally of up-to-date articles, at the end of each subdivision. To facilitate cross-referencing and ease of access a Synoptic Table has been included (see pp. xii–xviii) which precisely locates Treaty Articles and editorial matter on a page by page basis. The order adopted in the *Handbook* is normally that indicated by the Community's own version of the way the Treaty of Rome will be after consolidation within the TEU. The intention is to have as much consonance as possible between the *Handbook* and the Treaties as they appear in official versions.

The final subdivision looks at the wider contexts of the Union including relations with other European organizations together with issues and developments arising after the Maastricht Summit. The subdivision also considers the actors in European affairs, notably the Community's own present members, but also applicant and peripheral states. Here, and in the annexes, there are suggestions about how to take study further, whether by checking the meaning of technical terms, making comparisons with earlier forms of the Treaties or by further reading and contacts. A general bibliography is then annexed to the *Handbook* along with a glossary, details of the original treaties and a list of useful European addresses.

Using the Handbook

Clearly the *Handbook* is not meant to be read from start to finish as one would with a normal book. It makes the texts and their meaning available as and when needed, and not only at points picked out by others. Because it is designed to be available as a work of reference, to be consulted on specific points on which it will provide the text, a basic interpretation and explanation and a means of following up the subject, students, and others, need their own strategy for using it. Readers need to ask themselves why they are looking at the *Handbook*, what they are hoping to find, and what they are going to do with what they do find in it.

Reasons for using it will often determine what is read, and in what order. Sometimes it will be enough to consult the Treaties, and only look at the commentary or policy analysis afterwards. At other times, readers will need to work through the commentary and then consider the text, asking themselves whether they agree with what is said there and reflecting on any other points and questions which come to mind. This will require the development of the skills of close analysis needed by such a difficult text. Sometimes it may be necessary to consider the background sections or those dealing with events after Maastricht, either on their own or in conjunction with elements of the treaties. What needs to be remembered above all is that, first, what is really important is devising one's own plan of campaign, and, second, that the material essentially is there to stimulate personal understanding and assessment.

The reasons why people use it will also depend on the exercise they are engaged in at the time, whether essay writing, general study or seminar preparation. The first and last subdivisions are particularly aimed at essay writing because of their contextual nature. This is also true of the policy analysis sections and the references to periodical articles. The treaties are there to be searched and quoted in support of general arguments.

When it comes to general note-taking and study, the *Handbook* is there to save readers copying, whether electronically or by hand, the references from the Treaty of Rome and the TEU which they may need. Getting to know how it is organized by familiarity with its contents lists, index and prefaces is as important as it is for any other text. The *Handbook* can also serve as preliminary reading for lectures.

Finally, we hope that the *Handbook* and the way it is presented will also make it easier to utilize the actual Treaty texts, rather than the commentaries, in debate and seminars. By making them available as evidence to be cited, we hope it will give students more self-confidence in taking part in group discussions. As Burdess says, such preparation can prevent students being mere drones or noisy but 'empty vessels' in seminars. It may save on the highlighting!

Because it is intended to be helpful to students in finding out about the Union and making up their own minds about it, the compilers will be delighted to receive suggestions about how it could be improved from those who use it whether by corrections, additions, excisions or other developments.

So far the importance of the Treaties as constitutions has been stressed. However, constitutions do not emerge out of the blue. They are the product of particular times and circumstances, and have to be — in part — understood as such. Hence before setting out the treaties it is important to look at the way that the Treaty on European Union came about.

FURTHER READING

Caportarti, F., Jacobs, F. *et al.* (eds.), *The European Union Treaty: A commentary*, Clarendon, Oxford, 1986.

D'Ancona, M., 'A curse on Britain's lousy law-makers', *The Times*, 7 April 1993, p. 12.

EC, *Treaty on European Union, Together with the Complete Text of the Treaty establishing the European Community*, OJC 224, 31 August 1992.

Elazar, D., 'Constitution-making. The pre-eminently political act', in Banting, K. and Simeon, R. (eds.), *The Politics of Constitutional Change in Industrial Nations*, Macmillan, London, 1985, pp. 232–50.

Foreign and Commonwealth Office, *Britain in Europe: The European Community and Your Future*, Central Office of Information, London, 1992.

Gammie, G., 'Note by Counsel to the Speaker: the Treaty on European Union', in *Fifteenth Report from the Select Committee on European Legislation*, HMSO, London, 1992, pp. xl-lx.

Green, N. *et al. The Legal Framework of the Single European Market*, Oxford University Press, Oxford, 1992.

Kent, P., *European Community Law*, Pitmans/MLE, London, 1992.

Luff, P., *The Simple Guide to Maastricht*, European Movement, London, 1992.

Morgan, R., 'The EC: The Constitution of a Would Be Polity', in Bogdanor, V. (ed.), *Constitutions in Democratic Politics*, Gower, Aldershot, 1988, pp. 367–79.

Nelson O. and Pollard, S. *The Unseen Treaty: Treaty on European Union*, Nelson and Pollard, Oxford, 1992.

The European 'Maastricht Made Simple' *The European*, London, 1992.

The European 'Maastricht made simple: the essential guide to the Treaty that will shape Europe' (video), Screenpro, London, 1993.

The Independent on Sunday 'The Treaty of Maastricht: what it says and what it means', 11 October 1992.

The Independent on Sunday 'The Treaty of Maastricht:

what it says and what it means' (cassette), John Newton 1992.

The Sunday Times 'The Treaty on European Union: the full text and a step-by-step guide', 11 October 1992.

Wallace, M., 'Euopean governance in turbulent times', *JCMS*, 31 March 1993, pp. 293–304.

Wincott, D., *The Treaty of Maastricht: An adequate 'Constitution' for the European Union?*, European Public Policy Institute Occasional Paper 93/6, Warwick University, 1992.

STUDY SKILLS

Barnes, R., *Successful Study for Degrees*, Routledge, London, 1992.

Belsey, C., *Critical Practice*, Routledge, London, 1992.

Bradney, A. *et al. How to Study Law*, Sweet and Maxwell, London, 1992.

Burdess, N., *The Handbook of Student Skills*, Prentice Hall, Hemel Hempstead, 1991.

Casey, F., *How to Study. A Practical Guide*, Basingstoke, Macmillan, Basingstoke, 1991.

Clinch, P., *Using a Law Library*, Blackstone, London, 1992.

Cutts, M., *Making Sense of English in the Law*, Chambers, London, 1992.

Northedge, A., *The Good Study Guide*, Open University Press, Milton Keynes, 1992.

Pollard, D., and Hoyle, D., *Constitutional and Administrative Law*, Butterworth, London, 1992.

Rowntree, D., *Learn How to Study*, McDonald, London, 1990.

I. The Road to Maastricht

The Treaty on European Union did not come from nowhere. The final decisions taken by Heads of State and Government of the Twelve in Maastricht on the 9–10 December 1991 were, to begin with, simply the last stage of a series of debates inside the two intergovernmental conferences (IGCs) on Economic and Monetary Union and Political Union respectively. These had been convened in December 1990 and met throughout 1991. In turn, the arguments then deployed and the whole process of negotiation were themselves the product of earlier events and trends, not all of them restricted to the Community.

Three things really need to be remembered in understanding how the Community moved down the road to Maastricht. The first was the institutional and political legacy of early stages of European integration, notably that emerging from the so-called 'relaunching' of the Community in the mid-1980s. The Community's chequered past provided a constitutional patrimony on which integration could be built. A second aspect of the legacy was the emergence of political pressures for further integration. Disappointment that the SEA had not gone further in this, along with the inherent dynamic of the SEA and Single Market and the collapse of Communism together with the rapid reunification of Germany in 1989–90, provided some of the political impetus for further integration.

The second, and related, factor was the way the Community economy and thinking about the implications of the Single Market evolved in the 1980s. The mid-1980s had seen a return of economic stability and prosperity. However, although considerable convergence had been achieved there were still many problems while many also felt that monetary and social coordination were needed to complement the Single Market. This provided the first renewal of impulses towards Economic and Monetary Union, which led to the idea of an IGC on the subject.

The third main factor was the domestic one. Member state governments had always played a crucial part in encouraging the further development of the Community. Some continued to make the running at the turn of the decade, pushing for further integration because of the new political context in Europe. Yet they did so at a time when the European economy was sliding into a new crisis, and electorates were becoming increasingly restive and dissatisfied both with socio-economic conditions and government responses. This was to prove extremely important, especially in the response to the Treaty.

Very often these three factors were inextricably intertwined. The desire for further integration to consolidate what had been achieved inside the Community between 1985 and 1987 accelerated because of the end of the Cold War. Yet the post-Cold War era turned out to be a much less easy time, economically and politically, than had been assumed when the Berlin Wall came down. However, for the sake of simplicity this first section of the *Handbook* separates out the three elements and examines them one by one. An appreciation of this context is an indispensable background to understanding the Maastricht Treaty and the earlier, now revised, Treaties.

i. The legacy of European integration

The decision to negotiate a new treaty establishing a European union was conceived within the institutional framework the Community had inherited from the early stages of European integration. It was largely motivated by the continuing pressure for developing and democratizing that integration. While the *Handbook* is not the place for a detailed retelling of the general history of integration in post-war Europe it is important to show how the method of integration adopted by the ECSC, Euratom and the EEC proved successful and also generated a powerful movement in favour of such integration. It also developed a corpus of treaties and legislation known as the *acquis*, or patrimony, which is an aspect and incentive for further integration. Yet we should also be aware that things never proceeded smoothly. As Figure 2 shows, development came in fits and starts, some marked by the signing of new treaties and acts. Treaties and a genuine enthusiasm for integration provided the negotiators in the IGCs with an important double legacy.

Roots

Although there were practical and intellectual precedents for structured European cooperation going beyond mere collaboration between states, it was only in 1945, after Europe had, for a second time, been devastated by war that serious attempts to integrate Europe were made. The further undermining of Europe's position in the world, to the benefit of the United States and the USSR, the desperate need to prevent national conflicts causing a third 'European civil war', and the general desire for a freer, fairer and more prosperous Europe all encouraged such experiments. Resistance movements, in particular, were very keen on having some kind of overarching structure to achieve these ends.

Although the 'United States of Europe', which Winston Churchill urged on the continental powers in Zurich in 1946, did not emerge, by the 1950s several new European organizations had been created. These involved bilateral and

Figure 2. A chronology of Community development	1944		July	Draft Declaration on European Federation by European Resistance Movements

1944		July	Draft Declaration on European Federation by European Resistance Movements
1948	04	April	OEEC created
	05	June	Hague Conference: European Movement created
1949	04	April	NATO established
	05	June	Council of Europe founded
1950	09	May	Schuman Plan for ECSC
	20	June	Talks on Coal and Steel Community start
	24	October	Pleven Plan for EDC launched
1951	18	April	Treaty of Paris establishing ECSC signed by Six
1952	27	May	EDC Treaty signed
	23	July	ECSC comes into being
1954	30	August	French National Assembly refuses to ratify the EDC Treaty
	21	October	Western European Union established
1955	13	October	Action Committee for a United States of Europe created
	01–03	July	Messina Conference of Six agrees to further steps towards integration
1957	25	March	Treaties of Rome establishing Euratom and EEC signed by Six
1958	01	January	Treaties of Rome enter into force
1960	04	January	Stockholm Convention establishing EFTA signed by the Seven
1961	09	July	Greece becomes an Associate Member
	09	August	UK makes first application to join EC
1963	14	January	de Gaulle vetoes UK application
	12	September	Turkey becomes an Associate
		September	Negotiations on merging the institutions commence
1965	08	April	Merger Treaty signed
	30	June	'Empty Chair Crisis' begins
1966	29	January	'Luxembourg Compromise'
1967	10	May	UK makes second application
	01	July	Merger of Institutions of three Communities
1968	01	July	Completion of EEC Customs Union
1969	01–02	February	Hague Council agrees enlargement and union
1970	21	April	Council Decision on own resources
	22	April	Budgetary Treaty
	20	July	Davignon Report on EPC
		October	Werner Report on EMU
1972	22	January	Treaties of Accession with Denmark, Ireland, Norway and United Kingdom signed
	22	July	Agreement establishing a free trade area, between EC and EFTA countries (including Norway).
	21	October	Paris Summit
1973	01	January	Denmark, Ireland and UK become members 1975
	28	February	Lomé I Convention signed
	02	July	Second Budgetary Treaty
	29	December	Tindemans' Report
1978	06–07	July	Bremen Summit proposes the EMS
1979	09	March	EMS comes into operation
	28	May	Treaty on Greek Accession
	07–10	June	First direct elections to EP
1981	01	January	Greece becomes tenth member of EC
	09	July	EP creates Constitutional Committee
	08	October	French Memorandum on 'relance'
	04	November	Genscher–Colombo proposal for Union
1982		May	UK attempts to invoke veto
	21	June	EP resolution on institutional reform and political union
1983	19	June	Stuttgart Solemn Declaration on European Union
1984	14	February	Draft European Union Treaty
	14–17	June	Second direct elections to EP
	25–26	June	Fontainbleau Summit sets up Dooge Committee on institutional reform and agrees budgetary reform
1985	09	March	Dooge Committee reports

Figure 2 cont.

	12	June	Signature of Iberian Accession treaties
	14	June	Commission publishes Cockfield White Paper on the Completion of the Internal Market
	18–29	June	Milan Council sets up IGC to amend Treaty of Rome
	02–03	December	Luxembourg Summit and presentation of SEA proposals
1986	01	January	Spain and Portugal join the EC
	28	February	SEA signed
1987	15	February	Delors I Package to secure funding of EC proposed
	01	July	SEA comes into force
1988	11–12	February	Brussels Summit adopts Delors I financial package
	25	June	EC–COMECON Joint Declaration
	27–28	June	Hanover Summit sets up Delors Committee on EMU
1989	17	January	Delors proposes more structured relationship with EFTA
	12	April	Delors Committee Reports
	15–18	June	Third direct elections to EP
	26–27	June	Madrid Summit endorses Delors plan for EMU
	09	November	Fall of the Berlin Wall
	08	December	Strasbourg Summit proposes IGC on EMU
	15	December	Lomé IV Convention signed
1990	28–29	April	First Dublin Summit
	26	June	Second Dublin Summit
	01	July	German Economic and Monetary Union
	03	October	German Unification completed
	14–15	December	Rome Summit opens IGCs on EMU and EPU 1991
1991		April	Luxembourg Presidency draft
	19–21	August	August Coup in the Soviet Union
	24	September	Abortive Dutch Treaty draft
	10	December	Maastricht Summit accepts TEU
	16	December	Europe Agreements signed with Czechoslovakia, Hungary and Poland
1992	07	February	Treaty on European Union signed
	02	May	European Economic Area Agreement signed with the EFTA countries
	02	June	Danish Referendum says 'no' to the TEU
	31	December	Target date for the completion of the Internal Market
	31	December	Target date for the establishment of the EEA with EFTA
1993	01	February	Negotiations to begin on first round of enlargement
1994	01	January	Scheduled date for Stage II of EMU
		May	Channel Tunnel due to open
		June	Fourth direct elections to EP
1996			Intergovernmental Conference on Institutional Reform
1997	01	January	Earliest date for introduction of single currency
1999	01	January	Latest date for introduction of single currency

multilateral treaties. More significant were the Organization for European Economic Cooperation (OEEC) set up to coordinate the economic reconstruction of Europe using US aid, and the North Atlantic Treaty Organization (NATO) the military alliance created between the United States, Canada and the majority of European states not under Soviet control. Most of these were intergovernmental initiatives.

However, those continental activists and thinkers who believed in going further towards European unity were also active. A series of committees and congresses in 1946–7 climaxed in the 1948 Hague Conference which called for the creation of an economic union, a charter of human rights and a European parliament. Partly because of the creation of a 'European Movement' some governments, which previously had not been greatly moved by such ideas, came round to accepting the idea. Thus in May 1949 a new body, embracing ten western states including Britain, was established in Strasbourg.

Some had wanted to call this the European Union but British and other governments' objections led to it being called 'The Council of Europe', symbolizing its purely intergovernmental nature. Within its Committee of Ministers decisions could only be taken unanimously and the Parliamentary Assembly was merely consultative. Although it produced a Convention on Human Rights the next year and went on to attract new members and produce useful guidelines in the social and cultural fields this did not satisfy supporters of closer integration, some of whom were found inside western governments, including the United States.

Monnet and the new approach

Despite continuing economic difficulties and the outbreak of the Cold War the new organizations, in the view of Jean Monnet the head of the French Planning Commissariat and others, failed to make real practical progress in holding Europe together. Indeed he felt that the need to rehabilitate West Germany in order to strengthen Europe against the USSR could simply lead to new conflicts. His view was that the only solution was 'concrete, resolute action on a limited but decisive point, bringing about on this point a fundamental change, and gradually modifying the very terms of all the problems'. This approach, which envisaged unifying control of key economic sectors within those few countries willing to take part in such a supranational experiment, was seen as a means of starting an automatic process of integration which would eventually produce a wide federation of European States. This oblique approach to integration, which came to be known as 'neo-functionalism', proved to be more successful than earlier attempts to start by the direct, top-down creation of such a body.

Initially Monnet's ideas were embodied in the plan for joint control of Franco-German coal and steel resources put forward by the French Foreign Minister, Robert Schuman in May 1950. Though the British refused to have any part in such a supranational body, other countries — despite reservations on the far left and the far right — saw it as advantageous. Thus it treated Germany as an equal partner while at the same time controlling the industries which had previously sustained her military power. In particular it gave France an access to German resources, in line with the French Plan, which would not otherwise have been acceptable.

Hence after several months negotiation, a treaty establishing the European Coal and Steel Community (ECSC) was signed in April 1951 by Belgium, France, Germany, Italy, Luxembourg and the Netherlands, commonly referred to as the 'Six'. The Treaty of Paris prefigured later institutional patterns. After a Preamble, setting out the philosophy behind the ECSC, came four Titles dealing with aims, institutions, economic and social policies and generalities respectively. The institutional arrangements were very innovatory as they created a High Authority of nine independent members, able to act directly on the participating industries, and with its own financial resources. To check that this supranational body did not exceed its powers the Treaty also created a ministerial Council (assisted by a Liaison Committee of officials), a Parliamentary Assembly (drawn from delegates to the Council of Europe), a Consultative Committee representing the industries and a court.

Although it did not achieve all Monnet's hopes, the ECSC did two things. Firstly, it reduced customs duties, transport costs, discrimination and barriers to investment. Secondly, it generated experience of cooperation and a belief that it constituted a pointer for the future. Hence in 1950–1 there was a crop of projects for other communities, in agriculture, health, transport and, most significantly, defence. This emerged in response to the need to provide for German rearmament. Proposals for a European Army, controlled in a similar manner to the ECSC, were agreed in 1952. They encouraged an attempt to create an even wider Political Community which would have subsumed the ECSC and the European Defence Community (EDC) while providing the latter's common army with the political and foreign-policy direction it needed. However, all this went too far for many, and the French National Assembly refused to ratify the EDC Treaty, thereby ending the European Political Community as well. It was left to the Western European Union (WEU) to provide an umbrella for German rearmament along with NATO.

Messina and the Treaty of Rome

Although these failures, like difficulties in the OEEC, caused some pessimism among supporters of European integration, a number of Benelux politicians persevered, encouraged by the success of their own customs union. While they felt a purely sectoral approach was too restrictive and the idea of a United States of Europe, initially pushed by Monnet, too ambitious, their discussions showed there was a possibility of making progress by applying the ECSC method on a wider economic front. A resolution to this effect was passed by the Foreign Ministers of the Six at a meeting in Messina in June 1955. They set up a committee under the Belgian Foreign Minister, Paul-Henri Spaak, to examine the possibilities of further integration involving atomic energy and a common market. This met between July 1955 and March 1956 at the *Val Duchesse* in Brussels.

In its report, published in 1956, the Spaak Committee confirmed that mere sectoral integration within the ECSC would not work. It therefore proposed the creation of a separate customs union cum common market among the Six plus an Atomic Energy Community. Perhaps because of the way Jean Monnet's Action Committee lobbied political leaders, this met with approval from ECSC ministers and parliamentarians. The report formed the basis for negotiations in an intergovernmental conference again chaired by Spaak.

This met from June 1956 to February 1957 and, after some hard bargaining to ensure national interests, produced treaties establishing the European Economic Community (EEC) and the European Atomic Energy Community (Euratom). These were signed on 25 March 1957 in Rome. Along with the ECSC these were the first of the constitutional treaties which form the basis of Community law. Despite some opposition, ratification proceeded relatively smoothly and the Treaties came into operation on 1 January 1958.

The Treaties embodied the hope that 'by creating an economic community' they could lay 'the foundations of a deeper and wider community among peoples long divided by bloody conflict'. Economic means were again adopted in order to achieve essentially political ends. By 1987 the Treaty of Rome (see Annex, pp. 516–27) contained 248 Articles, divided into six Parts: Principles, Foundations, Policy, Association, Institutions and General and Final Provisions.

There were also 4 Annexes, 13 Protocols, 4 Conventions and 9 Declarations. The West German government also issued a unilateral, and so far unpublished, declaration stating its assumption that a revaluation of the two Treaties would be possible in the event of unification. Amongst the various additional materials the 'Convention on Certain Institutions' of 25 March 1957, which consolidated the various parliamentary bodies and courts, was another founding document. Its enactment was possible because the institutional structure of the new bodies replicated that of the ECSC although the Commission was given less power than the High Authority and member states correspondingly more. Many of the enthusiasts were therefore left dissatisfied.

The ups and downs of the EC

Despite this, the Communities settled down rapidly and effectively. Not merely did the EEC push ahead with tariff reductions but it forced Britain and other sceptical states to seek closer relationships with it, even though they had set up their own Free Trade Association (EFTA). This early success encouraged the Six to consider going further. However, French proposals in 1961 to create a political union failed because de Gaulle's strictly intergovernmental ideas were unacceptable to supporters of supranationalism. De Gaulle also twice vetoed British applications for membership, much to the annoyance of other member states.

Such disputes made it hard for the Six to agree necessary changes in the institutional arrangements of the Communities. Yet, following on the way the 1957 Convention combined the Assemblies, Courts and Economic and Social Committees of the three Communities, it seemed sensible to go on and unite the Commissions and Councils of Ministers. Much hard bargaining was needed, however, before the Merger Treaty was agreed in April 1965. This laid down the principles of a single Commission and Council while amending the relevant clauses of the three Treaties accordingly. The Merger Treaty also took tentative decisions on the relations of the two, the location of the various institutions, financing, and in a Protocol, on the status of officials of the merged Community. This was to come into effect on 1 July 1967. Some thought was given to merging the three Treaties themselves but, because this was not a statutory requirement, it did not happen.

Although the Commission was not turned into an embryo government responsible to the Parliament, as the supranationalists had wanted, such changes worried de Gaulle. This was especially so because the development of the

Common Agricultural Policy (CAP) would greatly increase the budget, and there was pressure for the Community to have its own resources rather than receive grants from the member states. He was also concerned by the way the Hallstein Commission was using its existing powers and by pressures for more power to be given to the Assembly. Since the Rome Treaty provided for majority voting on many issues after 1966 the French dug their heels in during 1965. They rejected both budgetary powers for the European Parliament and the principle of majority voting, and withdrew their delegates from Council meetings, thus halting progress within the Community.

This so-called 'Empty Chair Crisis' was partly resolved by the so-called 'Luxembourg Compromise' of January 1966. The Council then accepted the French view that, on issues which could be decided by majority voting, discussion should continue until unanimity was reached if a member state felt its vital national interests were at risk. The statement accepted that there was disagreement on what should happen if no compromise was reached, but said this need not hold up Community business. Although not a treaty as such, this was a constitutional milestone as it gave recalcitrant states an effective veto, within the letter of the Rome Treaty. This, following on the institutionalization of the Committee of Permanent Representatives in the Merger Treaty, increased intergovernmental tendencies in the Community.

q.v. Luxembourg Compromise pp. 531–2.

Hence it was not until de Gaulle had resigned that the Community moved forward again. A Summit of Heads of Government at the Hague not merely agreed to endow the Community with its own funds (subject to new controls by the Assembly) but looked forward to new policy initiatives, union in both monetary and political fields and enlargement. The Luxembourg Treaty on 'own resources', which modified both the Rome and the Merger Treaties, was agreed in 1970. Thinking on union was entrusted to two subcommittees under Davignon and Werner. The former led rapidly to the establishment of 'European Political Cooperation', whereas the latter's proposal of economic and monetary union by 1980 was never attempted.

q.v. European Political Cooperation pp. 344–55.

Enlargement did lead to a new treaty which, in turn, slightly modified the existing Treaties. Article 1 of the 1972 Treaty on Accession recognized the new member states after acceptance of conditions laid down in a special Act attached. The other two Articles provided for ratification procedures, allowing for it to become operative even if all applicants did not ratify. The Act specified the status of the new members and listed amendments to the Treaties and other Acts regulating the Community and finished by providing measures both for transition and implementation. This too was accompanied by a number of Protocols and Declarations. The 1979 Greek Accession Treaty was to take much the same form.

The enlarging Community looked forward to further development, and the 1972 Paris Summit thus endorsed the Hague ideas. The EC was then blown off course by the economic crises of the 1970s and the problems raised by British accession. However, in 1974 there was agreement on enhancing the status of the European Parliament, regular meetings of Heads of Government (nicknamed 'Summits' and later 'European Councils'), and the drawing-up of a report on Political Union by Leo Tindemans of Belgium. Despite some unease, a second budgetary treaty, strengthening parliamentary control, was agreed in 1975. Yet, with the European Councils strengthening intergovernmentalism, Tindemans' incremental proposals were not acted on. It took five years to bring in direct, universal suffrage, elections to the Parliament, partly due to British reticence.

While these, and the creation of the European Monetary System in the same year, gave hope to the supporters of integration, the Community was unhappy and ineffective in the 1970s and early 1980s. Arguments over budgetary contributions, the Common Agricultural Policy (CAP) and responses to the oil crises were at the root of this 'Eurosclerosis'. This also made it hard to respond to the desire of the Iberian countries to join the Community. None of this did much for its image.

The relaunch and the SEA

Many in the Community were unhappy about such disarray. Hence in 1979 'Three Wise Men' were invited to consider more effective operation. More significantly, in 1981 the French called for a 'relaunching' of the Community, and this was supported by the German—Italian Genscher—Colombo initiative. This called for a public political commitment rapidly to move to a more active and more accountable Community. The EC institutions were also pushing for change, the Commission for more effective decision-making, using the Community method, and the EP for a new and more federal constitution. The latter was to result in the 1984 EP Draft European Union Treaty. This was a short document envisaging the transition to a European Union, largely modelled on the Community but allowing decisions to be taken by cooperation or common action. Under it the Council of Ministers would have seen its role change, to the benefit of the EP to which the Commission would be responsible. New civic rights were also envisaged. The Treaty would have come into operation once states containing two-thirds of the EC's population accepted it.

Although this was never accepted, such pressures did tell on the national governments. Hence, in 1983 they responded to the Genscher—Colombo initiative by issuing a 'Solemn Declaration on Union'. This offered a new impetus to integration and a clarification of the role of the European Council. So, once the long wrangle over the British budgetary problem was resolved, as it finally was at Fontainbleau in 1984, the way opened for more decisive action. Two committees were set up to look at a People's Europe and institutional changes. The latter, chaired by Senator James Dooge of Ireland, had a difficult life but reported largely in favour of strengthening the Commission, enhancing the role of the EP, limiting the use of unanimous voting in the Council and regularizing the role of the European Council. With Franco-German support this led the 1985 Milan Council to take a majority vote to set up an intergovernmental conference to look at foreign policy, decision-making and Treaty amendments.

The Luxembourg Presidency then steered this through to the next Summit, encouraging even unwilling governments to put forward their ideas alongside those of the Commission. Because there were so many changes, it was agreed to group them together into a single document. Progress was possible because the decision to complete the Internal Market, taken in March 1985, was increasingly seen as needing such constitutional underpinning. Firm proposals were made to the December Summit and largely approved there, though the final details were not concluded and signed until the New Year. Both this and ratification were problematic because of the need to hold referenda in Denmark and Ireland.

None the less the SEA came into effect in the summer of 1987. It was a relatively short Treaty with 30 Articles divided into four Titles. The first set out the objectives and organization of the Treaty. The second, which covered Articles 4–29, amended the three Treaties. This included 18 amendments to the Rome Treaty bringing about a cooperation procedure involving the EP, a new Court of First Instance, more qualified majority voting, the timetable for the completion of the Internal Market, and new policy areas. As well as the Internal Market these included monetary cooperation, social policies, cohesion, research and development, and the environment. The third Title created an enhanced, but still separate, form of foreign policy cooperation (EPC), while the last Title provided for ratification and implementation. A number of Declarations were attached to the Treaty.

q.v. Annex
pp. 526–7.

Although reactions to the SEA were initially reserved and often sceptical, in practice it worked surprisingly well. Nonetheless some supporters of European Union still felt it had not gone far enough and was merely a tidying up of existing practices. So pressures for further change continued. Nonetheless the SEA, along with enlargement and the Internal Market programme, certainly gave the Community back its dynamism. It also drew other western countries into its orbit through the negotiations with the EFTA countries on the European Economic Area (EEA).

From Berlin to Maastricht

Following this re-establishment of momentum, events conspired to create further pressures for constitutional change inside the Community. There were five reasons for this. Firstly, the SEA did have an in-built dynamic. The way it worked encouraged people to think of developing it. Moreover many, including some governments, still felt it had not measured up to their ideals of an integrated and democratic Community. As awareness of how much more the Community was doing and how little parliamentary control there actually was, support for further democratization developed.

A related factor was that the Internal Market also seemed to need complementing with social and monetary measures. This led to the Social Charter. Before this, in 1988, the Twelve had set up a Committee under Jacques Delors to investigate the possibilities of moving towards monetary union. As will be seen, despite British unease, in the spring of 1989 this reported in favour of a three-stage timetable. Finally, the Strasbourg Council at the end of that year agreed to convene an Intergovernmental Conference (IGC) to produce the requisite

Treaty amendments to give effect to all this.

By then the Soviet Empire in Eastern Europe was beginning to unravel. This was to have a profound effect on thinking about integration. Thus a third factor was the growing belief that in order to respond to the needs of the former satellites the Community would have to become more effective and more democratic. The possible need for reform had already been noted in Article 30(12) of the SEA. This required the member states to re-examine the requirements of EPC during the early 1990s. The actual case for consolidation was argued first by the European Parliament in the autumn of 1989, and then by Delors and some member state governments in the spring of 1990. The idea also attracted the support of those who had been disappointed by the timidity of the SEA.

Two final pressures came from the international domain. Thus the unification of Germany in 1990 changed the balance of power inside the Community. Old fears of Germany were reawakened and many people saw the reinforcing of Community links as the best way of dealing with the problem. In essence, the central concern was to establish a European Germany, not a German Europe. Finally, the replacing of the Cold War by new ethnic and economic conflicts in the Gulf and southeastern Europe showed up the weaknesses in the diplomatic effectiveness of the Community.

The last two factors came together in the Kohl−Mitterrand initiative of April 1990 which called for a strengthening of the democratic legitimacy and coherence of the EC, notably in economic, political and security matters. The two Dublin conferences of 1990 endorsed this idea by agreeing to call a second IGC on Political Union. Foreign Ministers suggested that this should look at the scope of a European Union, political accountability, effectiveness and the coherence of international action. It was to meet alongside that on Economic and Monetary Union (EMU) which was brought forward. Both IGCs began to meet, normally separately, from December 1990 after the Rome Summit pushed ahead, despite British reservations about the agenda. They involved relevant ministers and advisers from the member states and met frequently right up until December 1991, sometimes in special 'retreats'.

Although member states, political groups and other lobbies all made their views known, the basis for both negotiations also derived in part from draft proposals put forward by the Commission. As far as economic and monetary union was concerned these were the conclusions of the so-called Delors' Report and the Draft Statute of the European System of Central Banks and the European Central Bank published in April 1989. These confirmed a three-stage approach to economic and monetary union culminating in the establishment of a single currency, the setting up of a European central bank, and the transfer of full economic and monetary competencies to the EC.

The proposals for political union, initially set out in a Commission Memorandum of October 1990, aimed primarily at providing the Community with a higher international profile through the establishment of a common foreign policy (including security and defence); extending the competencies of the EC; increasing the democratic legitimacy of the Community's institutions and decision-making processes; and establishing closer links with the people of Europe through the concepts of European citizenship and subsidiarity. This was supported both by the European and Italian Parliaments and the Belgian and Greek governments.

It soon became clear that few, if any, member states accepted the Commission proposals in their entirety. Divisions existed over the extent to which a common foreign policy should be extended to security and defence matters; over the extent to which the powers of the European Parliament should be increased; over the extension of qualified majority voting within the Council of Ministers; and over extending the competencies of the EC. On EMU, differences, albeit of a more technical nature, also emerged, primarily over the content of Stage II and the economic convergence criteria for moving towards a single currency.

Despite the clear differences which existed the Luxembourg Presidency, in April 1991, presented a 95-page 'non-paper' draft treaty. Although this was sharply criticized by the Commission and the EP, it won the grudging assent of most member states. Hence it opened the way for detailed bargaining. As a result of this a formal draft treaty on Political Union was tabled by the Luxembourg Presidency on 20 June.

This established the structure found in the final version. It was based on what were called 'pillars'. This meant, as will be seen, that some forms of integration would go on outside the main Community framework. Other elements were to be left to more intergovernmental cooperation, including through closer links with the WEU and developing the existing 'Trevi' mechanism of informal intergovernmental police cooperation. However, many changes in detail were to be introduced, in the idea of a federal aim for the Union, in policies (especially where EMU was concerned), and in the structure of the section on a common foreign and security policy.

Divisions between the member states meant that the Luxembourg Presidency was unable to conclude the IGCs before its term of office expired at the end of June 1991. Consequently, it was left to the Dutch Presidency to bring about agreement in the negotiations before the end of the year. However, the whole IGC process was almost put in jeopardy when, after a long silence over the summer, the Dutch government presented its own draft Treaty on 24 September 1991. The draft, which played down the concept of a Union but insisted on a single institutional structure, annoyed both member states and the EP. The Dutch were forced to withdraw it and revert to the Luxembourg draft. New versions were provided in late October and mid-November but these still gave rise to furious debate over federalism and other topics.

By then December had arrived and time was running out. Both the Commission and the Parliament were getting increasingly unhappy about the process. Despite these hiccups, the tortuous negotiations carried on although many questions were left unanswered until the Summit itself. Arguments on cohesion funds, commission powers, federalism, immigration, industrial policy, security, and social action continued until the Community leaders convened. Yet, despite fears that the British might not accept the emerging package, the European Council meeting at Maastricht on 9−10 December did reach agreement on a Treaty on European Union. However, this was only possible after long hours of negotiations and once significant 'opt-outs' on economic and monetary union and social policy had been granted to the United Kingdom. The founding document of the Union was therefore very much a reflection of the balance of force amongst the governments involved at the end of 1991.

It then remained to tidy up the agreements into a single treaty compatible with the existing versions. Article B thus had to be brought into line with J4(1). The Preamble was then added, along with Article 138a on the role of political parties in the Union, and Declaration 33. This process also involved two further conferences to amend the ECSC and Euratom treaties. The former did not take up the possibility, canvassed by the Commission early in 1991, of adding ECSC Articles to the Treaty of Rome, prior to the expiry of the ECSC Treaty in 2002 (subdivision VI).

q.v. Declaration 33 p. 441.

q.v. ECSC pp. 359–66.

The agreed and consolidated draft was then signed on 7 February 1992, again at Maastricht. A final addition was to be made in May 1992 as will be seen below. The Treaty was formally published by Brussels in the spring with the HMSO version appearing a little later. Nonetheless, a further stage along the road to closer integration had then been taken, thanks to the pressures which had always been there, and which had been reinforced by events after 1989.

However, this was far from being the end of the story. Both before and after the signing, other exogenous factors intervened. Life, as the saying goes, is what happens when you are making other plans! This was especially true of economic developments.

FURTHER READING

OFFICIAL TEXTS

The earlier treaties can be conveniently found in: *European Community Treaties*, 4th edn, Sweet & Maxwell, London, 1980; Rudden, B. and Wyatt, D., *Basic Community Laws*, 3rd edn, Clarendon Press, Oxford, 1986 or the EC *Treaties Establishing the EC*, OOPEC, Luxembourg, 1987, and *Documents Concerning Accessions to the EC II*, OOPEC, Luxembourg, 1987. See also *The Convoluted Treaties II*, Nelson & Pollard, Oxford, 1992. The Maastricht document appears both as *Treaty on European Union*, OOPEC, Luxembourg, 1992, and as *Treaty on European Union*, Cm 1934, HMSO, London, 1992. For the various drafts which prepared the way for the final version reference may be made to *Europe: Agence Presse Internationale* for 1991, e.g. special numbers 1722/3, 5 July 1991; 1733/4, 3 October 1991; 1746/7, 20 November 1991; and to European Parliament *1993 The New Treaties: European Parliament proposals*, OOPEC, Luxembourg, 1991.

SECONDARY WORKS

Arter, D., *The Politics of European Integration in the Twentieth Century*, Dartmouth, Aldershot, 1993.

Artis, M., 'The Maastricht road to monetary union', *Journal of Common Market Studies*, Vol. 30, no. 3, 1992, pp. 299–309.

Bogdanor, V., 'The June 1989 elections and the institutions of the EC', *Government and Opposition*, Vol. 24, no. 2, 1989, pp. 199–214.

Brivati, B. and Jones, H., *Reconstruction to Integration*, Leicester University Press, Leicester, 1993.

Church C.H. and Keogh, D. (eds.) *The Single European Act: A transnational study*, Erasmus Consortium, University College Cork, 1991.

Corbett, R. 'The Intergovernmental Conference on Political Union', *Journal of Common Market Studies*, Vol. 30, no. 3, 1992, pp. 279–98.

EC, *The Single European Act*, Supplement to Bulletin of the EC, 2/86.

George, S., *Britain and European Integration since 1945*, Blackwell, Oxford, 1991.

Hartley, A., 'Maastricht's problematical future', *The World Today*, Vol. 48, no. 10, 1992, pp. 179–82.

Heater, D., *The Idea of European Unity*, Pinter, London, 1992.

Laffan, B., *Integration and Co-operation in Europe*, Routledge, London, 1992.

Lane, P., *Europe since 1945: An introduction*, Batsford, London, 1985.

Laursen, F. and Vanhoonacker, S., *The Inter-governmental Conference on Political Union: Institutional Reform, New Policies and International Identity of the European Community*, Martinus Nijhoff, Dordrecht, 1992.

Lodge, J., 'The Single European Act: towards a new European dynamism?' *Journal of Common Market Studies*, Vol. 24, no. 3, 1986, pp. 203–24.

Lodge, J., 'Maastricht and Political Union', *European Access*, 1992/1, pp. 7–11.

Noël, E., 'The Single European Act', *Government and Opposition*, Vol. 24, no. 1, 1989, pp. 3–14.

Pinder, J., 'The Single Market: a step towards European Union', in Lodge, J. (ed.), *The European Community and the Challenge of the Future*, 2nd edn, Pinter, London. 1993, pp. 51–68.

Schermers, H. *et al.* 'The European Community', *Common Market Law Review*, Vol. 25, no. 3, 1988, pp. 541–616.

Stein, G., 'Lawyers, judges and the making of a transnational constitution', *American Journal of International Law*, Vol. 75, no. 1, 1981, pp. 1–27.

Urwin, D.W., *Western Europe since 1945: A political history*, 4th edn, Longman, London, 1989.

Urwin, D.W., *The Community of Europe: A history of European integration since 1945*, Longman, London, 1991.

Vaughan, R., *Twentieth Century Europe*, Croom Helm, London, 1979.

Wallace, H., 'Political reform in the European Community', *The World Today*, Vol. 47, no. 1, 1991, pp. 1–3.

Wallace, W., *The Transformation of Western Europe*, Pinter, London, 1990.

Wegs, J.R., *Europe since 1945: A concise history*, 3rd edn, St Martin's, London, 1991.

Williamson, D. *et al.* 'The Delors I package', *Common Market Law Review*, Vol. 13, no. 3, 1988, pp. 479–539.

ii. The evolution of the European economy

The second and related factor affecting the move to closer union at Maastricht was the way the Community economy and thinking about the implications of the Single Market evolved in the 1980s. By the mid-1980s, following a decade of slow economic growth if not recession, Europe was witnessing a return to economic stability and prosperity. At the same time the European Monetary System (EMS) was contributing to bringing about a convergence in the performance of the European economies. On the basis of this and the belief that a single currency was the natural complement to the Single Market, it was felt that the Community should proceed towards establishing an Economic and Monetary Union (EMU). Hence the idea of an intergovernmental conference and the inclusion in the TEU of provisions aimed at creating EMU and a single European currency. However, since the negotiations which led to Maastricht, much of Europe has seen the economic stability of 1985, give way first to slower growth and then to a new recession. The effect this will have on the process of European integration remains to be seen but the early signs were not encouraging.

Convergence in the 1980s

A fundamental factor in pushing the European Community down the road towards Maastricht was the degree to which the majority of European economies converged in the 1980s. Such convergence was evident not only in the policy objectives pursued by governments, but also in the levels of economic performance achieved. These developments were welcomed by the supporters of European Union since most accepted that economic convergence was necessary if the Community were to proceed towards EMU. As Figure 3 shows, this was

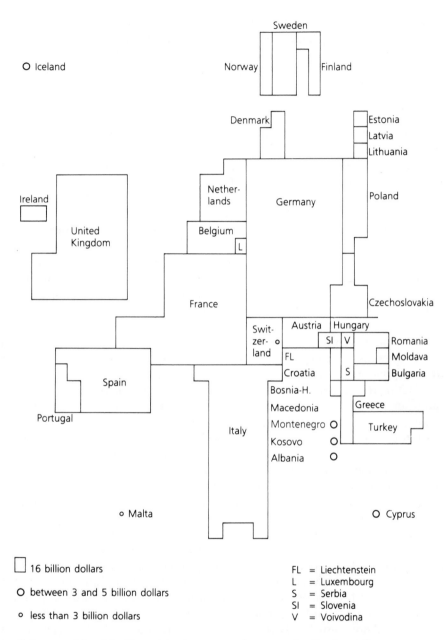

Figure 3. The economic strength of Europe (Source: European Free Trade Association. This map does *not* imply any political recognition of geographic entities mentioned therein.)

☐ 16 billion dollars

O between 3 and 5 billion dollars

∘ less than 3 billion dollars

FL = Liechtenstein
L = Luxembourg
S = Serbia
SI = Slovenia
V = Voivodina

needed because of the considerable disparities in economic strength. On the policy front, there was general agreement among governments that economic growth was dependent on low inflation and exchange-rate stability.

Consequently, although the low inflation policies adopted by governments increased already high levels of unemployment, the average level of inflation in Europe dropped from 13.5 per cent in 1980 to 5.9 per cent by 1985. Countries which were members of the Exchange Rate Mechanism (ERM) of the EMS fared particularly well. The original members of the ERM were Germany, France, Italy, Netherlands, Belgium, Luxembourg, Denmark and Ireland. Spain joined in June 1989, the United Kingdom in October 1990, and Portugal in April 1992, leaving only Greece still outside. By 1986 the average rate of inflation in these countries had fallen to below 3 per cent. Inflation in Italy, for example, fell, according to the OECD (Organization for Economic Cooperation and Development), from 21.2 per cent in 1980 to 4.7 per cent by 1987. This success was accompanied by increasing exchange-rate stability as the majority of member states accepted the disciplines of the ERM and agreed to maintain the level of their currencies. Although realignments were necessary during the period from when the EMS was set up in 1979 until January 1987, after this date only the move of the Italian lira from the wide to the narrow band in January 1990 caused any further realignments prior to the signing of the TEU.

The convergence in economic performance levels among EC member states in the 1980s was equally encouraging. Those countries which participated in the ERM experienced stabilizing prices and in several cases the narrowing of budget deficits. On average, the general government borrowing requirements of ERM participants were reduced from 5.5 per cent of GDP (Gross Domestic Product) in 1982 to 2.9 per cent by 1989. In addition, real unit labour costs in these countries declined thus improving investment profitability. However, excessive budget deficits in Belgium and Ireland prevented these countries from sharing in the economic convergence experienced by Germany, France, Denmark and the Netherlands to the same extent.

Of the remaining EC member states, Italy and Spain were also making significant economic progress during the second half of the 1980s although they showed much less favourable convergence positions. Inflation, although falling, was almost double the level of the group of countries mentioned above. Similarly unit labour costs were noticeably higher. Nevertheless, the commitment of both countries to reduce inflation and increase exchange-rate stability saw them draw closer to the core countries in the EMS. Spain joined the wider band of the ERM in June 1989, and in January 1990 Italy agreed to maintain the level of the lira within the limits of the Mechanism's narrow band. A similar commitment to the disciplines of the ERM was made by Portugal which, having reduced its high level of inflation, eventually joined the wider band in April 1992.

Meanwhile the United Kingdom, although enjoying relatively rapid economic growth after 1985, refused to join the ERM in either band until October 1990, and then more for reasons of political expediency than economic prudence. Essentially, despite the economic growth experienced prior to 1990, the UK economy did not enjoy levels of inflation and wage costs which suggested it was in any way converging with the economies of its European partners. Inflation at the turn of the decade was about double the average of the core ERM countries and increases in wage costs were in excess of 10 per cent. Similarly, the Greek economy was experiencing serious problems with inflation at 20 per cent in 1990 and public debt the equivalent of 90 per cent of GDP. As a result Greece decided that it could not take any part in the ERM.

Therefore, despite the economic problems experienced by some EC member states and a general but brief period of economic uncertainty which followed the stock market crashes of October 1987, the second half of the 1980s was none the less characterized by broad similarities in economic performance within the Community. This, and more particularly the success of the core ERM members in achieving greater convergence, encouraged many within the Community to push for further steps towards economic and monetary union.

Plans for EMU

The signing of the Single European Act opened up a new chapter for the Community with regard to economic and monetary union. For the first time the convergence of economic and monetary policies and the prospect of EMU were written into the EC's constitution. Indeed, provision was made for the Treaty of Rome to be revised to facilitate future developments in economic and monetary policies. In addition, the objective enshrined in the SEA of creating the Single Market, gave added impetus towards EMU since many regarded a single currency as the logical extension of such a project. As a result, and against the background of the ERM's perceived success in promoting economic convergence, as already noted, the Hanover European Council in June 1988 agreed to establish a Committee on Monetary Union, chaired by the Commission President, Jacques Delors, to draw up a plan for establishing full economic and monetary union.

The Committee's report, the so-called Delors' Report, was published in April 1989 and set out a three-stage approach to EMU. Stage I would involve all EC member states joining the ERM, while Stage II would see the gradual transfer of monetary competences to the EC and the creation of a European Central Bank. The final stage would involve setting irrevocably fixed exchange rates and the subsequent creation of a single currency and the transfer of full economic and monetary competences to the EC. Having received the report at its Madrid meeting in June 1989, the European Council agreed that revisions to the Treaty of Rome would have to be made to facilitate further progress to EMU. The decision thus taken to proceed towards EMU was soon reinforced by the revolutionary events of 1989 and the subsequent inevitability of German unification. French desires to see the new expanded Germany firmly secured economically and politically in the EC increased the political attraction of EMU. As a result, at the Dublin European Council in June 1990, it was agreed that an intergovernmental conference be convened to establish the necessary changes to the Treaty of Rome required for the Community to proceed towards EMU. The IGC duly began its work in December 1990, working initially on proposals from the Commission based on the recommendations of the Delors' Report.

The agreement on EMU reached in Maastricht in December 1991, and enshrined in the TEU, lays down a three-stage timetable for the creation of a single currency and the transfer of economic and monetary competences to the EC. More importantly from the point of view of the economies of the member states, the TEU also establishes a set of convergence criteria countries must satisfy if they are to proceed to the third stage and full economic and monetary union.

The five criteria require that the rate of inflation in the member state concerned be no more than 1.5 per cent of the average of the lowest three rates in the EMS; that its long-term interest rate be no more than 2 per cent above the lowest three rates in the EC; that the budget deficit be no larger than 3 per cent of GDP; that its national debt not exceed 60 per cent of GDP; and that the member state be a member of the narrow band of the ERM for at least two years without realignment. If during 1996 the European Council agrees that a majority of EC countries meet these criteria, the Council may then set a date for EMU to become operational. If this is not done (see below footnote 58 on p. 157), EMU will come into effect on 1 January 1999, irrespective of the number of countries satisfying the criteria.

With the convergence criteria for EMU now established, most national governments turned their attention towards meeting them. However, since the criteria were first set, the likelihood of member states meeting them has been reduced, in some instances significantly. This has been due mainly to the economic slowdown Europe has experienced since the turn of the decade. The fact that Britain and Italy were forced to leave the ERM in the autumn of 1992 added to the problems.

Economic slowdown at the turn of the decade

For most European countries the economic stability and prosperity of the late 1980s had come to end by 1991. Growth in GDP had often dropped to half that of 1990 and was still declining. In addition, demand was falling, forcing levels of industrial production to decline in all major European countries. On top of all this, unemployment was once again on the rise. Many countries appeared to be following the United Kingdom towards recession. This situation was made worse by economic difficulties in Germany, the economic motor of European growth in the 1980s and the dominant force within the ERM.

Although western Germany enjoyed a brief economic boom after the fall of the Berlin Wall, since 1990 its economy has been subjected to the increasing strains of unification. By 1992 the powerhouse of the European economy was running out of steam and serious doubts were being raised about its ability to meet the convergence criteria for EMU by the end of the decade. Similarly, concerns abounded that the German economy was about to enter into recession. Indeed, growth forecasts for 1993 were below 1 per cent, while those for production suggested a fall in output of 5 per cent.

The decline in the economic activity which accompanied this was compounded by the Bundesbank's policy aimed at reducing inflation to around 2 per cent. This kept interest-rate levels around 9–10 per cent thus discouraging investment and undermining confidence in the future of the economy. These high levels were exacerbated by the government's decision to keep to 1990 pre-election pledges and finance the unexpectedly high costs of unification by borrowing and not through taxation. The impact this had on the wider European economy was profound since high German interest rates had to be matched by other European countries if they wanted to maintain their currency's position in the ERM. Consequently, national governments throughout Europe found themselves unable to reduce interest rates in order to stimulate much needed economic growth.

The general economic slowdown which began to affect Europe in the early 1990s was to have profound effects on the Maastricht process. Negative economic growth undermined confidence in the European economy as a whole and led many people to question the Community's goal of increasing economic and monetary integration. Furthermore, while the Single Market project had promised economic growth, jobs and greater prosperity, the actual economic situation which people faced as 31 December 1992, the project's completion date, drew near increased already growing reservations about the merits of closer union within the EC, as well as the prospects for full economic and monetary union. The criteria set for the transition to Stage III, deemed by some, such as the German Bundesbank, as too liberal when they were agreed, were now becoming almost totally unrealistic. Such questions were to become an increasingly important theme in the ratification debate, threatening the permissive consensus on closer European integration on which political elites had counted.

q.v. ratification debate pp. 447–54.

FURTHER READING

Artis, M., 'The Maastricht Road to monetary union', *Journal of Common Market Studies*, Vol. 30, no. 3, 1992, pp. 299–309.

Barrell, R., *Macroeconomic Policy Coordination in Europe: The ERM and Monetary Union*, Sage, London, 1992.

Committee for the Study of EMU, *Report on Economic and Monetary Union in the European Community*, OOPEC, Luxembourg, 1989.

Crawford, M., *One Money for Europe? The Economies and Politics of Maastricht*, Macmillan, London, 1993.

Dyker, D. (ed.), *The National Economies of Europe*, Longman, London, 1992.

Dyker, D. (ed.), *The European Economy*, London, Longman, 1992.

EC Commission, *Economic and Monetary Union: Communication of the Commission of 21 August 1990*, OOPEC, Luxembourg, 1990.

Goni, E.Z., 'National budgeting for European convergence', *EIPAscope*, 199/1, pp. 4–6.

McDonald, F. and Dearden, S. (eds.), *European Economic Integration*, Longman, London, 1992.

OECD, *Economic Outlook*, no. 46, December 1989.

Thiel, E., 'From the Internal Market to an economic and monetary union', *Aussenpolitik*, Vol. 40, No. 1, 1989, pp. 66–75.

Thygesen, N., 'The Delors Report and European Economic and Monetary Union', *International Affairs*, Vol. 65, No. 4, 1989, pp. 637–52.

iii. Political trends in member states

The economic problems beginning to face Europe in 1991–2 were intimately linked to domestic politics. These had always had a significant effect on the evolution of the Community. For much of its history it had moved forward because such progress was in the national interest of most states. The citizens of member states had also been willing to accept this, there being, as has been said, a permissive consensus in favour of the Community. Such was the case in the mid-1980s when domestic politics ran relatively smoothly, giving rise to general agreement on Europe. The insertion of the Iberian countries, noted in Figure 4, did not disturb things.

Figure 4. The expansion of the Community

The Original Six

First enlargement to 9

Second enlargement to 10

Third enlargement to 12

This began to change towards the end of the decade as some governments decided to remodel their European policies because of post-Cold War pressures. Unfortunately they did so not just at a time when the European economy was sliding into a new crisis, but also when electorates were becoming increasingly dissatisfied politically. As a result popular reactions to Maastricht turned out to be more hostile than had been expected. The major reasons for such antagonism included not just the growing economic difficulties, but the related social pressures of the time, notably those deriving from migration and unemployment. Europe often provided opportunities for passing judgement on stale governments both inside and outside of the Community.

Equally, the hostility reflected the growing tendency of western electorates to question established politics, which were felt to be have performed poorly and to have been unresponsive to public needs and views. To some extent this was because politics had become so much more professional, and in a way, less representative than had previously been the case. The affluent society also provided far more diverting spectacles than those offered by politics. In any event, such views became more salient when Maastricht took integration into more sensitive areas than in the past.

In other words, the rather introverted world of Community affairs suffered because it was seen as another example of the structural gap between ordinary people and political and business elites. This did not produce any sweeping electoral change, at least in the run-up to Maastricht. However, it is clear that a political crisis was looming. As will be seen in the seventh sub-division of the *Handbook*, this was to explode during the ratification debate later in 1992.

Politics in the mid-1980s

The years of the European relaunch coincided with a period of economic revival and international stability. Thus the tensions generated by the New Freeze in East— West relations began to ease and, after 1985, relations with the East improved considerably. Domestically, the problems of terrorism and the conflicts arising from NATO's Dual Track policy also began to fade. And although there was increasing environmental concern, the overall tone of domestic politics was again set by right of centre forces. This showed itself in a variety of ways and varied as between countries.

In many northern Community states electorates turned increasingly to centre right parties, and left of centre parties often found the going very hard. This was true in Britain, where the Labour Party was humiliated electorally in 1983 and 1987, forcing it to rethink its strategy. Equally in Germany the Social Democratic party (SPD) was unable to profit from a slight decline in support for the Christian Democratic Union and its allies (CDU/CSU). In Denmark the Social Democrats lost votes consistently from 1979 to 1988 while, in the Netherlands, the Christian Democratic Appeal (CDA) held its own against an improving Labour party. France was at first an exception to the rule although in 1986 and 1988 the right-wing parties, the Rally for the Republic (RPR) and the Union for French Democracy (UDF), somewhat outpolled the *Parti Socialiste* (PS). Spanish and Greek socialists also lost votes over the decade though they continued in office.

Government, as a result, was either in the hands of the centre right or of parties which tended to adopt not dissimilar policies. Britain clearly fell into this category while Germany, Denmark and the Netherlands had coalition governments of the centre/right. By 1987 they had been joined by the Portuguese Social Democrats and *Fianna Fáil* in Ireland, both being returned on platforms of economic and financial restraint. The more mixed coalitions in Belgium, under Wilfrid Maertens, and in Italy, again led by the Christian Democrats, also moved in much the same direction.

Socialist governments like those in Spain, and to a lesser, later and much more limited extent, Greece, also found themselves forced to adopt more orthodox economic policies. The French example was notable since the Mitterrand administration was forced, by the discipline of the ERM, to abandon its attempt to stimulate growth by higher wages, nationalization and public investment. By 1983 it was forced to do a 'U'-turn in economic policy so as to maintain the franc. Thus many countries saw policies of cuts in public spending (especially subsidies), deregulation, industrial restructuring, privatization and tax reform. Generally such policies were a limited corrective to the budgetary deficits and feather-bedding caused by responses to the oil crises. They were neither as extreme nor as ideological as the policies followed in Britain.

Changing stances on Europe

This, limited, political convergence played a significant part in the evolution of the Community in the 1980s. Awareness of the need for greater competitiveness in a still difficult international economy pushed many governments into accepting the Single Market and the other provisions of the SEA even if this did not exactly coincide with their basic political outlook in the way it did with that of the Conservative government in Britain. A wider, freer market in Europe fitted the Thatcherite agenda exactly and, though there were doubts about the social and political arrangements necessary to support it, the price was felt worth paying. Hence the SEA occasioned little debate in Britain.

In Germany too, where there was concern about the costs of the Community to the Federal Republic, there was a desire for progress on the Internal Market. This was coupled with support for an extension in the scope of Community policy, notably in foreign affairs. Like Italy, Germany was also committed to increasing the powers of the European Parliament. This reflected Italian awareness that their own system was both unrepresentative and unable to implement much-needed reforms. For this reason it was against the Italian government that the ECJ was to allow appeals by individuals against non-implementation of EC law in the *Francovich* judgment. Under the Socialists France was keen on European Union and went along with the Internal Market and SEA package. However, the conservative government of Jacques Chirac in 1986–8 was slightly more reticent.

q.v.
Francovich
judgment
p. 291.

A similar situation was to be found in Ireland where the SEA had been pushed by the keenly pro-European *Fine Gael*/Labour coalition. However, although it was challenged by the *Fianna Fáil* opposition, the new government succeeded in steering through a referendum on the SEA caused by a challenge to its effects on Irish neutrality. Equally the Danish government — traditionally very cautious about further integration — successfully called a referendum to outflank opposition to the environmental and political implications of the Act. Of the other small states, Greece was in favour of the Community because it provided so much financial aid.

The Benelux powers were strongly supportive of further integration and rather regretted that the SEA had not gone further. The Belgians even saw Europe as a means of helping to hold their linguistically divided nation together. Spain and, to a slightly lesser extent, Portugal were also strong supporters of integration. Both looked to a stronger Community to support them in their transition away from authoritarianism and underdevelopment.

While the supporters of further integration did not immediately push for further change, this altered within a couple of years. The way the SEA worked encouraged the European Parliament to do so, while a referendum in June 1989 mandated the Italian government to campaign for further reform. Europe was also a key theme of Mitterrand's successful electoral campaigns in France in 1988. And, as has been noted, the belief that the Single Market needed financial, monetary and social underpinning encouraged further exploration of deeper union.

Pressure for such deepening was greatly encouraged by events in 1989. The rapid collapse of Soviet power in the former satellites had immediate effects on the Community. Not merely did it mean expanding the PHARE aid programme, which the Commission was administering for the G-24 group of industrialized countries but a special Summit was held in Paris in November 1989 to discuss events in the East. Subsequent European Councils also focused on relations with Eastern Europe. The Community continued to be a significant actor in the Conference on Security and Cooperation in Europe (CSCE) process, leading to the 1990 Paris Charter on peaceful relations in Europe.

While allowing the former satellites to draw closer was generally accepted in member states, there were differences of emphasis. France and the Iberian countries were thus rather reluctant to open their markets to the new democracies. As a result negotiation of improved trade and association deals with countries like Hungary and Poland proved quite difficult. There were also political debates about whether deepening the Community ought not to take precedence over widening it, not just to the East but also to the EFTA countries. Divergences were equally visible when it came to German unification. Margaret Thatcher in particular was hostile to this.

On the other hand France, initially even more cautious, was later willing to go along with rapid unification. This was to be a turning point. The French began to push for EMU, a restructuring of the EC which would strengthen Heads of State and Government, and help to control an 'over-mighty' Germany. Indeed President François Mitterrand adopted a conscious policy of drawing closer to Germany. In April 1990, in order to show gratitude and the continuing European bona fides of the united Germany, Chancellor Helmut Kohl joined him in successfully urging the EC to bring forward the IGC on EMU and to supplement it with a parallel conference on political union. The underlying aims of their initiative were to ensure that the Community would become more effective in dealing with the East and that Germany was firmly rooted in a more integrated Europe. By 'Europeanizing' Germany in this way, fears of German economic domination or actual expansionism could be limited.

Thus the pace of European unification was stepped up because it served the political ends of some key states. It was also supported by Italy and governments in some of the smaller states, although the Dutch were uneasy over the impact on NATO of a Franco-German mixed brigade. However, the Belgians gave the integration process a distinct shove by their March 1990 letter. Greek economic problems left the New Democracy government very dependent on Community aid. The Iberians continued to support the idea of European Union. Even the Danish government seemed to mellow, urging the EFTA countries to join the Community.

Only Britain differed, especially after Margaret Thatcher's abrupt change of tone and style after 1988, symbolized by the Bruges speech. Hence at the time that the eleven were deciding to move farther and faster, Britain was resisting the Social Charter and urging various alternatives to a single currency. Even though this changed somewhat with the pound's entry to the ERM and the election of John Major as Margaret Thatcher's successor, the Tory government continued to hold aloof because of its very different philosophies on sovereignty and economic policy. Nonetheless, the general consensus amongst governments was that integration had to be pushed forward. It was this belief which carried things forward to Maastricht.

Changes on the domestic scene

What was not realized at the time was that these developments were taking place simultaneously with changes in the general economic and political state of Europe. This was to produce an unexpected deviation in political attitudes during 1992. The continent was, in fact, entering a period of uncertainty. There were five main reasons for this.

To begin with, as has been seen, at the turn of the decade the United Kingdom began to lead Europe into a new recession, deriving from the impact of an internationalized economy and the mistakes made in responding to the stock market crisis of 1987. This was worsened by the way that membership of the ERM tied struggling economies to the higher interest and exchange rates inflicted on Germany, Europe's economic powerhouse, by the enormous costs of German unification. This dented confidence in the economic future, including EMU.

These costs began, secondly, to push up interest and unemployment rates, adding to government welfare costs and also to social tensions. This affected even those countries which had been able to ride out the unemployment of the 1970s. A property crisis also produced growing homelessness and massive problems of debt. Problems with falling birth rates, family structures, drugs and AIDS all added to social unease.

A third, related, consideration was that many people became increasingly worried about immigration into the West. This had greatly increased as the boom of the 1980s had attracted large numbers of migrants from the increasingly economically unsuccessful countries of south-eastern Europe, North Africa and elsewhere in the Third World. Governments were often felt to be too lax in dealing with this threat to cultural identity and security. So extreme right forces began to profit from such worries in a much more striking way than previously.

Furthermore, dealing with such problems would have been difficult for governments in any circumstances. In practice things were even harder because they were already being sanctioned by electorates dissatisfied both with their performance and with their remoteness. The elections to the European Parliament in 1989 were notable for the way that all parties in power, whether of the left or the right, lost votes. Similar trends were also visible in ordinary national elections. Parties which had been in power for a long time, were felt to have grown stale, and this weakened their ability to take decisive action.

This was part of a final problem, the emerging moroseness towards political elites, a trend called *Politikverdrossenheit* in Germany and, for many, symbolized by the Perot candidature in the United States. Because of the political trends already noted, established parties were often seen as cynical, dishonest and prone to put their own and sectional interests above those of the electorate. And if parties have become 'enterprises in search of power', state machines were felt too bureaucratic and distant, especially from regions in need. Consequently people increasingly voted against governments rather than for opposition parties. However, small formations both on the alternative/Green Left and on the far Right did benefit from this. This meant less identification with parties and increasing willingness to switch votes between elections. People were also willing to vote in new ways, in line with individual self-interest. Paradoxical results could follow as people might favour more government action but not the taxes needed to pay for them.

Thus there was no clear change in political complexion, although there was something of a retreat from narrow fiscal orthodoxy in the face of recession. In the Netherlands the CDA won the 1989 election and decided to form a coalition with Labour rather than their erstwhile Liberal allies. Yet if left of centre opposition parties in Germany and Britain saw their standing in the polls rise they were unable to capitalize on this in elections. Equally the Danish Social Democrats re-established their electoral base in 1990 but remained in opposition partly because not all the governing parties did better than others. Even the collapse of Communist parties did not really help the left. The French Socialist Party suffered major erosion of its support in local elections even though the orthodox centre and right have not been able to capitalize on this. Much the same was true in Spain where the continuing weakness of the centre right enabled the Spanish Socialist Workers Party (PSOE) to ride out its losses.

Similarly conservative governments found the going hard. *Fianna Fáil* discovered in 1989 that it could not govern without the centrist Progressive Democrats, New Democracy in Greece came under increasing pressure because of its austerity policies. In Germany the CDU failed to capitalize on its general-election success in 1990. Then, in 1991, virtually all parties involved in the Maertens government lost ground in Belgium. Even more strikingly the parties in the Italian coalition suffered heavy losses in the April 1992 elections, at which the populist regional *Leghe* won nearly 10 per cent of the vote. They went on to record up to 30 per cent in local elections.

Apart perhaps from Portugal, most governments in the Community had weakened and were under pressure by the early 1990s. In other words they were already at odds with their electorates even before Maastricht opened up a range of issues which inflamed exactly those sensibilities which governments and elites had already offended. While this political moroseness did not always lead to anti-European sentiments, it is clear that some elements of public opinion saw Maastricht as another example of elites going their own way. It also says something about the increasing interaction of domestic and European issues, especially as integration had begun to move into more sensitive areas such as citizenship, control and currency.

So, as will be seen, once the shouting over the signing of Maastricht died down, these underlying trends were to make themselves felt. The powerful and volatile domestic feelings need to be borne in mind in assessing the Treaty and its precise contents. This is partly because they affected the rocky road to ratification. Even more so it is because they helped to shape the way that the Treaty itself came to be interpreted and understood.

FURTHER READING

Adam-Schwatzer, I., 'Germany, France and European Integration', *Studia Diplomatica*, Vol. 41, No. 1, 1988, pp. 37–44.

Cafruny, A.W. and Rosenthal, G.G., *The State of the European Community: Maastricht and beyond*, Longman, London, 1993.

Church C.H. and Keogh D. (eds.) *The Single European Act: A transnational study*, Erasmus Consortium, University College Cork, 1991.

Dorfman, G.A. and Duignan, P., *Politics in Western Europe*, 2nd edn, Hoover Institution Press, Stanford, 1992.

Fry E. and Raymond G., *The Other Western Europe: A political analysis of the smaller democracies*, ABC-Clio, Santa Barbara, 1983.

George, S., *An Awkward Partner: Britain in the EC*, Oxford University Press, Oxford, 1990.

Goodman, S.F., *The European Community*, 2nd edn, Macmillan, London, 1993.

Griffiths, A., *European Community Survey: The European Community*, Longman, London, 1992.

Hancock M., *et al. Politics in Western Europe*, Macmillan, London, 1992.

Haywood, E., 'The European Policy of François Mitterrand', *Journal of Common Market Studies*, Vol. 31, No. 2, 1993, pp. 269–82.

Hendriks, G.E., 'West Germany's role in the EC', *European Access*, 1990/2, pp. 10–12.

Hine, D., *Governing Italy: The politics of bargained pluralism*, Oxford University Press, Oxford, 1993.

Kielinger, T., 'Waking up with a headache', *International Affairs*, Vol. 66, No. 2, 1990, pp.

249–63.

Koole, R. and Mair, P., (eds.) 'Political data handbook 1992', *European Journal of Political Research*, Vol. 22, No. 4, 1992.

Laffan, B., *Integration and Co-operation in Europe*, Routledge, London, 1992.

Peters, B.G., *European Politics Reconsidered*, Holmes and Meier, London, 1990.

Peterson K.S., 'Denmark and 1992: Why the Danes "drag their feet"', *European Access*, 1990/2, pp. 15–16.

Rehfelt, U., 'France' in Seers, D. and Vaitsos, C. (eds.), *Integration and Unequal Development: The experience of the EEC*, Macmillan, London, 1980, pp. 135–75.

Schweitzer, C.C. and Karsten, D., *Federal Republic of Germany and EC Membership Evaluated*, Pinter, London, 1990.

Sharp, P., *Irish Foreign Policy and the European Community*, Dartmouth, Aldershot, 1990.

Smith, G., *West European Politics*, 5th edition, Heinemann, London, 1989.

Stevens, A., *The Government and Politics of France*, Macmillan, London, 1992.

Turner, B. and Nordquist, G., *The Other European Community*, Weidenfeld and Nicolson, London, 1982.

Western Europe 1994, Europa Publications, London, 1993.

Williams, A. (ed.), *Southern Europe Transformed: Political and economic change in Greece, Italy, Portugal and Spain*, Harper and Row, London, 1984.

II. The Union Treaty A:
General Axioms

Even when seen against the background of recent trends in European economics and politics, the Treaty on European Union remains a complex and difficult document, especially for one intended to serve as the constitution of an altered and possibly enlarged European entity. This is not just a matter of the 'turgid Eurospeak' in which it is written, a style which defies interpretation according to Schmitter. Other difficulties emerge at the very start of the Treaty since its opening sections encapsulate many of the key elements of the overall Maastricht Agreements. In other words, many of the general axioms of the settlement are to be found here. However, before analysing these it is necessary to consider three things: the overall structure of the Treaty; the nature of the Union it is expected to define and serve; and the often politically motivated ways in which people have so far appraised and interpreted the Treaty.

This subdivision of the *Handbook* therefore starts with these preliminary considerations. It then goes on to comment upon and to print the first, general, sections of the Treaty, beginning with all the Preambles relevant to the Union. These lead directly into the Common Provisions of the TEU which are the kernel of the new entity. The subdivision also highlights a number of innovations and policy developments which arise. One of the key innovations here is the new role given to the European Council and this calls for special comment.

The TEU also involved large-scale changes to the existing Treaty of Rome (as amended by the Single European Act). So the revised Principles of the Treaty of Rome are set out and examined. They involve two more major innovations: subsidiarity and citizenship. The idea of subsidiarity has become increasingly central both to the ratification process and to the way that the TEU is likely to be operated. Hence it too demands detailed attention. Equally, the addition of Union citizenship is another major, and controversial, difference between the Community and the Union, which also needs to be thought about carefully. This is especially so since citizenship relates both to the democratic legitimacy of the Union and to the evolution of policies on a 'People's Europe'.

As already suggested, these first sections although relatively short, are extremely significant. The opening elements of such Treaties as the TEU are not just scene-setting. They establish the context, justifications and objectives of the European Community and Union. They also define the nature of these bodies and set out the mechanisms, processes, institutions, timetables and principles by which they are to work. Hence they sum up the very essence of the enterprise and raise fundamental questions both for students and for the public at large. It is hardly surprising that they have been at the heart of post-Maastricht debates.

The structure of the Treaty

The fact that the initial sections of the Treaty are so significant is partly a reflection of the structure traditionally adopted by continental treaties. As Box 3 shows, the TEU starts with a Preamble which sets out what the signatories believed they were doing in signing the Treaty. These are then followed by seven Titles or divisions. This structure was implicit in the drafts used in negotiating the TEU, up to and including Maastricht. However, the actual use of specific Title numbers only began with the consolidation of the two draft Treaties on EMU and EPU.

In using this particular structural approach the TEU follows the ECSC, EAEC (European Atomic Energy Community) and SEA Treaties, all of which have Titles as their primary division. The Treaty of Rome, on the other hand, uses Parts as its main division with Titles as the next subdivision down. In both cases Titles can be divided into Chapters and these, in turn, into Sections. The SEA, like the Accession Treaties, follows this model although it also further divides some Sections into Subsections. The two earlier founding Treaties, like the Merger and Budgetary Treaties, are somewhat simpler in structure.

Running through the various divisions of the TEU are a series of individual Articles or clauses. Because the Treaty is so much a series of amendments to existing Treaties, which already have their own numerical series of Articles, the drafters eschewed a new series of numbers, opting instead for capital letters. In the first and last Titles each Article gets a letter of its own. However, elsewhere the lettered Articles are subdivided numerically. This practice is taken to its most extreme extent in Article G, which accounts for 80 of the 253 pages in the Community version of the Treaty. The Article contains 86 detailed and numbered

| **Box 3.**
The basic structure of
the Treaty on
European Union | Preamble

Title I Common provisions (Articles A–F)
    II 86 Changes to Treaty of Rome (G)
    III Changes to ECSC Treaty (H)
    IV Changes to EAEC Treaty (I)
    V CFSP (J)
    VI Justice and Home Affairs (K)
    VII Final provisions (L–S)

Protocols
Final Act/Declarations
1 May 92 Declaration on abortion |

amendments to the Rome Treaty.[1] As will be seen the structure of the Treaty of Rome is altered by the TEU in order both to replace 'the EEC' by 'the EC'[2] and to accommodate new policy responsibilities.

All told there are 136 amendments to the three main founding Treaties. To add to the confusion many of these amendments introduce new clauses, denoted by lower-case additions to the numbered Articles. For example Article 130 is followed by Articles 130a to 130x, which spread across a number of Titles of the revised Rome Treaty.[3] This was done in order to save too much alteration to the numbering of the Treaty of Rome to which people are now accustomed.

Of the seven Titles of the Treaty on European Union, the first, as Box 3 has shown, deals essentially with the establishment of the Union as such. The next three list the amendments to the three main Treaties. These are then followed by the two so-called 'pillars' on foreign and internal affairs which, with the Community, constitute the Union. The last Title combines further basic statements about the judicial nature of the Union, with provisions for amendment, application and ratification.

To this is then added a series of Protocols and Declarations. Protocols are Treaty documents which contain material which adds and expands provisions of the Treaty. They are slightly separate from the Treaty being underwritten by the Final Act on 7 February 1992 at the same time as the TEU itself was finalized. A formal decision was then taken to annex them to the various Treaties. They are subject to ratification by member states. As such they are a largely binding part of normal international law, since they, to some extent, modify or supplement the Treaty. However, they have no force outside the Treaty. The Protocols to the TEU establish guidelines for implementing and operating the Treaty, detailed rules for specific institutions (some of which are fairly long), details of opt-outs and other special national provisions, the agreement on implementing the Social Chapter, and commitments of principle such as that on cohesion.

q.v. Social Chapter pp. 423–5

The Final Act, done in Maastricht in February 1992, also contains the list of Declarations which were agreed by the IGCs in December and after.[4] These deal with a whole range of procedural and policy issues and, in contrast to the Protocols, are more expressions of interpretation and intent. Consequently, they are of significantly lesser standing. In fact they are explanatory statements made by those attending the IGC rather than by the Treaty makers as such. Hence they are not really binding and they cannot be ratified in their own right as can a Protocol. And although, like Protocols they are justiciable by the ECJ, they are much harder to enforce. Hence, they are directly attached to the Final Act rather

q.v. Final Act pp. 427–9

---

1. To avoid confusion with the numbered provisions of the Treaty of Rome, the amendment numbers are not used in the *Handbook*, except where they introduce changes relevant to the entire Treaty (Article G(1)); to Annex III to the Treaty (Article G(85)); and to the Protocol on the European Investment Bank (Article G(86)).

2. Article G(1) of the TEU states that throughout the Treaty of Rome, 'The term "European Economic Community" shall be replaced by the term "European Community".'

3. There is, however, no Article 130q in the revised Treaty of Rome although this number had been used previously for material dealing with consultation of EcoSoc.

4. Later, as already seen, an interpretation of Protocol 17 on Irish Abortion Law was agreed on 1 May 1992. This was attached to the TEU as such rather than to the Final Act (see p. 536). See subdivision VI of the *Handbook* for a further discussion of the status and significance of the TEU's Protocols and Declarations.

than to the Treaty. Consequently they are printed after the Final Act and not before it as are the Protocols. Both the Treaty of Rome and the SEA have similar appendices, as already noted, although the SEA has no Protocols. With all these add-ons, the whole package comes to 61,351 words.

The nature of the Union

So what does the TEU actually involve? Although this is now often overlooked in the British debate the essential aim of the TEU is to create a new entity the 'European Union'. In this it goes beyond both mere cooperation and the SEA. It is not easy, at this stage, to say exactly what the Union involves because when it is considered (and the recent British government booklet pays it virtually no attention) it is often approached obliquely. Some see it as a notional and ramshackle construction, owing more to MFI than Montesquieu. Other authorities accept that its exact legal status is both unclear and undefined, partly because it is evolving and not a finished structure. Nowhere in the TEU is Union fully and satisfactorily defined. However the seven aspects signalled in Box 4 deserve to be noted. Yet none of these is wholly straightforward, as will be seen.

Box 4.
Nature of the Union

1. Superior status
2. No legal personality and depends on the *acquis*
3. Specific aims of its own
4. New characteristics
5. Threefold pillared structure
6. Dual working methods
7. Not fixed but part of an ongoing process

1. Because of its structure the Union lacks what is called a 'legal personality'. For this reason many of the new tasks and activities it sets itself have to be carried out inside the EC pillar where they are subject to judicial supervision. However, some feel that the Maastricht settlement does not make for good law and could, in fact, damage the *acquis*. This need for the Community to give effect to so many of the Union's tasks shows that, as Article A implies, the Community and its *acquis* is its essential foundation. The Council and the Commission are responsible for giving consistency to the Union, even the vitally important EMU being left to the Community to implement.

q.v. legal personality p. 328

2. The Union, like the TEU, is partly superior to its predecessors. It brings the other Community Treaties into its purview and restructures them, notably by transforming the EEC into the EC. Yet it neither abolishes them nor coordinates them into a single new treaty. Indeed the integrity of the other Treaties, including those on Coal and Steel and Euratom, is specifically upheld. And there are still questions about the Treaties' status in national law.

3.   Moreover, the Union is a specific political entity with distinct aims which relate both to its new and its old elements. On the one hand it aims at enhancing the relations between the economies, peoples and states involved. On the other it seeks to improve the working of existing institutions and processes, providing them with elevated aims together with a new dynamic and ability to act. However, many of the Union's activities are not new in themselves but simply codify what was already happening in the Community.

4.   As a political entity the Union embodies new characteristics. Thus it has its own citizenship, a new organizing principle in subsidiarity and the recognition of national identity, and new forms of diplomatic and police cooperation. Yet the first is supplementary to existing forms, the second was implicit in the Treaty of Rome and the third builds on what was already being done on the margins of the Community.

5.   The structure of the Union is threefold. As Figure 5 shows, the European Council acts as a directing body for three pillars.[5] Indeed, it is the Union's only institution as such. On the one hand the Union is based on an enhanced

Figure 5. The institutional structure of the Union and its 'pillars'

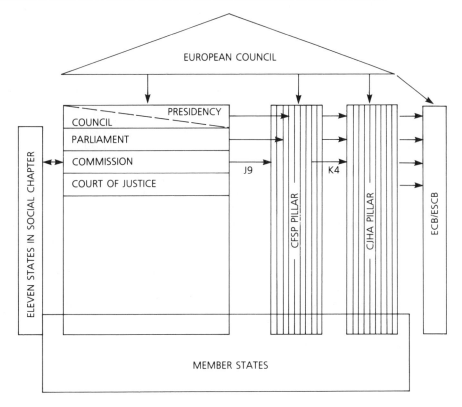

5. Quermone, J. P., 'Trois lectures de la Traité de Maastricht', *Revue française de science politique*, Vol. 42, No. 5, 1992, pp. 802–17, suggests that the independence given to the proposed European Central Bank means that EMU really deserves to be considered as a fourth pillar of the Union.

European Community which acts largely in a supranational or integrationist mode. It is also based on two separate pillars, for foreign and security policy, and home and judicial policy respectively. This suggests that it will be, as Schmitter says, 'a dispersed polity'. However, other provisions, and notably the reference to a single institutional framework, suggest the actual *modus operandi* of the Union will not be as distinct as the pillar image suggests. Nonetheless, the overall structure is comparable to the façade of a Greek temple and not to a single skyscraper or a tree.

6. The Union involves two methods of operation. In the EC pillar the normal Community methods are to be found. In the other two pillars, although the Community institutions play a part, the mode of operation is essentially intergovernmental and the ECJ has no built-in jurisdiction. This may allow for what Schmitter calls 'selective defection'. In any case, the Union derives its authority from the intermeshing of national and Community levels. However Articles B, 228a and K.9 provide some links between the two modes.

7. So the Union is neither a beginning nor a fixed and final construction but part of a process. The Union is a compromise stage in the continuing evolution of European integration. And, as well as being the latest stage in the evolution of integration, that is 'a new stage in the process of creating an ever closer union', the TEU sets up further timetables and targets. As the Treaty is concluded for an unlimited period, the Union opens the way to whatever form of political unity is chosen in the future.

All this means that the TEU has not created a wholly fixed and new United States of Europe. Exactly what it has created remains both complex and unclear. Delors has understandably talked of it as 'an unidentified political object'. Clearly the Union goes beyond the status quo and is a new body with its own aims and characteristics. Yet it lacks means, stability and clarity. Indeed it is replete with contradictions, in conception and expression. Thus Union is sometimes a structure and sometimes a way of working. In other words it echoes the two senses of the word in English: 'uniting' and 'being united'.[6]

Being both a larger Community and a system of collaboration between states, the Union, like the EC itself, is a *sui generis* body in which intergovernmental and supranational elements are linked through a modest form of cooperative federalism. As Sbragia says, it has 'the political dimension of federalism without its constitutional dimension'. And like the EC its compromise nature may well create difficulties in application as well as ratification. It is another incremental stage in the development of integration, which does not wholly address the political and constitutional nature and balance of the institutions of integration.

---

6. This may be another reason why the British government preferred the term Union to that of federalism, even though, in the British context of 1707 and 1801 'Union' suggests the creation of a single national state. And, in the late 1980s the concept of 'Union' was itself often attacked by Margaret Thatcher as being meaningless and unnecessary. There is thus a certain irony in its reappearance in the TEU.

Box 5. Innovations brought about by Maastricht	1. New policy responsibilities 2. Increased role for the EP 3. Clarification of institutional structure 4. Increased budgetary and financial controls 5. Further judicial controls 6. Common Foreign and Security Policy 7. EMU and single currency 8. Social Chapter 9. Cooperation in judicial and home affairs 10. Deadlines for further action

Because the Union builds on the existing Communities it is important not to overlook the other changes brought about by the TEU. If the Union is defined in Titles I and VII and its new pillars established in Titles V and VI, the bulk of the Treaty deals with amendments to the three earlier Treaties, especially to the Rome Treaty document. Commentators have varied in their appreciations of what are the significant changes, some pointing to EMU and others to the general extension of Community competence.

In fact, the TEU, as well as redefining the nature of the Community, and extending its institutions and authority, partially tidies up the Treaty of Rome. As Box 5 indicates, there are also ten areas where important changes have been made to the pattern of integration as a whole. These are new or enhanced policy responsibilities for the EC; a new recognition and powers for the Parliament; a clarification of the institutional structure; enhanced budgetary and financial control; further constitutional jurisdiction; a new common foreign and security policy; EMU and single currency; the development of the Social Chapter; judicial cooperation; and a timetable for further consolidation and development. These, together with the alterations in the structure of the Treaty of Rome will be examined in subsequent subdivisions.

In doing all this, the authors of Maastricht have gone some way to bringing the Treaty of Rome into line with the new order. However, it leaves a number of obsolete Articles and infelicities untouched. So it is more of a grafting operation than a systematic rewriting of the old Treaty. Hence, even with all these changes, the Treaty remains something of a skeleton, lacking flesh and muscle. At present it is a matter of political signals as much as of practical outcomes. As has been suggested, only time and circumstances will tell how this flexible framework will actually be applied and, hence, how it will evolve. Some authorities believe that, because of this incomplete nature, it all needs to be simplified and redrafted into a more genuine constitution.

Approaches to the Union Treaty

To suggest that the TEU is an uncertain and unclear document is to differ from many views of the Maastricht Agreements. Attitudes to the Treaty and the Union have been very disparate and increasingly vigorously expressed, even if they are

1. An undemocratic and non-integrated botch
2. A shift towards decentralization and member state interests
3. An anti-Keynesian and anti-social accord
4. A limited integrationist deal to be defended
5. A curate's egg settlement
6. A wrong turning taken for historical reasons
7. A great achievement by the Community
8. A threat to democratic small states
9. A step on the road to a federalist perdition

usually rather general and rarely get to grips with the detailed contents. They have also changed with circumstances. As Box 6 suggests there have been at least nine main approaches.

1)   At the outset many proponents of closer integration were extremely disappointed with the Treaty. They saw it as a technocratic and intergovernmental arrangement, with many negative features. Rather than resting on the kind of detailed preparation found in the past it was cobbled together by civil servants who did not worry about the quality of their texts provided that they were agreeable to the Twelve. This forced them to be vague and very protective of national interests, often to the point of threatening the integrity of the *acquis* and the uniqueness of the Community in the view of some. Nor were such critics willing to see it as held together by effective Community institutions.

Moreover, the settlement was seen as largely limited to confirming what was already happening. Lord Cockfield told the House of Lords that there was little that was new and that the whole thing had been 'greatly exaggerated'. Thus the TEU emerged as incoherent (in the way it borrowed from here and there) and insufficiently democratic (in not giving the Parliament or the Court sufficient control). It also, for the critics, failed to address the main issues facing the Community. Finally, there was the possibility that the deal would open the way to the renationalization of Community operations. Hence, there were several calls for a new start on a proper democratic constitution for an integrated Europe.

2)   In a way this paralleled the interpretation advanced by the UK government. The latter sees the TEU as ending the possibility of a federal Europe not just because it refused to include the word federalism but because of seven other facets. These are, to begin with, the fact that the Treaty lays down clear legal boundaries for Community action (thereby ending the creeping extension of unclear competences); the insistence on intergovernmental cooperation in the two pillars (which provides a way forward where individual national action no longer suffices); the introduction of opt-outs; the clear statements on the rights of member states; the stress on better housekeeping and the repression of fraud; the provision for more accountability amongst recalcitrant member states; and the increasing stress on subsidiarity and decentralization.

Thus the TEU is seen as a change of direction away from ineluctable supranationalism towards voluntary intergovernmentalism while, at the same time, producing other changes of use to Britain. Kenneth Clarke described it as the 'most conservative step taken by the Community in twenty years'. And Philippe Schmitter talks of it being marked by 'ostentatious statism'. Some supporters of further integration indeed see it as threatening to subvert the *acquis* in order to advance national interests. The thought has also occurred that while it is fallible, not having the TEU might lead to something much worse, whether at Community level or through German-dominated bilateral deals.

3)   It is worth noting that some critics on the extreme left seem to share something of such views. Far from welcoming the TEU as a step forward in creating a social Europe they see it as making this totally impossible. They denounce the Treaty as being the work of monetarists. In their opinion the primacy accorded to price and currency stability will prevent any socially progressive developments whether at national or Community level. In particular they see it as a barrier to Keynesian economic policies. They therefore demand its rejection.

4)   Despite such claims, many of the original integrationist doubters have now come round to defending Maastricht in case it gives way to something even more decentralized and in line with Anglo-Danish 'Euroscepticism' than what they see as a 'minimalist' agreement. Political pragmatism has made them now see it as marking an integrationist step forward, albeit of an evolutionary nature. They are comforted here by the spillover of much of the Community model into the new Union, with elements of the J and K sets of Articles seen as opening a breach in intergovernmentalism, and encouraging further spillover. And, whatever its weaknesses, failure to ratify it would be a damaging defeat for closer European integration. It could lead to the unravelling of what has been achieved so far. Norman Lamont similarly accused it of having too much rhetoric and too much vision.

5)   Many authorities have agreed with the Counsel to the Speaker of the House of Commons that, because the attitudes taken by drafters varied so much from one part of the Treaty to another, any global pro- or anti- stance is a dangerous simplification. Indeed some authorities see conflicting centralist (or supranational) and decentralist (or intergovernmental) trends inside the Treaty. The TEU, in other words, is 'good in parts', just like the infamous bad egg which, according to a *Punch* cartoon in the last century, a humble curate was offered at a bishop's dining table. Thus it is not a single, coherent and fully engineered change of direction, but a piecemeal compromise which had to be complex and unclear in order to cover up the very different views of the drafters. It might even be called a fog built on a marsh. Hence it leaves a very ambiguous entity whose real nature has still to be worked out, whether by the European Court of Justice (ECJ) or others. On the other hand, it is more significant than the SEA and than John Major has admitted. And it is federal in the continental sense of the word and not that usually used in British debate.[7]

---

7. Many continental traditions, as in France in 1793, Switzerland after 1848, and post-war Germany understand 'federalism' to mean a political system which seeks to protect regional autonomy within a framework of mutually advantageous cooperation. Hence a 'federalist' is one who *opposes* centralization and not the reverse as in the British use of the term. This British usage probably springs from the American experience in which, during the American Civil War, the Federal side upheld the view of the Union as constituting a single state from which there

6)   More recently it has been suggested that the TEU needs to be understood historically as a reaction, whether quixotic or panic stricken, to the end of the Cold War and German unification. Douglas Hurd has remarked that it was carried through under pressure of events. Jacques Attali called it the last act of the Cold War. Others have gone farther and seen it as a Treaty too far or too fast. Impelled by fears that European security needed to be restored and German predominance restrained, Community leaders moved to a German-style New Europe, based on German economic and financial power held in check by institutions copied from those of Germany: an independent bank; subsidiarity rights like those of the *Länder*; and similar social policy stances. In so doing, it is now claimed, they took a 'wrong turning' because Germany is not strong enough to sustain the new role and because it was all done too soon and against national interests, prevailing conditions and popular readiness.

7)   On the other hand some schools of thought have seen it as marking a much more integrationist tendency in the Community. To begin with, the majority of the negotiators in December 1991 hailed it as a great breakthrough, a famous victory which gave the Community an irreversible dynamic to move closer together. It was seen as a cornerstone for the completion of European Union based on an augmented Community, a flawed and incomplete Union perhaps, but a Union none the less. Despite the fact that federalism was not mentioned the principle was inherent in innovations like the banking system, citizenship and enhanced judicial powers. Article F could even be seen as forcing member states to remain democratic in the way that Swiss cantons are obliged to be by their Federal Constitution. Claims that Britain had succeeded in impeding such a quantum leap were indignantly rejected. The Luxembourg Prime Minister thus told the College of Europe that it was a commitment to press on down the difficult road to a cooperative and fraternal Europe.

8)   Such a view was shared by many Danes who were sceptical about the Union partly because of its policy limitations and partly because of its lack of democracy. Greens and other political radicals also offered a similar, unflattering, assessment. Thus, while the Danes did not like its currency provisions, they felt it did not go far enough where environmental controls and social security provision were concerned. At the same time it elevated a bureaucratic Commission at the expense both of small states and of individuals. They were often alarmed by the possibility of enforced enlistment in a Union army. Yet they were happy to continue with the European Community hence their slogan 'Europe "Yes", Maastricht "No"'. Yet

9)   It is not clear that this was wholly true for some British critics. For many in the United Kingdom the TEU was an unnecessary Treaty, partly because it involved constitution mongering at a time of economic crisis. It was also something which threatened to create an uncompetitive, protectionist economic

---

could be no secession. So, while it is clear that the Union is a 'federal' structure, this does not mean that it has to be seen as an embryo United States of Europe. Those who desire the latter are best described as 'institutionalist centralists' or 'federationists' rather than as federalists. It is worth noting here that *The Times* oscillates between the two conflicting senses of the word, using 'federal' to mean centralizing when talking about the Community and as decentralizing in most other contexts. A further irony is that many British eurosceptics use classic decentralist federal arguments and instruments to oppose a federal Brussels.

and monetary straitjacket in which unelected bankers would usurp power from democratically elected parliaments and their members. Furthermore, there were fears that the City would lose its flexibility by too close integration, while the Social Chapter, contrary to some Danish thinking, was seen as a further burden on industry. Generally, the Treaty was seen as leading to total social and economic perdition, an 'iron collar' as Charles Pasqua called it in France.

Even more insistently was the TEU depicted as an attack on British, and other national, sovereignties. This was because it involved illegitimate weakening of the rights of UK citizens, of the UK legal system and especially of the UK Parliament. Danish (and other) sympathies for strengthening the European Parliament in order to democratize the Community were usually rejected, as were thoughts of increasing the rights of citizens, save through a referendum on the Treaty. This became an increasingly insistent theme. Subsidiarity and the creation of pillars were seen as quite illusory defences against allegedly 'federalist' encroachment on the British constitution. However, although many saw the agreements as a too rapid and too far-reaching constitutional break in the gradualist evolution of an essentially economic Community, there is a case for saying that some of the British 'Europhobes' attacked Maastricht not just for what was in it, but because it is a symbol of further (if not, indeed, of all) European integration.[8]

All these views can claim some justification because the TEU does point in different directions. Hence, the Treaty should not be viewed as the victory of any single strategy or opinion. Being both a framework agreement and a complex compromise between governments and other interests, it is clearly a contradictory document full of 'messy ambiguities', fudging crucial issues and capable of supporting more than one interpretation. Indeed, it is difficult to see what else any such agreement could be, given its ambiguous institutional foundations, the way it was devised and the competing forces at work. It had to be flexible, not to say elastic, to satisfy all those involved. There are therefore legitimate differences of opinion as to what it means. No one approach can provide a full understanding of the meaning of the TEU.

Moreover, the way that the Treaty is understood depends not just on the political views of those concerned, but also on the time at which they are expressed. The way that a constitution is read can change over time. Thus the French Act of 1958 has sometimes been read as setting up a Presidential regime, at other times as more of a parliamentary one. In the case of the TEU its reading will depend on how member states choose to use it as well as on the way that other political forces react to its half-hearted invocation of democratization. These reactions depend in turn on the internal political complexion of the member states, a point explored in subdivision VII below.

---

8. Although criticism of the TEU has been very trenchant, it rarely spelled out a realistic alternative course to be followed. Given the fact that the British view was a minority one in Europe this stance logically points to leaving the EC, as the Danish authorities have become aware. The references made to a more open (and internally competitive) European Economic Community, in which there would be no further powers for the Commission and Parliament and all decisions would be subject to an initial national veto, ignore likely continental opposition to such a course of action. Hence more considered critics of Maastricht have come round to seeing the value of ratifying the Treaty and then exploiting internal possibilities of change.

The *Handbook* is not concerned, therefore, to advance any particular committed opinion. It starts from the acceptance that there is no single, right way of understanding the Treaty, given its compromise nature. Many elements of the TEU are best understood as the input of the competing forces. The *Handbook* also accepts that even these understandings of the Treaty change over time. So it tries to take the analysis a little deeper in order to allow readers to make their own judgements, rather than confining them to the rather general, ideologically motivated, and partial appraisals noted here.[9]

FURTHER READING

Attali, J., *The Times*, 29 June 1993.

Commons Select Committee on European Legislation, *Fourth Report 1992–93*: Treaty on European Union, HMSO, London, HC 79-iv, 8 July 1992.

Corbett, R., 'The Inter-Governmental Conference on Political Union', *Journal of Common Market Studies*, Vol. 30, No. 3, 1992, pp. 271–98.

Everling, U., 'Reflections on the structure of the European Union', *Common Market Law Review*, vol. 29, no. 5, 1992, pp. 1053–77.

Foreign and Commonwealth Office, *Britain and Europe*, Central Office of Information, London, 1992.

Hampton, C., 'Legal maze of Maastricht', *Financial Times*, 8 September 1992.

Howe, M., *Europe and the Constitution after Maastricht*, Nelson and Pollard, Oxford, 1992.

Hurd, D., 'A good deal of British Sense', *The Times*, 6 August 1993.

Lodge, J., 'Maastricht and Political Union', *European Access*, 1992/1, pp. 7–10.

Ludlow, P., *The Treaty of Maastricht and the Future of Europe*, CEPS Working Documents 68, Brussels, 1992.

Melchior, F., 'Le Traité de Maastricht sur l'union européenne (essai de présentation synthétique)', *Actualités du droit*, 1992/4, pp. 1209–1254.

Noël, E., 'Reflections on the Maastricht Treaty', *Government and Opposition*, Vol. 27, No. 2, 1992, pp. 148–57.

Pliakos, A., 'La nature juridique de l'Union européenne', *Revue trimestrielle de droit européen*, Vol. 29, No. 2, 1993, pp. 187–224.

Quermone, J. P., 'Trois lectures de la Traité de Maastricht', *Revue française de science politique*, Vol. 42, No. 5, 1992, pp. 802–17.

Sandholtz, W., 'Choosing Union', *International Organization*, Vol. 47, No. 1, 1993, pp. 1–40.

Santer, J., 'L'Europe après Maastricht', in *The College in 1992*, College of Europe, Bruges, 1993.

Sbragia, A. M. (ed.) *Euro-Politics: Institutions and policymaking in the 'New' European Community*, Brookings Institution, Washington, 1992.

Schmitter, P.C., 'Interests, powers and functions', Working paper, Centre for Advanced Study in the Behavioral Science, Stanford, April 1992.

Weilemann, P., 'European Union gains stature', *German Comments*, Vol. 26, No. 4, 1992, pp. 64–70.

i. Preambles

As already mentioned, the first elements of the Maastricht Treaty — the Preamble, the Common Provisions and the revised Principles of the Treaty of Rome — are extremely significant despite their relative shortness. They are more than mere scene-setting. However, there is much debate over the status of the Preambles. John Major and others have been known to dismiss them as 'Eurobabble' or 'waffle' because they make high-sounding, but very imprecise, declarations and, as such, are thought not to have any binding legal status. They were drafted after

---

9. This view owes a good deal to Philippe Schmitter. He also argues that whatever the Eurocrats sought, the TEU has allowed for the institutionalization of diversity because of its contradictory nature. Moreover, the outcome may be a *sui generis* polity and not the Federation or intergovernmental league.

the rest of the Treaty and not at Maastricht itself. For this reason the House of Lords felt that the vague, and in their view essentially political, concept of 'subsidiarity' ought to be relegated to the Preamble.

This is not a universally accepted view and many continental jurists accept them as meaningful commitments. They clearly provide evidence of the intentions of the drafters of a Treaty and this would be considered significant by the ECJ as it did in the 1963 *Van Gend en Loos* case. The Court then used the Treaty of Rome's commitment to union to show that a new legal order had been created. The official Community version of the collected Treaties, moreover, includes the Preambles as part of the 'Text' of the various Treaties. They are lofty statements of what the signatories wish to achieve by their agreement. They do not, in themselves, create rights but pave the way for them to appear in specific and binding Treaty Articles. For this reason the Danes sought to escape from any commitment to the reference to Union contained in the Preamble.

So, it would not be wise to dismiss them out of hand even if they are less binding than the later parts of treaties which they introduce and prefigure. Preambles are, after all, a common element in legislative enactments in many countries. They can be used to justify or summarize the legislation. Continental practice often also involves specifying the various texts and decisions which have led the legislators to this new step. So they are useful in helping readers to situate the new treaties.

This is particularly important with the Treaties constituting the Union because these have several Preambles. Obviously the TEU has its own. And, since its Title II is a series of amendments to the Treaty of Rome, the Preamble to the latter remains effective and is printed in the consolidated version. Moreover, the other two major Treaties, the ECSC and Euratom Treaties, still have a life of their own, so that their Preambles, along with that to the SEA need to be remembered.[10]

They all start by listing the Heads of State involved in signing the Treaty in question. These illustrous personages are then described, in a series of staccato statements, as collectively sharing various feelings about what they wish to do. The TEU has twelve of these statements which can be divided into five types. The first notes that they are embarked on a new stage in a continuing process and at a new time, following the fall of the Iron Curtain. The second reaffirms their political principles of democracy on the one hand and diversity in unity on the other. This highlights the limits to centralization. The third set of statements are commitments to improve existing processes of integration: institutional, economic and social, the last being balanced against the needs of the Internal Market. The fourth set spells out the new elements added: citizenship, foreign policy and judicial cooperation, while the last points up the need for further

---

10. The Preamble to the ECSC Treaty contains five statements. These stress the desire of the member states to maintain and safeguard peace by substituting age-old rivalries for the merging of essential interests. This is to be achieved through the establishment of an organized Europe and common bases for economic development. Emphasis is also placed on the desire to raise living standards. The Preamble to the Euratom Treaty also contains five statements. These stress the importance of nuclear energy for industry and the need to undertake joint efforts to realize its potential. Emphasis is also placed on the development of the nuclear industry to the benefit of the people. Finally, a commitment is made to cooperation with third countries and international organizations.

integration through the means of a 'Union' based on responsiveness and subsidiarity.

The Treaty of Rome Preamble is equally a product of its times, making it clear that the Treaty is an initial stage in what it hopes will be an ongoing process, and a stage in which it hopes the various divisions in Europe would be overcome. This explains the invitations to other states to join what is, significantly, described as 'an ever closer union among the peoples of Europe'. This is not an addition made at Maastricht, as is sometimes imagined, but something which has been implicit throughout the life of the EC. All member states tacitly accepted this aim when they ratified the Rome Treaty in which they first appeared.

The latter has eight statements in its Preamble, most of them dealing with specific economic objectives: improved social conditions; ending obstacles to free trade (both internally and internationally); strengthening unity and cohesion; and aiding former colonies. These economic commitments remain valid even though some critics have carped at the way the EEC is transformed into a general Community by the TEU. The means by which the new body is to work are also, interestingly, described as a pooling of resources rather than a transfer to a wholly new body.

The Preamble to the SEA, which is included here partly for illustrative purposes, is again concerned to situate the Treaty in context. In this case the context is that of decisions taken at various European Councils, and especially Stuttgart in 1983, to create a European Union. However, although this is defined here as consisting of the Community and EPC, little attention was actually paid to the concept of Union thereafter. There is also a reference to EPC as an innovative element of 'Union'.

The bulk of the Preamble is given over to justifying the SEA by the need for the Community to speak with one voice, by the results of earlier integration and by the need to improve existing activities. The strengthening of the objectives of the Community are also significant from a judicial point of view. Another significant point is that the SEA Preamble introduces the first Treaty references to the democratic nature of the Community, building on the April 1978 Copenhagen Declaration.

Perhaps because of the 1958 and 1967 mergers of institutions, the Community's initial consolidated version of the Treaty does not include the Preambles to the two other founding Treaties. That for the ECSC spells out the political need for integration and the neo-functionalist methodology adopted. That for Euratom concentrates on the value of nuclear power and the requirements to be met in developing it. Like all the Preambles they both then return to the Heads of State. The latter are said to have designated listed people as 'plenipotentiaries', that is people with full powers, to act for them, without reference back. The Preamble ends with proof that the individuals involved are duly and fully authorized to agree a Treaty. This is no doubt a hangover from earlier times when such information was not flashed around the world by the media and delegates needed assurance, in the form of parchment 'full powers' that those with whom they were dealing were who, and what, they claimed to be.

Preamble to the Treaty on European Union

RESOLVED to mark a new stage in the process of European integration undertaken with the establishment of the European Communities,

RECALLING the historic importance of the ending of the division of the European continent and the need to create firm bases for the construction of the future Europe,

CONFIRMING their attachment to the principles of liberty, democracy and respect for human rights and fundamental freedoms and of the rule of law,

DESIRING to deepen the solidarity between their peoples while respecting their history, their culture and their traditions,

DESIRING to enhance further the democratic and efficient functioning of the institutions so as to enable them better to carry out, within a single institutional framework, the tasks entrusted to them,

RESOLVED to achieve the strengthening and the convergence of their economies and to establish an economic and monetary union including, in accordance with the provisions of this Treaty, a single and stable currency,

DETERMINED to promote economic and social progress for their peoples, within the context of the accomplishment of the internal market and of reinforced cohesion and environmental protection, and to implement policies ensuring that advances in economic integration are accompanied by parallel progress in other fields,

RESOLVED to establish a citizenship common to the nationals of their countries,

RESOLVED to implement a common foreign and security policy including the eventual framing of a common defence policy, which might in time lead to a common defence, thereby reinforcing the European identity and its independence in order to promote peace, security and progress in Europe and in the world,

REAFFIRMING their objective to facilitate the free movement of persons while ensuring the safety and security of their peoples, by including provisions on justice and home affairs in this Treaty,

RESOLVED to continue the process of creating an ever closer union among the peoples of Europe, in which decisions are taken as closely as possible to the citizen in accordance with the principle of subsidiarity,

IN VIEW of further steps to be taken in order to advance European integration,

HAVE DECIDED to establish a European Union and to this end have designated as their plenipotentiaries:[11]

Preamble to the Treaty of Rome

DETERMINED to lay the foundations of an ever closer union among the peoples of Europe,

RESOLVED to ensure the economic and social progress of their countries by common action to eliminate the barriers which divide Europe,

AFFIRMING as the essential objective of their efforts the constant improvement of the living and working conditions of their peoples,

---

11. Here follow the names of the government ministers who signed the TEU on behalf of their states. Their names can be found, if required, in the official versions of the TEU.

RECOGNIZING that the removal of existing obstacles calls for concerted action in order to guarantee steady expansion, balanced trade and fair competition,
ANXIOUS to strengthen the unity of their economies and to ensure their harmonious development by reducing the differences existing between the various regions and the backwardness of the less favoured regions,
DESIRING to contribute, by means of a common commercial policy, to the progressive abolition of restrictions on international trade,
INTENDING to confirm the solidarity which binds Europe and the overseas countries and desiring to ensure the development of their prosperity, in accordance with the principles of the Charter of the United Nations,
RESOLVED by thus pooling their resources to preserve and strengthen peace and liberty, and calling upon the other peoples of Europe who share their ideal to join in their efforts,
HAVE DECIDED to create a European Economic Community and to this end have designated as their Plenipotentiaries

Preamble to the Single European Act

MOVED by the will to continue the work undertaken on the basis of the Treaties establishing the European Communities and to transform relations as a whole among their States into a European Union, in accordance with the Solemn Declaration of Stuttgart of 19 June 1983,
RESOLVED to implement this European Union on the basis, firstly, of the Communities operating in accordance with their own rules and, secondly, of European Cooperation among the Signatory States in the sphere of foreign policy and to invest this union with the necessary means of action,
DETERMINED to work together to promote democracy on the basis of the fundamental rights recognized in the constitutions and laws of the Member States, in the Convention for the Protection of Human Rights and Fundamental Freedoms and the European Social Charter, notably freedom, equality and social justice,
CONVINCED that the European idea, the results achieved in the fields of economic integration and political cooperation, and the need for new developments correspond to the wishes of the democratic peoples of Europe, for whom the European Parliament, elected by universal suffrage, is an indispensable means of expression,
AWARE of the responsibility incumbent upon Europe to aim at speaking ever increasingly with one voice and to act with consistency and solidarity in order more effectively to protect its common interests and independence, in particular to display the principles of democracy and compliance with the law and with human rights to which they are attached, so that together they may make their own contribution to the preservation of international peace and security in accordance with the undertaking entered into by them within the framework of the United Nations Charter,
DETERMINED to improve the economic and social situation by extending common policies and pursuing new objectives, and to ensure a smoother functioning of the Communities by enabling the institutions to exercise their powers under conditions most in keeping with Community interests,
WHEREAS at their Conference in Paris from 19 to 21 October 1972 the Heads of State or of Government approved the objective of the progressive realization of Economic and Monetary Union,
HAVING REGARD to the Annex to the conclusions of the Presidency of the European Council in Bremen on 6 and 7 July 1978 and the Resolution of the European Council in Brussels on 5 December 1978 on the introduction of the

European Monetary System (EMS) and related questions, and noting that in accordance with that Resolution, the Community and the Central Banks of the Member States have taken a number of measures intended to implement monetary cooperation,

HAVE DECIDED to adopt this Act and to this end have designated as their plenipotentiaries:

ii. Union Treaty Common Provisions

While there is uncertainty about the status of Preambles, this is not so with the next section of the Treaty on European Union. This carries forward the scene-setting, by establishing objectives and setting the overall tone.[12] Whereas the Preamble deals with the why of the Treaty, Title I deals with what is to be done and how. With Title VII, it thus goes a long way to defining the basic aims and principles of the new Union. The provisions of Title I are said to be 'common' in the sense that they refer to all the various Titles and institutions. The term should not be taken to indicate low status.

The first Article is really a corollary of the last statement of the Preamble. It is included not just to establish continuity but, as already explained, to give full legal force to the Preamble's aim of making the creation of a Union the first and crucial achievement of the Treaty. The insistence on the fact that the Union is established by a Treaty points to the essential role of the member states in the process of closer integration. The reference in Article A to an ever closer union taken, as already seen, from the Treaty of Rome, replaces an earlier suggested commitment to 'a process leading gradually to a Union with a federal goal'. This was rejected by the British as too threatening, although some authorities feel that in fact 'an ever closer union', the version accepted by Britain, could, as already noted, actually be seen as more redolent of inexorable centralism.

It is followed by the new insistence on decisions being taken as closely as possible to the citizen. Intended as a blow against Brussels this could also be read as a desire to take integration beyond nation states to the ordinary people. However, it is not really developed in Title II of the Treaty. The institutional foundations and aims of the Union are also spelled out in Article A with pride of place being given to the Community dimension.

The next Article (B) expands the aims of the Union by identifying five sets of more precise objectives: reinforcing economic freedom and progress; creating a more effective international presence; protecting human and civil rights; cooperating on judicial and related affairs; and developing the *acquis*. The reference to the *acquis* has been seen as making for inflexibility, but it can equally be seen as stressing the continuity between the Union and the pre-TEU Community.

---

12. The Danish government stated that it wished to have it established that not all these 'objectives', as set out in the common provisions, should apply to Denmark after any settlement prior to a second referendum. This included the defence policy dimension, the single currency, citizenship, and supranationalization of justice and police cooperation.

The last paragraph involves both a general commitment to review the effectiveness of the Union and a specific undertaking to convene a new IGC in 1996. This has proved controversial, because it has been seen as a potential hostage to further centralization by moving from cooperation to integration in some elements of the other pillars. The choice of citizenship as the way to achieve the otherwise unobjectionable aim of strengthening the protection of the rights of the peoples of the Union has also proved controversial. Equally, the possibility that a more effective international presence might lead to a common defence has worried both pacifists and supporters of national military rights.

Article C has been seen as undermining the intergovernmental element of the Union because it insists, by referring to 'a single institutional framework', on the role of the Brussels institutions in all the activities of the Union, even the intergovernmental pillars. The renewed stress on consistency, following on that in Article A, might also be seen as pointing in the same direction although the legal limits on the institutions' powers are also noted. And the institutions include the intergovernmental Council of Ministers.

Equally, the stress on the *acquis* points to continuity with the past. However, some authorities like Curtin believe that the stress is belied by other elements of the Treaty. The new role of the European Council as set out in Article D may be crucial to the structure of the Union as has been said, but is even more ambiguous. Not only is the Council made out to be the overriding and dynamic force of the Union (thus stressing its ultimate intergovernmental nature) but it is also required to report to the European Parliament. However, it is unlikely that this is meant to imply any presumption of accountability to the Parliament. In any case, because the European Council does not figure amongst the EC institutions in Title II it is examined at greater length at the end of this section.

Of the last two Articles, the next, Article E, makes it clear that the status of the other institutions is somewhat different from that of the European Council, because their powers are clearly subject to the modified Treaty of Rome as well as to the TEU. This is no doubt intended to establish the legal basis of their authority. Finally Article F combines two rather different elements. On the one hand it makes a further binding commitment to national identities (providing that the member states remain democratic) and human rights, thereby again stressing the limits to supranationalism. This is echoed later in Article 128(1). On the other *q.v. Article 128(1) p. 203* it finishes with a 'catch-all' clause which could be used to allow the Union to develop new institutions, policies and especially financial resources, should these be deemed necessary to fulfil the objectives listed in Article B which go beyond those of the EC and may require extra finance. British Eurosceptics would see all this as a threat although it will certainly make flexible adjustment of the Union easier.

The original Luxembourg draft on European Union added a reference to a Conference of National Parliaments to Title I. In the event the only references *q.v. Declarations pp. 434–5.* to national parliaments are in the Declarations where greater involvement through increased contact and exchanges of information between the EP and national parliament are urged, along with talk of consulting the shadowy Conference of National Parliaments on the main features of the Union. In other words, even here the Treaty is ambiguous as to the exact nature of the Union and how it combines supranationalism and intergovernmentalism. There are also many unanswered questions such as whether the identities of member states which cease to be democratic should be respected.

Title I (TEU) Common provisions

ARTICLE A

By this Treaty, the High Contracting Parties establish among themselves a European Union, hereinafter called 'the Union'.
This Treaty marks a new stage in the process of creating an ever closer union among the peoples of Europe, in which decisions are taken as closely as possible to the citizen.

The Union shall be founded on the European Communities, supplemented by the policies and forms of cooperation established by this Treaty. Its task shall be to organize, in a manner demonstrating consistency and solidarity, relations between the Member States and between their peoples.

ARTICLE B

The Union shall set itself the following objectives:

— to promote economic and social progress which is balanced and sustainable, in particular through the creation of an area without internal frontiers, through the strengthening of economic and social cohesion and through the establishment of economic and monetary union, ultimately including a single currency in accordance with the provisions of this Treaty;[13]
— to assert its identity on the international scene, in particular through the implementation of a common foreign and security policy including the eventual framing of a common defence policy, which might in time lead to a common defence;
— to strengthen the protection of the rights and interests of the nationals of its Member States through the introduction of a citizenship of the Union;
— to develop close cooperation on justice and home affairs;
— to maintain in full the 'acquis communautaire' and build on it with a view to considering, through the procedure referred to in Article N(2), to what extent the policies and forms of cooperation introduced by this Treaty may need to be revised with the aim of ensuring the effectiveness of the mechanisms and the institutions of the Community.

The objectives of the Union shall be achieved as provided in this Treaty and in accordance with the condition and the timetable set out therein while respecting the principle of subsidiarity as defined in Article 3b of the Treaty establishing the European Community.

ARTICLE C

The Union shall be served by a single institutional framework which shall ensure the consistency and the continuity of the activities carried out in order to attain its objectives while respecting and building upon the 'acquis communautaire'.

The Union shall in particular ensure the consistency of its external activities as a whole in the context of its external relations, security, economic and

---

13. It has been pointed out by Bill Nicoll that the UK government accepted this objective without any specific reserve beyond the reference to 'the provisions of the Treaty' which, of course, includes the opt-out on Economic and Monetary Union.

development policies. The Council and the Commission shall be responsible for ensuring such consistency. They shall ensure the implementation of these policies, each in accordance with its respective powers.

ARTICLE D

The European Council shall provide the Union with the necessary impetus for its development and shall define the general political guidelines thereof.

The European Council shall bring together the Heads of State or of Government of the Member States and the President of the Commission. They shall be assisted by the Ministers for Foreign Affairs of the Member States and by a Member of the Commission. The European Council shall meet at least twice a year, under the chairmanship of the Head of State or of Government of the Member State which holds the Presidency of the Council.

The European Council shall submit to the European Parliament a report after each of its meetings and a yearly written report on the progress achieved by the Union.

ARTICLE E

The European Parliament, the Council, the Commission and the Court of Justice shall exercise their powers under the conditions and for the purposes provided for, on the one hand, by the provisions of the Treaties establishing the European Communities and of the subsequent Treaties and Acts modifying and supplementing them and, on the other hand, by the other provisions of this Treaty.

European Convention for the Protection of Human Rights and Fundamental

ARTICLE F

1. The Union shall respect the national identities of its Member States, whose systems of government are founded on the principles of democracy.

2. The Union shall respect fundamental rights, as guaranteed by the European Convention for the Protection of Human Rights and Fundamental Freedoms signed in Rome on 4 November 1950 and as they result from the constitutional traditions common to the Member States, as general principles of Community law.

3. The Union shall provide itself with the means necessary to attain its objectives and carry through its policies.

FURTHER READING

Baldassarri, M. and Mundell, R., *Building the New Europe*, Macmillan, London, 1993.

Belmont European Policy Centre, *The New Treaty on European Union I*, Belmont European Policy Centre, Brussels, 1992.

Commons Select Committee on European Legislation, *Fifteenth Report 1991–92*: Treaty on European Union, HMSO, London, HC 24-x, 11 March 1992.

Coombes, D., *Understanding European Union*, Longman, London, 1994.

Curtin, D., 'The constitutional structure of the Union: a Europe of bits and pieces', *Common Market Law Review*, Vol. 30, No. 1, 1993, pp. 17–69.

EPP Group, *The Maastricht Treaty: Analysis and commentary*, EPP Research and Documentation Service, Brussels, June 1992.

Fielding, L., 'More of the same, or more of more? The

EC after Maastricht', lecture to the University of Sussex, 3 March 1992.

Laffan, B., 'The Treaty of Maastricht: A quantum leap forward or SEA mark II?', unpublished Paper, Department of Politics, University College Dublin, 1991–2.

Nicoll, W. and Salmon, T., *Understanding the New European Community*, 2nd edn, Harvester Wheatsheaf, Hemel Hempstead, 1993.

Padoa-Schioppa, A., 'Sur les institutions politiques de l'Europe nouvelle', *Commentaire*, Vol. 15, No. 58, 1992, pp. 283–92

Schmitter, P., *Interests, Process and Function. Emergent Properties and Unintended Consequences*, Centre for Advanced Study in the Behavioural Sciences Working Papers, Stanford University, April 1992.

iii. The European Council

As already suggested, the European Council occupies a somewhat anomalous position amongst EC institutions. This is true where its origins, its composition, its rules, its status and its operations are concerned. Nonetheless, it has now moved beyond being simply a 'Summit' into a more complex and influential body. Yet it still remains somewhat ambiguous in nature.

Neither the European Council nor Summit meetings are mentioned in the Treaty of Rome. In fact the idea of such a body emerged in the 1960s out of the Library Group and the informal meetings made necessary by the growing importance of the Communities and Gaullist fears of supranationalism. Because informal meetings often produced little more than rhetorical flourishes, Helmut Schmidt and Valery Giscard d'Estaing persuaded their colleagues to place them on a more regular footing in 1975. Since then the European Council, as the body was thereafter called, has been responsible for most of the major decisions (and non-decisions) of the Community: primarily economic in the 1970s, and more political and international since. This was to be a prelude to an increasingly important role in the 1980s, notably in the defining of the 1992 Project. This then led to formalization in the SEA.

Its membership is partly defined in Article D as being Heads of State or of Government of the member states and the President and one other member of the Commission. This represents both an increase and a greater precision about the Commission's role than in the past. Ministers for Foreign Affairs regularly join the Heads in a supportive capacity while the Presidency can, according to Declarations 3 and 4, invite Economic and Finance Ministers to attend when EMU matters are under discussion. Hardly any advisers are allowed to be present and the European Council's agenda is drawn up by the secretarial services of the Presidency and not by a special body, as was once envisaged.

q.v. Declarations 3 and 4 p. 432

Not surprisingly, its rules are relatively simple and evolved at Summits in 1974, 1977 and 1983. Thus the number of meetings per year was laid down, though this has changed and has not always been observed. Member states holding the Presidency have not always been able to resist the temptation of gaining publicity by holding extra meetings. Like the Council of Ministers, the European Council does not produce formal minutes, so as to encourage free and constructive debates. Instead Presidency communiqués or 'conclusions' are drawn up.

Because it was, at first a somewhat informal body, it developed outside the Treaty of Rome framework and was only given constitutionalized status in the Treaties after 1987. In Title I (Common Provisions) of the SEA Article 2 states that

> The EC shall bring together the Heads of State or of Government of the member States and the President of the Commission of the European Communities. They shall be assisted by the Ministers for Foreign Affairs and by a Member of the Commission. The European Council shall meet at least twice a year.

This says little of its powers, role or tasks. The fact that, as in the past, its decisions are sent to the Council of Ministers for action, means both that its conclusions eventually become decisions of the latter and that it has no formal powers. Hence, even now its status as a proper European institution remains somewhat unclear and disputed. The Parliament's new draft Union constitution gives it the status of an institution but does not change its limited, inspirational, role.

Because, as Delors has pointed out, it represents the ultimate dominance of intergovernmentalism, the European Council has not always been so popular with the Parliament and other supporters of closer integration. Indeed some have claimed that its predominance owes something to a desire to encourage the development of French-style Presidential regimes in Europe. Hence Parliament's 1984 European Union Treaty (EUT) accorded the European Council rather less status than it has here. Such feelings might seem to explain why Article D requires it to report to Parliament not merely on its meetings but on the progress of the Union. However, since this has been going on in Stuttgart since 1983, this should not be read as a hint that the European Council is answerable for its stewardship.

The political role of the European Council has changed with time. At first it was designed to overcome the inertia of the other institutions and chart a new course for the Community by using informal meetings. So key roles have been launching, and then supervising, both constitutional and institutional reform as well as new policy initiatives. It has also found itself having to act as a kind of appeal court and monitoring agency at times, although this has lessened of late. Equally, it has a role in improving policy coordination. As such its Declarations can be read as guides to good practice. Thus it has been the place where political consensus has been built enabling new initiatives, whether in policy or enlargement, to be taken. Maastricht was a good example of its constitutional and institutional effectiveness, as was the Edinburgh Summit which saw it devise a hitherto unknown (and undefined) form of enactment to enshrine Danish reservations on the TEU.[14] And beyond all this it has a foreign policy role in summarizing and publicizing Community stances on major issues, thereby laying down the frameworks within which EPC (and now the CFSP (Common Foreign and Security Policy)) and EC can operate.

In other words the European Council has brought a vital political dynamic and legitimacy to the Community and this role seems likely to be enhanced after Maastricht when it will become the main coordinating body for the three pillars. Article 103 also makes it the body to which changes in EMU will be reported and from which guidelines on EMU will emerge for the Council of Ministers to formally adopt. This might suggest an increased role for the European Council and some observers believe that it has already started to play its new role before the Treaty has been ratified.[15] In fact, this merely continues existing practice, so it is doubtful whether the European Council will emerge as the embryo of a European government. Indeed, when Article 109k(4) wants the Heads of State and Government actually to decide on moving to the third stage of EMU, they have to do this as a special meeting of the Council of Ministers.

---

14. The Conference Declaration is a somewhat uncertain instrument said to be derived from practice in non-Community international law. Hence its exact status within the Community context has been much debated.

15. Emmanuel Gazzo made this point in an editorial in *Agence Presse Europe* of 22 October 1992 apropos of the Birmingham Summit's promise to ensure that the fundamental principles of the Union would be observed in dealings over Denmark.

In line with the vision of Helmut Kohl and François Mitterrand, in other words, who saw the European Council as the brains of the Union, the TEU certainly makes it clear that its task is to devise and drive all the Union's activities. It is to do this not by precise legislation but by defining its general political guidelines. This political emphasis is emphasized by Article J8 which entrusts it with defining the principles and guidelines for the common foreign and security policy. Events subsequent to Maastricht have confirmed that it retains the political initiative and that this is usually exercised on the side of intergovernmentalism. So it is, in Bulmer's words, an 'indispensable agency'.

q.v. Article J8 pp. 380–1

FURTHER READING

Bonomi, G. and Regelsberger, E., 'Decision making in the EC European Council', *International Spectator*, Vol. 22, No. 3, 1987.

Bulmer, S., *The Council of Ministers and the European Council*, European Political Research Unit, Manchester, 1992.

Bulmer, S. and Wessels, W., *The European Council*, Macmillan, London, 1987.

'Comprendre le Traité de Maastricht — La France au coeur de l'Europe', *Lettre de Matignon*, numero hors série, July 1992.

European Parliament, *Maastricht — The Treaty on European Union: The position of the European Parliament*, OOPEC, Luxembourg, 1992.

Johnston, M. T., *The European Council: Gatekeeper of the European Community*, Westview, Boulder, 1993.

Taulegne, B., *Le Conseil européen*, Presses Universitaires de France, Paris, 1993.

iv. a) Principles

Although Title II of the TEU takes us back into the Treaty of Rome, and replaces new provisos with the first series of amending Articles, its opening Articles (contained in Parts One and Two of the Rome Treaty) still deserve to be treated as part of the general axioms of the Union. Whereas the TEU's common provisions indicate what the Union is, the revised Principles of the Treaty of Rome tell us much more about what its main pillar actually does, and how it does it. Thus, Part One spells out the principle of subsidiarity which has only been hinted at so far. Part Two goes on to supplement the description of the Union by adding the concept of Citizenship to the Community, thereby building on the hesitant beginnings of Community policy on a 'People's Europe'.

Before looking at these changes in more detail it is helpful to introduce the overall changes made to the Treaty of Rome by Title II of the TEU. Such changes are often cosmetic and involve a certain amount of tidying up and reshuffling. However, there are two complications. Firstly, where any change is made Community versions of the Treaty indicate this as being wholly new material. This can give an exaggerated impression of the changes actually made at Maastricht.[16] On the other hand substantial changes are made through this long

---

16. Thus the Counsel to the Speaker observed that 'a drafting idiosyncrasy, particularly noticeable in the institutional and general provisions, is that if any amendment is needed in any Article, even a minor or consequential amendment, that Article is re-enacted as a whole, So the amount of substantive amendment is less than may appear'. As already suggested, italic is here used to indicate such changes.

and not terribly stimulating list of alterations, both to the scope of the Community and to its nature.

The Title — Provisions amending the Treaty establishing the European Economic Community — has no Preamble. However, Article G does provide that 'The Treaty establishing the European Economic Community shall be amended in accordance with the provisions of this Article, in order to establish a European Community.' Some Eurosceptics and others suggest that this is a substantive change, involving moving away from the essential nature of the 'Economic' Community which Britain entered in the 1970s. In fact, it can be seen as partly a piece of tidying up since, after the Merger Treaty, the EEC became part of the European Communities, for which it provided the institutional structure. The term EEC was never removed from the Treaties although, in practice, 'EC' came to replace 'EEC' in day-to-day continental usage. Hence prior to Maastricht the European Parliament asked for the term to be changed. In agreeing this the TEU changed the name rather than the nature of the Community since, as already suggested, non-economic dimensions were fully involved in the establishment of the Communities. And there are still three separate Communities not just one. However, new countries (see below pp. 344−5) cannot join them direct as entry will, in future, be to the Union.

After this provision relating to the Treaty of Rome as a whole come the many individually specified alterations. These are listed under seven lettered subheadings. The first of these (A) provides that '1: Throughout the Treaty: 1) The term "European Economic Community" shall be replaced by the term "European Community".' The more specific changes are then listed numerically. Thus B covers the changes to Part Two (Principles) which are listed as numbers 2−9. Subheading C, which defines Citizenship, creates a new Part II for the Rome Treaty but does not have an amendment number in the TEU series.

Changes under D also restructure the Treaty of Rome by amalgamating its old subheadings of Parts Two and Three into a new Part Three on 'Community Policies'. As will be seen, new Titles are also created within this Part. The specific policy changes introduced are listed as amendments D10−39 and those to Part Five as 39−77 under subheading E. Part Four (Overseas Territories), is not amended in any way but there are further changes under E to Part Six (General Provisions), numbered 78 to 84. The majority of the Annexes and protocols of the Treaty of Rome are unchanged. However, subheading F/85 introduces changes to Annex III as does G(86) to the EIB (European Investment Bank) Protocol. This Completes Article G of the TEU. Articles H onward deal with other elements of the Maastricht settlement.

q.v. EIB protocol pp. 544−53

Turning to the Principles themselves, these can be seen as performing five functions for the Community and, by implication, for the Union. Thus they specify the Community's tasks and, secondly, provide further detailed justifications for them. Thirdly, they lay down legal principles and means by which these tasks are to be carried out: working within constitutional law; accepting obligations on member states; enacting required policies; and respecting subsidiarity. The last two functions are providing an indication of the timetables by which the agenda is to be fulfilled (notably for the post-1985 version of the Single Market) and specifying the single institutional framework on which the TEU rests. Though many of these points are gone into in more detail later in the Treaties, without such an initial statement of general provisions and axioms, the rest of the Treaty would be both hard to understand and somewhat imperfect in itself. These principles can also be used to query existing or proposed Community legislation.

More specifically, Article 1, consecrates the general change from EEC to EC. Article 2 carries this further forward by extending the tasks of the Community from a common market and gradual approximation of policies to a common market, the implementation of common policies and the creation of monetary union. The purposes which these tasks are to achieve are also widened and made more specific. The clause is rather significant because it both sums up the very nature of the EC and provides a base for much legislative activity.

Nonetheless, in the next Article the drafters have continued to spell out the activities which the Community is required to undertake. These now move from eleven, focused on the common market and selected concerns, to twenty which bring in provisions agreed in the SEA and go further into social, cultural and other fields. However, these activities are not all of the same type or standing. Three are, as before, designated as common policies, thereby giving them an enhanced status, as compared to the three ordinary policies. Six are required actions, to some of which specific objectives are attached, and five require measures to be taken or systems to be established. Finally three are described as contributions since the activities involved are not primarily matters where the Community has responsibility.

There is a cross reference to the new Article 100c although references to opportunities for workers and the EIB have been dropped. The points made in Article 3 are then enlarged in 3a by the inclusion of references to policy coordination, EMU and new governing principles for monetary matters. The last can be read as elevating price stability over the solidarity and social progress referred to in Articles A and B. Equally there is no reference to the new objectives of maintaining employment and increasing standards of living which are set out in Article 2.

Presumably because Article 3a seems to subject member states to binding obligations in economic and financial policy, subsidiarity is made a further sub-article rather than giving it an Article of its own. Indeed precisely why it is included under Article 3b rather than under the TEU's Common Provisions is unclear as will be shown below. The Article does three things. It obliges the Community as a whole to act within the same kind of legal restraints to be found in Article 4. It also spells out the bones of the principle of subsidiarity which are to be used in deciding where, in areas in which the EC does not have sole power, it can still take action on behalf of larger Community interests. Hence, as will be shown below, it can be read both as a new restraint on Brussels, which is the British view, and as a justification for further interventionism.

The changes and expansions to Article 4 start by raising the Court of Auditors to the status of a Community institution, eliminating an earlier subparagraph on its powers in the process, and thereby giving it more authority to control expenditure. They also create a new consultative body in the shape of the previously informal Committee of the Regions, and list the economic and financial organs of the Community. The reference to the EIB is thus transferred here from Article 3. Otherwise the institutions remain as before.

The task of the unchanged Article 5 is to specify what the expectations of member states as components of the Community actually are. It is thus an important statement of principle. Of the other Articles, Article 7 (after a procedural change to bring it into line with the cooperation procedure involving the Parliament) moves down to 6 replacing an Article on the financial and economic policy obligations of member states made redundant by the new Article 3a and other provisions on EMU. Articles 8–8c then also move down one place to become Articles 7–7c, continuing to specify the timetable and procedures for completing the Single Market. This move leaves room for the new Articles 8–8e which make up Part Two of the amended Treaty on Citizenship, building on the implicit ban on discrimination on grounds of nationality in the new Article 6.

Overall the effect of the changes to the Principles can be summed up under five headings. First, they leave the common market as a central, indeed an enhanced, concern of the Community. Second, they increase the objectives of the Community both through the commitment to EMU and the new policies areas. Third, they make the Principles more specific, more cross referenced and, perhaps, even a little simpler in expression if not in status. Fourth, they tend to treat the Treaty and the Community more as ends in themselves than was the case with the Treaty of Rome, thereby increasing the impression that the EC is seen as an autonomous force. On the other hand, fifth, the obligations on member states are not really changed, and their position may be said to be strengthened by the mere fact (if not the contents) of the reference to subsidiarity. Once again, the conflicting tendencies within the TEU show up clearly. Subsidiarity is anything but an exception to this general rule.

Title II (TEU)/Part One (TOR): Principles

ARTICLE 1

By this Treaty, the High Contracting Parties establish among themselves a European Community.

ARTICLE 2

The Community shall have as its task, by establishing a common market and **an economic and monetary union and by implementing the common policies or activities referred to in Articles 3 and 3a,** to promote throughout the Community a harmonious and balanced development of economic activities, **sustainable and non-inflationary growth respecting the environment, a high degree of convergence of economic performance, a high level of employment and of social protection, the** raising of the standard of living and **quality of life, and economic and social cohesion and solidarity among Member States.**

ARTICLE 3

For the purposes set out in Article 2, the activities of the Community shall include, as provided in this Treaty and in accordance with the timetable set out therein:

(a) the elimination, as between Member States, of customs duties and quantitative restrictions on the import and export of goods, and of all other measures having equivalent effect;

(b) *a common commercial policy;*

(c) **an internal market characterized by** the abolition, as between Member States of obstacles to the free movement of **goods**, persons, services and capital;

(d) **measures concerning the entry and movement of persons in the internal market as provided for in Article l00c;**

(e) *a common policy in the sphere of agriculture* **and fisheries;**

(f) *a common policy in the sphere of transport;*

(g) *a system ensuring that competition in the internal market is not distorted;*

(h) the approximation of the laws of Member States to the extent required for the functioning of the common market;

(i) **a policy in the social sphere comprising** *a European Social Fund;*

(j) **the strengthening of economic and social cohesion;**

(k) **a policy in the sphere of the environment;**

(l) **the strengthening of the competitiveness of Community industry;**

(m) **the promotion of research and technological development;**

(n) **encouragement for the establishment and development of trans-European networks;**

(o) **a contribution to the attainment of a high level of health protection;**

(p) **a contribution to education and training of quality and to the flowering of the cultures of the Member States;**

(q) **a policy in the sphere of development cooperation;**

(r) *the association of the overseas countries and territories in order to increase trade and promote jointly economic and social development;*

(s) **a contribution to the strengthening of consumer protection;**

(t) **measures in the spheres of energy, civil protection and tourism.**

ARTICLE 3a

1. For the purposes set out in Article 2, the activities of the Member States and the Community shall include, as provided in this Treaty and in accordance with the timetable set out therein, the adoption of an economic policy which is based on the close coordination of Member States' economic policies, on the internal market and on the definition of common objectives, and conducted in accordance with the principle of an open market economy with free competition.

2. Concurrently with the foregoing, and as provided in this Treaty and in accordance with the timetable and the procedures set out therein, these activities shall include the irrevocable fixing of exchange rates leading to the introduction of a single currency, the ECU, and the definition and conduct of a single monetary policy and exchange rate policy the primary objective of both of which shall be to maintain price stability and, without prejudice to this objective, to support the general economic policies in the Community, in accordance with the principle of an open market economy with free competition.

3. These activities of the Member States and the Community shall entail compliance with the following guiding principles: stable prices, sound public finances and monetary conditions and a sustainable balance of payments.

ARTICLE 3b

The Community shall act within the limit of the powers conferred upon it by this Treaty and of the objectives assigned to it therein.

In areas which do not fall within its exclusive competence, the Community shall take action, in accordance with the principle of subsidiarity, only if and in so far as the objectives of the proposed action cannot be sufficiently achieved by the Member States and can therefore, by reason of the scale or effects of the proposed action, be better achieved by the Community.

Any action by the Community shall not go beyond what is necessary to achieve the objectives of this Treaty.

ARTICLE 4

1. The tasks entrusted to the Community shall be carried out by the following institutions:

— a EUROPEAN Parliament,
— a COUNCIL,
— a COMMISSION,
— a COURT OF JUSTICE,
— **a COURT OF AUDITORS.**

Each institution shall act within the limits of the powers conferred upon it by this Treaty.

2. The Council and the Commission shall be assisted by an Economic and Social Committee **and a Committee of the Regions** acting in an advisory capacity.

ARTICLE 4a

A European System of Central Banks (hereinafter referred to as 'ESCB') and a European Central Bank (hereinafter referred to as 'ECB') shall be established in accordance with the procedures laid down in this Treaty; they shall act within the limits of the powers conferred upon them by this Treaty and by the Statute of the ESCB and of the ECB (hereinafter referred to as 'Statute of the ESCB') annexed thereto.

ARTICLE 4b

A European Investment Bank is hereby established, **which shall act within the limit of the powers conferred upon it by this Treaty and the Statute annexed thereto.**

ARTICLE 5

Member States shall take all appropriate measures, whether general or particular, to ensure fulfilment of the obligations arising out of this Treaty or resulting from action taken by the institutions of the Community. They shall facilitate the achievement of the Community's tasks.

They shall abstain from any measure which could jeopardize the attainment of the objectives of this Treaty.

ARTICLE 6

Within the scope of application of this Treaty, and without prejudice to any special provisions contained therein, any discrimination on grounds of nationality shall be prohibited.
The Council, acting in accordance with the procedure referred to in Article 189c, may adopt rules designed to prohibit such discrimination.

ARTICLE 7

1. The common market shall be progressively established during a transitional period of twelve years.

This transitional period shall be divided into three stages of four years each; the length of each stage may be altered in accordance with the provisions set out below.

2. To each stage there shall be assigned a set of actions to be initiated and carried through concurrently.

3. Transition from the first to the second stage shall be conditional upon a finding that the objectives specifically laid down in this Treaty for the first stage have in fact been attained in substance and that, subject to the exceptions and procedures provided for in this Treaty, the obligations have been fulfilled.

This finding shall be made at the end of the fourth year by the Council, acting unanimously on a report from the Commission. A Member State may not, however, prevent unanimity by relying upon the non-fulfilment of its own obligations. Failing unanimity, the first stage shall automatically be extended for one year. At the end of the fifth year, the Council shall make its finding under the same conditions.

Failing unanimity, the first stage shall automatically be extended for a further year. At the end of the sixth year, the Council shall make its finding, acting by a qualified majority on a report from the Commission.

4. Within one month of the last-mentioned vote any Member State which voted with the minority or, if the required majority was not obtained, any Member State shall be entitled to call upon the Council to appoint an arbitration board whose decision shall be binding upon all Member States and upon the institutions of the Community. The arbitration board shall consist of three members appointed by the Council acting unanimously on a proposal from the Commission.

If the Council has not appointed the members of the arbitration board within one month of being called upon to do so, they shall be appointed by the Court of Justice within a further period of one month.

The arbitration board shall elect its own Chairman.

The board shall make its award within six months of the date of the Council vote referred to in the last subparagraph of paragraph 3.

5. The second and third stages may not be extended or curtailed except by a decision of the Council, acting unanimously on a proposal from the Commission.

6. Nothing in the preceding paragraphs shall cause the transitional period to last more than fifteen years after the entry into force of this Treaty.

7. Save for the exceptions or derogations provided for in this Treaty, the expiry of the transitional period shall constitute the latest date by which all the rules laid down must enter into force and all the measures required for establishing the common market must be implemented.

ARTICLE 7a

The Community shall adopt measures with the aim of progressively establishing the internal market over a period expiring on 31 December 1992, in accordance with the provisions of this Article and of Articles 8b, 8c, 28, 57(2), 59, 70(1), 84, 99, 100a and 100b and without prejudice to the other provisions of this Treaty.

The internal market shall comprise an area without internal frontiers in which the free movement of goods, persons, services and capital is ensured in accordance with the provisions of this Treaty.

ARTICLE 7b

The Commission shall report to the Council before 31 December 1988 and again before 31 December 1990 on the progress made towards achieving the internal market within the time limit fixed in Article 8a.

The Council, acting by a qualified majority on a proposal from the Commission, shall determine the guidelines and conditions necessary to ensure balanced progress in all the sectors concerned.

ARTICLE 7c

When drawing up its proposals with a view to achieving the objectives set out in Article 8a, the Commission shall take into account the extent of the effort that certain economies showing differences in developments will have to sustain during the period of establishment the internal market and it may propose appropriate provisions.

If these provisions take the form of derogations, they must be of a temporary nature and must cause the least possible disturbance to the functioning of the common market.

FURTHER READING

Belmont European Policy Centre, *The New Treaty on European Union 1*, Belmont European Policy Centre, Brussels, 1992.

Cafruny, A. W. and Rosenthal, G. G., *The State of the European Community: Maastricht and beyond*, Longman, London, 1993.

Commons Select Committee on European Legislation, *Fifteenth Report 1991–92: Treaty on European Union*, HMSO, London, HC 24-x, 11 March 1992.

Corbett, R., *The Treaty of Maastricht*, Longman, London, 1993.

Curtin, D., 'The constitutional structure of the Union: a Europe of bits and pieces', *Common Market Law Review*, Vol. 30, No. 1, 1993, pp. 17–69

EC Commission, *The Maastricht Agreement*, Background Report ISEC/B25/92, London, 29 September 1992.

European Parliament, *Maastricht The Treaty on European Union: The position of the European Parliament*, OOPEC, Luxembourg, 1992.

EPP Group, *The Maastricht Treaty: Analysis and commentary*, EPP Research and Documentation Service, Brussels, 1992.

Martin, D., *Maastricht in a Minute*, David Martin, Edinburgh, 1992.

Millar, D., *Draft Treaty on European Union: Synopsis of section on European Political Union*, Europa Institute, Edinburgh, 1991.

Padoa-Schioppa, T. 'Sur les institutions politiques de l'Europe nouvelle', *Commentaire* Vol. 15, No. 58, 1992, pp. 283–92.

Rideau, J., 'Le Traité de Maastricht. Aspects institutionnels', *Revue des affaires européennes*, 1992/2, pp. 21–48.

Seidel, M., 'Zur Verfassung der Europäische Gemeinschaft nach Maastricht', *Europarecht*, Vol. 27, No. 2, 1992, pp. 125–44.

Wincott, D., *The Treaty of Maastricht: An adequate 'Constitution' for the European Union?*, European Public Policy Institute Occasional Paper 93/6, University of Warwick, 1993.

iv. b) Subsidiarity

The principle of subsidiarity has become so central to the debate on the TEU, its ratification and long-term future, that it calls for specific comment. Two very different views about it have emerged. Some authorities see it as a worthwhile innovation, introduced partly at German behest, exemplifying real limits to collective action and setting legal boundaries to any loss of national identity. It thus helps to provide a more democratically controlled, transparent Community closer to its citizens. Others say it is meaningless and misleading gobbledegook designed to disguise the actual increase in central powers at the expense of national rights brought about by the TEU. Indeed it is seen by some as a spur to 'centralizing federalism' and not a barrier to it. Other Articles, like 5 and 235, are held to rob it of real effect.

Such opposed, and passionately held, opinions reflect the way the concept has become obscured by the post-Maastricht crisis of the Community. This resulted in the Edinburgh Declaration which has significantly changed the way the actual Treaty provisions are likely to be 'read'. Hence, as well as looking at the origins of the concept and the problems presented by the Treaty text, a proper understanding of subsidiarity, requires some consideration of the Edinburgh reformulation.

q.v.
Edinburgh
Declaration
pp. 532–5

The broad idea can be traced back into medieval political thought[17]. It was

---

17. The actual word derives from Latin military usage which described troops being held in reserve as being a 'subsidium' or reinforcement, available to support the main unit. From this a broader meaning of helping out emerged, and it was this which was taken up by theologians. For them a 'subsidiary' action is one taken in support of a basic community, and not one which replaces communal decisions. Pius XI said 'Of its very nature, the true aim of all social activity should be to help individual members of the social body, but never to absorb or destroy them.' Hence subsidiarity became the political principle that decisions should be taken at the lowest appropriate level. In federal systems a similar principle guides the distribution of powers between national and local authorities.

then used in a bottom-up way by German Calvinists to defend their autonomy. Similar ideas then appear in nineteenth-century Dutch Calvinism as a means of defending social independence against a secular state. However, its modern rise is due more to Catholic opponents of ultra-montanism who borrowed it from the way nineteenth-century federal states distributed power to various levels, as a means of limiting Papal power. It was still used in this way in the 1980s when liberals challenged the imposition of conservative bishops against the wishes of local diocesan communities.

By then it had passed into the mainstream of catholic social thought, acquiring a new sense in the process. Thus it occurred in the Encyclicals Rerum Novarum of 1891 and, especially, Quadragesimo Anno of 1931. The latter actually coined the term from German secular usage when trying to set limits to Fascist governmental interference in society. In Italy, for example, Mussolini's regime was encroaching on what the Church felt was its own autonomous sphere of influence. This idea of defending the rights of vulnerable groups against repression from above by rules on the distribution of power was reasserted by the Second Vatican Council and taken up particularly by Christian Democratic parties in Europe. For some of them subsidiarity was part of the divine order and thus a principle of natural law.

In Community circles it was first mentioned, apropos of European Union, in the mid-1970s. It seemed a way of facilitating the development of the Community with the rights of states and other political actors in a pyramid structure. Hence it appeared in Spinelli's proposals on which the European Parliament's 1984 EUT was based and, in a vaguer sense, in the new environmental Article 134r(4) added to the Rome Treaty by the SEA. It was also echoed in the Council of Europe's 1988 Charter on Local Autonomy and the Community's Social Charter of December 1989. By then it was being invoked all the time. Jacques Delors used it partly as a means of countering some of Margaret Thatcher's criticisms of Brussels, as did the German *Länder*, worried that they were losing power to Brussels. It was also seen as offering a counter to the impact of the Single Market on local economic interests.

So, once it was decided to hold two IGCs the European Parliament, on the basis of a detailed report drawn up by Giscard d'Estaing, took up the issue. In 1990 it passed two resolutions urging that the principle both be enshrined in the Maastricht Treaty and be subject to ECJ rulings in case of dispute. Its suggested formulation was:

> The Community shall act only to fulfil the tasks conferred on it by the Treaties and to achieve the objectives defined therein. Where powers have not been exclusively or completely assigned to the Community, it shall, in carrying out its tasks, take action wherever the achievement of these objectives requires it because, by virtue of their magnitude or effects, they transcend the frontiers of the Member States or because they can be undertaken more effectively by the Community than by the Member States acting separately.

The TEU version only partly followed this. The wording of the Articles was, in fact, changed at the last moment, to take account of German sensibilities, giving more stress to the right of member states to undertake new actions.[18] However, it is clear that in building subsidiarity into the Treaties, the TEU was not really innovating. It was making explicit earlier understandings about the operation of federal-type bodies such as the Community without using the more emotive term of federalism. Moreover, it did not require the difficult process of deciding which powers belonged to the Community and which to the member states, which is the way that federal systems normally deal with the problem of the division of powers.[19] No doubt such considerations appealed to the present UK government. This was despite the fact that the TEU elsewhere expressly protects national identities.

Yet, despite becoming the buzz word of the moment, subsidiarity remains an abstract and difficult concept. It has little meaning for most ordinary people, particularly those who, like the British, are unfamiliar with constitutional thought. British unease about the term seems to reflect three things: suspicion of Brussels inspired constitution mongering; a different semantic understanding of the term; and even a trace of anti-Catholicism.[20] The fact that it raises two different questions about political action from above, of whether such action is actually necessary and whether the kind of action taken is appropriate and effective, does not make it any easier to grasp. Nor does the fact that it has existed in a Protestant bottom-up form as well as a top-down Catholic one.[21] This means that there are problems about definition as well as of enforcement of the principle.

In any case it is more a moral and political consideration than a legal one. Its history suggests that it has been used more as a political weapon than an objective tool of analysis. And people have changed its meaning to suit new needs and circumstances. Hence many lawyers still see it as an essentially political concept, if not a state of mind. As such it is not susceptible of easy definition let alone effective legal enforcement.

Given all this it is not surprising that the Maastricht formulation proved so opaque and unconvincing. Though Article 3b innovates by giving explicit expression and a new legal significance to subsidiarity, which becomes a general principle of EC and Union law which can be applied on the basis of the TEU it also poses at least seven problems. To begin there is a problem as to why the provision is included in the amended Treaty of Rome, which implies that it does

---

18. Wincott, D., *The Treaty of Maastricht: An adequate 'constitution' for the European Union?*, European Public Policy Institute Occasional Paper 93/6, University of Warwick, 1993, pp. 11–12. John Temple Lang of the Competition Directorate also provides a luminous discussion of the reasons why the idea was introduced in *What Powers should the European Community Have?*, Institute of European Public Law, Hull University, 1992. He singles out the German *Länder*, the need to counterbalance new powers given to the Commission (in part by restricting its workload to manageable proportions), and the need to start some kind of definition of functions which would give assurance to member states about their role.

19. Federal constitutions like that of Switzerland lay down general rules on this subject. Thus Article 3 of the Swiss Constitution provides that all powers not specifically given to the Confederation remain with the cantons, so that any new policy areas which emerge can be dealt with locally unless the cantons consciously allow them to be referred upwards. The German *Grundgesetz*, at Articles 70 and 71, puts things rather the other way round.

20. In English usage subsidiary can often mean 'tributary' or 'of lesser importance' as with a subsidiary subject studied at university and, in business terms, a dependent and controlled company. The related term 'subsidy' has also acquired a somewhat pejorative ring. The supportive element essential to the term in other European languages seems to play a much diminished role.

21. Thalmann, J., 'Subsidiarität–katholisch oder protestantisch?', *EGMagazin*, 1992/12, p. 28.

not relate to the Union, or at least to its other two pillars. However, this is clearly not the case because the Preamble describes it as part of the process of developing an ever closer union. This is echoed in the second paragraph of Article A while Article B makes it clear that the Union as a whole must reflect subsidiarity. It is included in the Community pillar because of the insubstantial nature of the Union. This ensures the possibility of enforcement by the ECJ.

q.v. Article A p. 57

q.v. Article B p. 57

Second, this vagueness is compounded by the drafting. The actual Article eschews the clear statements of principle about who does what, such as are found in the Swiss or, to a lesser extent, the American Constitution or even in the 1984 draft European Union Treaty (EUT).[22] It always opts for a reference to the 'principle' without defining either its meaning or its precise status. Thus, rather than setting out a simple statement about minimum interference or decentralization it adopts a very complex formulation. This is because the first approach would have threatened both the Community *acquis* and reopened the question of federalism. Nor is the TEU clear whether subsidiarity is an overriding principle or not.

Article 3b in fact begins with a general statement about the limits on Community action, copied from Article 4 of the 1984 Parliamentary draft, and then goes on to say — in a way which could possibly be read as an exception to this rule — that subsidiarity shall apply to action outside the Community's areas of exclusive competence. Here the Community may only act when member states cannot or when the scale and effects of the problem require it. The third element seems to be a warning that the Community must not merely stay within the set bounds but must never go beyond them. So, while Article 3b spells out the key principles of subsidiarity, it does not resolve their complications.[23] Some believe that this obfuscation was deliberate and politically motivated. However, the nature of the concept and the very variant understandings of what it means, suggests that agreed simplicity was probably impossible.

The third problem is that there is a profound ambiguity about using subsidiarity as a barrier to federalism. This is because, in so far as it is a general principle about the exercise of power, it presupposes, as Martin Bangemann pointed out, the existence of a larger structure within which power is deployed. And though the British government rejected this claim, it is clear that subsidiarity is having to serve as a quasi-constitutional principle because critics of the TEU do not want to tackle the constitutional issue directly. In other words it is a federal principle in the continental sense of the term. If the British did not have such a hang-up over the term it is arguable that greater safeguards (as well as simplicity)

22. Amendment 10 to the US Constitution provides that: 'The powers not delegated to the United States by the Constitution, nor prohibited by it to the States, are reserved to the States respectively, or to the people.' The EUT avoids the issue by providing for individual allocation of duties subject to a clarification in Article 12. This view is echoed in Article 9 of the new EP draft. The latter seems, however, to allow less room to member states and, in Article 11, offers a definition of subsidiarity to which is coupled proportionality. Temple Lang points out that, in fact, subsidiarity is better as a means of regulating the exercise of power than it is of allocating responsibilities. It provides a test of need for individual measures and provides a choice of means. It thus makes for a clearer definition of aims but does not limit EC competence. In other words, it is concerned with questions of degree rather than of kind.

23. These are attribution, i.e. deciding who is to act; necessity i.e. whether action is actually required; and proportionality i.e. ensuring that any Brussels action taken is not excessively disproportionate to the end sought. In other words, Community sledgehammers should not be used to crack national nuts.

could have come from a proper federal statement on the sharing of powers despite the challenges that this might have posed.

A fourth, and related problem, is that the TEU formulation is, as previously noted, actually more about the exercise of power than about its distribution. Because, in theory, it only applies to areas where the Community does not have full competence, it does nothing to define, let alone reduce, the existing powers of the Community. It only really deals with the management and implementation of power. This is not how it is understood by those for whom subsidiarity is a code word for an attack on the Commission.

Narrowly, the term means deciding how Community objectives should best be met, but in the real world the concept is often used by those who would deny that the Community should have any such objectives. They would like to see powers repatriated whether in order to protect industries as in France or to protect parliamentary defence of free market principles as in Britain. This would allow larger states to distort markets at the expense of poorer states and threaten the *acquis*. Equally it might allow states to paralyse Community action in general if it is used in a kneejerk anti-Brussels way.

Fifth, because subsidiarity is invoked as an undefined principle as well as a set of guidelines on the exercise of community competences, it has wider implications than sometimes assumed. British government sources see it as something which brings power back from Brussels to the member states. This it clearly can do. However, as a general principle, if not as a TEU Title, it can also be invoked to justify allowing decisions, where appropriate, to be taken below national level. If the idea of subsidiarity is that action is best taken as near as possible to those whom it effects, then this is logically valid sub-nationally. The addition of a Committee of the Regions points in this direction.

Indeed many local authorities are already appealing to the principle, at the European level, in large communities like Scotland or Wales, or even more locally. Jacques Delors has also been heard to talk of using subsidiarity to devolve the execution of some Community responsibilities to the private sector. So far this view has received a very cool response from the British government which tends to think that the answer to unresponsive local authorities is to transfer more power to Whitehall.[24] Other governments with active regions who are, as yet, not fully subject to Community rules, could also find this an expensive possibility given the new provisions for fining recalcitrant member states. The relationship of subsidiarity to a Union 'in which decisions are taken as closely as possible to its citizens' has, as will be seen, yet to be explored.[25]

A sixth problem is that the Treaty does not make it very clear by whom, or how, the principle is to be put into operation. There has been much argument about which body should see to it. Some solutions might slow down the Community's operation even further, others might lead to no real change. Other problems of making the principle operational include the fact that applying a

---

24. It was only reluctantly that the government conceded, during the ratification debate, that British representatives on the Committee of the Regions should be elected councillors.

25. The extent of the application of the principle to Euratom and ECSC also remains unclear. Some authorities think that subsidiarity may also be useful within the context of the CFSP.

simple 'best level test', as Leon Brittan has called it, may not work. Questions of need, comparative efficiency, of proportionality and value added may all need to be considered.

Equally, subsidiarity may not do much for policy coordination and integration. Subsidiarity in environmental policy may require a different approach from something like the Structural Funds. And it will clearly take different forms in different countries. The fear has already been expressed that too much subsidiarity might jeopardize the maintenance of the uniform and fair standards which the Single Market project is seeking to establish.

Finally, in this context, while some believe that Article 3b does not change much in Community law, enforcing it is generally seen as a problem. As a vague political statement of intent it appears to many lawyers that it cannot be effectively justiciable. This is despite the fact that it appears to be cast in legalese and, as part of the Treaty of Rome, must be subject to the ECJ. However, some German opinion has suggested that there could be a legal code which might make it easier for the ECJ to assess whether or not the rules had been broken. In other words, Maastricht's treatment of subsidiarity was as capable of as many interpretations as the TEU itself, and the political motivations for such diverse readings are equally evident.

These problems have only been partly resolved by developments subsequent to Maastricht. For while some of these problems were solved, new ones emerged. Thus the institutions began work on developing and operationalizing the concept. A first report was given at Lisbon, at which Delors said that the Commission was willing to justify all its future actions in the light of the principle and also to review past legislation. Later the Birmingham Summit equated 'subsidiarity' with 'nearness' which, as already suggested, would not be accepted by all defenders of the former. However, the British Presidency's ideas were rejected as too negative, while the Commission's own proposals, which emerged in an October paper, were immensely detailed and obscure.

q.v.
Birmingham
Summit p.
451

Nonetheless, an agreement was reached at Edinburgh in an annex to the Presidency conclusions on the application of the principle of subsidiarity and of Article 3b. This did three things. Firstly, it made subsidiarity the basic principle of the Union. It also reinforced the enhanced legal explicitness and significance which the TEU gives the concept. However, it defined subsidiarity not just as a contribution to respect for national identities but also, because of the nature of the concept, to taking Union decisions as close as possible to its citizens. This raises questions about democracy, notably at sub-national levels.

q.v. Article
3b pp.
63–6

Second, it provides a gloss on Article 3b by explaining it as the answer to three questions: can the Community act? Should it act? And, if so, how? On the first, by pointing out that the Community can only act where it has Treaty power to do so, it claims that national action is the norm and Community action the exception. By slightly fudging the question of exclusive competence, it implicitly raises the first paragraph of Article 3b almost to a rule of federal division of activity, if not of power.

Third, in the light of the new emphasis and understanding, it makes implementing Article 3b an obligation on all Community institutions. An interinstitutional accord will lay down how they should carry out their responsibilities in this context. However, here it does make clear both that the principle can only apply where the Community does not have full competence and that implementation must respect the legal *acquis*, the institutional balance and the provisions of the TEU, notably Article F(3). Member states are sternly warned that they cannot use it to escape existing obligations notably because it does not have direct effect. However, the Court of Justice will police observance of the principle.

q.v. Article F(3) pp. 56–8

More precise guidelines and procedures for fulfilling the guidelines are then set out. In areas of non-exclusive competence a series of questions have to be answered before the Community can act. Hence future action will have to rest on an argued justification of the legal right, the practical need and the inappropriateness of other options. At the same time, it expands the third paragraph of Article 3b into more general instructions for all Community action. This has to be limited, proportionate and simple. Neither must it limit member states' scope for cooperation, execution and interpretation.

To ensure that all this is done the Commission will have to present an annual report on its monitoring of the application of the principle. The Council is also to present its own thoughts on whether Commission appraisals and proposals are effective, thus allowing member states a limited right of challenge on the grounds of subsidiarity. Finally, details are given both of a preliminary review by the Commission of existing and proposed legislation which does not meet the new tests, and of its determination to resist Council pressures for new measures.

All this is now being put into practice. However, while the outcome is generally unclear, it is certain that subsidiarity will remain both an essential element of Community politics and a continuing subject of debate.[26] The fact that it is not a universal panacea but a contradictory political compromise to dig Maastricht out of its hole ensures this. Edinburgh has compounded its contradictions by making it a matter of democracy as well as of federal balance and the execution of power.

So, the three competing forces and understandings still have much on which to feed. Thus the British government continues to defend subsidiarity as a mechanism for resisting further centralization in the interests of nation states. On the other hand, many others insist that subsidiarity can work both ways preventing unnecessary central action but also allowing appropriate measures. While mainstream opinion sees this as a sensible piece of federalist common sense, British Eurosceptics stress the fact that the redefined principle does not prevent the acquisition of new powers by the Community, guarantee member states' autonomy, or provide real means for ensuring that Brussels actually acts in a devolutionist way. In other words, it does not live up to the claims made for it even if it does not positively encourage further centralization. Essentially it leaves Maastricht untouched.

---

26. The new draft EP Treaty takes things further by making subsidiarity subordinate to the objectives of the Union. But it extends it from the exercise to the extension of Union power. It also takes more note of 'proportionality', as defined in note 23 above.

At the same time, there are those who say that the new formulation is fallible because it does not do anything for the autonomy of natural communities whose interests subsidiarity was originally meant to protect. As a territorial delimitation between Brussels and national governments, it does nothing to bring decisions closer to the people. The Community as a whole, as Declaration 17 suggests, tends to think of this simply in terms of better information and publicity rather than really addressing the democratic deficit.[27] Edinburgh would seem to provide a new opportunity to push this line.

q.v.
Declaration
17 p. 435

So, while the attempt to develop the idea is a genuine one, and has led to a not insignificant rethinking of the Community's aims and modes of operation, it is not clear that the present messy political compromise will hold. Its impact on the Community *acquis* is particularly problematical. Subsidiarity may partially shape the evolution of Community politics but in the end what really counts will be the changing political balance in the Community and the extent to which the ECJ is willing to tackle so politically contentious an issue, as and when it is put to it. So it could therefore be a somewhat transitional concept.

Depending on how things evolve, subsidiarity is likely to be reconsidered in 1996. Perhaps then a simpler and more honestly federalist approach might be adopted, even if this did not have the flexibility and sophistication of subsidiarity. As it is, the insistence on using the problematic concept of subsidiarity to solve what are essentially federalist problems has probably given rise to more ambiguities and difficulties, not to mention to less certain protection of national and other rights than would a federal solution.

FURTHER READING

Adonis A., 'Subsidiarity: myth and the Community's future', *IEA Inquiry* 19/1990.

Cass, D. Z., 'The word that saves Maastricht? The principle of subsidiarity and the division of powers within the European Community', *Common Market Law Review*, Vol. 29, No. 5, 1992, pp. 1107–36.

Christophe-Tchakaloff, M. F. 'La subsidiarité: du vice de la vertu de l'ambiguïté', *Revue Politique et Parlementaire*, no. 964, 1993, pp. 70–78

Constantinesco, Vlad, 'La subsidiarité comme principe constitutionnel de l'intégration européenne', *Aussenwirtschaft*, Vol. 46, Nos. 3–4, 1991, pp. 207–28.

Delhombre, Jean, 'La subsidiarité et son "péche" originel', *Revue Politique et parlementaire*, No. 961, 1992, pp. 54–65.

EC, 'Subsidiarity', *Bulletin of the EC*, 10/1992, pp. 116–26.

Emilou, Nicholas, 'Subsidiarity: an effective barrier against "the enterprise of ambition"', *European Law Review*, Vol. 17, No. 5, 1992, pp. 383–407.

Federal Trust, *Subsidiarity: A report*, Federal Trust, London, 1993/4.

Gallacher, J., 'Subsidiarity and political union: an opportunity for local government', *European Information Service*, No. 134, 1992, pp. 3–5.

Hoetjes, B. J. S., 'The European tradition of federalism: the Protestant dimension', in Burgess, M. and Gagnon, A., (eds.) *Comparative Federalism and Federations*, Harvester Wheatsheaf, Hemel Hempstead, 1993, pp. 131–33.

Perissich, Riccardo, 'La principe de subsidiarité fil conducteur de la politique de la Communauté dans les annés à venir', *Revue du marche unique européen*, 1992/3, pp. 5–12

Teasdale, Anthony L., 'Subsidiarity in post-Maastricht Europe', *The Political Quarterly*, Vol. 64, No. 2, 1993, pp. 187–97.

Temple Lang, J., *What Powers should the European Community Have?*, Institute of European Public Law, Hull University, 1992.

Toth, A. G., 'The Principle of subsidiarity in the Maastricht Treaty', *Common Market Law Review*, Vol. 29, No. 5, 1992, pp. 1079–105.

Tyrie, A. and Adonis, A., *Subsidiarity: No panacea*, European Policy Forum, London, 1992.

Wallace, H. and Wilke, M., *Subsidiarity: Approaches to power sharing*, RIIA, London, 1990.

27. By this is meant the fact that executive decisions in the Community are not subject to the scrutiny, amendment and formal acceptance normal in parliamentary democracies. See below pp. 253–9.

v. a) Citizenship

Attempts to make subsidiarity the means of bringing decision-making as close to the ordinary citizen as possible have clearly not got very far. However, ordinary citizens do appear in the TEU in other ways notably through the new Part on Union Citizenship. This too has proved very controversial although the provisions are not wholly new. The Treaty of Rome did create certain rights for individuals, including free movement, the ban on discrimination on grounds of nationality and access to the ECJ. These rights were derived essentially from the economic activities with which the Treaty was concerned. They had been strengthened by ECJ jurisprudence which, since *Van Gend en Loos*, has sought both to empower and involve individuals in Community affairs. The 1991 *Francovich* judgment has allowed member states to be fined for infringing the rights of individuals.

Nonetheless, such rights were limited in number and scope. They were also scattered throughout the Treaties which meant that they were never very prominent. What the new Part of the Treaty does therefore is not to present an innovative new Bill of Rights (though Article F(2) invokes other European codes of rights) but to formalize and extend the concept of citizenship by going beyond the economic rights of workers. In other words, although this is called Union citizenship and represents an attempt to give more reality to the Union by encouraging the population at large to feel themselves part of it, it can equally well be understood as Community citizenship.

The essential reason for its inclusion is an attempt to make the Community more democratic. The negotiators wished to involve the 'people' in Community affairs, by gaining their support, bringing them into contact with decision-making and freeing them from unnecessary interference. In Jacques Delors' words, it is to give people 'a feeling of belonging to a collective adventure'. As suggested below, its inclusion is linked to thinking about policy on a 'People's Europe'. This had given a large place to civic rights in the Community context. There was also a certain anomaly in that human rights should not be formally entrenched in a Community based on law.

Activity in this field had originally been the concern of the Council of Europe. However, such considerations began to appear on the agendas of European Summits in the early 1970s, partly because of German pressures. At the same time the ECJ also began to extend its protection to various minority groups through its rulings. In the 1980s this widened into the beginnings of a policy on a People's Europe, which involved developing civic rights. These became a major concern of the European Parliament, figuring as Article 3 of the draft EUT in 1984, which defined citizenship as something open only to citizens of member states and involving rights of participation and acceptance of the rule of law. This was followed by the Bindi Report and the April 1989 Declaration on Rights and Freedoms. Similar ideas also figured in the Social Charter, in thinking in the House of Lords and elsewhere about the need for uniform protection of rights after 1992 and in the pressures for the Community to subscribe to the Council of Europe's European Convention on Human Rights and Fundamental Freedoms (ECHR).

The concept of citizenship was therefore taken up by others during the run-up to the IGCs. President Mitterrand made a statement in June 1990. Three months later the Spanish government submitted a considered plea for a statement of the rights, freedoms and obligations of citizens in the new Community. This was taken up by the Commission and others in the IGC on Political Union and ultimately included in the Treaty.

Despite this pre-history, the proposals did not go as far as some wished. They are largely restricted to setting out what was already being done, so that they embody a limited view of what civic rights actually are. Rather than creating new rights within a separate genus of citizenship the provisions reflect the fact that citizens of member states already have rights mainly directly but also through the ECHR which is referred to in Articles F(2) and K.2. The normal gamut of political rights does not appear here. Equally there is no explanation of the duties of Union citizenship though these are said to exist.

q.v. Article F(2) p. 58

q.v. Article K.2 pp. 384–5

These minimal provisions are not specifically underwritten by reference to the ECJ. However, the fact that Part Two appears within the Community division of the TEU, rather than as something purely to do with the Union, clearly reflects the fact that, since the Union does not have a legal personality, it has to be in the Community pillar, if the ECJ is to have any chance of supervising their working. It will no doubt judge this against the ECHR. In any case, being intergovernmental the other pillars exclude civic participation. The present formulation may also have something to do with the desire not to push the idea too far. Clearly, despite the desire of using citizenship to bring the TEU closer to the people, there was no thought of actually consulting them.

The aim was simply to add a new dimension to the rights already enjoyed by citizens of member states. It sought neither to add things and certainly not to take anything away. The acceptance of ultimate national sovereignty in this area was underlined by Declaration 2. This reaffirms the sole right of states to decide questions of nationality and citizenship.[28]

q.v. Declaration 2 p. 432

The actual proposals thus start by making the link between Union citizenship and prior possession of member state nationality. Union citizenship cannot be enjoyed directly since most opinion holds that only a state can create citizenship. Nor is Union citizenship an inherent right but something conferred by member states through the Treaty. However, Union citizenship applies automatically and cannot be rejected by unwilling national citizens. On the other hand the rights themselves are such that there would be no obligation to actually make use of them. And many people would not be able to do so anyway.

The first paragraph of Article 8a begins spelling out this limited range of rights. Here, although there is a clear continuity with the Single Market as defined in the Treaty, there is also an innovation. Article 8a(1) provides an autonomous right of circulation and establishment. This had only existed in restricted form in the jurisprudence deriving from the Rome Treaty. Yet, as Jacques Bourrinet says, it is a prerequisite for the efficient working of the Single Market, at least where

---

28. The Declaration stresses that decisions on who should enjoy national citizenship can be taken only by national, and not EC, law. States can register the criteria they will use by depositing a document with the Presidency of the day but this deposit can, in no way, bind their hands. The Declaration is thus an attempt at reassuring doubting nationalists that they are not losing any rights. However, it was not very successful in its aims.

ordinary individuals are concerned. Moreover, the institutions can intervene to maintain and develop these economic rights and the way they are exercised. Timetables for doing this and confirming the whole range of civic rights are laid down in Articles 8b, 8c and 8e. Such changes would, of course, require unanimous approval in the Council of Ministers.

The other rights in Articles 8b, c and d are essentially political: free movement and establishment; voting and standing in municipal and European elections in whichever member state a citizen resides; the right to diplomatic protection in a third country where the citizen's nation is not represented; and the right directly to address grievances to the Parliament and the Ombudsman. The political rights are to be exercised whether or not the European Parliament comes up with proposals for a uniform method of election, as required under Article 138(3). More generally, Article 8e provides for regular triennial reviews on whether the development of the Union requires civic rights to be strengthened or extended. At present they do not constitute a full endowment of primary political rights, partly because they can be legally withheld in certain circumstances.

Although these clauses were designed to give the population a share in the Union by offering additional and complementary rights, while safeguarding national interests, they proved very controversial. The clauses therefore figured in the ratification and referendum debates, and on the agendas of the various Summits. Thus the Birmingham Summit stressed that the new proposals took nothing away from national citizenship. The Edinburgh Decisions and Declarations on Denmark reiterated that Union citizenship was a political matter entirely different from what was contained in the Danish Constitution. It was an addition to Danish citizenship and did not imply any replacement of national citizenship by Union citizenship.

Nor, it was pointed out, did the provisions diminish the Danish right to decide who obtained Danish citizenship. In any case any changes to the existing TEU provisions would require a five-sixths majority in the Folketing. However, the Schengen states have taken a different line, inviting candidates for Community membership to follow their precedents in enforcing Article 8a. This suggests a more constraining reading of Part Two. The European Parliament's new draft Constitution for Europe also suggests a significant development of Union citizenship and civic rights, placing these at the core of the Union's legitimacy.[29]

q.v.
Schengen
pp. 125–6

The reasons why all this is so controversial seem to lie less in the practice than in the principle. Thus the Danes are prepared to accept much of the former but as a national decision and not as an externally imposed legal obligation. Indeed they already allow EC citizens to vote in local elections. Such facilities also exist, on a limited scale in Belgium, Britain (for Irish nationals), Ireland, Italy and the Netherlands.

There seem to be three main objections to TEU citizenship even though there is no obligation on individuals to accept the new rights. Firstly, citizenship is a very symbolic and sensitive matter in today's world. Constitutions, like that

---

29. The draft talks only of citizens and not of peoples and declares that all powers emanate from the former. Its Article 3 also commits the Union to recognizing and protecting their rights. Article 7 continues to make Union citizenship dependent on national citizenship. This largely restates the political rights confirmed by Maastricht whereas Article 8 lists 24 human rights which the Union is called on to uphold.

of Switzerland, give it a very high prominence and make special arrangements for policing it. This reflects the important role that citizenship is seen to play in building and defining nationality. By creating a feeling of belonging, citizenship plays an important role in forming national identity. And, in some federal systems, the development of citizenship has been a centralizing force. Citizenship, in other words, symbolizes the existence of a state which can impose duties like conscription on people.

So many people feared that the citizenship clauses would be used by citizens and Brussels to diminish the member states and build up the Union as a rival state. The fact that constitutions have had to be altered to allow for ratification is significant in this context. Even the Spaniards who proposed the idea, no doubt to help the many Spaniards working abroad as *Gastarbeiter*, have had problems in amending their constitution to give effect to Part Two. Opening up the question thus seems to threaten both national sovereignty and demographic integrity, since the provisions embody a non-ethnic view of citizenship.

Secondly, Article 8b(1) allows foreigners to stand in local elections. This is an equally emotional issue. In some countries this opens the way to election of foreigners as mayors, which would give them executive authority. Put another way Article 8b(1) threatens the nationalness of the state rather than the nation. France, in particular, was very hostile to this possibility, partly on ethnic grounds, and Eurobarometer polls showed this to be the most unpopular aspect of the proposals.

Thirdly, TEU citizenship is clearly intended to be a dynamic concept. This means that although member states rights are initially upheld in the TEU as against Union citizenship, the latter could be enhanced by review or other action (including that provided by Article K.9), thereby making them both more attractive and more of a rival to national citizenship. Even though this would require a new treaty pressures to accede to such changes could be hard to resist. The fact that there is no real opting-out of this, even after Edinburgh, makes many people fearful of the future. Because civic rights are often seen as encouraging integration and a sense of community, nationalists see TEU citizenship as a threat despite apparent constitutional safeguards.[30]

British Eurosceptics share this view. However, although the government has not been so worried about it, possibly since the Irish can already vote in British elections. It may also be because the concept promises to help open up the workings of the Community to public scrutiny. Nonetheless, there is another problem. While the Labour Party has stuck to an essentially political view of civic rights much recent conservative thinking has moved to a more consumerist interpretation.[31] This could conceivably make for future argument.

30. Recently Lady Thatcher has also proposed a general Magna Carta of freedom in elections, law, market access, property and worship for the new world order.

31. Recent debate on citizenship in Britain has tended to focus on the delivery and audit of public services rather than on political rights. Indeed the UK government uses citizen, consumer and customer almost interchangeably. Thus the Citizen's Charter has no references to elections in it. And empowering the citizen is often portrayed as participation in things like Neighbourhood Watch schemes and School Governors' meetings. Some critics, in Britain and beyond, say that this is a deliberate move to depoliticize the concept while weakening the citizenry by dividing them up according to concrete interests. It offers no upward or outward accountability for the citizen.

On the other hand, there are those, notably in the European Parliament, who believe that these provisions are fallible and ambiguous. They do not make allowance for the role of the Parliament as the representative of the citizenry and the author of a Declaration of Fundamental Rights and Freedoms of its own. Nor do the provisions refer to the member states' own rich tradition of human rights legislation. Finally, they offer no protection for residents of Europe who are not nationals of EC states. So, as with subsidiarity, citizenship remains untidy, restricted and problematical. This is less for what it is in the Treaty than for what it represents. It remains to be seen whether policies on a Citizens' Europe will succeed in redressing matters.

Part two: Citizenship of the Union

ARTICLE 8

1. Citizenship of the Union is hereby established.

Every person holding the nationality of a Member State shall be a citizen of the Union.

2. Citizens of the Union shall enjoy the rights conferred by this Treaty and shall be subject to the duties imposed thereby.

ARTICLE 8a

1. Every citizen of the Union shall have the right to move and reside freely within the territory of the Member States, subject to the limitations and conditions laid down in this Treaty and by the measures adopted to give it effect.

2. The Council may adopt provisions with a view to facilitating the exercise of the rights referred to in paragraph 1; save as otherwise provided in this Treaty, the Council shall act unanimously on a proposal from the Commission after obtaining the assent of the European Parliament.

ARTICLE 8b

1. Every citizen of the Union residing in a Member State of which he is not a national shall have the right to vote and to stand as a candidate at municipal elections in the Member State in which he resides, under the same conditions as nationals of that State. This right shall be exercised subject to detailed arrangements to be adopted before 31 December 1994 by the Council, acting unanimously, on a proposal from the Commission and after consulting the European Parliament; these arrangements may provide for derogations where warranted by problems specific to a Member State.

2. Without prejudice to Article 138(3) and to the provisions adopted for its implementation, every citizen of the Union residing in a Member State of which he is not a national shall have the right to vote and to stand as a candidate in elections to the European Parliament in the Member State in which he resides, under the same conditions as nationals of that State. This right shall be exercised subject to detailed arrangements to be adopted before 31 December 1993 by the Council, acting unanimously on a proposal from the Commission and after consulting the European Parliament; these arrangements may provide for derogations where warranted by problems specific to a Member State.

ARTICLE 8c

Every citizen of the Union shall, in the territory of a third country in which the Member State of which he is a national is not represented, be entitled to protection by the diplomatic or consular authorities of any Member State, on the same conditions as the nationals of that State. Before 31 December 1993, Member States shall establish the necessary rules among themselves and start the international negotiations required to secure this protection.

Article 8d   Every citizen of the Union shall have the right to petition the European Parliament in accordance with Article 138d.
Every citizen of the Union may apply to the Ombudsman established in accordance with Article 138e.

ARTICLE 8e   The Commission shall report to the European Parliament, to the Council and to the Economic and Social Committee before 31 December 1993 and then every three years on the application of the provisions of this Part.

This report shall take account of the development of the Union.

On this basis, and without prejudice to the other provisions of this Treaty, the Council, acting unanimously on a proposal from the Commission and after consulting the European Parliament, may adopt provisions to strengthen or to add to the rights laid down in this Part, which it shall recommend to the Member States for adoption in accordance with their respective constitutional requirements.

v. b) Policies on a People's Europe

The introduction of provisions for TEU citizenship must, as already indicated, be seen against a wider policy background. The Community has long been aware that it needs to appeal more to ordinary citizens. So while in theory all EC policies may be of interest to all citizens they are rarely seen as such. Hence attempts have been made to develop practical and symbolic activities which will develop the implications of the Treaties, provide concrete gains to citizens and encourage them to identify with the Community.

The roots of this concern can be traced to Summits in 1973–4. However, it really developed in the mid-1980s as part of the post-Fontainebleau moves to end 'Eurosclerosis'. These led to the SEA and 1992. They fitted in with British views that concrete gains such as cheap air fares to Europe made the Community more real than high-sounding declarations. The 1984 Dublin Summit then set up a Committee under the Italian politician Adonnino to look into the questions. Its first report made concrete recommendations on things like border crossings, rights of establishment and residence and recognition of diplomas.

The Second Report, which was endorsed by the June 1985 Milan Council, looked to eight specific areas for action. These involved political and general rights, some of which were to finish up in the TEU provisions on citizenship. However, talk of simplification and codification of EC law so as to make it more accessible to the citizen has not come about. The other areas were culture and communications; information; youth, education and sport; volunteer work in the Third World; and training and strengthening the image of Europe. The last called for more use of the European anthem, flag and passport. It also proposed special stamps and Community signs at border crossings. The overall aim of this extremely disparate list was to give citizens a clearer view of the Community's existence and dimensions.

This was followed up by the Commission which reported on voting rights and was faintly echoed in the SEA's references to social justice. In 1988 the Commission issued a new report on the subject which again stressed symbols, consciousness raising, and the European identity. It also talked of a European cultural area, an idea which had already led to encouragement of joint TV programmes and made 1988 a European TV Year just as the previous year had been European Environment Year. This was to lead to the Media 92 and BABEL programmes on language.

Within the realm of youth and exchanges things were also beginning to happen with the ERASMUS, COMETT and YES schemes. These were to bring thousands of young people and firms into contact with their colleagues in other Community countries. TEMPUS has also extended such possibilities to the east of Europe. Thought was also given to improving language skills since some educational matters, which had originally been regarded as outside the Community's competence were accepted as being a legitimate interest. The Commission was especially anxious to promote a European dimension in education, notably in higher education, through the Jean Monnet Action Programme to support courses, posts, research and special open modules.

q.v.
Exchange
Pro-
grammes
pp.
199–201

There was also talk of dealing with current problems (such as health, the environment and civil protection), and preparing for 1992. This led the Commission to suggest simpler border facilities with fewer checks, in line with what is happening under the Schengen Agreement. As part of a proposed dialog on matters related to People's Europe it also tabled a draft directive on voting rights. While not all of these initiatives came to fruition, the Community can count on some achievements in giving Europe a 'more human face', as it puts it. Consumer protection, data protection, encouragement of the media, environmental activity, free circulation, greater interchangeability of social security and health cover, and provision for migrants, the disabled and the elderly are all regarded in this light. However, other ideas have not been acted upon while others, such as action on works of art and support for museums, are only now being tackled.

Nonetheless, the Community feels that it is developing an overall policy, and a set of practical programmes, which take provision beyond the merely symbolic to create real active citizenship and participation. Some of these like ERASMUS, have been remarkably successful. This, Brussels hopes, will both make 'Europe' mean something in its citizens' daily lives encouraging them to vote in its elections and generally support it.

Such ambitions are no doubt laudable but there are problems to be faced. First, the programme itself is very bitty and often slightly superficial. This is due to the fact that the Community's potential is limited by its nature. Second, the evidence on turnout in European Parliamentary elections and identification is not very promising. Over half those sampled recently claim 'never' to feel European. Participation in a successful programme does not always have a spill-over effect. Third, even with the stress laid on respecting national cultures and identities at Maastricht and Birmingham, activities in this field tend to alarm fervent nationalists. Fourth, the visa provisions of the TEU, combined with the use of new technology in the Schengen area, suggest to some people that there are threats to individual liberties. Finally, the idea of making the Community more transparent avoids some of the real issues of citizenship and participation as already suggested. This is despite the Declaration on the right of access to information.

q.v.
Declaration
17 p. 435

Hence this area, like much else in the General Axioms sub-subdivision, illustrates the contrasting approaches to the Maastricht agreements. While the reasons for the settlement, the objectives laid down in the Common Provisions and the enabling principles given to the EC are all less extreme than either supporters or opponents tend to claim, their compromise characteristics create uncertainties and ambiguities. These allow all schools of thought to find something in these opening sections which they can use to defend their positions, especially when it comes to innovations such as subsidiarity and citizenship.

However, the Treaty is not all axioms. It contains highly detailed enactments as well. The next Parts and Titles are a mass of specific provisions and policies with characteristics of their own. And it is to these that the *Handbook* now turns.

FURTHER READING

Blumann, C., 'Europe des citoyens', *Revue du marché commun et de l'union européenne*, No. 346, 1991, pp. 283–92

Bourrinet, J., 'Vers une citoyenneté européenne: aspects économiques', *Revue du Marché commun et de l'union européenne*, No. 362, 1992, pp. 772–6

Closa, C., 'The concept of citizenship in the Treaty on European Union', *Common Market Law Review*, Vol. 29, No. 5, 1992, pp. 1137–69

Coenen, H. and Leisink, P., *Work and Citizenship in the New Europe*, Edward Elgar, Aldershot, 1993.

EC Commission, *A Community with a Human Face*, OOPEC, Luxembourg, 1990.

EC Commission, *A Citizen's Europe*, OOPEC, Luxembourg, 1993.

European Parliament, *Declaration of Fundamental Rights and Freedoms*, EP Information Office, London, 12 April 1989.

Garcia, S., *European Identity and the Search for Legitimacy*, Pinter, London, 1993.

Heater, D., *Citizenship: The civic Ideal in world history, politics and education*, Longman, London, 1990.

Laffan, B., *Integration and Co-operation in Europe*, Routledge, London, 1992.

Meehan, E., *Citizenship and the European Community*, Sage, London, 1993.

Meehan, E., 'Citizenship and the European Community', *The Political Quarterly*, Vol. 64, No. 2, 1993, pp. 172–86.

Oldfield, A., *Citizenship and Community*, Routledge, London, 1990.

Roche, M.C., *Rethinking Citizenship: Welfare, ideology and change in modern societies*, Polity, Oxford, 1992.

Spencer, M., *1992 and All That. Civil Liberties in the Balance*, Civil Liberties Trust, London, 1990.

III. The Union Treaty B: Commercial and Monetary Policies

Having examined in the preceding pages the opening Articles of both the TEU and the amended Treaty of Rome, the *Handbook* now turns to the policies of the Community. Initially, when the Treaty of Rome was signed, these covered only a limited number of areas. However, as a result of subsequent revisions of the Treaty, the number and scope of policy areas given legal basis in the Treaty has increased drastically. This is reflected, in part, by the fact that following amendments and additions introduced by the TEU, provisions governing the policies of the Community account for approximately 60 per cent of the text of the present Treaty of Rome.

Following the entry into force of the TEU, all the provisions for EC policies, with the sole exception of the association of overseas countries and territories (OCTs), are to be found in the new Part Three of the amended Treaty of Rome, appropriately entitled 'Community Policies'. The provisions relating to the OCTs are found, as before, in Part Four of the Treaty. Essentially, the new Part Three brings together under one heading the provisions contained in the original pre-TEU Parts Two and Three, entitled 'Foundations of the Community' and 'Policy of the Community' respectively, and the relevant amendments and insertions provided for in the TEU. The one exception relates to the provisions for the European Investment Bank which under the TEU have been transferred to Part Five of the amended Treaty of Rome.

The new Part Three of the amended Treaty of Rome contains a total of 180 Articles which are divided up into seventeen Titles (Titles I–XVII). This subdivision of the *Handbook* deals with the first seven of these (Titles I–VII). The remaining ten Titles (Titles VIII–XVII), along with Part Four of the Treaty of Rome, are the subject of the *Handbook*'s next subdivision, The European Union C: Social and General Policies.

As the title of this sub-division indicates, the seven Titles under discussion contain provisions relating to the Community's commercial and monetary policies. For the sake of convenience, the *Handbook* deals with these by placing them into three sub-subdivisions numbered (i–iii). The first of these concerns itself with the foundation stones of the Community — the Customs Union and the Single Market. In doing so, the sub-subdivision offers the reader an introduction to the provisions relating to the four freedoms contained in Titles I and III followed by an analysis of the progress the Community has made to date in implementing these and creating a single market. It also deals with the provisions relating to agriculture within the Community (Title II) and, by implication, contains an analysis of the Common Agricultural Policy and the Common Fisheries Policy.

The second sub-subdivision examines the provisions contained in Titles IV and V of the amended Treaty of Rome. These relate to transport, competition and the approximation of laws, as well as the new Community competence for visa policy. However, an examination of possibly the most debated and most complex provisions in the amended Treaty comes in the third sub-subdivision. This is dedicated to the central element of the TEU, the provisions for economic and monetary union (Title VI). Here, as throughout the *Handbook*, all relevant provisions contained in the Treaty of Rome, as well as those agreed on at Maastricht, are reproduced in full. Furthermore, in the introduction to the provisions, cross-references are made to all the appropriate Protocols and Declarations. This is then followed by an analysis of the Community's policy relating to economic and monetary union. Also included at the end of this sub-subdivision are the provisions relating to the Community's Common Commercial Policy (Title VIII) and a brief analysis of the commercial policy the EC has implemented to date.

i. The Customs Union and the Single Market

As noted above, this sub-subdivision of the Handbook deals with the first three Titles of Part Three of the amended Treaty of Rome. It starts by considering the provisions relating to the establishment of the Customs Union — the original centrepiece of the Community. It then proceeds to examine one of the most established, yet often divisive EC policy areas — agriculture. Thereafter, following a discussion of the Common Fisheries Policy, the sub-subsection discusses the provisions for and the substance of the Single Market. It thus covers some of the most prominent and indeed significant areas of Community activity.

The free movement of goods

The first Title of Part Three of the amended Treaty of Rome contains a total of 29 Articles (Articles 9–37). None of these was amended by the TEU, nor were any additional Articles inserted. In many respects, this reflects the centrality of the Articles and the concepts contained in them to the Treaty. However, one of the Articles, Article 28, had already been amended by the SEA. The Articles provide for the free movement of goods within the Community and the establishment of the Customs Union, the foundation on which the Community is built. The Title is divided into two Chapters covering the Customs Union and the elimination of quantitative restrictions between member states.

However, three Articles without a chapter heading precede these two Chapters and act as an introduction to the often detailed provisions which follow. The first of these introductory Articles establishes the Customs Union as the basis of the Community. Thus, the Article prohibits customs duties on all trade between the member states — effectively creating a free trade area; and calls for the adoption of a Common Customs Tariff to be imposed on trade with third countries — turning the free trade area into a customs union (Article 9). Provision is then made for the free circulation within the Community of goods originating from a third country and for a reduction in the administrative formalities involved in such trade (Article 10). The last of these three introductory Articles is more general, calling on member states to enable governments to carry out all their obligations with regard to customs duties as laid down in the Treaty (Article 11).

The first Chapter of Title I deals with the creation of the Customs Union. Divided into two Sections, the Chapter first addresses the elimination of customs duties between the member states (Articles 12−17) and then provides for the setting up of a Common Customs Tariff, also referred to as the Common External Tariff (Articles 18−29). Most of the provisions contained in these Articles have little relevance to the Community's activities today. For the most part, they relate to the twelve-year transitional period during which the Customs Union was set up; lay down timetables for the abolition of customs duties; and set out methods for calculating the Common External Tariff. Nevertheless, certain points should still be noted.

The first Article of note is Article 12 since it requires member states to refrain from introducing new customs duties or measures having equivalent effect or from increasing existing charges on trade with other member states. This is, of course, a fundamental principle for the maintenance of free trade within the Community. Secondly, there is Article 18. This is essentially a declaration of commitment by the member states to the goal of freer international trade. Here, the member states express their willingness to develop such trade through the conclusion of agreements designed to reduce customs duties between the Community and the third state concerned. This declaration is backed up by the guidelines laid down in Article 29 concerning the Commission's responsibilities in setting up the Common Customs Tariff (CCT). Here the Commission, in carrying out its obligations under Articles 18−29, is encouraged to promote trade with non-EC countries. In addition, the guidelines require the Commission to develop fair competition within the Community; ensure that EC requirements of raw materials and semi-finished goods are met; and avoid disturbances to the economies of the member states thus facilitating increased productivity and consumption.

q.v. Common Commercial Policy pp. 180−7.

With more direct regard to the CCT, the Treaty provides for certain exceptions to be made in the Community-wide application of the tariff. According to Article 25, these may be made in three instances. Firstly, the Council, acting by a qualified majority, may grant member states tariff quotas at a reduced rate or duty free on products where domestic production is insufficient to supply demand. Secondly, the Commission may grant similar exceptions on certain products where there is a shortage of supply within the Community or where the source for these products has changed.[1] Finally, the Commission may authorize the suspension of duty collection or indeed grant duty-free access to the EC market for certain agricultural goods listed in the second annex to the Treaty of Rome,[2] provided that this does not distort trade between the member states. All such exceptions are to be periodically re-examined by the Commission.

Finally, having established the CCT, Article 28 empowers the Council, on a proposal from the Commission, to alter duties as part of the tariff or to suspend their application. Since the introduction of the amendments to the Treaty of Rome contained in the SEA, such a decision has been made on the basis of a qualified majority. However, prior to this, during the transitional period, the Council was required to act unanimously. Indeed, once the CCT had been established the Council could only vote by a qualified majority on limited alterations or suspensions lasting no longer than twelve months. The changes introduced by the SEA thus provide the Community with greater flexibility in applying the CCT.

The second Chapter of Title I deals with the elimination of quantitative restrictions (QRs) on trade within the Community (Articles 30−37). Articles 30 and 34 prohibit all QRs and measures having equivalent effect on imports and exports between member states. The prohibition of QRs on imports is reinforced by the requirement that member states refrain from introducing new QRs (Article 31) and making existing QRs more restrictive (Article 32). Indeed, according to the Treaty, all QRs and measures having equivalent effect, both on imports and exports between member states, were to be eliminated during the first four years of the Community's existence (Articles 32 and 34(2)).

Although the provisions of this Chapter would appear to outlaw QRs entirely, Article 36 does allow for restrictions to be placed on imports, exports or goods in transit, provided that such measures are justified on the grounds of public health, public morality or public policy. Similarly, restrictions can be introduced to protect the health and life of humans, animals and plants; to protect the national heritage of a member state; and to protect industrial and commercial property. However, member states are not allowed to introduce any such restrictions if they are designed to act as an obstacle to trade.

Title I   Free movement of goods/Part Three: Community policies

ARTICLE 9

1. The Community shall be based upon a customs union which shall cover all trade in goods and which shall involve the prohibition between Member States of customs duties on imports and exports and of all charges having equivalent effect, and the adoption of a common customs tariff in their relations with third countries.

---

1. These products are identified in Lists E and G of Annex 1 to the original Treaty of Rome. The Lists are reproduced in *Treaties establishing the European Communities*, OOPEC, Luxembourg, 1973, on p. 373 and pp. 384−9 respectively.

2. Annex 2 to the original Treaty of Rome is reproduced in *Treaties establishing the European Communities*, OOPEC, Luxembourg, 1973, pp. 391−5.

2. The provisions of Chapter 1, Section 1, and of Chapter 2 of this Title shall apply to products originating in Member States and to products coming from third countries which are in free circulation in Member States.

ARTICLE 10

1. Products coming from a third country shall be considered to be in free circulation in a Member State if the import formalities have been complied with and any customs duties or charges having equivalent effect which are payable have been levied in that Member State, and if they have not benefited from a total or partial drawback of such duties or charges.

2. The Commission shall, before the end of the first year after the entry into force of this Treaty, determine the methods of administrative cooperation to be adopted for the purpose of applying Article 9(2), taking into account the need to reduce as much as possible formalities imposed on trade.

Before the end of the first year after the entry into force of this Treaty, the Commission shall lay down the provisions applicable, as regards trade between Member States, to goods originating in another Member State in whose manufacture products have been used on which the exporting Member State has not levied the appropriate customs duties or charges having equivalent effect, or which have benefited from a total or partial drawback of such duties or charges.

In adopting these provisions, the Commission shall take into account the rules for the elimination of customs duties within the Community and for the progressive application of the common customs tariff.

ARTICLE 11

Member States shall take all appropriate measures to enable Governments to carry out, within the periods of time laid down, the obligations with regard to customs duties which devolve upon them pursuant to this Treaty.

Chapter 1   The Customs Union

Section 1   Elimination of customs duties between member states

ARTICLE 12

Member States shall refrain from introducing between themselves any new customs duties on imports or exports or any charges having equivalent effect, and from increasing those which they already apply in their trade with each other.

ARTICLE 13

1. Customs duties on imports in force between Member States shall be progressively abolished by them during the transitional period in accordance with Articles 14 and 15.

2. Charges having an effect equivalent to customs duties on imports, in force between Member States, shall be progressively abolished by them during the transitional period. The Commission shall determine by means of directives the timetable for such abolition. It shall be guided by the rules contained in Article 14(2) and (3) and by the directives issued by the Council pursuant to Article 14(2).

ARTICLE 14

1. For each product, the basic duty to which the successive reductions shall be applied shall be the duty applied on 1 January 1957.

2. The timetable for the reductions shall be determined as follows:

(a) during the first stage, the first reduction shall be made one year after the date when this Treaty enters into force; the second reduction, eighteen months later; the third reduction, at the end of the fourth year after the date when this Treaty enters into force;

(b) during the second stage, a reduction shall be made eighteen months after that stage begins; a second reduction, eighteen months after the preceding one; a third reduction, one year later;

(c) any remaining reductions shall be made during the third stage; the Council shall, acting by a qualified majority on a proposal from the Commission, determine the timetable therefor by means of directives.

3. At the time of the first reduction, Member States shall introduce between themselves a duty on each product equal to the basic duty minus 10 per cent.

At the time of each subsequent reduction, each Member State shall reduce its customs duties as a whole in such manner as to lower by 10 per cent its total customs receipts as defined in paragraph 4 and to reduce the duty on each product by at least 5 per cent of the basic duty.

In the case, however, of products on which the duty is still in excess of 30 per cent, each reduction must be at least 10 per cent of the basic duty.

4. The total customs receipts of each Member State, as referred to in paragraph 3, shall be calculated by multiplying the value of its imports from other Member States during 1956 by the basic duties.

5. Any special problems raised in applying paragraphs 1 to 4 shall be settled by directives issued by the Council acting by a qualified majority on a proposal from the Commission.

6. Member States shall report to the Commission on the manner in which effect has been given to the preceding rules for the reduction of duties. They shall endeavour to ensure that the reduction made in the duties on each product shall amount:

— at the end of the first stage, to at least 25 per cent of the basic duty;
— at the end of the second stage, to at least 50 per cent of the basic duty.

If the Commission finds that there is a risk that the objectives laid down in Article 13, and the percentages laid down in this paragraph, cannot be attained, it shall make all appropriate recommendations to Member States.

7. The provisions of this Article may be amended by the Council, acting unanimously on a proposal from the Commission and after consulting the European Parliament.

ARTICLE 15

1. Irrespective of the provisions of Article 14, any Member State may, in the course of the transitional period, suspend in whole or in part the collection of duties applied by it to products imported from other Member States. It shall inform the other Member States and the Commission thereof.

2. The Member States declare their readiness to reduce customs duties against the other Member States more rapidly than is provided for in Article 14 if their general economic situation and the situation of the economic sector concerned so permit.

To this end, the Commission shall make recommendations to the Member States concerned.

ARTICLE 16

Member States shall abolish between themselves customs duties on exports and charges having equivalent effect by the end of the first stage at the latest.

ARTICLE 17

1. The provisions of Articles 9 to 15(1) shall also apply to customs duties of a fiscal nature. Such duties shall not, however, be taken into consideration for

the purpose of calculating either total customs receipts or the reduction of customs duties as a whole as referred to in Article 14(3) and (4).

Such duties shall, at each reduction, be lowered by not less than 10 per cent of the basic duty. Member States may reduce such duties more rapidly than is provided for in Article 14.

2. Member States shall, before the end of the first year after the entry into force of this Treaty, inform the Commission of their customs duties of a fiscal nature.

3. Member States shall retain the right to substitute for these duties an internal tax which complies with the provisions of Article 95.

4. If the Commission finds that substitution for any customs duty of a fiscal nature meets with serious difficulties in a Member State, it shall authorize that State to retain the duty on condition that it shall abolish it not later than six years after the entry into force of this Treaty. Such authorization must be applied for before the end of the first year after the entry into force of this Treaty.

Section 2 Setting up of the Common Customs Tariff

ARTICLE 18

The Member States declare their readiness to contribute to the development of international trade and the lowering of barriers to trade by entering into agreements designed, on a basis of reciprocity and mutual advantage, to reduce customs duties below the general level of which they could avail themselves as a result of the establishment of a customs union between them.

ARTICLE 19

1. Subject to the conditions and within the limits provided for hereinafter, duties in the common customs tariff shall be at the level of the arithmetical average of the duties applied in the four customs territories comprised in the Community.

2. The duties taken as the basis for calculating this average shall be those applied by Member States on 1 January 1957.

In the case of the Italian tariff, however, the duty applied shall be that without the temporary 10 per cent reduction. Furthermore, with respect to items on which the Italian tariff contains a conventional duty, this duty shall be substituted for the duty applied as defined above, provided that it does not exceed the latter by more than 10%. Where the conventional duty exceeds the duty applied as defined above by more than 10%, the latter duty plus 10% shall be taken as the basis for calculating the arithmetical average.

With regard to the tariff headings in List A, the duties shown in that List shall, for the purpose of calculating the arithmetical average, be substituted for the duties applied.

3. The duties in the common customs tariff shall not exceed:

(a) 3 per cent for products within the tariff headings in List B;
(b) 10 per cent for products within the tariff headings in List C;
(c) 15 per cent for products within the tariff headings in List D;
(d) 25 per cent for products within the tariff headings in List E; where, in respect of such products, the tariff of the Benelux countries contains a duty not exceeding 3 per cent, such duty shall, for the purpose of calculating the arithmetical average, be raised to 12 per cent.

4. List F prescribes the duties applicable to the products listed therein.

5. The Lists of tariff headings referred to in this Article and in Article 20 are set out in Annex I to this Treaty.

ARTICLE 20

The duties applicable to the products in List G shall be determined by negotiation between the Member States. Each Member State may add further products to this List to a value not exceeding 2 per cent of the total value of its imports from third countries in the course of the year 1956.

The Commission shall take all appropriate steps to ensure that such negotiations shall be undertaken before the end of the second year after the entry into force of this Treaty and be concluded before the end of the first stage.

If, for certain products, no agreement can be reached within these periods, the Council shall, on a proposal from the Commission, acting unanimously until the end of the second stage and by a qualified majority thereafter, determine the duties in the common customs tariff.

ARTICLE 21

1. Technical difficulties which may arise in applying Articles 19 and 20 shall be resolved, within two years of the entry into force of this Treaty, by directives issued by the Council acting by a qualified majority on a proposal from the Commission.

2. Before the end of the first stage, or at latest when the duties are determined, the Council shall, acting by a qualified majority on a proposal from the Commission, decide on any adjustments required in the interests of the internal consistency of the common customs tariff as a result of applying the rules set out in Article 19 and 20, taking account in particular of the degree of processing undergone by various goods to which the common tariff applies.

ARTICLE 22

The Commission shall, within two years of the entry into force of this Treaty, determine the extent to which the customs duties of a fiscal nature referred to in Article 17(2) shall be taken into account in calculating the arithmetical average provided for in Article 19(1). The Commission shall take account of any protective character which such duties may have.

Within six months of such determination, any Member State may request that the procedure provided for in Article 20 should be applied to the product in question, but in this event the percentage limit provided in that Article shall not be applicable to that State.

ARTICLE 23

1. For the purpose of the progressive introduction of the common customs tariff, Member States shall amend their tariffs applicable to third countries as follows:

(a) in the case of tariff headings on which the duties applied in practice on 1 January 1957 do not differ by more than 15 per cent in either direction from the duties in the common customs tariff, the latter duties shall be applied at the end of the fourth year after the entry into force of this Treaty;

(b) in any other case, each Member State shall, as from the same date, apply a duty reducing by 30% the difference between the duty applied in practice on 1 January 1957 and the duty in the common customs tariff;

(c) at the end of the second stage this difference shall again be reduced by 30%;

(d) in the case of tariff headings for which the duties in the common customs tariff are not yet available at the end of the first stage, each Member State shall, within six months of the Council's action in accordance with Article 20, apply such duties as would result from application of the rules contained in this paragraph.

2. Where a Member State has been granted an authorization under Article 17(4), it need not, for as long as that authorization remains valid, apply the preceding provisions to the tariff headings to which the authorization applies. When such authorization expires, the Member State concerned shall apply such duty as would have resulted from application of the rules contained in paragraph 1.

3. The common customs tariff shall be applied in its entirety by the end of the transitional period at the latest.

ARTICLE 24

Member States shall remain free to change their duties more rapidly than is provided for in Article 23 in order to bring them into line with the common customs tariff.

ARTICLE 25

1. If the Commission finds that the production in Member States of particular products contained in Lists B, C and D is insufficient to supply the demands of one of the Member States, and that such supply traditionally depends to a considerable extent on imports from third countries, the Council shall, acting by a qualified majority on a proposal from the Commission, grant the Member State concerned tariff quotas at a reduced rate of duty or duty free.

Such quotas may not exceed the limits beyond which the risk might arise of activities being transferred to the detriment of other Member States.

2. In the case of the products in List E, and of those in List G for which the rates of duty have been determined in accordance with the procedure provided for in the third paragraph of Article 20, the Commission shall, where a change in sources of supply or a shortage of supplies within the Community is such as to entail harmful consequences for the processing industries of a Member State, at the request of that Member State, grant it tariff quotas at a reduced rate of duty or duty free.

Such quotas may not exceed the limits beyond which the risk might arise of activities being transferred to the detriment of other Member States.

3. In the case of the products listed in Annex II to this Treaty, the Commission may authorize any Member State to suspend, in whole or in part, collection of the duties applicable or may grant such Member State tariff quotas at a reduced rate of duty or duty free, provided that no serious disturbance of the market or the products concerned results therefrom.

4. The Commission shall periodically examine tariff quotas granted pursuant to this Article.

ARTICLE 26

The Commission may authorize any Member State encountering special difficulties to postpone the lowering or raising of duties provided for in Article 23 in respect of particular headings in its tariff.

Such authorization may only be granted for a limited period and in respect of tariff headings which, taken together, represent for such State not more than 5 per cent of the value of its imports from third countries in the course of the latest year for which statistical data are available.

ARTICLE 27

Before the end of the first stage, Member States shall, in so far as may be necessary, take steps to approximate their provisions laid down by law, regulation or administrative action in respect of customs matters. To this end, the Commission shall make all appropriate recommendations to Member States.

ARTICLE 28

Any autonomous alteration or suspension of duties in the common customs tariff shall be decided by the Council, acting by a qualified majority on a proposal from the Commission.

ARTICLE 29

In carrying out the tasks entrusted to it under this Section the Commission shall be guided by:

(a) the need to promote trade between Member States and third countries;
(b) developments in conditions of competition within the Community in so far as they lead to an improvement in the competitive capacity of undertakings;

(c) the requirements of the Community as regards the supply of raw materials and semi-finished goods; in this connection the Commission shall take care to avoid distorting conditions of competition between Member States in respect of finished goods;

(d) the need to avoid serious disturbances in the economies of Member States and to ensure rational development of production and an expansion of consumption within the Community.

Chapter 2   Elimination of quantitative restrictions between member states

ARTICLE 30

Quantitative restrictions on imports and all measures having equivalent effect shall, without prejudice to the following provisions, be prohibited between Member States.

ARTICLE 31

Member States shall refrain from introducing between themselves any new quantitative restrictions or measures having equivalent effect.

This obligation shall, however, relate only to the degree of liberalization attained in pursuance of the decisions of the Council of the Organization for European Economic Co-operation of 14 January 1955. Member States shall supply the Commission, not later than six months after the entry into force of this Treaty, with lists of the products liberalized by them in pursuance of these decisions. These lists shall be consolidated between Member States.

ARTICLE 32

In their trade with one another Member States shall refrain from making more restrictive the quotas and measures having equivalent effect existing at the date of the entry into force of this Treaty.

These quotas shall be abolished by the end of the transitional period at the latest. During that period, they shall be progressively abolished in accordance with the following provisions.

ARTICLE 33

1. One year after the entry into force of this Treaty, each Member State shall convert any bilateral quotas open to any other Member States into global quotas open without discrimination to all other Member States.

On the same date, Member States shall increase the aggregate of the global quotas so established in such a manner as to bring about an increase of not less than 20 per cent in their total value as compared with the preceding year. The global quota for each product, however, shall be increased by not less than 10 per cent.

The quotas shall be increased annually in accordance with the same rules and in the same proportions in relation to the preceding year.

The fourth increase shall take place at the end of the fourth year after the entry into force of this Treaty; the fifth, one year after the beginning of the second stage.

2. Where, in the case of a product which has not been liberalized, the global quota does not amount to 3 per cent of the national production of the State concerned, a quota equal to not less than 3 per cent of such national production shall be introduced not later than one year after the entry into force of this Treaty. This quota shall be raised to 4 per cent at the end of the second year, and to 5 per cent at the end of the third. Thereafter, the Member State concerned shall increase the quota by not less than 15 per cent annually.

Where there is no such national production, the Commission shall take a decision establishing an appropriate quota.

3. At the end of the tenth year, each quota shall be equal to not less than 20 per cent of the national production.

4. If the Commission finds by means of a decision that during two successive years the imports of any product have been below the level of the quota opened, this global quota shall not be taken into account in calculating the total value of the global quotas. In such case, the Member State shall abolish quota restrictions on the product concerned.

5. In the case of quotas representing more than 20 per cent of the national production of the product concerned, the Council may, acting by a qualified majority on a proposal from the Commission, reduce the minimum percentage of 10 per cent laid down in paragraph 1. This alteration shall not however, affect the obligation to increase the total value of global quotas by 20 per cent annually.

6. Member States which have exceeded their obligations as regards the degree of liberalization attained in pursuance of the decisions of the Council of the Organization for European Economic Cooperation of 14 January 1955 shall be entitled, when calculating the annual total increase of 20 per cent provided for in paragraph 1, to take into account the amount of imports liberalized by autonomous action. Such calculation shall be submitted to the Commission for its prior approval.

7. The Commission shall issue directives establishing the procedure and timetable in accordance with which Member States shall abolish, as between themselves, any measures in existence when this Treaty enters into force which have an effect equivalent to quotas.

8. If the Commission finds that the application of the provisions of this Article, and in particular of the provisions concerning percentages, makes it impossible to ensure that the abolition of quotas provided for in the second paragraph of Article 32 is carried out progressively, the Council may, on a proposal from the Commission, acting unanimously during the first stage and by a qualified majority thereafter, amend the procedure laid down in this Article and may, in particular, increase the percentages fixed.

ARTICLE 34

1. Quantitative restrictions on exports, and all measures having equivalent effect, shall be prohibited between Member States.

2. Member States shall, by the end of the first stage at the latest, abolish all quantitative restrictions on exports and any measures having equivalent effect which are in existence when this Treaty enters into force.

ARTICLE 35

The Member States declare their readiness to abolish quantitative restrictions on imports from and exports to other Member States more rapidly than is provided for in the preceding Articles, if their general economic situation and the situation of the economic sector concerned so permit.

To this end, the Commission shall make recommendations to the Member States concerned.

ARTICLE 36

The provisions of Articles 30 to 34 shall not preclude prohibitions or restrictions on imports, exports or goods in transit justified on grounds of public morality, public policy or public security: the protection of health and life of humans, animals or plants; the protection of national treasures possessing artistic, historic or archaeological value; or the protection of industrial and commercial property. Such prohibitions or restrictions shall not, however, constitute a means of arbitrary discrimination or a disguised restriction on trade between Member States.

ARTICLE 37

1. Member States shall progressively adjust any State monopolies of a commercial character so as to ensure that when the transitional period has ended no discrimination regarding the conditions under which goods are procured and marketed exists between nationals of Member States.

The provisions of this Article shall apply to any body through which a Member State, in law or in fact, either directly or indirectly supervises, determines or appreciably influences imports or exports between Member States. These provisions shall likewise apply to monopolies delegated by the State to others.

2. Member States shall refrain from introducing any new measure which is contrary to the principles laid down in paragraph 1 or which restricts the scope of the Articles dealing with the abolition of customs duties and quantitative restrictions between Member States.

3. The timetable for the measures referred to in paragraph 1 shall be harmonized with the abolition of quantitative restrictions on the same products provided for in Articles 30 to 34.

If a product is subject to a State monopoly of a commercial character in only one or some Member States, the Commission may authorize the other Member States to apply protective measures until the adjustment provided for in paragraph 1 has been effected; the Commission shall determine the conditions and details of such measures.

4. If a State monopoly of a commercial character has rules which are designed to make it easier to dispose of agricultural products or obtain for them the best return, steps should be taken in applying the rules contained in this Article to ensure equivalent safeguards for the employment and standard of living of the producers concerned, account being taken of the adjustments that will be possible and the specialization that will be needed with the passage of time.

5. The obligations on Member States shall be binding only in so far as they are compatible with existing international agreements.

6. With effect from the first stage the Commission shall make recommendations as to the manner in which and the timetable according to which the adjustment provided for in this Article shall be carried out.

Agriculture

The second Title of Part Three contains the provisions of the Treaty of Rome relating to agriculture (Articles 38–47). The fact that agriculture appears so early in the Treaty is an indication of the importance the original six member states attached to it as a vital area of economic activity and as a vehicle for promoting integration. This is highlighted by the fact that the Title on agriculture appears immediately after the provisions relating to the free movement of goods and the Customs Union, but before the remaining three 'freedoms' which today are widely held to be the fundamental economic principles of the Community. However, despite the predominance of free market principles within the last decade and a half, the contents of Title II were left untouched by the TEU. Indeed, the provisions contained within the Title have remained unamended since the Treaty was signed in 1957. Hence, there are no amendments or additions made to the Title by the TEU.

The actual purpose of the Title is to set out the Community's aims with regard to agriculture and provide for the creation of a common policy, as originally required under Article 3(d),[3] to replace those of the member states. As such,

---

3. The TEU renumbered the provisions contained in Article 3. As a result, the reference to a common policy for agriculture now appears in Article 3(e) as opposed to Article 3(d), as was previously the case.

therefore, the Title does not contain details of how the Community's Common Agricultural Policy (CAP) operates. Instead, it establishes what the Community should and may include when formulating such a policy.

The opening Article of the Title states firmly that the common market created by the Community is to cover agricultural products as defined in the second Annex to the Treaty of Rome (Article 38).[4] This Annex contains 25 chapter headings and may be added to by the Council voting by a qualified majority on a proposal from the Commission. In addition, Article 38 requires that the Community establish a common agricultural policy among the member states as part of the common market for agricultural goods, thus replacing individual national policies on agriculture.

The objectives to be included in the Community's policy are set out in Article 39(1) and, for the most part, reflect the desire of the Community's founder members to become self-sufficient in agricultural production by maintaining and developing the agricultural sector within the economy. The first two objectives require that the common policy promotes increased agricultural productivity and ensures a fair standard of living for the agricultural community, while the third and fourth objectives involve the stabilization of markets and the guaranteed availability of supplies. The fifth objective relates more to the consumer in that the common policy is to ensure that agricultural products are available at reasonable prices.

As indicated, Title II does not lay down detailed rules for the operation of a common agricultural policy. Instead it provides guidelines setting out what a common organization for agriculture might involve. Such guidelines are contained in Articles 40 and 41. The first of these proposes that the common organization take one of the three forms indicated in Article 40(2). It then suggests that price regulation, production and marketing aids, storage arrangements, and a mechanism for stabilizing trade with third countries all be part of the common organization. Provision is also made for the establishment of one or more guidance and guarantee funds to help the Community achieve the objectives set out in Article 39. Finally, Article 41 proposes that the Community's common policy for agriculture include the coordination of vocational training programmes and of research into agricultural production, as well as the promotion of consumer consumption.

Although Article 38 states that the Community's common market includes agriculture, it is clear from the provisions of Title II that the principles of free trade which underpin the common market are not applicable to agriculture to the same extent as they are to industrial products. Indeed, as far as competition is concerned, Article 42 effectively allows the Council to maintain a non-competitive market organization for agricultural products. Furthermore, the authorization of state aid by the Council is actively encouraged where it maintains or furthers the economic development of businesses involved in the agricultural sector.

---

4. Annex II to the Treaty of Rome is reproduced in *Treaties establishing the European Communities*, OOPEC, Luxembourg, 1973, pp. 391–5.

The procedure and timetable for the formulation and development of a common agricultural policy is laid down in Article 43. Given that the Community has developed a common policy in the sphere of agriculture, the majority of the provisions contained in this Article are now redundant. However, the Article does contain, in the third subparagraph of paragraph 2, a description of the decision-making procedure to be adopted by the Community in relation to the common policy on agriculture. Here, it is stated that the Council, on a proposal from the Commission, is to make regulations, issue directives and take decisions by a qualified majority. The EP has only a consultative role in the procedure.

The three Articles which follow on from Article 43 contain provisions relating to the abolition of customs duties, quantitative restrictions, and minimum prices; national organizations; and countervailing charges during the period prior to the establishment of the common Community organization (Articles 44−6). As such they are now redundant. Similarly, the provisions on the EcoSoc contained in Article 47 have no direct relevance today since they relate to the Committee's role in formulating the original common policy under Article 43. However, this does not mean to say that the EcoSoc, or similarly the EP, refrains from issuing opinions on the EC's agricultural policy. The high profile of agriculture within the EC means that EC institutions and organs, along with member state governments and pressure groups, are constantly monitoring and assessing the effectiveness of the common policy.

Title II Agriculture

ARTICLE 38

1. The common market shall extend to agriculture and trade in agricultural products. 'Agricultural products' means the products of the soil, of stock-farming and of fisheries and products of first-stage processing directly related to these products.

2. Save as otherwise provided in Articles 39 to 46, the rules laid down for the establishment of the common market shall apply to agricultural products.

3. The products subject to the provisions of Articles 39 to 46 are listed in Annex II to this Treaty. Within two years of the entry into force of this Treaty, however, the Council shall, acting by a qualified majority on a proposal from the Commission, decide what products are to be added to this list.

4. The operation and development of the common market for agricultural products must be accompanied by the establishment of a common agricultural policy among the Member States.

ARTICLE 39

1. The objectives of the common agricultural policy shall be:
(a) to increase agricultural productivity by promoting technical progress and by ensuring the rational development of agricultural production and the optimum utilization of the factors of production, in particular labour;
(b) thus to ensure a fair standard of living for the agricultural community, in particular by increasing the individual earnings of persons engaged in agriculture;
(c) to stabilize markets;
(d) to assure the availability of supplies;
(e) to ensure that supplies reach consumers at reasonable prices.

2. In working out the common agricultural policy and the special methods for its application, account shall be taken of:

(a) the particular nature of agricultural activity, which results from the social structure of agriculture and from structural and natural disparities between the various agricultural regions;
(b) the need to effect the appropriate adjustments by degrees;
(c) the fact that in the Member States agriculture constitutes a sector closely linked with the economy as a whole.

ARTICLE 40

1. Member States shall develop the common agricultural policy by degrees during the transitional period and shall bring it into force by the end of that period at the latest.

2. In order to attain the objectives set out in Article 39 a common organization of agricultural markets shall be established.

This organization shall take one of the following forms, depending on the product concerned:

(a) common rules on competition;
(b) compulsory coordination of the various national market organizations;
(c) a European market organization.

3. The common organization established in accordance with paragraph 2 may include all measures required to attain the objectives set out in Article 39, in particular regulation of prices, aids for the production and marketing of the various products, storage and carry-over arrangements and common machinery for stabilizing imports or exports.

The common organization shall be limited to pursuit of the objectives set out in Article 39 and shall exclude any discrimination between producers or consumers within the Community.

Any common price policy shall be based on common criteria and uniform methods of calculation.

4. In order to enable the common organization referred to in paragraph 2 to attain its objectives, one or more agricultural guidance and guarantee funds may be set up.

ARTICLE 41

To enable the objectives set out in Article 39 to be attained, provision may be made within the framework of the common agricultural policy for measures such as:

(a) an effective coordination of efforts in the spheres of vocational training, of research and of the dissemination of agricultural knowledge; this may include joint financing of projects or institutions;
(b) joint measures to promote consumption of certain products.

ARTICLE 42

The provisions of the Chapter relating to rules on competition shall apply to production of and trade in agricultural products only to the extent determined by the Council within the framework of Article 43(2) and (3) and in accordance with the procedure laid down therein, account being taken of the objectives set out in Article 39.

The Council may, in particular, authorize the granting of aid:

(a) for the protection of enterprises handicapped by structural or natural conditions;
(b) within the framework of economic development programmes.

ARTICLE 43

1. In order to evolve the broad lines of a common agricultural policy, the Commission shall, immediately this Treaty enters into force, convene a conference of the Member States with a view to making a comparison of their agricultural policies, in particular by producing a statement of their resources and needs.

2. Having taken into account the work of the conference provided for in paragraph 1, after consulting the Economic and Social Committee and within two years of the entry into force of this Treaty, the Commission shall submit proposals for working out and implementing the common agricultural policy, including the replacement of the national organizations by one of the forms of common organization provided for in Article 40(2), and for implementing the measures specified in this Title.

These proposals shall take account of the interdependence of the agricultural matters mentioned in this Title.

The Council shall, on a proposal from the Commission and after consulting the European Parliament, acting unanimously during the first two stages and by a qualified majority thereafter, make regulations, issue directives, or take decisions, without prejudice to any recommendations it may also make.

3. The Council may, acting by a qualified majority and in accordance with paragraph 2, replace the national market organizations by the common organization provided for in Article 40(2) if:

(a) the common organization offers Member States which are opposed to this measure and which have an organization of their own for the production in question equivalent safeguards for the employment and standard of living of the producers concerned, account being taken of the adjustments that will be possible and the specialization that will be needed with the passage of time;

(b) such an organization ensures conditions for trade within the Community similar to those existing in a national market.

4. If a common organization for certain raw materials is established before a common organization exists for the corresponding processed products, such raw materials as are used for processed products intended for export to third countries may be imported from outside the Community.

ARTICLE 44

1. In so far as progressive abolition of customs duties and quantitative restrictions, between Member States may result in prices likely to jeopardize the attainment of the objectives set out in Article 39, each Member State shall, during the transitional period, be entitled to apply to particular products, in a non-discriminatory manner and in substitution for quotas and to such an extent as shall not impede the expansion of the volume of trade provided for in Article 45(2), a system of minimum prices below which imports may be either:

— temporarily suspended or reduced; or

— allowed, but subjected to the condition that they are made at a price higher than the minimum price for the product concerned.

In the latter case the minimum prices shall not include customs duties.

2. Minimum prices shall neither cause a reduction of the trade existing between Member States when this Treaty enters into force nor form an obstacle to progressive expansion of this trade. Minimum prices shall not be applied so as to form an obstacle to the development of a natural preference between Member States.

3. As soon as this Treaty enters into force the Council shall, on a proposal from the Commission, determine objective criteria for the establishment of minimum price systems and for the fixing of such prices.

These criteria shall in particular take account of the average national production costs in the Member State applying the minimum price, of the position of the various undertakings concerned in relation to such average production costs, and of the need to promote both the progressive improvement of agricultural practice and the adjustments and specialization needed within the common market.

The Commission shall further propose a procedure for revising these criteria in order to allow for and speed up technical progress and to approximate prices progressively within the common market.

These criteria and the procedure for revising them shall be determined by the Council acting unanimously within three years of the entry into force of this Treaty.

4. Until the decision of the Council takes effect, Member States may fix minimum prices on condition that these are communicated beforehand to the Commission and to the other Member States so that they may submit their comments.

Once the Council has taken its decision, Member States shall fix minimum prices on the basis of the criteria determined as above.

The Council may, acting by a qualified majority on a proposal from the Commission, rectify any decisions taken by Member States which do not conform to the criteria defined above.

5. If it does not prove possible to determine the said objective criteria for certain products by the beginning of the third stage, the Council may, acting by a qualified majority on a proposal from the Commission, vary the minimum prices applied to these products.

6. At the end of the transitional period, a table of minimum prices still in force shall be drawn up. The Council shall, acting on a proposal from the Commission and by a majority of nine votes in accordance with the weighting laid down in the first subparagraph of Article 148(2), determine the system to be applied within the framework of the common agricultural policy.

ARTICLE 45

1. Until national market organizations have been replaced by one of the forms of common organization referred to in Article 40(2), trade in products in respect of which certain Member States:

— have arrangements designed to guarantee national producers a market for their products; and
— are in need of imports,

shall be developed by the conclusion of long-term agreements or contracts between importing and exporting Member States.

These agreements or contracts shall be directed towards the progressive abolition of any discrimination in the application of these arrangements to the various producers within the Community.

Such agreements or contracts shall be concluded during the first stage; account shall be taken of the principle of reciprocity.

2. As regards quantities, these agreements or contracts shall be based on the average volume of trade between Member States in the products concerned during the three years before the entry into force of this Treaty and shall provide for an increase in the volume of trade within the limits of existing requirements, account being taken of traditional patterns of trade.

As regards prices, these agreements or contracts shall enable producers to dispose of the agreed quantities at prices which shall be progressively approximated to those paid to national producers on the domestic market of the purchasing country. This approximation shall proceed as steadily as possible and shall be completed by the end of the transitional period at the latest.

Prices shall be negotiated between the parties concerned within the framework of directives issued by the Commission for the purpose of implementing the two preceding subparagraphs.

If the first stage is extended, these agreements or contracts shall continue to be carried out in accordance with the conditions applicable at the end of the fourth year after the entry into force of this Treaty, the obligation to increase quantities and to approximate prices being suspended until the transition to the second stage.

Member States shall avail themselves of any opportunity open to them under their legislation, particularly in respect of import policy, to ensure the conclusion and carrying out of these agreements or contracts.

3. To the extent that Member States require raw materials for the manufacture of products to be exported outside the Community in competition with products of third countries, the above agreements or contracts shall not form an obstacle to the importation of raw materials for this purpose from third countries. This provision shall not, however, apply if the Council unanimously decides to make provision for payments required to compensate for the higher price paid on goods imported for this purpose on the basis of these agreements or contracts in relation to the delivered price of the same goods purchased on the world market.

ARTICLE 46

Where in a Member State a product is subject to a national market organization or to internal rules having equivalent effect which affect the competitive position of similar production in another Member State, a countervailing charge shall be applied by Member States to imports of this product coming from the Member State where such organization or rules exist, unless that State applies a countervailing charge on export.

The Commission shall fix the amount of these charges at the level required to redress the balance; it may also authorize other measures, the conditions and details of which it shall determine.

ARTICLE 47

As to the functions to be performed by the Economic and Social Committee in pursuance of this Title, its agricultural section shall hold itself at the disposal of the Commission to prepare, in accordance with the provisions of Articles 197 and 198, the deliberations of the Committee.

The Common Agricultural Policy

Undoubtedly the most widely known, and indeed contentious of the EC's common policies, is the Common Agricultural Policy (CAP). This was first formulated in the 1960s in line with the requirements laid down in the then Article 3(d) and in Articles 38–47. At the time, and up until the 1980s, the CAP was held up as a shining example of how national policies could be successfully integrated into a common Community policy administered at the EC rather than national level. However, the policy in achieving its objectives has since become more a symbol of disunity within the Community as the need for an overhaul of the policy has become increasingly apparent.

The CAP, as developed in the 1960s, has as its aims those laid down in Article 39(1) of the Treaty of Rome. These require the policy to increase agricultural productivity, ensure a fair standard of living for agricultural communities within the EC, stabilize markets, assure the availability of supplies and guarantee reasonable prices to the consumer. The essential purpose of these aims was to overcome traditional difficulties with regard to supplies by promoting agricultural self-sufficiency within the Community. Three principles, agreed upon by the Six when developing the policy, govern the attainment of these objectives. The first of these is the principle of a single agricultural market, i.e. the free movement of agricultural goods within the Community. This is complemented by the second principle of Community preference. This affords protection to EC producers by restricting imports into the Community of cheaper agricultural goods from third countries. The final principle, that of joint financial responsibility, emphasizes the common nature of the policy and highlights the continued acceptance by the member states of the need to provide financial assistance to the agricultural sector.

The common policy which emerged in line with these principles, the CAP, is based upon a common market organization for agricultural goods. The central element of this is a price support mechanism which, in effect, provides agricultural producers with guaranteed prices for their produce and protects them from cheaper agricultural imports. In short, the mechanism works on the basis of a set of target, intervention and threshold prices. These are set annually by the Council and apply to a majority of agricultural products produced within the EC. As its name suggests, the target price is an estimate of the price a producer may expect to obtain in the market place. The intervention price is set below the level of the target price, and is, in effect, the price producers are guaranteed under the CAP. That is to say, if the market price within the EC for a given product falls below the level of the intervention price, the producer may withdraw the product from the market and sell it to an intervention agency which will pay the producer the equivalent of the intervention price.

Once produce is sold to the intervention agency, it is the responsibility of the agency to dispose of it. This it can do in a variety of ways. Firstly, it may place the produce in storage until the market price rises to or above the level of the intervention price and the produce can be sold within the Community. The costs of storage are paid by the EC through the Guarantee Section of the European Agricultural Guidance and Guarantee Fund (EAGGF). Secondly, the agency may attempt to sell the produce on the world markets, usually at a price well below the intervention price. Here the difference between the price received by the agency and that originally paid to the producer is once again met by the EC. If the agency is unsuccessful in pursuing either of these options, then the surplus produce is either bought up by the Community and sold at a reduced rate to needy social groups; used as food aid to developing countries; or destroyed. In each case the costs are borne by the Community.

Clearly, if ever the market price for a particular product falls below the level of the intervention price, the EC will assume any financial implications. In theory, however, any costs to the Community of supporting producers may be offset, in part at least, by the levy imposed on 25 per cent of agricultural products imported from third countries. This levy raises the world market price of the imported product to the level of the threshold price set by the Community and accrues directly to the EC budget. However, the extent to which theory has been translated into practice is marginal. In 1991, agricultural levies offset

q.v. EC budget pp. 322–7.

approximately only 5 per cent of Community expenditure under the Guidance Section of the EAGGF.

As this last figure suggests, the CAP's price support mechanism is enormously costly to the EC. Indeed, in 1991 the Community spent over ECU 31 billion in guaranteeing prices to agricultural producers. Overall, this figure represented in excess of 53 per cent of overall EC budgetary expenditure for 1991 and, as such, reflects the extent to which expenditure on the CAP has dominated Community expenditure and thus restricted the EC's ability to invest financial resources in other policy areas.

The main reason for the predominance of CAP expenditure in the budget may be attributed to the success of the policy in achieving the objectives laid down in Article 39(1). Since the 1960s, agricultural production within the EC has increased to such an extent that the Community is now guaranteed supplies of most products as the result of domestic production, and has an essentially stable market for agricultural goods. However, the price support mechanism which has helped bring about this situation has also promoted, through guaranteed prices, excessive overproduction. For example, whereas by the mid-1970s increased production meant that the Community was almost 100 per cent self-sufficient as far as cereals, beef, dairy produce, poultry and vegetables were concerned, by the 1980s increased production had led to sizeable surpluses. Indeed, the Community was up to 120 per cent self-sufficient in some areas. Under the price support mechanism producers were guaranteed prices for all produce even if this was in excess of demand.

As this situation persisted throughout the 1980s the need for a reform of the CAP was widely accepted. However, with national governments hesitant to offend often highly organized and vocal farming lobbies, negotiating a reform package to cut surplus production and reduce the costs of CAP expenditure to the EC budget was an extremely slow progress. Nevertheless, in 1988 a series of measures was agreed. These included the introduction of so-called stabilizers — automatic reductions in the level of price support if production exceeds a predetermined level; so-called co-responsibility levies, whereby producers would contribute to the storage and or disposal of excess production; and set-aside schemes under which producers would be paid to take land out of production.[5]

However, any success the reform package may have had in reducing overproduction was short-lived. By the early 1990s surpluses had returned and the Community was forced to address the issue of CAP reform once again. Pressure for reform was also coming from other agricultural producers in non-EC member states, particularly the United States, within the Uruguay Round of GATT talks on reducing barriers to international trade. Here it was argued that the EC, through the CAP, was distorting competition in agricultural trade by unfairly subsidizing its agricultural producers. In addition, the Community was being encouraged to open up its markets to agricultural imports from the countries of Central and

---

5. *Council Decision (88/377/EEC) of 24 June 1988 concerning budgetary expenditure. Interinstitutional Agreement on budgetary discipline and improvement of the budgetary procedure*, OJL 185, 15 July 1988.

Eastern Europe in an attempt to assist them in developing their fledgling market economies.

As a result of these pressures a further reform package was agreed in June 1992 on the basis of proposals put forward by the Commissioner responsible for agriculture, Ray MacSharry, the previous year.[6] The package centred around a sharp reduction in the guaranteed prices offered to cereal and beef producers. In addition, the reforms introduced a shift away from subsidies for production to income support for agricultural producers. Henceforth more land would be taken out of production under the set-aside scheme with producers receiving direct payments for doing so. Finally, measures were also introduced to encourage early retirement, and reduce the intensity of farming methods, thereby promoting more environmentally friendly agricultural production.[7]

The carefully negotiated reforms eventually met with the approval of the EC's critics in the GATT negotiations. However, well organized and often violent opposition to the reforms within national EC farming communities, particularly in France, has remained high, emphasizing the great difficulties the EC faces in bringing about any effective reform to a policy which since its introduction has clearly protected the interests of producers. While the 1992 reform package offered some hope that surpluses would be reduced and that the future survival of agricultural communities throughout the EC would be more secure, continued pressure for greater access to the Community market to be afforded to the countries of Central and Eastern Europe will ensure that reform of the CAP will remain on the EC's political agenda. Indeed, as the Community moves closer towards widening its membership to take in countries such as Austria, Finland, Sweden and Norway, some of which provide their agricultural producers greater protection than the EC does its, further reform of the CAP will be vital. However, given the difficulties faced in reforming the CAP in the past and the reluctance of producers to see their guaranteed markets and prices further reduced does not bode well. The need for a radical overhaul of the CAP has been widely accepted, yet the likelihood of it happening remains, as always, decidedly slim.

FURTHER READING

Aubin, C., 'Comprendre la politique agricole commune: éléments d'analyse positive', *Revue du Marché commun et de l'Union européenne*, No. 356, 1992, pp. 224–30.

Bartola, A. and Sotte, F., 'Riforma della PAC e agricolture nella CEE', *Rivista di Economica Agraria*, Vol. 47, No. 2, 1992, pp. 89–122.

Blumann, C., 'La réforme de la PAC', *Revue trimestrielle de droit européen*, Vol. 29, No. 2, 1993, pp. 187–224.

Butler, F., 'The EC's Common Agricultural Policy', in Lodge, J. (ed.), *The European Community and the Challenge of the Future*, 2nd edn, Pinter, London, 1993, pp. 112–130.

---

6. *European Commission Guidelines for the Reform of the Common Agricultural Policy*, COM(91)100, final, Brussels, 1 February 1991.

7. Details of the reforms can be found in Council Regulations (EEC) 1738/92–1761/92 dated 30 June 1992, (OJL 180, Brussels, 1 July 1992); Council Regulations (EEC) 1765/92–1766/92 dated 30 June 1992 (OJL 181, Brussels, 1 July 1992); Council Regulations (EEC) 2046/92–2080/92 dated 30 June 1992 (OJL 215, Brussels, 30 July 1992); Commission Regulations (EEC) 2289/92–2296/92 dated 31 July 1992 and 4 August 1992 (OJL 221, Brussels, 6 August 1992).

Charles-Le-Bihan, D. and Gadbin, D., 'New trends in the Common Agricultural Policy', in Hurwitz, L. and Lequesne, C. (eds.), *The State of the European Community: Policies, institutions and debates in the transition years*, Longman, London, 1991, pp. 167–81.

EC Commission, *The Agricultural Situation in the Community*, OOPEC, Luxembourg, annually.

EC Commission, *Our Farming Future*, OOPEC, Luxembourg, 1993.

EC Commission, *Green Europe*, periodically.

EC Commission, *Possible Developments in the Policy of Arable Land Set Aside*, COM(93)226 final, Brussels, 18 May 1993.

EcoSoc, *Reform of the Common Agricultural Policy*, OOPEC, Luxembourg, 1992.

European Review of Agricultural Economics, quarterly.

Gadbin, D., 'Le réforme de la politique agricole commune: le piège des quotas', *Revue du marché commun et de l'Union européenne*, No. 358, 1992, pp. 389–96.

Gibbons, J., 'The Common Agricultural Policy', in McDonald, F. and Dearden, S. (eds.), *European Economic Integration*, Longman, London, 1992, pp. 131–45.

Guyomard, H. and Mayé, L.P., 'La réforme de la PAC — Une Révolution ou un grand pas dans la bonne direction?', *Revue du marché commun et de l'Union européenne*, No. 366, 1993, pp. 222–36.

Hendriks, G., *Germany and European Integration: The Common Agricultural Policy — an area of conflict*, Berg, Oxford, 1992.

House of Lords, *The Implementation of the Reform of the Common Agricultural Policy*, Select Committee on the European Communities, 9th Report, 1992–3, HL-28, 27 October 1992.

Koester, U. and Cramon-Taubadel, S. von 'EC agricultural reform ad infinitum?', *Intereconomics*, Vol. 27, No. 4, 1992, pp. 151–6.

Marsh, J. (ed.), *The Changing Role of the Common Agricultural Policy: The future of farming in Europe*, Pinter, London, 1992.

Olmi, G., *Politique agricole commun*, Editions de l'Université de Bruxelles, Brussels, 1991.

Rollo, J.M.C., 'Reform of the CAP: the beginning of the end or the end of the beginning?', *The World Today*, Vol. 48, No. 1, 1992, pp. 4–7.

Swinbank, A., 'CAP reform, 1992', *Journal of Common Market Studies*, Vol. 31, No. 3, 1993, pp. 359–72.

Urff, W. von 'Der Agrarhandel in der Uruguay-Runde des GATT — Irritationen zwischen der EG und der USA', *Integration*, Vol. 16, No. 2, 1993, pp. 80–94.

Warley, T.K., 'Europe's agricultural policy in transition', *International Journal*, Vol. 47, No. 1, 1992, pp. 112–35.

The Common Fisheries Policy

Alongside the CAP, the Community has, since the 1960s, gradually been developing a Common Fisheries Policy (CFP). This is despite the fact that no provision was made in the Treaty of Rome for such a policy until the TEU introduced an amendment to this effect.[8] The main legal basis for the current policy has therefore been Article 38(1) which extends the scope of the Community's common policy for agriculture (CAP) to fisheries. However, central to the policy has also been the freedom of establishment as laid down in Articles 52–58.

q.v. CAP pp. 101–4.

q.v. freedom of establishment pp. 110–14.

Initial agreement on a common fisheries policy was reached by the original six members of the Community in 1970. It was agreed that a common market organization similar to that operated under the CAP for agricultural produce should be established for fisheries as well. This involved a price support mechanism; the setting of various standards governing product quality, handling arrangements and packaging; and is supplemented with financial aid to help reduce the economic and social disparities which exist between the various fishing communities in the EC. In addition, in 1970 it was agreed that in setting up the

---

8. Article 3(e) of the amended Treaty of Rome states that the Community shall include 'a common policy in the sphere of agriculture and fisheries'. Prior to the TEU no mention was made of fisheries in the article, then numbered Article 3(d).

common market for fisheries, national territorial waters would become Community waters and free and equal access to them would be granted to all vessels registered in the Community.

While this was generally acceptable to the Six, since the Community has widened to include first the United Kingdom and then Spain, two countries with sizeable fisheries industries, agreement on the CFP has often proved elusive. In part this stems from the reluctance of member states, particularly the United Kingdom, to grant access to their traditional territorial waters. However, the Community has also been forced to recognize the need to conserve rapidly declining stocks within its waters. This has proved almost impossible to reconcile with the principle of free and equal access as member states have striven to protect the interests of their own national fisheries industries.

In 1983 the then ten member states agreed to a series of reforms to the existing CFP. These aimed at overcoming the problems associated with free and equal access and the need for conservation, while maintaining the economic viability of the EC's fisheries industry. The central element of the CFP, the common market organization, was retained, yet free and equal access to EC waters was subjected to certain restrictions. Firstly, it was agreed that the existing international principle of nation states operating a 12-mile exclusion zone around their coastline, in which only nationally registered vessels or traditional users could fish, should be upheld within the EC. Secondly, in order to conserve stocks a limit was imposed on overall annual catches of certain fish in areas most affected by overfishing. This system of total allowable catches (TACs) is based on national quotas agreed on annually by the Community.

While the reform package appeared to resolve most of the problems facing the CFP at the time, there was still scope for disagreement among the member states particularly over the level of national quotas, and over compliance with them. Similarly, conflict was to emerge over who should be covered by whose national quotas. Following Spain's accession to the EC, many Spanish vessels registered in the United Kingdom in order to access the country's 12-mile exclusion zone, yet with the introduction of the 1988 UK Merchant Shipping Act, restrictions were placed on the registration of foreign-owned vessels. However, the Act was successfully challenged in the ECJ on the basis that it contravened the principle of non-discrimination on the grounds of nationality then contained in Article 7 of the Treaty of Rome.[9] As a consequence, the United Kingdom was forced to amend its legislation accordingly.

The main problem which the Community has, however, been forced to deal with has been a combination of overfishing and overcapacity. This is a result of the widely recognized need to conserve fish stocks in EC waters in the face of increased demand for fisheries products, and the need to reduce the 40 per cent overcapacity which exists in the EC's fisheries industry. These issues were addressed in a series of measures adopted by the Council in 1991 and 1992. The most significant of these included a requirement that the mesh of fishing nets be widened to allow younger fish to avoid being caught, and a prohibition on

---

9. Under the TEU, Article 7 was renumbered Article 6.

the use of drag nets. In addition, vessels were required to remain in port for prescribed periods of time to reduce overfishing, and the Community agreed to increase efforts to enforce TACs and national quotas.[10] Finally, to help reduce the socio-economic impact of restructuring the fishing industry, a decision was adopted in late 1992 to establish a Financial Instrument for Fisheries Guidance (FIFG) as part of the EC's Structural Funds.

q.v.
Structural
Funds pp.
221–5.

While the reforms helped reduce overproduction within the EC, the Community was eager to meet domestic demand for fisheries products and reduce the impact of the reduced fishing opportunities domestically by maintaining and improving existing EC access to the territorial waters of non-member states. However, with demand in the EC high, producers from third countries were eager to exploit export opportunities. As a result, since 1992 the EC has enjoyed an influx of cheap imports of fish from Russia, Iceland, Norway and Poland. Naturally, this has caused domestic EC prices to fall, in some cases by up to 15–20 per cent, leading ultimately to the introduction of minimum prices in early 1993. The fall in prices was exacerbated by devaluations of sterling and the peseta in 1992 and the subsequent increase in cheaper UK and Spanish products circulating within the EC market. Since, unlike the CAP, the CFP has never offered any compensation to producers for changes in exchange rates, there was violent resistance to falling prices in many parts of the Community.[11]

The future of the CFP, although ensured given the formal requirement of a common policy for fisheries inserted into the Treaty of Rome by the TEU, is likely to be fraught with disagreements as the Community persists in attempting to reconcile free and equal access with the need to reduce capacity. Unfortunately, any solution to the problems is likely to be more elusive as a result of recession in Europe and the increased sensitivity of national governments to the prospects of job losses as a consequence of the much needed restructuring of the fisheries industry. Furthermore, the future of the CFP is likely to be the subject of intense debate during the negotiations with Sweden, Finland and particularly Norway, as they proceed towards full membership of the EC by the mid-1990s.

FURTHER READING

Churchill, R.R. 'Quota hopping: the Common Fisheries Policy wrongfooted?', *Common Market Law Review*, Vol. 27, No. 2, 1990, pp. 209–48.

EC Commission *European Fisheries Report: Current position and prospects*, COM(93)95 final, Brussels, 16 March 1993.

European Parliament *Manuel sur la Politique Commune de la Pêche*, OOPEC, Luxembourg, 1992.

House of Lords, *Review of the Common Fisheries Policy*, Select Committee on the European Communities, 2nd Report, 1992–3, HL-9, 23 June 1992.

Wise, M., *The Common Fisheries Policy of the European Community*, Methuen, London, 1984.

10. For details of the reforms see *Council Regulation (EEC) 3687/91 of 28 November 1991 on the Common Organisation of the Market in Fishery Products*, OJL 354, Brussels, 23 December 1991, and *Council Regulation (EEC) 3759/92 of 17 December 1992 on the Common Organization of the Market for Fishery and Aquaculture Products*, OJL 388, Brussels, 31 December 1992.

11. Since the collapse of the Bretton Woods system of fixed exchange rates in the late 1960s, the EC has administered and financed a system of so-called Monetary Compensatory Amounts (MCAs) to compensate farmers for a loss in income as a result of currency fluctuations.The MCAs subsidize or tax imports or exports, where appropriate, so as to rectify the real value if the common support prices in the light of changes in the value of the national currency. MCAs were to be officially abolished at the beginning of 1993.

Free movement of persons, services and capital

Title III of the new Part Three of the amended Treaty of Rome consists of four Chapters covering the free movement of persons, services and capital. As such, the provisions contained within this Title, in conjunction with Title I concerning the free movement of goods, provide the legal basis for the four freedoms which are fundamental to the Community's Single Market. Given the centrality of the latter to the development of the EC since the mid-1980s, the importance for the Community of the provisions in Title III should not be underestimated.

q.v. free movement of goods pp. 85–95.

q.v. Single Market pp. 122–30.

Of the four Chapters contained in the Title, the first two, those relating to workers (Articles 48–51) and the right of establishment within the Community (Articles 52–58), are dedicated to the free movement of persons. The two remaining Chapters contain provisions relating to the free movement of services (Articles 59–67) and the free movement of capital and payments (Articles 67–73h). With the exception of the last Chapter on capital and payments, the majority of the provisions contained in Title III have not been amended by the TEU. Where amendments have been made in Chapters 1–3, these relate solely to decision-making procedures and not to the substance of the provisions.

The free movement of workers

The shortest of the four Chapters in Title III, Chapter 1, concerns the free movement of workers within the Community. According to its provisions, such freedom of movement should have been secured by the end of the transitional period, i.e. by the end of 1969 (Article 48(1)). However, the free movement of workers was still being sought even after the deadline for the completion of the Single Market at the end of 1992 had passed.

The definition of free movement used with regard to workers is laid down in Article 48(2–3). Here, free movement involves the abolition of any discrimination against workers of another Community member state with regard to employment, pay and working conditions. It is envisaged that this will confer on workers the right to accept offers of employment and move freely anywhere in the Community; to stay in a member state for the purpose of finding employment; and to remain in a member state having been employed there. Limitations may, however, be applied on the grounds of public health and security. Similarly, it is stated that the provisions of Article 48 do not apply to those employed in public services (Article 48(4)).

The role of the Community in ensuring the free movement of workers involves the issuance of directives and the making of regulations in a variety of areas, as laid down in Articles 49 and 51. The first of these Articles requires the Community to promote cooperation between national employment services; abolish administrative restrictions on qualifying periods for and on the choice of employment for workers from other member states; and establish mechanisms for making information regarding employment opportunities available throughout the Community. Article 51, meanwhile, requires the Community to adopt measures relating to the transferability of social security payments and benefits between member states as necessary in providing for the free movement of workers. The Community is also requested, under Article 50, to encourage the exchange of young workers.

Prior to the introduction of the amendments to the Treaty of Rome contained in the SEA, measures under Articles 49 and 51 were all adopted by the Council acting unanimously on the basis of a proposal from the Commission. However, the procedure by which directives are issued and regulations are made under Article 49 has since changed significantly. Following the entry into force of the SEA, the Council began adopting measures under Article 49 on the basis of a qualified majority in accordance with the cooperation procedure now laid down in Article 189c and after consulting the EcoSoc. The procedure was further amended by the TEU. As a result, the Council still acts by a qualified majority and in consultation with the EcoSoc, but in dealing with the EP is now obliged to use the conciliation procedure laid down in Article 189b. However, any measures adopted under Article 51 still require unanimity within the Council and do not involve either the EP or the EcoSoc in the decision-making process. Finally, although Article 50 calls on the member states to encourage the exchange of workers within the framework of a joint programme, no indication is given as to the role of either the Community in developing such a programme, or the decision-making procedures to be adopted.

q.v. vocational training and youth policies pp. 190–203.

q.v. Article 189c pp. 304–5.

q.v. Article 189b pp. 302–4.

Title III Free movement of persons, services and capital

Chapter 1 Workers

ARTICLE 48

1. Freedom of movement for workers shall be secured within the Community by the end of the transitional period at the latest.

2. Such freedom of movement shall entail the abolition of any discrimination based on nationality between workers of the Member States as regards employment, remuneration and other conditions of work and employment.

3. It shall entail the right, subject to limitations justified on grounds of public policy, public security or public health:

(a) to accept offers of employment actually made;
(b) to move freely within the territory of Member States for this purpose;
(c) to stay in a Member State for the purpose of employment in accordance with the provisions governing the employment of nationals of that State laid down by law, regulation or administrative action;
(d) to remain in the territory of a Member State after having been employed in that State, subject to conditions which shall be embodied in implementing regulations to be drawn up by the Commission.

The provisions of this Article shall not apply to employment in the public service.

ARTICLE 49

As soon as this Treaty enters into force, the Council shall, **acting in accordance with the procedure referred to in Article 189b** and after consulting the Economic and Social Committee, issue directives or make regulations setting out the measures required to bring about, by progressive stages, freedom of movement for workers, as defined in Article 48, in particular:

(a) by ensuring close cooperation between national employment services;

(b) by systematically and progressively abolishing those administrative procedures and practices and those qualifying periods in respect of eligibility for available employment, whether resulting from national legislation or from agreements previously concluded between Member States, the maintenance of which would form an obstacle to liberalization of the movement of workers;

(c) by systematically and progressively abolishing all such qualifying periods and other restrictions provided for either under national legislation or under agreements previously concluded between Member States as impose on workers of other Member States conditions regarding the free choice of employment other than those imposed on workers of the State concerned;

(d) by setting up appropriate machinery to bring offers of employment into touch with applications for employment and to facilitate the achievement of a balance between supply and demand in the employment market in such a way as to avoid serious threats to the standard of living and level of employment in the various regions and industries.

ARTICLE 50   Member States shall, within the framework of a joint programme, encourage the exchange of young workers.

ARTICLE 51   The Council shall, acting unanimously on a proposal from the Commission, adopt such measures in the field of social security as are necessary to provide freedom of movement for workers; to this end, it shall make arrangements to secure for migrant workers and their dependants:

(a) aggregation, for the purpose of acquiring and retaining the right to benefit and of calculating the amount of benefit, of all periods taken into account under the laws of the several countries;

(b) payment of benefits to persons resident in the territories of Member States.

The right of establishment

Closely linked with the free movement of workers is the right of establishment. Such a right within the Community is provided for in the second Chapter of Title III (Articles 52−58). Essentially, the right of establishment confers on individuals and companies the right to set up business anywhere in the Community. Hence, the Chapter, which consists of seven Articles, deals not only with the rights of companies and firms, as defined in Article 58, but also with those of self-employed people, who are not covered by the provisions of the previous Chapter on the free movement of workers.

The aim of the Community is to guarantee the freedom of establishment to nationals[12] of other member states by progressively abolishing existing and prohibiting new restrictions (Articles 52 and 53). The abolition of existing restrictions, according to Article 52, should have taken place during the transitional period from 1 January 1958 to 31 December 1969. However, total

---

12. For details of nationality see Declaration 2, p. 432.

freedom of establishment within the Community has yet to be achieved, although significant progress has been made as a result of directives issued under the Single Market programme.

q.v. Single Market programme pp. 122–30.

According to the Treaty of Rome, the Community is to promote the freedom of establishment on the basis of a general programme for the abolition of restrictions drawn up by the Commission. These and the necessary implementing directives should have been adopted by the Council during the first years of the Community's existence (Article 54(1)). Needless to say, this goal was not achieved. Instead, the Community is still legislating today in order to achieve the original objectives of the Treaty. According to Article 54(3) special attention is to be paid to certain areas listed. Thus, directives are to be issued which have as their objective the prioritization of the freedom of establishment in areas which contribute to the development of trade and production; cooperation between member states in ascertaining business activity within the Community; the guaranteeing of certain rights for self-employed workers; the abolition of restrictive administrative procedures; the enabling of nationals from one member state to acquire and use land and buildings situated in another member state;[13] the enabling of companies to establish branches in other Community countries; the coordination of safeguards required of companies and firms; and fair competition. However, no activity connected with the exercise of official authority is subject to any directives issued by the Council. Likewise, the Council may, acting by a qualified majority on a proposal from the Commission, exempt other areas from the provisions contained in Articles 52–58 (Article 55). Further exemptions from the provisions contained in the Chapter may be granted on the grounds of public policy, public security and public health (Article 56). However, national legislation in this respect is to be coordinated in line with directives currently issued by the Council in accordance with the conciliation procedure laid down in Article 189b. This change of decision-making procedure introduced by the TEU replaces the previous SEA requirement that the Council act by a qualified majority in line with the cooperation procedure, rather than simply in consultation with the EP, as was previously the case under the original Treaty of Rome.

q.v. Article 189b pp. 302–4.

q.v. cooperation procedure pp. 300–2.

Directives issued under Article 54 are adopted by the Council in accordance with the conciliation procedure laid down in Article 189b and in consultation with the EcoSoc (Article 54(2)). Thus the Council acts by a qualified majority. However, this will only be the case once the TEU comes into force. Prior to this, and after the transitional period had expired, directives were issued by the Council on the basis of a qualified majority in the Council once it had consulted the EP and the EcoSoc. However, it was not until the SEA introduced the cooperation procedure that the EP became fully involved in the decision-making process with regard to the freedom of establishment.

A similar development in the decision-making process has taken place with regard to the directives relating to the mutual recognition of diplomas and other

---

13. The *Protocol on the Acquisition of Property in Denmark* (see p. 394), attached to the Treaty of Rome by the TEU, allows Denmark to maintain existing legislation on the acquisition of second homes.

formal qualifications issued by the Council on the basis of Article 57. The provisions of this Article are aimed at promoting the free movement of self-employed workers within the Community not only through the mutual recognition of diplomas, but also through the coordination of national training requirements for the professions. As far as mutual recognition and the coordination of national legislation relating to the rights of establishment of self-employed workers are concerned, the Council is to act in accordance with the conciliation procedure laid down in Article 189b. This procedure, introduced by the TEU, supersedes the procedure followed under the SEA whereby the Council acted on the basis of a qualified majority and in accordance with the cooperation procedure. This had itself replaced the previous requirement for the Council to act solely in consultation with the EP, as originally provided for in the Treaty of Rome when it first entered into force. Hence it became an essential element of the Single Market programme, speeding up decision-making in an area where progress prior to the SEA had been decidedly slow. A similar procedure is to be adopted where directives involve a member state amending existing principles laid down by law in relation to professional training requirements and other conditions of access, except that here the Council must always act unanimously. Such a procedure was previously required, prior to the introduction of the SEA, for directives relating to the protection of savings, and to the pharmaceutical, medical and allied professions.

q.v. Article 189b pp. 302–4.

q.v. cooperation procedure pp. 300–2.

Chapter 2   Right of establishment

ARTICLE 52

Within the framework of the provisions set out below, restrictions on the freedom of establishment of nationals of a Member State in the territory of another Member State shall be abolished by progressive stages in the course of the transitional period. Such progressive abolition shall also apply to restrictions on the setting up of agencies, branches, or subsidiaries by nationals of any Member State established in the territory of any Member State.

Freedom of establishment shall include the right to take up and pursue activities as self-employed persons and to set up and manage undertakings, in particular companies or firms within the meaning of the second paragraph of Article 58, under the conditions laid down for its own nationals by the law of the country where such establishment is effected, subject to the provisions of the Chapter relating to capital.

ARTICLE 53

Member States shall not introduce any new restrictions on the right of establishment in their territories of nationals of other Member States, save as otherwise provided in this Treaty.

ARTICLE 54

1. Before the end of the first stage, the Council shall, acting unanimously on a proposal from the Commission and after consulting the Economic and Social Committee and the European Parliament, draw up a general programme for the abolition of existing restrictions on freedom of establishment within the Community. The Commission shall submit its proposal to the Council during the first two years of the first stage.

The programme shall set out the general conditions under which freedom of establishment is to be attained in the case of each type of activity and in particular the stages by which it is to be attained.

2. In order to implement this general programme or, in the absence of such programme, in order to achieve a stage in attaining freedom of establishment as regards a particular activity, the Council, **acting in accordance with the procedure referred to in Article 189b** and after consulting the Economic and Social Committee, shall act by means of directives.

3. The Council and the Commission shall carry out the duties devolving upon them under the preceding provisions, in particular:

(a) by according, as a general rule, priority treatment to activities where freedom of establishment makes a particularly valuable contribution to the development of production and trade;

(b) by ensuring close cooperation between the competent authorities in the Member States in order to ascertain the particular situation within the Community of the various activities concerned;

(c) by abolishing those administrative procedures and practices, whether resulting from national legislation or from agreements previously concluded between Member States, the maintenance of which would form an obstacle to freedom of establishment;

(d) by ensuring that workers of one Member State employed in the territory of another Member State may remain in that territory for the purpose of taking up activities therein as self-employed persons, where they satisfy the conditions which they would be required to satisfy if they were entering that State at the time when they intended to take up such activities;

(e) by enabling a national of one Member State to acquire and use land and buildings situated in the territory of another Member State, in so far as this does not conflict with the principles laid down in Article 39(2);

(f) by effecting the progressive abolition of restrictions on freedom of establishment in every branch of activity under consideration, both as regards the conditions for setting up agencies, branches or subsidiaries in the territory of a Member State and as regards the conditions governing the entry of personnel belonging to the main establishment into managerial or supervisory posts in such agencies, branches or subsidiaries;

(g) by coordinating to the necessary extent the safeguards which, for the protection of the interests of members and others, are required by Member States of companies or firms within the meaning of the second paragraph of Article 58 with a view to making such safeguards equivalent throughout the Community;

(h) by satisfying themselves that the conditions of establishment are not distorted by aids granted by Member States.

ARTICLE 55

The provisions of this Chapter shall not apply, so far as any given Member State is concerned, to activities which in that State are connected, even occasionally, with the exercise of official authority.

The Council may, acting by a qualified majority on a proposal from the Commission, rule that the provisions of this Chapter shall not apply to certain activities.

ARTICLE 56

1. The provisions of this Chapter and measures taken in pursuance thereof shall not prejudice the applicability of provisions laid down by law, regulation or administrative action providing for special treatment for foreign nationals on grounds of public policy, public security or public health.

2. Before the end of the transitional period, the Council shall, acting unanimously on a proposal from the Commission and after consulting the European Parliament, issue directives for the coordination of the aforementioned provisions laid down

by law, regulation or administrative action. After the end of the second stage, however, the Council shall, acting **in accordance with the procedure referred to in Article 189b**, issue directives for the coordination of such provisions as, in each Member State, are a matter for regulation or administrative action.

ARTICLE 57

1. In order to make it easier for persons to take up and pursue activities as self-employed persons, the Council shall, **acting in accordance with the procedure referred to in Article 189b**, issue directives for the mutual recognition of diplomas, certificates and other evidence of formal qualifications.

2. For the same purpose, the Council shall, before the end of the transitional period, *issue directives for the coordination of the provisions laid down by law, regulation or administrative action in Member States concerning the taking up and pursuit of activities as self-employed persons. The Council, acting unanimously on a proposal from the Commission and after consulting the European Parliament, shall decide on directives* the implementation of which involves in at least one Member State amendment of the existing principles laid down by law governing the professions with respect to training and conditions of access for natural persons. In other cases the Council shall act **in accordance with the procedure referred to in Article 189b**.

3. In the case of the medical and allied and pharmaceutical professions, the progressive abolition of restrictions shall be dependent upon coordination of the conditions for their exercise in the various Member States.

ARTICLE 58

Companies or firms formed in accordance with the law of a Member State and having their registered office, central administration or principal place of business within the Community shall, for the purposes of this Chapter, be treated in the same way as natural persons who are nationals of Member States.

'Companies or firms' means companies or firms constituted under civil or commercial law, including cooperative societies, and other legal persons governed by public or private law, save for those which are non-profit making.

The free movement of services

The third Chapter of Part Three, Title III concerns the free movement of services within the Community (Articles 59–66). The provisions contained in the eight Articles which make up the Chapter apply to services as defined in Article 60. Hence, they cover areas of economic activity such as insurance, banking, information technology and telecommunications. These services are also subject to the provisions of the previous Chapter on the right of establishment. The provisions do not, however, apply to transport services. These are covered by the provisions of Title IV. Nor, according to Article 61, do the provisions apply to the free movement of capital in banking and insurance services, as this falls under the provisions of Title III, Chapter 4 concerning capital and payments.

q.v. provisions of Title IV pp. 131–3.

The essential aim of the Community in respect of services is to abolish all restrictions on companies and nationals[14] of EC member states providing services within the EC (Article 59) and prohibit the introduction of new restrictions (Article

q.v. Title III, Chapter 4 pp. 119–22.

---

14. For details of nationality see Declaration 2, p. 432.

62). Originally, it was intended that this would be completed during the transitional stage (Article 59) in line with a general programme for liberalization to be put forward by the Commission (Article 63), and with the Community moving beyond the general programme where the economic situation allowed (Article 64). Yet, as indicated below, it was not until the Community embarked on the Internal Market programme in the mid-1980s that substantial progress was made in this direction. In the meantime, member states were to be prohibited from applying restrictions on the freedom to provide services on the grounds of nationality or residence (Article 65), and where proposals were put forward, these were to prioritize liberalization in services which affect production costs or promote trade in goods (Article 63).

q.v.
Internal
Market pp.
120–30.

Although the Treaty aims at free movement for all within the Community, preference is given to promoting greater freedom for EC nationals to provide services. As such, although the Council, after the first stage and prior to the SEA, adopted directives implementing Commission proposals on the basis of a qualified majority, if the provisions of Chapter 3 were to be extended to nationals of third countries, a unanimous vote was required. With the introduction of the amendments introduced by the SEA, however, the Council is now only required to vote by a qualified majority (Article 59).

Chapter 3   Services

ARTICLE 59

Within the framework of the provisions set out below, restrictions on freedom to provide services within the Community shall be progressively abolished during the transitional period in respect of nationals of Member States who are established in a State of the Community other than that of the person for whom the services are intended.

The Council may, acting by a qualified majority on a proposal from the Commission, extend the provisions of this Chapter to nationals of a third country who provide services and who are established within the Community.

ARTICLE 60

Services shall be considered to be 'services' within the meaning of this Treaty where they are normally provided for remuneration, in so far as they are not governed by the provisions relating to freedom of movement for goods, capital and persons.

'Services' shall in particular include:

(a) activities of an industrial character;
(b) activities of a commercial character;
(c) activities of craftsmen;
(d) activities of the professions.

Without prejudice to the provisions of the Chapter relating to the right of establishment, the person providing a service may, in order to do so temporarily pursue his activity in the State where the service is provided, under the same conditions as are imposed by that State on its own nationals.

ARTICLE 61

1. Freedom to provide services in the field of transport shall be governed by the provisions of the Title relating to transport.

2. The liberalization of banking and insurance services connected with movements

of capital shall be effected in step with the progressive liberalization of movement of capital.

ARTICLE 62

Save as otherwise provided in this Treaty, Member States shall not introduce any new restrictions on the freedom to provide services which have in fact been attained at the date of the entry into force of this Treaty.

ARTICLE 63

1. Before the end of the first stage, the Council shall, acting unanimously on a proposal from the Commission and after consulting the Economic and Social Committee and the European Parliament, draw up a general programme for the abolition of existing restrictions on freedom to provide services within the Community. The Commission shall submit its proposal to the Council during the first two years of the first stage.

The programme shall set out the general conditions under which and the stages by which each type of service is to be liberalized.

2. In order to implement this general programme or, in the absence of such programme, in order to achieve a stage in the liberalization of a specific service, the Council shall, on a proposal from the Commission and after consulting the Economic and Social Committee and the European Parliament, issue directives, acting unanimously until the end of the first stage and by a qualified majority thereafter.

3. As regards the proposals and decisions referred to in paragraphs 1 and 2, priority shall as a general rule be given to those services which directly affect production costs or the liberalization of which helps to promote trade in goods.

ARTICLE 64

The Member States declare their readiness to undertake the liberalization of services beyond the extent required by the directives issued pursuant to Article 63(2), if their general economic situation and the situation of the economic sector concerned so permit.

To this end, the Commission shall make recommendations to the Member States concerned.

ARTICLE 65

As long as restrictions on freedom to provide services have not been abolished, each Member State shall apply such restrictions without distinction on grounds of nationality or residence to all persons providing services within the meaning of the first paragraph of Article 59.

ARTICLE 66

The provisions of Articles 55 to 58 shall apply to the matters covered by this Chapter.

The free movement of capital and payments

The final Chapter of Part Three, Title III concerns the objective of establishing the free movement of capital and payments throughout the Community (Articles 67–73h). Thus the Chapter covers not only the removal of restrictions on cross-border investment, but also those on the movement of money within the Community. As such the full implementation of the provisions of the Chapter is a necessary prerequisite for EMU.

q.v. EMU pp. 150–80.

As a result of amendments introduced by the TEU, the Chapter brings together under one heading the existing provisions of the Chapter, a slightly amended version of the original Article 106 of the Treaty of Rome as the new Article 73h, and several entirely new Articles. The effect of this on the Chapter is that its title has changed under the TEU from simply 'Capital' to 'Capital and Payments'. A more profound effect of the amendments is that, according to Article 73a, from 1 January 1994 the first seven Articles and the final Article of the Chapter cease to be valid. This date signals the start of Stage II of EMU and the abolition of all restrictions on the free movement of capital within the EC. The affected Articles will then be replaced by Articles 73b–73g which were inserted into the Treaty by the TEU. However, until 1 January 1994 the provisions of Articles 67–73 and Article 73h are applicable. It is these provisions which are discussed first.

As provisions contained in the Treaty of Rome when it was first signed, Articles 67–73 and Article 73h set out the Community's original aims with regard to the free movement of capital and payments within the EC. As with services, the essential aim of the Community is progressively to remove all restrictions on free movement within its borders (Article 67). With regard to capital and payments, this is to be achieved through the issuance of directives by the Council,[15] acting by a qualified majority, on a proposal from the Commission, which under Article 69 is required to consult the Monetary Committee set up under Article 105 of the Treaty of Rome before amendments were introduced to the Article by the TEU. Member states are encouraged not to introduce new restrictions on capital movements (Article 71 and Article 73(3)) and, at the same time, be as liberal as possible in granting authorization for exchanges where this is still required (Art 68(1)). Similarly, according to the second paragraph of Article 68, member states are not allowed to apply in a discriminatory fashion domestic rules governing capital markets. Finally, Articles 71 and 73h(1) state that capital movements and payments may be liberalized beyond the level prescribed in the Treaty where the economic situation in the member states allows it.

q.v. Monetary Committee pp. 153–4.

With regard to the exchange policies of the member states, the Commission may propose measures to coordinate these. Such measures are, since the end of the second stage of the transitional period, to be adopted by the Council on the basis of a qualified majority. However, where they involve a restriction on liberalization they may only be adopted by the Council acting unanimously (Article 70). In addition, the Commission may authorize member states to introduce measures to protect the functioning of their capital markets if they are being disrupted by movements of capital. Such authorization may, however, be amended or revoked by the Council acting by a qualified majority (Article 73(1)). A similar procedure exists for difficulties in applying exchange rules as a result of measures introduced to coordinate exchange policies (Article 70(2)).

However, the procedure adopted when a member state, for reasons of urgency or secrecy, is forced to adopt measures on its own initiative is significantly different. Such measures must be communicated to the Commission and the other member states, yet it is the Commission which, in consultation with the Monetary

---

15. In line with the Declaration 3 (see p. 432), the Council, as required by Articles 67–73h, comprises Economic and Financial Ministers.

Committee, decides whether the measures should be abolished or amended (Article 73(2)). The Commission is also responsible for delivering opinions on capital movements to and from third countries communicated to it by the member states (Article 72). However, this has not been a greatly used power.

As indicated above, the provisions contained in Articles 67–73 and 73h only apply until 31 December 1993. After this date they are replaced by Articles 73b–73g, as introduced to the Treaty by the TEU, thus ensuring a qualitative improvement of facilities for capital movements. According to the provisions contained in these Articles, all restrictions on the movement of capital and on payments within the Community and with third countries will be prohibited (Article 73b). However, all member states which, on 31 December 1993, enjoy derogations from existing Community law in this respect may be allowed to maintain these for a maximum of a further two years. In addition, any restrictions relating to capital movements involving third countries which have been adopted as part of national or Community law prior to 31 December 1993 will still be applicable. Similarly, the Council may, acting unanimously and on a proposal from the Commission, introduce additional measures restricting such capital movements. Where measures do not constitute a reversal of existing liberalization measures with regard to capital movements involving third countries, these may be adopted by the Council acting by a qualified majority (Article 73c).

Furthermore, the prohibition of restrictions may not prevent member states either from applying the relevant provisions of existing tax law, or from taking measures to combat tax evasion. However, no measures may be used in a discriminatory fashion. Similarly, according to Article 73d, the provisions of Articles 73b–73g may not prejudice the applicability of restrictions on the right of establishment.

q.v. right of establish-ment pp. 110–14.

As with Article 73, the new Article 73f makes provision for the Community to act when capital movements cause serious difficulties within the EC. However, from 1 January 1994 the Community may only act in instances where capital movements to or from third countries affect the operation of the economic and monetary union. In such cases, the Council, acting on a proposal from the Commission and in consultation with the European Monetary Institute and subsequently, when established, the European Central Bank, may take safeguard measures which can last up to six months (Article 73f). Similarly, under Article 73g, the Council may take measures concerning the movement of capital as part of the Common Foreign and Security Policy (CFSP), as provided for in Article 228a. Member states may also, for so-called 'serious' political reasons and on grounds of urgency, take unilateral action against third countries with regard to capital movements. However, contrary to what was previously provided for in Article 73, it is now left to the Council, not the Commission, to amend or abolish these measures. Any decision taken by the Council in this respect is to be reported to the EP (Article 73g). Finally, where the Council is to act under Articles 73f and 73g, the preparatory work is to be carried out by the Monetary Committee prior to the beginning of Stage III of EMU, and by the Economic and Financial Committee thereafter (Article 109c).

q.v. European Central Bank pp. 158–9.

q.v. Article 228a p. 339.

q.v. Article 109c pp. 168–9.

Chapter 4   Capital and payments

ARTICLE 67

1. During the transitional period and to the extent necessary to ensure the proper functioning of the common market, Member States shall progressively abolish between themselves all restrictions on the movement of capital belonging to persons resident in Member States and any discrimination based on the nationality or on the place of residence of the parties or on the place where such capital is invested.

2. Current payments connected with the movement of capital between Member States shall be freed from all restrictions by the end of the first stage at the latest.

ARTICLE 68

1. Member States shall, as regards the matters dealt with in this Chapter, be as liberal as possible in granting such exchange authorizations as are still necessary after the entry into force of this Treaty.

2. Where a Member State applies to the movements of capital liberalized in accordance with the provisions of this Chapter the domestic rules governing the capital market and the credit system, it shall do so in a non-discriminatory manner.

3. Loans for the direct or indirect financing of a Member State or its regional or local authorities shall not be issued or placed in other Member States unless the States concerned have reached agreement thereon. This provision shall not preclude the application of Article 22 of the Protocol on the Statute of the European Investment Bank.[16]

ARTICLE 69

The Council shall, on a proposal from the Commission, which for this purpose shall consult the Monetary Committee provided for in Article 105, issue the necessary directives for the progressive implementation of the provisions of Article 67, acting unanimously during the first two stages and by a qualified majority thereafter.

ARTICLE 70

1. The Commission shall propose to the Council measures for the progressive coordination of the exchange policies of Member States in respect of the movement of capital between those States and third countries. For this purpose the Council shall issue directives, acting by a qualified majority. It shall endeavour to attain the highest possible degree of liberalization. Unanimity shall be required for measures which constitute a step back as regards the liberalization of capital movements.

2. Where the measures taken in accordance with paragraph 1 do not permit the elimination of differences between the exchange rules of Member States and where such differences could lead persons resident in one of the Member States to use the freer transfer facilities within the Community which are provided for in Article 67 in order to evade the rules of one of the Member States concerning the movement of capital to or from third countries, that State may, after consulting the other Member States and the Commission, take appropriate measures to overcome these difficulties.

Should the Council find that these measures are restricting the free movement of capital within the Community to a greater extent than is required for the purpose of overcoming the difficulties, it may, acting by a qualified majority on a proposal from the Commission, decide that the State concerned shall amend or abolish these measures.

---

16. The *Protocol on the Statute of the European Investment Bank* is reproduced on pp. 544–53.

ARTICLE 71

Member States shall endeavour to avoid introducing within the Community any new exchange restrictions on the movement of capital and current payments connected with such movements, and shall endeavour not to make existing rules more restrictive.

They declare their readiness to go beyond the degree of liberalization of capital movements provided for in the preceding Articles in so far as their economic situation, in particular the situation of their balance of payments, so permits.

The Commission may, after consulting the Monetary Committee, make recommendations to Member States on this subject.

ARTICLE 72

Member States shall keep the Commission informed of any movements of capital to and from third countries which come to their knowledge. The Commission may deliver to Member States any opinions which it considers appropriate on this subject.

ARTICLE 73

1. If movements of capital lead to disturbances in the functioning of the capital market in any Member State, the Commission shall, after consulting the Monetary Committee, authorize that State to take protective[17] measures in the field of capital movements, the conditions and details of which the Commission shall determine.

The Council may, acting by a qualified majority, revoke this authorization or amend the conditions or details thereof.

2. A Member State which is in difficulties may, however, on grounds of secrecy or urgency, take the measures mentioned above, where this proves necessary, on its own initiative. The Commission and the other Member States shall be informed of such measures by the date of their entry into force at the latest. In this event the Commission may, after consulting the Monetary Committee, decide that the State concerned shall amend or abolish the measures.

ARTICLE 73a

As from 1 January 1994, Articles 67 to 73 shall be replaced by Articles 73b, c, d, e, f and g.

ARTICLE 73b

1. Within the framework of the provisions set out in this Chapter, all restrictions on the movement of capital between Member States and between Member States and third countries shall be prohibited.

2. Within the framework of the provisions set out in this Chapter, all restrictions on payments between Member States and between Member States and third countries shall be prohibited.

ARTICLE 73c

1. The Provisions of Article 73b shall be without prejudice to the application to third countries, of any restrictions which exist on 31 December 1993 under national or Community law adopted in respect of the movement of capital to or from third countries involving direct investment — including investment in real estate — establishment, the provision of financial services or the admission of securities to capital markets.

2. Whilst endeavouring to achieve the objective of free movement of capital between Member States and third countries to the greatest extent possible and without prejudice to the other Chapters of this Treaty, the Council may, acting by a qualified majority on a proposal from the Commission, adopt

17. In OJC 224 of 31 August 1992, the word 'protective' appears in italics. There would appear to be no firm reason for this. Earlier versions of the Treaty of Rome have not highlighted the word in any way.

measures on the movement of capital to or from third countries involving direct investment — including investment in real estate — establishment, the provision of financial services or the admission of securities to capital markets. Unanimity shall be required for measures under this paragraph which constitute a step back in Community law as regards the liberalization of the movement of capital to or from third countries.

ARTICLE 73d

1. The provisions of Article 73b shall be without prejudice to the right of Member States:

(a) to apply the relevant provision of their tax law which distinguish between tax-payers who are not in the same situation with regard to their place of residence or with regard to the place where their capital is invested;[18]

(b) to take all requisite measures to prevent infringement of national law and regulations, in particular in the field of taxation and the prudential supervision of financial institutions, or to lay down procedures for the declaration of capital movements for purposes of administrative or statistical information, or to take measures which are justified on grounds of public policy or public security.

2. The provisions of this Chapter shall be without prejudice to the applicability of restrictions on the right of establishment which are compatible with this Treaty.

3. The measures and procedures referred to in paragraphs 1 and 2 shall not constitute a means of arbitrary discrimination or a disguised restriction on the free movement of capital and payments as defined in Article 73b.

ARTICLE 73e

By way of derogation from Article 73b, Member States which, on 31 December 1993, enjoy a derogation on the basis of existing Community law, shall be entitled to maintain, until 31 December 1995 at the latest, restrictions on movement of capital authorized by such derogations as exist on that date.

ARTICLE 73f

Where, in exceptional circumstances, movement of capital to or from third countries cause, or threaten to cause, serious difficulties for the operation of economic and monetary union, the Council, acting by a qualified majority on a proposal from the Commission and after consulting the ECB, may take safeguard measures with regard to third countries for a period not exceeding six months if such measures are strictly necessary.

ARTICLE 73g

1. If, in the cases envisaged in Article 228a, action by the Community is deemed necessary, the Council may, in accordance with the procedure provided for in Article 228a, take the necessary urgent measures on the movement of capital and on payments as regards the third countries concerned.

2. Without prejudice to Article 224 and as long as the Council has not taken measures pursuant to paragraph 1, a Member State may, for serious political reasons and on grounds of urgency, take unilateral measures against a third country with regard to capital movements and payments. The Commission and the other Member States shall be informed of such measures by the date of their entry into force at the latest.

The Council may, acting by a qualified majority on a proposal from the Commission, decide that the Member State concerned shall amend or abolish

18. See also Declaration 7, p. 433.

such measures. The President of the Council shall inform the European Parliament of any such decision taken by the Council.

ARTICLE 73h   **Until 1 January 1994, the following provisions shall be applicable:**

1) Each Member State undertakes to authorize, in the currency of the Member State in which the creditor or the beneficiary resides, any payment connected with the movement of goods, services or capital, and any transfers of capital and earnings, to the extent that the movement of goods, services, capital and persons between Member States has been liberalized pursuant to this Treaty.

The Member States declare their readiness to undertake the liberalization of payments beyond the extent provided in the preceding subparagraph, in so far as their economic situation in general and the state of their balance of payment in particular so permit.

2) In so far as movement of goods, services and capital are limited only by restrictions on payments connected therewith, these restrictions shall be progressively abolished by applying, mutatis mutandis, the provisions of this Chapter and the Chapters relating to the abolition of qualitative restrictions and to the liberalization of services.

3) Member States undertake not to introduce between themselves any new restrictions on transfers connected with the invisible transactions listed in Annex III to this Treaty.

The progressive abolition of existing restrictions shall be effected in accordance with the provisions of Articles 63 to 65, in so far as such abolition is not governed by the provisions contained in paragraphs 1 and 2 or by the other provisions of this Chapter.

4) If need be, Member States shall consult each other on the measures to be taken to enable the payment and transfers mentioned in this Article to be effected; such measures shall not prejudice the attainment of the objectives set out in this Treaty.

The Customs Union and the Single Market[19]

When the EEC was set up in 1958 the primary aims of the then six members were the promotion of free trade between themselves and the creation of a customs union. Since then, as the principle of free trade has become more widely accepted and trade tariffs have been reduced, particularly within Western Europe, the emphasis on the removal of tariffs and quantitative restrictions on trade, has been replaced by the desire to develop the Customs Union into a 'single' market. As such, a decade and a half after the Customs Union was formally established in 1968, the aim of the Community moved beyond the abolition of tariff barriers on trade between its member states to the removal of all non-tariff barriers, thus creating a single EC market. It is this single internal EC market, like the Customs Union before it, which today is the cornerstone of the Community's existence. Its importance therefore cannot be underestimated. Before discussing the Single

---

19. Here, the terms 'Single Market', 'Internal Market' and '1992' are used interchangeably to indicate the efforts of the Community from the mid-1980s onwards to realize the free movement of goods, capital, services and people.

Market, however, it is necessary first to understand what is meant by a customs union.

The essential nature of a customs union is free trade between the union's members and the establishment of a common external tariff on trade with non-member states. Thus, the creation of a customs union involves the abolition of all import and export duties, and of quantitative restrictions on trade between the member states. In addition, it involves the harmonization of national tariffs on trade with third countries and their subsequent replacement with an external tariff common to all member states. However, as far as the EC is concerned, the Customs Union provided for in the Treaty of Rome forms part of a 'common' market. Thus, it is supplemented by provisions in the Treaty for the free movement of persons, services and capital, as well as a common policy for agriculture. Furthermore, the effective functioning of the Customs Union is promoted internally through a common competition policy, and externally through a common commercial policy. Both these are administered centrally by the supranational institutions of the Community.

q.v. free movement pp. 108–22.

q.v. competition policy pp. 137–45.

q.v. common commercial policy pp. 180–7.

While the Six were slow to implement the majority of the provisions which accompanied the establishment of the Customs Union — the major exception being the Common Agricultural Policy — the actual removal of tariff barriers on trade between the member states and the setting up of the common external tariff proceeded at a faster rate than provided for in the Treaty of Rome. Thus the EEC's Custom Union was formally established eighteen months ahead of schedule on 1 July 1968.

However, although the establishment of the Customs Union was accompanied by a steady increase in trade between the then six member states, what little progress which had been made in abolishing non-tariff barriers and thus liberalizing trade further, was to be stifled by the general economic downturn and recession which Europe suffered in the 1970s and the problems resulting from the first enlargement of the Community in 1973. The ensuing stagnation in the development of the Community meant that only limited additional progress was made in consolidating the achievements of the Six in establishing the Customs Union. Indeed, as member states sought to overcome the problems of inflation, unemployment and industrial restructuring, forced upon governments by the recession, by pursuing nationally orientated economic policies, the attraction of developing the Common Market and common Community policies was limited. Consequently, as the Community entered the 1980s, the market which its members constituted was essentially as fragmented as it had been in 1968. This was largely due to the proliferation of non-tariff barriers.

While the fragmented state of the Community's supposed Common Market may have led some to believe that the future of the EC was in doubt, overcoming the fragmentation was seized upon by supporters of the Community, and by the Commission in particular, as the means to promote the economic rejuvenation of the European economy and the political renaissance of the Community itself. Ranged alongside the pro-EC lobby were several member states traditionally sceptical about closer integration, most notably the United Kingdom under Margaret Thatcher. Decidedly less enthused about the Commission's political motives for a barrier-free EC, these governments supported the idea since it was very much in line with the free market principles which had become central to their economic policies (see The Road to Maastricht, pp. 13–25). It was argued that by removing all the non-tariff barriers to trade within the EC, thus realizing the Community's Internal Market, producers would gain access to a consumer market of approximately 320 million people. Such an opportunity, if seized upon by industry, would, it was believed, boost the recession-hit European economy, thus promoting economic growth and creating more jobs. Indeed, the 1988 Cecchini Report into the costs of not completing the Internal Market produced for the Commission, suggested that the project could create as many as 5 million new jobs and add as much as 5 per cent to Community GDP.[20] Furthermore, the enforced modernization and greater efficiency which increased competition within a single EC market would promote, would improve the competitive position of EC industry on world markets and thus allow Community producers to challenge and hopefully displace US and Japanese competitors. Hence, the much voiced support for the proposals from EC-based multinationals.

Meanwhile, politically, by agreeing to embark on such an ambitious project, the member states would create a new *raison d'être* for the Community. In addition, if the Single Market were to function effectively and fairly, powers of administration and monitoring would have to be passed to the independent supranational authorities. Thus, not only would the Community gain recognition as the essential framework for the Single Market, its powers would also be strengthened. Similarly, the need to complement the Single Market with minimum health, safety, and environmental standards would give added political substance to the Community.

The ideas behind the completion of the Internal Market were first formulated in two Commission reports issued in June 1981 and December 1982.[21] There then followed a series of political pronouncements by the European Council and member state governments in favour of the idea, culminating in a formal request that the Commission draw up a detailed list of the necessary measures. This task was duly undertaken under the direction of Lord Cockfield, and resulted in the publication of the Commission's so-called White Paper on the Internal Market.[22] This was formally presented to the European Council at its Summit in Milan in June 1985.

The essential aim of completing the Internal Market, as laid down in the White Paper, was the realization within the EC of the four so-called 'freedoms': the free movement of goods; the free movement of people; the free movement of services; and the free movement of capital. Thus, the White Paper contained 289 legislative

20. The full report of Cecchini and his team is contained in EC Commission, *Research on the 'Cost of Non-Europe' Basic Findings*, 16 vols., OOPEC, Luxembourg, 1988. A summary of the findings is contained in Cecchini, P., *1992 The European Challenge: The benefits of a single market*, Gower, Aldershot, 1988. However, not all authorities accept Cecchini's findings.

21. *The State of the Internal Market*, COM(81)313 final, Brussels, 17 June 1981; *Strengthening the Internal Market*, COM(82)399 final, Brussels, 24 June 1982.

22. *Completing the internal market — White Paper from the Commission to the European Council (Milan, 28 and 29 June 1985)*, COM(85)310 final, Brussels, 14 June 1985.

proposals, the adoption of which the Commission believed would be vital if such an objective were to be attained. These were subsequently accepted by the member states as the basis on which the necessary Single Market legislation would be introduced. In addition, the European Council agreed to set up an intergovernmental conference (IGC) to amend the Treaty of Rome so that the completion of the Internal Market could become an explicit aim of the Community. Moreover, the IGC was empowered to introduce a new decision-making process giving a greater legislative role to the EP and allowing the Council to adopt most Single Market legislation by a qualified majority. The resulting treaty, the Single European Act, thus provided the legislative framework through which the proposals in the White Paper could be translated into legislation. As such, the SEA set out the EC's goal as establishing the Internal Market by 31 December 1992 (Article 8a, now Article 7a); introduced qualified majority voting in the Council of Ministers for the majority of measures required to achieve this (Article 100a);[23] and provided the EP, through the so-called 'cooperation procedure', with a significant role in the adoption of Single Market legislation (Article 149, now Article 189c).

q.v. Article 7a p. 67.

q.v. Article 100a pp. 148–9.

q.v. Article 189c pp. 304–5.

Once the SEA had entered into force in July 1987 work formally began on realizing the four freedoms. The White Paper identified three types of non-tariff barriers which would have to be abolished if the Single Market were to be worthy of its name. These were the various physical, technical and fiscal barriers which reduced opportunities for trade within the Community.

The most visible and clearly identifiable of these barriers to free movement are physical barriers, the most obvious being the Community's internal frontier posts and the administrative paperwork involved in transporting goods from one member state to another. The White Paper proposed that all internal EC frontier posts be abolished by 31 December 1992. As a result goods being transported within the Community would not be subjected to any border controls, thus reducing the time spent by traders and carriers crossing borders, and removing the administrative costs borne by the member states in maintaining internal border controls. For the individual citizen, the abolition of border controls would, in theory, reduce the cost of imported goods. More significantly, however, individuals would be allowed to move freely throughout the Community without having to present a passport.

Although the principle of promoting free movement through the abolition of physical barriers was generally welcomed by the member states, concerns were voiced over the impact the removal of the EC's internal border controls would have on illegal immigration, drug trafficking, and international terrorism. For the majority of member states the answer to the problem lay in moving towards common immigration and visa policies and increasing cross-border police cooperation. Indeed, the commitment of the Benelux states, Germany and France to remove border controls led the governments of the five countries to sign the

---

23. Under Article 100a(2) of the Treaty of Rome, measures relating to fiscal matters, those relating to the free movement of persons, and those relating to the rights and interests of employed people require unanimity in the Council of Ministers if they are to be adopted.

so-called 'Schengen Agreement' of 14 June 1985.[24] Under the agreement, the signatories endeavoured to remove all controls on individuals, where possible, by 1 January 1990. This would be accompanied by increased cooperation in matters related to justice and home affairs and a tightening of external border controls. However, while the Schengen signatories moved, albeit unsuccessfully, towards the early removal of border controls, the UK government remained resolute in its opposition to the total abolition of controls, arguing forcibly for their maintenance to control illegal immigration, drug trafficking and terrorism. Consequently, many controls were still in place when the proposed date for the completion of the Internal Market passed on 31 December 1992.[25]

q.v. justice and home affairs pp. 381–90.

While physical barriers to trade are clearly the most visible of the three barriers the White Paper set out to abolish, it is arguably technical barriers which are the most effective in maintaining the fragmentation of the EC's Internal Market. Such barriers take a variety of forms, ranging from product specifications and quotas on the transportation of goods within the EC, to the non-recognition of educational and professional qualifications and the maintenance of restrictions on the establishment of companies in the Community.

As far as the free movement of goods is concerned, technical barriers mainly involve minimum standards which a product must meet before it can be sold in a given member state. For the most part these specifications relate to health, safety, the environment and consumer protection, and, in principle, are widely accepted. Nevertheless, differences between national specifications do act as barriers to trade and in many cases afford national producers an element of protection against imports from third countries, whether they be other EC member states or not. However, although prior to the mid-1980s efforts had been made to overcome such differences by harmonizing legislation throughout the Community, these had often been thwarted by the need to obtain unanimous agreement within the Council. Therefore, when the Court of Justice issued its judgment in the so-called 'Cassis de Dijon' case in 1979[26] and established the principle of 'mutual recognition', a significant landmark for the development of the Internal Market had been passed.

The principle of mutual recognition provides that where a product is legally manufactured and marketed according to existing regulations in one member state,

---

24. The text of the Schengen Agreement can be found in *Report of the House of Lords Select Committee on the European Communities, 1992: Border control of people*, Session 1988–9, 22nd Report (H.L. Paper 90). An Implementing Convention was later signed on 19 June 1990 in Dublin. Italy became a signatory to this agreement on 27 November 1990, followed by Spain, Portugal on 15 June 1991 and Greece on 6 November 1992. When enlargement negotiations began in February 1993 with Austria, Finland and Sweden, these countries were invited to adhere to the Schengen Agreement and its Implementing Convention, *Agence Presse Europe*, 5 February 1993.

25. Despite initial enthusiasm among the signatories to the Schengen Agreement, the dates for the total abolition of internal border controls have been revised on a number of occasions. Having initially opted for 1 January 1990, the date was first changed to 31 December 1992, and then to 1 July 1993 generally and to 1 January 1994 for controls at airports. However, fears concerning insufficient Dutch controls on drug trafficking and Italian failings *vis-à-vis* the Mafia, led the incoming Balladur government in France to freeze implementation of the Agreement. Most recently, political agreement was reached among Schengen signatories on removing all controls by 1 December 1993, providing sufficient progress on improving checks on people entering the EC was made, action against drug trafficking increased, and the Schengen Information System (SIS) established. 'Date set to end passport in most of EC', *Financial Times*, 1 July 1993.

26. The 'Cassis de Dijon' case, more formally known as Case 120/78 *Rewe-Zentral AG* v. *Bundesmonopolverwaltung für Branntwein*, can be found in *European Court Reports*, 1979, pp. 649–75.

this product may be sold freely in each of the other member states, irrespective of whether it complies with existing legislation in that member state or not. While such a principle clearly demands that minimum EC-wide standards with regard to health and safety, consumer protection and the environment be adopted by the member states, hence the insertion of Article 100a into the Treaty of Rome by the SEA, it nevertheless means that national regulations which restrict the domestic sale of goods produced elsewhere in the EC can no longer be applied. Similarly, provided agreement can be reached on the minimum requirements of professional and educational qualifications, the principle of mutual recognition should enable EC citizens to move more freely within the Community, particularly when seeking employment.

q.v. Article 100a pp. 148–9.

In addition to mutual recognition, however, free movement, particularly of services and capital, can only be achieved if existing restrictions are actually removed. Hence, proposals were contained in the White Paper to abolish controls on capital movements between the member states, a move integral to the establishment of economic and monetary union, as well as to remove national restrictions on the freedom to provide insurance and banking services. In addition, measures were put forward to liberalize public procurement and transport services.

q.v. transport policy pp. 130–6.

As far as fiscal barriers were concerned, the primary aim of the White Paper was to bring national indirect taxation (i.e. VAT) levels and systems closer in line with one another. The argument here is that the Single Market cannot function effectively if there are significant variations in the levels of excise duties and indirect taxation imposed on goods and services by each of the member states. However, although the harmonization of taxes is provided for in Article 99 of the Treaty of Rome, the Commission in drafting legislative proposals for the implementation of the White Paper eventually sought instead to approximate member states' VAT levels within two bands. These proposals were later shelved as a result of UK resistance to EC involvement in taxation and the Commission's opposition to zero-rating certain products. Consequently, further discussions on the approximation of VAT were postponed until 1996.

q.v. Article 99 p. 146.

While this clearly represented a setback for the Community in its efforts to complete the Internal Market, it has not detracted from the general success of the Single Market programme in relaunching the EC. Indeed, had it not been for the success of the '1992' project in regenerating and subsequently promoting the image and development of the Community, it is debatable whether the negotiations which led to the signing of the TEU would ever have taken place. However, while the basic concepts behind the Single Market, such as the free movement of people, have been widely understood by the general public, and thus led to a greater awareness of, and in some cases a greater identification with, the EC, by 31 December 1992 the Internal Market was far from complete. This was most visible in the continued existence of border controls.

Indeed, ever since the proposals contained in the Commission's White Paper were first translated into legislation, progress towards the completion of the Internal Market has consistently been slower than originally planned. Consequently, when the envisaged completion date for the '1992' project, 31

Box 7.
Implementation of EC
Single Market
legislation by the
member states as of
31 December 1992

	Applicable measures implemented	Derogations	Applicable measures not yet implemented	Percentage of measures adopted implemented
Denmark	165		22	88.2
France	152		37	80.4
Portugal	147	1	44	77.0
Netherlands	142		46	75.5
Spain	143		48	74.9
Greece	140		49	74.1
Ireland	138		49	73.8
United Kingdom	138	1	49	73.8
Germany	137		51	72.9
Luxembourg	131		54	70.8
Italy	131	1	59	68.9
Belgium	129		59	68.6

Sources: Compiled from information contained in EC Commission (London Office), *The Internal Market after 1992*, Background Report, ISEC/B7/93, 4 March 1993.

December 1992, arrived, there were few people who were surprised to learn that not all the envisaged legislation was in place.[27] Indeed, although over 90 per cent of the proposals contained in the White Paper had been adopted by the Council, only 79 of the measures adopted had actually entered into force in all member states of the EC.[28] The discrepancy here results from the fact that the vast majority of measures relating to the Single Market are adopted by the Council in the form of Directives, and must therefore be translated into national legislation according to the respective legislative procedures in each of the member states. Thus, although a measure may have been adopted at the EC level by the Council, national implementing measures have to be adopted before the directive enters into force. Nevertheless, as Box 7 shows, three-quarters of the member states had, by 31 December 1992, implemented over 70 per cent of the measures so far adopted by the Council. Somewhat surprisingly, given the 'No' vote in June 1992, Denmark has by far the best record for implementation. Italy and Belgium, meanwhile, both staunch supporters of the EC, have only a paltry record.

q.v. Article 7a p. 67.

27. Although widely assumed to be a legally binding date for the completion of the Internal Market, the Community only *aimed* to establish the Internal Market by this date (see Article 8a, now Article 7a). This was confirmed by the Declaration on Article 8a of the EEC Treaty annexed to the Final Act of the SEA. This Declaration states:

The Conference wishes by means of the provisions in Article 8a to express its firm political will to take before 1 January 1993 the decisions necessary to complete the internal market defined in those provisions, and more particularly the decisions necessary to implement the Commission's programme described as the White Paper on the Internal Market.
    Setting the date of 31 December 1992 does not create an automatic legal effect.

It should be noted, however, that Declarations attached to Community treaties are not legally binding, see Toth, A.G., 'The legal status of the Declarations annexed to the Single European Act', *Common Market Law Review*, vol. 23, No. 4, 1986, pp. 803–12.

28. Of the 282 Commission proposals, the Council had, by 31 December 1992, fully adopted 261 and had adopted its so-called 'common position' on a further 3. Of the 18 proposals awaiting adoption by the Council, 13 had been given a high priority.

In the light of these figures on the implementation of Single Market legislation, it is hardly surprising that a report for the Commission into the future of the Internal Market after 1992 presented by the former Commissioner, Peter Sutherland,[29] stressed the importance of ensuring that the relevant EC laws be effectively and equally enforced throughout the Community. Indeed, the success of the Internal Market will very much rest on the four freedoms being realized. This is particularly so given that the economic benefits projected in the Cecchini Report may not emerge in the short-term as a result of the current economic recession in the Community. However, to argue on the basis of the figures relating to implementation that the Single Market has failed would be to underestimate the significance of the 1992 project for the development of the EC. As well as reaffirming the free trade principles originally laid down in the Treaty of Rome, the Single Market provided the EC in the 1980s with a sense of purpose. As a result, the Community has gained in stature and in confidence. Moreover, the Single Market has had the knock-on effect of promoting closer cooperation in a variety of areas. Most significantly, the Single Market has helped revive the prospect of economic and monetary union. Thus, the importance of the Single Market, although it may not be complete, and even though it may have been overshadowed by recent economic and financial upheavals (see The Road from Maastricht, pp. 446–59), should not be understated.

q.v.
Cecchini
Report p.
124.

q.v.
economic
and
monetary
union pp.
150–80.

FURTHER READING

Butt Philip, A., *Dismantling Border Controls*, Pinter, London, 1993.

Cameron, D.R., 'The 1992 Initiative: causes and consequences', in Sbragia, A.M. (ed.), *Euro-Politics: Institutions and policymaking in the 'New' European Community*, Brookings Institution, Washington, 1992, pp. 23–74.

Cecchini, P., *The European Challenge 1992: The benefits of a Single Market*, Gower, Aldershot, 1988.

Cox, A. and Watson, G., *The Restructuring of European Industry: The impact of the Single Market project on concentration and merger activity in the EC*, Earlsgate Press, Winteringham, 1993.

Daly, M., 'Harmonization of direct taxes in the European Community', *Rivista di Politica Economica*, Vol. 82, No. 6, 1992, pp. 5–48.

Department of Trade and Industry, *The Single Market: The facts*, 11th edn, DTI, London, February 1993.

EC Commission, *Completing the Internal Market — white paper from the Commission to the European Council (Milan, 28 and 29 June 1985)*, COM(85)310 final, Brussels, 14 June 1985.

EC Commission, *Opening up the Internal Market*, OOPEC, Luxembourg, 1991.

EC Commission, *Reinforcing the Effectiveness of the Internal Market: Working document of the Commission on a Strategic Programme on the Internal Market*, COM(93)256 final, Brussels, 2 June 1993.

EC Commission, *Research on the 'Cost of Non-Europe' Basic Findings*, 16 vols., OOPEC, Luxembourg, 1988.

EC Commission, *Strengthening the internal market*, COM(82)399 final, Brussels, 24 June 1982.

EC Commission, *The Single Market in Action*, OOPEC, Luxembourg, 1992.

EC Commission, *The State of the Internal Market*, COM(81)313 final, Brussels, 17 June 1981.

EC Commission, *Guide to VAT in 1993: The new VAT system in the frontier-free Community*, OOPEC, Luxembourg, 1992.

Furlong, P. and Cox, A., *The European Community at the Crossroads: The problems of implementing the Single Market Project*, Earlsgate Press, Winteringham, 1994.

Helm, D. (ed.), 'European Internal Market', *Oxford*

29. The Sutherland Report was presented to the Commission on 26 October 1992. Details of the report can be found in EC Commission (London Office), *The Internal Market after 1992*, Background Report, ISEC/B7/93, 4 March 1993. See also *Reinforcing the Effectiveness of the Internal Market: Working document of the Commission on a Strategic Programme on the Internal Market*, COM(93)256 final, Brussels, 2 June 1993.

Review of Economic Policy, Vol. 9, No. 1, 1993.

McDonald, F., 'The Single European Market', in McDonald, F. and Dearden, S. (eds.), *European Economic Integration*, Longman, London, 1992, pp. 16–38.

Owen, R. and Dynes, M., *The Times Guide to the Single European Market*, Times Books, London, 1992.

Palmer, J., *1992 and Beyond*, OOPEC, Luxembourg, 1989.

Penketh, K., 'The Customs Union', in McDonald, F. and Dearden, S. (eds.), *European Economic Integration*, Longman, London, 1992, pp. 1–15.

Pinder, J., 'The Single Market: a step towards union', in Lodge, J. (ed.), *The European Community and the Challenge of the Future*, 2nd edn, Pinter, London, 1993, pp. 51–68.

Schwarze, J., Becker, U. and Pollack, C. (eds.), *The 1992 Challenge at National Level*, Nomos Verlagsgesellschaft, Baden-Baden, 1991.

Swann, D. (ed.), *The Single European Market and Beyond: A study of the wider implications of the Single European Act*, Routledge, London, 1992.

Thomson, I., 'Internal Market developments', *European Access*, bi-monthly.

ii. Transport and common rules

Having looked at the foundation stones of the Community as it currently stands — the Customs Union and the Internal Market — and examined in brief the most prominent of EC policies, the CAP, this next sub-subdivision deals with several policy areas included in the Treaty of Rome to assist in the effective functioning of the common market. The most prominent of these is competition policy, an area of EC activity which has received much attention since the launching of the Single Market programme. The provisions relating to competition are contained in Title V, along with various general, yet often highly significant provisions, particularly as far as the Single Market is concerned. However, before analysing and reproducing these and examining recent developments in EC competition policy, the *Handbook* turns to the provisions in the Treaty of Rome relating to transport and the Community's attempts to adopt a common transport policy.

q.v. Single Market programme pp. 122–30.

Transport

The provisions relating to transport in the EC are found in Part Three, Title IV of the amended Treaty of Rome (Articles 74–84). With the exception of Articles 75 and 84, these remained unchanged following the introduction of the amendments contained in both the SEA and the TEU. However, the TEU did force a renumbering of the Title; prior to the TEU's entry into force, Articles 74–84 were found in Title IV of Part Two of the Treaty of Rome.

The aim of the Community with regard to transport is the formulation and implementation of a Common Transport Policy (CTP), as called for in both Article 74 and Article 3(f).[30] The policy is to cover rail, road and inland waterway transport, although it may be extended by the Council, acting, since the SEA, by a qualified majority, to include the sea and air sectors (Article 84). Such a policy is to include the establishment during the transitional period of common rules on international transport within the Community and of operating conditions

q.v. Article 3(f) p. 65.

---

30. Prior to the TEU, the reference to a common transport policy in the principles of the Community was contained in Article 3(e).

for non-EC carriers. While these, plus a general facility for 'other appropriate provisions', were laid down in the original Treaty of Rome, the TEU introduces a fourth element to the CTP: measures to improve transport safety (Article 75(1−2)).

As with other areas for Community action, until measures are adopted at the EC level, member states may maintain existing rules governing transport, provided they are not used to discriminate against other EC carriers (Article 76). Indeed, Article 79 provides the Commission with a monitoring role to ensure that discrimination is abolished. Furthermore, free competition is to be promoted through the prohibition of charges or conditions favourable to one or more undertakings (Article 80), and the gradual reduction of charges imposed for border crossings (Article 81). However, Article 80(2) does allow the Commission to assess the extent to which charges and conditions are necessary to meet the requirements of transport in underdeveloped areas of the Community. Similarly, member states are allowed to grant state aid where this is used to coordinate transport services or is used to fund a public service obligation (Article 77). Finally, Article 82 exempts the Federal Republic of Germany from the provisions of Articles 74−84 in respect of measures designed to redress the economic disadvantages caused to certain regions affected by the division of the country (see also Article 92(2)(c)). *q.v. Article 92(2)(c) p. 141.* Prior to German unification in October 1990, this effectively allowed the German government to adopt an independent transport policy with regard to the areas of the country bordering on the German Democratic Republic.[31]

For the most part decisions relating to the CTP are to be taken by the Council acting by a qualified majority, on a proposal from the Commission. Originally, after the second stage of the transitional period, the Council was required to consult both the EP and the EcoSoc before acting. However, with the entry into force of the TEU the EP's role is elevated as the Council is forced to act in accordance with the cooperation procedure laid down in Article 189c (Article 75(1)). *q.v. Article 189c pp. 304−5.* However, where the effect of the measures under consideration is likely to have serious effects on the standard of living and employment in particular areas of the EC, the Council is required to act unanimously and only, since the TEU, in consultation with the EP and EcoSoc (Article 75(3)). No amendments have been introduced, however, regarding the rules governing discrimination under Article 79. Here, it is still the Council, acting by a qualified majority and in consultation with the EcoSoc, but not the EP, that is responsible for decision-making. Throughout the decision-making process, the Commission may consult a special Advisory Committee on transport matters set up under Article 83.

Title IV   Transport

ARTICLE 74

The objectives of this Treaty shall, in matters governed by this Title, be pursued by Member States within the framework of a common transport policy.

---

31. The fact that the TEU did not delete Article 82 suggests that the German government may still make use of its provisions. However, to do so would require a liberal interpretation if the measures referred to were to be applied to the former GDR. (See also note 38 on p. 138).

ARTICLE 75

1. For the purpose of implementing Article 74, and taking into account the distinctive features of transport, the Council shall, **acting in accordance with the procedure referred to in Article 189c** and after consulting the Economic and Social Committee, lay down:

(a) common rules applicable to international transport to or from the territory of a Member State or passing across the territory of one or more Member States;

(b) the conditions under which non-resident carriers may operate transport services within a Member State;

(c) **measures to improve transport safety;**

(d) *any other appropriate provisions.*

2. The Provisions referred to in (a) and (b) of paragraph 1 shall be laid down during the transitional period.

3. By way of derogation from the procedure provided for in paragraph 1, where the application of provisions concerning the principles of the regulatory system for transport would be liable to have a serious effect on the standard of living and on employment in certain areas and on the operation of transport facilities, they shall be laid down by the Council acting unanimously **on a proposal from the Commission, after consulting the European Parliament and the Economic and Social Committee**. In so doing, the Council shall take into account the need for adaptation to the economic development which will result from establishing the common market.

ARTICLE 76

Until the provisions referred to in Article 75 (1) have been laid down, no Member State may, without the unanimous approval of the Council, make the various provisions governing the subject when this Treaty enters into force less favourable in their direct or indirect effect on carriers of other Member States as compared with carriers who are nationals of that State.

ARTICLE 77

Aids shall be compatible with this Treaty if they meet the needs of coordination of transport or if they represent reimbursement for the discharge of certain obligations inherent in the concept of a public service.

ARTICLE 78

Any measures taken within the framework of this Treaty in respect of transport rates and conditions shall take account of the economic circumstances of carriers.

ARTICLE 79

1. In the case of transport within the Community, discrimination which takes the form of carriers charging different rates and imposing different conditions for the carriage of the same goods over the same transport links on grounds of the country of origin or of destination of the goods in question, shall be abolished, at the latest, before the end of the second stage.

2. Paragraph 1 shall not prevent the Council from adopting other measures in pursuance of Article 75(1).

3. Within two years of the entry into force of this Treaty, the Council shall, acting by a qualified majority on a proposal from the Commission and after consulting the Economic and Social Committee, lay down rules for implementing the provisions of paragraph 1.

The Council may in particular lay down the provisions needed to enable the institutions of the Community to secure compliance with the rule laid down in paragraph 1 and to ensure that users benefit from it to the full.

4. The Commission shall, acting on its own initiative or on application by a Member State, investigate any cases of discrimination falling within paragraph 1 and, after consulting any Member State concerned, shall take the necessary

decisions within the framework of the rules laid down in accordance with the provisions of paragraph 3.

ARTICLE 80

1. The imposition by a Member State, in respect of transport operations carried out within the Community, of rates and conditions involving any element of support or protection in the interest of one or more particular undertakings or industries shall be prohibited as from the beginning of the second stage, unless authorized by the Commission.

2. The Commission shall, acting on its own initiative or on application by a Member State, examine the rates and conditions referred to in paragraph 1, taking account in particular of the requirements of an appropriate regional economic policy, the needs of underdeveloped areas and the problems of areas seriously affected by political circumstances on the one hand, and of the effects of such rates and conditions on competition between the different modes of transport on the other.

After consulting each Member State concerned, the Commission shall take the necessary decisions.

3. The prohibition provided for in paragraph 1 shall not apply to tariffs fixed to meet competition.

ARTICLE 81

Charges or dues in respect of the crossing of frontiers which are charged by a carrier in addition to the transport rates shall not exceed a reasonable level after taking the costs actually incurred thereby into account.

Member States shall endeavour to reduce these costs progressively.

The Commission may make recommendations to Member States for the application of this Article.

ARTICLE 82

The provisions of this Title shall not form an obstacle to the application of measures taken in the Federal Republic of Germany to the extent that such measures are required in order to compensate for the economic disadvantages caused by the division of Germany to the economy of certain areas of the Federal Republic affected by that division.

ARTICLE 83

An Advisory Committee consisting of experts designated by the Governments of Member States, shall be attached to the Commission. The Commission, whenever it considers it desirable, shall consult the Committee on transport matters without prejudice to the powers of the transport section of the Economic and Social Committee.

ARTICLE 84

1. The provisions of this Title shall apply to transport by rail, road and inland waterway.

2. The Council may, acting by a qualified majority, decide whether, to what extent and by what procedure appropriate provisions may be laid down for sea and air transport.

The procedural provisions of Article 75(1) and (3) shall apply.[32]

32. This subparagraph was added to Article 84 by the SEA to ensure that the procedure for adopting legislation relating to sea and air transport would be the same as that used for existing areas of EC transport policy.

Transport policy

Of the three spheres of economic activity (agriculture, commerce and transport), singled out for common policies in the original Treaty of Rome, transport has received the least attention. Despite efforts by the Commission in the 1960s and 1970s to develop a global approach for the EC towards transport, the member states, through the council, paid only limited attention to the proposals being put forward. Indeed, it was not until the programme to complete the Internal Market had been launched in the mid-1980s, and the EP had taken the Council to the Court of Justice over its failure to act on transport, that any significant measures were adopted in line with the responsibilities placed on the Community by the Treaty of Rome. Since then a series of directives and regulations relating to transport have been adopted or issued by the Council. However, the extent to which the Community has developed a coherent and comprehensive common transport policy as a result remains open to question.

The main thrust of the EC's transport policy to date has been deregulation. As such, the measures that have been adopted have been a response to attempts, central to the Single Market programme, to implement the four freedoms and create a barrier-free Community market. For the most part, the directives and regulations have been aimed at deregulating the road haulage and air transport sectors of the EC transport industry. As regards road haulage, an agreement was reached in 1988 to abolish all permits and quotas on the transport of goods between member states by 31 December 1992, while in June 1990 a transitional road haulage *cabotage*[33] regime was introduced. This was designed to prepare the road haulage sector for full liberalization at a later date. However, given German demands for compensation for the environmental and infrastructural burden of being geographically at the centre of the EC, a date for full liberalization was only agreed in June 1993. This followed a decision to introduce a licence, the so-called *vignette*, for lorries using EC roads, and to distribute the funds raised from the licence among those member states most affected by transport. However, the *vignette* will not become fully operative until 1 July 1998.[34] The gradual introduction of *cabotage* within the road passenger transport sector began on 1 January 1993.

Within the air transport sector a degree of deregulation comparable with that in the road haulage sector has yet to be achieved. Nevertheless, the Community has agreed on three packages of liberalization measures as part of its 'open skies' policy for Europe. The most recent of these, adopted by the Council in July 1992, envisages full deregulation of scheduled, non-scheduled and air cargo services within the EC by 1 January 1997. Existing legislation is also to be extended to six EFTA countries within the framework of the EEA (European Economic Area) Agreement signed in 1992.

q.v. EEA Agreement pp. 479–85.

---

33. *Cabotage* is the right to ply for hire in another country. Traditionally, road hauliers have normally only been able to transport goods from their own country, requiring a permit if they wish to carry goods on the return journey.

34. 'EC agree on common system for road haulage', *Financial Times*, 21 June 1993.

In addition to the road and air transport sectors of the industry, limited measures have been introduced to deregulate shipping and rail transport. In 1991 a directive was adopted opening up access to railway infrastructure in each of the member states for undertakings wishing to run passenger and freight services, while in 1992 a regulation was agreed liberalizing *cabotage* on coastal shipping within the Community. This built upon earlier agreements establishing the freedom within the Community to provide shipping services between, to and from member states. However, in contrast to the deregulatory bias of most legislation, the Council has also agreed to exempt certain shipping consortia from the EC's competition rules. Proposals have also been put forward for an EC system of vessel registration.

Beyond liberalization and deregulation, several measures relating to the transport industry have been agreed by the Council which suggest that a common EC policy of sorts is beginning to emerge. For the most part, the proposals and directives which have so far been put forward or adopted reflect the EC's concerns over transport's impact on the environment and society; the need to promote transport safety within the Community; and the advantages for the Single Market and economic and social cohesion of a European transport infrastructure.

While legislation has been proposed on transport safety, few regulations have been adopted to date. However, with the express provision included in the TEU for transport safety to be made a Community competence (Article 75(1)(c)), it is likely that the trickle of relevant legislation emanating from Brussels will increase. Indeed, the proposals relating to the future development of the Community's transport policy put forward by the Commission in December 1992 highlighted safety in transport as one of the top priorities for the EC.[35] Similarly, the Commission's proposals encouraged EC action minimizing the environmental impact of transport, thus building on existing legislation restricting emissions of harmful gasses, noise pollution, and dumping at sea.[36] As far as infrastructure and economic and social cohesion are concerned, ECU 240 million was made available in 1990–2 through the European Regional Development Fund (ERDF) for infrastructure projects linking and thus integrating peripheral regions into the Community. These included financing for the Scanlink in Denmark and the rail and road links into the Channel Tunnel. This area of transport policy was given a boost by the TEU which introduced into the Treaty of Rome a Title dedicated to trans-European networks.[37]

A further area of importance when considering the EC's policy on transport is external relations. These are of particular importance since good relations with countries such as Switzerland and Austria, given their geographical location in the centre of the EC, are vital to the effective functioning of the Internal Market.

q.v. Article 75(1)(c) p. 132.

q.v. ERDF p. 222.

q.v. trans-European networks pp. 211–14.

---

35. *The Future Development of the Common Transport Policy: A global approach to the construction of a Community framework for sustainable mobility*, COM(92)494 final, Brussels, 2 December 1992. See also, *A Common Policy on Safe Seas*, COM(93)66 final, Brussels, 24 February 1993; *An action programme on road safety*, COM(93)246 final, Brussels, 9 June 1993.

36. *Green Paper on the Impact of Transport on the Environment: A Community strategy for* 'sustainable mobility', COM(92)46 final, Brussels, 20 February 1992.

37. See also *Transport Infrastructure*, COM(92)231 final, Brussels, 11 June 1992; *The Creation of a Combined Network and its Operating Conditions*, COM(92)230, Brussels, 11 June 1992.

In 1991 agreements were signed with both countries, in association with the later agreement on the EEA, increasing the number of transit permits available to EC lorries. In addition, the Swiss agreed to construct two new combined rail tunnels suitable for larger combined road-rail vehicles under the Alps to improve north-south Community transport links. The Swiss non-ratification of the EEA means that further negotiations are likely to be needed.

FURTHER READING

Button, K., 'The liberalization of transport services', in Swann, D. (ed.) *The Single European Market and Beyond: A study of the wider implications of the Single European Act*, Routledge, London, 1992, pp. 146–61.

Cafruny, A.W., 'Toward a Maritime Policy', in Hurwitz, L. and Lequesne, C. (eds.), *The State of the European Community: Policies, institutions and debates in the transition years*, Longman, London, 1991, pp. 285–99.

EC Commission, *Air Transport Relations with Third Countries*, COM(92)434 final, Brussels, 21 October 1992.

EC Commission, *Communication for a Common Policy on Safe Seas*, COM(93)66 final, Brussels, 24 February 1993.

EC Commission, *Communication for an Action Plan on Road Safety*, COM(93)66 final, Brussels, 9 June 1993.

EC Commission, *Green Paper on the Impact of Transport on the Environment: A Community strategy for* 'sustainable mobility', COM(92)46 final, Brussels, 20 February 1992.

EC Commission, *The Future Development of the Common Transport Policy: A global approach to the construction of a Community framework for sustainable mobility*, COM(92)494 final, Brussels, 2 December 1992.

EC Commission, *Transport Infrastructure*, COM(92)231 final, Brussels, 11 June 1992.

EcoSoc, *Transport Policy in the EC*, EcoSoc, Brussels, 1991.

Mason, K. and Gray, R., 'The liberalisation of civil aviation in the European Community — an overview', *European Research*, Vol. 2, No. 4, 1992, pp. 11–15.

Reh, W., 'Die Verkehrspolitik der Europäischen Gemeinschaft: Chance oder Risiko für eine umweltgerechte Mobilität', *Aus Politik und Zeitgeschichte*, B5/93, 1993, pp. 34–44.

Thomson, I., 'European air transport liberalization — bibliographic snapshot', *European Access*, 1992/4, pp. 39–41.

Whitelegg, J., *Transport for a Sustainable Future*, Belhaven Press, London, 1993.

Common rules on competition, taxation and approximation of laws

Title V of Part Three of the amended Treaty of Rome contains, under a new and more accurate heading, the provisions previously found in Title I of Part Three on Common Rules. These rules, unless otherwise specified, relate to all areas of Community activity provided for in the Treaty of Rome. However, as the new Title indicates, the common rules fall into three distinct categories, each of which has its own Chapter heading within the Title. These appear in the Treaty in what might be regarded as a descending order of importance with regard to the Customs Union and the Internal Market. The first Chapter of the Title contains extensive rules governing competition between undertakings within the EC (Articles 85–94). The second Chapter then addresses the framework in which undertakings operate by providing for the harmonization of taxation (Articles 95–99), thus complimenting those in Articles 85–94 promoting free and fair competition. The final Chapter then provides a general set of rules for the approximation of laws in all areas not covered elsewhere in the Treaty (Articles 100–102), as well as provisions specific to the Internal Market and, since the entry into force of the TEU, visa policy. The overall effect of the TEU has been to bring about changes to the provisions contained in each of these Chapters, amending five and introducing two new Articles.

Competition

As indicated, the first Chapter of the new Title V is dedicated to competition within the Community. As such, its provisions cover all areas of EC activity, except for competition within the transport and agricultural sectors. The provisions contained within it fall into three Sections. The first of these comprises rules applying to undertakings (Articles 85–90), while the two remaining Sections contain provisions relating to dumping (Article 91) and state aids (Articles 92–94). The two amendments introduced to this Chapter by the TEU affect provisions in this last Section.

q.v. transport pp. 130–6.

q.v. agriculture pp. 95–105.

As stated in the Principles, the aim of the Community is 'an open market with free competition' (Article 3a). Consequently, the Treaty of Rome prohibits 'the prevention, restriction or distortion of trade' (Article 85), and the abuse by undertakings of 'a dominant position' within the Internal Market (Article 86). In order to ensure that companies (Article 87) and the member states (Article 90) adhere to this, the Council is required to adopt, on the basis of proposals from the Commission, and in consultation with the EP, appropriate directives and regulations. During the first three years of the Community's existence the Treaty of Rome required that such directives and regulations were adopted on the basis of unanimity within the Council. Since then, however, a qualified majority in the Council is all that is required. Once adopted, it is the responsibility of the Commission to ensure that the directives and regulations are adhered to (Articles 89(1) and 90(3)). Where infringements occur, the Commission, not the Council, may insist that the company or member state concerned take certain measures necessary to remedy the situation (Article (89(2)). However, until measures are adopted by the Council with regard to competition, it is left to the member states to ensure that the principles contained in Articles 85 and 86 are complied with (Article 88).

q.v. Article 3a p. 65.

The second Section, containing only one Article, Article 91, deals with dumping during the transitional stage of the Community's development. For the original six member states the Article became redundant once the Customs Union was established in 1968. However, when a new member is granted a transitional period in which to adapt to EC rules, the provisions become valid once again. In such cases, where dumping is found to be taking place, it is left to the Commission to determine what measures are to be taken to alleviate the situation.

q.v. Customs Union pp. 122–3.

Section 3 of Chapter 1 concerns the granting of state aid to industry by member states. In theory, under Article 92(1) all forms of aid which distort or threaten to distort competition are deemed to be incompatible with the Internal Market. However, the remainder of the Article sets out certain forms of aid which are compatible (Article 92(2)), and certain forms which may be considered as compatible (Article 92(3)). For the most part, aid which is deemed acceptable is that granted for social purposes and for rectifying damage caused by natural disasters.[38] As for state aid under Article 92(3), this may be granted to promote economic development in areas of high unemployment, and to fund projects of common European interest. It may also be granted to certain, unspecified economic areas, and, in line with an amendment introduced by the TEU, to promote cultural and heritage conservation within the Community. Additional categories of aid may be proposed to the Council by the Commission. Such proposals can be adopted by the Council acting by a qualified majority, as provided for in Article 92(3)(e).[39] Furthermore, a member state may apply to the Council for permission to grant aid in derogation from the provisions of Article 92. Such a derogation may be granted by the Council acting unanimously (Article 93(2)). In all cases where a member state proposes granting aid, details must be communicated to the Commission (Article 93(3)). Detailed rules governing the application of Articles 92 and 93 are to be adopted by the Council in line with the provisions laid down in Article 94. This, following an amendment introduced by the TEU, requires the Council to consult the EP before acting by a qualified majority on a proposal from the Commission. Prior to the amendment the EP was excluded from the decision-making procedures governing competition within the Community.

Although provision is made for state aids to be granted, Article 93 requires the Commission in cooperation with the member states to keep all such aids under constant review. Where it is believed that aid is being misused or is no longer compatible with the principles laid down in Article 92, the Commission, as opposed to the Council, may require that the aid be abolished or altered. If the member state concerned fails to comply with the Commission's ruling the matter may be referred to the Court of Justice, which in turn may impose a fine on the member state under Article 171.

q.v. Article 171 pp. 286–7.

Title V Common rules on competition, taxation and approximation of laws

Chapter 1 *Rules on competition*

Section 1 Rules applying to undertakings

ARTICLE 85

1. The following shall be prohibited as incompatible with the common market: all agreements between undertakings, decisions by associations of undertakings and concerted practices which may affect trade between Member States and which have as their object or effect the prevention, restriction or distortion of competition

---

38. Article 92(2) also makes provision for aid to be granted to areas of the Federal Republic of Germany affected economically by the division of the country. Given the unification of Germany in October 1990, the status of this provision is unclear (see also Article 82, p. 133). It would appear that no effort was made during the IGC negotiations to delete either Article 92(2) or Article 82, nor either of the two Protocols on Germany attached to the Treaty of Rome when it was signed in 1957.

39. As a result of the insertion of a new subparagraph (d) to Article 92(3) by the TEU, the existing subparagraph (d) is renumbered (e).

within the common market, and in particular those which:

(a) directly or indirectly fix purchase or selling prices or any other trading conditions;
(b) limit or control production, markets, technical development, or investment;
(c) share markets or sources of supply;
(d) apply dissimilar conditions to equivalent transactions with other trading parties, thereby placing them at a competitive disadvantage;
(e) make the conclusion of contracts subject to acceptance by the other parties of supplementary obligations which, by their nature or according to commercial usage, have no connection with the subject of such contracts.

2. Any agreements or decisions prohibited pursuant to this Article shall be automatically void.

3. The provisions of paragraph 1 may, however, be declared inapplicable in the case of:

— any agreement or category of agreements between undertakings;
— any decision or category of decisions by associations of undertakings;
— any concerted practice or category of concerted practices;

which contributes to improving the production or distribution of goods or to promoting technical or economic progress, while allowing consumers a fair share of the resulting benefit, and which does not:

(a) impose on the undertakings concerned restrictions which are not indispensable to the attainment of these objectives;
(b) afford such undertakings the possibility of eliminating competition in respect of a substantial part of the products in question.

ARTICLE 86

Any abuse by one or more undertakings of a dominant position within the common market or in a substantial part of it shall be prohibited as incompatible with the common market in so far as it may affect trade between Member States.

Such abuse may, in particular, consist in:

(a) directly or indirectly imposing unfair purchase or selling prices or unfair trading conditions;
(b) limiting production, markets or technical development to the prejudice of consumers;
(c) applying dissimilar conditions to equivalent transactions with other trading parties, thereby placing them at a competitive disadvantage;
(d) making the conclusion of contracts subject to acceptance by the other parties of supplementary obligations which, by their nature or according to commercial usage, have no connection with the subject of such contracts.

ARTICLE 87

1. Within three years of the entry into force of this Treaty the Council shall, acting unanimously on a proposal from the Commission and after consulting the European Parliament, adopt any appropriate regulations or directives to give effect to the principles set out in Articles 85 and 86.

If such provisions have not been adopted within the period mentioned, they shall be laid down by the Council, acting by a qualified majority on a proposal from the Commission and after consulting the European Parliament.

2. The regulations or directives referred to in paragraph 1 shall be designed in particular:

(a) to ensure compliance with the prohibitions laid down in Article 85(1) and in Article 86 by making provision for fines and periodic penalty payments;
(b) to lay down detailed rules for the application of Article 85(3), taking into

account the need to ensure effective supervision on the one hand, and to simplify administration to the greatest possible extent on the other;

(c) to define, if need be, in the various branches of the economy, the scope of the provisions of Articles 85 and 86;

(d) to define the respective functions of the Commission and of the Court of Justice in applying the provisions laid down in this paragraph;

(e) to determine the relationship between national laws and the provisions contained in this Section or adopted pursuant to this Article.

ARTICLE 88

Until the entry into force of the provisions adopted in pursuance of Article 87, the authorities in Member States shall rule on the admissibility of agreements, decisions and concerted practices and on abuse of a dominant position in the common market in accordance with the law of their country and with the provisions of Article 85, in particular paragraph 3, and of Article 86.

ARTICLE 89

1. Without prejudice to Article 88, the Commission shall, as soon as it takes up its duties, ensure the application of the principles laid down in Articles 85 and 86. On application by a Member State or on its own initiative, and in cooperation with the competent authorities in the Member States, who shall give it their assistance, the Commission shall investigate cases of suspected infringement of these principles. If it finds that there has been an infringement, it shall propose appropriate measures to bring it to an end.

2. If the infringement is not brought to an end, the Commission shall record such infringement of the principles in a reasoned decision. The Commission may publish its decision and authorize Member States to take the measures, the conditions and details of which it shall determine, needed to remedy the situation.

ARTICLE 90

1. In the case of public undertakings and undertakings to which Member States grant special or exclusive rights, Member States shall neither enact nor maintain in force any measure contrary to the rules contained in this Treaty, in particular to those rules provided for in Article 7 and Articles 85 to 94.[40]

2. Undertakings entrusted with the operation of services of general economic interest or having the character of a revenue-producing monopoly shall be subject to the rules contained in this Treaty, in particular to the rules on competition, in so far as the application of such rules does not obstruct the performance, in law or in fact, of the particular tasks assigned to them. The development of trade must not be affected to such an extent as would be contrary to the interests of the Community.

3. The Commission shall ensure the application of the provisions of this Article and shall, where necessary, address appropriate directives or decisions to Member States.

Section 2 Dumping

ARTICLE 91

1. If, during the transitional period, the Commission, on application by a Member State or by any other interested party, finds that dumping is being practised within the common market, it shall address recommendations to the person or persons with whom such practices originate for the purpose of putting an end to them.

---

40. It would appear that in drafting the TEU, the IGC overlooked the need to alter the reference to 'Article 7' in this paragraph to read 'Article 6' in line with the renumbering of Article 7 provided for in Article G(8) of TEU. Nevertheless, in the unofficial version of the consolidated version of the Treaty of Rome contained in OJC 224, the renumbering was carried out, albeit without an acknowledgement that a change had taken place. See also the oversight with regard to Article 207, p. 321.

Should the practices continue, the Commission shall authorize the injured Member State to take protective measures, the conditions and details of which the Commission shall determine.

2. As soon as this Treaty enters into force, products which originate in or are in free circulation in one Member State and which have been exported to another Member State shall on reimportation be admitted into the territory of the first-mentioned State free of all customs duties, quantitative restrictions or measures having equivalent effect. The Commission shall lay down appropriate rules for the application of this paragraph.

Section 3 Aids granted by States

ARTICLE 92

1. Save as otherwise provided in this Treaty, any aid granted by a Member State or through State resources in any form whatsoever which distorts or threatens to distort competition by favouring certain undertakings or the production of certain goods shall, in so far as it affects trade between Member States, be incompatible with the common market.

2. The following shall be compatible with the common market:

(a) aid having a social character, granted to individual consumers, provided that such aid is granted without discrimination related to the origin of the products concerned;

(b) aid to make good the damage caused by natural disasters or other exceptional occurrences;

(c) aid granted to the economy of certain areas of the Federal Republic of Germany affected by the division of Germany, in so far as such aid is required in order to compensate for the economic disadvantages caused by that division.

3. The following may be considered to be compatible with the common market:

(a) aid to promote the economic development of areas where the standard of living is abnormally low or where there is serious underemployment;

(b) aid to promote the execution of an important project of common European interest or to remedy a serious disturbance in the economy of a Member State;

(c) aid to facilitate the development of certain economic activities or of certain economic areas, where such aid does not adversely affect trading conditions to an extent contrary to the common interest. However, the aids granted to shipbuilding as of 1 January 1957 shall, in so far as they serve only to compensate for the absence of customs protection, be progressively reduced under the same conditions as apply to the elimination of customs duties, subject to the provisions of this Treaty concerning common commercial policy towards third countries;

(d) **aid to promote culture and heritage conservation where such aid does not affect trading conditions and competition in the Community to an extent that is contrary to the common interest**.

(e) *such other categories of aid as may be specified by decision of the Council acting by a qualified majority on a proposal from the Commission.*

ARTICLE 93

1. The Commission shall, in cooperation with Member States, keep under constant review all systems of aid existing in those States. It shall propose to the latter any appropriate measures required by the progressive development or by the functioning of the common market.

2. If, after giving notice to the parties concerned to submit their comments, the Commission finds that aid granted by a State or through State resources is not compatible with the common market having regard to Article 92, or that such

aid is being misused, it shall decide that the State concerned shall abolish or alter such aid within a period of time to be determined by the Commission.

If the State concerned does not comply with this decision within the prescribed time, the Commission or any other interested State may, in derogation from the provisions of Articles 169 and 170, refer the matter to the Court of Justice direct.

On application by a Member State, the Council may, acting unanimously, decide that aid which that State is granting or intends to grant shall be considered to be compatible with the common market, in derogation from the provisions of Article 92 or from the regulations provided for in Article 94, if such a decision is justified by exceptional circumstances. If, as regards the aid in question, the Commission has already initiated the procedure provided for in the first subparagraph of this paragraph, the fact that the State concerned has made its application to the Council shall have the effect of suspending that procedure until the Council has made its attitude known.

If, however, the Council has not made its attitude known within three months of the said application being made, the Commission shall give its decision on the case.

3. The Commission shall be informed, in sufficient time to enable it to submit its comments, of any plans to grant or alter aid. If it considers that any such plan is not compatible with the common market having regard to Article 92, it shall without delay initiate the procedure provided for in paragraph 2. The Member State concerned shall not put its proposed measures into effect until this procedure has resulted in a final decision.

ARTICLE 94

The Council may, acting by a qualified majority on a proposal from the Commission **and after consulting the European Parliament**, make any appropriate regulations for the application of Articles 92 and 93 and may in particular determine the conditions in which Article 93(3) shall apply and the categories of aid exempted from this procedure.

Competition policy

q.v. Single Market pp. 120–30.

While the essence of the Single Market is the abolition of physical, technical and fiscal barriers to trade so that the free movement of goods, services, capital and persons can be realized, the market would not be able function effectively if free and fair competition were not guaranteed. This was implicit in the inclusion of Articles 85–94 in the Treaty and was indeed recognized by the EC as early as 1962 when the powers of the Commission in developing and implementing a Community competition policy were first laid down. However, until the mid-1980s the Commission refrained from exercising in full the powers which had been conferred on it. Since then, the free market principles of the Single Market have gained widespread acceptance within the EC. Also, the Commission has become more confident in carrying out its obligations under the Treaty of Rome. As a result, the Community has witnessed, particularly when Leon Brittan was Commissioner responsible for competition policy, the development in Brussels of a coherent and comprehensive competition policy.

The recent development of the Community's competition policy has taken a variety of forms. Firstly, the Commission has been quick to seize the opportunity to develop its judge and jury powers under Articles 85–94. This has resulted in the Commission intensifying its investigations into malpractice and imposing more stringent fines on those found guilty of pursuing anti-competitive practices. However, the Commission is by no means judge and jury over all agreements between companies. Its powers do not normally extend to agreements between small or medium-sized companies (SMEs) with an aggregate annual turnover of less than ECU 200 million and a market share of less than 5 per cent.[41] Furthermore, agreements between companies involved in certain areas such as franchising, patent and know-how licensing, R&D, and intra-EC air services have been exempted from EC competition law as a result of either individual or bloc exemptions under Article 85(3). Nevertheless, it is likely that these will all be reviewed within the foreseeable future. Indeed, the liberalization of air transport services within the Community has become a major plank of the EC's transport policy for the 1990s. On state aids, the Commission has taken steps to tighten up the requirements for all member states to notify and report state aids, and to restrict the terms and levels of assistance granted. However, Commission scrutiny policy relating to state aids received a setback in June 1993 when the Court of Justice overturned existing Commission rules on the transparency of financial relations between member states and public companies in the manufacturing sector.[42] Non-compliance with EC rules has led several state owned undertakings, such as the French car maker, Renault, and the UK engineering company, British Aerospace, being forced to repay state aid — a matter which has caused enormous embarrassment for the national governments affected.

q.v. transport policy pp. 134–6.

Second, competition policy has developed as a result of a series of legislative acts which have extended the powers of the Commission in ensuring free and fair competition in the Single Market. The most significant of these was the 1989 Merger Regulation. This entered into force in September 1990 and requires all proposed mergers with an aggregate world turnover of ECU 5 billion and an EC turnover of ECU 250 million which are likely to impede competition to be assessed by the Commission before they are allowed to take place.[43] Proposed mergers involving a turnover of less than ECU 5 billion, as with all areas of competition policy not covered by EC-level rules, remain under the control of national authorities and subject to national rules. Unlike existing rules on competition which allowed the Commission to examine alleged abuses of a dominant position in the market, the Merger Regulation grants the Commission, through its Merger Task Force, substantial powers to pre-empt anti-competitive practices. However, although this enhancement of the Commission's powers suggests a commitment by the member states to promoting free and fair competition within the EC, reactions to the implementation and possible extension of the Merger Regulation

---

41. However, EC competition laws do not apply exclusively to companies based in, or having a branch or subsidiary in, the Community. Following a Court of Justice ruling in 1988, all companies selling in the Internal Market are subject to EC competition rules, *Common Market Law Reports*, No. 4, 1988, p. 901.

42. 'Setback for EC state aid controls', *Financial Times*, 22 June 1993; 'EC loses state aid case', *Financial Times*, 17 June 1993.

43. *Council Regulation (EEC) 4064/89 of 21 December 1989 on the Control of Concentrations Between Undertakings*, OJL 395, 30 December 1989.

have been mixed. Thus, although the speed and efficiency with which the Merger Task Force has dealt with the over 300 cases referred to it since 1990 has been widely praised, when the proposed Franco-Italian takeover of the Canadian aircraft maker De Havilland was blocked in 1991 — the only proposed merger to have been rejected — the Commission was subjected to intense criticism from both the French and the Italians.[44] Furthermore, there appeared to be little support from national governments for initial Commission suggestions in 1992–3 that the threshold for merger investigations be lowered. Proposals for the establishment of an EC competition authority independent of both the Commission and the member states would, however, receive a more favourable hearing, particularly from Germany.[45]

A third area in which the EC's competition policy has developed as a result of the Single Market programme has been public procurement. Although not specifically referred to in the Treaty of Rome, open tendering for public contracts has been promoted by the EC for several years. The result of this has been the introduction of a series of directives, covering services (1992) and utilities (1990), such as water, energy and telecommunications, which require all public contracts with a value in excess of an EC-wide threshold, in some cases as low as ECU 125,000, to be opened up to competitive tendering throughout the EC. These new directives have also been accompanied by amendments to existing directives on supplies and works, first adopted in 1977 and 1971 respectively. While the principle of free and fair competition may have been instrumental in pushing governments to open up public procurement, equally significant were the perceived gains this would bring. According to the Cecchini Report, by promoting competition in awarding public contracts, which annually account for around ECU 400 billion (15 per cent of EC GDP), total savings within the EC could reach ECU 17.5 billion (0.5 per cent of EC GDP).[46]

q.v. Cecchini Report p. 124.

These three examples clearly indicate that increasing competition within the EC has become a clear policy objective of the Community. This is reinforced by the emphasis placed on the promotion of competition between undertakings as a central plank of the Community's industrial policy. However, this apparent commitment to free and fair competition may come under strain if economic recession in Europe persists. Indeed, initial reactions to developing competition policy further, particularly within sensitive industries, and the degree of hostility which greeted the Commission's first vetoing a proposed merger, suggest that the commitment may not, in reality, be as strong as member states make out.

q.v. industrial policy pp. 214–18.

44. A report in June 1993 did, however, cast doubt over the consistency of the Commission's vetting procedures. See Neven, D., Nuttall, R. and Seabright, P., *Merger in Daylight*, Centre for Economic Policy Research, London, 1993; also 'Getting away with merger', *The Economist*, 12 June 1993.

45. 'Shaken Europe's pillar of strength', *Financial Times*, 28 September 1992; 'Marriage made in Brussels', *Financial Times*, 19 January 1993; 'Expanded EC merger powers will face opposition', *Financial Times*, 1 March 1993.

46. Cecchini, P., *The European Challenge 1992: The Benefits of a Single Market*, Gower, Aldershot, 1988, p. 17.

FURTHER READING

Brittan, L., *European Competition Policy: Keeping the playing field level*, Brassey's, Brussels, 1992.

Brittan, L., 'The future of EC Competition Law', *European Business Law Review*, Vol. 27, No. 4, 1993, pp. 27–31.

Curwen, P. and Gale, J., 'Implementing EC Merger Control Regulation', *European Business and Economic Development*, Vol. 2, No. 1, 1993, pp. 8–13.

Davies, J. and Lavoie, C., 'EEC Merger Control: a half-term report before the 1993 review', *Butterworths Journal of International Banking and Financial Law*, Vol. 8, No. 1, 1993, pp. 22–5.

EC Commission, *Report on Competition Policy*, OOPEC, Luxembourg, annually.

Ehlermann, C.D., 'Deux ans d'application du contrôle des concentrations: bilan et perspectives', *Revue du Marché commun et de l'Union européenne*, No. 366, 1993, pp. 242–9.

European Competition Law Review (bi-monthly).

Halverson, J.T., 'EC Merger Control: Competition Policy or Industrial Policy', *Legal Issues of European Integration*, 1992/2, pp. 49–66.

Jacobs, D.M. and Stewart-Clark, J., *Competition Law in the European Community*, 2nd edn, Kogan Page, London, 1991.

Jacquemin, A., 'The international dimension of European Competition Policy', *Journal of Common Market Studies*, Vol. 31, No. 1, 1993, pp. 91–101.

Jones, C., Van der Woudes, M. and Lewis, X., *EEC Competition Law Handbook*, Butterworths, London, 1991.

Kamburoglou, P., 'EWG-Wettbewerbspolitik und Subsidiarität', *Wirtschaft und Wettbewerb*, Vol. 43, No. 4, April 1993, pp. 273–83.

Kemp, J., 'Competition Policy', in McDonald, F. and Dearden, S. (eds.), *European Economic Integration*, Longman, London, 1992, pp. 59–81.

McClellan, A. and Jambrun, P., 'Fusions, enterprises communes et autres acquisitions dans le Marché commun', *Revue du Marché commun et de l'Union européenne*, No. 356, 1992, pp. 231–9.

Neven, D., Nuttall, R. and Seabright, P., *Merger in Daylight: The economics and politics of European Merger Control*, Centre for Economic Policy Research, London, 1993.

Rowen, D., *Competition Policy in the Community*, European Policy Forum, London, 1992.

Stehn, J., 'Wettbewerbsverfälschungen im Binnenmarkt: Ungelöste Probleme nach Maastricht', *Die Weltwirtschaft*, 1993/1, pp. 43–60.

Swann, D., 'Standards, procurement, mergers and state aids', in Swann, D. (ed.), *The Single European Market and Beyond: A study of the wider implications of the Single European Act*, Routledge, London, 1992, pp. 53–80.

Weiss, F., *Public Procurement in European Community Law*, Athlone Press, London, 1993.

Woolcock, S., 'Public procurement', in Hurwitz, L. and Lequesne, C. (eds.), *The State of the European Community: Policies, institutions and debates in the transition years*, Longman, London, 1991, pp. 127–36.

Woolcock, S. *et al. Britain, Germany and 1992: The limits of deregulation*, RIIA/Pinter, London, 1991.

Taxation

The second Chapter of Title V contains five Articles relating to taxation (Articles 95–99). These, as with those in the first Chapter of Title V, have as their aim the promotion of fair competition within the Community. Thus, Articles 95 and 96 require member states not to afford domestic products any indirect protection through either the imposition of taxation on goods imported from elsewhere in the Community or the repayment of excess internal taxation on exports. Similarly, the imposition of countervailing charges, unless approved for a limited period by the Council is prohibited (Article 98). Despite this, turnover taxes may be retained and simplified, provided they do not infringe the principles laid down in Articles 95–96. Where an infringement does occur, it is left to the Commission to instruct the member state concerned on how it should proceed (Article 97).

The most significant and often contentious provision of Chapter 2, however, is contained in Article 99. This Article requires the Council to adopt measures aimed at harmonizing indirect taxation within the Community so as to ensure the establishment and functioning of the Internal Market. To many, such a

q.v.
Internal Market pp. 122–30.

competence, if exercised, undermines the sovereign right of national governments to tax its citizens. Moreover, from the consumer's point of view, harmonizing indirect taxation is often opposed as it would undoubtedly lead to taxes being levied on previously tax-exempted items. This is particularly so in the United Kingdom where VAT is not levied on books, food and children's clothing. Nevertheless, the objective of the Community remains unchanged post-Maastricht. However, the TEU did introduce an amendment requiring the Council, on the basis of a proposal from the Commission and acting unanimously, to adopt the necessary harmonization measures in consultation with the EP and the EcoSoc. Previously the EcoSoc had not been consulted at all. Indeed, it was not until the entry into force of the SEA that the Council was obliged, under Article 99, to consult the EP.

Chapter 2   Tax provisions

ARTICLE 95

No Member State shall impose, directly or indirectly, on the products of other Member States any internal taxation of any kind in excess of that imposed directly or indirectly on similar domestic products.

Furthermore, no Member State shall impose on the products of other Member States any internal taxation of such a nature as to afford indirect protection to other products.

Member States shall, not later than at the beginning of the second stage, repeal or amend any provisions existing when this Treaty enters into force which conflict with the preceding rules.

ARTICLE 96

Where products are exported to the territory of any Member State, any repayment of internal taxation shall not exceed the internal taxation imposed on them, whether directly or indirectly.

ARTICLE 97

Member States which levy a turnover tax calculated on a cumulative multi-stage tax system may, in the case of internal taxation imposed by them on imported products or of repayments allowed by them on exported products, establish average rates for products or groups of products, provided that there is no infringement of the principles laid down in Articles 95 and 96.

Where the average rates established by a Member State do not conform to these principles, the Commission shall address appropriate directives or decisions to the State concerned.

ARTICLE 98

In the case of charges other than turnover taxes, excise duties and other forms of indirect taxation, remissions and repayments in respect of exports to other Member States may not be granted and countervailing charges in respect of imports from Member States may not be imposed unless the measures contemplated have been previously approved for a limited period by the Council acting by a qualified majority on a proposal from the Commission.

ARTICLE 99

The Council shall, acting unanimously on a proposal from the Commission and after consulting the European Parliament **and the Economic and Social Committee**, adopt provisions for the harmonization of legislation concerning turnover taxes, excise duties and other forms of indirect taxation to the extent that such harmonization is necessary to ensure the establishment and the functioning of the internal market within the time-limit laid down in Article 7a.

The approximation of laws

The purpose of Chapter 3 of the new Title V is to provide for the approximation, where deemed necessary for the functioning of the Internal Market and not provided for elsewhere in the Treaty, of the laws of the member states. Hence, the EC is competent to require member states to amend national legislation in line with Community-wide directives relating to the Single Market. The actual Treaty Chapter on the approximation of laws consists of seven Articles (Articles 100−102), four of which have been inserted into the Treaty of Rome by either the SEA or the TEU (Articles 100a−100d). These additions specify new areas for the approximation of laws, such as the Internal Market and visas. They thus complement the general provisions for approximation contained in the three Articles which originally made up the Chapter when the Treaty of Rome entered into force in 1958 (Articles 100, 101 and 102).

These three Articles contain provisions which empower the Council to adopt directives approximating the laws of the member states to ensure the establishment and functioning of the Common Market on which the Community is based. Commission proposals for such directives, while originally requiring only a unanimous decision within the Council before being adopted, now, following an amendment introduced by the TEU, have to be presented to the EP and the EcoSoc for consultation before adoption (Article 100). However, there is no EP or EcoSoc involvement in the decision-making procedure in cases where differences in national laws are deemed to cause distortions to competition within the Common Market. Here, it is left to the Council, acting by a qualified majority on a proposal from the Commission, to issue the directives necessary to remedy the situation (Article 101). Finally, where a member state proposes to amend a national law, the effect of which might be a distortion of competition, the Commission is required to advise the member state concerned on measures to avoid any distortion. Where a member state ignores the recommendations of the Commission, other member states are not required to amend their own national laws to remedy the situation (Article 102).

q.v. Common Market p. 123.

As indicated, the Articles inserted into the Chapter by the SEA (Articles 100a and 100b) make specific provision for the approximation of national laws with regard to the establishment and functioning of the Internal Market. Under these Articles, when originally inserted, directives could be issued by the Council acting by a qualified majority on a proposal from the Commission and in accordance with the cooperation procedure now found in Article 189c, and in consultation with the EcoSoc. However, following the introduction of an amendment by the TEU to Article 100a, the role of the EP is enhanced now that the Council is required to issue directives in accordance with the conciliation procedure laid down in Article 189b (Article 100a(1)). For the most part, the Council is required to use this procedure for the approximation of all national laws relating to the Internal Market, providing, in doing so, for high levels of health and safety, and consumer and environmental protection (Article 100a(3)). However, the procedure does not apply to fiscal matters, the free movement of people, and workers' rights (Article 100a(2)). Instead, any measures aimed at harmonizing legislation in these areas have to be adopted in accordance with the procedure

q.v. Article 189c pp. 304−5.

q.v. Article 189b pp. 302−4.

laid down in Article 100, the main effect of which is that the Council must vote unanimously. By way of derogation, member states may, if it is deemed necessary apply national provisions for the protection of the environment or working conditions, or to protect public morality or health and safety levels as laid down in Article 36. However, where these are deemed by the Commission or another member state to constitute discrimination or a disguised restriction on trade, they may be referred to the Court of Justice (Article 100a(4)). Finally, where the appropriate national laws have not been harmonized by the end of 1992, provision is made for the Council, acting in accordance with the procedures laid down in Article 100a, to recognize these laws as having equivalent effect to those applied by another member state (Article 100b).

q.v. Article 36 p. 94.

The second specific area where the amended Treaty of Rome provides for harmonization under Chapter 3 of Title V is visa policy. Provisions to this effect were inserted into the Treaty by the TEU (Articles 100c and 100d). Here, the immediate aim of the Community is to develop a common visa policy *vis-à-vis* nationals from third countries, although provision is made in Article 100c(6) for the adoption of common policies in any of the areas currently covered by Article K of the TEU on justice and home affairs, provided a decision to this effect is taken under Article K.9. The common visa policy is to be agreed upon within the Council, acting unanimously on a proposal from the Commission and after consulting the EP (Article 100c(1)). The Council is, however, to be assisted in its work by the Coordinating Committee set up under Article K.4 of the TEU (Article 100d). However, from 1 January 1996, policy decisions will only require a qualified majority in the Council, a procedure to be adopted prior to this date for adopting a common format to visas (Article 100c(3)). While this will effectively result in a common EC visa policy, provision is also made for member states to be granted temporary national restrictions, limited initially to a maximum of six months (Article 100c(2)). Similarly, the common policy will not prevent member states from carrying out their responsibilities with regard to internal security and the maintenance of law and order (Article 100c(5)).

q.v. Article K.9 p. 386.

q.v. Article K.4 p. 385.

Chapter 3 Approximation of laws

ARTICLE 100

The Council shall, acting unanimously on a proposal from the Commission **and after consulting the European Parliament and the Economic and Social Committee**, issue directives for the approximation of such *laws, regulations or administrative provisions of the* Member States as directly affects the establishment or functioning of the common market.

ARTICLE 100a

1. By way of derogation from Article 100 and save where otherwise provided in this Treaty, the following provisions shall apply for the achievement of the objectives set out in Article *7a*. The Council shall, acting **in accordance with the procedure referred to in Article 189b** and after consulting the Economic and Social Committee, adopt the measures for the approximation of the provisions laid down by law, regulation or administrative action in Member States which have as their object the establishment and functioning of the internal market.

2. Paragraph 1 shall not apply to fiscal provisions, to those relating to the free

movement of persons nor to those relating to the rights and interests of employed persons.

3. The Commission, in its proposals envisaged in paragraph 1 concerning health, safety, environmental protection and consumer protection, will take as a base a high level of protection.

4. If, after the adoption of a harmonization measure by the Council acting by a qualified majority, a Member State deems it necessary to apply national provisions on grounds of major needs referred to in Article 36, or relating to protection of the environment or the working environment, it shall notify the Commission of these provisions.

The Commission shall confirm the provisions involved after having verified that they are not a means of arbitrary discrimination or a disguised restriction on trade between Member States.

By way of derogation from the procedure laid down in Articles 169 and 170, the Commission or any Member State may bring the matter directly before the Court of Justice if it considers that another Member State is making improper use of the powers provided for in this Article.

5. The harmonization measures referred to above shall, in appropriate cases, include a safeguard clause authorizing the Member States to take, for one or more of the non-economic reasons referred to in Article 36, provisional measures subject to a Community control procedure.

ARTICLE 100b

1. During 1992, the Commission shall, together with each Member State, draw up an inventory of national laws, regulations and administrative provisions which fall under Article 100a and which have not been harmonized pursuant to that Article.

The Council, acting in accordance with the provisions of Article 100a may decide that the provisions in force in a Member state must be recognized as being equivalent to those applied by another Member state.

2. The provisions of Article 100a(4) shall apply by analogy.

3. The Commission shall draw up the inventory referred to in the first subparagraph of paragraph 1 and shall submit appropriate proposals in good time to allow the Council to act before the end of 1992.

ARTICLE 100c

1. The Council, acting unanimously on a proposal from the Commission and after consulting the European Parliament, shall determine the third countries whose nationals must be in possession of a visa when crossing the external borders of the Member States.

2. However, in the event of an emergency situation in a third country posing a threat of a sudden inflow of nationals from that country into the Community, the Council, acting by a qualified majority on a recommendation from the Commission, may introduce, for a period not exceeding six months, a visa requirement for nationals from the country in question. The visa requirement established under this paragraph may be extended in accordance with the procedure referred to in paragraph 1.

3. From 1 January 1996, the Council shall adopt the decisions referred to in paragraph 1 by a qualified majority. The Council shall, before that date, acting by a qualified majority on a proposal from the Commission and after consulting the European Parliament, adopt measures relating to a uniform format for visas.

4. In the areas referred to in this Article, the Commission shall examine any request made by a Member State that it submit a proposal to the Council.

5. This Article shall be without prejudice to the exercise of the responsibilities incumbent upon the Member States with regard to the maintenance of law and order and the safeguarding of internal security.

6. This Article shall apply to other areas if so decided pursuant to Article K.9 of the provisions of the Treaty on European Union which relate to cooperation in the fields of justice and home affairs, subject to the voting conditions determined at the same time.

7. The provisions of the conventions in force between the Member States governing areas covered by this Article shall remain in force until their content has been replaced by directives or measures adopted pursuant to this Article.

ARTICLE 100d **The Coordinating Committee consisting of senior officials set up by Article K.4 of the Treaty on European Union shall contribute, without prejudice to the provisions of Article 151, to the preparation of the proceedings of the Council in the fields referred to in Article l00c.**

ARTICLE 101 Where the Commission finds that a difference between the provisions laid down by law, regulation or administrative action in Member States is distorting the conditions of competition in the common market and that the resultant distortion needs to be eliminated, it shall consult the Member States concerned.

If such consultation does not result in an agreement eliminating the distortion in question, the Council shall, on a proposal from the Commission, acting unanimously during the first stage and by a qualified majority thereafter, issue the necessary directives. The Commission and the Council may take any other appropriate measures provided for in this Treaty.

ARTICLE 102 1. Where there is reason to fear that the adoption or amendment of a provision laid down by law, regulation or administrative action may cause distortion within the meaning of Article 101, a Member State desiring to proceed therewith shall consult the Commission. After consulting the Member States, the Commission shall recommend to the States concerned such measures as may be appropriate to avoid the distortion in question.

2. If a State desiring to introduce or amend its own provisions does not comply with the recommendation addressed to it by the Commission, other Member States shall not be required, in pursuance of Article 101, to amend their own provisions in order to eliminate such distortion. If the Member State which has ignored the recommendation of the Commission causes distortion detrimental only to itself, the provisions of Article 101 shall not apply.

iii. Economic and monetary policies

Economic and monetary union

The third Title of Part Three is one of the most significant Titles in the amended Treaty of Rome. It contains the provisions (Articles 102a–109m) which form the basis of the future economic and monetary union (EMU) of the EC. This proposed union is the major objective of the TEU, involving not only the eventual introduction of a single currency, but also the transfer of monetary competences away from national authorities to a newly created European Central Bank. It thus represents a qualitative step away from existing intergovernmental cooperation to supranational integration on economic and monetary matters.

Except where indicated below, all the provisions relating to EMU contained in Part Three, Title III are new to the Treaty of Rome. The Title also contains possibly the most detailed and complex provisions inserted into the Treaty by the TEU. This is highlighted by the fact that 11 of the Protocols attached to the amended Treaty of Rome, one of which consists of 53 Articles, and 6 Declarations relate directly to the provisions contained in Title III. The potential confusion this may cause the reader is heightened by the fact that, as a result of the decision by the member states to proceed towards EMU in a series of three stages, the majority of the provisions do not have immediate effect once the TEU enters into force. Instead, certain provisions are only valid for a limited period of time, while others may only become valid once the transition has been made to the final stage of EMU (see Article 109e(3)). Furthermore, the fact that member states may be granted derogations from various elements of the EMU process makes it even more complex.

q.v. Article 109e(3) p. 169.

In an attempt to clarify this, the analysis of the Treaty provisions contained in this sub-subdivision of the *Handbook* will first examine the general aims of the EC's economic and monetary policy and the provisions contained in Part Three, Title III of the amended Treaty of Rome which have immediate effect once the TEU enters into force (i.e. those relating to Stage I of EMU). It will then discuss the provisions relevant to Stage II of EMU, and finally those which will apply once the Community has embarked on Stage III and achieves full economic and monetary union.

The Title is actually divided into four Chapters. These replace the first three Chapters of Part Three, Title II of the post-SEA Treaty of Rome.[47] The first of these (Articles 102a–104c) deals with the economic policy of the Community, while the remaining three are devoted to monetary matters (Articles 105–109m). As such, the second Chapter outlines the nature of Community monetary policy during the final stage of EMU (Articles 105–109). The third Chapter then describes the role of the institutions involved in the conduct of monetary policy (Articles 109a–109d), while Chapter 4 contains the arrangements for the transition through the three stages to full EMU (Articles 109e–109m). It is the provisions contained in these last three Chapters which are the most complex in the Title. An indication of the various stages to which all the provisions in the Title apply is given in Box 8.

As indicated, Chapter 1 concerns the Community's economic policy. However, the actual economic objectives of the Union and the tasks the Community is to fulfil with regard to economic policy are not specifically mentioned in the Articles contained in the Chapter, although reference is made

---

47. Prior to the SEA, this title consisted of three Chapters numbered accordingly: '1. Conjunctural Policy', '2. Balance of Payments', and '3. Commercial Policy'. With the introduction of the amendments to the Treaty of Rome contained in the SEA a new Chapter 1, 'Cooperation in Economic and Monetary Policy (Economic and Monetary Union)', was inserted, forcing the existing Chapters to be renumbered 2–4 respectively. Under the TEU, the first three Chapter Titles were dropped, while Commercial Policy was transferred to an entirely new Title (see pp. 180–3).

Box 8. The provisions of Part Three, Title III of the Amended Treaty of Rome and their applicability to the three stages of Economic and Monetary Union

Article	Description	I	II	III
102a	Objectives and principles of economic policy	X	X	X
103	Formulation of economic policy, ensuring its implementation	X	X	X
103a(1)	Rules governing severe supply difficulties	X	X	X
103a(2)	Rules governing severe economic difficulties			X
104	Rules governing credit facilities		X	X
104a(1)	Rules governing privileged access to financial institutions		X	X
104a(2)	Defining application of Art. 104a(1)	X		
104b	Financial liability of the Community		X	X
104c(1, 9, 11)	Rules governing government deficits			X
104c(2–8, 10, 12–13)	Rules governing government deficits		X	X
104c(14)	Rules governing government deficits	X	X	X
105	Tasks and objectives of ESCB			X
105a	Issuance of notes and coins			X
106	Composition of ESCB		X	X
107	Independence of ESCB			X
108	Independence of central banks		X	X
108a	ECB regulatory instruments			X
109	Relations with non-Community currencies			X
109a	Composition of ECB			X
109b	ECB relations with other EC institutions			X
109c(1)	Tasks and composition of the Monetary Committee	X	X	X
109c(2–4)	Tasks and composition of the Economic and Financial Committee			X
109d	Role of Commission, Council and member states	X	X	X
109e	General details concerning Stage II	X	X	X
109f	Tasks, composition and regulatory instruments of EMI		X	
109g	Currency composition of ECU	X	X	X
109h	Rules governing balance of payments difficulties	X	X	
109i	Rules governing balance of payments crises	X	X	
109j	Transition to Stage III		X	
109k	Derogations from Stage III		X	X
109l(1–3)	Details concerning composition and tasks of ECB.		X	X
109l(4–5)	ECU value			X
109m(1)	Exchange rate policy	X	X	
109m(2)	Exchange rate policy			X

to them (Article 102a). Instead, they are to be found among the objectives of the Union as laid down in Article B of the TEU. They involve promoting 'balanced and sustainable economic and social progress', and 'strengthening economic and social cohesion'. This is to be done through the establishment of economic and monetary union and the introduction of a single currency.

q.v. Article B p. 59.

However, while it is stated that these are the objectives of the Union, it is left to the Community, in line with Article 2 of the amended Treaty of Rome, to achieve them. This the Community must do by promoting balanced economic development; sustainable and non-inflationary growth; a high degree of convergence of economic performance; a high standard of living; and economic and social cohesion and solidarity among the member states. In doing so, the Community is required to act in accordance with certain principles. These are

q.v. Article 2 p. 64.

laid down in Articles 102a and 3a of the amended Treaty, and include stable prices; sound public finances and monetary conditions; a sustainable balance of payments; an efficient allocation of resources; and the principle of an open market economy with free competition.

q.v. Article 3a p. 65.

While references to the Community's economic policy and the economic objectives of the Union suggests that the TEU heralds a supranational economic policy, the actual conduct of economic policy remains in the hands of the member states (Articles 102a and 103(1)). However, Article 103(1) does require member states to regard their economic policies as a matter of common concern and to coordinate them with a view to achieving the general objectives indicated above and in line with broad guidelines set out by the Council of Ministers.[48] Such guidelines are to be adopted by a qualified majority on the basis of an agreement reached within the European Council (Article 103(2)).[49] The degree of economic convergence achieved and member states' compliance with the guidelines laid down is to be regularly monitored by the Council under Article 103(3). A report containing the results of the monitoring is to be presented to the EP. Indeed, where a member state's economic policy is considered by the Commission to be inconsistent with the broad guidelines laid down by the Council, the Council may, by a qualified majority make and publicize a recommendation to the member state concerned (Article 103(4−5)).[50] The aim of this is to compel member states to meet their obligations not only with regard to the Union's economic objectives, but also in preparing for economic and monetary union.

As noted earlier, EMU is to be achieved in three stages (see Figure 6). However, there is no explicit mention of Stage I in the amended Treaty of Rome. This is because the first stage of EMU actually began, prior to the signing of the TEU, on 1 July 1990 following a decision taken by the European Council at its Madrid Summit in June 1989. Nevertheless, the amended Treaty of Rome does contain provisions governing the first stage. Essentially, these provide the Community with the opportunity to put into place certain basic prerequisites for economic and monetary union. As such, Stage I involves the removal of all restrictions on payments and the free movement of capital within the EC in line with the provisions contained in Article 73b of the amended Treaty of Rome (Article 109e(2)). However, where a member state is in difficulty with regard to its balance of payments and this may affect the functioning of the Single Market, Articles 109h and 109i do provide for mutual assistance and protective measures to be taken.[51] In addition, Stage I involves the so-called Monetary Committee promoting the coordination of member states' policies in these and all other areas

q.v. Article 73b p. 120.

---

48. In line with the Declaration 3, the Council will continue to comprise Economic and Finance ministers, see p. 432.

49. In line with the Declaration 4, the President of the Council is to ask the Economic and Finance ministers to participate in the European Council when the latter discusses matters related to economic and monetary union, see p. 432.

50. However, the Council is empowered, under Article 103a(1), to decide upon appropriate economic measures to combat any severe difficulties in the supply of certain products.

51. The provisions contained in Articles 109h and 109i are slightly amended versions of the provisions contained in Articles 108 and 109 of the Treaty of Rome in its pre-TEU form. Both Articles will cease to apply once the Community has moved to Stage III of EMU (Articles 109h(4) and 109i(4)).

Figure 6. EMU
structures

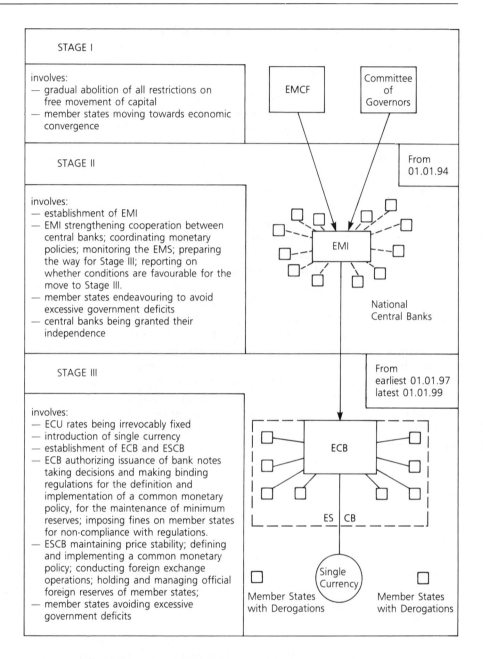

STAGE I

involves:
— gradual abolition of all restrictions on
  free movement of capital
— member states moving towards economic
  convergence

EMCF

Committee
of
Governors

STAGE II

From
01.01.94

involves:
— establishment of EMI
— EMI strengthening cooperation between
  central banks; coordinating monetary
  policies; monitoring the EMS; preparing
  the way for Stage III; reporting on
  whether conditions are favourable for the
  move to Stage III.
— member states endeavouring to avoid
  excessive government deficits
— central banks being granted their
  independence

EMI

National
Central Banks

STAGE III

From
earliest 01.01.97
latest 01.01.99

involves:
— ECU rates being irrevocably fixed
— introduction of single currency
— establishment of ECB and ESCB
— ECB authorizing issuance of bank notes
  taking decisions and making binding
  regulations for the definition and
  implementation of a common monetary
  policy, for the maintenance of minimum
  reserves; imposing fines on member states
  for non-compliance with regulations.
— ESCB maintaining price stability; defining
  and implementing a common monetary
  policy; conducting foreign exchange
  operations; holding and managing official
  foreign reserves of member states;
— member states avoiding excessive
  government deficits

ECB

ES CB

Single
Currency

Member States
with Derogations

Member States
with Derogations

necessary for the effective functioning of the Internal Market. The Monetary
Committee was originally set up in 1958 in accordance with provisions then found
in Article 105(2) of the Treaty of Rome. These now appear in a slightly amended
form in Article 109c(1). The Committee will, however, be dissolved at the
beginning of Stage III (Article 109c(2)).

With the entry into force of the TEU, the content of Stage I is further defined.

Thus, the amended Treaty of Rome requires that, during the first stage, credit facilities with central banks and measures establishing privileged access to financial institutions favouring EC, government, or public bodies be abolished (Articles 104 and 104a). Secondly, member states are requested, where necessary, to adopt multiannual programmes to promote the lasting economic convergence required for progress towards economic and monetary union, paying particular attention to the maintenance of price stability and sound public finances (Article 109e(2)(a)). Member states are also required during Stage I, as well as Stage II, to treat their exchange rate policies as a matter of common concern, taking into account cooperation within the European Monetary System (Article 109m(1)). This provision reflects traditional practice as previously provided for in Articles 107(1) and 102a(1) of the Treaty of Rome prior to the TEU. Finally, the Council is required during Stage I to assess the progress made towards achieving economic and monetary convergence and in the implementation of EC law relating to the completion of the Internal Market (Article 109e(2)).

q.v. European Monetary System pp. 176–9.

Unlike Stage I, Stage II is explicitly mentioned in the amended Treaty of Rome. Indeed, it is firmly stated that the second stage of EMU begins on 1 January 1994 (Article 109e(1)). From this date onwards, the Community is to intensify the preparations for full economic and monetary union. Firstly, the governments of member states will be required to improve budgetary discipline and endeavour to avoid excessive budget deficits (Article 109e(4)). Their performance will be monitored by the Commission and assessed with reference to values laid down in the Protocol on the Excessive Deficit Procedure (Article 104c(2)). These require that the planned or actual government deficit is no greater than 3 per cent, and total government debt does not exceed 60 per cent of the member state's GDP. If a member state fails, or risks failing, to fulfil one or both of these criteria, the Commission will produce a report, followed by an opinion, which will be forwarded to the Council. If the Council decides that an excessive deficit does exist, it may, acting by a qualified majority, make recommendations to the member state concerned to rectify the situation (Article 104c(3–7 and 12)).[52] If the member state fails to reduce its budget deficit sufficiently, the Council may make its original recommendations public (Article 104c(8)). However, the member state concerned may not be referred to the Court of Justice under Article 169 or Article 170 as a result of non-compliance (Article 104c(10)). In line with the principle of budgetary discipline, from 1 January 1994 the EC and its member states can no longer be liable for or assume the financial commitments of government or public bodies, except where these commitments involve the joint execution of specific projects (Article 104b).

q.v. Protocol on the Excessive Deficit Procedure pp. 416–17.

A second area where preparations for Stage III are to be made is in developing the institutional and legal framework for full economic and monetary union. As such, Stage II involves member states gradually granting national central banks their full independence, and amending national legislation so that it complies with

---

52. When acting by a qualified majority under Article 104c, the Council votes by a two-thirds majority of the votes as weighted in accordance with Article 148(2) (see p. 268). The member state to which the recommendations are addressed is excluded from the vote (Article 104c(13)).

the relevant provisions of the amended Treaty of Rome and of the Statute of the European System of Central Banks (Articles 108 and 109e(5)).

In addition, Stage II is to involve the establishment of the European Monetary Institute (EMI). This will comprise the governors of the national central banks, be presided over by an appointee of the member states (Article 109f(1)), and will operate in accordance with the EMI Statute, as contained in the Protocol on the Statute of the European Monetary Institute attached to the amended Treaty of Rome. The tasks of the EMI cover several areas as laid down in Article 109f(2). These include the promotion of cooperation between national central banks; the monitoring of the European Monetary System (EMS); and the coordination of the monetary policies of the member states. The EMI is also charged with preparing the ground for Stage III. This involves developing the necessary procedures and instruments for the successful functioning of a single monetary policy, and, by 31 December 1996, specifying the framework required for the European System of Central Banks (ESCB) to function effectively during Stage III (Article 109f(3)). Additional tasks may also be assigned to the EMI by the Council in accordance with Article 109f(7). In executing the tasks conferred on it, the EMI may, on the basis of a two-thirds majority, formulate opinions and recommendations relating to monetary and exchange rate policies within the EC (Article 109f(4–5)). It is also to be consulted by the Council regarding any legislative proposal within the former's competences, and may similarly be consulted by member states where required by the Council (Article 109f(6)). Finally, the EMI is required to assume any consultative role provided for in the amended Treaty of Rome for the European Central Bank (ECB) prior to the latter being set up (Article 109f(8–9)).[53] Similarly, prior to the establishment of the EMI, any consultative role assigned to it under in Article 109f will be carried out by the Committee of Governors (Article 109f(8)).

Undoubtedly the most significant task entrusted to the EMI is the drawing up, along with the Commission, of the reports which will form the basis of the European Council's decision as to when Stage III of EMU will begin.[54] The reports will first of all examine the extent to which each member state's national legislation relating to the independence of central banks is compatible with that of the Treaty of Rome and the Statute of the ESCB. This presumes that member states are at least in the process of drafting appropriate legislation. However, as far as the transition to Stage III is concerned, the most important aspect of the reports will be the assessment of each member state's fulfilment of the so-called convergence criteria, since only those member states which meet all of the convergence criteria will be eligible to participate in the final stage of EMU (Article 109j(1)).

The convergence criteria which member states must meet are outlined in Article 109j(1) and given more detail in Protocols 5 and 6 attached to the amended Treaty of Rome. In short, a member state must have a sustainable rate of inflation

q.v. Statute of the European System of Central Banks and the Statute of the European Monetary Institute pp. 394–416.

q.v. Protocols 5 and 6 pp. 416–18.

---

53. No indication is given here as to whether the EMI is to assume the consultative role assigned to the ECB under Article N of the TEU. For the implications of this see footnote 17 on p. 265 below.
54. See footnote 58.

which is no greater than 1.5 percentage points above that of the three lowest rates in the EC; its government's budgetary deficit must be less than 3 per cent of the country's GDP; the overall public debt of the member state must not exceed 60 per cent of its GDP;[55] the member state's currency must have maintained its position within the narrow band of the ERM for at least two years without a devaluation; and average long-term interest rates in the country must not have exceeded the level of the three lowest rates in the Community by more than 2 percentage points over a period of least one year. In addition to assessing whether member states meet the convergence criteria, the Commission-EMI reports are also to consider the development of the ECU (European Currency Unit), the results of the integration of markets, balance of payments, and the development of various price indices such as unit labour costs (Article 109j(1)).

On the basis of the reports the Council will assess, acting by a qualified majority, which member states meet the convergence criteria. It will then present its findings to the heads of state and government, meeting as the Council of Ministers (Article 109j(2)).[56] This extraordinary Council, meeting before 31 December 1996, and having received the opinion of the EP, will decide whether the Community should embark on Stage III of EMU. The heads of state or of government are to take three decisions. Firstly, they are required to decide whether a majority of member states meet the convergence criteria. Secondly, they are required to decide whether it is actually appropriate for the Community to proceed to Stage III. If so, they are, thirdly, to set the date for that move. Each of these decisions is to be taken on the basis of a qualified majority, thus preventing any member state from vetoing the move (Article 109j(3)). Indeed, member states agreed at Maastricht to respect the will of the Community to enter into Stage III and not to prevent this from taking place.[57]

However, if by 31 December 1997 the heads of state or of government have failed to set a date for the beginning of Stage III, this final stage of EMU will begin on 1 January 1999, irrespective of how many member states are in a position to meet the necessary conditions for the adoption of a single currency.[58] Nevertheless, it is left to the heads of state or of government, on a recommendation from the Council and having received the opinion of the EP,

---

55. As far as the two criteria relating to government debt are concerned, Article 104c(6) leaves it to the Council to decide exactly what constitutes an 'excessive deficit'. The figures of 60 per cent and 3 per cent of GDP laid down in Protocol 5 on the excessive deficits (see pp. 416–17) are reference values only (Article 104c(2)). The 1.5 percentage points referred to with regard to the rate of inflation is laid down in Protocol 6 relating to convergence criteria (see pp. 417–18).

56. It is worth noting that the decision to proceed to Stage III does not lie, *de jure*, with the European Council. Instead, it lies with the Council of Ministers 'meeting in the composition of the Heads of State or of Government' (Article 109j(2–4)). This reflects the fact that the European Council has no legislative powers. Thus, if the final decision as to whether the Community should proceed to Stage III is to be taken at the highest level, the heads of state or of government must take it acting as the Council of Ministers. Of even greater significance is the fact that the Commission will not formally be involved in the decision. Although it is an active participant in European Councils, the Commission does not take part in the deliberations of the Council.

57. See Protocol 10, reproduced on p. 419.

58. It is widely assumed that Stage III will begin at the latest on 1 January 1999. Indeed, this is the suggestion made in Article 109j(4). However, this is based on the assumption that the Council by the end of 1997 has not set a date for the beginning of Stage III in accordance with Article 109j(3). Yet, it does not take into account the possibility of the Council agreeing, prior to 31 December 1997, on starting Stage III at a date after 1 January 1999. This option is likely to be taken up by the Council given the events of August 1993 (see pp. 454–9).

to decide, before 1 July 1998, which member states will take part in Stage III (Article 109j(4)). While most member states will automatically participate if it is agreed that they meet the necessary conditions, Protocols attached to the amended Treaty of Rome provide for the United Kingdom and for Denmark to be exempted from inclusion in Stage III. In the case of the United Kingdom, a separate decision specifically committing the country to move to Stage III must be taken by the United Kingdom government and Parliament before the country can take part in the adoption of the single currency.[59] Denmark, meanwhile, must notify the Council in advance of the assessment, as provided for in Article 109j(2), if it wishes to exempt itself from Stage III. Such an exemption may, however, be abrogated.[60]

Once the decision to begin the final stage of EMU has been made, or immediately after 1 July 1998, whichever is sooner, measures are to be taken to establish the European System of Central Banks (ESCB) and the European Central Bank (ECB) (Article 109l(1)). Once established, the ECB will take over the tasks of the EMI which will then be dissolved (Article 109l(2)). In addition, the Council is to confirm which member states do not meet the conditions for the move to Stage III and thus confer on them the status of 'Member State with a derogation' (Article 109k(1)).

When Stage III actually begins the conversion rate against the ECU of the currencies of the member states without derogations will be fixed irrevocably and the ECU will become a legal currency. It will then be the responsibility of the Council to take the necessary measures to ensure the rapid introduction of the ECU as the single currency of those member states participating in Stage III (Article 109l(4). See also Article 109g). Also, member states will be required henceforth to maintain budgetary discipline and avoid excessive government deficits (Article 104c(1)). Where a member state is adjudged to be running an excessive deficit and fails to put into practice the advice of the Council provided for in Article 104c(7), during Stage III, the Council may require that the member state concerned take specific measures to remedy the situation (Article 104c(9)). If the member state fails to comply with such a requirement, the Council may impose a fine (Article 104c(11)). However, where a member state is faced with severe economic difficulties, financial assistance may be granted by the Council in line with Article 103a(2).[61]

In addition, the ECB and the ESCB, as established towards the end of Stage II, will become fully operational at the start of Stage III.[62] The ECB will be headed by a Governing Council comprising the governors of the national central

---

59. Protocol 11, more commonly referred to as the 'UK Opt-out', is reproduced below on pp. 419–21. It should be noted that the Protocol also exempts the United Kingdom from adopting measures in preparation for Stage III. Consequently, there is no obligation on the UK government to grant the Bank of England its independence in line with Article 108.

60. Protocol 12 (see pp. 421–2). Denmark did, in fact, notify the Council of its wish not to participate in Stage III in December 1992 as part of an agreement reached at the Edinburgh Summit of the European Council, before the TEU actually entered into force (see pp. 532–5).

61. This echoes previous provisions in the Treaty of Rome. No indication was given there either as to the source of the financial assistance mentioned.

62. Detailed provisions relating to the ECB and the ESCB are contained in Protocol 3, see pp. 394–409.

banks and the members of the Executive Board of the ECB. This board will consist of six professional bankers or monetary experts, each nominated by the member states for a single eight-year term of office (Article 109a). All members of the Executive Board and of the ECB in general are to act totally independently (Article 107). Thus, neither the Council, the Commission or the EP will be directly involved in any decisions taken by the ECB. Provision is made, however, for the Council and the Commission to be represented, without having the right to vote, at meetings of the Executive Council. In addition, the ECB must present an annual report to the Community institutions, and appear before the competent committees of the EP when requested (Article 109b).

The powers and tasks of the ECB are highly significant. The Bank is exclusively responsible for authorizing the issuance of ECU bank notes (Article 105a(1)). Measures necessary for the harmonization of denominations of coins will be adopted by the Council, having consulted the ECB, in accordance with the cooperation procedure laid down in Article 189c (Article 105a(2)). The ECB will also be able to make legally binding and directly applicable regulations on the minimum level of reserves to be held by national central banks, the efficiency of clearing and payment systems, and on the supervision of credit institutions. And, where an undertaking fails to comply with a ECB regulation or decision, the Bank will be able to impose a fine (Article 108a). Finally, the ECB is to be consulted by other Community institutions and national authorities, and indeed may itself issue opinions to them on matters within its competences (Article 105(4)).

q.v. Article 189c pp. 304–5.

The ESCB, meanwhile, will also be totally independent (Article 107), although certain provisions contained in its statute are to developed, and may be amended, by the Council (Article 106(5−6)). The ESCB will comprise the ECB and the national central banks (Article 106(1)), and will be governed by the decision-making bodies of the ECB (Article 106(3)). Its primary objective will be the maintenance of price stability. It will also be responsible for defining and implementing the EC's monetary policy and be required to support the Community in the attainment of its economic objectives. In doing so, it is to act in accordance with the principles laid down in Articles 3a and 102a of the amended Treaty of Rome. In addition, the ESCB will hold and manage the official foreign reserves of the member states; promote the smooth operation of payments within the EC; and conduct foreign exchange operations (Article 105(1−3)). However, as far as agreements on the establishment of exchange rate systems with third countries are concerned, these are to be concluded by the Council in accordance with the procedure laid down in Article 109.[63] Finally, the ESCB and, where agreed by the Council, the ECB, are responsible for ensuring the adequate supervision of credit institutions and the stability of the financial system (Article 105(5−6)).

A third institution which will begin functioning at the start of Stage III is

---

63. This is the first and only explicit mention of monetary relations with non-EC member states. Nevertheless, in Declaration 5, the Community's aim is deemed to be the promotion of stable international monetary relations, see p. 432. See also Declaration 6 on pp. 432–3.

the Economic and Financial Committee. This will replace the Monetary Committee and assume the latter's duties in so far as they relate to the financial situation in the EC. It will not, however, be required to review the monetary situation in the Community, as this will be the responsibility of the ESCB and ECB. Instead it will be responsible for monitoring the economic situation in the EC and for submitting regular reports on it to the Council (Article 109c(2), see also Article 109c(4)). The composition of the Economic and Financial Committee is to be decided by the Council (Article 109c(3)).

Finally, for those member states who fail to meet the necessary criteria for move to Stage III and the adoption of a single currency, provision is made for their progress in meeting the conditions laid down in Article 109j(1) to be reviewed at least every two years after Stage III has formally begun (Article 109k(2)). Until such a time as the heads of state or of government, meeting as the Council, decide by a qualified majority to abrogate the derogation granted, the member state concerned will not be subject to the provisions governing Stage III. As such, therefore, the national central banks of member states with derogations will not participate in the decision-making procedures of the ECB and ESCB or those of the Council in matters relating to the single monetary policy (Articles 109k(3—6), 109l(3), 109m(2)).[64]

To summarize, the provisions contained in Title III of Part Three of the amended Treaty of Rome set out the principles according to which and the mechanisms by which the Community is to achieve its and the Union's economic and monetary objectives. Central to this is the establishment, over a series of three stages, of an economic and monetary union. The final stage, which may begin as early as 1997, will involve a European Central Bank assuming responsibility for EC monetary policy and will lead to the introduction of a single European currency. Given the criteria for the move to Stage III of EMU, the actual timing of the move will be determined as much by the economic convergence of the member states' economies as by political will. To a significant extent, an indication of if and when the move to the final stage is to take place will become evident in the success of the existing route being followed by the EC in promoting economic and monetary integration. It is to this, the European Monetary System, which the *Handbook*, following the text of Articles 102a—109m, turns.

Title VI Economic and monetary policy

Chapter 1 Economic policy

ARTICLE 102a   Member States shall conduct their economic policies with a view to contributing to the achievement of the objectives of the Community, as defined in Article 2, and in the context of the broad guidelines referred to in Article 103(2). The Member States and the Community shall act in

---

64. See also Article 43 of Protocol 3, below on pp. 406—7, and Articles 3—9 of Protocol 11, below on pp. 420—1.

accordance with the principle of an open market economy with free competition, favouring an efficient allocation of resources, and in compliance with the principle set out in Article 3a.

ARTICLE 103

1. *Member States shall regard their* economic *policies as a matter of common concern* and shall coordinate them within the Council, in accordance with the provisions of Article 102a.

2. The Council shall, acting by a qualified majority on a recommendation from the Commission, formulate a draft for the broad guidelines of the economic policies of the Member States and of the Community, and shall report its findings to the European Council.

The European Council shall, acting on the basis of the report from the Council, discuss a conclusion on the broad guidelines of the economic policies of the Member States and of the Community.

On the basis of this conclusion, the Council shall, acting by a qualified majority, adopt a recommendation setting out these broad guidelines. The Council shall inform the European Parliament of its recommendation.

3. In order to ensure closer coordination of economic policies and sustained convergence of the economic performances of the Member States, the Council shall, on the basis of reports submitted by the Commission, monitor economic developments in each of the Member States and in the Community as well as the consistency of economic policies with the broad guidelines referred to in paragraph 2, and regularly carry out an overall assessment.

For the purpose of this multilateral surveillance, Member States shall forward information to the Commission about important measures taken by them in the field of their economic policy and other information as they deem necessary.

4. Where it is established, under the procedure referred to in paragraph 3, that the economic policies of a Member State are not consistent with the broad guidelines referred to in paragraph 2 or that they risk jeopardizing the proper functioning of economic and monetary union, the Council may, acting by a qualified majority on a recommendation from the Commission, make the necessary recommendations to the Member State concerned. The Council may, acting by a qualified majority on a proposal from the Commission, decide to make its recommendations public.

The President of the Council and the Commission shall report to the European Parliament on the result of multilateral surveillance. The President of the Council may be invited to appear before the competent Committee of the European Parliament if the Council has made its recommendations public.

5. The Council, acting in accordance with the procedure referred to in Article 189c, may adopt detailed rules for the multilateral surveillance procedure referred to in paragraphs 3 and 4 of this Article.

ARTICLE 103a

1. Without prejudice to any other procedures provided for in this Treaty, the Council may, acting unanimously on a proposal from the Commission, decide upon the measures appropriate to the economic situation, in particular if severe difficulties arise in the supply of certain products.

2. *Where a Member State is in difficulties or is seriously threatened with* severe *difficulties* caused by exceptional occurrences beyond its control, the Council may, acting unanimously on a proposal from the Commission, grant, under certain conditions, Community financial assistance to the Member State

concerned. Where the severe difficulties are caused by natural disasters, the Council shall act by qualified majority. The President of the Council shall inform the European Parliament of the decision taken.

ARTICLE 104

1. Overdraft facilities or any other type of credit facility with the ECB or with the central banks of the Member States (hereinafter referred to as 'national central banks') in favour of Community institutions or bodies, central governments, regional, local or other public authorities, other bodies governed by public law, or public undertakings of Member States shall be prohibited, as shall the purchase directly from them by the ECB or national central banks of debt instruments.

2. Paragraph 1 shall not apply to publicly-owned credit institutions which, in the context of the supply of reserves by central banks, shall be given the same treatment by national central banks and the ECB as private credit institutions.

ARTICLE 104a

1. Any measure, not based on prudential considerations, establishing privileged access by Community institutions or bodies, central governments, regional, local or other public authorities, other bodies governed by public law, or public undertakings of Member States to financial institutions shall be prohibited.

2. The Council, acting in accordance with the procedure referred to in Article 189c, shall, before 1 January 1994, specify definitions for the application of the prohibition referred to in paragraph 1.

ARTICLE 104b

1. The Community shall not be liable for or assume the commitments of central governments, regional, local or other public authorities, other bodies governed by public law, or public undertakings of any Member State, without prejudice to mutual financial guarantees for the joint execution of a specific project. A Member State shall not be liable for or assume the commitments of central governments, regional, local or other public authorities, other bodies governed by public law or public undertakings of another Member State, without prejudice to mutual financial guarantees for the joint execution of a specific project.

2. If necessary, the Council, acting in accordance with the procedure referred to in Article 189c, may specify definitions for the application of the prohibitions referred to in Article 104 and in this Article.

ARTICLE 104c

1. Member States shall avoid excessive governmental deficits.

2. The Commission shall monitor the development of the budgetary situation and of the stock of government debt in the Member States with a view to identifying gross errors. In particular it shall examine compliance with budgetary discipline on the basis of the following two criteria:

(a) whether the ratio of the planned or actual government deficit to gross domestic product exceeds a reference value, unless
   — either the ratio has declined substantially and continuously and reached a level that comes close to the reference value;
   — or, alternatively, the excess over the reference value is only exceptional and temporary and the ratio remains close to the reference value;
(b) whether the ratio of government debt to gross domestic product exceeds a reference value, unless the ratio is sufficiently diminishing and approaching the reference value at a satisfactory pace.

The reference values are specified in the Protocol on the excessive deficit procedure annexed to this Treaty.

3. If a Member State does not fulfil the requirements under one or both of these criteria, the Commission shall prepare a report. The report of the Commission shall also take into account whether the government deficit exceeds government investment expenditure and take into account all other relevant factors, including the medium term economic and budgetary position of the Member State.

The Commission may also prepare a report if, notwithstanding the fulfilment of the requirement under the criteria, it is of the opinion that there is a risk of an excessive deficit in a Member State.

4. The Committee provided for in Article 109c shall formulate an opinion on the report of the Commission.

5. If the Commission considers that an excessive deficit in a Member State exists or may occur, the Commission shall address an opinion to the Council.

6. The Council shall, acting by a qualified majority on a recommendation from the Commission, and having considered any observations which the Member State concerned may wish to make, decide after an overall assessment whether an excessive deficit exists.

7. Where the existence of an excessive deficit is decided according to paragraph 6, the Council shall make recommendations to the Member State concerned with a view to bringing that situation to an end within a given period. Subject to the provisions of paragraph 8, these recommendations shall not be made public.

8. Where it establishes that there has been no effective action in response to its recommendations within the period laid down, the Council may make its recommendations public.

9. If a Member State persists in failing to put into practice the recommendations of the Council, the Council may decide to give notice to the Member State to take, within a specified time limit, measures for the deficit reduction which is judged necessary by the Council in order to remedy the situation.

In such a case, the Council may request the Member State concerned to submit reports in accordance with a specific timetable in order to examine the adjustment efforts of that Member State.

10. The right to bring actions provided for in Articles 169 and 170 may not be exercised within the framework of paragraphs 1 to 9 of this Article.

11. As long as a Member State fails to comply with a decision taken in accordance with paragraph 9, the Council may decide to apply or, as the case may be, intensify one or more of the following measures:
— to require the Member State concerned to publish additional information, to be specified by the Council, before issuing bonds and securities;
— to invite the European Investment Bank to reconsider its lending policy towards the Member State concerned;
— to require the Member State concerned to make a non-interest-bearing deposit of an appropriate size with the Community until the excessive deficit has, in the view of the Council, been corrected;
— to impose fines of an appropriate size.

The President of the Council shall inform the European Parliament of the decisions taken.

12. The Council shall abrogate some or all of its decisions referred to in

paragraphs 6 to 9 and 11 to the extent that the excessive deficit in the Member State concerned has, in the view of the Council, been corrected. If the Council has previously made public recommendations, it shall, as soon as the decision under paragraph 8 has been abrogated, make a public statement that an excessive deficit in the Member State concerned no longer exists.

13. When taking the decisions referred to in paragraphs 7 to 9, 11 and 12, the Council shall act on a recommendation from the Commission by a majority of two thirds of the votes of its members weighted in accordance with Article 148(2), excluding the votes of the representative of the Member State concerned.

14. Further provisions relating to the implementation of the procedure described in this Article are set out in the Protocol on the excessive deficit procedure annexed to this Treaty.

The Council shall, acting unanimously on a proposal from the Commission and after consulting the European Parliament and the ECB, adopt the appropriate provisions which shall then replace the said Protocol.

Subject to the other provisions of this paragraph the Council shall, before 1 January 1994, acting by a qualified majority on a proposal from the Commission and after consulting the European Parliament, lay down detailed rules and definitions for the application of the provisions of the said Protocol.

Chapter 2 Monetary policy

ARTICLE 105

1. The primary objective of the ESCB shall be to maintain price stability. Without prejudice to the objective of price stability, the ESCB shall support the general economic policies in the Community with a view to contributing to the achievement of the objectives of the Community as laid down in Article 2. The ESCB shall act in accordance with the principle of an open market economy with free competition, favouring an efficient allocation of resources, and in compliance with the principles set out in Article 3a.

2. The basic tasks to be carried out through the ESCB shall be:
— to define and implement the monetary policy of the Community;
— to conduct foreign exchange operations consistent with the provisions of Article 109;
— to hold and manage the official foreign reserves of the Member States;
— to promote the smooth operation of payment systems.

3. The third indent of paragraph 2 shall be without prejudice to the holding and management by the government of Member States of foreign exchange working balances.

4. The ECB shall be consulted:
— on any proposed Community act in its fields of competence;
— by national authorities regarding any draft legislative provision in its fields of competence, but within the limits and under the conditions set out by the Council in accordance with the procedure laid down in Article 106(6).

The ECB may submit opinions to the appropriate Community institutions or bodies or to national authorities on matters in its fields of competence.

5. The ESCB shall contribute to the smooth conduct of policies pursued by the competent authorities relating to the prudential supervision of credit institutions and the stability of the financial system.

6. The Council may, acting unanimously on a proposal from the Commission and after consulting the ECB and after receiving the assent of the European

Parliament, confer upon the ECB specific tasks concerning policies relating to the prudential supervision of credit institutions and other financial institutions with the exception of insurance undertakings.

ARTICLE 105a

1. The ECB shall have the exclusive right to authorize the issue of bank notes within the Community. The ECB and the national central banks may issue such notes. The bank notes issued by the ECB and the national central banks shall be the only such notes to have the status of legal tender within the Community.

2. The Member States may issue coins subject to approval by the ECB of the volume of the issue. The Council may, acting in accordance with the procedure referred to in Article 189c and after consulting the ECB, adopt measures to harmonize the denominations and technical specifications of all coins intended for circulation to the extent necessary to permit their smooth circulation within the Community.

ARTICLE 106

1. The ESCB shall be composed of the ECB and of the national central banks.

2. The ECB shall have legal personality.

3. The ESCB shall be governed by the decision-making bodies of the ECB which shall be the Governing Council and the Executive Board.

4. The Statute of the ESCB is laid down in a Protocol annexed to this Treaty.

5. Articles 5.1, 5.2, 5.3, 17, 18, 19.1, 22, 23, 24, 26, 32.2, 32.3. 32.4, 32.6, 33.l(a) and 36 of the Statute of the ESCB may be amended by the Council, acting either by a qualified majority on a recommendation from the ECB and after consulting the Commission or unanimously on a proposal from the Commission and after consulting the ECB. In either case, the assent of the European Parliament shall be required.

6. The Council, acting by a qualified majority either on a proposal from the Commission and after consulting the European Parliament and the ECB or on a recommendation from the ECB and after consulting the European Parliament and the Commission, shall adopt the provisions referred to in Articles 4, 5.4, 19.2, 20, 28.1, 29.2, 30.4 and 34.3 of the Statute of the ESCB.

ARTICLE 107

When exercising the powers and carrying out the tasks and duties conferred upon them by this Treaty and the Statute of the ESCB, neither the ECB, nor a national central bank, nor any member of their decision-making bodies shall seek or take instructions from Community institutions or bodies, from any government of a Member State or from any other body. The Community institutions and bodies and the governments of the Member States undertake to respect this principle and not to seek to influence the members of the decision-making bodies of the ECB or of the national central banks in the performance of their tasks.

ARTICLE 108

Each Member State shall ensure, at the latest at the date of the establishment of the ESCB, that its national legislation including the statutes of its national central bank is compatible with this Treaty and the Statute of the ESCB.

ARTICLE 108a

1. In order to carry out the tasks entrusted to the ESCB, the ECB shall, in accordance with the provisions of this Treaty and under the conditions laid down in the Statute of the ESCB:
— make regulations to the extent necessary to implement the tasks defined in Article 3.1, first indent, Articles 19.1, 22 and 25.2 of the Statute of

the ESCB and in cases which shall be laid down in the acts of the Council referred to in Article 106(6);

— take decisions necessary for carrying out the tasks entrusted to the ESCB under this Treaty and the Statute of the ESCB;

— make recommendations and deliver opinions.

2. A regulation shall have general application. It shall be binding in its entirety and directly applicable in all Member States.

Recommendations and opinions shall have no binding force.

A decision shall be binding in its entirety upon those to whom it is addressed.

Articles 190 to 192 shall apply to regulations and decisions adopted by the ECB.

The ECB may decide to publish its decisions, recommendations and opinions.

3. Within the limits and under the conditions adopted by the Council under the procedure laid down in Article 106(6), the ECB shall be entitled to impose fines or periodic penalty payments on undertakings for failure to comply with obligations under its regulations and decisions.

ARTICLE 109

1. By way of derogation from Article 228, the Council may, acting unanimously on a recommendation from the ECB or from the Commission, and after consulting the ECB in an endeavour to reach a consensus consistent with the objective of price stability, after consulting the European Parliament, in accordance with the procedure in paragraph 3 for determining the arrangements, conclude formal agreements[65] on an exchange rate system for the ECU[66] in relation to non-Community currencies. The Council may, acting by a qualified majority on a recommendation from the ECB or from the Commission, and after consulting the ECB in an endeavour to reach a consensus consistent with the objective of price stability, adopt, adjust or abandon the central rates of the ECU within the exchange rate system. The President of the Council shall inform the European Parliament of the adoption, adjustment or abandonment of the ECU central rates.

2. In the absence of an exchange rate system in relation to one or more non-Community currencies as referred to in paragraph 1, the Council, acting by a qualified majority either on a recommendation from the Commission and after consulting the ECB or on a recommendation from the ECB, may formulate general orientations for exchange rate policy in relation to these currencies. These general orientations shall be without prejudice to the primary objective of the ESCB to maintain price stability.

3. By way of derogation from Article 228, where agreements concerning monetary or foreign exchange regime matters need to be negotiated by the Community with one or more States or international organizations, the Council, acting by a qualified majority on a recommendation from the Commission and after consulting the ECB, shall decide the arrangements

65. The use of the term 'formal agreement' is not intended to create a new category of international agreement under EC law. See Declaration 8, p. 433.

66. Although all versions of the TEU are supposed to be identical, the format of 'ECU' often differs from one version to the next. The UK government's version of the Treaty uses 'ECU' (Cm 1934, May 1992), as does the EC Official Journal versions found in OJC 191, 29 July 1992 and OJC 224, 31 August 1992. Such a format is also to be found in German versions of the TEU (*Bulletin*, No. 16, 21 February 1992). However, the EC Council/EC Commission version of the TEU published in February 1992 originally contained the format 'ecu'. A list of corrigendum was later issued replacing 'ecu' with 'ECU'. Such an attempt to harmonize the format throughout the Community did not, however, prevent the French government from using the format 'écu' in copies of the Treaty issued in advance of the country's referendum in September 1992.

for the negotiation and for the conclusion of such agreements. These arrangements shall ensure that the Community expresses a single position. The Commission shall be fully associated with the negotiations.

Agreements concluded in accordance with this paragraph shall be binding on the institutions of the Community, on the ECB and on Member States.

4. Subject to paragraph 1, the Council shall, on a proposal from the Commission and after consulting the ECB, acting by a qualified majority decide on the position of the Community at international level as regards issues of particular relevance to economic and monetary union and, acting unanimously, decide its representation in compliance with the allocation of powers laid down in Articles 103 and 105.

5. Without prejudice to Community competence and Community agreements as regards economic and monetary union, Member States may negotiate in international bodies and conclude international agreements.

Chapter 3   Institutional provisions

ARTICLE 109a

1. The Governing Council of the ECB shall comprise the members of the Executive Board of the ECB and the Governors of the national central banks.

2. (a) The Executive Board shall comprise the President, the Vice-President and four other members.
   (b) The President, the Vice-President and the other members of the Executive Board shall be appointed from among the persons of recognized standing and professional experience in monetary or banking matters by common accord of the Governments of the Member States at the level of Heads of State or of Government, on a recommendation from the Council, after it has consulted the European Parliament and the Governing Council of the ECB.

Their term of office shall be eight years and shall not be renewable.

Only nationals of Member States may be members of the Executive Board.

ARTICLE 109b

1. The President of the Council and a member of the Commission may participate, without having the right to vote, in meetings of the Governing Council of the ECB.

The President of the Council may submit a motion for deliberation to the Governing Council of the ECB.

2. The President of the ECB shall be invited to participate in Council meetings when the Council is discussing matters relating to the objectives and tasks of the ESCB.

3. The ECB shall address an annual report on the activities of the ESCB and on the monetary policy of both the previous and current year to the European Parliament, the Council and the Commission, and also to the European Council. The President of the ECB shall present this report to the Council and to the European Parliament, which may hold a general debate on that basis.

The President of the ECB and the other members of the Executive Board may, at the request of the European Parliament or on their own initiative, be heard by the competent Committees of the European Parliament.

ARTICLE 109c   *1. In order to promote coordination of the policies of Member States to the full extent needed for the functioning of the internal market, a Monetary Committee with advisory status is hereby set up.*

It shall have the following tasks:
— *to keep under review the monetary and financial situation of the Member States and of the Community and the general payments system of the Member States and to report regularly thereon to the Council and to the Commission;*
— *to deliver opinions at the request of the Council or of the Commission, or on its own initiative for submission to those institutions;*
— **without prejudice to Article 151, to contribute to the preparation of the work of the Council referred to in Articles 73f, 73g, 103(2), (3), (4) and (5), 103a, 104a, 104b, 104c, 109e(2), 109f(6), 109h, 109i, 109j(2) and 109k(1);**
— **to examine, at least once a year, the situation regarding the movement of capital and the freedom of payments, as they result from the application of this Treaty and of measures adopted by the Council; the examination shall cover all measures relating to capital movements and payments; the Committee shall report to the Commission and to the Council on the outcome of this examination.**

The Member States and the Commission shall each appoint two members of the Monetary Committee.[67]

2. At the start of the third stage, an Economic and Financial Committee shall be set up. The Monetary Committee provided for in paragraph 1 shall be dissolved.

The Economic and Financial Committee shall have the following tasks:
— **to deliver opinions at the request of the Council or of the Commission, or on its own initiative for submission to those institutions;**
— **to keep under review the economic and financial situation of the Member States and of the Community and to report regularly thereon to the Council and to the Commission, in particular on financial relations with third countries and international institutions;**
— **without prejudice to Article 151, to contribute to the preparation of the work of the Council referred to in Article 73f, 73g, 103(2), (3),(4) and (5), 103a, 104a, 104b, 104c, 105(6), 105a(2), 106(5) and (6), 109, 109h, 109i(2) and (3), 109k(2), 109l(4) and (5), and to carry out other advisory and preparatory tasks assigned to it by the Council;**
— **to examine, at least once a year, the situation regarding the movement of capital and the freedom of payments, as they result from the application of this Treaty and of measures adopted by the Council; the examination shall cover all measures relating to capital movements and payments; the Committee shall report to the Commission and to the Council on the outcome of this examination.**

The Member States, the Commission and the ECB shall each appoint no more than two members of the Committee.

3. The Council shall, acting by qualified majority on a proposal from the Commission and after consulting the ECB and the Committee referred to in this Article, lay down detailed provisions concerning the composition of the Economic and Financial Committee. The President of the Council shall inform the European Parliament of such a decision.

---

67. The provisions italicized in Article 109c(1) were originally contained in Article 105(2) of the Treaty of Rome.

4. In addition to the tasks set in paragraph 2, if and as long as there are Member States with a derogation as referred to in Articles 109k and 109l, the Committee shall keep under review the monetary and financial situation and the general payments system of those Member States and report regularly thereon to the Council and to the Commission.

ARTICLE 109d   For matters within the scope of Articles 103(4), 104c with the exception of paragraph 14, 109, 109j, 109k and 109(4) and (5), the Council or a Member State may request the Commission to make a recommendation or a proposal, as appropriate. The Commission shall examine this request and submit its conclusions to the Council without delay.

Chapter 4   Transitional provisions

ARTICLE 109e   **1.** The second stage for achieving economic and monetary union shall begin on 1 January 1994.

2. Before that date

(a) each Member State shall:

— adopt, where necessary, appropriate measures to comply with the prohibitions laid down in Article 73b, without prejudice to Article 73e, and in Articles 104 and 104a(1);

— adopt, if necessary, with a view to permitting the assessment provided for in subparagraph (b), multiannual programmes intended to ensure the lasting convergence necessary for the achievement of economic and monetary union, in particular with regard to price stability and sound public finances;

(b) the Council shall, on the basis of a report from the Commission, assess the progress made with regard to economic and monetary convergence, in particular with regard to price stability and sound public finances, and the progress made with the implementation of Community law concerning the internal market.

3. The provision of Articles 104, 104a(1), 104b(1), and 104c with the exception of paragraphs 1, 9, 11 and 14 shall apply from the beginning of the second stage.

The provision of Articles 103a(2), 104c(1), (9) and (11), 105, 105a, 107, 109, 109a, 109b and 109c(2) and (4) shall apply from the beginning of the third stage.

4. In the second stage, Member States shall endeavour to avoid excessive government deficits.

5. During the second stage, each Member State shall, as appropriate, start the process leading to the independence of its central bank, and in accordance with Article 108.

ARTICLE 109f   **1.** At the start of the second stage, a European Monetary Institute (hereinafter referred to as 'EMI') shall be established and take up its duties; it shall have legal personality and be directed and managed by a Council, consisting of a President and the Governors of the national central banks, one of whom shall be Vice-President.

The President shall be appointed by common accord of the Governments of the Member States at the level of Heads of State or of Government, on a recommendation from, as the case may be, the Committee of Governors of the central banks of the Member States (hereinafter referred to as 'Committee of Governors') or the Council of the EMI, and after consulting the European Parliament and the Council. The President shall be selected from among persons of recognized standing and professional experience in monetary or banking matters. Only nationals of Member States may be President of the EMI. The Council of the EMI shall appoint the Vice-President.

The Statute of the EMI is laid down in a Protocol annexed to this Treaty.

The Committee of Governors shall be dissolved at the start of the second stage.

2. The EMI shall:
— strengthen cooperation between the national central banks;
— strengthen the coordination of monetary policies of the Member States, with the aim of ensuring price stability;
— monitor the functioning of the European Monetary System;
— hold consultations concerning issues falling within the competence of the national central banks and affecting the stability of financial institutions and markets;
— take over the tasks of the European Monetary Cooperation Fund, which shall be dissolved; the modalities of dissolution are laid down in the Statute of the EMI;
— facilitate the use of the ECU and oversee its development, including the smooth functioning of the ECU clearing system.

3. For the preparation of the third stage, the EMI shall:
— prepare the instruments and procedures necessary for carrying out a single monetary policy in the third stage;
— promote the harmonization, where necessary, of rules and practices governing the collection, compilation and distribution of statistics in the areas within its field of competence;
— prepare the rules for operations to be undertaken by the national central banks within the framework of the ESCB;
— promote the efficiency of cross-border payments;
— supervise the technical preparation of ECU bank notes.
At the latest by 31 December 1996, the EMI shall specify the regulatory, organizational and logistical framework necessary for the ESCB to perform its tasks in the third stage. This framework shall be submitted for decision to the ECB at the date of its establishment.

4. The EMI, acting by a majority of two thirds of the members of its Council, may:
— formulate opinions or recommendations on the overall orientation of monetary policy and exchange rate policy as well as on related measures introduced in each Member State;
— submit opinions or recommendations to Governments and to the Council on policies which might affect the internal or external monetary situation in the Community and, in particular, the functioning of the European Monetary System;
— make recommendations to the monetary authorities of the Member States concerning the conduct of monetary policy.

5. The EMI, acting unanimously, may decide to publish its opinions and its recommendations.

6. The EMI shall be consulted by the Council regarding any proposed Community act within its field of competence.

Within the limits and under the conditions set out by the Council, acting by a qualified majority on a proposal from the Commission and after consulting the European Parliament and the EMI, the EMI shall be consulted by the authorities of the Member States on any draft legislative provision within its field of competence.

7. The Council may, acting unanimously on a proposal from the Commission and after consulting the European Parliament and the EMI, confer upon the EMI other tasks for the preparation of the third stage.

8. Where this Treaty provides for a consultative role for the ECB, references to the ECB shall be read as referring to the EMI before the establishment of the ECB.

Where this Treaty provides for a consultative role for the EMI, references to the EMI shall be read, before 1 January 1994, as referring to the Committee of Governors.

9. During the second stage, the term 'ECB' used in Articles 173, 175, 176, 177, 180 and 215 shall be read as referring to the EMI.

ARTICLE 109g

The currency composition of the ECU basket shall not be changed.

From the start of the third stage, the value of the ECU shall be irrevocably fixed in accordance with Article 109l(4).

ARTICLE 109h

1. Where a Member State is in difficulties or is seriously threatened with difficulties as regards its balance of payments either as a result of a overall disequilibrium in its balance of payments, or as a result of the type of currency at its disposal, and where such difficulties are liable in particular to jeopardize the functioning of the common market or the progressive implementation of the common commercial policy, the Commission shall immediately investigate the position of the State in question and the action which, making use of all the means at its disposal, that State has taken or may take in accordance with the provisions of **this Treaty.** *The Commission shall state what measures it recommends the State concerned to take.*

If the action taken by a Member States and the measures suggested by the Commission do not prove sufficient to overcome the difficulties which have arisen or which threaten, the Commission shall, after consulting the Committee **referred to in Article 109c,** *recommend to the Council the granting of mutual assistance and appropriate methods therefor.*

The Commission shall keep the Council regularly informed of the situation and of how it is developing.

2. The Council, acting by a qualified majority, shall grant such mutual assistance; it shall adopt directives or decisions laying down the conditions and details of such assistance, which may take such forms as:

(a) a concerted approach to or within any other international organizations to which Member States may have recourse;

(b) measures needed to avoid deflection of trade where the State which is in difficulties maintains or reintroduces quantitative restrictions against third countries;

(c) the granting of limited credits by other Member States, subject to their agreement.

3. If the mutual assistance recommended by the Commission is not granted by the Council or if the mutual assistance granted and the measures taken are insufficient, the Commission shall authorize the State which is in difficulties to take protective measures, the conditions and details of which the Commission shall determine.

Such authorization may be revoked and such conditions and details may be changed by the Council acting by a qualified majority.

4. Subject to Article 109k(6), this Article shall cease to apply from the beginning of the third stage.

ARTICLE 109i

1. Where a sudden crisis in the balance of payments occurs and a decision within the meaning of **Article 109h(2)** *is not immediately taken, the Member State concerned may, as a precaution, take the necessary protective measures. Such measures must cause the least possible disturbance in the functioning of the common market and must not be wider in scope than is strictly necessary to remedy the sudden difficulties which have arisen.*

2. The Commission and the other Member State shall be informed of such protective measures not later than when they enter into force. The Commission may recommend to the Council the granting of mutual assistance under **Article 109h.**

3. After the Commission has delivered an opinion and the Committee **referred to in Article 109c has been consulted,** *the Council may, acting by a qualified majority, decide that the State concerned shall amend, suspend or abolish the protective measures referred to above.*

4. Subject to Article 109k(6), this Article shall cease to apply from the beginning of the third stage.

ARTICLE 109j

1. The Commission and the EMI shall report to the Council on the progress made in the fulfilment by the Member States of their obligations regarding the achievement of economic and monetary union. These reports shall include an examination of the compatibility between each Member State's national legislation, including the statutes of its national central bank, and Articles 107 and 108 of this Treaty and the Statute of the ESCB. The report shall also examine the achievement of a high degree of sustainable convergence by reference to the fulfilment by each Member State of the following criteria:
— **the achievement of a high degree of price stability; this will be apparent from rate of inflation which is close to that of, at most, the three best performing Member States in terms of price stability;**
— **the sustainability of the government financial position; this will be apparent from having achieved a government budgetary position without a deficit that is excessive as determined in accordance with Article 104c(6);**
— **the observance of the normal fluctuation margins provided for by the Exchange Rate Mechanism of the European Monetary System, for at least two years, without devaluing against the currency of any other Member State;**
— **the durability of convergence achieved by the Member State and of its participation in the Exchange Rate Mechanism of the European Monetary System being reflected in the long-term interest rate levels.**

The four criteria mentioned in this paragraph and the relevant periods over which they are to be respected are developed further in a Protocol annexed to this Treaty. The reports of the Commission and the EMI shall also take account of the development of the ECU, the results of the integration of markets, the situation and development of the balances of payments on current account and an examination of the development of unit labour costs and other price indices.

2. On the basis of these reports, the Council, acting by a qualified majority on a recommendation from the Commission, shall assess:
— **for each Member State, whether it fulfils the necessary conditions for the adoption of a single currency;**

— whether a majority of the Member States fulfil the necessary conditions for the adoption of a single currency;

and recommend its findings to the Council, meeting in the composition of the Heads of State or of Government. The European Parliament shall be consulted and forward its opinion to the Council, meeting in the composition of the Heads of State or of Government.

3. Taking due account of the reports referred to in paragraph 1 and the opinion of the European Parliament referred to in paragraph 2, the Council, meeting in the composition of Heads of State or of Government, shall, acting by a qualified majority, not later than 31 December 1996:

— decide, on the basis of the recommendations of the Council referred to in paragraph 2, whether a majority of the Member States fulfil the necessary conditions for the adoption of a single currency;
— decide whether it is appropriate for the Community to enter the third stage,

and if so

— set the date for the beginning of the third stage.

4. If by the end of 1997 the date for the beginning of the third stage has not been set, the third stage shall start on 1 January 1999. Before 1 July 1998, the Council, meeting in the composition of Heads of State or of Government, after a repetition of the procedure provided for in paragraphs 1 and 2, with the exception of the second indent of paragraph 2, taking into account the reports referred to in paragraph 1 and the opinion of the European Parliament, shall, acting by a qualified majority and on the basis of the recommendations of the Council referred to in paragraph 2, confirm which Member States fulfil the necessary conditions for the adoption of a single currency.

ARTICLE 109k

1. If the decision has been taken to set the date in accordance with Article 109j(3), the Council shall, on the basis of its recommendation referred to in Article 109j(2), acting by a qualified majority on a recommendation from the Commission, decide whether any, and if so which, Member States shall have a derogation as defined in paragraph 3 of this Article. Such Member States shall in this Treaty be referred to as 'Member States with a derogation'.

If the Council has confirmed which Member States fulfil the necessary conditions for the adoption of a single currency, in accordance with Article 109j(4), those Member States which do not fulfil the conditions shall have a derogation as defined in paragraph 3 of this Article. Such Member States shall in this Treaty be referred to as 'Member States with a derogation'.

2. At least once every two years, or at the request of a Member State with a derogation, the Commission and the ECB shall report to the Council in accordance with the procedure laid down in Article 109j(1). After consulting the European Parliament and after discussion in the Council, meeting in the composition of the Heads of State or of Government, the Council shall, acting by a qualified majority on a proposal from the Commission, decide which Member States with a derogation fulfil the necessary conditions on the basis of the criteria set out in Article 109j(1), and abrogate the derogations of the Member States concerned.

3. A derogation referred to in paragraph 1 shall entail that the following Articles do not apply to the Member State concerned: Articles 104c(9) and (11), 105(1), (2), (3) and (5), 105a, 108a, 109, 109a(2)(b). The exclusion of such a Member State and its national central bank from rights and obligations within the ESCB is laid down in Chapter IX of the Statute of the ESCB.

4. In Articles 105(1), (2), and (3), 105a, 108a, 109 and 109a(2)(b), 'Member States' shall be read as 'Member States without a derogation'.

5. The voting rights of Member States with a derogation shall be suspended for the Council decisions referred to in the Articles of this Treaty mentioned in paragraph 3. In that case, by way of derogation from Articles 148 and 189a(1), a qualified majority shall be defined as two thirds of the votes of the representatives of the Member States without derogation weighted in accordance with Article 148(2), and unanimity of those Member States shall be required for an act requiring unanimity.

6. Articles 109h and 109i shall continue to apply to a Member State with a derogation.

ARTICLE 109l

1. Immediately after the decision on the date for the beginning of the third stage has been taken in accordance with Article 109j(3), or, as the case may be, immediately after 1 July 1998:
— the Council shall adopt the provisions referred to in Article 106(6);
— the governments of the Member States without a derogation shall appoint, in accordance with the procedure set out in Article 50 of the Statute of the ESCB, the President, the Vice-President and the other members of the Executive Board of the ECB. If there are Member States with a derogation, the number of members of the Executive Board may be smaller than provided for in Article 11.1 of the Statute of the ESCB, but in no circumstances shall it be less than four.

As soon as the Executive Board is appointed, the ESCB and the ECB shall be established and shall prepare for their full operation as described in this Treaty and the Statute of the ESCB. The full exercise of their powers shall start from the first day of the third stage.

2. As soon as the ECB is established, it shall, if necessary, take over tasks of the EMI. The EMI shall go into liquidation upon the establishment of the ECB; the modalities of liquidation are laid down in the Statute of the EMI.

3. If and as long as there are Member States with a derogation, and without prejudice to Article 106(3) of this Treaty, the General Council of the ECB referred to in Article 45 of the Statute of the ESCB shall be constituted as a third decision-making body of the ECB.

4. At the starting date of the third stage, the Council shall, acting with the unanimity of the Member States without a derogation, on a proposal from the Commission and after consulting the ECB, adopt the conversion rates at which their currencies shall be irrevocably fixed and at which irrevocably fixed rate the ECU shall be substituted for these currencies, and the ECU will become a currency in its own right. This measure shall by itself not modify the external value of the ECU. The Council shall, acting according to the same procedure, also take the other measures necessary for the rapid introduction of the ECU as the single currency of those Member States.

5. If it is decided, according to the procedure set out in Article 109k(2), to abrogate a derogation, the Council shall, acting with the unanimity of the Member States without a derogation and the Member State concerned, on a proposal from the Commission and after consulting the ECB, adopt the rate at which the ECU shall be substituted for the currency of the Member State concerned, and take the other measures necessary for the introduction of the ECU as the single currency in the Member State concerned.

ARTICLE 109m

1. Until the beginning of the third stage, each Member State shall treat its exchange rate policy as a matter of common interest. In doing so, Member

States *shall take account of the experience acquired in cooperation within the framework of the European Monetary System (EMS) and in developing the ECU, and shall respect existing powers in this field.*[68]

2. From the beginning of the third stage and for as long as a Member State has a derogation, paragraph 1 shall apply by analogy to the exchange rate policy of that Member State.

Economic and monetary policy

Economic and monetary union (EMU) is widely recognized by supporters and opponents of the TEU alike as the Treaty's central element. Indeed for many, when the TEU was signed, EMU became for the 1990s what the Internal Market had been for the 1980s: the essential *raison d'être* of the Community. Such an assessment may be exaggerated. Indeed, as events have shown the likelihood of EMU being realized has decreased dramatically (see the Economic Standing of Maastricht). However, the firm commitment to a single currency in the TEU and the amended Treaty of Rome does, nevertheless, serve as a useful indicator of how far the Community had developed by the early 1990s beyond the expectations of the founder members.

q.v. the Economic Standing of Maastricht pp. 454–9.

When the Treaty of Rome was signed in 1957, no mention was made of the then EEC developing into an economic and monetary union, nor of the member states forsaking their national currencies for a single European currency. Indeed, the Treaty of Rome originally provided only limited scope for economic and monetary integration beyond that involved in the establishment of the Customs Union and the realization of the four freedoms. Nevertheless, by the late 1960s the possibility of a single currency was firmly on the political agenda of the Community. Once the Customs Union had been established in 1968, the Six were keen to identify new areas for closer integration. Given the gradual collapse of the Bretton Woods system of internationally fixed exchange rates at the time, and the need to address the problems of creeping economic recession collectively, economic and monetary union was seized upon as an appropriate policy objective. Thus, following a declaration on EMU made at the Hague Summit of heads of state and government in 1969, proposals were put forward by the Luxembourg Prime Minister and Finance Minster, Pierre Werner, for the creation of an economic and monetary union within the EC by 1980.

The proposals contained in the Werner Report, which was presented to the Council and the Commission in October 1970, advocated a three-stage approach to EMU based around the development of a so-called currency snake, the establishment of a European central bank, and the coordination and harmonization of economic policies within the EC. As such, this reflected the French preference for a more structured approach to economic union, with the goal, and indeed the reality, of EMU acting as a locomotive for economic convergence. Introduced

---

68. The provisions italicized in Article 109m(1) were originally inserted into the Treaty of Rome as Article 102a by the SEA.

in 1972, the snake was a system of limited exchange rate flexibility in which the value of participant currencies could fluctuate by ±1.125% of a centrally fixed parity. However, soon after the Six had embarked on the road to EMU the international currency crises of 1971–3, the oil crisis of 1973, the subsequent onset of recession in Europe, and differences between the French and the Germans on how the Community should progress towards economic and monetary union forced plans for EMU to be abandoned. In addition, the inability of member states with weaker currencies to maintain their position in the snake meant that this attempt to induce exchange rate stability in the EC also had to be abandoned by the late 1970s.

While the collapse of the Werner Plan was clearly a setback for those advocating full EMU for the EC, by 1978 plans to develop a less ambitious system of stable exchange rates were already being drawn up. The drive behind the plans came in the form of a Franco-German initiative designed to provide Germany with the exchange rate stability in the EC it required to maintain its export-led economy, and to provide France with a degree of influence over German monetary policy to compensate for the *de facto* linkage of the franc to the Deutschmark. Indeed, following an agreement reached at the Bremen European Council Summit in July 1978, the European Monetary System (EMS) was launched at the beginning of 1979. It is through this system that the signatories to the TEU envisaged the Community moving towards full economic and monetary union. Unlike the Werner Plan, the EMS reflects more the German preference for economic and monetary union to be achieved through the gradual and almost total convergence of economies. This approach stands in contrast to that of the French, in that it regards EMU as the crowning point, rather than the locomotive, of the convergence process.

The EMS consists of three elements: the European Currency Unit; the Exchange Rate Mechanism; and the European Monetary Cooperation Fund. The first of these, the European Currency Unit (ECU), is a notional Eurocurrency based on a trade-weighted basket of all EC currencies. Given its strong trading position within the EC, Germany's Deutschmark (DM) is the most significant currency in the basket, accounting for over 30 per cent of the ECU's value. A further 30 per cent of the value is made up by the French franc and the pound sterling (see Box 9). The ECU has several functions, most prominent among which is its role as an accounting and reference value in the transfer of credits within the EMS (see below). It is also used as an accounting unit, both for the EC's budget and for currency transactions between many European companies, and as a form of credit security through the issuance of ECU bonds on international currency markets. However, the ECU does not circulate as a hard currency.

q.v. EC's budget pp. 322–7.

The second element of the EMS, and undoubtedly the most important as far as progress to economic and monetary union is concerned, is the Exchange Rate Mechanism (ERM). This, like its predecessor, the snake, is a system of semi-fixed exchange rates in which the value of a currency may fluctuate within a prescribed margin of a centrally fixed rate of exchange. The central rate is set when a currency joins the ERM, although it may be altered as part of a realignment of currency values agreed upon unanimously by the Council of Ministers. Within the ERM,

Box 9. Composition of ECU and EMS central rates

Currency	Central rate per ECU (14 June 1993)*	Composition of ECU % Currency (14 June 1993)	Composition of ECU Value of currency (21 September 1989)
Belgian franc	40.2123	8.21	3.301
Danish krone	7.43679	2.66	0.1976
German mark	1.94964	32.02	0.6242
Spanish peseta	154.250	4.46	6.885
French franc	6.53883	20.37	1.332
Irish punt	0.808828	1.06	0.0008552
Luxembourg franc	40.2123	0.32	0.13
Dutch guilder	2.19672	10.01	0.2198
Portuguese escudo	192.854	0.72	1.393
Italian lira†	1793.19	8.47	151.8
UK pound†	0.786749	11.16	0.08784
Greek drachma†	264.513	0.54	1.44

* Date of last realignment
† Presently outside ERM
Source: EC Commission, *ECU-EMS Information*, No. 5–6/1993, p. 10.

most participating currencies (membership for EC currencies is not compulsory) may fluctuate within ± 2.25% of an agreed central rate against the ECU. Other, often weaker currencies, are allowed to operate within a broader ± 6.00% band, although they may move to the narrower band. In both cases where a currency approaches the upper or lower limit of its band, the relevant national central bank is obliged to intervene to ensure that the currency's value against the ECU is maintained. This a national central bank can do either by selling or buying the appropriate currency when that currency reaches the upper or lower limits of its band. Intervention may also involve the raising or lowering of domestic interest rates where appropriate.

The third element of the EMS is the European Monetary Cooperation Fund (EMCF). This provides a variety of credit facilities to member states' central banks, the most significant of which is the Very Short-Term Financing Facility (VSTF). This allows national central banks to borrow on a short-term basis foreign currencies in order to finance an intervention within the ERM.

Despite large adjustments to central rates and a series of realignments during the first five years of its operation, from the mid-1980s to the early 1990s the EMS achieved notable success in creating monetary and exchange rate stability among members of the ERM. During the period inflation rates declined significantly and exchange rates remained stable. Moreover, it appeared that the ERM was contributing effectively to increased economic convergence within the Community.

q.v. Convergence in the 1980s pp. 26–9.

Several factors lay behind this apparent success, not least of which was the leading role of the DM. Such a role was naturally assumed by the DM given the dominant position among EC currencies it held on international currency and capital markets. However, this had political implications for other member states. By conferring on the DM the role of stabilizing anchor within the ERM, member states were forced to bring their national monetary policies more in line with the anti-inflationary policy pursued by the Bundesbank, Germany's independent central bank. While this clearly met with the approval of Germany, which had always argued that any EC-based economic and monetary union should only come about as the result of a high degree of economic convergence among the economies of the EC, it made the success of the ERM dependent on the ability and willingness of member states with weaker currencies to introduce and maintain monetary stability in line with what were ultimately the domestic requirements of the German economy. Indeed, once it became clear that the Deutschmark was the dominant currency within the ERM, demands were made, particularly by the French, for closer cooperation between member states and central banks in maintaining the effective operation of the mechanism. By implication, this would involve a greater say for the other member states in determining German monetary policy. While any external involvement in the Bundesbank's policy was unacceptable to Germany, agreement was reached on closer cooperation between member states within the ERM in 1987.

A second factor contributing to the success of the ERM in the second half of the 1980s, and one linked to the anchor role assumed by the DM, was the widespread adoption of economic austerity packages by governments in the early 1980s, most evident in the economic policy reversal of the French Socialist government in 1983–4. While ideological motives lay behind the shift in some European countries, the commitment to the ERM in others undoubtedly contributed to the abandonment of inflationary policies.

Finally, the general Europe-wide period of economic growth in the mid- to late 1980s, whether or not facilitated by the exchange rate and monetary stability resulting from the ERM, in no way undermined the effective functioning of the mechanism. Indeed, the association of economic growth with price stability and low inflation guaranteed that the ERM maintained widespread support within the EC, even to the extent of the United Kingdom, the traditional sceptic of the ERM, eventually joining the mechanism in October 1990. The perceived benefits of membership also attracted Portugal and Spain into the wider band of the ERM by April 1992, while several members of EFTA began pegging their currencies to the ECU and restricting fluctuations to a minimum. While this may have suggested a firm political, as well as economic, commitment to the ERM, it also convinced those in charge of the mechanism that the ERM was working adequately. Hence, the mechanism and attitudes towards it in the early 1990s became more rigid, thus reducing the scope for minor reforms and realignments were they to become necessary. Moreover, the symbolic value of the ERM as the barometer of progress towards European Union meant that supporters of the TEU, particularly France and Germany, were loath to see the mechanism and the EMS as a whole as anything other than a success.

As indicated above in The evolution of the European economy, the success of the ERM in bringing about economic convergence within the EC led to calls

q.v. The evolution of the European economy pp. 26–31.

for steps to be taken in the direction of establishing full economic and monetary union. As a result, the TEU introduced extensive amendments to the Treaty of Rome and provided for a three-stage approach to EMU. According to the timetable governing the stages, the transition to the final stage, the creation of a European Central Bank, and the introduction of a single currency, will come about provided a significant degree of economic convergence has been achieved within the Community. As such, this mix of convergence- and timetable-led approaches to EMU represents a compromise between German and French preferences.

q.v. EMU pp. 150–60.

However, although on paper EMU appears inevitable, whether the EC moves to Stage III at some time between 1997 and 1999 will depend on the political and economic situation of the day. While in December 1991 when the European Council Summit in Maastricht approved the TEU, the prospects for EMU seemed favourable, as seen below in the Economic Standing of Maastricht, the outlook by late 1993 had become decidedly bleak. The EMS and, in particular, the ERM had come under enormous strain, teetering at times on the verge of collapse as a result of turbulence on international currency markets. All the same, given the support voiced by many member states in favour of EMU, the prospect of a single European currency, explicit in the TEU, will not disappear from the Community's agenda in the 1990s.

q.v. Economic Standing of Maastricht pp. 454–9.

FURTHER READING

Agleitta, M. and Ghymers, C., 'Monetary integration in Europe', *Recherches Economiques de Louvain*, Special Issue, Vol. 59, No. 1–2, 1993.

Bank of England 'The Maastricht agreement on economic and monetary union', *Bank of England Quarterly Bulletin*, Vol. 32, No. 1, 1992, pp. 64–9.

Bean, C.R., 'Economic and monetary Union in Europe', *Journal of Economic Perspectives*, Vol. 6, No. 4, 1992, pp. 31–52.

Bishop, G., *Is There a Rapid Route to EMU of the Few?*, Salomon Brothers, London, 11 May 1993.

Bundesbank, 'Die Beschlüsse von Maastricht zur Europäischen Wirtschafts- und Währungsunion', *Monatsbericht der Deutschen Bundesbank*, Februar 1992.

Burdekin, R.C.K., Whilbourg, C. and Willett, T.D., 'A monetary constitution case for an independent central bank', *The World Economy*, Vol. 15, No. 2, 1992, pp. 231–49.

Butler, M., 'Europe's currency tangle: the way ahead', *The Economist*, 30 January 1993, pp. 21–3.

Committee for the Study of Economic and Monetary Union, *Report on Economic and Monetary Union in the European Community*, OOPEC, Luxembourg, 1989.

de Drauwe, P. and Papademos, L. (eds.), *The European Monetary System in the 1990s*, Longman, London, 1990.

Dornbusch, R. and Jacquest, P., 'La France et l'Union économique et monétaire européenne',

Observations et diagnostics économiques, No. 39, 1992, pp. 31–73.

EC Commission, 'One market, one money', *European Economy*, Vol. 44, 1990, pp. 63–178.

Emerson, M. and Huhne, C., *The ECU Report*, Pan, London, 1991.

Fratianni, M. and von Hagen, J., *The European Monetary System and European Monetary Union*, Westview, Oxford, 1992.

Gäckle, T. *Die Weiterentwicklung des Europäischen Währungssystems zur Europäischen Währungsunion: Geld- und budgetpolitische Voraussetzungen*, Nomos Verlagsgesellschaft, Baden-Baden, 1992.

Gnos, C., 'La transition vers l'Union Économique et Monétaire: les vertus négligées de la monnaie commune', *Revue du Marché commun et de l'Union européenne*, No. 360, 1992, pp. 621–6.

Gretschmann, K., (ed.), *Economic and Monetary Union: Implications for national policy-makers*, European Institute of Public Administration, Maastricht, 1992.

Gros, D. and Thygesen, N., *European Monetary Integration: From the European Monetary System to European Monetary Union*, Longman, London, 1992.

Jochimsen, R., 'Die europäischen Wirtschafts- und Währungsunion — Chancen und Risikien', *Europa-Archiv*, Vol. 48, No. 13–14, 1993, pp. 377–88.

Jochimsen, R., 'European Economic and Monetary Union: the do's and dont's', *The World Today*, Vol. 49, No. 6, 1993, pp. 115–21.

Johnson, C. (ed.), *ECU: The currency of Europe*, Euromoney Books, London, 1991.

Kaufmann, H. and Overturf, S., 'Progress within the European Monetary System', in Hurwitz, L. and Lesquene, C. (eds.), *The State of the European Community: Policies, institutions and debates in the transition years*, Longman, London, 1991, pp. 183–205.

Kenen, P.B., 'The European Central Bank and monetary policy in Stage III of EMU', *International Affairs*, Vol. 68, No. 3, 1992, pp. 457–74.

Lastra, R.M., 'The independence of the European system of central banks', *Harvard International Law Journal*, Vol. 33, No. 2, 1992, pp. 475–519.

Lehment, H. and Scheide, J., 'Die Europäische Wirtschafts- und Währungsunion: Probleme des Übergangs', *Die Weltwirtschaft*, No. 1, 1992, pp. 50–67.

Lieberman, S., *The Long Road to European Monetary Union*, University Press of America, Lanham, 1992.

Louw, A., 'The ecu and its role in the process towards monetary union', *European Economy*, No. 48, 1991, pp. 115–48.

Mehnert, R.J., 'Beyond 1992: one central bank, one currency', in Hurwitz, L. and Lequesne, C. (eds.), *The State of the European Community: Policies, institutions and debates in the transition years*, Longman, London, 1991, pp. 81–94.

Minford, P., 'The path to monetary union in Europe', *The World Economy*, Vol. 16, No. 1, 1993, pp. 1–15.

Minford, P., *The Price of EMU Revisited*, Centre for Economic Policy Research Discussion Paper 656, CEPR, London, 1992.

Minikin, R., *The ERM Explained: A straightforward guide to the Exchange Rate Mechanism and the European currency debate*, Kogan Page, London, 1993.

Nölling, W., *Monetary Policy in Europe after Maastricht*, Macmillan, Basingstoke, 1993.

Nyahoho, E., 'L'accord monétaire de Maastricht et ses implications de politiques économiques', *Études Internationales*, Vol. 24, No. 2, 1993, pp. 355–83.

O'Donnel, R. (ed.), *Economic and Monetary Union*, Studies in European Union No. 2, Institute of European Affairs, Dublin, 1991.

Pauly, L.P., 'The politics of European monetary union: national strategies, international implications', *International Journal*, Vol. 47, No. 1, 1992, pp. 93–111.

Portes, R. 'EMS and EMU after the fall', *The World Economy*, Vol. 16, No. 1, 1993, pp. 17–27.

Qvigstad, J.F., *Economic and Monetary Union (EMU): A survey of the EMU and empirical evidence on convergence for the EC and the EFTA countries*, EFTA Occasional paper No. 36, EFTA, Geneva, 1992.

Sandholtz, W., 'Choosing Union — monetary politics and Maastricht', *International Organization*, Vol. 47, No. 1, 1993, pp. 1–39.

Thiel, E. 'Europäische Wirtschafts- und Währungsunion — Von der Marktintegration zur politischen Integration', *Aus Politik und Zeitgeschichte*, B7-8/92, 1992, pp. 3–11.

Thygesen, N. 'L'Union économique et monétaire: notes critiques sur le traité de Maastricht', *Commentaire*, Vol. 15, No. 58, 1992, pp. 293–305.

Treasury and Civil Service Committee, *Prospects for Monetary Union*, HMSO, London, 1993.

Treaty on European Union: Synopsis of the provisions on Economic and Monetary Union, Europa Institute, Edinburgh, 1992.

Vibert, F., *The Independence of the Bank of England and the Maastricht Treaty*, European Policy Forum, London, 1993.

Wincott, D., 'The European Central Bank: constitutional dimensions and political limits', *International Relations*, Vol. 11, No. 2, 1992, pp. 111–26.

Woolley, J.T., 'Policy credibility and European monetary institutions', in Sbragia, A.M. (ed.), *Euro-Politics: Institutions and Policymaking in the 'New' European Community*, Brookings Institution, Washington, 1992, pp. 157–90.

Zis, G., 'European Monetary Union: the case for complete monetary integration', in McDonald, F. and Dearden, S. (eds.), *European Economic Integration*, Longman, London, 1992, pp. 39–49.

Common commercial policy

The final Title to be dealt with in this subdivision of the *Handbook* is the new Title VII of Part Three of the amended Treaty of Rome. This Title contains provisions concerning the Community's Common Commercial Policy (CCP) (Articles 110–116). Such a policy was originally provided for in the Treaty of Rome (Article 3(b)) since it complimented the Customs Union on which the Community was to be based. As the EC has since progressed towards completing the Single Market and establishing an economic and monetary union, the

q.v. Article 3(b) p. 64.

importance of the CCP has not diminished. Today, it forms as much a complement to the Single Market and to EMU as it did to the original Customs Union.

Prior to the entry into force of the TEU, the provisions for the CCP were to be found in the fourth Chapter of the Title dedicated to economic policy. Since the entry into force of the TEU, they have been accorded a Title of their own. However, whereas the original Treaty of Rome contained seven Articles dedicated to the CCP, following the introduction of amendments by the TEU only four of the Articles survive (Articles 110, 112, 113 and 115). The other three (Articles 111, 114 and 116) were repealed.[69] Of the Articles which remain, two were amended by the TEU (Articles 113 and 115).

The aims of the Community's CCP are laid down in Article 110. This confirms the desire of the member states to contribute to the development of world trade through the abolition of trade barriers. As such, the Article reinforces what is stated earlier in the Treaty in Article 18. The principle of uniformity, on which the CCP is to be based, and which covers tariff rates, the conclusion of tariff and trade agreements, trade liberalization, export policy, and anti-dumping measures, is set out in Article 113(1). Hence, all member states conform to common EC policy in these areas. Article 113 also lays down the procedures by which the CCP is to be implemented, and by which tariff and trade agreements concluded. In each case it is the responsibility of the Commission to put forward proposals to the Council, which then acts by a qualified majority. However, as far as agreements with third states or international organizations are concerned, it is the Commission which negotiates on behalf of the Community in line with mandates issued by the Council. During the negotiations, the Commission is assisted by a special committee appointed by the Council. The agreement reached is then concluded by the Council acting by a qualified majority. However, following the introduction of an amendment to Article 113 inserted by the TEU, certain provisions of the amended Article 228 and the new Article 228a apply to tariff and trade agreements. For the most part these relate to the right of member states, the Council and the Commission to refer any agreement to the ECJ to ensure that it is compatible with the Treaty of Rome, and to the suspension of economic relations as part of the Common Foreign and Security Policy. This is also relevant to the EC's general external relations as discussed in subdivisions V and VII below.

Beyond the conclusion of tariff and trade agreements, the CCP also involves

q.v. Article 18 p. 90.

q.v. Articles 228–228a pp. 338–9.

q.v. Common Foreign and Security Policy pp. 373–81.

---

69. Of the three Articles relating to the CCP which were repealed by the TEU, Article 111 concerned the adoption of the CCP and tariff negotiations with third countries during the transitional period; Article 114 laid down the Council's voting procedure for concluding agreements under Articles 111(2) and 113 during the transitional period; and Article 116 required the Community, from the end of the transitional period, to proceed by common action in international fora of an economic character. The deletion of this third Article from the amended Treaty of Rome reflects the agreement in the TEU to develop a Common Foreign and Security Policy (see pp. 373–81). However, despite the transitional nature of Article 112, this was neither repealed nor amended. Rather, it was retained since negotiators agreed that the Community had not reached the stage where it could claim to have implemented a genuine common policy on export aid. In addition to the repeal of the three Articles mentioned, amendments introduced by the TEU to Articles 113 and 115 removed all references to the transitional period. For details of the discussions in the negotiations, see Devuyst, Y., 'The EC's Common Commercial Policy and the Treaty on European Union — an overview of the negotiations', *World Competition*, Vol. 16, No. 2, 1992, pp. 67–80. While this rationalization process clearly removes several redundant sentences and thus makes reading the Treaty easier, it would appear that it was only carried out with regard to the CCP, albeit not fully, and not to otner parts of the Treaty of Rome.

the harmonization of export grants based on directives issued by the Council acting by a qualified majority (Article 112). Furthermore, Article 115 provides for cooperation between member states in implementing the CCP so as to avoid trade deflection. However, in certain instances the Commission may authorize member states to take protective measures. In cases of urgency, member states are now required, following an amendment introduced by the TEU, to seek authorization from the Commission to take whatever measures are deemed necessary to reduce any economic difficulties resulting from application of the CCP. Prior to the entry into force of the TEU, member states could act unilaterally. The Commission may nevertheless decide that any of the measures adopted should be amended or abolished. In selecting appropriate measures, priority is to be given to those which cause least disturbance to the functioning of the Internal Market (Article 115).

Title VII   Common commercial policy

ARTICLE 110

By establishing a customs union between themselves Member States aim to contribute, in the common interest, to the harmonious development of world trade, the progressive abolition of restrictions on international trade and the lowering of customs barriers.

The common commercial policy shall take into account the favourable effect which the abolition of customs duties between Member States may have on the increase in the competitive strength of undertakings in those States.

ARTICLE 111   **Repealed**

ARTICLE 112

1. Without prejudice to obligations undertaken by them within the framework of other international organizations, Member States shall, before the end of the transitional period, progressively harmonize the systems whereby they grant aid for exports to third countries, to the extent necessary to ensure that competition between undertakings of the Community is not distorted.

On a proposal from the Commission, the Council shall, acting unanimously until the end of the second stage and by a qualified majority thereafter, issue any directives needed for this purpose.

2. The preceding provisions shall not apply to such drawback of customs duties or charges having equivalent effect nor to such repayment of indirect taxation including turnover taxes, excise duties and other indirect taxes as is allowed when goods are exported from a Member State to a third country, in so far as such drawback or repayment does not exceed the amount imposed, directly or indirectly, on the products exported.

ARTICLE 113

1. *The* common commercial policy shall be based on uniform principles, particularly in regard to changes in tariff rates, the conclusion of tariff and trade agreements, the achievement of uniformity in measures of liberalization, export policy and measures to protect trade such as those to be taken in *the event* of dumping or subsidies.

2. The Commission shall submit proposals to the Council for implementing the common commercial policy.

3. Where agreements with **one or more States or international organizations** need to be negotiated, the Commission shall make recommendations to the Council, which shall authorize the Commission to open the necessary negotiations.

The Commission shall conduct these negotiations in consultation with a special committee appointed by the Council to assist the Commission in this task and within the framework of such directives as the Council may issue to it.

The relevant provisions of Article 228 shall apply.

4. In exercising the powers conferred upon it by this Article, the Council shall act by a qualified majority.

ARTICLE 114   Repealed

ARTICLE 115   In order to ensure that the execution of measures of commercial policy taken in accordance with this Treaty by any Member State is not obstructed by deflection of trade, or where differences between such measures lead to economic difficulties in one or more Member States, the Commission shall recommend the methods for the requisite cooperation between Member States. Failing this, the Commission **may** authorize Member States to take the necessary protective measures, the conditions and details of which it shall determine.

In case of urgency, Member States **shall request authorization to** take the necessary measures *themselves* **from the Commission, which shall take a decision as soon as possible;** *the Member States concerned* shall **then** notify the *measures* to the other Member States. *The Commission* may decide **at any time** *that the Member* States concerned shall amend or abolish *the measures in question*.

In the selection of such measures, priority shall be given to those which cause the least disturbance to the functioning of the common market.

ARTICLE 116   Repealed

The Common Commercial Policy

Community relations with third, i.e. non-member, countries are regulated through a variety of mechanisms. Several of these, such as the association of overseas countries and territories and association under Article 238, have been part of the Treaty of Rome since it was signed. Others, which include monetary matters with third countries under Article 109 and Development Cooperation have been added since. However, the most developed mechanism for relations with other countries is the Common Commercial Policy (CCP).

The existence of the CCP is a natural extension of both the Customs Union, on which the EC is based, and the Common External Tariff, which is a central element of that union. Operational since the late 1960s, the CCP covers trade relations with third countries in all areas where the EC has competence to regulate. Thus, the CCP covers trade in goods, services and payments. However, it does not directly cover trade in agricultural goods as these are governed by the CAP, nor does it cover trade in coal and steel since both these products are regulated by the European Coal and Steel Community. Nevertheless, the Combined Nomenclature, published annually by the Commission, contains over 16,000 tariff headings for which the EC is responsible.

On the basis of this nomenclature the Community, under the CCP, operates a trade policy common to all its member states. This policy has in most respects

q.v. association of overseas countries and territories pp. 246–8.

q.v. Article 109 pp. 166–7.

q.v. Customs Union pp. 88–93.

q.v. European Coal and Steel Community pp. 359–66.

replaced all national trade policies. As such, the CCP, alongside the CAP, is one of the most highly integrated of the Community's policies. Indeed, it is the EC, not the member states, which is responsible for determining, in the form of the Common External Tariff (CET), tariff levels on trade with third countries, and for concluding international tariff and trade agreements. However, member states are allowed, under Article 115 to impose restrictions, whether in the form of quotas or voluntary export restraints (VERs), on imports from third countries. In addition, member states are not excluded from concluding economic cooperation agreements with third countries, provided they do not affect the CET or CCP trade agreements. As a supplement to national policies and initiatives, the Community is also responsible for promoting EC exports to non-member states.

The extent to which the EC has carried out its responsibilities is reflected in the array of trade-based agreements it has signed with third countries since the Community was established. These vary in both form and content. Several of the agreements concluded by the EC are done so on a multilateral basis with the Community being one signatory among several. Others are concluded on a purely bilateral basis with one partner. As far as content is concerned, agreements may be non-preferential, essentially creating a formal basis for dialogue between the parties, or alternatively they may be of a preferential nature. Such preferential trade agreements, which cover three-quarters of the EC's external trade, allow exports from the partner country to enter the Community market at a reduced tariff rate. However, where the EC does provide preferential access, the agreement must conform to rules laid down in the General Agreement on Tariffs and Trade (GATT). Thus all preferential trade agreements must eventually lead to the creation of a free trade area or customs union covering substantially all goods. One exception is the Community's General System of Preferences (GSP). This scheme, sanctioned by GATT and reviewed annually, allows the EC to grant tariff preferences on certain goods exported to the EC by over 120 developing countries.

Prominent among the trade-based agreements signed by the EC since it was set up have been the Yaoundé and Lomé Conventions concluded with the so-called ACP (African, Caribbean and Pacific) countries, most recently in 1989; the free trade agreements signed with the member states of EFTA in 1972−3;[70] the trade and cooperation agreements with the countries of the Maghreb (Algeria, Morocco and Tunisia) and the Mashreq (Egypt, Lebanon, Jordan and Syria) in 1976−7;[71] those with the countries of the ASEAN in 1980;[72] and the Andean

q.v. ACP countries pp. 242−5.

q.v. EFTA pp. 481−5.

---

70. *Agreement between the European Economic Community and the Republic of Austria*, OJL 300, 31 December 1972; *Agreement between the European Economic Community and the Kingdom of Sweden*, OJL 300, 31 December 1972; *Agreement between the European Economic Community and the Swiss Confederation*, OJL 300, 31 December 1972; *Agreement between the European Economic Community and the Republic of Iceland*, OJL 301, 31 December 1972; *Agreement between the European Economic Community and the Kingdom of Norway*, OJL 171, 27 June 1973; *Agreement between the European Economic Community and the Republic of Finland*, OJL 328, 28 November 1973.

71. *Cooperation Agreement between the European Economic Community and the People's Democratic Republic of Algeria*, OJL 263, 27 September 1978; *Cooperation Agreement between the European Economic Community and the Kingdom of Morocco*, OJL 264, 27 September 1978; *Cooperation Agreement between the European Economic Community and the Republic of Tunisia*, OJL 265, 27 September 1978; *Cooperation Agreement*

Pact in 1983;[73] and more recently in 1989—93 the trade and cooperation and interim agreements with the countries of the countries of the former Soviet bloc.[74] While not all these agreements are based entirely on Article 113, the basis on which the Community negotiates tariff and trade agreements with third countries, they each have as the central element tariff and trade concessions. Indeed, apart from the United States and Japan, there are few countries with which the EC has not signed, either directly or through a regional trading bloc, a formal agreement as part of the CCP (see Community external relations).

q.v. Community external relations pp. 340—9.

In addition to these agreements, the Community acts as a single entity within international trade organizations such as GATT, the Organization for Economic Cooperation and Development (OECD), and the United Nations Conference on Trade and Development (UNCTAD), and is a signatory to international trade agreements such as the 1975 Multi-Fibre Agreement (MFA) which regulates trade in textiles. Finally, the Community has exclusive responsibility under the CCP for imposing anti-dumping measures on third-country producers exporting goods into the EC at prices below what is considered to be a fair and reasonable price.

However, while the Community may appear to pursue a common trade policy, this does not mean to say that the policy is all embracing. This has been highlighted by moves to complete the Internal Market. For, if the Internal Market is to involve the free movement of goods, purely national restrictions on imports, such as Japanese cars, become somewhat anachronistic. This situation is compounded by the fact that the abolition of internal border controls makes enforcement of national restrictions by the member states almost impossible. The logical consequence of this would be to replace the 6,500 national restrictions with global EC quotas or EC negotiated VERs. Indeed, pressure has been such that, once the EC has successfully removed all its internal borders, it is envisaged that all national restrictions will be abolished.

Although the CCP gained much attention in the first twenty years of the EC's existence, its prominence on the Community's policy agenda has since declined. This has been due to a variety of factors, not least of which has been the gradual

---

between the European Economic Community and the Arab Republic of Egypt, OJL 266, 27 September 1978; *Agreement between the European Economic Community and the Lebanese Republic*, OJL 18, 22 January 1974; *Cooperation Agreement between the European Economic Community and the Hashemite Kingdom of Jordan*, OJL 268, 27 September 1978; *Cooperation Agreement between the European Economic Community and the Syrian Arab Republic*, OJL 269, 27 September 1978.

72. *Cooperation Agreement between the European Economic Community and Indonesia, Malaysia, the Philippines, Singapore and Thailand — member countries of the Association of South East Asian Nations*, OJL 144, 10 June 1980.

73. *Cooperation Agreement between the European Economic Community, of the one part, and the Cartegna Agreement and the member countries thereof — Bolivia, Colombia, Ecuador, Peru and Venezuela — of the other part*, OJL 153, 8 June 1984.

74. *Interim Agreement on trade and trade-related matters between the European Economic Community and the European Coal and Steel Community, of the one part, and the Republic of Poland, of the Other Part*, OJL 114, 30 April 1992; *Interim Agreement on trade and trade-related matters between the European Economic Community and the European Coal and Steel Community, of the one part, and the Czech and Slovak Federal Republic, of the other part*, OJL 115, 30 April 1992; *Interim Agreement on trade and trade-related matters between the European Economic Community and the European Coal and Steel Community, of the one part, and the Republic of Hungary, of the other part*, OJL 116, 30 April 1992; *Interim Agreement on trade and trade-related matters between the European Economic Community and the European Coal and Steel Community, of the one part, and the Romania, of the other part*, OJL 81, 2 April 1993; *Cooperation Agreement between the European Economic Community and the Republic of Slovenia*, OJL 189, 29 July 1993.

liberalization of world trade through successive GATT agreements, and the establishment in 1977 of free trade in industrial goods with the EFTA countries, the EC's main trading partners. Nevertheless, the CCP did gain a higher political profile in the 1980s as the member states of the EC introduced sanctions on trade with countries such as South Africa as part of their efforts to develop a coordinated EC foreign policy within the framework of European Political Cooperation.

q.v. European Political Cooperation pp. 340–5.

However, with the emergence of the new democracies of Central and Eastern Europe and their demands for greater access to EC markets, the Community has been forced to reassess its overall trade policy objectives. While on the one hand the EC has to fulfil its obligations under existing trade and trade-based agreements with various developing countries, it is also responsible for ensuring that the fledgeling market economies of Central and Eastern Europe have every opportunity to develop (see Towards a Wider Western Europe). This, the Community has agreed, should be done through an increase in trade, thus requiring the EC to increase access to its domestic market. By implication, however, increased access reduces the significance of the trade preferences granted to existing and often long-standing EC partners. More significant from a domestic political point of view is that trade liberalization produces challenges for EC producers, particularly those in sensitive and thus traditionally protected industries, such as textiles, clothing, steel and agriculture. While one of the aims of the Single Market programme has been to promote domestic competition among EC producers, to date there appears to be only limited evidence to suggest that trade liberalization will also be used to such an end.

q.v. Towards a Wider Western Europe pp. 479–88.

Despite these challenges which the Community is being forced to meet in implementing and developing the CCP, the policy is firmly established. Similarly, it is widely accepted and supported by the member states, although differences over the negotiating stance adopted by the Community in international negotiations, such as the Uruguay Round of GATT talks, do occasionally vary. Nevertheless, commercial policy is one of the most integrated EC policy areas. Indeed, the apparent coherence of the EC's external trade relations was not an insignificant factor in the proposals realized in part in the TEU for the development of a Common Foreign and Security Policy (CFSP). However, the attention which the CFSP attracts as one of the main pillars of the European Union, threatens to overshadow the importance of the CCP, particularly for those countries in the process of economic reform and development.

q.v. CFSP pp. 373–81.

FURTHER READING

Cremona, M., 'The completion of the Internal Market and the incomplete Commercial Policy of the European Community', *European Law Review*, Vol. 15, No. 4, 1990, pp. 283–97.

Devuyst, Y., 'The EC's common Commercial Policy and the Treaty on European Union — an overview of the negotiations', *World Competition*, Vol. 16, No. 2, 1992, pp. 67–80.

Ecalle, F. and Paquier, O., 'Le commerce extérieur des

pays de la Communauté européenne — Les effets de la progression vers le Marché Unique', *Économie et statistique*, No. 253, 1992, pp. 49–59.

Heidensohn, K., *Europe and World Trade*, Pinter, London, 1994.

Maresceau, M. (ed.), *The European Community's Commercial Policy after 1992: The legal dimension*, Martinus Nijhoff, Dordrecht, 1993.

Nicolaides, P. and Wijngaarden, R. van 'Reform of anti-dumping regulations — the case of the EC', *Journal of World Trade*, Vol. 27, No. 3, 1993, pp. 31–53.

O'Cleireacain, S., 'Europe 1992 and gaps in the EC's Common Commercial Policy', *Journal of Common Market Studies*, Vol. 28, No. 3, 1990, pp. 201–18.

Oppermann, T. and Beise, M., 'GATT-Welthandelsrunde und kein Ende? — Die EG Handelspolitik auf dem Prüfstand', *Europa Archiv*, Vol. 48, No. 1, 1993, pp. 1–11.

Penketh, K., 'External trade policy', in McDonald, F. and Dearden S. (eds.), *European Economic Integration*, Longman, London, 1992, pp. 146–58.

Sturma, P., 'La participation de la Communauté européenne à des «sanctions» internationales', *Revue du Marché commun et de l'Union européenne*, No. 366, 1992, pp. 250–64.

Woolcock, S., 'Trade diplomacy and the European Community', in Story, J. (ed.), *The New Europe: Politics, government and economy since 1945*, Blackwell, Oxford, 1993, pp. 292–313.

IV. **The Union Treaty C:**
Social and General Policies

As mentioned above the TEU brings together all Community policies within Part Three of the amended Treaty of Rome. It then subdivides Part Three into a series of seventeen Titles each containing provisions on specific policy areas. The first seven of these Titles were dealt with in the previous subdivision of the *Handbook*. This next subdivision completes the presentation of the Treaty provisions contained in Part Three of the amended Treaty of Rome by examining the contents of Titles VIII–XVII. In addition, it examines the contents of Part Four of the Treaty which deals with the association of overseas countries and territories, the only Part of the Treaty to survive unamended under the TEU.

This subdivision of the *Handbook* has been given the title 'Social and General Policies' since the contents of Titles VIII–XVII cover a wide range of often diverse policy areas. For the sake of convenience it is split into a further three sub-subdivisions numbered i–iii. These are introduced for purely practical reasons providing the reader with manageable reference points when using the *Handbook*. As such they are not terms employed by the drafters of the Treaty. The first of these sub-subdivisions deals with the social and cultural policies of the Community including the provisions relating to public health and consumer protection introduced to the Treaty by the TEU (Titles VIII–XI). The second sub-subdivision addresses a range of policy areas reflecting the Community's competences with regard to economic and social cohesion, European industry, and the environment (Titles XII–XVI). The third sub-subdivision brings together the final Title of Part Three, that relating to development and cooperation with less developed countries (Title XVII), and the provisions contained within Part Four of the Treaty.

With the exception of the majority of provisions relating to social policy and those relating to the association of overseas countries and territories few of the Articles dealt with in this subdivision can be found in the original Treaty of Rome. Most were first inserted into the Treaty by the SEA. These include the provisions on economic and social cohesion, research and technological development, and the environment. However, few of these provisions have remained unamended as a result of the TEU. Amendments and additions have been made to the provisions covering each of the three policy areas as well as to the provisions governing social policy. In addition, the Title numbers originally used have been changed as a result of the merger of the original Parts Two and Three of the Treaty of Rome. Consequently, whereas previously after the SEA, social policy, economic and social cohesion, research and technological development, and the environment were numbered Titles III, V, VI and VII, they are now Titles VIII, XIV, XV and XVI respectively. Furthermore the TEU has actually removed the contents of one Title, Title IV The European Investment Bank, and relocated it under Chapter 5 of Part Five, Title I.

*q.v.
European
Investment
Bank pp.
312–13.*

The remaining changes introduced by the TEU concern the introduction to the Treaty of Rome of several new policy competences. These include Education, Vocational Training and Youth (Title VIII, Chapter 3), Culture (Title IX), Public Health (Title X), Consumer Protection (Title XI), Trans-European Networks (Title XII), Industry (Title XIII), and Development Cooperation (Title XVII). However, as will be seen in the policy analyses in this subdivision of the *Handbook*, it is questionable as to whether it is appropriate to recognize these new Titles as new policy areas *per se*. For the most part the provisions inserted by the TEU into the part of the Treaty of Rome under discussion here give a firm legal basis for activities which have already become part of the Community's sphere of action. As one commentator puts it, as far as the new short Titles are concerned, the TEU is 'a case of making new bottles into which to pour old wine so as to make it more drinkable'.[1] Although in many respects it is difficult to disagree with this conclusion,[2] there are cases where the provisions inserted into the Treaty do provide the Community with competences which go beyond those already held. Consequently, the TEU does extend the competences of the Community into new areas, but to a much lesser extent than may initially seem the case.

What follows, therefore, is an analysis of the second half of the new Part Three of the Treaty of Rome as constituted in its post-TEU form. As in the previous subdivision, the provisions of each Title are reproduced with an indication of which are new to the Treaty and which have been amended by the TEU. This is accompanied by an analysis of these provisions followed by an analysis of Community policy in the particular area under consideration. In the case of the policy analyses which relate to social policy contained in Chapters 1 and 2 of Title VIII this includes a brief analysis of the so-called Social Chapter, the agreement on social policy signed at Maastricht by eleven of the twelve member

---

1. Buchan, D., *Europe: The strange superpower*, Dartmouth, Aldershot, 1993, p. 51.
2. Indeed, despite the claims of several ministers that the contents of the short Titles (Education, Vocational Training and Youth; Culture; Public Health; Consumer Policy; Trans-European Networks; Industry; Development Cooperation) contain significant new competences for the EC, the UK government appears to accept Buchan's argument, suggesting even that the TEU limits existing EC action (House of Commons Foreign Affairs Committee, *Europe After Maastricht, Second Report*, vol. I, 642–II, pp. 55–6). A Foreign Office memorandum states:

> In all areas except visas the Community has been able to take action in the past using other Treaty articles, and has done so. In each case, the Commission played its usual role under the Treaties — sole right of initiative and responsibility for following up legislation — as it will in the future. There has been no change to the nature of the Commission's involvement except that in some areas of policy the Maastricht Treaty codifies, and therefore limits, the extent of Community action — for example prescriptions that there shall be no harmonising measures in areas like public health, education and training.

(House of Commons Foreign Affairs Committee, *Europe After Maastricht, Second Report*, vol. II, 642–II, p. 225).

states with the exception of the United Kingdom. Furthermore, the policy analyses which might normally be expected to follow the provision analyses for the Social Fund (Title VIII, Chapter 2) and for Trans-European Networks (Title XII) are grouped together under The Structural Funds analysis following the commentary on the provisions contained in Title XV on Economic and Social Cohesion.

i. Social and cultural policies

As already noted, this sub-subdivision of the Handbook deals with the provisions contained in Titles VIII–XI of the amended Treaty of Rome. The majority of these relate to what may be loosely termed 'social policies', i.e. relating to society. The provisions are not, as a UK reader might suspect recipes for socialist policies. Rather, they relate to matters such as working conditions, education and vocational training, public health and consumer protection.

Social policy, education, vocational training and youth

The first Title to be dealt with in this sub-subdivision of the *Handbook* is Title VIII of Part Three of the amended Treaty of Rome. This contains a total of 13 Articles, the initial eleven of which (Articles 117–125) were previously found in Title III of the Treaty in its post-SEA form. This was simply entitled Social Policy. However, following the amendments introduced by the TEU, it has now gained two extra Articles and hence a new Title reflecting these additions: Social Policy, Education, Vocational Training and Youth.

This new Title is divided into three Chapters. The first Chapter contains those provisions of the Treaty which set out the aims and objectives of the Community's social policy, and lay down the procedure by which these may be achieved. For the most part the aims and objectives (Articles 117, 118, 119 and 120) are identical to those which were contained in the Treaty of Rome when it entered into force in 1958. Essentially, these are the improvement of working conditions and living standards for workers and equal pay for men and women. However, additions have been made. The SEA of 1986, in an attempt to provide the Internal Market programme with what is referred to as a 'human face', introduced two new Articles which encouraged improvements in the health and safety of workers (Articles 118a) and the development of a European-level dialogue between management and workers (Article 118b). The need to promote health and safety in the Internal Market was also identified in the provisions relating to the approximation of laws contained in Article 100a(3). Article 118a also introduced qualified majority voting in the Council and the involvement of the EP through the cooperation procedure for matters contained within the Article. Although this did not change the requirement of unanimity within the Council for measures aimed at achieving the original aims and objectives of the Community social policy (Article 121), it did represent a qualitative step forward in speeding up the passage of social legislation and in reducing the so-called democratic deficit. Moreover,

q.v. Article 100a(3) p. 148.

it opened up the possibility, challenged in the Court of Justice by the UK government, of draft social policy legislation being framed to emphasize its benefits for health and safety, thus facilitating adoption by a qualified majority in the Council under Article 118a. While the SEA may have enhanced the Community's competences in the field of social policy, the open hostility of the UK government to the idea of extending the SEA reforms and expanding the scope of Community social policy, meant that further progress under the TEU was restricted to an agreement on social policy between the other eleven member states annexed to the Protocol on Social Policy, itself annexed to the amended Treaty of Rome, and to a restriction on the definition of remuneration under Article 119 contained in Protocol 2 also annexed to the Treaty.

q.v.
Protocol on Social Policy pp. 422–3.

This agreement on Social Policy, the so-called 'Social Chapter',[3] consists of seven Articles and provides for cooperation between the eleven member state signatories in promoting a variety of objectives. These objectives go beyond those laid down in Article 118 of the Treaty of Rome by using as their benchmark the Social Charter adopted by the same eleven member states in 1989.[4] As such, they involve the promotion of dialogue between management and labour, and proper social protection for workers. Although not a Community-based agreement, the measures under the Social Chapter are to be adopted using traditional EC decision-making procedures and implementing measures. Given its opt-out, the United Kingdom is not to be party to the decision making. However, it is required to pay its share of the administrative costs involved.

q.v.
Protocol 2 p. 394.

The second Chapter of Title VIII contains three Articles (Articles 123–125) which relate to the establishment of the European Social Fund. The aim of the Fund is to improve employment opportunities by increasing worker mobility within the Community (Article 123). The means by which this aim is to be achieved were extended under the TEU to include the vocational training and retraining of workers. The fund itself is administered by the Commission with the assistance of a committee of governmental, trade union and employers' representatives (Article 124). A second amendment introduced by the TEU increases the role of the EP in adopting implementing decisions relating to Article 123 by subjecting such decisions to the cooperation procedure as described in Article 189c (Article 125). The activities of the ESF are discussed below in the policy analysis of the Structural Funds.

q.v. Article 189c pp. 304–5.

q.v.
Structural Funds pp. 221–5.

Despite the implications of its title, Education, Vocational Training and Youth, Title VIII, Chapter 3 contains only two Articles: Article 126 on education, and Article 127 on vocational training. The reference to Youth in the name of the Title appears simply to emphasize the priority the Community gives to youth in implementing measures related to education and vocational training. The

---

3. The Social Chapter's formal title is the *Agreement on social policy concluded between the Member States of the European Community with the exception of the United Kingdom of Great Britain and Northern Ireland*, see pp. 423–5.

4. *Community Charter of the Fundamental Social Rights of Workers*, COM(89) 471 final, Brussels, 22 October 1989. This should not be confused with the Council of Europe's European Social Charter signed in 1961, which sets out a series of fundamental rights relating to work, pay, training, social welfare, and to the social legal and economic protection of the family.

provisions contained in Article 126, which under the TEU appear for the first time in the Treaty of Rome, empower the Community to encourage cooperation between the member states in developing what is referred to as 'quality education' (Article 126). As far as the competences of the Community are concerned, these involve promoting language learning, student and teacher mobility, educational exchanges and the development of distance learning.

The second Article of Chapter 3, Article 127, contains provisions for an EC vocational training policy. This builds on the provisions, deleted under the TEU, contained within Articles 125 and 128 of the pre-TEU Treaty of Rome.[5] Here, the aims of the Community are essentially the promotion of vocational training opportunities, particularly where this will facilitate adaptation to industrial change, cooperation between training establishments, and mobility among young people and instructors. This last aim reinforces the existing requirement laid down in Article 50 that the member states encourage the exchange of youth workers.

q.v. Article 50 p. 100.

Both Articles also provide for cooperation with third countries and international organizations, and describe the decision-making procedures under which 'incentive measures' and 'recommendations' relating to education (Article 126) and 'measures' relating to vocational training (Article 127) are to be adopted. In the case of education this involves the cooperation procedure described in Article 189c, while measures relating to vocational training are to involve the conciliation procedure described in Article 189b. Finally, it is made explicitly clear in both Articles that any measures taken are not to include the harmonization of national legislation and that, in pursuing the aims laid down, the Community is to respect fully the responsibility of member states for their own education and vocational training policies. Thus, while the TEU may appear to provide the EC with new competences, the predominant role of the member states with regard to education and vocational training is maintained.

q.v. Article 189c pp. 304–5.

q.v. Article 189b pp. 302–4.

Title VIII Social policy, education, vocational training and youth

Chapter 1 Social provisions

ARTICLE 117[6] Member States agree upon the need to promote improved working conditions and an improved standard of living for workers, so as to make possible their harmonization while the improvement is being maintained.

They believe that such a development will ensue not only from the functioning of the common market, which will favour the harmonization of social systems, but also from the procedures provided for in this Treaty and from the approximation of provisions laid down by law, regulation or administrative action.

---

5. The new provisions appear to provide the Community with a more sharply defined role in vocational training policy than was previously the case. Article 128 of the original Treaty of Rome allowed the Community free rein in defining the principles of vocational training policy — a situation resented by less integrationist member states who recognized in the provisions what they termed a 'creeping competence'. However, only limited use was actually made of it.

6. See also Declaration 23, p. 436.

ARTICLE 118   Without prejudice to the other provisions of this Treaty and in conformity with its general objectives, the Commission shall have the task of promoting close cooperation between Member States in the social field particularly in matters relating to:

— employment;
— labour law and working conditions;
— basic and advanced vocational training;
— social security;
— prevention of occupational accidents and diseases;
— occupational hygiene;
— the right of association, and collective bargaining between employers and workers.

To this end, the Commission shall act in close contact with Member States by making studies, delivering opinions and arranging consultations both on problems arising at national level and on those of concern to international organizations.

Before delivering the opinions provided for in this Article, the Commission shall consult the Economic and Social Committee.

ARTICLE 118a   1. Member States shall pay particular attention to encouraging improvements, especially in the working environment, as regards the health and safety of workers, and shall set as their objective the harmonization of conditions in this area, while maintaining the improvements made.

2. In order to help achieve the objective laid down in the first paragraph the Council, acting *in accordance with the procedure referred to in Article 189c* and after consulting the Economic and Social Committee, shall adopt, by means of directives minimum requirements for gradual implementation, having regard to the conditions and technical rules obtaining in each of the Member States.

Such directives shall avoid imposing administrative, financial and legal constraints in a way which would hold back the creation and development of small and medium-sized undertakings.

3. The provisions adopted pursuant to this Article shall not prevent any Member State from maintaining or introducing more stringent measures for the protection of working conditions compatible with this Treaty.

ARTICLE 118b   The Commission shall endeavour to develop the dialogue between management and labour at European level which could, if the two sides consider it desirable, lead to relations based on agreement.

ARTICLE 119   Each Member State shall during the first stage ensure and subsequently maintain the application of the principle that men and women should receive equal pay for equal work.

For the purpose of this Article, 'pay' means the ordinary basic or minimum wage or salary and any other consideration, whether in cash or in kind, which the worker receives, directly or indirectly, in respect of his employment from his employer.

Equal pay without discrimination based on sex means:

(a) that pay for the same work at piece rates shall be calculated on the basis of the same unit of measurement;
(b) that pay for work at time rates shall be the same for the same job.

ARTICLE 120   Member States shall endeavour to maintain the existing equivalence between paid holiday schemes.

ARTICLE 121 The Council may, acting unanimously and after consulting the Economic and Social Committee, assign to the Commission tasks in connection with the implementation of common measures, particularly as regards social security for the migrant workers referred to in Articles 48 to 51.

ARTICLE 122 The Commission shall include a separate chapter on social developments within the Community in its annual report to the European Parliament.

The European Parliament may invite the Commission to draw up reports on any particular problems concerning social conditions.

Chapter 2 The European Social Fund

ARTICLE 123 In order to improve employment opportunities for workers in the **internal** market and to contribute thereby to raising the standard of living, a European Social Fund is hereby established in accordance with the provisions set out below; it shall *aim to render the* employment of workers easier and *to increase* their geographical and occupational mobility within the Community, **and to facilitate their adaptation to industrial changes and to changes in production systems, in particular through vocational training and retraining.**

ARTICLE 124 The Fund shall be administered by the Commission.

The Commission shall be assisted in this task by a Committee presided over by a member of the Commission and composed of representatives of Governments, trade unions and employers' organizations.

ARTICLE 125 *The Council,* **acting in accordance with the procedure referred to in Article 189c and** *after consulting the Economic and Social Committee,* **shall adopt implementing decisions relating to the European Social Fund.**

Chapter 3 Education, vocational training and youth

ARTICLE 126 **1. The Community shall contribute to the development of quality education by encouraging cooperation between Member States and, if necessary, by supporting and supplementing their action, while fully respecting the responsibility of the Member States for the content of teaching and the organization of education systems and their cultural and linguistic diversity.**

2. Community action shall be aimed at:

— developing the European dimension in education, particularly through the teaching and dissemination of the languages of the Member States;
— encouraging mobility of students and teachers, inter alia by encouraging the academic recognition of diplomas and periods of study;
— promoting cooperation between educational establishments;
— developing exchanges of information and experience on issues common to the education systems of the Member States;
— encouraging the development of youth exchanges and of exchanges of socio-educational instructors;
— encouraging the development of distance education.

3. The Community and the Member States shall foster cooperation with third countries and the competent international organizations in the field of education, in particular the Council of Europe

4. In order to contribute to the achievement of the objectives referred to in this Article, the Council:

— acting in accordance with the procedure referred to in Article 189b, after consulting the Economic and Social Committee and the Committee of the Regions, shall adopt incentive measures, excluding any harmonization of the laws and regulations of the Member States;
— acting by a qualified majority on a proposal from the Commission, shall adopt recommendations.

ARTICLE 127

1. The Community shall implement a vocational training policy which shall support and supplement the action of the Member States, while fully respecting the responsibility of the Member States for the content and organization of vocational training.

2. Community action shall aim to:

— facilitate adaptation to industrial changes, in particular through vocational training and retraining;
— improve initial and continuing vocational training in order to facilitate vocational integration and reintegration into the labour market;
— facilitate access to vocational training and encourage mobility of instructors and trainees and particularly young people;
— stimulate cooperation on training between educational or training establishments and firms;
— develop exchanges of information and experience on issues common to the training systems of the Member States.

3. The Community and the Member States shall foster cooperation with third countries and the competent international organizations in the sphere of vocational training.

4. The Council, acting in accordance with the procedure referred to in Article 189c and after consulting the Economic and Social Committee, shall adopt measures to contribute to the achievement of the objectives referred to in this Article, excluding any harmonization of the laws and regulations of the Member States.

Social policy

Although the original Treaty of Rome did contain a Title dedicated to social policy, the scope of the provisions contained within it was limited. Indeed, whereas social policy at a national level covers matters such as social security and health care, EC social policy is confined to matters relating to employment and working conditions. This, needless to say, causes confusion in the United Kingdom when the merits of granting more powers to the EC on social affairs are being debated.

The aim of EC social policy is the promotion of improved living and working conditions throughout the Community. The means to such an end were originally strictly limited and confined to the promotion of greater cooperation between member states on matters such as health and safety and labour law. Consequently, it was not until the late 1980s and the entry into force of amendments introduced by the SEA that significant advances were made in developing a Community social policy. Prior to this period, EC involvement in social policy was restricted primarily to the activities of the European Social Fund and the implementation

q.v.
European
Social Fund
pp. 221–5.

of a Community vocational training policy. Nevertheless, advances were made
with respect to equal pay for men and women.

q.v.
vocational
training
policy pp.
201–5.

In accordance with the provisions of Article 119 which required the
application of the principle that men and women should receive equal pay for
equal work, the Community in 1975 agreed the first of several directives relating
to the principle of the equal treatment of men and women. These directives
required member states to introduce legislation to guarantee men and women
equal pay, equal access to employment, vocational training and promotion, and
equal treatment in matters of social security.[7] While these directives were
significant in that they asserted the Community's legislative rights under the
Treaty's provisions on social policy, they did not herald the introduction of EC
legislation in other areas such as working conditions and employer–employee
relations. Instead the EC had to wait until the Internal Market programme had
been launched before any further significant progress was made.

As already noted, the SEA introduced amendments to the Treaty of Rome
Title on social policy. These gave the Community explicit competences to
introduce measures designed to encourage improvements in health and safety
in the workplace and encouraged the Commission to promote dialogue between
management and labour at a European level. As such these amendments provided
a boost for EC social policy. However, concerns were raised that these new
competences would not afford workers sufficient protection within the emerging
Single Market.

These concerns centred around the need to provide protection to those
workers taking advantage of the opportunity to move freely throughout the EC,
and to prevent so-called 'social dumping' — the movement of capital to areas
where labour is less protected, thus triggering downward pressure on working
conditions and workers' rights elsewhere. In addition, once assessments of the
likely benefits of the Single Market had shown that these would predominantly
accrue to businesses, it was felt that a 'human face' should be given to the 1992
project. Consequently, following pressure from the European Trade Union
Congress (ETUC), the EP and the EcoSoc, the Commission produced a draft social
charter in May 1989.

Officially entitled the 'Community Charter of Fundamental Social Rights of
Workers,[8] the Social Charter, as it became known, put forward a series of
proposals as the basis for Community social legislation to accompany the move
towards the Single Market. The proposals concentrated on employment-related
issues, listing areas such as fair pay, adequate social security benefits, freedom
of association and increased dialogue between management and labour. The
response to the Charter was generally favourable, although outright opposition

---

7. *Council Directive (75/117/EEC) of 10 February 1975 on the approximation of the laws of the Member States relating to the application of the principle of equal pay for men and women*, OJL 45, 19 February 1975; *Council Directive (76/207/EEC) of 9 February 1976 on the implementation of the principle of equal treatment for men and women as regards access to employment, vocational training and promotion, and working conditions*, OJL 39, 14 February 1976; *Council Directive (79/7/EEC) of 19 December 1986 on the progressive implementation of the principle of equal treatment for men and women in matters of social security*, OJL 6, 10 January 1979.

8. *Community Charter of the Fundamental Social Rights of Workers*, COM(89)471 final, Brussels, 22 October 1989.

from the UK government meant that at the Strasbourg Summit in December 1989 only eleven member states accepted the Charter as the basis for future Community legislation.

Nevertheless, the Commission was quick to make proposals for legislation aimed at realizing the objectives laid down in the Social Charter. Indeed, prior to the Strasbourg Summit it had already produced a Social Action Programme containing 47 pieces of draft legislation.[9] Since 1989, these proposals, 17 of which are directives, have gradually come before the Council, although the original aim of having the Social Charter implemented by the end of 1992 has proved somewhat elusive. Indeed, at the start of 1993, only just over half of the Commission's proposals had been adopted by the Council. This was primarily due to the reluctance of the UK government to accept any substantive legislation relating to maximum working hours and a minimum wage. Nevertheless, by June 1993 progress had been made. A directive on a 48-hour week had been adopted, alongside legislation concerning health and safety matters, employment contracts, collective redundancies, and the protection of young workers.

This apparent acceptance of increased Community involvement in social policy was further evidenced by the extended competences originally envisaged as part of the amendments to be introduced into the Treaty of Rome by the TEU. However, as noted above, following resistance from the United Kingdom's Conservative government, the eleven member states which supported increased Community competences were forced into relegating such competences to an Agreement on Social Policy annexed to Protocol 14 attached to the amended Treaty of Rome. Consequently, there were no significant increases in EC social policy competences within the Treaty of Rome as part of the TEU. Indeed, the provisions contained in the so-called Social Chapter merely formalized the aims and objectives of the Social Action Programme.

q.v. Agreement on Social Policy pp. 423–5.

q.v. Protocol 14 pp. 422–3.

Although it may be argued that there has been a significant increase in social policy initiatives emanating from Brussels since 1989, the opposition to new legislation from the UK government and its unwillingness to accept the Social Chapter, as evidenced most clearly in the latter stages of the ratification debate in the United Kingdom, have substantially limited the progress which might have been expected. However, despite the general political will to proceed with increased social legislation, signalled by the determination of the eleven — and indeed by opposition parties in the United Kingdom — to see new competences included somewhere in the TEU, the onset of recession in Europe since the early 1990s and the need to regenerate the European economy have cast doubts over the future implementation of the existing Social Action Programme. In addition, the new Commission which took office in January 1993 appears to favour a more flexible approach towards social legislation preferring to consolidate existing policy achievements.[10] Similarly, in line with the principle of subsidiarity, the Commission seems likely to move away from the more prescriptive approach

q.v. ratification debate pp. 446–54.

9. *Action Programme of the European Commision aimed at the Implementation of the Community Charter of Workers' Fundamental Social Rights*, COM(89)568 final, Brussels, 29 November 1989.
10. 'Flynn opts for the strategic course', *Financial Times*, 29 January 1993.

towards the social policy previously pursued, in favour of allowing national governments to define more the details of legislation. Nevertheless, while less social regulation may be favoured by business and some governments as a necessary prerequisite for a return to economic growth in Europe, the development of EC social policy is unlikely to disappear from the political agenda. The commitment of the majority of right of centre governments in the EC to a social market economy, and the progress with the implementation of the Social Action Programme will ensure that social policy continues to develop. Indeed, progress will undoubtedly be facilitated given that legislation may now be adopted under the Social Chapter without the involvement of the UK government, due to its opt-out, in the decision-making process.

FURTHER READING

Addison, J.T. and Siebert, W.S., *Social Engineering in the European Community: The Social Charter, Maastricht and beyond*, Institute of Economic Affairs, London, 1993.

Baldwin, R. and Daintith, T. (eds.) *Harmonisation and Hazard. Regulating Workplace Health and Safety in the European Community*, Graham and Trotman, London, 1992.

Birk, R. (ed.), *Die soziale Dimension des Europäischen Binnenmarktes*, Nomos Verlagsgesellschaft, Baden-Baden, 1991.

Butt Philip, A., 'European Social Policy after Maastricht', *Journal of European Social Policy*, vol. 2, no. 2, 1992, pp. 121–4.

Carter, S., 'EC Equal Opportunities Policy — bibliographical review', *European Access*, 1991/5, pp. 39–46.

Corona-Viron, P., 'Social protection', in Hurwitz, L. and Lequesne, C. (eds.), *The State of the European Community: Policies, institutions and debates in the transition years*, Longman, London, 1991, pp. 229–41.

Crovitz, S. P., 'Equal pay in the European Community — practical and philosophical goals', *University of Chicago Legal Forum*, 1992, pp. 477–96.

Cunningham, S., 'The development of equal opportunities theory and practice in the European Community', *Policy and Politics*, vol. 20, no. 3, 1992, pp. 177–89.

Curwen, P., 'Social policy in the European Community in the light of the Maastricht Treaty', *European Business Journal*, vol. 4, no. 4, 1992, pp. 17–26.

Dearden, S., 'Social policy', in McDonald, F. and Dearden, S. (eds.), *European Economic Integration*, Longman, London, 1992, pp. 82–99.

Doogan, K., 'The Social Chapter and the Europeanisation of employment and social policy', *Policy and Politics*, vol. 20, no. 3, 1992, pp. 167–76.

Dowling, D. C. Jr. 'EC Employment Law after Maastricht: "Continental Social Europe"?', *The International Lawyer*, vol. 27, no. 1, 1993, pp. 1–26.

EC Commission, 'First Report on the application of the

Community Charter of the Fundamental Social Rights of Workers', *Social Europe*, 2/91.

EC Commission, *Second Report . . . on the application of the Community Charter of the Fundamental social rights of workers*, COM(92)562 final, Brussels, 23 December 1992.

EC Commission, *Social Europe*, (periodically).

EC Commission, *Towards A Europe of Solidarity: Intensifying the fight against social exclusion, fostering integration*, COM(92)542 final, Brussels, 23 December 1992.

European Industrial Relations Review, 'The social-dialogue — Euro-bargaining in the making?', no. 220, 1992, pp. 25–9.

Fitzpatrick, B., 'Community Social Law after Maastricht', *Industrial Law Journal*, vol. 21, no. 3, 1992, pp. 199–213.

Foschi, F., 'La dimensione sociale nel processo integrativo europeo', *Rivista di studi politici internazionali*, vol. 59, no. 3, 1992, pp. 393–404.

Gold, M., 'Social Policy: the UK and Maastricht', *National Institute Economic Review*, 1992/1, pp. 95–103.

Gold, M., *The Social Dimension: Employment Policy in the European Community*, Macmillan, Basingstoke, 1993.

House of Lords, *Social Policy after Maastricht, Select Committee on the European Communities*, 7th Report, 1991–2, HL-48, 18 February 1992.

Journal of European Integration, 'Social Europe', Special edn, vol. 13, no. 2–3, 1990.

Journal of European Social Policy, 'European Social Policy after Maastricht', Special edn, vol. 2, no. 2, 1992

Lange, P., 'The politics of the social dimension', in Sbragia, A. M. (ed.), *Euro-Politics: Institutions and policymaking in the New European Community*, Brookings Institution, Washington, 1992, pp. 225–56.

Majone, G., 'The European Community between social policy and social regulation', *Journal of Common*

Market Studies, vol. 31, no. 2, 1993, pp. 153–70.

Moxon-Browne, E., 'Social Europe', in Lodge, J. (ed.), *The European Community and the Challenge of the Future*, 2nd edn, Pinter, London, 1993, pp. 152–62.

Nielsen, R. and Szyszczak, E., *The Social Dimension of the European Community*, Handelshøjskolens Forlag, Copenhagen, 1991.

Petersen, J.H., 'Harmonization of social security in the EC revisited', *Journal of Common Market Studies*, vol. 29, no. 5, 1991, pp. 505–26.

Pillinger, J., *Feminising the Market: Women's pay and employment in the European Community*, Macmillan, Basingstoke, 1993.

'Rechtsfragen der Maastrichter Vereinbarungen zur Sozialpolitik', *Europäischer Zeitschrift für Wirtschaftsrecht*, vol. 3, no. 6, 1992, pp. 178–87.

Rhodes, M., 'The future of the 'social dimension': labour market Regulation in the post-1992 Europe', *Journal of Common Market Studies*, vol. 30, no. 1, 1992, pp. 23–51.

Rhodes, M., 'The social dimension of the Single European Market: national versus transnational regulation', *European Journal of Political Research*, vol. 19,

no. 2–3, 1991, pp. 245–80.

Ryan, J., 'The effects of European integration on the social policy of the European communities', *European Research*, vol. 2, no. 4, 1991, pp. 16–21.

Springer, B., *The Social Dimension of 1992: Europa faces a new EC*, Adamantine Press, London, 1992.

Stewart, T. P. and Abellard, D. A., 'Labor laws and social policies in the European Community after 1992', *Law and Policy in International Business*, vol. 23, no. 3, 1992, pp. 508–91.

Teague, P., 'Coordination or decentralization? EC social policy and industrial relations', in Lodge, J. (ed.), *The European Community and the Challenge of the Future*, 2nd edn, Pinter, London, 1993, pp. 163–77

Watson, P., 'Social policy after Maastricht', *Common Market Law Review*, vol. 30, no. 3, 1993, pp. 481–513.

Whiteford, E.A., 'Social policy after Maastricht', *European Law Review*, vol. 18, no. 3, 1993, pp. 202–22.

Wise, M. and Gibb, R., *Single Market to Social Europe*, Longman, London, 1993.

Education policy

Neither the Treaty of Rome nor the SEA mentions education in any of its provisions. It can therefore be argued that the insertion of Article 126 in the Treaty of Rome by the TEU represents a new departure for the Community into the field of education. However, as many students in higher education are aware, since the mid-1980s the Community, through its ERASMUS (European Action Scheme for the Mobility of University Students) programme, has become instrumental in facilitating student exchanges throughout the EC. As such, therefore, the provisions contained within Article 126 effectively give recognition to existing practice. However, apart from the Community's LINGUA (Action Programme to Promote Foreign Language Competence in the Community) programme to promote the exchange of foreign language teachers within the EC, very little attention has been paid to non-vocational education at secondary levels and below, other than efforts to promote the so-called 'European dimension' within education. Therefore, since Article 126 makes no exclusive reference to higher education as the sole beneficiary of future Community action, it can be assumed that in the limited areas where the Community does have competence under the TEU, these extend to all levels of education.

The Community's ERASMUS programme was set up in 1987 to provide top-up funds to enable students in higher education to embark on a period of study at another EC higher education institution. By 1991–2 over 1,200 institutions had become involved and over 59,000 students were annually taking advantage of the opportunity to study in another EC country. The success of the programme meant that in 1991–92 it was extended to include institutions and students in the EFTA countries. However, its popularity has meant that the overall costs of the programme have risen at a time when member states are looking to cut back on Community expenditure wherever possible. Proposals have even been made to reduce the proposed target of involving 10 per cent of all students in higher education in ERASMUS exchanges down to 5 per cent. This concern with the costs of financing such exchanges is evidenced by the fact that Article 126 stresses the academic recognition of diplomas and period studies as the basis for exchanges, not simply the opportunity to study abroad.

While the success of ERASMUS has certainly been the crowning achievement of the EC's forays into education, it has by no means been the only initiative which the Community has embarked on or considered.[11] Alongside ERASMUS the late 1980s saw the creation of the LINGUA programme for the exchange of language teachers and the COMETT (Programme of the Community in Education and Training for Technologies) programme for the creation of industrial and business placements for university students. Both programmes have proved successful, with COMETT during its first three years of operation (1987–90) initiating over 1,300 projects involving 6,000 companies, 1,500 universities and 1,000 other organizations. More recently, the Community has set up a combined ERASMUS/LINGUA-type programme known as TEMPUS (Trans-European Mobility Scheme for University Studies) with the countries of Central and Eastern Europe.

Among other initiatives to come under discussion since the late 1980s have been the questions of open and distance learning, the latter specifically encouraged under Article 126, and the creation of academic credit transfer systems and a Community computerized database for student information purposes. Beyond Europe, on the basis of the Transatlantic Declaration signed in November 1990, plans have also been put forward to encourage educational exchanges with the United States.

FURTHER READING

EC Commission, *Annual Report . . . on the Scheme for Cooperation and Mobility in Higher Education between Central/Eastern Europe and the European Community (Tempus)*, COM(93)30 final, Brussels, 3 February 1993.

EC Commission, *Community Education and Training — Achievements since 1986 and Guidelines for the Future*, Background Report ISEC/B22/93, London, 28 June 1993.

EC Commission, *EC Education and Training Programmes 1986–1992 — Results and Achievements: an overview*, COM(93)151 final, Brussels, 5 May 1993.

EC Commission, *ERASMUS Programme (European Community Action Scheme for the Mobility of Students) 1992 Annual Report*, COM(93) 268 final, 25 June 1993.

EC Commission, *European Higher Education–Industry Cooperation: Advanced training for competitive advantage*, COM(92)457 final, 9 December 1992.

EC Commission, *Evaluation of the Tempus Programme (May 1992)*, COM(93)29 final, 3 February 1993.

EC Commission, *Guidelines for Community Action in the Field of Education and Training*, COM(93)183 final, Brussels, 5 May 1993.

EC Commission, Lingua Programme: 1992 activity report, COM(93)194 final, Brussels, 10 May 1993.

EC Commission, *Memorandum on Higher Education in the European Community*, COM(91)349 final, Brussels, 5 November 1991.

EC Council, *Conclusion of the Council and of the Ministers for Education Meeting within the Council of 11 June 1993 on Furthering an Open European Space for Cooperation within Higher*

---

11. EC Commission, *Community Education and Training — Achievements since 1986 and Guidelines for the Future*, Background Report, ISEC/B22/93, London, 28 June 1993.

Education, OJC 186, 8 July 1993.

Neave, G., *The EEC and Education*, Trentham Books, Stoke, 1986.

Rosenthal, G. G., 'Education and Training Policy', in Hurwitz, L. and Lequesne, C. (eds.), *The State of the European Community: Policies, institutions*

and debates in the transition years, Longman, London, 1991, pp. 273–83.

Sprokkereef, A., 'Developments in European Community education policy', in Lodge, J. (ed.), *The European Community and the Challenge of the Future*, 2nd edn, Pinter, London, 1993, pp. 340–47.

Vocational training policy

Unlike education, vocational training was specifically referred to in the original version of the Treaty of Rome under the Chapter devoted to the European Social Fund (ESF).[12] As such much of what the Community does in the field of vocational training is coupled together with ESF programmes. Although a set of principles for a Community vocational policy were formulated as early as 1963,[13] it was not until 1975 that a European Centre for the Development of Vocational Training (CEDEFOP) was set up to advise the Commission when formulating EC policy. And, indeed, it was not until the TEU that vocational training gained any prominence as a Community policy competence.

Although originally directed at the workforce in general, the EC's vocational training policy has, since the economic crises of the 1970s, become more and more involved with youth training as the problem of youth unemployment in the Community, particularly since the early 1980s, has persisted. Recently, in 1989, the Community introduced its first PETRA (Community Action Programme on the Vocational Training of Young People and their Preparation for Adult and Working Life) programme to supplement national policies in providing at least one year's vocational training to young people in addition to full time compulsory education. The programme also encouraged Community-wide cooperation on vocational guidance and allowed young people to take advantage of short-term work placements in other EC countries. Its success has led to the launch, in January 1992, of a second action programme, PETRA II.

In addition to PETRA, the Community has also developed an action programme for the development of continuing vocational training in the EC (FORCE) which came into force in 1991. More recently the Commission has put forward extensive proposals for the development of an EC vocational policy for the 1990s,[14] and steps have been taken to open up access to vocational training throughout the Community through the adoption of open and distance learning techniques. The Commission proposals on developing the existing vocational policy stress the need for increased investment in vocational training, thus making it available to all young people; for better quality training, particularly where skills are in short supply; and for what is referred to as 'transparency': equal access

---

12. Provision is also made in Article 57(2) for the coordination of national training programmes, see p. 114.

13. *Council Decision 63/226/EEC laying down principles for implementing a common vocational training policy*, OJL 63, 20 April 1963.

14. EC Commission, *Memorandum on Vocational training in the European Community in the 1990s*, COM(91)397 final, Brussels, 12 December 1991.

to training, the recognition of qualifications, and the establishment of trans-European information exchange networks. Such proposals suggest that the Community is already well advanced in developing an EC vocational training policy.

FURTHER READING

EC Commission, *Guidelines for Community Action in the Field of Education and Training*, COM(93)183 final, Brussels, 5 May 1993.

EC Commission, *Memorandum on Vocational Training in the European Community in the 1990s*, COM(91)397 final, Brussels, 12 December 1991.

EC Commission, *Report from the Commission on the Implementation of the PETRA Programme (1988–91)*, COM(93)48 final, Brussels, 11 February 1993.

EC Commission, *Third Report ... on the Third Joint Programme for the Exchange of Youth Workers 1985–91*, COM(92)512 final, Brussels, 7 December 1992.

EC Council, *Resolution of the Council of 11 June 1993 on Vocational Training in the 1990s*, OJC 186, 8 July 1993.

Youth policy

Despite the prominence of the word 'youth' in the titles of Title VIII and Title VIII, Chapter 3, there is, as already noted, no mention of an explicit policy for youth in the provisions which follow. This runs counter to the usual practice of a Title indicating the inclusion of specific provisions for Community action in the area mentioned in the Articles which follow. Instead, the Treaty addresses the question of youth by promoting the development of quality education and implementing an EC vocational training policy, making direct reference to 'young people' only once (Article 127(2)). The exchange of youth workers is, however, referred to in Article 50.

q.v. Article 50 p. 100.

q.v. European Social Fund pp. 221–5.

Nevertheless, the Community has been active in promoting youth employment opportunities under the European Social Fund, and in providing exchange opportunities for 15–25 year olds through the establishment of a Youth for Europe action programme (YES). First set up in 1988, the programme entered its second phase in 1991 with a total of ECU 25 million funding from the EC.[15] The aim of the programme is to promote bilateral and multilateral project-centred youth exchanges, transnational projects, and the further training of youth workers. Particular emphasis is placed on drawing together young people from different social, economic, and cultural backgrounds. However, even when the numbers of young people participating in the Youth for Europe and the various educational and vocational training programmes are added together, only 0.07 per cent of young people have actually been involved in EC initiatives. Despite the commitment of the Commission to increase this number, financial constraints are unlikely to result in any significant increase in participation levels.

---

15. *Youth for Europe Programme Phase II*, OJL 217, 6 August 1991.

FURTHER READING

EC Commission, *Youth Information Action Plan*, COM(92)297 final, Brussels, 2 September 1992.

Laffan, B., *Integration and Cooperation in Europe*, Routledge, London, 1992.

Culture

Title IX introduces a Community competence for culture to the Treaty of Rome for the first time. The Title itself consists of only one Article (Article 128) and as such is one of four single Article Titles inserted into the Treaty of Rome by the TEU. The Article sets out the role of the Community as contributing to 'the flowering of cultures of the member states' while bringing to the fore 'the common cultural heritage of the Community'. The emphasis here is clearly on promoting national cultures, thus maintaining cultural diversity within the Community. This is reinforced by the insertion by the TEU of a new paragraph (d) into Article 92(3) of the Treaty of Rome. The new paragraph permits member state governments to grant state aid to promote culture and heritage conservation. Fears that the EC is attempting to impose cultural homogeneity on the member states would appear, therefore, to be unjustified

q.v. Article 92(3) p. 141.

    Having described the EC's role relating to culture, Article 128 then lists the general aims of Community action in the cultural sphere. Essentially, these involve encouraging cooperation between the member states in improving people's cultural awareness, safeguarding Europe's cultural heritage, promoting creativity and facilitating cultural exchanges. Following on from this, the Article makes provision for the Community and its member states to foster cultural links with third countries and international organizations, as well as requiring the Community to take into account cultural aspects when pursuing action in other areas where it is competent. The final paragraph of the Article describes the decision-making procedure for adopting so-called 'incentive measures' and recommendations through which Community action is to be implemented. Both are to be adopted on the basis of unanimity within the Council, although incentive measures also require the assent of the EP in accordance with the new conciliation procedure described in Article 189b and consultation with the Committee of the Regions.

q.v. Article 189b pp. 302–4.

Title IX Culture

ARTICLE 128

1. The Community shall contribute to the flowering of the cultures of the Member States, while respecting their national and regional diversity and at the same time bringing the common cultural heritage to the fore.

2. Action by the Community shall be aimed at encouraging cooperation between Member States and, if necessary, supporting and supplementing their action in the following areas:

— improvement of the knowledge and dissemination of the culture and history of the European peoples;
— conservation and safeguarding of cultural heritage of European significance;
— non-commercial cultural exchanges;
— artistic and literary creation, including in the audiovisual sector.

3. The Community and the Member States shall foster cooperation with third countries and the competent international organizations in the sphere of culture, in particular the Council of Europe.

4. The Community shall take cultural aspects into account in its action under other provisions of this Treaty.

5. In order to contribute to the achievement of the objectives referred to in this Article, the Council:

— acting in accordance with the procedure referred to in Article 189b and after consulting the Committee of the Regions, shall adopt incentive measures, excluding any harmonization of the laws and regulations of the Member States. The Council shall act unanimously throughout the procedures referred to in Article 189b;
— acting unanimously on a proposal from the Commission, shall adopt recommendations.

Cultural policy

As with many of the new competences granted to the Community under the TEU, the measures relating to culture the Community is likely to adopt in the future will not emerge out of a vacuum. Although not an early concern of the Community, since the early 1980s culture has been recognized as an area where the Community might make a positive contribution. Indeed, the 1983 Solemn Declaration on European Union identified culture as an area where the Community should become more active. However, although 1985 saw Athens first awarded the title of European City of Culture, attempts to create a 'European Cultural Area' involving the promotion of an EC audiovisual industry, increased cultural awareness within education, and the removal of barriers to cultural exchanges, made only slow progress. Primarily, this was due to fears among and within member states that the Commission was intent on imposing cultural uniformity on the Community.

Nevertheless, Community action in the cultural sphere has occurred. Support has been given to the EC Youth and Baroque Orchestras, annual awards have been made for literary and translation work, and funding made available for innovative conservation projects aimed at protecting Europe's architectural heritage and art treasures. Furthermore, the Community has adopted a media programme providing funding for a media business school, a European Film Distribution Office and a European Script Fund. Financial assistance has also been granted to various independent film production units and R&D projects aimed at developing film technology. However, possibly the most controversial element of the EC's attempts to promote European culture so far has been the so-called

'TV Without Frontiers' Directive which entered into force in 1991.[16] This affords EC television producers a degree of protection against non-European programmes, and applies the concept of free movement to television broadcasting. Finally, the Community has been active in developing cultural links with third countries, particularly those in Central and Eastern Europe and Latin America, through the signing of cultural agreements.

As such therefore, it can be argued that the introduction to the Treaty of Rome by the TEU of the competences in the sphere of culture contained in Article 128 effectively gives recognition to existing practice. In broad terms, this may be true. However, Article 128 does provide for a more defined Community role in cultural matters. Hence a more structured EC approach towards culture is now likely. Indeed, in April 1992, the Commission put forward its first set of proposals for Community cultural action.[17] These stressed the need to conserve Europe's common cultural heritage; create an environment conducive to the development of culture in line with the provisions of the amended Article 128; and promote the influence of European culture abroad through cooperation with non-member countries.

However, the extent to which the Community will be able to achieve these aims is likely to be constrained by two factors. Firstly, although Article 128 gives prominence to the flowering of national culture, fears that the Community will eventually try to impose cultural uniformity on its citizens are unlikely to abate. Secondly, the emphasis of Community action is to be placed on non-commercial activities. Thus a central element of any future action will be financing. Consequently, while the desire to preserve cultural heritage and promote cultural development may be strong, scepticism and a lack of funds may see Community cultural action proceed at a pace not dissimilar to that which has characterised progress to date.

FURTHER READING

EC Commission, *Communication . . . on evaluation of the Action Programme to promote the development of the European Audiovisual Industry (MEDIA) (1991–1993)*, COM(93)364 final, Brussels, 23 July 1993.

EC Commission, *New Prospects for Community Cultural Action*, COM(92)149 final, Brussels, 29 April 1992.

Roberts, E. L., 'Cultural policy in the European Community: A case against extensive national retention', *Texas International Law Journal*, vol. 28, no. 1, 1993, pp. 191–28.

Weber, R., 'La coopération culturelle européenne, enjeux et perspectives', *Cadmos*, vol. 15, no. 58–9, 1992, pp. 63–88.

16. *Council Directive 89/552/EEC of 3 October 1989 on the coordination of certain provisions laid down by law, regulation or administrative action in Member States concerning the pursuit of television broadcasting activities*, OjL 298, 17 October 1989.

17. *New Prospects for Community Cultural Action*, COM(92)149 final, Brussels, 29 April 1992.

Public health

As with the previous Title, Title X is one of four single Article Titles introduced to the Treaty of Rome by the TEU. It sets out, in a new Article 129, provisions relating to public health within the EC. The previous Article 129 concerned the establishment of the European Investment Bank (EIB), the amended provisions for which can now be found in Article 198d. In many respects, the new Article 129 provides a legal basis for existing Community action in the field of public health. It lays down the aims of Community action, the means by which such action is to be achieved and the decision-making procedures to be adopted in formulating the appropriate measures. It also encourages the Community and the member states to foster cooperation in public health matters with international organizations and third countries.

q.v. Article 198d p. 313.

It does not, however, provide for a centralized regulation of public health or public health systems throughout the EC. Rather, according to Article 129, the aim of the Community with regard to public health is 'to contribute to ensuring a high level of human health protection' among its citizens.[18] This involves the prevention of diseases; the promotion of research into their causes and transmission; and the promotion of health information and education provision. Particular emphasis is placed on combating drug abuse. Thus, the remit of the Community covers a substantial part of what is traditionally regarded as public health.

In pursuing these objectives, the essence of Community action is the coordination of national policies and programmes by the member states. Thus, competence for the administration of public health remains firmly in the hands of the individual member states. Indeed, it is made explicitly clear in paragraph 4 that any measures taken at the EC level are not to involve the harmonization of national laws. As such, therefore, no provision is made for an EC public health policy *per se*. Nevertheless, Community institutions are involved in the implementation of the provisions of Article 129. Firstly, it is left to the Commission to promote the coordination of national policies. And, secondly, the so-called 'incentive measures' provided for in Article 129(4) are to be adopted by the Council in close cooperation with the EP under the conciliation procedure, as described in Article 189b, with both the EcoSoc and the Committee of Regions being consulted before measures are adopted. Finally, the importance of promoting public health at an EC level is ensured by the provision that the Community meet the requirements of health protection in developing other policies. It would appear therefore, that the TEU ascribes to the EC a general promotional rather than a significant legislative or administrative role with regard to public health.

q.v. Article 189b pp. 302–4.

18. See also Article 3(o), p. 65.

Title X   Public health

ARTICLE 129

1. The Community shall contribute towards ensuring a high level of human health protection by encouraging cooperation between the Member States and, if necessary, lending support to their action.

Community action shall be directed towards the prevention of diseases, in particular the major health scourges, including drug dependence, by promoting research into their causes and their transmission, as well as health information and education.

Health protection requirements shall form a constituent part of the Community's other policies.

2. Member States shall, in liaison with the Commission, coordinate among themselves their policies and programmes in the areas referred to in paragraph 1. The Commission may, in close contact with the Member States, take any useful initiative to promote such coordination.

3. The Community and the Member States shall foster cooperation with third countries and the competent international organizations in the sphere of public health.

4. In order to contribute to the achievement of the objectives referred to in this Article, the Council:

— **acting in accordance with the procedure referred to in Article 189b, after consulting the Economic and Social Committee and the Committee of the Regions, shall adopt incentive measures, excluding any harmonization of the laws and regulations of the Member States;**

— **acting by a qualified majority on a proposal from the Commission, shall adopt recommendations.**

Public health policy

As indicated above, public health, like culture, is an area in which the Community has been active in recent years despite the fact that it has had no explicit competence to do so. As such, one of the functions of the TEU in inserting a new Article 129 into the Treaty of Rome is to give existing practice a firm Treaty basis. The second function, is to set out clearly what the purpose of Community action is.

To date, EC activity in the sphere of public health has taken three forms. Firstly, the Community has been active, since the entry into force of the SEA, in promoting health and safety in the workplace in accordance with the provisions laid down in Article 118a. This has led to a series of directives being adopted mainly aimed at creating a safe working environment. Secondly, the Community has been active in improving living and working conditions on a more global scale by increasing controls over environmental pollution as part of its action on the environment. As such, public health is catered for under existing policy headings. However, it is in the third area, that of promoting health awareness that the new policy competences are likely to be applied.

Here, Community activity has revolved around a series of coordination programmes in the field of medical and health research, and the funding of extensive publicity campaigns increasing public awareness of diseases such as AIDS

q.v. Article 118a p. 193.

q.v. environment pp. 323–9.

and cancer. These campaigns have included the development of the 1991–3 'Europe against AIDS' programme and a similar venture for 1990–4 entitled 'Europe against Cancer'. However, the EC has also been active in advocating legislation on public health matters. Most controversial has been the attempt, strongly supported by the EP and EcoSoc, to ban tobacco advertising. However, for the most part these initiatives have been *ad hoc* and not part of any overall Community strategy for public health.

Nevertheless, shortly before the TEU was agreed upon at the Maastricht Summit in December 1991, the Council of Ministers made several declarations and resolutions regarding Community action on health policy choices, health and the environment and drug abuse.[19] While most of the areas identified in the documents produced are deemed to warrant joint consideration and regular discussion, the aim is to assist member states in the framing of their own health policies. As such, therefore, the scope of future Community action appears to be limited to data collection and making information relating to health in the EC available to member state governments. Nevertheless, it can be expected that the Community will develop existing public awareness campaigns, and indeed promote measures linked to public health through other policies.

FURTHER READING

EC Commission, *Communication . . . concerning an assessment of the European Drug Prevention Week*, COM(93)353 final, Brussels, 27 July 1993.

EC Commission, *Communication . . . on collaboration between the Commission of the European Communities and the World Health Organization*, COM(93)224 final, Brussels, 24 May 1993.

EC Commission, 'Europe Against Cancer; public health: initiatives and texts adopted in 1990 *Social Europe*, 1/91.

EC Commission, *Programme 1991–1993 'Europe against AIDS'*, COM(93)42 final, Brussels, 10 March 1993.

EC Commission, *Report on the evaluation of the effectiveness of Community action taken in the context of the 'Europe against Cancer' programme (1987–1992)*, COM(93)93 final, Brussels, 15 March 1993.

EC Council, *Resolution of the Council and the Ministers for Health, meeting within the Council of 27 May 1993 on future action in the field of public health*, OJC 174, 25 June 1993.

EC Council, *Public Health: Framework for future cooperation and Community action*, OJC 174, 25 June 1993.

Normand, C. E. M. and Vaughan, J.P., *Europe without Frontiers: The Implications for Health*, John Wiley, Chichester, 1993.

Consumer protection

The third single Article Title introduced by the TEU into the Treaty of Rome is Title XI which contains provisions for consumer protection within the Community. While the inclusion may appear to grant the Community a new competence, consumer protection was mentioned in Article 100a(3) when

q.v. Article 100a(3) p. 149.

---

19. *Declaration by the Council and the Ministers for Health of the Member States, meeting within the Council of 4 June 1991 on action to combat the use of drugs, including the abuse of medicinal products, in sport*, OJC 170, 29 June 1991; *Resolution of the Council and the Ministers for Health, Meeting within the Council of 11 November 1991 concerning fundamental health-policy choices*, OJC 304, 23 November 1991.

introduced to the Treaty of Rome by the SEA as an area where the EC could adopt legislation as part of the Internal Market. The impetus, therefore, for including a Title dedicated to consumer protection in the post-TEU Treaty of Rome stems in the main from the drive in the second half of the 1980s towards the completion of the Internal Market. Indeed, paragraph 1(a) makes direct reference to ensuring consumer protection within the context of measures adopted under Article 100a. However, the EC has long been active in promoting consumer interests as part of its aim of improving living and working conditions in the Community. Consequently Article 129a contains a further provision extending the Community's competence beyond the attainment of a high level of consumer protection solely within the context of Internal Market legislation. Paragraph 1(b) provides the Community with the competence to adopt, in accordance with Article 189b and after consulting the EcoSoc, specific actions to protect the health, safety and economic interests of consumers as well as to provide them with adequate information about goods they wish to purchase. Such action, which remains unspecified, is not, however, to prevent member states from maintaining or introducing stricter measures, provided they are compatible with the provisions of the Treaty of Rome. This type of provision is characteristic of Community policy in other areas, such as the environment, where member states with high levels of protection do not wish to see them watered down by those members less enthusiastic about EC-level regulation.

q.v. Article 189b pp. 302–4.

q.v. environment pp. 232–9.

Title XI Consumer protection

ARTICLE 129a

1. The Community shall contribute to the attainment of a high level of consumer protection through:

(a) measures adopted pursuant to Article 100a in the context of the completion of the internal market;

(b) specific action which supports and supplements the policy pursued by the Member States to protect the health, safety and economic interests of consumers and to provide adequate information to consumers.

2. The Council, acting in accordance with the procedure referred to in Article 189b and after consulting the Economic and Social Committee, shall adopt the specific action referred to in paragraph 1(b).

3. Action adopted pursuant to paragraph 2 shall not prevent any Member State from maintaining or introducing more stringent protective measures. Such measures must be compatible with this Treaty. The Commission shall be notified of them.

Consumer protection policy

As indicated above, the Community was already in the process of developing a consumer protection policy before launching itself into the Internal Market programme. Indeed, as early as 1972 five fundamental consumer rights were laid down as the basis for Community action. These included the protection of consumers' health and safety; their economic interests; their right to information; their right to redress; and their right to representation and participation in the decision-making processes of the EC. Implementing measures aimed at ensuring these five rights have been a central element of EC consumer protection policy.

As a result the Community already has in place a body of law relating to consumer protection, as well as structures monitoring the requirements of consumers. Indeed within the Commission, there is not only a specific consumer policy portfolio, but also, since 1989, a special Consumer Policy Service unit. Furthermore, a Consumer Consultative Council, made up of representatives of the main consumer groups including the disabled and the elderly, exists to deliver opinions on relevant legislative proposals. The Community is also prominent in providing funding for national consumer organizations.

To date most consumer protection legislation has been introduced as part of Community 'Plans of Action', first launched in 1975. However, the need for unanimity within the Council of Ministers meant that, until the switch to qualified majority voting under the SEA in 1987, few directives were successfully adopted. Important legislation relating to product safety, misleading advertising and consumer credit was agreed upon, yet it was not until the second half of the 1980s and the launching in 1986 of the Third Consumer Programme that the bulk of present EC consumer protection legislation was adopted.

This legislation extends existing directives, particularly those related to product safety, and in many cases increases minimum standards. In addition, legislation has been introduced relating to unfair terms in consumer contracts, the liability of providers of services, and advertising. However, although EC action to date has been successful in increasing the level of protection afforded consumers in the Community, the emphasis has been on introducing legislation. Consequently, there is a recognized need to increase efforts to ensure its implementation, partly through increased monitoring of products, and partly through providing consumers with better opportunities for legal redress. Nevertheless, it is also recognized that existing legislation needs to be regularly updated to take into account scientific and technological advances and to ensure that it fulfils the aims of the EC's consumer protection policy. However, while the TEU may appear to facilitate such developments the debate surrounding the application of the principle of subsidiarity may not lead to the increase in consumer protection activity at EC level for which consumer groups wish.

FURTHER READING

Argiros, G., 'Consumer safety and the Single European Market: some observations and proposals', *Legal Issues of European Integration*, 1990/1, pp. 139–55.

EC Commission, *Consumer Policy in the European Community — An Overview*, Background Report, ISEC/B2/93, London, 1 January 1993.

EC Commission, *Consumer Policy: Second Commission three-year action plan 1993–1995 placing the single market at the service of European consumers*, COM(93)378 final, Brussels, 28 July 1993.

Goyens, M., 'Consumer protection in a Single European Market: what challenge for the EC agenda?', *Common Market Law Review*, vol. 29, no. 1, 1992, pp. 71–92.

Micklitz, H. -W. and Reich, N., 'Verbraucherschutz im Vertrag über die Europäische Union —

Perspektiven für 1993', *Europäische Zeitschrift für Wirtschaftsrecht*, vol. 3, no. 19, 1992, pp. 593—8.

Reich, N., *Europäisches Verbraucherschutzrecht*, Nomos Verlagsgesellschaft, Baden-Baden, 1993.

Thomson, I., 'The consumer and Europe — bibliographical review', *European Access*, 1991/5, pp. 44—53.

ii. Industrial and technical policies

This second sub-subdivision concerns itself with Titles XII—XVI of Part Three of the amended Treaty of Rome. It thus covers the Titles dedicated to Trans-European Networks (Title XII) and Industry (Title XIII), as inserted into the Treaty by the TEU, as well as amended versions of the Titles dedicated to Economic and Social Cohesion (Title XIV), Research and Technological Development (Titles XV) and the Environment (Title XVI).

Trans-European networks

Title XII contains three Articles (Articles 129b—129d) inserted into the Treaty of Rome by the TEU. These Articles set out the means by which the Community is to establish and develop trans-European networks covering transport, telecommunications and energy, as encouraged in Article 3(n). As such they provide a firm Treaty base for existing moves towards the creation of a trans-European transport network, the opening up of access to energy resources within Europe as proposed in the European Energy Charter of 1991, and give an impetus to plans to develop a Single Market in telecommunications. Such networks will involve linking together national infrastructures and opening up access to them. According to Article 129b, there will be two outcomes of this: firstly, the creation of trans-European networks will allow the citizens of the Union, businesses and local communities to benefit fully from the establishment of the Internal Market; and secondly, the networks will help promote economic and social cohesion within the Community as set out in Articles 130a-130e.

q.v. Article 3(n) p. 65.

q.v. Energy Charter p. 371.

In order to facilitate the establishment of such networks, the Community is made responsible for identifying the necessary infrastructure projects of common interest and for ensuring the inter-operability of national networks. To these ends it may, through the Cohesion Fund, support member states in the financing of transport infrastructure projects such as the European high-speed rail network (see Figure 7). The Community is also called on to support member states in developing projects of common interest by guaranteeing loans and providing interest rate subsidies. In addition, member states, encouraged by the Commission, are required to coordinate national infrastructure projects which are likely to have an impact on the creation of trans-European networks. Finally, in line with the trans-European nature of the networks being sought, provision is made for cooperation with third countries in the promotion of projects of mutual interest and in ensuring the inter-operability of their networks with those of the Community (Article 129c).

q.v. Articles 130a—130e pp. 220—1.

q.v. Cohesion Fund p. 223.

As far as decision-making procedures are concerned, the guidelines covering

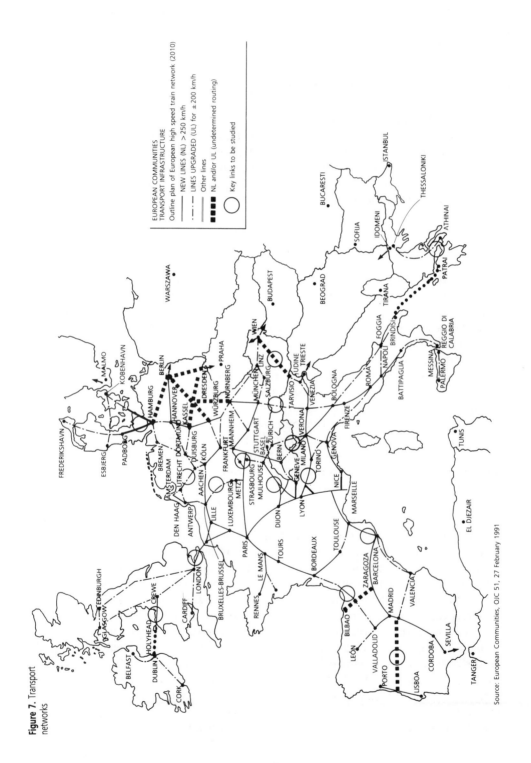

Figure 7. Transport networks

EUROPEAN COMMUNITIES
TRANSPORT INFRASTRUCTURE
Outline plan of European high speed train network (2010)

— NEW LINES (NL) >250 km/h
—·—· LINES UPGRADED (UL) for ±200 km/h
····· Other lines
▪▪▪▪ NL and/or UL (undetermined routing)
◯ Key links to be studied

Source: European Communities, OJC 51, 27 February 1991

the objectives and priorities of the Community with regard to trans-European networks and the broad lines of measures to be taken are to be adopted by the Council in accordance with the conciliation procedure laid down in Article 189b. Other measures aimed at ensuring inter-operability and providing financial assistance are to be adopted by the Council under the cooperation procedure as described in Article 189c. In all cases the Council is required to consult both the EcoSoc and the Committee of the Regions before making its final decision. Similarly, where the guidelines or a project relate to the territory of a member state, they must have the approval of the member state concerned (Article 129d).

q.v. Article 189b pp. 302–4.

q.v. Article 189c pp. 304–5.

Title XII Trans-European networks

ARTICLE 129b

1. To help achieve the objectives referred to in Articles 7a and 130a and to enable citizens of the Union, economic operators and regional and local communities to derive the full benefit from the setting up of an area without internal frontiers, the Community shall contribute to the establishment and development of trans-European networks in the areas of transport, telecommunications and energy infrastructures.

2. Within the framework of a system of open and competitive markets, action by the Community shall aim at promoting the interconnection and inter-operability of national networks as well as access to such networks. It shall take account in particular of the need to link island, landlocked and peripheral regions with the central regions of the Community.

ARTICLE 129c

1. In order to achieve the objectives referred to in Article 129b, the Community:

— shall establish a series of guidelines covering the objectives, priorities and broad lines of measures envisaged in the sphere of trans-European networks; these guidelines shall identify projects of common interest;
— shall implement any measures that may prove necessary to ensure the inter-operability of the networks, in particular in the field of technical standardization;
— may support the financial efforts made by the Member States for projects of common interest financed by Member States, which are identified in the framework of the guidelines referred to in the first indent, particularly through feasibility studies, loan guarantees or interest rate subsidies; the Community may also contribute, through the Cohesion Fund to be set up no later than 31 December 1993 pursuant to Article 130d, to the financing of specific projects in Member States in the area of transport infrastructure.

The Community's activities shall take into account the potential economic viability of the projects.

2. Member States shall, in liaison with the Commission, coordinate among themselves the policies pursued at national level which may have a significant impact on the achievement of the objectives referred to in Article 129b. The Commission may, in close cooperation with the Member States, take any useful initiative to promote such coordination.

3. The Community may decide to cooperate with third countries to promote projects of mutual interest and to ensure the inter-operability of networks.

ARTICLE 129d　　　The guidelines referred to in Article 129c(1) shall be adopted by the Council, acting in accordance with the procedure referred to in Article 189b and after consulting the Economic and Social Committee and the Committee of the Regions.

Guidelines and projects of common interest which relate to the territory of a Member State shall require the approval of the Member State concerned.

The Council, acting in accordance with the procedure referred to in Article 189c and after consulting the Economic and Social Committee and the Committee of the Regions, shall adopt the other measures provided for in Article 129c(1).

Industry

The fourth single Article Title in Part Three is Title XIII. This contains a new Article 130, as introduced to the Treaty of Rome by the TEU, replacing the second of two Articles which originally contained provisions relating to the European Investment Bank. These have now been renumbered as Articles 198d and 198e. The new Article 130 contains the first provisions to be included in the Treaty of Rome for what can loosely be termed an EC industrial policy, although no reference is made to a policy as such. Instead, the Article sets out in paragraph 1 four areas in which the Community and the member states may take action to ensure that the conditions necessary for the competitiveness of the Community's industry exist. This emphasis on competition is reflected in the fact that none of the four areas mentioned contains any reference to the maintenance of traditional industries or heavy government involvement in industry. In addition, it is made explicitly clear in the final paragraph of the Article that no measure may be introduced on the basis of Article 130 that could lead to the distortion of competition. Instead, the four areas stress the adjustment of industry to structural change, initiative, cooperation and innovation. As such, the essential role of the Community is the creation of an environment in which undertakings may benefit from the opportunities which exist.

q.v. Articles 198d and 198e p. 313.

However, the creation of such an environment is not a matter solely for the Community to pursue. Rather, the onus is placed on the member states to proceed by way of consultations with one another and only where necessary to coordinate their action. Furthermore, where the Community as a whole is to contribute to the achievement of the objectives set out in paragraph 1, it is to do so through policies pursued under other provisions in the Treaty. The only decisions the Community may take on the basis of Article 130 are specific measures designed to support action taken in the member states. Such decisions are to be taken on the basis of unanimity within the Council with only a consultative role for the EP and the EcoSoc.

Title XIII Industry

ARTICLE 130　　　1. The Community and the Member States shall ensure that the conditions necessary for the competitiveness of the Community's industry exist.

For that purpose, in accordance with a system of open and competitive markets, their action shall be aimed at:

— speeding up the adjustment of industry to structural changes;
— encouraging an environment favourable to initiative and to the development of undertakings throughout the Community, particularly small and medium-sized undertakings;
— encouraging an environment favourable to cooperation between undertakings;
— fostering better exploitation of the industrial potential of policies of innovation, research and technological development.

2. The Member States shall consult each other in liaison with the Commission and, where necessary, shall coordinate their action. The Commission may undertake any useful initiative to promote such coordination.

3. The Community shall contribute to the achievement of the objectives set out in paragraph 1 through the policies and activities it pursues under other provisions of this Treaty. The Council, acting unanimously on a proposal from the Commission, after consulting the European Parliament and the Economic and Social Committee, may decide on specific measures in support of action taken in the Member States to achieve the objectives set out in paragraph 1.

This Title shall not provide a basis for the introduction by the Community of any measure which could lead to a distortion of competition.

Industrial policy

Although the Community has never claimed to have had an industrial policy as such, this does not mean to say that it has not been heavily involved with the various branches of industry which exist within the EC economy. Indeed, the first of the Communities to be established, the European Coal and Steel Community, was created with the express purpose of ensuring the continued existence of both the coal and steel industries of the original six member states. Moreover, there has often been pressure from some member states, particularly France, for the Community to adopt a *dirigiste* attitude towards industry. However, under both the ECSC Treaty and the Treaty of Rome, the emphasis is on the promotion of market liberalization and free trade, rather than protectionism and state intervention. Hence, as opposed to any specific provision for an industrial policy based on state or Community-level involvement in industry, the bias of the Treaty of Rome is towards guaranteeing competition and abolishing state aids and monopolistic practices.

q.v. ECSC pp. 359–66.

Consequently, despite the perception of the Conservative government in the United Kingdom, Community action with regard to industry, particularly of late with the moves to complete the Internal Market, has been aimed at removing uncompetitive practices within industry in the EC. This, it is believed, will improve the competitiveness of European industry and provide it with a competitive domestic market from which it can compete effectively on world markets. Indeed, in the early 1980s, it was the fear that European industry as a result of its uncompetitiveness was in danger of finding itself forever lagging behind the United States and Japan in the pursuit of world markets that helped prompt the EC into launching its Internal Market programme and promoting R&D as part of the SEA. With the initial success of the Internal Market in regenerating European industry, marred albeit by the general economic downturn of the early 1990s, the Community's emphasis on competition would appear to have been justified.

The underlying liberal, free market ethos of the Community is reflected in the Commission's most recent proposals on the future of industry within the EC. The 1990 paper, entitled *Industrial Policy in an Open and Competitive Environment — Guidelines for a Community Approach*,[20] stresses the need to increase the competitive nature of industry. In the paper, the Commission rejects an interventionist approach towards the future development of industry within the Community, favouring instead the further liberalization of markets and the positive adjustment of industries through diversification and modernization. Such an approach has been reinforced by other Commission papers adopting similar approaches for the future of individual industrial sectors such as information technology, biotechnology, the maritime industry, and clothing and textiles.

The basic thrust, therefore, of Community policy with regard to industry is to force each sector to become more efficient, and thus more competitive, by creating a competitive environment. However, more direct assistance is provided through a variety of channels. The most prominent of these are the Community-backed R&D programmes, such as EUREKA, BRITE, ESPRIT and RACE, which involve not only the provision of financial assistance towards research projects, but also help promote cooperation between undertakings and the dissemination of information. Equally, assistance is given to industry through the retraining of workers as part of the Community's vocational training programmes.

q.v. R&D programmes pp. 229–32.

q.v. vocational training programmes pp. 201–2.

The aim of creating a liberalized domestic market as the means to increase the competitive nature of European Industry is mirrored, in part, by the Community's efforts to open up access to the EC market for third countries. Of significance here is the proposal that the motor industry and the market for motor vehicles be completely liberalized by 1992 and that the protection from Japanese competition afforded EC companies be gradually reduced. On the other hand, in the case of sensitive products, such as coal, steel and textiles, there has been little progress in liberalizing the domestic market. Indeed, the use of anti-dumping legislation by the Community has often come in for widespread criticism, both from within the EC and from abroad. Similarly, the Community has been heavily criticized for adopting overly protectionist stances in bilateral trade negotiations, particularly with regard to the countries of Central and Eastern Europe.

Despite the protection afforded the more sensitive industries, the essence of the Community's policy towards industry is non-intervention and market liberalization. However, with the economic downturn which has affected Europe since the early 1990s, there have been indications that the enthusiasm for competition and liberal market policies may be receding as several sectors of European industry struggle to survive the onset of recession. Indeed, as recession spread more widely through the Community in 1992, the European Council at

---

20. *Industrial Policy in an Open and Competitive Environment — Guidelines for a Community Approach*, COM(90)556 final, Brussels, 16 November 1990.

Edinburgh adopted a package of measures aimed at stimulating economic growth.[21] Although for the most part the measures were directed towards improving the infrastructure of the European economy, they nevertheless suggest that the Community is becoming more willing to consider more direct assistance to support industry.[22] However, any action contemplated will be tempered by the lack of funds available.

Indeed, two further developments in 1992–3 point towards a more pro-industry and less free-market orientated thinking within the Community, particularly within the Commission. The first of these is the appointment of Karel Van Miert as competition Commissioner. Unlike his predecessor, Leon Brittan, Van Miert appears less committed to a vigorous enforcement of Community legislation on state aids and mergers, and more inclined to adopt a softer approach towards industries seeking assistance from governments as they struggle in a recessionary economic climate. Such an approach would also appear to be in line with the views held by the industry Commissioner Martin Bangemann who, while insisting on the need to create a strong and competitive domestic EC market, has in the past opposed Brittan's more zealous attempts to promote competition within the Internal Market.

q.v. competition policy pp. 142–5.

The second development concerns the apparent feeling in several of the member states that the Commission should become less involved in what are deemed to be national affairs, employing more the principle of subsidiarity, thus allowing more decisions to be taken at the national level. If the Commission pursues such an option, it is likely that it will refrain from taking controversial decisions promoting competition within industry. Instead, it is possible that the Commission will leave national governments to adopt industrial policies of their own, provided that they are broadly in line with provisions of the Treaty of Rome.

In summary, it would appear that the provisions contained in the new Article 130 will not bring about a fundamental shift in EC policy towards industry. Indeed, it can be argued that the provisions reflect more the economic promise of the late 1980s than the recessionary realities of the early 1990s. Consequently, as the importance of industrial competitiveness is replaced by the need for economic survival, the emphasis of industrial policies in Europe may become less non-interventionist. Yet, even if intervention were to regain government support, it is unlikely that the EC will be at the centre of developing an appropriate Community-wide policy. Article 130 neither provides it with such a competence, nor are governments wary of Brussels likely to sanction one.

FURTHER READING

Bangemann, M., *Meeting the Global Challenge: Establishing a successful European Industrial Policy*, Kogan Page, London, 1992.

EC Commission, *Industrial Policy in an Open and Competitive Environment — Guidelines for a Community Approach*, COM(90)556 final, Brussels, 16 November 1990.

EC Commission, *Panorama of EC Industry*, (Annually).

---

21. *Promoting Economic Recovery in Europe (The Edinburgh Growth Initiative)*, COM(93)164 final, Brussels, 22 April 1993.

22. 'In sickness and in health', *Financial Times*, 26 March 1993.

EC Commission, *Promoting Economic Recovery in Europe (The Edinburgh Growth Initiative)*, COM(93)164 final, Brussels, 22 April 1993.

EC Commission, *The European Aircraft Industry: First assessment and possible Community actions*, COM(92)164 final, Brussels, 29 April 1992.

EC Commission, *The European Maritime Industries: Further steps for strengthening their competitiveness*, COM(92)490 final, Brussels, 18 November 1992.

EC Commission, *The Motor Vehicle Industry: Situation, issues at stake and proposals for action*, COM(92)166 final, Brussels, 8 May 1992.

Geroski, P. A., 'European Industrial Policy and industrial policy in Europe', *Oxford Review of Economic Policy*, vol. 5, no. 2, 1989, pp. 20–36.

Klodt, H., 'Europäische Industriepolitik nach Maastricht', *Die Weltwirtschaft*, 1992/3, pp. 263–73.

Lehner, S. and Meiklejohn, R., 'Fair competition in the Internal Market: Community state aid policy', *European Economy*, no. 48, September 1991, pp. 7–114.

Nicolaides, P. (ed.) *Industrial policy in the European Community: A necessary response to economic integration?*, European Institute of Public Administration, Maastricht, 1992.

Economic and social cohesion

Part Three, Title XIV of the amended Treaty of Rome contains an amended version of the provisions relating to economic and social cohesion (Articles 130a–130e). These were originally inserted into the Treaty of Rome as Part Three, Title V by the SEA. Under the TEU they have also been added to. However, this has not resulted in an increase in the number of Articles within the Title since the TEU merely replaced the provisions of the existing, and by then defunct, Article 130d with new provisions.[23] The TEU also added two new paragraphs to Article 130b and gave added recognition to the strengthening of economic and social cohesion by including it as an explicit area of EC activity (Article 3(j)).

 q.v. Article 3(j) p. 65.

The insertion of Articles 130a–130e into the Treaty by the SEA reflected the concern of the Community for its less-developed areas as the EC embarked on the completion of the Internal Market. Consequently, the provisions set out the means by which the Community would attempt to strengthen its economic and social cohesion. That is to say, the Community committed itself to reducing the economic and social disparities (See Box 10) which existed between its various regions (Article 130a). As such, the provisions, along with a commitment to double budgetary expenditure on promoting economic and social cohesion, represented a concession by the richer to the less-developed member states (Greece, Ireland, Portugal and Spain) for acceptance of the Internal Market programme. A similar trade-off occurred with respect to the TEU. Here, the richer member states agreed to the creation of a Cohesion Fund (Article 130d) in exchange for the poorer member states' acceptance of the provisions relating to Economic and Monetary Union. The purpose of the new fund is to provide financial assistance for projects involving the environment, transport infrastructure and trans-European networks.[24]

 q.v. budgetary expenditure pp. 322–7.

 q.v. Economic and Monetary Union pp. 150–80.

---

23. The original provisions of Article 130d, as introduced to the Treaty of Rome by the SEA, called on the Community to clarify and to rationalize the tasks of the Structural Funds, and to increase the efficiency of and cooperation between the funds.

24. In line with Declaration 9, the EC is asked to consider nature conservation in promoting economic and social cohesion (see p. 433). A second declaration, Declaration 26, draws attention to the structural problems of the French overseas departments, the Azores, Madeira and the Canary Islands (see p. 437).

Box 10.
GDP per capita in the
EC in 1990 (in ECU)

Greece	6 823
Portugal	8 136
Ireland	9 885
Spain	10 925
United Kingdon	14 582
Netherlands	14 614
Italy	14 848
Belgium	15 207
Denmark	15 539
France	16 157
West Germany	16 954
Luxembourg	17 928
EC(12)	*14 488*

Source: Eurostat, *Basic Statistics of the Community*, 29th Edition, OOPEC, Luxembourg, 1992, p. 40.

The means by which the Community is to achieve the goal of economic and social cohesion are described in Article 130b. They include the coordination of economic policies and action taken through the Structural Funds and the European Investment Bank. As a result of the amendments introduced by the TEU, progress in attaining the objectives set out in Article 130a is to be monitored by the Commission. Where necessary a triennial report by the Commission is to be accompanied by a list of appropriate proposals to improve the situation. Essentially, such proposals are to be implemented through the Structural Funds, although provision is made for specific action to be taken independently of them. The Structural Funds, as Article 130b points out, are the European Agricultural Guidance and Guarantee Fund (EAGGF), Guidance Section; the European Social Fund (ESF); and the European Regional Development Fund (ERDF).

q.v. Structural Funds pp. 221–5.

q.v. European Investment Bank pp. 312–14.

q.v. Articles 43 p. 99.

With the exception of the ERDF, the aims of each of the funds have been pointed out earlier in the analysis of Articles 43 and 125. The aims of the ERDF, however, appear in Article 130c. Essentially, the aim of the Fund is to help redress the main regional imbalances within the EC, particularly with regard to those regions whose development is deemed to be lagging, and to those regions affected by industrial decline. The process by which the Fund's implementing decisions are to be taken is outlined in Article 130e. This involves the Community's cooperation procedure and as such remains unchanged under the TEU, except that the Council, must now consult with the EcoSoc and the Committee of the Regions before finally adopting a proposal.

q.v. Article 125 p. 194.

As far as the overall organization of the Structural Funds and the rules governing their activities are concerned, the new Article 130d states that these are to be determined by the Council, on the basis of a Commission proposal, in consultation with the EcoSoc and the Committee of the Regions, and having gained the assent of the EP. Provision is also made for the grouping of the Structural Funds, furthering the idea of rationalization previously an integral part of Article 130d under the SEA.

Title XIV Economic and social cohesion

ARTICLE 130a

In order to promote its overall harmonious development, the Community shall develop and pursue its actions in leading to the strengthening of its economic and social cohesion.

In particular, the Community shall aim at reducing the disparities between **the levels of development of** the various regions and the backwardness of the least-favoured regions, **including rural areas.**

ARTICLE 130b

Member States shall conduct their economic policies and shall coordinate them is such a way as, in addition, to attain the objectives set out in Article 130a. The **formulation and** implementation of the **Community's** policies **and actions and the implementation of** the internal market shall take into account the objectives set out in Article 130a and shall contribute to their achievement. The Community shall *also* support the achievement of these objectives by the action it takes through the Structural Funds (European Agricultural Guidance and Guarantee Fund, Guidance Section; European Social Fund; European Regional Development Fund), the European Investment Bank and other existing financial instruments.

The Commission shall submit a report to the European Parliament, the Council, the Economic and Social Committee and the Committee of the Regions every three years on the progress made towards achieving economic and social cohesion and on the manner in which the various means provided for in this Article have contributed to it. This report shall, if necessary, be accompanied by appropriate proposals.

If specific actions prove necessary outside the Funds and without prejudice to the measures decided upon within the framework of the other Community policies, such actions may be adopted by the Council acting unanimously on a proposal from the Commission and after consulting the European Parliament, the Economic and Social Committee and the Committee of the Regions.

ARTICLE 130c

The European Regional Development Fund is intended to help to redress the *main* regional imbalances in the Community through *participation* in the development and structural adjustments of regions whose development is lagging behind and in the conversion of declining industrial regions.

ARTICLE 130d

Without prejudice to Article 130e, the Council, acting unanimously on a proposal from the Commission and after obtaining the assent of the European Parliament and consulting the Economic and Social Committee and the Committee of the Regions, shall define the tasks, priority objectives and the organization of the Structural Funds, which may involve grouping the Funds. The Council, acting by the same procedure, shall also define the general rules applicable to them and the provisions necessary to ensure their effectiveness and the coordination of the Funds with one another and with the other existing financial instruments.

The Council, acting in accordance with the same procedure, shall before 31 December 1993 set up a Cohesion Fund to provide a financial contribution to projects in the fields of environment and trans-European networks in the area of transport infrastructure.

ARTICLE 130e

Implementing decisions relating to the European Regional Development Fund shall be taken by the Council, acting *in accordance with the procedure referred to in Article 189c* **and after consulting the Economic and Social Committee and the Committee of the Regions.**

With regard to the European Agricultural Guidance and Guarantee Fund — Guidance Section, and the European Social Fund, Articles 43 *and 125 respectively shall continue to apply.*

The Structural Funds and regional policy

The original version of the Treaty of Rome made no mention of structural funds or of a Community regional policy. Indeed, the Treaty made no mention at all of the regions. Consequently, it was not until the Community was faced with its first enlargement and the economic crises of the 1970s, that its attention was seriously turned to the problems facing the regions and proposals were put forward for developing a policy towards them. However, the Treaty of Rome did make provision for the establishment of two funds which now form part of the so-called structural funds and assist in implementing the Community's regional policy.

The first of these is the European Social Fund (ESF), as provided for in Articles 123–126. This was set up in 1960 with the aim of promoting employment and increasing the geographical and occupational mobility of workers within the Community. During its early years of operation, the Fund concentrated its efforts on the redeployment and retraining of workers within the original Community of six. However, following a reform of the fund in 1970 and the introduction of the first Social Action Programme in 1974, the emphasis of ESF activities was redefined to take account of the rising levels of unemployment resulting from the decline of traditional industries in Europe in the 1970s. Consequently, the Fund began to concentrate its efforts on retraining redundant workers and promoting vocational skills in young people. At the same time, the Fund also devoted resources to opening up job opportunities for women and the disabled.

However, the persistent increases in unemployment in the late 1970s and early 1980s forced a further reform of the ESF. As a result, ESF funding was refocused on educational retraining and the development of employment skills among young people, with particular attention being paid to the long-term unemployed and women. Thus, by 1989, 75 per cent of ESF aid (ECU 3,580 million) was being spent on projects for the under-25s, including in excess of ECU 250 million in 1991 on the Euroform initiative to develop new qualifications, new skills and new employment opportunities among the young. Despite this shift in emphasis, the ESF is still active in promoting equal opportunities in employment and vocational training for women and the disabled through programmes such as NOW and Horizon respectively. Finally, with the unification of Germany in 1990, the ESF has become heavily involved in dealing with the problem of unemployment in the five new *Länder*, allocating in 1991 over ECU 900m to projects there.

q.v. Article 40(4) p. 98.

The second structural fund, set up in line with provisions laid down in the Treaty of Rome, is the Guidance Section of the European Agricultural Guarantee and Guidance Fund (EAGGF). This was eventually set up in 1970, in accordance with Article 40(4), once the Community's Common Agricultural Policy was in operation. Its essential task was and remains the modernization and rationalization of agricultural production methods. However, as the lesser section of the two

q.v. Common Agricultural Policy pp. 95–104.

which make up the EAGGF, its finances are considerably less than those of the Guarantee Section. Consequently, although it was originally envisaged that funds available to the EAGGF would be allocated on a 2:1 ratio between the Guarantee Section and the Guidance Section, the latter has rarely had more than 7 per cent of total funding made available to it. Nevertheless, this figure, which in 1991 equalled over ECU 2.25 billion, represented almost 20 per cent of the total financing available to the Structural Funds.

q.v. EAGGF Guarantee Section pp. 102–3.

Although the activities of both the ESF and the Guidance Section of the EAGGF have gradually developed a clear emphasis on promoting assistance to the less developed areas of the Community, it was not until 1975 that a fund was created with the specific aim of reducing the economic and social disparities between various regions of the EC. This fund, the European Regional Development Fund (ERDF), did not emerge out of the Treaty of Rome. Instead, in response to the economic difficulties being experienced in the 1970s and in an attempt to provide some form of assistance to the declining industrial regions of the United Kingdom, the Community made use of the catch-all Article 235 to establish the Fund in order to redistribute aid to its struggling and less developed regions.

q.v. Article 235 p. 340.

The primary aim of the ERDF, as now laid down in Article 130c of the Treaty of Rome, is to help redress the principal regional imbalances in the Community. This it does by jointly funding programmes and projects with local and national authorities in each of the member states in order to stimulate economic development in the poorest areas of the Community. Finance is provided by the ERDF in accordance with the principle of *additionality* — all funding being additional to that made available by local and national governments. This is meant to ensure that the member states contribute to the financing of projects, something which the UK government is not always willing to do. Projects and programmes co-financed by the ERDF are normally aimed at improving industrial infrastructure and promoting job creation on the basis of a Commission proposal, since the agricultural sector is covered by the EAGGF.

While the establishment of the ERDF essentially heralded the emergence of an EC regional policy, it was not until after the second and third enlargements of the Community in 1981 and 1986 respectively, and the adoption of the Internal Market programme as part of the SEA, that regional policy was given a high profile among the activities of the Community. Indeed, not only was the ERDF formally recognized by the SEA through the insertion of Articles 130b–130e into the Treaty of Rome, but the aim of increasing economic and social cohesion within the Community as a counter to the possible economic implications of the Internal Market on the more remote and less developed regions was firmly established as a policy objective of the EC. As laid down in Article 130a of the amended Treaty, this was to involve reversing the backwardness of the so-called least favoured regions as well as tackling disparities between the various regions within the Community. While this clearly boosted the standing of the three funds mentioned, the commitment of the member states to economic and social cohesion was further reinforced by the decision to double in real terms the finances available to the funds by 1993. As a result, in 1991 over ECU 14.5 billion were allocated to the Structural Funds compared to a figure of only ECU 5.5 billion in 1985.

Under the TEU, the regions gained a further boost in that provision was made for the establishment of a Cohesion Fund (Article 130d,). Following an agreement reached at the Lisbon Summit in June 1992, the fund was set up on 1 April 1993 before ratification of the TEU had actually been completed.[25] In addition, the new Title XII concerning Trans-European Networks makes specific reference to the need to link up peripheral with central areas of the Community. Furthermore, the entry into force in late 1994 of the Agreement establishing the European Economic Area, the less-developed regions of the Community will benefit from the availability of extra funds provided by the member states of EFTA.

q.v. Article 130d p. 220.

q.v. European Economic Area pp. 479–82.

While the creation of new funds and the insertion of economic and social cohesion into the Treaty of Rome by the SEA provided the Community with instruments to develop a regional policy, the actual objectives of such a policy long remained unclear and, given the number of funds, often uncoordinated. This was recognized in the SEA, and later in the TEU, where provision was made for a rationalization of the funds and a clarification of the aims of EC's regional policy. As a result, in 1988, the Council agreed on a series of reforms for the funds, including the formulation of specific regional policy objectives.[26] These objectives were numbered 1–5 with Objective 5 being subdivided into (a) and (b).

The first and second objectives require the Community to promote the development and structural adjustment of the regions whose development is lagging behind that of the rest of the Community (Objective 1), and to convert regions seriously affected by industrial decline (Objective 2). Therefore, along with Objective 5(b) which seeks the promotion of rural areas, these two objectives require the application of Community funds to specific areas where economic and social development are below 75 per cent of the EC average. Thus the regions identified under Objective 1, include significant parts of Spain and Italy, and the whole of Greece, Northern Ireland and Portugal, while various regions scattered throughout the Community are eligible under Objectives 2 and 5(b).

The remaining objectives promote the combating of unemployment (Objective 3), the occupational integration of young people (Objective 4), and the speeding up of adjustments to agricultural structures (Objective 5(a)). As such these objectives correspond with the activities of the ESF and the Guidance Section of the EAGGF, and have a more horizontal dimension. Thus they are pursued throughout the EC.

The success of the Structural Funds since the 1988 reforms has been difficult to gauge particularly with the slowdown in economic growth experienced by the Community since the early 1990s. Nevertheless, statistics produced in 1993 suggested that a degree of economic convergence among the regions had been

---

25. Following discussions at the Edinburgh Summit of the European Council in December 1992, final agreement on the establishment of the Cohesion Fund was reached in March 1993. See *Council Regulation (EEC) No 792/93 of 30 March 1993 establishing a cohesion financial instrument*, OJL 79, 1 April 1993; *Communication and draft proposal for a Council Regulation (EC) establishing a Cohesion Fund*, COM(92)339 final, Brussels, 31 July 1992; *Revised draft proposal for a Council Regulation (EEC) establishing a Cohesion Fund*, COM(92)599 final, Brussels, 23 December 1992.

26. *Council Regulation (EEC) No 2052/88 of 24 June 1988 on the tasks of the Structural Funds and their effectiveness and on coordination of their activities between themselves and with the operations of the European Investment Bank and the other existing financial instruments*, OJL 185, 15 July 1988.

achieved in the period 1980–90.[27] On some criteria, such as average per capita income, 40 per cent of EC regions had moved closer to the Community average. However, such a large percentage reflects the fact that several richer regions had moved closer to the mean as a result of a fall in income. Nevertheless, from a Community perspective the overall convergence was a welcome sign that the activities of the Structural Funds were bearing fruit.

All the same, with the need to create improved economic and social conditions in the less developed areas of the EC in order to increase the prospects of EMU, it has been accepted that existing regional policy objectives will have to undergo further revision in the near future. Steps in this direction were taken in March 1993 when the Commission presented a set of proposals for a revision of the Structural Funds.[28] However, the scope for change is limited given the financial constraints placed on regional policy expenditure as a result of the decision of the European Council at Edinburgh in December 1992 to limit the increase in funding to approximately half that originally envisaged in the Delors II proposals. Nevertheless, changes in the distribution of structural monies were agreed in mid-1993, although a fundamental revision of the Funds did not take place. While at present the existing arrangements may suffice, a complete overhaul of EC regional policy will be unavoidable once the Community expands to take in the countries of Central and Eastern Europe. Consequently, regional policy and the Structural Funds are likely to retain their current position towards the top of the EC's policy agenda.

*q.v. Delors
II proposals
pp. 325–7.*

FURTHER READING

Armstrong, H., 'Community regional policy', in Lodge, J. (ed.), *The European Community and the Challenge of the Future*, 2nd edn, Pinter, London, 1993, pp. 131–51.

Begg, I., 'European integration and regional policy', *Oxford Review of Economic Policy*, vol. 5, no. 2, 1989, pp. 90–114

Chabert, J. 'La vocation des Régions dans l'Europe de l'An 2000', *Studia Diplomatica*, vol. 44, no. 6, 1991, pp. 13–28.

Coombes, D. and Rees, N., 'Regional and Social Policy', in: Hurwitz, L. and Lequesne, C. (eds.), *The State of the European Community: Policies, institutions and debates in the transition years*, Longman, London, 1991, pp. 207–28.

Day, G. and Rees, G. (eds.), *Regions, National and Regional Integration*, University of Wales Press, Cardiff, 1991.

EC Commission, *Community Structural Policies: Assessment and outlook*, COM(92)84 final, Brussels, 18 March 1992.

EC Commission, *Europe 2000 — Outlook for the Development of the Community's Territory*, OOPEC, Luxembourg, 1991.

EC Commission, *Reform of the Structural Funds: A tool to promote economic and social cohesion*, OOPEC, Luxembourg, 1992.

EC Commission, *Regional Development Studies*, periodically.

EC Commission, *The Community's Structural Fund Operations 1994–1999*, COM(93)67 final, Brussels, 10 March 1993.

EC Commission, 'The European Social Fund', *Social Europe*, 2/91.

EC Commission, *The Future of Community Initiatives under the Structural Funds*, COM(93)282 final, Brussels, 16 June 1993.

EC Commission, *The Regions in the 1990s*, OOPEC, Luxembourg, 1991.

EC Commission, *Third Annual Report on the Implementation of the Reform of the Structural Funds*, OOPEC, Luxembourg, 1992.

---

27. 'For richer for poorer', *The Economist*, 30 January 1993.
28. *The Community's Structural Fund Operations 1994–99*, COM(93)67 final, Brussels, 10 March 1993; EC Commission, *The Structural Funds for 1994–99*, Background Report, ISEC/B16/93, London, 28 May 1993.

Éthier, D., 'La réforme des fonds structurels de la Communauté européenne: enjeux et perspectives', *Études internationales*, vol. 23, no. 3, 1992, pp. 517–29.

Franzmeyer, F., 'Die Europäische Wirtschafts- und Währungsunion: Ausbau der gemeinschaftlichen Kohäsionspolitik', *Integration*, vol. 16, no. 2, 1993, pp. 95–102.

Gallizioli, G., *I Fondi Strutturali delle Comunità europee*, Casa Editrice Dott. Antonio Milani, 1992.

Hannequart, A. (ed.), *Economic and Social Cohesion in Europe: A new objective for integration*, Routledge, London, 1992.

Leonardi, R. (ed.), *The Regions and the European Community: The regional response to the Single Market in the underdeveloped areas*, Frank Cass, London, 1993.

MacKay, R., '1992 and the Regions', *European Access*, 1989/5, pp. 12–15.

Mair, D., 'European regional development: an analysis of the reformed Structural Funds', *European Research*, vol. 2, no. 3, 1991, pp. 1–3.

Marks, G., 'Structural policy in the European Community', in Sbragia, A.M. (ed.), *Euro-Politics:*

Institutions and policymaking in the 'New' European Community, Brookings Institution, Washington, 1992, pp. 191–224.

Marques Mendes, A. J., 'Economic cohesion in Europe: the impact of the Delors Plan', *Journal of Common Market Studies*, vol. 29, no. 1, 1990, pp. 17–36.

Marx, F., *EG-Regionalpolitik: Fortschritt und Stagnation im Spannungsfeld von Integrationsziel und nationalstaatlichen Interessen*, Alano Verlag, Aachen, 1992.

Ridinger, R., 'Wirtschaftlicher und sozialer Zusammenhalt in der EG — Die zukünftige Gestaltung der EG-Regionalpolitik', *Europa-Archiv*, vol. 47, no. 5, 1992, pp. 133–40.

Scott, J. and Mansell, W., 'European regional development policy: confusing quality with quantity', *European Law Review*, vol. 18, no. 2, 1993, pp. 87–108.

Tomkins, J. and Twomey, J., 'Regional policy', in: McDonald, F. and Dearden, S. (eds.), *European Economic Integration*, Longman, London, 1992, pp. 100–17.

Research and technological development

The Treaty of Rome made no explicit provision for the development of a Community Research and Development (R&D) policy. Consequently, it was not until the mid-1980s, when the modernization of European industry was deemed vital if Europe were to compete successfully with the United States and Japan on world markets, that R&D was introduced into the Treaty of Rome as part of the SEA. A new Title containing 11 Articles (Title VI, Articles 130f–130q) was thus inserted into the Treaty. This was then renumbered and amended by the TEU. Consequently, the provisions relating to R&D policy, themselves renumbered to make use of the previously unused Article 130j as Articles 130f–130p, are now found in Title XV.[29] Despite the renumbering of the Title and several of the Articles, the actual content of the provisions remains, in substance, for the most part unaltered. However, the status of EC responsibility for R&D was raised by the TEU's inclusion of R&D as an area of EC activity singled out in the new Article 3(m) of the Treaty.

q.v. Article 3(m) p. 65.

The main objective of the Community's R&D policy is the strengthening of the scientific and technological bases of Community industry and of its competitiveness at international level. Such an objective is to be achieved by encouraging research cooperation between companies and research bodies and

---

29. When the original provisions for R&D were introduced to the Treaty of Rome by the SEA no Article 130j was included. Consequently the 11 Articles contained within the then Title VI were numbered 130f–130i and 130k–130q. This situation was changed by the TEU which renumbered the existing R&D provisions to make use of the previously omitted Article 130j. As a result, the R&D provisions contained in the new Title XV are now numbered sequentially as Articles 130f–130p. Article 130q, thus being made redundant, no longer appears in the amended Treaty of Rome.

opening up opportunities in the Internal Market (Article 130f). In essence, therefore, despite a rewording of the provisions, the objectives of the Community remain unchanged following the amendments introduced by the TEU. However, a subtle change was introduced in that, where previously the Community had concerned itself with the scientific and technological base of '*European*' industry, under the TEU it now contents itself solely with that of '*Community*' industry. A more evident change to Article 130f brought about by the TEU is the replacement of the existing paragraph 3 concerning R&D and the Internal Market, with a provision for all R&D activities pursued under the Treaty to be adopted in accordance with the provisions laid down in Title XV.

According to the amended Treaty, Community action in the area of R&D, as under the SEA, is to complement the activities of the member states in promoting research cooperation, the dissemination of the results of such research, and the mobility and training of researchers (Article 130g). This is to be achieved through the coordination of R&D activities so that national and Community policies are mutually consistent (Article 130h). As with Article 130f, the provisions of Article 130h remain almost unaltered, despite a reformatting and a rewording of the Article under the TEU. However, once again a subtle change has taken place in that the Commission is no longer mentioned as a participant in the actual coordinating of national and Community policies. Furthermore, the Commission's role in taking initiatives to promote coordination is redefined so that it must now, as a result of the TEU, work in '*cooperation*' with the member states rather than simply in close '*contact*' with them.

Less subtle changes are evident in the rewording of Article 130i. The provisions of this Article, which now contains the amended provisions of the previous Articles 130i and the unamended first paragraph of 130k, concern the adoption of a multi-annual framework programme setting out the objectives and broad guidelines of EC R&D activity and the maximum financial contribution to be made by the Community. Such a programme is to be adopted by the Council, having consulted the EcoSoc, in accordance with the conciliation procedure laid down in Article 189b, except that all Council decisions are to be taken on the basis of unanimity. While the need for the Council to act unanimously mirrors the post-SEA practice regarding the adoption of the multi-annual framework programme as previously laid down in Article 130q, the involvement of the EP via Article 189b in the adoption procedure represents a welcome shift away from the purely consultative role previously afforded the Parliament under the SEA.

q.v. Article 189b pp. 302–4.

The actual implementation of the framework programmes is to be carried out through specific programmes adopted by the Council, in consultation with the EP and EcoSoc, on the basis of a qualified majority. While this corresponds to the original provisions contained in Articles 130k and 130q, the TEU does introduce an element of financial discipline to the programmes in that the funding required may not exceed that of the framework programme overall. Further provisions regarding the implementation of the framework programme are found in the new Articles 130j–130o. The first of these (Article 130j) contains a reworded version of the second paragraph of the original Article 130k relating to the dissemination of research results, as well as a new provision regarding the rules governing participation in the framework programmes. The new Articles 130k–130o contain the provisions originally found in Articles 130l–130p respectively. With the exception of the new Article 130k, whose provisions are identical to those of the original Article 130l, all have undergone some form of rewording. In all cases, none of the rewording affects the content of the provisions. Thus Articles 130k and 130l concern supplementary R&D programmes involving only a limited number of EC member states; Article 130m cooperation with third countries and competent international organizations; Article 130n the establishment of structures to carry out Community R&D programmes; and Article 130o the decision-making procedures governing Articles 130j, 130k, 130l and 130n. The final provision contained in Title XV, and one introduced by the TEU, requires the Commission to present an annual report to the EP and the Council on R&D activities (Article 130p).

Title XV Research and technological development

ARTICLE 130f

1. The *Community shall have the objective of strengthening* the scientific and technological bases of **Community** industry and *encouraging* it to become more competitive at international level, **while promoting all the research activities deemed necessary by virtue of other chapters of this Treaty.**

2. *For this purpose the Community shall,* **throughout the Community,** encourage undertakings, research centres and universities in their research and technological development activities **of high quality**; it shall support their efforts to cooperate with one another, aiming, notably, at enabling undertakings to exploit the internal market potential to the full, in particular through the opening up of national public contracts, the definition of common standards and the removal of legal and fiscal obstacles to that cooperation.

3. **All community activities under this Treaty in the area of research and technological development, including demonstration projects, shall be decided on and implemented in accordance with the provisions of this Title.**

ARTICLE 130g

In pursuing these objectives, the Community shall carry out the following activities, complementing the activities carried out in the Member States:

(a) implementation of research, technological development and demonstration programmes, by promoting cooperation with **and between** undertakings, research centres and universities;

(b) promotion of cooperation in the field of Community research, technological development and demonstration with third countries and international organizations;

(c) dissemination and optimization of the results of activities in Community research, technological development and demonstration;

(d) stimulation of the training and mobility of researchers in the Community.

ARTICLE 130h

1. **The Community and the Member States shall coordinate their research and technological development activities so as to ensure that national policies and Community policy are mutually consistent.**

2. In close **cooperation** with the Member States, the Commission may take any useful initiative to promote *the coordination referred to in paragraph 1.*

ARTICLE 130i

1. *A multiannual framework programme, setting out all activities of the Community, shall be adopted* by the Council, acting in accordance with the procedure referred to in Article 189b after consulting the Economic and Social Committee. The Council shall act unanimously throughout the procedures referred to in Article 189b.

The framework programme shall:

— *establish* the scientific and technological objectives *to be achieved by the activities provided for in Article 130g and fix the relevant priorities;*
— *indicate the broad* lines of *such* activities;
— fix the **maximum overall** amount and the detailed rules for *Community* financial participation in the *framework* programme and *the respective shares in each of the activities provided for.*

2. The framework programme **shall** be adapted or supplemented as the situation changes.

3. *The framework programme shall be implemented through specific programmes developed within each activity. Each specific programme shall define the detailed rules for implementing it, fix its duration and provide for the means deemed necessary.* The sum of the amounts deemed necessary, fixed in the specific programmes, may not exceed the overall maximum amount fixed for the framework programme and each activity.

4. The Council, acting by a qualified majority on a proposal from the Commission and after consulting the European Parliament and the Economic and Social Committee, shall adopt the specific programmes.

ARTICLE 130j

For the implementation of the multiannual framework programme the Council shall:

— determine the rules for the participation of undertakings, research centres and universities;
— lay down the rules governing the dissemination of research results.

ARTICLE 130k

In implementing the multiannual framework programmes, supplementary programmes may be decided on involving the participation of certain Member States only, which shall finance them subject to possible Community participation.

The Council shall adopt the rules applicable to supplementary programmes, particularly as regards the dissemination of knowledge and access by other Member States.

ARTICLE 130l

In implementing the multiannual framework programme the Community may make provision, in agreement with the Member States concerned, for participation in research and development programmes undertaken by several Member States, including participation in the structures created for the execution of those programmes.

ARTICLE 130m

In implementing the multiannual framework programme the Community may make provision for cooperation in Community research, technological development and demonstration with third countries or international organizations.

The detailed arrangements for such cooperation may be the subject of agreements between the Community and the third parties concerned, which shall be negotiated and concluded in accordance with Article 228.

ARTICLE 130n

The Community may set up joint undertakings or any other structure necessary for the efficient execution of Community research, technological development and demonstration **programmes.**

ARTICLE 130o

The Council, acting unanimously on a proposal from the Commission and after consulting the European Parliament and the Economic and Social Committee, shall adopt the provisions referred to in Article 130n.

The Council, acting in accordance with the procedure referred to in Article 189c and after consulting the Economic and Social Committee, shall adopt the provisions referred to in Articles 130j to l. Adoption of the supplementary programmes shall require the agreement of the Member States concerned.

ARTICLE 130p

At the beginning of each year the Commission shall send a report to the European Parliament and the Council. The report shall include information on research and technological development activities and the dissemination of results during the previous year, and the work programme for the current year.

Research and technological development policy

Although Euratom and the ECSC have both traditionally been involved in promoting research and technological development (R&D) within the atomic energy, and coal and steel industries respectively, it was not until the early 1980s that the EC began to develop a R&D policy of its own by encouraging European industry to develop coherent and long-term R&D strategies. Since then, the Community has set up and partially financed a variety of research programmes centred mainly around new technologies. Indeed, its emerging involvement in R&D was recognized in the SEA's insertion of a new Title dedicated to research and technological development and the subsequent confirmation by the TEU that the promotion of R&D is an area of EC activity (Article 3(m)).

q.v. Article 3(m) p. 65.

One of the Community's motives for promoting R&D in the 1980s was the belief that Europe's poor competitive position *vis-à-vis* the United States and Japan in world markets stemmed, in part at least, from the fact that Europe was seriously lagging behind its major competitors in the pursuit of new technologies. Indeed, of the 37 technological sectors of the future identified by the Commission in 1986, Europe was only dominant in two. This did not necessarily mean that Europe spent significantly less of its GDP on R&D, although large differences did exist between countries. Rather, it was believed that much of the R&D being undertaken in one EC member state often merely duplicated that being carried out in another. Hence, often valuable resources were being wasted. In addition, it was believed that many companies in the EC were too small to fund R&D projects.

To remedy the situation, the EC launched a variety of R&D programmes, providing the necessary finance through the adoption of global framework programmes of four to five years' duration. The essential aims of the programmes launched were the development of European expertise in the new computer-based technologies; the promotion of collaborative and pre-competitive research between companies; the dissemination of research results throughout the Community; the coordination of national R&D policies; and the development of R&D activities in the poorer member states. To these ends, ECU 3,800 million was made available for the period 1984–7. This was increased to ECU 5,400 million for the period 1987–91, and then to ECU 5,700 million for 1990–4. While seemingly large, these sums represent less than 5 per cent of total government spending on R&D within the EC.

The first EC programme to be launched was ESPRIT (European Strategic Programme for Research and Development in Information Technology) in early 1984. This seeks to promote research into micro-electronics and other areas of information technology. As with the majority of later programmes, under ESPRIT the EC helps finance cooperation between companies, research institutes and universities, on specific projects vetted by the Community. Initially, during its first phase, (1984–7) ESPRIT received ECU 1,500 million in assistance from the EC. However, this was increased slightly to ECU 1,660 million for the period 1987–91.

The second programme to be launched was BRITE (Basic Research in Industrial Technologies for Europe). This was set up in 1985 to encourage traditional industries to make optimum use of technological developments in improving production techniques and product reliability. While the thrust of the programme is to develop technologies common to more than one industry, a second element of the programme concentrates on flexible material products such as textiles.

The third major EC programme is RACE (Research and Development in Advanced Communications Technologies for Europe). As its title suggests, the programme, which began in 1987, is concerned with promoting research into telecommunications. As such, its primary aim is to establish an independent European communications network during the 1990s. In order to achieve this ECU 550 million were granted to the programme for the period 1987–91.

While these three programmes form the central core of the Community's R&D policy, the EC is also active in promoting several industry-specific projects and encouraging research on a more Europe-wide basis through the EUREKA (European Research Coordination Agency) programme. The Community's involvement in industry-specific projects is determined by the Framework Programme currently in operation. Consequently, the projects which the Community presently helps finance focus on the areas laid down in the Third R&D Framework Programme adopted in 1990. This identified 15 specific areas and resulted in both the continued funding of existing projects and the launching of new programmes. However, EC contributions to these projects are aimed at facilitating R&D coordination, rather than providing full funding. Thus, Community involvement is on a much lesser scale than with ESPRIT, BRITE and RACE. Among the programmes the EC is involved in are BAP (Biotechnology Action Programme), CUBE (Concertation Unit for Biotechnology in Europe), BRAIN (Basic Research in Adaptive Intelligence and Neurocomputing), BRIDGE (Biotechnology Research for Innovation, Development and Growth in Europe), FAST (Forecasting and Assessment in the Field of Science and Technology), and SPRINT (Strategic Programme for Innovation and Technology Transfer).

EUREKA, meanwhile, was launched in 1985 to encourage industry-led collaborative research projects aimed at producing hi-tech goods and services. Its membership, however, is not restricted to EC member states alone. Indeed, at present all the member states of EFTA as well as Turkey are members of the

q.v. EFTA pp. 479–85.

agency. While such a wide membership may suggest that more government funds are available for EUREKA-backed projects, most of the finance required has to be raised from private sources and international capital markets. Despite this, by mid-1991, the agency had managed to back 520 projects involving over ECU 8,000 million. The major projects supported by EUREKA have been JESSI (Joint European Submicron Silicon Initiative) and HDTV (High Definition Television).

With recession hitting the Community from the early 1990s onwards, the success of the EC's efforts to develop European industry's competitive position in international markets has been difficult to gauge. Indeed, given the size of the Community's R&D budget compared to that of member state governments overall, it can be argued that the EC could only hope to have a marginal impact in improving the market position of EC companies — a point apparent in the 1992 Delors II proposals for increasing the size of the Community budget. However, while EC programmes have helped industry to develop some new technologies and provided valuable research results, doubts have been raised concerning the effectiveness of certain projects, particularly the flagship EUREKA projects, JESSI and HDTV.[30] Consequently, the proposals put forward by the Commission for the Fourth R&D Framework Programme in 1992–3 proposed greater coordination of research activities within the Community and a concentration on generic technologies which might benefit a larger proportion of industry.[31] Such coordination is vital given that the funds to be made available for the new framework programme are unlikely to be increased to the ECU 13,100 million requested by the Commission.[32] However, if as noted earlier in the *Handbook*, the EC intends to pursue an industrial policy based on promoting competitiveness through modernization and the exploitation of new technologies, and if as proposed by the Commission, Community R&D policy is to be extended to cover areas such as transport systems, the urban environment, social exclusion and education, the substantial increase in funds the Commission has called for may have to be given serious consideration by the member states.

q.v.
industrial
policy pp.
215–18.

FURTHER READING

EC Commission, 'Research after Maastricht — an assessment — a strategy', *Bulletin of the European Communities*, Supplement 2/92.

EC Commission, *Second Commission Working Document concerning RTD Policy in the Community and the Fourth Framework Programme (1994–98) of Community RTD Activities*, COM(93)158 final, Brussels, 22 April 1993.

EC Commission, *Working Document of the Commission concerning the Fourth Framework Programme of Community Activities in the Field of Research and Technological Development 1994–8*, COM(92)406 final, Brussels, 9 October 1992.

Elizalde, J., 'Legal aspects of Community policy on research and technological development (RTD)', *Common Market Law Review*, vol. 29, no. 2, 1992, pp. 309–46.

30. 'Europe's technology policy', *The Economist*, 9 January 1993; 'Flagship on the rocks' *Financial Times*, 9 February 1993.

31. *Working Document of the Commission concerning the Fourth Framework Programme of Community activities in the field of research and technological development 1994–8*, COM(92)406 final, Brussels, 9 October 1992; *Second Commission Working Document concerning RTD Policy in the Community and the Fourth Framework Programme (1994–8) of Community RTD Activities*, COM(93)158 final, Brussels, 22 April 1993.

32. 'Brussels wants £10 billion for R&D', *Financial Times*, 23 April 1993.

Fels, X. *et al.* 'La télévision à haute définition: L'Europe dans la compétition mondiale', *Revue du Marché commun et de l'Union européenne*, special issue, no. 355, 1992.

Gaster, R., 'Research and technology policy', in Hurwitz, L. and Lequesne, C. (eds.), *The State of the European Community: Policies, institutions and debates in the transition years*, Longman, London, 1991, pp. 243–58.

Kay, N., 'Industrial collaborative activity and the completion of the Internal Market', *Journal of Common Market Studies*, vol. 29, no. 4, 1991, pp. 347–62.

Peterson, J., 'Technology policy in Europe: explaining the framework programme and EUREKA in theory and practice', *Journal of Common Market Studies*, vol. 29, no. 3, 1991, pp. 269–90

Sandholtz, W., 'ESPRIT and the politics of international collective action', *Journal of Common Market Studies*, vol. 30, no. 1, 1992, pp. 1–21.

Sharp, M., 'The Community and new technologies', in Lodge, J. (ed.), *The European Community and the Challenge of the Future*, 2nd edn, Pinter, London, 1993, pp. 200–23.

Sharp, M. and Pavitt, K., 'Technology policy in the 1990s: old trends and new realities', *Journal of Common Market Studies*, vol. 31, no. 2, 1993, pp. 129–51.

The Economist, 'Europe's Technology Policy', 9 January 1993, pp. 21–3.

Williams, R., 'The EC's technology programme as an engine for Integration', *Government and Opposition*, vol. 24, no. 2, 1989, pp. 158–76.

Environment

The provisions on the environment contained within Title XVI, like many of the provisions dealt with in this subdivision of the *Handbook*, are relative, if not total newcomers to the Treaty of Rome. Indeed, although the Community became active in legislating on the environment from the early 1970s onwards, it was not until the SEA that the EC gained any formal competences for action on environmental matters. Since then, with the introduction of the TEU, the Community has seen these competences extended, both qualitatively and quantitatively.

q.v. Environmental Policy pp. 235–9.

When originally introduced to the Treaty of Rome by the SEA, the provisions relating to the environment were found in Articles 130r–130t, contained in the then new Title VII. These were accompanied by a requirement that the Commission promote environmental protection when proposing Single Market legislation under Article 100a. While the provisions as amended have retained the same Article numbers under the TEU, they are now found in the new Title XVI. In addition, the environment is now explicitly mentioned in Article 3(k) as an area of EC activity.

q.v. Article 100a pp. 148–9.

q.v. Article 3(k) p. 65.

The most striking difference between the provisions on the environment introduced by the SEA and those which appear as a result of the TEU is qualitative. Under the SEA, the Community was only competent to pursue 'action' relating to the environment, whereas in the post-TEU Treaty of Rome, the Community is to have a true 'policy' on the environment. The objectives of Community policy are set out in Article 130r. These include, albeit in a slightly reworded form, the three objectives originally introduced into the Treaty of Rome by the SEA. These relate to the quality of the environment, the protection of human health, and the non-exploitation of natural resources. They are then supplemented by a fourth, objective inserted by the TEU, encouraging the Community to promote measures for dealing with global environmental problems.

The second paragraph of Article 130r expands on these aims by listing the aims of Community policy. This paragraph, while retaining all of the original aims introduced by the SEA, includes additional objectives inserted by the TEU. The original aims emphasize preventive action, the principle that the polluter pays and that environmental damage should be rectified at source. The TEU goes beyond these by introducing the precautionary principle, and by stressing the need for the high level of environmental protection sought to take into account regional economic diversity in Community. More significantly, the TEU strengthens the requirement of the Community to integrate environmental protection measures into the definition and implementation of other policies.[33]

While the first two paragraphs of Article 130r set out the objectives and aims of EC environmental policy, Article 130r, paragraph 3 presents a list of matters to be taken into consideration during the preparatory stages of Community policy. These are identical, except for a cosmetic change to the wording of line 3, to those contained in the existing provisions, and relate to scientific data, the regions, and the cost-benefit ratio of any measures. Paragraph 4, meanwhile, contains, with the addition of the word 'competent', the provisions for cooperation with third countries and international organizations previously contained in Article 130r(5). This replaces the subsidiarity clause relating to the environment now incorporated into the general subsidiarity provision covering all Community policies found in Article 3b.

q.v. Article 3b p. 65.

Whereas Article 130r sets out the essential nature of Community policy on the environment, Article 130s lays down the procedures by which action is to be taken and measures are to be adopted. Under the SEA decisions on what action the Community should pursue were taken by the Council on the basis on unanimity following consultation with the EP and EcoSoc, although the Council could if it wished vote on the basis of a qualified majority. Following the amendments to the Treaty introduced by the TEU, measures are now to be taken in accordance with the cooperation procedure as described in Article 189c. However, the existing rules introduced by the SEA will still apply to certain measures, such as planning and energy, as indicated in Article 130s(2). The implementation and financing of such measures are for the most part to be carried out by the member states (Article 130s(4)).

q.v. Article 189c pp. 304–5.

While the thrust of a Community policy is to ensure EC-wide standards, the provisions of Article 130s(5) and Article 130t make two exceptions to this rule. Firstly, with the introduction of Article 130s(5), a member state may for financial reasons be granted a derogation from a measure or receive financial support to help implement it. This is specifically aimed at assisting the less-developed regions of the Community in coping with the costs of Community policy. Secondly, in line with the original provision under the SEA, Article 130t allows a member state to introduce more stringent environmental measures provided that they are compatible with the Treaty and, under the TEU, are communicated to the Commission.

---

33. In Declaration 20, the Commission undertakes to take full account of the environmental impact of any proposals it puts forward (see pp. 435–6).

Title XVI Environment

ARTICLE 130r

1. Community **policy** *on the environment shall contribute to pursuit of the following objectives:*

— *preserving, protecting and improving* the quality of the environment;
— *protecting human health;*
— *prudent and rational utilization of natural resources;*
— **promoting measures at international level to deal with regional or world-wide environmental problems.**

2. Community **policy** *on the environment shall* **aim at a high level of protection taking into account the diversity of situations in the various regions of the Community. It** shall be based on *the precautionary principle and on* the principles that preventative action should be taken, that environmental damage should as a priority be rectified at source and that the polluter should pay. Environmental protection requirements **must be integrated into the definition and implementation** *of other Community policies.*

In this context, harmonization measures answering these requirements shall include, where appropriate, a safeguard clause allowing Member States to take provisional measures, for non-economic environmental reasons, subject to a Community inspection procedure.

3. In preparing its **policy** *on the* environment, the Community shall take account of:

— available scientific and technical data;
— environmental conditions in the various regions of the Community;
— the potential benefits and costs of action or lack of action;
— the economic and social development of the Community as a whole and the balanced development of its region.

4. Within their respective spheres of competence, the Community and the Member States shall cooperate with third countries and with the **competent** *international organizations. The arrangements for Community cooperation may be the subject of agreements between the Community and the third parties concerned, which shall be negotiated and concluded in accordance with Article 228.*

The previous subparagraph shall be without prejudice to Member States' competence to negotiate in international bodies and to conclude international agreements.

ARTICLE 130s

1. The Council, acting **in accordance with the procedure referred to in Article 189c** and after consulting the Economic and Social Committee, shall decide what action is to be taken by the Community *in* **order to achieve the objective referred to in Article 130r.**

2. By way of derogation from the decision-making procedure provided for in paragraph 1 and without prejudice to Article 100a, the Council, acting unanimously on a proposal from the Commission and after consulting the European Parliament and the Economic and Social Committee, shall adopt:

— **provisions primarily of a fiscal nature;**
— **measures concerning town and country planning, land use with the exception of waste management and measures of a general nature, and management of water resources;**
— **measures significantly affecting a Member State's choice between different energy sources and the general structure of its energy supply.**

The Council may, under the conditions laid down in the preceding

subparagraph, define those matters referred to in this paragraph on which decisions are to be taken by a qualified majority.

3. In other areas, general action programmes setting out priority objectives to be attained shall be adopted by the Council, acting in accordance with the procedure referred to in Article 189b and after consulting the Economic and Social Committee.

The Council, acting under the terms of paragraph 1 or paragraph 2 according to the case, shall adopt the measures necessary for the implementation of these programmes.

4. Without prejudice to certain measures of a Community nature, the Member States shall finance and implement the environment policy.

5. Without prejudice to the principle that the polluter should pay, if a measure based on the provisions of paragraph 1 involves costs deemed disproportionate for the public authorities of a Member State, the Council shall, in the act adopting that measure, lay down appropriate provisions in the form of:

— temporary derogations and/or
— financial support from the Cohesion Fund to be set up no later than 31 December 1993 pursuant to Article 130d.

ARTICLE 130t

The protective measures adopted pursuant to Article 130s shall not prevent any Member State from maintaining or introducing more stringent protective measures. *Such measures* **must be** compatible with this Treaty. **They shall be notified to the Commission.**

Environmental policy

As indicated above, the Treaty of Rome, when signed, made no specific provision for the development of a Community environmental policy. Instead, the EC had to wait until the introduction of the SEA in 1987 before it was granted an explicit competence to pursue action on the environment. Nevertheless, from the early 1970s onwards the Community began to play an active role in producing legislation to protect the environment. As such, the inclusion of a Title dedicated to the environment in the Treaty of Rome as it now stands is more an acknowledgement of the status quo than a positive step forward in providing the Community with a new area of competence.

Increased awareness of the environment in the 1960s and 1970s forced governments and international organizations alike to address such issues as pollution control and environmental protection. In 1972 the first United Nations Conference on the Environment took place and was soon followed in the same year by an agreement among the then six heads of state and government of the EC to lay down certain principles regarding future Community action on the environment. These principles required the Community to treat environmental issues at source; ensure that the polluter pays; promote research into environmental protection; and encourage the coordination and harmonization of national policies. As such, these principles were the forerunners of those now enshrined in Article 130r(2) of the amended Treaty of Rome. Somewhat surprisingly, given the economic pressures the Community came under in the 1970s, the agreement on a set of principles was accompanied by Community action with the establishment in 1973 of the first in a series of five Environmental Action Programmes, the most recent of which came into operation in 1993. The first four of these programmes (1973, 1977, 1983 and 1987) dealt with a wide variety of areas and were often supplemented by Community involvement in the signing of multilateral environmental conventions.

The actual scope of Community action on the environment is large with over 300 directives, regulations and decisions currently in force covering issues from pollution control to wildlife protection. High on the agenda is pollution. Here the Community has been active in reducing levels of lead in petrol; restricting harmful emissions from many vehicles through legislation on the compulsory fitting of catalytic converters to certain types of new cars and vans; limiting emissions from power stations; and reducing the use of chlorofluorocarbons (CFCs) in an attempt to prevent further damage to the ozone layer. In the case of CFCs, the Community has actually gone beyond its obligations under international agreements, such as the Vienna Convention on the Protection of the Ozone Layer (1985) and the follow-up Montreal Protocol (1987), by committing itself to reduce emissions of CFCs by 85 per cent by 2000.[34] Furthermore, the Commission in June 1993 proposed that the Community phase out hydrochlorofluorocarbons by 2014, 16 years earlier than agreed under the Montreal Protocol. In addition, in an attempt to reduce further the negative impact the emission of harmful gases has on the atmosphere, the Community has been discussing since 1991 Commission proposals for the introduction of a carbon/energy tax.

q.v. carbon/ energy tax pp. 370–2.

Early Community legislation often dealt with water pollution, with the Community adopting several directives in the 1970s concerning drinking and bathing water, the latter of which has led to numerous battles between the Commission and member states over the cleanliness of beaches. Under pollution control, the Community has also been active in legislating on waste management. As a result legislation has been introduced to limit the levels of chemicals which can be discharged into Community waters; on the disposal of sewage; on the transportation and disposal of industrial and radioactive waste; and on the recycling of waste materials.

Beyond matters related to pollution control, the Community has been active in protecting endangered species whether they be of the flora or fauna kind. As such the Community is a signatory to, among others, the 1974 Washington Convention on Trade in Endangered Species (CITES). Consequently, the EC has introduced legislation protecting migratory birds and following public pressure banned the import of whale products and certain pelts.

Although the legislation which has been adopted as part of the Community's first four Environmental Action Programmes has essentially been reactive in

---

34. However, the derogations granted to Spain and Portugal under a 1988 Council Directive on emission limitations are not to be affected by any future Community legislation according to the Declaration 11 (see p. 433).

nature, the Community has made an attempt to reduce the potential future impact on the environment of projects aimed at improving the Community's industrial base and infrastructure. As a result, all major construction projects in the EC are subject to an Environmental Impact Assessment before they may proceed. In addition, the Community proposes to set up its own European Environment Agency (EEA) responsible for providing reliable scientific data on the environment, thus enabling a more effective control over environmental problems, and providing a sounder scientific base for new legislation. Furthermore, in 1993 steps were taken to set up a voluntary Community-wide Eco-Management and Audit Scheme (EMAS) designed to promote responsible environmental management in industry.[35]

The 5th Environmental Action Programme (1993–2000),[36] while recognizing the importance of the measures and programmes already adopted by the Community, has been designed so that EC action on the environment becomes more proactive, embracing the thesis of 'sustainable development' proposed by the 1987 Brundland Report of the World Commission on Environment and Development. As such, the emphasis of future environmental policy will be placed on dealing with the root causes of environmental problems rather than responding to problems as they occur. Consequently, the aim of the programme will be to raise public awareness of the environment and develop more environmentally friendly attitudes among industry, business and the general public.

The proposals put forward as part of the new programme vary. They involve improving resource management within industry; decreasing demand and thus emissions for pollutants such as carbon and sulphur dioxide; curbing demand for transport and encouraging greater use of public rather than private transport. Furthermore, the programme includes proposals for minimizing the impact of agriculture on the environment by encouraging the use of more environmentally friendly farming methods, and proposals for improving the management of mass tourism to prevent its adverse environmental impact.

However, the new emphasis on proactive measures does not exclude the consolidation of existing measures and activities. Indeed, legislation is proposed which would set targets for further reductions in the emission of pollutants into the atmosphere and for acceptable pollution levels in water sources. Furthermore, improved waste management is sought through recycling and the safe disposal of dangerous substances, while measures are proposed which concentrate on improving the urban environment through better planning and a more efficient allocation of resources. Beyond these proposed measures, the programme also encourages further action in the effective management of risks and accidents. This is to include additional legislation on health and safety; the establishment of European task forces to deal with environmental accidents; and the development of the eco-labelling system introduced in June 1993.

---

35. 'EC agrees scheme for voluntary ecological audits', *Financial Times*, 24 March 1993; 'The green time bomb', *Financial Times*, 31 March 1993.

36. *'Towards Sustainability'* — *A European Community Programme of Policy and Action in Relation to the Environment and Sustainable Development*, COM(92)23 final, 3 Vols., Brussels, 27 March 1992.

Beyond legislation, the new programme also recognizes the opportunities involved in using other instruments to achieve the sustainability of the environment envisaged. Such instruments centre around research and data availability, and integrating environmental costs and risks into all areas of economic activity. However, it is the emphasis on creating public awareness of society's responsibilities towards the environment which has the potential of being the most significant contributory factor in the preservation of the environment. Nevertheless, since the programme was launched, the Commission has also been active in promoting discussions on remedying environmental damage, thus maintaining the development of the traditional responsive policy approach.[37]

Unlike many policy areas, the environment is one of few which enjoys widespread support for action at the Community level. Indeed, when in the aftermath of the 'No' vote in the first Danish referendum on the TEU the environment was suggested as an area of EC competence which could be handed back to national governments, the idea was quickly dismissed out of hand. Consequently, it is not surprising that the TEU should have upgraded the environment to an area of Community policy. However, despite the clear acceptance of the need to pursue measures to protect the environment at the European and international levels, the general reluctance of the Community to avoid being regarded as over-active and interfering may result in environmental matters not receiving the attention at the EC level many would deem vital.

FURTHER READING

Aubin, A., *La Communauté européenne face à la pollution atmosphérique*, edns Apogée, Rennes, 1993.

EC Commission, *A Community Strategy to Limit Carbon Dioxide Emissions and Improve Energy Efficiency*, COM(92)246 final, Brussels, 1 June 1992.

EC Commission, *European Community Environmental Legislation*, 7 vols., OOPEC, Luxembourg, 1992.

EC Commission, *Green Paper on Remedying Environmental Damage*, COM(93)47 final, Brussels, 14 May 1993.

EC Council, *Resolution (93/C 138/01) of the Council and the Representatives of the Governments of the Member States, Meeting within the Council of 1 February 1993 on a Community Programme of policy and Action in Relation to the Environment and Sustainable Development*, OJC 138, 17 May 1993.

EC Commission, 'The climate challenge — economic aspects of the Community's strategy for limiting CO_2 emissions', *European Economy*, no. 51, 1992.

EC Commission, *'Towards Sustainability'* — A

European Community Programme of Policy and Action in Relation to the Environment and Sustainable Development, COM(92)23 final, 3 vols., Brussels, 27 March 1992.

EcoSoc, *Environment and the Single Market*, EcoSoc, Brussels, 1991.

Epiney, A. and Furrer, A., 'Umweltschutz nach Maastricht: Ein Europa der drei Geschwindigkeiten', *Europarecht*, vol. 27, no. 4, 1992, pp. 369–408.

Feeley, M. S. and Gilhuly, P. M., 'Green law-making: a primer on the European Community's environmental legislative process', *Vanderbilt Journal of Transnational Law*, vol. 24, no. 4, 1991, pp. 653–88.

Freestone, D., 'European Community environmental policy and law', *Journal of Law and Society*, vol. 18, no. 1, 1991, pp. 135–54.

Hagland, P., 'Environmental Policy', in Hurwitz, L. and Lequesne, C. (eds.), *The State of the European Community: Policies, institutions and debates in the transition years*, Longman, London, 1991, pp. 259–72.

Haigh, N. *EEC Environmental Policy and Britain*, 2nd

37. EC Commission, *Green Paper on Remedying Environmental Damage*, COM(93)47 final, Brussels, 14 May 1993.

edn, Longman, London, 1990.

Haigh, N., *Manual of Environmental Policy: The EC and Britain*, Longman, London, 1992.

Hassan, J., 'Environment policy', in McDonald, F. and Dearden, S. (eds.), *European Economic Integration*, Longman, London, 1992, pp. 118–30.

Höll, O. (ed.), *Environmental Cooperation in Europe: The political dimension*, Westview, Oxford, 1993.

House of Lords, *A Community Eco-Audit Scheme*, Select Committee on the European Communities, 12th Report, 1991–2, HL-42, 8 December 1992.

House of Lords, *Environmental Aspects of the Reform of the Common Agricultural Policy*, Select Committee on the European Communities, 14th Report, 1992–3, HL-45, 16 December 1992.

House of Lords, *Fifth Environmental Action Programme: Integration of Community policies*, Select Committee on the European Communities, 8th Report, 1992–3, HL-27, 27 October 1992.

House of Lords, *Implementation and Enforcement of Environmental Legislation*, Select Committee on the European Communities, 9th Report, 1991–2, HL-53, 10 March 1992.

Huelshoff, M. G. and Pfeiffer, T., 'Environmental policy in the EC: neo-functionalist sovereignty transfer or neo-realist gate-keeping', *International Journal*, vol. 47, no. 1, 1992, pp. 136–58.

Jachtenfuchs, M. and Struebel, M. (eds.) *Environmental Policy in Europe: Assessment, challenges and perspectives*. Nomos Verlagsgesellschaft, Baden-Baden, 1992.

Johnson, S. and Corcelle, G., *The Environmental Policy of the European Communities*, Graham and Trotman, London, 1989.

Judge, D. (ed.), *A Green Dimension for the European Community: Political issues and processes*, Frank Cass, London, 1993.

Kramer, L., 'Environmental Protection and Article 30 EEC Treaty', *Common Market Law Review*, vol. 30, no. 1, 1993, pp. 111–43.

Liberatore, A., 'Problems of transnational policymaking: environmental policy in the *European Community*', *European Journal of Political Research*, vol. 19, no. 2–3, 1991, pp. 281–305.

Liefferink, J.D., Mol, A. P. J. and Lowe, P. O. (eds). *European Integration and Environmental Policy*, Belhaven Press, London, 1993.

Sola, N. F., 'Incidence interne de la participation de la Communauté européenne aux accords multilatéreaux de protection de l'environnement', *Revue du Marché commun et de l'Union européenne*, no. 363, 1992, pp. 793–806.

Thieffry, P., 'Les nouveaux instruments juridiques de la politique communautaire de l'environnement', *Revue trimestrielle de droit européen*, vol. 28, no. 4, 1992, pp. 669–85.

Thomson, I. 'The environment and Europe — bibliographical review', *European Access*, 1991/6, pp. 36–46.

Verhoeve, G. *et al.*, *Maastricht and the Environment*, Institute for European Environmental Policy, London, 1992.

Wagenbaur, R. 'Regulating the European environment — The EC experience', *University of Chicago Legal Forum*, 1992, pp. 17–40.

Wurzel, R., 'Environmental policy', in Lodge, J. (ed.), *The European Community and the Challenge of the Future*, 2nd edn, Pinter, London, 1993, pp. 178–99

iii. Development and association policies

The last Title of Part Three (130u–130y) and the whole of Part Four (Articles 131–136a) of the amended Treaty of Rome are dedicated to the EC's relations with the developing countries of the world. While the provisions of Article 130u–130y can be applied to any country, the Treaty imposes restrictions on which countries may become associates under Part Four. Essentially, only those countries or territories which belong to a member state are eligible. This special status is also reflected in the fact that the provisions for association contained in Part Four date from the founding of the Community. Those relating to Development Cooperation in Title XVII, however, were only inserted into the Treaty by the TEU. This does not mean to say the Community has neglected those developing countries not covered by the criteria for relations under Part Four. Rather, the insertion of Articles 130u–130y provides a formal Treaty base for existing policy.

Development cooperation

The aims of Community policy, as laid down in Title XVII, are to foster sustained economic and social development in developing countries, particularly in the disadvantaged countries of the world; to promote the integration of these countries into the world economy; and to campaign against poverty. Moreover, the Community is to help develop and consolidate democracy and contribute towards the respect for human rights and fundamental freedoms. This is to be done while complying with international commitments, such as those entered into within the framework of the United Nations (Article 130u). Furthermore, Article 130v requires the Community to take into account the objectives set out in Article 130u when implementing other EC policies which may affect developing countries. This suggests that the TEU is providing the EC with extensive new competences for conducting relations with developing countries. However, the reference in Article 130w to the African, Caribbean and Pacific (ACP) countries and the ACP-EEC Convention implies that cooperation available under Title XVII may not be as extensive as that pursued with the ACP countries.

q.v. ACP-EEC Convention pp. 242–5.

The procedure for adopting measures to further the objectives of development cooperation is laid down in Article 130w. This involves the Council acting in accordance with the cooperation procedure as described in Article 189c. Where necessary, appropriate measures may be adopted in the form of multiannual programmes and involve contributions from the European Investment Bank. However, it is made clear in Articles 130u(1) and 130x that Community action is to complement not replace the policies pursued by the member states. In particular, the provisions of the Title emphasize the coordination of national and Community policies. Moreover, Article 130y urges the EC and the member states to cooperate with third countries and international organizations in promoting development. However, here the right of member states to act unilaterally is stressed.

q.v. European Investment Bank pp. 313–15.

Title XVII Development cooperation

ARTICLE 130u

1. Community policy in the sphere of development cooperation, which shall be complementary to the policies pursued by the Member States, shall foster:

— **the sustainable economic and social development of the developing countries, and more particularly the most disadvantaged among them;**
— **the smooth and gradual integration of the developing countries into the world economy;**
— **the campaign against poverty in the developing countries.**

2. Community policy in this area shall contribute to the general objective of developing and consolidating democracy and the rule of law, and to that of respecting human rights and fundamental freedoms.

3. The Community and the Member States shall comply with the commitments and take account of the objectives they have approved in the context of the United Nations and other competent international organizations.

ARTICLE 130v   The Community shall take account of the objectives referred to in Article 130u in the policies that it implements which are likely to affect developing countries.

ARTICLE 130w   1. Without prejudice to the other provisions in this Treaty the Council, acting in accordance with the procedure referred to in Article 189c, shall adopt the measures necessary to further the objectives referred to in Article 130u. Such measures may take the form of multiannual programmes.

2. The European Investment Bank shall contribute, under the terms laid down in its Statute, to the implementation of the measures referred to in paragraph 1.

3. The provisions of this Article shall not affect cooperation with the African, Caribbean and Pacific countries in the framework of the ACP-EEC Convention.

ARTICLE 130x   1. The Community and the Member States shall coordinate their policies on development cooperation and shall consult each other on their aid programmes, including in international organizations and during international conferences. They may undertake joint action. Member States shall contribute if necessary to the implementation of Community aid programmes.

2. The Commission may take any useful initiative to promote the coordination referred to in paragraph 1.

ARTICLE 130y   Within their respective spheres of competence, the Community and the Member States shall cooperate with third countries and with the competent international organizations. The arrangements for Community cooperation may be the subject of arrangements between the Community and the third parties concerned, which shall be negotiated and concluded in accordance with Article 228.

The previous paragraph shall be without prejudice to Members States' competence to negotiate in international bodies and to conclude international agreements.

Development and cooperation policy

Although the insertion of Title XVII into the Treaty of Rome by the TEU finally provides the Community with an explicit competence to formulate and implement an EC development and cooperation policy to complement the policies of the individual member states, this does not mean to say that the Community has traditionally neglected the less-developed regions of the world. Indeed, as noted above, when the Treaty of Rome was signed provision was made for the establishment of close economic and political ties with the overseas countries and territories of the original member states. However, as many of these countries gained full independence new relationships had to be developed. Consequently, the Community has developed an array of multilateral, bilateral and regional agreements which cover almost all developing countries in the world.

As a result of these agreements the EC currently distributes in excess of ECU 3 billion of aid annually to developing countries throughout the world and provides these countries with access to one of the most important export markets in the world. Beyond this, the Community has also been one of the main providers of emergency humanitarian and relief aid throughout the world, establishing in 1992 its own European Office for Urgent Humanitarian Aid to coordinate more effectively disaster relief operations. Equally, the Community has been active in contributing to the work of various United Nations organizations such as the Conference on Trade and Development (UNCTAD), the Industrial Development Organization (UNIDO) and the World Food Programme (WFP). Such contributions have been accompanied by the Community's own food-aid programmes and support for several non-governmental organizations working in developing countries.

However, the main vehicle to date for promoting Community cooperation with developing countries has been the series of Yaoundé and Lomé conventions signed by the EC and various countries from Africa, the Caribbean and the Pacific region, commonly referred to as the ACP countries. Although technically association agreements concluded on the basis of Article 238, the conventions form the central plank of Community action in promoting cooperation with developing countries. The first two conventions, Yaoundé I and Yaoundé II, were signed in 1963 and 1969 respectively and involved the granting of trade concessions and aid to over 18 countries. However, it was not until 1975 and the signing of the first Lomé Conventions that the Community became actively involved with the development of the signatory countries. Since Lomé I was signed, the number of developing countries which have become part of the Lomé system of cooperation has risen significantly. Forty-nine developing countries signed Lomé I (1975), 58 Lomé II (1980), 66 Lomé III (1984), and 69 Lomé IV (1989) (see Figure 8).[38]

q.v. Article 238 p. 340.

The essence of EC development cooperation under the Lomé conventions has been and remains the economic development of the signatory countries through the granting of aid for structural adjustment and the promotion of trade. For the period 1990–5 the total amount of aid allocated to the Lomé countries was set at ECU 12 000 million (see Box 11). This aid, which is administered through the European Development Fund (EDF), covers infrastructure projects of both a national and regional nature; projects aimed at economic diversification; and technical assistance in a variety of forms. Alongside the medium- to long-term aims of promoting the economic development of the ACP countries, the Lomé system also provides for more immediate short-term assistance from the Community in the form of emergency and refugee aid.

On the trade side, EC assistance comes in a variety of forms. Firstly, the Community grants to the ACP countries non-reciprocal trade preferences. That

38. *Fourth ACP-EEC Convention signed at Lomé on 15 December 1989*, OJL 229, 17 August 1991. The following ACP countries were signatories: Angola, Antigua and Barbuda, Bahamas, Barbados, Belize, Bénin, Botswana, Burkina Faso, Burundi, Cameroon, Cape Verde, Central African Republic, Comoros, Congo, Côte d'Ivoire, Djibouti, Dominica, Dominican Republic, Ethiopia, Fiji, Gabon, Gambia, Ghana, Grenada, Guinea, Guinea-Bissau, Equatorial Guinea, Guyana, Haïti, Jamaica, Kenya, Kiribati, Lesotho, Liberia, Madagascar, Malawi, Mali, Mauritania, Mauritius, Mozambique, Niger, Nigeria, Uganda, Papua New Guinea, Rwanda, Saint Christopher and Nevis, Saint Lucia, Saint Vincent and the Grenadines, Western Samoa, São Tomé and Príncipe, Senegal, Seychelles, Sierra Leone, Solomon Islands, Somalia, Sudan, Suriname, Swaziland, Tanzania, Chad, Togo, Tonga, Trinidad and Tobago, Tuvalu, Vanuatu, Zaire, Zambia, Zimbabwe. Eritrea became the 70th signatory in October 1993.

Figure 8. Lomé countries

(Source: European Communities, *The Courier*, No. 142, Nov–Dec 1993)

is, the ACP countries enjoy preferential access to EC markets for their exports yet do not have to grant EC goods equal access to their own markets. Secondly, the EC contributes to two stabilizing funds, STABEX and SYSMIN, which provide cash transfers to offset losses in export earnings on various agricultural and mining exports where an ACP country depends heavily on such revenue. Thirdly, under the Lomé conventions, the EC agrees to purchase a minimum amount of sugar from the ACP countries at a guaranteed price, sugar being one of the most significant export products of several ACP states.

On the political side, EC involvement with the ACP countries in promoting their economic development has been increased through the creation of institutions to promote political dialogue and cooperation. These mirror in

Box 11.
Lomé IV — financial
resources

Lomé IV (1990–1995)	million ECU
EDF grants	6 215
Structural adjustment	1 150
STABEX	1 500
SYSMIN	480
Emergency aid	350
Refugee aid	100
Interest rate subsidies	280
Risk capital	825
EIB loans	1 200
TOTAL	12 000

structure the institutions of the EC itself in that there exists an ACP Council of Ministers, comprising EC and ACP ministers as well as senior members of the EC Commission, a Committee of Ambassadors which supports the Council in its work; and an EC–ACP Consultative Assembly with members drawn from the EP and the parliaments of the ACP states. However, the role of the Assembly is entirely consultative. Decision-making powers rest entirely with the Council of Ministers. Here decisions on all matters relating to EC–ACP relations are taken on the basis of a unanimous vote.

In addition to the series of Lomé conventions, the Community also has strong relations with several other developing countries. However, these tend to be concentrated around the Mediterranean. Thus, the Community has concluded cooperation agreements with the countries of the Maghreb (Algeria, Morocco and Tunisia) and the Mashreq (Egypt, Jordan, Lebanon and Syria). The aim of these is to promote closer relations with the EC as well as sustained economic development. Indeed, a fourth financial aid package was successfully negotiated in 1991 following the end of the Gulf War, reflecting the willingness of the EC to increase relations with the region, not only in an attempt to restore effective relations in the aftermath of the Gulf War, but also in an attempt to promote even further the economic development of these countries where population growth threatens to lead to increased immigration into the EC.

*q.v.
Maghreb
and
Mashreq
pp. 494–7.*

Relations with other developing countries throughout the world, although evolving, are not as extensive, concentrating more on trade matters. Nevertheless, initial Commission proposals put forward in 1992 in response to the inclusion of Title XVII in the amended Treaty of Rome set out quantitative as well as qualitative steps forward to be taken by the Community in developing a European development cooperation policy.[39] These include increased humanitarian aid; technical assistance; refugee aid; increased political dialogue; economic cooperation; assistance for environmental measures; and a reform of the Community's Common Agricultural Policy (CAP) so as to promote opportunities for trade. However, although such a policy is intended to be implemented globally, the Commission does single out certain areas for particular attention. These

*q.v. CAP
pp. 101–5.*

39. *Development Cooperation Policy in the Run Up to 2000. The Community's relations with the developing countries viewed in the context of political union*, SEC(92)915, 16 September 1992.

include sub-Saharan Africa and the Mediterranean, areas where the Community already has strong ties but where additional assistance is deemed necessary; Latin America; and Asia.

In many respects the new provisions contained in Articles 130u–130y inserted into the Treaty of Rome by the TEU reflect the content of existing Community policy towards the signatories of the Lomé conventions. Thus, in addition to sanctioning existing practice, they encourage the EC to develop similar degrees of cooperation with other developing countries. However, the extent to which the Community is likely to promote closer cooperation is likely to be conditioned by financial constraints. Nevertheless, by gaining an explicit competence to formulate and implement a policy on development cooperation the Community's existing efforts in this direction and the interests of developing countries in maintaining close ties with the EC are at least safeguarded.

FURTHER READING

Davenport, M., *Europe: 1992 and the Developing World*, Westview, Oxford, 1992.

Dearden, S., 'The European Community and the Third World', in McDonald, F. and Dearden, S. (eds.), *European Economic Integration*, Longman, London, 1992, pp. 159–74.

EC Commission, *Development*, periodically.

EC Commission, *Development Cooperation Policy in the Run Up to 2000. The Community's Relations with the Developing Countries Viewed in the Context of Political Union*, SEC(92)915, 16 September 1992.

EC Commission, *The Courier*, bi-monthly.

EC Commission, *The European Community's Relations to French Overseas Departments, European Autonomous Regions, Independent Countries within EC Boundaries, and Overseas Countries and Territories*, Background Report ISEC/B20/93, London, 28 June 1993.

EC Commission, *The Run Up to 2000: Identifying priority areas for the coordination of development cooperation policies between the Community and the Member States*, COM(93)123 final, Brussels, 24 March 1993.

Edye, D. and Lintner, V., *The Lomé Convention: New dawn or neo-colonialism?*, University of North London Press, London, 1992.

Flaescg-Mougin, C. and Raux, J., 'From Lomé III to Lomé IV: EC–ACP Relations', in: Hurwitz, L. and Lequesne, C. (eds.), *The State of the European Community: Policies, institutions and debates in the transition years*, Longman, London, 1991, pp. 343–57.

Grilli, E.R., *The European Community and the Developing Countries*, Cambridge University Press, Cambridge, 1992.

Grilli, E. R. and Riess, M., 'EC Aid to associated countries: distribution and determinants', *Review of World Economics*, vol. 128, no. 2, 1992, pp. 202–15.

Gruhn, I. V., 'Eurafrica reconsidered: the road beyond Lomé', *Mediterranean Quarterly*, vol. 3, no. 3, 1992, pp. 55–76.

Handouni, S., 'Les tentatives d'intégration des pays du Maghreb face à l'élargissement de la Communauté économique européenne', *Études Internationales*, vol. 23, no. 12, 1992, pp. 319–48.

Hewitt, A., 'Development Assistance Policy and the ACP', in Lodge, J. (ed.), *The European Community and the Challenge of the Future*, 2nd edn, Pinter, London, 1993, pp. 300–11.

House of Lords, *EC Development Aid*, Select Committee on the European Communities, 21st Report, 1992–3, HL-86, 11 May 1993.

Journal of *Common Market Studies*, 'Special issue on Europe 1992 and the developing countries', vol. 29, no. 2, 1990.

Maganza, G., *La Convention de Lomé*, edns de l'Université de Bruxelles, Brussels, 1990.

Notzold, J., 'Lomé IV: a chance for black Africa's return to the world economy?, *Aussenpolitik*, vol. 41, no. 2, 1990, pp. 181–92.

Nuscheler, F. and Schmuck, O. (eds.), *Die Süd-Politik der EG; Europas Entwicklungsverantwortung in der veränderten Weltordnung*, Europa Union Verlag, Bonn, 1992.

Weidmann, K., *Die EG-Entwicklungspolitik in Afrika*, Nomos Verlagsgesellschaft, Baden-Baden, 1991.

Weidmann, K. (ed.), *EC Agricultural Policy and Development Cooperation*, Nomos Verlagsgesellschaft, Baden-Baden, 1992.

Part Four: overseas countries and territories

Part Four of the Treaty of Rome contains provisions for the association of overseas countries and territories (OCT) with the Community (Articles 131–136a). With the exception of Article 136a, the Articles have been part of the Treaty of Rome since it was signed in 1957. Their inclusion reflected French demands that the Treaty should allow for the benefits of the Community to be extended to Algeria and France's overseas *départements*. The countries and territories eligible for association were then listed in Annex IV to the Treaty of Rome.[40] With the accession of the United Kingdom to the Community in 1973 this list was extended, although since 1957 the list has shortened as more territories have gained independence and become signatories to the Lomé Conventions.

The purpose of association under Part Four, not to be confused with association under Article 238, is to promote the economic and social development of the countries and territories eligible and to establish close economic relations between them and the Community (Article 131). The objectives of association are laid down in Article 132. These include equal trade status to member states; equal right to participate in tenders and supplies for investment financed by the Community; and equal rights of establishment as laid down in the Treaty of Rome. On trade, provision is made for customs duties to be abolished on imports from the overseas countries and territories and for each overseas country and territory to levy customs duties which meet the needs of their development and industrialization or produce revenue for their budgets. Nevertheless, these duties are to be progressively reduced (Article 133). Moreover, where they cause deflections of trade to the detriment of an EC member state, the Commission may be called upon to propose measures to remedy the situation (Article 134). Finally, association is to involve the free movement of workers between the Community and the overseas countries and territories subject to provisions relating to public health, public security and public policy (Article 135). The final two Articles of Part Four provide for the continued regulation of relations between the Community and the overseas countries and territories (Article 136) and for the extension of Articles 131–136 to Greenland (Article 136a).[41]

q.v. Article 238 p. 340.

Part Four Association of the overseas countries and territories

ARTICLE 131

The Member States agree to associate with the Community the non-European countries and territories which have special relations with Belgium, Denmark, France, Italy, the Netherlands and the United Kingdom. These countries and

---

40. The countries and territories to which the provisions of Articles 131–136a currently apply are: Saint Pierre and Miquelon, Mayotte, New Caledonia and Dependencies, French Polynesia, Wallis and Futuna Islands, French Southern and Antarctic Territories, Aruba, Netherlands Antilles (Bonaire, Curaçao, Saba, Saint Eustatius, Saint Martin), Anguilla, Cayman Islands, Falkland Islands, South Georgia and the Sandwich Islands, Turks and Caicos Islands, British Virgin Islands, Montserrat, Pitcairn, St Helena and Dependencies, British Antarctic Territory, British Indian Ocean Territory, Greenland. See *Council Decision 91/482/EEC of 25 July 1991 on the association of the overseas countries and territories with the European Economic Community*, OJL 263, 19 September 1991.

41. Article 136a was added to the Treaty of Rome by Article 3 of the *Treaty amending, with regard to Greenland, the Treaties establishing the European Communities*, OJL 29, 1 February 1985.

territories (hereinafter called the 'countries and territories') are listed in Annex IV to this Treaty.

The purpose of association shall be to promote the economic and social development of the countries and territories and to establish close economic relations between them and the Community as a whole.

In accordance with the principles set out in the Preamble to this Treaty, association shall serve primarily to further the interests and prosperity of the inhabitants of these countries and territories in order to lead them to the economic, social and cultural development to which they aspire.

ARTICLE 132

Association shall have the following objectives:

1. Member States shall apply to their trade with the countries and territories the same treatment as they accord each other pursuant to this Treaty.

2. Each country or territory shall apply to its trade with Member States and with the other countries and territories the same treatment as that which it applies to the European State with which it has special relations.

3. The Member States shall contribute to the investments required for the progressive development of these countries and territories.

4. For investments financed by the Community, participation in tenders and supplies shall be open on equal terms to all natural and legal persons who are nationals of a Member State or of one of the countries and territories.

5. In relations between Member States and the countries and territories the right of establishment of nationals and companies or firms shall be regulated in accordance with the provisions and procedures laid down in the Chapter relating to the right of establishment and on a non-discriminatory basis, subject to any special provisions laid down pursuant to Article 136.

ARTICLE 133

1. Customs duties on imports into the Member States of goods originating in the countries and territories shall be completely abolished in conformity with the progressive abolition of customs duties between Member States in accordance with the provisions of this Treaty.

2. Customs duties on imports into each country or territory from Member States or from the other counties or territories shall be progressively abolished in accordance with the provisions of Articles 12,13,14,15 and 17.

3. The countries and territories may, however, levy customs duties which meet the needs of their development and industrialisation or produce revenue for their budgets.

The duties referred to in the preceding subparagraph shall nevertheless be progressively reduced to the level of those imposed on imports of products from the Member State with which each country or territory has special relations. The percentages and the timetable of the reductions provided for under this Treaty shall apply to the differences between the duty imposed on a product coming from the Member State which has special relations with the country or territory concerned and the duty imposed on the same product coming from within the Community on entry into the importing country or territory.

4. Paragraph 2 shall not apply to countries and territories which, by reason of the particular international obligations by which they are bound, already apply a non-discriminatory customs tariff when this Treaty enters into force.

5. The introduction of or any change in customs duties imposed on goods imported into the countries and territories shall not, either in law or in fact give rise to any direct or indirect discrimination between imports from the various Member States.

ARTICLE 134   If the level of the duties applicable to goods from a third country on entry into a country or territory is liable, when the provisions of Article 133 (1) have been applied, to cause deflections of trade to the detriment of any Member State, the latter may request the Commission to propose to the other Member States the measures needed to remedy the situation.

ARTICLE 135   Subject to the provisions relating to public health, public security or public policy, freedom of movement within Member States for workers from the countries and territories, and within the countries and territories for workers from Member States, shall be governed by agreements to be concluded subsequently with the unanimous approval of Member States.

ARTICLE 136   For an initial period of five years after the entry into force of this Treaty, the details of and procedure for the association of the countries and territories with the Community shall be determined by an Implementing Convention annexed to this Treaty.

Before the Convention referred to in the preceding paragraph expires, the Council shall, acting unanimously, lay down provisions for a further period, on the basis of the experience acquired and of the principles set out in this Treaty.

ARTICLE 136a   The provisions of Articles 131 to 136 shall apply to Greenland subject to the special provisions for Greenland set out in the Protocol on special arrangements for Greenland, annexed to this Treaty.

Part Four: association policy

The essence of Part Four association with the Community is not dissimilar to that found in the Lomé conventions. Thus relations between the Community and the OCTs are aimed at promoting economic, cultural and social development and strengthening economic ties. The main vehicles for this are trade promotion via preferential trade arrangements; the SYSMIN and STABEX systems of financial assistance; and the funding by the EC of various development projects. Agreements to date have also involved the creation of an institutional framework to promote cooperation and political dialogue. Similarities with the Lomé Conventions are also evident in the most recent association agreement, which was concluded for a ten-year period in 1991.[42] This, like Lomé IV, encourages a decentralization of cooperation, and places greater emphasis than before on the protection of the environment and the role of women.

q.v. Lomé conventions pp. 242–5.

42. See *Council Decision (91/482/EEC) of 25 July 1991 on the association of the overseas countries and territories with the European Economic Community*, OJL 263, 19 September 1991.

V. The Union Treaty D:
Institutions, Finance, External Relations and Final Provisions

After dealing with links between the Community and overseas territories, the Treaty of Rome moves on to institutional matters. This order is significantly different from that in national constitutions where institutions appear early on as an expression of state sovereignty. The Treaty of Rome implies that what really matters are the functions which member states have agreed to carry out in common so that institutions are simply a means to carry them out. The reality is, however, more complex.

The institutional and related provisions, even in the consolidated Treaty, are both slimmer and less numerous than those which have occupied previous subdivisions of the *Handbook*. Although the nominal numbering rather obscures this, the opening parts of the Treaty account for over 200 Articles, compared to the 130 plus of the institutional provisions.[1] Hence this fourth analytical subdivision brings these institutional questions together with consideration of Community financing and law, plus two other elements of the Rome and Maastricht Treaties: the Rome Treaty's General and Final Provisions and the Final Provisions of the TEU. These are logically related, not just by their appellation, but also because they both contain similar elements.

The Treaty of Rome's concluding elements fall into three categories: legal principles and obligations; questions of the applicability of the Treaty; and transitional arrangements. If the last are now redundant, the first two remain of considerable importance, covering material on the liability of the Community and, especially, on the main frameworks for relations between the Community and other bodies and states. This leads to a consideration of the nature of recent Community external relations. The final element of the subdivision is the rather disparate provisos of the Final Provisions of the TEU which provide new insights

---

1. In the Community's own preliminary consolidated treaties the initial policy elements account for 49 pages of text compared to 19 pages devoted to the institutions and 26 pages covering the pillars and final elements. This version, of course, excludes the Declarations.

into the Union's nature and relations with the Community as reformulated by the TEU. It also deals with questions of amendment and reform which had been included in the Rome Treaty. Thus, these provisions neatly round off consideration of the Treaty of Rome and help to lead into the Pillars and Protocols attached to the Maastricht Treaty.

i. Institutional provisions

The Community's institutions are a key, not merely to this subdivision of the *Handbook*, but also to an understanding of the Union in general. To begin with, while the initial Articles of the TEU refer to the Union being 'served by a single institutional framework', virtually all the detailed discussion of actual institutions appears within the Community pillar. Indeed, Article 4 of the latter sets out the list of Community institutions. Even the independent European Central Bank appears within the provisions of the revised Treaty of Rome. In other words, with the somewhat anomalous exception of the European Council the Union has no institutions of its own. It has to borrow those of the Community.

q.v.
European
Council pp.
58–61.

Moreover, institutions remind us that one cannot just have 'powers' in a body like the Community. Laws and other kinds of rules are not self-implementing. They need somebody to apply them, especially in an organism whose range of members and policies is expanding in the way those of the Community are doing. Some people go as far as to argue that the institutions are essential to developing the future of the Community.

Certainly the institutions are highly significant. Thus, as Box 12 implies, they distinguish the Community from the many intergovernmental organizations which do not have such institutions. Secondly, as noted above, they provide a unifying factor in the Union. They also provide an attractive decision-making framework, participation in which has been much sought after by would-be member states. Fourth, the balance between the institutions points to the importance of the various interests inside the Community. In fact, Pescatore and others see the major institutions as each having a different legitimacy: the Parliament representing the people; the Council the member states as such; the Commission the 'European interest'; and the ECJ the rule of law.[2] With the addition of the Court of Auditors it might be argued that another principle of legitimacy has been added to the Union.

Equally, some of the non-intergovernmental institutions also represent an interest of their own in decision-making. Sixth, their competences and rules, notably in finance and Council voting procedures, exemplify the balance of power between the Union and its member states. Finally, the institutions are symbolic of the debate about widening and deepening the Community.

Yet, despite this, it is probably true to say that they have attracted less attention in the United Kingdom than other elements of Maastricht such as

---

2. Pescatore, P., 'La Constitution, son contenu, son utilité', *Zeitschrift für Schweizerische Recht*, vol. 111, no. 1, 1992, pp. 54–5.

Box 12.
Institutional problems
and roles

Perceived institutional problems prior to Maastricht

(a) Lack of legitimacy
(b) Encroachment on national sovereignty
(c) Democratic deficit
(d) Lack of balance
(e) Low effectiveness

Roles of institutions

1. Mark Union out as supranational
2. Unify the Union
3. Provide means of decision-making
4. Express balance of interests inside Union
5. Represent a specific 'legitimacy'
6. Exemplify balance of power between Union and its member states
7. Symbolize debate between widening and deepening

citizenship, EMU and the extension of Community policy powers. This is partly because the institutions and their interrelations highlight UK difficulties in comprehending constitutions. It is also partly due to a UK tendency to see the Community as simply 'a free trade area with a few common rules' as Lord Young once said.

It is also because the apparently bland texts do not always make clear the real role of the institutions. Indeed sometimes it seems that the text is as important for what it leaves unsaid as for what it actually says. Some of the references to institutions, moreover, like those in Articles 241–246, are now redundant and could well have been edited out by the IGC. And, of course, many of the Articles which specify what the institutions should do appear elsewhere in the Treaty. Like many constitutions, in other words, the TEU just lists the institutions rather than spelling out the last 'jot and tittle' of the way they are to function.

The institutions as they emerge from the consolidated Treaties have to be seen against the background of a good deal of criticism during the IGCs. Despite the fact that their structure and way of operating is very similar to that found in most Western democracies with its division of powers and multiple legitimacies, they have been subject to a number of contradictory criticisms.[3] These are, as Box 12 has suggested, that they lacked real legitimacy and popular acceptance; that they were overweening and overcentralized, thereby threatening national sovereignty; that they lacked accountability and transparency, the so-called democratic deficit; that they were internally unbalanced, to the benefit of Commission and Court; and that they provided only slow, ineffective and costly action.

The Maastricht negotiators went some way towards redressing these problems

---

3. Thus the Community has what can be seen as an executive, a legislature and a judiciary: the three main branches of Western states. However, this is not universally accepted, partly because of technical roles played by EC institutions, and partly because it confers too much of a state-like character on the EC. Pescatore also suggests that the EC rests on the four legitimacies of people, states, Community and law. Others would argue that the institutions can be divided either into political and judicial or into principal, auxiliary and secondary.

and certainly gave institutional questions more attention than perhaps the SEA had done. Specifically they claimed they wanted to bring the institutions closer to the Union's citizens; to make them more accountable to the member states and their parliaments; to make them more democratic and open; to change the institutional balance in favour of the European Parliament, Council of Ministers and European Council; and to make their working more effective, more financially responsible and simpler. How seriously they actually took these aims remains a moot point.

So, how far, and how successfully, did the TEU go in trying to remedy these defects? David Martin, MEP, observed that the institutional provisions were flawed, deficient and incomplete, yet none the less they did help to constitute a new Union. Hence on legitimacy the Treaty establishes the right of petition, an Ombudsman and the Committee of the Regions. In terms of their powers there are new references to national parliaments and subsidiarity. Yet the European Central Bank, or ECB, escapes accountability. The democratic deficit has been partially addressed by new powers and procedures involving the European Parliament. Yet this still lacks many of the powers of a real legislature.

q.v. European Central Bank pp. 158–9.

Equally, while the balance has been changed by making the European Council the guarantor of unity inside the Union, and by other minor changes, the essential ambiguity remains. The European Council does not figure in this section of the Treaty, although it is a highly significant body for the Community, as well as for the Union. Moreover, the Commission occurs in areas where the pillar structure suggests it should not as it does in Articles B, K.9 and M. And whether Declaration 17 about providing better public access to information will lead to any real change remains to be seen.

q.v. Declaration 17 p. 435.

Finally, there have been some moves towards greater efficiency and financial responsibility, such as more qualified majority voting, more concern for enforcement, and the upgrading of the Court of Auditors. Yet, at the same time, there is no tidy list of powers to be exercised by specific institutions or levels. The half-hearted attempts to upgrade the role of the European Parliament have made decision-making much more complex. So, overall, many institutional questions remained unresolved and it is not surprising that the TEU commits the Community to a further IGC in 1996.

The changes made at Maastricht seem more a matter of ratifying existing but unrecognized practices, and tidying up and reordering, than of radical innovation. They also involve increasing the formal status of some institutions, something which has a considerable significance in Community terms. Being a Community institution, rather than an advisory organ implies a certain independence and importance.[4] Community institutions thus enjoy greater standing and authority, including a share in decision-making; the ability to bring legal actions for failure to act under Article 175; and a wide range of responsibilities, including in external

4. In practice the Community has at least five different types of organizations within its structure. There are the institutions, the advisory bodies, and autonomous sectoral bodies like the ECB, all of which are established by Treaty. Then there are administrative agencies which derive from institutional standing orders such as the Secretariat General. Finally there are the many non-treaty advisory and consultative committees.

relations. So, by upgrading to the status of an institution, the negotiators were saying something about the Community itself as well as about the leading position of the body in question. The changed status of the Court of Auditors can be regarded in this light. On the other hand the ECB and, to a lesser extent the EMI, seem, as already noted, to have been given a semi-autonomous status.

The institutional givens of the Community, and ultimately of the Union, thus remain contradictory and transitional. It is, moreover, too early to assess how well they will work. In any case neither the institutions themselves, nor the rules and financial provisions that go with them to make up the framework, determine how they are used. This depends on outside pressures and the outcome of planned discussions in 1996.

This subdivision therefore only takes us some way towards understanding how the institutions either presently do, or will, work. This is particularly because there are institutional provisions elsewhere in the Treaty, for instance in Articles C, D, and E. Here the discussion follows the new order beginning, in Chapter 1 of Title I of Part Five with a batch of established institutions: Parliament, Council of Ministers, COREPER (Committee of Permanent Representatives), Commission, ECJ and Court of Auditors. Each institution has a Section of its own, numbered from 1 to 5.[5] However, significantly the Treaty provides much more detail on the ECJ than it does on the EP and the Commission.

Some of their interrelations are then the subject of a second Chapter. However, this is only part of the broader political process of the Community which is sketched in Figure 9. The legislative interrelations are followed by Chapter 3 on the Economic and Social Committee; Chapter 4 on the upgraded Committee of the Regions; and Chapter 5 on the European Investment Bank (EIB). Part V then ends with Title II which is devoted to the financial rules and procedures of the Union. This has no further internal divisions.

(a) The European Parliament

As in previous Community Treaties, the European Parliament is the first institution to be listed in the consolidated Treaty. This can be taken to imply a certain primacy in line both with the essential democratic role of parliaments in Western societies and with the Parliament's claim to represent the people of Europe.[6] However, while Maastricht has upgraded the role of the Parliament to some extent, it still remains in many, if not all, ways less esteemed and influential than most national

---

5. Part Five thus contains a Title I with five Chapters as follows. Chapter 1 covering Articles 137–188c is divided into Sections: 1 on the European Parliament (Articles 137–144); 2 on the Council (Articles 145–154); 3 on the Commission (Articles 155–163); 4 on the Court of Justice (Articles 164–188); and 5 on the Court of Auditors (Articles 188a–188c). Then follow four further Chapters without Sections e.g. 2 on Provisions Common to Several Institutions (Articles 189–192); 3 on the Economic and Social Committee (Articles 193–198); 4 on the Committee of the Regions (Articles 198a–198c); and 5 on the EIB (Articles 198d–198e). Title II, dealing with Financial Provisions, and covering Articles 199–209a then follows. These various elements are covered in successive units of this subdivision of the *Handbook* which also includes the final elements of both the Treaties of Rome and of Maastricht.

6. At the outset, the Assembly as it then was, did not have anything like the status which the Parliament was to gain in later years.

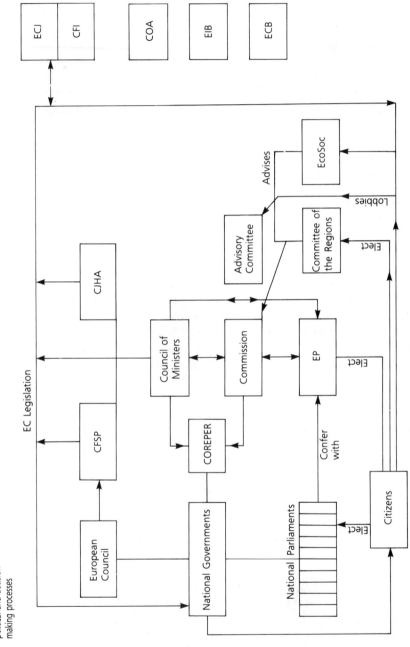

Figure 9. Community political and decision-making processes

parliaments. Although the Members of the European Parliament (MEPs) used the title European Parliament from 1962 onward, it was only legally conceded in the SEA. If, under the TEU, it has got new teeth thanks to Articles 137, 138a, 158 and 189−90, it still suffers from many weaknesses. François Mitterrand's unwillingness 'to be controlled by Egon Klepsch', the President of the EP, was upheld by the negotiators, at the expense of the Parliament's own aims prior to the IGC. Hence there remains what, as has been seen, is called the 'democratic deficit'.[7] At best the gap has been marginally narrowed rather than closed by the new Treaty.

The TEU begins by assuming the existence of the Parliament in Article 137. However its powers, although no longer advisory and consultative, continue to be clearly derived from the Treaty and not from any inherent democratic rights. Article 138 then spells out the principles and processes by which MEP's are to be elected and their number.[8] The TEU then inserts a new Article 138a which recognizes the roles which political parties can and should play within the Union, and by implication in the Parliament. The equally new Article 138b next lists five different ways in which the Parliament can now share in the Community's legislative process. These are assent, conciliation, cooperation, consultation and by inviting the Commission to act.

The Parliament's rights to set up committees of enquiry into maladministration are then formalized in Article 138c and detailed provisions are laid down for the appointment of an Ombudsman to act for it and individuals in the same way at Articles 138d. The rights of individual citizens are then reinforced by Article 138e which formalizes the existing unofficial right of petition to the Parliament. The Section does not mention however, as is shown on p. 260, either the extensions of the Parliament's existing rights or all the new ones created by the Treaty. The previous discussion of the Parliament's right to cooperate in policy-making has now been transferred to Chapter II of the Title.

The remaining Articles here deal with questions of organization. By Article 139 the Parliament thus has to hold at least one session per year, though in reality it holds many more. Articles 140−142 allow it to decide on its own officers and procedures. The same series of Articles also allows it to hear both the Council and the Commission. But whereas the Council can, according to Article 140, determine how this must be done, the amendments introduced by TEU mean that the Commission has to reply and is open to a collective dismissal under Article 144.

Despite these opportunities many people think that this does not make the European Parliament the complete equal of national parliaments. As Box 13 indicates, there are several reasons for this. If we regard parliaments as fulfilling

---

7. By this is meant the fact that the executive institutions and the processes of decision-making etc., are not subject to proper parliamentary accountability and scrutiny as they are supposed to be in Western states. The idea assumes that the European Parliament is the natural representative of the peoples of Europe to whom the institutions should ultimately be responsible.

8. Paragraph 26 of Part A of the Edinburgh Declaration gave 1 new MEP to Belgium, Greece, and Portugal; 4 to Spain, and 6 each to Britain, France, Italy and the Netherlands. This was in order to preserve political harmony by balancing the 18 new seats given to Germany to reflect the incorporation of the former German Democratic Republic. The fact that Germany now has 99 seats may also be symbolic. All this brings the total seats in the EP to 567.

Box 13.
Roles of Parliaments

1. Legitimation
2. Representation
3. Legislation [decision-making]
   EP = informed
        consulted
        gives assent
        cooperates
        codecides
4. Scrutiny and control of the Executive
5. Recruitment and socialization

five roles, the European Parliament only scores patchily on four and not at all on the fifth. Thus the European Parliament is not yet a body which provides full *legitimation* of democratic acceptability on behalf of the Union. It has to approve most treaties, enlargements, and association agreements thanks to Articles such as 238. Article 175 also allows the EP to defend its prerogatives if these are challenged. However, as noted it cannot define its own powers, have a government to support, and it can only play a minor consultative part in revising the Treaties under Article N. In most Parliaments such constitutional revision is a major function and one subject to special rules on the majority needed to validate agreed changes. Equally the EP needs to conciliate national parliaments.[9] And people do not automatically look to it, even if the number of petitions has been increasing of late.

q.v. Articles 238 p. 340.

q.v. Article N p. 356.

Its *representative* character is also new, dating only from 1979 when it became directly elected rather that merely nominated. It is also somewhat fallible. This is partly because its compromise formulae for allocating seats means that small states are overrepresented at the expense of those with large populations. In addition it has not been able to achieve a uniform electoral system. At present the United Kingdom accounts for more constituencies than the rest of the Union, and excludes proportional representation outside Northern Ireland. This gives the United Kingdom a disproportionate influence on the composition of the Parliament, while denying fair representation to its own citizens.[10] It remains to be seen whether the new provisions for majority decision on a uniform electoral provision in Article 138(3) will bear fruit. Electorates' habit of using EP elections to vent their spleen on their governing parties for faults committed at home does not help this role. Neither is the fact that only about 200 MEPs are regular attenders helpful in this context. Finally, the reference to political parties sees them as much

---

9. Declaration 13 (see p. 434) thus provides for greater involvement of national parliaments including through the exchange of facilities and information between them and the EP, now that dual mandates are much less common than in the past. Declaration 14 (see p. 434) invites the EP and national parliaments to meet as a Conference, as happened in Rome in 1990, to discuss the development of the Union. This reflects feelings that real legitimacy resides in national parliaments and that allowing them a say is the best way of avoiding conflict. Sir Leon Brittan and others would like to see their role given more formality and influence.

10. The United Kingdom has experienced considerable conceptual difficulty in adjusting to the six extra seats awarded to it at Edinburgh and has been forced to bypass the normal processes of boundary revision. The idea of allocating the six extra seats on a nation-wide proportional representation basis was turned down flatly.

as a means of persuading citizens to support Europe as a vehicle for representing the latter.

The *legislative and decision-making* role of the Parliament has been enhanced by the TEU. As already noted, there are now five ways in which the Parliament can influence and participate in legislation under Article 138b. The TEU introduced what is described in the Treaty itself as 'the procedure referred to in Article 189b'. This is often called a codecision procedure. However, since joint decisions can only occur at specific points in the procedure, it is better called the conciliation procedure. Others, like HMG, call it the 'negative assent' procedure. Whatever the title, the complex process allows the Parliament to veto acts in certain fields when agreement cannot be reached with the Council through a new Conciliation Committee.

Then there is the SEA cooperation procedure, now transferred to Article 189c; the right to assent to treaties and other international agreements, and the old right to give advisory opinions, or the right of 'consultation'. The TEU also now makes it possible for the Parliament to submit proposals deemed necessary to implement the Treaty, which is the nearest the Parliament gets to a right to initiate legislation.

q.v.
Conciliation
Committee
pp. 298–9.

The amended Treaty of Rome also provides for the Parliament to be informed and consulted on a large number of issues, although this does not always mean that the Council has to secure parliamentary approval. It should also be noted that the Parliament has a right of information on a number of other matters.[11] This also allows it to exert some influence. Equally, the Commission often uses statements to Parliament to float ideas of its own. And, as will be seen, the Parliament has a special role in the budgetary process. However, for the most part the Council continues to make the key decisions while the decision-making procedures involving the Parliament are complex and have yet to prove their effectiveness.[12]

The Parliament's tasks of *scrutiny and control* have also been increased by the TEU. It now has the formal right to set up committees of enquiry as it has done in the past. It can also use the new Ombudsman as a means of parliamentary control since, although the Ombudsman is independent, he is to report to Parliament. The office offers something both to those who wish to see the Community develop further and those who wish to halt its growth. This may explain why it has proved hard to get agreement on the way to implement the provisions of Article 138(4). The Parliament continues to be able to dismiss the Commission as a whole. It will now, by implication, share in confirming the President under the amended Article 158. Equally, it will also debate the Commission's programme and report (Article 154).

The Commission is also increasingly responsible to the Parliament for its financial management to the Parliament through Article 206, as well as through the Parliament's other roles in the budgetary process. The TEU here also allows the Parliament to invite the Court of Auditors to produce a special report on

---

11. This is the case, *inter alia*, in Articles 73g(2), 103(2), 103(4), 104n(2), 107n(2), 109 and 130p.
12. See below pp. 298–301 for a discussion of those areas of the Treaty to which the main decision-making modes apply, and notably Box 17 there.

financial activities about which there are doubts in the Chamber. Much of EMU also escapes parliamentary control as do most of the activities of the other pillars of the Union. On a day-to-day basis the Parliament can continue to quiz the Commission through written and oral questions under Article 140.

However, it cannot interrogate or control the Council of Ministers in any meaningful way. And the Parliament plays but little of the role of *recruitment and socialization* played by other parliaments. Admittedly some MEPs have gone on to become Ministers for European Affairs in their national governments, but it is more common for former Commissioners and others to take up seats in Parliament. This can give it something of the nature of an Upper House. The Parliament has been pressing for such rights but Maastricht only allowed it a consultative role in appointments to the ECB.

The earlier drafts of the TEU did not offer much more than that provided in the final version. This removed the reference to it as an 'advisory' body, recognized that the Parliament must approve the new electoral procedure, introduced the negative assent and Commission invitation procedures, accepted the Ombudsman and brought the selection of the Commission into line with the timing of parliamentary elections. Other changes were made in other parts of the Treaty. There was also a degree of tidying up existing practices.

The actual working of the Parliament has not been affected by the Treaty. It remains able, under Article 142, to lay down its own rules of procedure which provide for legislation to be discussed by some 18 committees of 25 to 56 members who meet in public. Their recommendations are then laid before the plenary session of Parliament by a *rapporteur*. Plenary sessions take place in Strasbourg, in a building shared with the Council of Europe, and in Brussels where Committees also meet. There are also special sessions where matters of current interest are debated and outside speakers address the Parliament. The 2,000 strong Secretariat is based in Luxembourg. The existence of such multiple locations is a matter of great controversy because of the costs and dislocation it causes. However, as a result of recent Summit decisions, it seems likely to continue.

The Parliament is chaired by a President elected from its own ranks. He, or she, is a significant figure with more of political influence than the Speaker of the House of Commons. The President is assisted by a number of Vice-Presidents and others who make up its Steering Committee or Bureau. It is this which is consulted about the appointment of the President of the Commission. A large role is also played by the ten political groups which bring together the members of the seventy or more parties represented in the Parliament. These provide a structure for contribution to parliamentary debates and organizations. The Socialist and Christian Democratic groups in the Parliament are the two largest. However, the EP does not work in the confrontational right versus left style practised at Westminster, partly because national links can cut across ideological ones. Rather it builds different coalitions according to different issues and seeks a degree of consensus.

So, as already suggested, the Parliament has gained in influence and status, but only incrementally. There has been no revolution in its standing or symbolism such as the Parliament has been pressing for since 1961. Before the IGC's met it sought a say in more appointments, real codecision and the right to initiate legislation. It has got only a little of the first, something of the second, and virtually nothing of the last.

However, the size of the Parliament has recently been increased. There are also proposals for further changes to cater for enlargement and to redress what is seen as the emphasis on intergovernmentalism in the TEU. These are contained in Declaration 15 while the conciliation procedure can be reviewed in 1996. Hence arguments about the nature and role of the Parliament are likely to continue.

q.v. Declaration 15 p. 434

Part Five   Institutions of the Community

Title I   Provisions governing the institutions

Chapter 1   The institutions

Section 1   The European Parliament

ARTICLE 137

The European Parliament, which shall consist of representatives of the peoples of the States brought together in the Community, shall exercise the powers conferred upon it by this Treaty.

ARTICLE 138[13]

1. The representatives in the European Parliament of the peoples of the State brought together in the Community shall be elected by direct universal suffrage.

2. The number of representatives elected in each Member State shall be as follows:

Belgium	24
Denmark	16
Germany	81
Greece	24
Spain	60
France	81
Ireland	15
Italy	81
Luxembourg	6
Netherlands	25
Portugal	24
United Kingdom	81

3. The European Parliament shall draw up proposals for elections by direct universal suffrage in accordance in accordance with a uniform procedure in all Member States.

The Council shall, acting unanimously **after obtaining the assent of the European Parliament, which shall act by a majority of its component members,** lay down the appropriate provision, which it shall recommend to Member States for adoption in accordance with their respective constitutional requirements.

---

13. This Article is still noted as coming from clause 14 of the Act on Direct Elections which came into effect in 1979 and has not been given ordinary status as have many other inheritances from other treaties in Part V of the Treaty of Rome. For the post-Edinburgh division of seats see above at footnote 8.

ARTICLE 138a[14] Political parties at European level are important as a factor for integration within the Union. They contribute to forming a European awareness and to expressing the political will of the citizens of the Union.

ARTICLE 138b In so far as provided in this Treaty, the European Parliament shall participate in the process leading up to the adoption of Community acts by exercising its powers under the procedures laid down in Articles 189b and 189c and by giving its assent or delivering advisory opinions.

The European Parliament may, acting by a majority of its members, request the Commission to submit any appropriate proposal on matters on which it considers that a Community act is required for the purpose of implementing this Treaty.

ARTICLE 138c In the course of its duties, the European Parliament may, at the request of a quarter of its members, set up a temporary Committee of Inquiry to investigate, without prejudice to the powers conferred by this Treaty on other institutions or bodies, alleged contraventions or maladministration in the implementation of Community law, except where the alleged facts are being examined before a court and while the case is still subject to legal proceedings.

The temporary Committee of Inquiry shall cease to exist on the submission of its report.

The detailed provisions governing the exercise of the right of inquiry shall be determined by common accord of the European Parliament, the Council and the Commission.

ARTICLE 138d Any citizen of the Union, and any natural or legal person residing or having his registered office in a Member State, shall have the right to address, individually or in association with other citizens or persons, a petition to the European Parliament on a matter which comes within the Community's fields of activity and which affects him, her or it directly.

ARTICLE 138e 1. The European Parliament shall appoint an Ombudsman empowered to receive complaints from any citizen of the Union or any natural or legal person residing in or having his registered office in a Member State concerning instances of maladministration in the activities of the Community institutions or bodies, with the exception of the Court of Justice and the Court of First Instance acting in their judicial role.

In accordance with his duties, the Ombudsman shall conduct inquiries for which he finds grounds, either on his own initiative or on the basis of complaints submitted to him direct or through a member of the European Parliament, except where the alleged facts are or have been the subject of legal proceedings. Where the Ombudsman establishes an instance of maladministration, he shall refer the matter to the institution concerned, which shall have a period of three months in which to inform him of its views. The Ombudsman shall then forward a report to the European Parliament and the institution concerned. The person lodging the complaint shall be informed of the outcome of such inquiries.

The Ombudsman shall submit an annual report to the European Parliament on the outcome of his inquiries.

---

14. This Article was not included in the December version of the Treaty but emerged when the IGC returned to Maastricht in February 1992. By then consultations had taken place on appropriate wording.

2. The Ombudsman shall be appointed after each election of the European Parliament for the duration of its term of office. The Ombudsman shall be eligible for reappointment.

The Ombudsman may be dismissed by the Court of Justice at the request of the European Parliament if he no longer fulfils the conditions required for the performance of this duties or if he is guilty of serious misconduct.

3. The Ombudsman shall be completely independent in the performance of his duties. In the performance of those duties he shall neither seek nor take instructions from any body. The Ombudsman may not, during his term of office, engage in any other occupation, whether gainful or not.

4. The European Parliament shall, after seeking an opinion from the Commission and with the approval of the Council acting by a qualified majority, lay down the regulations and general conditions governing the Ombudsman's duties.

ARTICLE 139

The European Parliament shall hold an annual session. It shall meet, without requiring to be convened, on the second Tuesday in March.
The European Parliament may meet in extraordinary session at the request of a majority of its members or at the request of the Council or of the Commission.

ARTICLE 140

The European Parliament shall elect its President and its officers from among its members.

Members of the Commission may attend all meetings and shall, at their request, be heard on behalf of the Commission.

The Commission shall reply orally or in writing to questions put to it by the European Parliament or by its members.

The Council shall be heard by the European Parliament in accordance with the conditions laid down by the Council in its rules of procedure.

ARTICLE 141

Save as otherwise provided in this Treaty, the European Parliament shall act by an absolute majority of the votes cast.

The rules of procedure shall determine the quorum.

ARTICLE 142

The European Parliament shall adopt its rules of procedure, acting by a majority of its members.

The proceedings of the European Parliament shall be published in the manner laid down in its rules of procedure.

ARTICLE 143

The European Parliament shall discuss in open session the annual general report submitted to it by the Commission.

ARTICLE 144

If a motion of censure on the activities of the Commission is tabled before it, the European Parliament shall not vote thereon until at least three days after the motion has been tabled and only by open vote.

If the motion of censure is carried by a two-thirds majority of the votes cast, representing a majority of the members of the European Parliament, the members of the Commission shall resign as a body. They shall continue to deal with current business until they are replaced in accordance with Article 158.

In this case, the term of office of the members of the Commission appointed to replace them shall expire on the date which the term of office of the members of the Commission obliged to resign as a body would have expired.

FURTHER READING

GENERAL

Bradshaw, J., 'Institutional reform in the EC beyond Maastricht', *European Trends*, 4/1991, pp. 82–93.

Burley, A.M., 'Democracy and judicial review in the European Community', *University of Chicago Legal Forum*, 1992, pp. 81–92.

Dehousse, R., '1992 and beyond: the institutional dimension of the Internal Market programme', *Legal Issues of European Integration*, 1989/1 , pp. 109–36.

EC Commission, *The Treaty on European Union: The meaning of Maastricht*, Fact Sheet 3, Brussels, October 1992.

Foakes, J., *Tolleys' European Community Institutions*, Tolley, London, 1982.

Garcia, S., *European Identity and the Search for Legitimacy*, Pinter, London, 1993.

Goodman, S.F., *The European Community*, 2nd edn, Macmillan, London, 1993.

Griffiths, A., *European Community Survey: The European Community*, Longman, London, 1992.

Hailsham, Lord and Vaughan, D. (eds.), *The Law of the European Communities*, Butterworth, London, 1986.

Henig, S., *Power and Politics in the European Community*, Europotentials, London, 1983.

Holland, M., *European Community Integration*, Pinter, London, 1992.

Kangis, P., 'How democratic is the EC?', *European Access* 1989/6, pp. 10–11.

Martin D., *Maastricht in a Minute*, David Martin, Edinburgh, 1992.

Nicoll, W. and T. Salmon, *Understanding the New European Community*, 2nd edn, Harvester Wheatsheaf, Hemel Hempstead, 1993.

Nugent, N., *The Government and Politics of the European Community*, 2nd edn, Macmillan, London, 1991.

Pescatore P., 'La Constitution, son contenus, son utilité', *Zeitschrift für Schweizerische Recht*, vol. 111, no. 1, 1992, pp. 41–72.

Regards sur l'actualité — 180: Special Maastricht, La Documentation Française, Paris, 1992.

Rideau, J., 'Le Traité de Maastricht du Février 1992 sur l'Union Européenne — aspects institutionels', *Revue des affaires européennes*, 1992/2, pp. 21–48.

Sloot, T. and Vershuren, P., 'Decision making speed in the EC', *Journal of Common Market Studies*, vol. 30, no. 1, 1990, pp. 75–85.

Weidenfeld, W. (ed.), *The Shaping of a European Constitution*, Bertelsmann Foundation, Gütersloh, 1990.

Williams, S., 'Sovereignty and accountability in the EC', *The Political Quarterly*, vol. 61, no. 3, 1990, pp. 299–317.

Wincott D., *The Treaty of Maastricht: An adequate 'constitution' for the European Union?*, European Public Policy Institute Occasional Paper 93/6, University of Warwick, 1992.

EUROPEAN PARLIAMENT

Attina, F., 'The voting behaviour of MEPs and the problems of the Europarties', *European Journal of Political Research*, vol. 18, no. 5, 1990, pp. 557–79.

European Parliament, *Maastricht: The Treaty on European Union: The position of the European Parliament*, OOPEC, Luxembourg, 1992.

European Parliament, *Projet de Document de Travail sur La Constitution de L'Union Européenne*, Commission Institutionelle, 15 February 1993, pp. 203–601.

Fitzmaurice, J., 'An analysis of the European Community's co-operation procedure', *Journal of Common Market Studies*, vol. 26, no. 4, 1988, pp. 389–400.

Jacobs, F. and Corbett, R., *The European Parliament*, Longman, London, 1992.

Kangis, P., 'Decision making and dissolution of the EP', *European Access*, 1990/3, pp. 12–13.

Lodge, J., 'The European Parliament in Election year', *European Access* 1989/2, pp. 10–13.

Palmer, M., *The European Parliament*, Pergamon, Oxford, 1981.

Plumb, H., 'Building a democratic Community: the role of the EP', *The World Today*, vol. 45, no. 7, 1989, pp. 112–17.

Reich, C., 'Le traité sur l'Union européenne et le Parlement européen', *Revue du Marché commun et de l'Union européenne*, no. 357, 1992, pp. 287–92.

Robinson, A. and Webb, A., *The European Parliament in the EC Policy Process*, Policy Studies Institute, London, 1985.

Stepat, S., 'Execution of functions by the EP', *Journal of European Integration*, vol. 12, no. 1, 1988, pp. 5–36.

(b) The Council of Ministers

The Council of Ministers, which is the subject of Section 2 of the Chapter, represents the member states and is often regarded as the intergovernmental element in the Community. However, the Council is a Community institution. It has to take the Community interest into account and not just seek the lowest common denominator. The TEU has not really changed this.

However, the Treaty does make two major changes where the Council is concerned. One deals with its Secretariat. The other relates to its composition. Maastricht was also responsible for a certain amount of tidying up. Thus rather than treating changes made by the Merger Treaty, when it created one instead of three commissions, as a kind of parenthesis, the Treaty makes them a full part of the Treaty of Rome. This was the case with Articles 146, 147 and 154. The TEU also moves the old Article 149 to Article 189c but leaves nothing in its place. The Community's own exposition of exactly what changes have been made has not always been clear. The order of Article 151 is also changed as well as extended to cover the Council Secretariat.

The Treaty's discussion of the Council of Ministers thus begins in a very low-key way by stressing its responsibility for ensuring that the objectives of the Treaty are attained. Thus it neither affirms its existence, which had been done in Article 4, nor asserts its status as the representative of the member states and hence of the intergovernmental element in the Union. Indeed, Maastricht made no change to the existing text, even though some readings of the TEU see it as strengthening the hands of the member states at the expense of both democracy and the cooperative federalism which had been developing inside the Council. Nor do the powers of the Council amount to a complete right for member states to do what they like. Their authority is limited by the Treaties. Nonetheless, the Council's role, and with it the intergovernmental elements in the Community, has already grown much more than had been expected in the 1950s, thanks to the Empty Chair Crisis.

q.v. Article 4 pp. 63–5.

q.v. Empty Chair Crisis p. 20.

The Council's duties are spelled out relatively broadly and in a number of places. Thus there is no clear delimitation of tasks as between it and other institutions. Article 145 accords it three types of role: ensuring coordination of member states' economic policies; taking decisions; and conferring power on the Commission to act. Council influence over the latter also includes scrutinizing its activities and, according to Article 152, inviting it to undertake research. This can be seen as allowing the Council a role in policy initiation. Article 154 also gives the Council powers over the salaries of both the Commission and the Court. Although the Treaty does not say so here, it also has responsibilities in the budgetary process, in international relations, and in responding to the Parliament and other institutions. These appear in a whole range of other Treaty Articles.

Of all these tasks those of legislating and decision-making are the most important, since it is these which give member states, and the intergovernmental element, their ultimate control over the destinies of the Community. There can be no Community legislation without Council approval. This can involve laying down broad guidelines, turning the general ideas of the European Council into

q.v. European Council pp. 58–61.

legally viable forms, and issuing a whole range of opinions. Interestingly the draft constitutions now circulating, such as that produced by the European Policy Forum of London, do not suggest much change to these duties, though the European Parliament would like to share in more of them.

The membership of the Council, according to Article 146, has to be of ministerial rank and has to have the authority to take decisions without referring back to the national governments. This marks a change on the previous situation in the Treaty of Rome which can be read as seeing the members as simple delegates of governments with no freedom of action. At various times the Germans would like to have had *Länder* delegates representing them, and this was largely conceded. In practice, and in contrast to the European Council, each member state sends a delegation to ensure that national interests can be properly defended. So there can be as many as a hundred people present.

The Council decides for itself how it operates thanks to Articles 147 and 151(3). Formal meetings are held mainly in Brussels, at present in the Charlemagne Building but soon in state of the art new offices opposite the Berlaymont. However, it often meets in Luxembourg, because this was the seat of the ECSC Council, and at places in the member state holding the Presidency. This is especially the case for informal, 'brain-storming' meetings. Although Article 147 suggests infrequent meetings, in practice there can be as many as 90 meetings of the Council in any year, according to an agreed cycle. This is normally laid down well in advance but Presidencies can, and do, alter things to suit their own sense of priorities.[15] So many meetings mean a considerable burden on individuals and on national governments in general especially when the various standing committees and working groups are taken into account.

Because the Council is seen as the body enjoying ultimate power within the Union, its voting procedures are of great importance. Article 148 envisages three forms of decision-making: unanimity (which is not described here), straightforward majority voting, and qualified majority voting. The last provides a defence against domination by large states since the requirement for 54 votes, sometimes coming from eight states, means that the four main states must have the support of at least three other medium or small states if their proposals are to go through. This means that decisions are not taken by sheer weight of numbers.

The tradition established by the Luxembourg Compromise also provides that, on issues where a member state feels that its vital interests are at issue, the Council should continue discussion until agreement can be reached. If this did not happen then the state in question had a quasi-veto on Community decision making. States like Britain and Denmark have placed much stress on this precedent. However, it has proved harder to utilize than its supporters imagine because vital interests can be narrowly defined. The rights of individual states are also assisted by the habit of 'going round the table' at the outset of every meeting, allowing each

q.v.
Luxembourg
Compromise
pp. 531–2.

---

15. In other words Article 147, which actually derives from the Merger Treaty and not from the original Rome Treaty, is purely formal and does not describe existing practice.

minister to speak for up to ten minutes, setting out his government's views.[16] The casting of proxy votes, foreseen in Article 150, seems to be a very uncommon practice.

Whatever the Treaty of Rome says, many authorities believe that the Council seeks to work by consensus because it works best this way. Hence, the Presidency rarely pushes things to a vote, ensuring that nobody wishes to continue the decision or to object to what seems to be the 'sense of the meeting'.[17] However, since votes are not recorded and the Council's meetings are confidential, it is not easy to be certain of what actually happens. The Council is unlikely to give way to calls for its operations to be more open since this could reveal the way that political pressures can be brought to bear on recalcitrant ministers in Council. They may well give way because of the need to preserve gains in other areas of Community activity, even though they know that opinion at home would not approve such concessions. This is especially the case where negotiating positions are subject to scrutiny such as that applied by the European Committee of the Danish *Folketing*.

Although the Treaty always speaks of the Council in the singular, this has been a legal fiction since at least 1964. The Council, like the French Council of Ministers under the *ancien régime*, can take a variety of forms depending on the subjects it is discussing, with different ministers attending at different times. Thus it can be a General Affairs Council with Foreign Ministers in attendance dealing with external relations, institutional questions and general matters, including preparing the agenda for Summit meetings. This is often regarded as the Senior Council but there is no legal basis for this.

It can also meet as ECOFIN when Finance Ministers discuss economic and related matters. And Declarations 3 and 4 of the TEU provide for them to join the European Council to form the special Council of Ministers for EMU. However, the Agricultural Council meets the most frequently of all. Other important Councils are the Budgetary, the Internal Market and the Technological and Industrial. Indeed, with the exception of Defence, virtually all the Ministries found in most governments are now involved in Council affairs. The discontinuous and hydra-headed nature of the Council means that there can be inconsistencies between different meetings, whatever the theory suggests. Because of this the European Parliament has often called for a single, permanent minister to represent governments at the Council. Some governments, like that of France, have already moved somewhat in this direction.

q.v. *Declara-* *tions 3 and* *4 p. 432.*

Irrespective of the nature of the Council, the Treaty allows for three kinds of Council officers to help it fulfil its duties. These are the Presidency (Article 146), COREPER and the Council Secretariat (both Article 151). Such offices have become increasingly important, much more so than the Treaty text would suggest.

---

16. The Belgian Presidency was, in July 1993, talking of trying to do away with this on the grounds of efficiency. It hoped to limit initial statements to those who genuinely wanted to speak. This may be an optimistic aspiration. The size of the blocking minority will also be reconsidered as part of the enlargement negotiations.

17. Since 1987, the Rules of Procedure allow any member state to call for a vote. Previously it was left to the Presidency. This meant that votes were less likely to be taken and made the Luxembourg Compromise easier to uphold.

Article 153 also allows the Council to set up various committees in order to liaise with the Commission on policy. These range from the consultative to the regulatory (See below pp. 275–7.) The Council also proceeds through a number of working parties of its own which examine the proposals submitted by the Commission.

According to the amended Treaty of Rome the Presidency is an office whose only duty is to share in calling meetings. It is to be held in turn by the member states according to two cycles which ensure that no state is always in office during the first half of the year when the workload can be lighter and less significant. In practice, the office has grown considerably since 1966, albeit as much by default as by design. It has become a key manager of Community business a position which is seen as conferring a certain status on the state which holds it, especially for the smaller states. The Presidency thus attends world meetings, enjoys two seats at the Council of Ministers and can host one or more European Councils on its own territory.

As Kirchner shows, the Presidency has become responsible for steering the Community, setting out an agenda of things to be achieved over the coming six months and the themes to be dealt with.[18] Equally, it has an important administrative role: chairing COREPER; liaising with the Secretariat of the Council and EPC to draw up agendas; and moving business along. At the same time the Presidency has a third representative function: receiving Ambassadors; attending international gatherings; and generally speaking for the Community. Thus it is the Presidency which draws up the European Council Conclusions after Summit meetings. To enable it do this the Presidency has to be politically very sensitive, seeking to exemplify the Community interest, negotiating, and doing a whole range of deals in order to get agreement.

States have varied in the way they have handled their Presidencies. Some have been much more active than others, but all have a style of their own although, increasingly, Presidencies have worked with their predecessor and successor states in what has become known as the Troika. Nonetheless, the load can be a heavy one for some, mainly smaller, states. A six-month tenure is also very short and does not make it easy to achieve either real consistency or major projects. Partly for this reason, key decisions are more often taken at the end of a Presidency rather than at the beginning.

The Council also needs the support of its Committee of Permanent Representatives, known as COREPER after its initials in French. This goes back a long way but was only given full Treaty recognition at Maastricht. Previously its authority derived from the Council's Rules of Procedure. Its task is to seek for preliminary agreement to save overburdening the Council as such. It has two levels: COREPER 2, which brings together member states' ambassadors to the EC and deals with any sensitive and politically unresolved matters; and COREPER 1 which is composed of deputy representatives and deals with technical matters,

---

18. Kirchner, E., *Decision Making in the European Communities: The Council of Ministers and the Presidency*, Manchester University Press, Manchester, 1993.

including agriculture, on which there is a measure of agreement. Only the first can take decisions.

COREPER also relies on other specialized bodies such as the Special Committee on Agriculture; the Committee of Political Directors; and the Monetary Committee. These are composed of national representatives and can exercise real authority. Thus the Monetary Committee takes decisions on changes in the ERM. Some feed, as already seen, into Commission committees. There is also the *Antici* group which prepares Summit meetings. All these are supported by anything up to 200 working groups. Together they provide the Council with the means of processing its business so that agreed decisions can be reached without too much difficulty.

The third supporting element of the Council is its Secretariat. Its role seems to be essentially one of administrative support. It prepares agenda and minutes, advises the Presidency and maintains both continuity and liaison with other institutions. To do this it employs some 2,000 staff, including many translators, and is divided into six Directorates. This makes it both an important defence for the Council and something of a power broker. Its present institutionalization and legitimization by Article 151(2) of the Treaty is probably, in the personal view of Nicoll, due to the need to ensure that it controls the secretarial support for the other two Pillars of the union, thereby ensuring that these do not become autonomous. Hence Declaration 28 talks of a possible merger between the two, as well as of a better division of responsibility between COREPER and the Political Committee where the CFSP is concerned.

q.v. Declaration 28 p. 437.

Even though these changes are somewhat cosmetic and do not go very far to meet the demands of some reformers, they have been seen as making the Council even less accountable. Although there is pressure for the creation of a unified permanent Council, operating openly, through majority voting and sharing decision-making with Parliament, Wincott argues that the TEU limits the control of national parliaments.[19] With the implicit recognition, in Article 146, that ministers can bargain and the ability to conceal votes taken by majority and in secret governments have gained a new freedom of action, escaping from parliamentary control.[20] This reduces the democratic legitimacy of the Council. One might also add that the amended Rome Treaty does not do a great deal to ensure greater consistency or efficiency, especially where implementation is concerned. The Council remains one of the few bodies which legislates only in secrecy. Nor does it really resolve the ambiguities of the Council's relations with the European Council.

19. Wincott, D., 'A troublesome legacy? Some implications of the political development of the European Community', unpublished paper presented to the April 1993 PSA Annual Conference in Leicester, January 1993.
20. On the other hand it has been argued that, when ministers were not recognized as having the right to commit their governments, it was possible for one or two powers to block agreement by insisting on referring back for instructions.

Section 2   The Council

ARTICLE 145

To ensure that the objectives set out in this Treaty are attained, the Council shall, in accordance with the provisions of this Treaty:
— ensure coordination of the general economic policies of the Member States;
— have power to take decisions;
— confer on the Commission, in the acts which the Council adopts, powers for the implementation of the rules which the Council lays down. The Council may impose certain requirements in respect of the exercise of these powers. The Council may also reserve the right, in specific cases, to exercise directly implementing powers itself. The procedures referred to above must be consonant with principles and rules to be laid down in advance by the Council, acting unanimously on a proposal from the Commission and after obtaining the Opinion of the European Parliament.

ARTICLE 146

The Council shall consist of **a representative of each Member State at ministerial level, authorized to commit the government of that Member State.**

The office of President shall be held in turn by each Member State in the Council for a term of six months, in the following order of Member States:
— for a first cycle of six years: Belgium, Denmark, Germany, Greece, Spain, France, Ireland, Italy, Luxembourg, Netherlands, Portugal, United Kingdom;
— for the following cycle of six year: Denmark, Belgium, Greece, Germany, France, Spain, Italy, Ireland, Netherlands, Luxembourg, United Kingdom, Portugal.

ARTICLE 147

The Council shall meet when convened by its President on his initiative or at the request of one of its members or of the Commission.

ARTICLE 148

1. Save as otherwise provided in this Treaty, the Council shall act by a majority of its members.

2. Where the Council is required to act by a qualified majority, the votes of its members shall be weighted as follows:

Belgium	5
Denmark	3
Germany	10
Greece	5
Spain	8
France	10
Ireland	3
Italy	10
Luxembourg	2
Netherlands	5
Portugal	5
United Kingdom	10

For their adoption, acts of the Council shall require at least:
— fifty four votes in favour where this Treaty requires them to be adopted on a proposal from the Commission,
— fifty four votes in favour, cast by at least eight members, in other cases.

3. Abstentions by members present in person or represented shall not prevent the adoption by the Council of acts which require unanimity.

Article 149 is repealed[21]

---

21. Although the TEU, at G(45), states that this Article is repealed, the reality is slightly more complicated. Certainly there is now no Article 149, but most of the contents of the old Article, which deal with the SEA derived cooperation procedure of decision-making, are now to be found in Article 189. See pp. 301–2 below.

ARTICLE 150   Where a vote is taken, any member of the Council may also act on behalf of not more than one other member.

ARTICLE 151   1. *A committee consisting of the Permanent Representatives of the Member States shall be responsible for preparing the work of the Council and for carrying out the tasks assigned to it by the Council.*

2. The Council shall be assisted by a General Secretariat, under the direction of a Secretary-General. The Secretary-General shall be appointed by the Council acting unanimously.
The Council shall decide on the organization of the General Secretariat.

3. *The Council shall adopt its rules of procedure.*

ARTICLE 152   The Council may request the Commission to undertake any studies which the Council considers desirable for the attainment of the common objectives, and to submit to it any appropriate proposals.

ARTICLE 153   The Council shall, after receiving an opinion from the Commission, determine the rules governing the committees provided for in this Treaty.

ARTICLE 154   *The Council shall, acting by a qualified majority, determine the salaries, allowances and pensions of the President and members of the Commission, and of the President, Judges, Advocates-General and Registrar of the Court of Justice. It shall also, again by a qualified majority, determine any payment to be made instead of remuneration.*

FURTHER READING

Archer, C. and Butler, F., *The European Community: Structure and Process*, Pinter, London, 1992.

Brittan, L., 'The institutional development of the EC', Henry Street Memorial Lecture, University of Manchester, 16 October 1992.

EC Council, *Guide to the Council of the European Communities*, OOPEC, Luxembourg, 1992.

Hayes, F. *et al.* 'The Permanent Representatives of the member states', *Journal of Common Market Studies*, vol. 28, no. 1, 1989, pp. 119–38.

Keohane R. and Hoffman, S. (eds.), *The New European Community: Decisionmaking and institutional change*, Westview, Boulder, 1991.

Kirchner, E., *Decision-making in the European Community: The Council Presidency and European Integration*, Manchester University Press, Manchester, 1992.

Noël, E., *Working Together: The institutions of the EC*, OOPEC, Luxembourg, 1991.

O'Nuallain, C., *The Presidency of the European Council of Ministers*, Croom Helm, London, 1985.

Sabsoub, J.-P., *The Council of the European Community*, OOPEC, Luxembourg, 1990.

Vasey, M., 'Decision making in the Agricultural Council and the "Luxembourg Compromise"', *Common Market Law Review*, vol. 25, no. 4, 1988, pp. 725–32.

Wessels, W., 'The EC Council', in Keohane, R. and Hoffman, S. (eds.), *The New European Community: Decisionmaking and institutional change*, Westview, Boulder, 1991, pp. 133–54.

Whitton, J., 'The Council of the European Communities — Bibliographical review', *European Access*, 1991/2, pp. 39–47.

Wincott, D., 'A troublesome legacy? Some "legal" implications of the political development of the European Community', *PSA Annual Conference Paper*, 1993.

(c) The Commission

The Commission of the European Community is a very unusual kind of body. While not having quite the power of the High Authority of the Coal and Steel Community, it is still an important body whose legitimacy is that of the Community interest itself. Not surprisingly the Commission has therefore been described as the 'conscience of the Community'. Jean Monnet once described it as the 'Platonic embodiment of Communitarian spirit, with gallic *élan*, self confidence and expertise'.

Itself a hybrid of executive, legislative and enforcement agency, it has also generated a series of related offices such as the Community Secretariat General. Equally, it has come to symbolize the whole administrative apparatus of the Community. Yet, it is not a self-contained body. It is not the Community's only executive instrument. Rather it works in tandem with the Council which, as already seen, both controls it and sets it tasks.

Despite this, the Commission has become perhaps the most controversial of all the Community institutions. This is because it is unelected, activist and pro-Community. It is also a reflection of the fact that it is a good deal more able and skilful than its opponents care to concede. For, if de Gaulle clipped its wings during Walter Hallstein's Presidency, so that it was much less active in the 1970s, by the late 1980s external and internal forces had conspired to renew its dynamism. Such changes in pace and style owed very little to changes in the Treaty of Rome. Even with the TEU there were no really dramatic changes to the Articles regulating the Commission. So, as well as looking at the changes that were made, it is necessary to look beyond the Treaty to understand the roles played by the Commission, its membership, *modus operandi* and actual significance for the Community and the Union.

The TEU makes seven kinds of change to the rules governing the Commission. To begin with, it tidies up the existing text of the Treaty of Rome mainly by giving fuller status to the amendments introduced by the Merger Treaty (e.g. Articles 156 and 157). Second it provides a new mode of appointment for the President and the Commission, including what has been called 'double investiture' by Parliament as well as by member states (Article 158). Thirdly, in other Articles such as 103, 104c, 109c, 109h and 128–130, it confers other powers of investigation and initiative in new policy areas such as EMU and social policy. Here its position *vis-à-vis* member states seems to have been strengthened. Fourth, it is described in Articles J.9 and K.4(2) as being fully associated with the work of the two intergovernmental pillars of the Union. As well as establishing its right to be fully informed of what is happening within the pillars it can also innovate as in Article J.8 and even suggest, under Article K.9, that certain actions be transferred to the Community pillar.

q.v. conciliation procedure pp. 298–300.

On the other hand, a further change is that the new conciliation procedure may make it less independent of the Parliament, and more involved in political management both inside the Council and the Parliament. A sixth consideration is that it is now subject to somewhat stricter financial controls and accountability. In particular it has, under Article 201a together with Declarations 18 and 20, to establish that the existing budget can finance new activities and that environmental implications are considered. Finally, it will have to operate under new policy guidelines which often make it clear that primary responsibility lies with the member states. This has already made itself felt in educational policy. Moreover, subsidiarity may become an even more telling constraint.[22]

q.v. Declarations 18 and 20 pp. 435–6.

q.v. subsidiarity pp. 68–75.

---

22. This is apparent in the Commission's May 1993 Working Paper, *Guidelines for Community Action in the Field of Education and Training*, COM(93)183 final, Brussels, 5 May 1993. On subsidiarity see pp. 68–75.

Box 14.
What the Commission does

1. Upholds the Treaties, which implies
   (a) monitoring and
   (b) enforcement

2. Advises on matters in the Treaties, as required, of its own volition and when innovations are felt necessary

3. Takes Decisions whether in its own right or on a shared basis. This can also involve
   (a) information gathering and research;
   (b) taking quasi-legislative action: and
   (c) political management

4. Carries out duties bestowed upon it by the Council

5. Manages
   (a) the Community civil service; and
   (b) the Community's finances

6. Represents the Community in
   (a) diplomatic negotiations and missions; and
   (b) by providing information, etc.

7. Deals with any residual tasks

As a result of such changes the Treaty starts in Article 155 by repeating the existing statement of the Commission's four duties. These, however, are by no means a full description of the Commission's actual functions, such as the informational and the political. In particular, they omit the Commission's managerial, representational and residual roles. Hence the European Parliament's constitutional drafts have been much more explicit about what the Community can do. Box 14 takes this further.

The first constitutional duty of the Commission is to *uphold the Treaties* and the acquis of legislation passed under their authority. Hence the Commission is often described as the 'Guardian of the Treaties'. However, this duty involves two separate functions: monitoring the activities of other institutions as a kind of watchdog; and then seeking to ensure implementation by persuasion or, at worst bringing a case before the ECJ. Here it acts as a kind of prosecutor.[23]

The second duty is to *advise on matters in the Treaty*, either where required to do so by the Treaty or a Community institution, or of its own volition. Here too the duty requires more than one function. Thus it requires a kind of research function, whether through seeking advice from the Economic and Social and Regional Committees; consulting expert interests, commissioning academic studies (of which it does a lot), or of remembering exactly what the Community has been doing, or trying to do. Article 152 and others actually force the Commission to prepare such opinions. This leads into the fact that the Commission has a quasi-monopoly of policy initiation and innovation inside the Community. This is not because of a single Article, although Article 189a points in this direction, but

---

23. Despite the belief in the United Kingdom that the Commission is all pervasive, many authorities consider that it is actually lax and weak when it comes to dealing with member states who fail to implement the Treaties. Hence there is said to be 'an implementation deficit'.

because a host of Articles require the Council to act on a proposal from the Commission.

The third duty is *to take decisions*, whether in its own rights as permitted by Articles 89–93 and 115 on competition, and the CAP, or as a partner with Council and Parliament, in the passage of legislation. This again requires the informational function, while conferring quasi-legislative and judicial roles. Indeed, as has already been seen, the Commission has been described as being both judge and jury in competition matters. It also requires a very political function, of negotiating with other institutions and interests, putting together deals, and using its powers of persuasion to drive the policy process along. This shades off into the fourth duty of *exercising powers conferred on it* by the last paragraph of Article 145. Such duties are usually subject to the special scrutiny of committees of Council and other representatives. This process, which is very important to decision-making, is known as *comitology*.[24]

However, in practice the Commission does rather more than this. Indeed, these duties do scant justice to the Commission's actual role as an executive agency. Thus, to begin with, the Commission, in order to carry out all these functions, needs both human and financial resources. So it is a manager of the Community's administration and of its budget. Secondly, it is responsible for representing the Community. It does this by negotiating international agreements and by maintaining Community offices and envoys in other countries. Equally, at home, it is the body to whom all others turn because of its permanence and consistency. It is always there and hence people turn to it either to find out about the Community through its information and publication services, or to incite or query Community action.

As the Community's counsellor, receptionist and troubleshooter in fact, the Commission has a final residual role. It is the body called on to do the jobs that nobody else can really do. Without such a body, with a life of its own, it is likely that Community functioning would be rather less efficient than it presently is. Because of this, some proposed redrafts of the Treaties make this odd-jobbery a specific duty of the Commission. Article 156, which derives from the Merger Treaty, could be regarded as a further duty, that of reporting to the Parliament. However, this is probably best understood as a gesture towards the idea of accountability. In practice the Annual Report is debated but the Commission cannot really be made to answer for what is essentially a description of what has happened throughout the Community.

The first definition of what the Commission actually is comes in Article 157. This derives from both the Merger Treaty and Accession Treaties up to those with the Iberian states, and is essentially a code of good practice. The Treaty's definition of the Commission is restricted to the seventeen competent, independent,[25]

---

24. Comitology involves a range of bodies attached to the Commission. Some are management committees with executive powers, as in agriculture, others are advisory, whether expert or consultative. Presence on these committees gives a real access to decision-making which is why, during the EEA negotiations, the EFTA states were so keen to seek places within the system.

25. The two references to independence in Article 157(1) and (2) could be taken to imply that Commissioners should have been independent of the national government or other interests before nomination as well as in the

nationals of the member states who actually make up the Commission proper. Their independence comes from their oath not to accept directions, an undertaking by member states not to pressure them, and the threat of the loss of their pensions and other privileges and immunities. The fact that so many fail to win a second term of office suggests that most Commissioners remain more independent than some governments wish.

However, this does not stop members of the Commission maintaining close links with their own, national, political systems. Many, of course, have been cabinet ministers there. So, they can act as powerful links and advocates for the Community interest, a process sometimes called 'going native' by Margaret Thatcher. This is in line with the perception that they are political figures with their own views and contribution to make and not mere executant civil servants as some UK Europhobes would prefer.

The Commission meets without translators, votes by majority, and has a quorum of eight. Members are expected to defend the decisions taken collectively. It works as much by written procedures as by oral ones and is tightly controlled by its rules of procedure. The Court of Justice has thus established that the original text of its proposals must be attached to its minutes.

While the TEU does not alter this, it does make significant changes to the nomination of the Commission and its President. Previously the Commission as a whole were appointed by 'the common accord' of the governments of the member states, and for five years. The amended Article 158 provides for a five-year term of office, save where a Commission is dismissed by a censure vote in the Parliament under Article 144. Moreover, not merely is their installation in office dependent on approval by the Parliament, in what is known as 'negative approval', but, from 1995, terms of office will begin after a new Parliament has been elected and will coincide with the length of the Parliament. This does not make the Commission fully responsible to the Parliament. However, it does imply an enhanced accountability.

Prior to the TEU, the President of the Commission was only mentioned as one of the officers of the Commission in Article 161. Following on the TEU the rules have been brought into line with reality. The amended Article 158 gives precedence to his/her nomination and this requires consultation with the Parliament, probably represented by its Enlarged Bureau. The latter also has to endorse the new President along with the rest of the Commission.

The President also gains a formal, consultative role in the selection of the other members of the Commission. The revised Article 161 reduces the number of the previously largely symbolic Vice-Presidents. This too can be regarded as a move towards a clearer leadership role. However, Maastricht did not go as far as the Parliament's new draft constitution which specifies the role of the President and extends it to dismissing both other Commissioners and the Parliament itself.

exercise of their duties. This has never been the case and seems to be either a reflection of the importance given to independence of the Commissioners or, less likely, of poor drafting. The TEU did not adopt the suggestions of the Luxembourg and Dutch Presidencies to establish Deputy Commissioners and to restrict the number to twelve. However, Declaration 15 (see p. 434) commits them to examine the number of Commissioners in the future.

As suggested, these changes reflect the way the Presidency has, since the time of Roy Jenkins, taken on a more active role. This role has been marked by the personal style of the incumbent, particularly under Jacques Delors. The authority of the Presidency has emerged partly from the general context, partly from personality especially with Delors' long tenure of office, and partly from the fact that, by custom, the President has a seat at the European Council as well as at international meetings such as those of the G7. The fact that the President also presents the Commission's programme to the Parliament, as well as reporting to it, is also significant.

Nonetheless, the President has only limited powers. He/she can neither dismiss other Commissioners, only define and redistribute portfolios, nor be outvoted by colleagues, some of whom may be more experienced and dug in than the President. The Commission is essentially a collegiate body, taking decisions in common at their weekly meeting, even though its members have specific responsibilities of their own. Hence conflicts are not unknown.

Articles 159 and 160 provide for the ending of Commissioners' tenure, whether by resignation or dismissal. In the first case, the TEU confirms the existing rule, as originally laid down in the Merger Treaty, that a replacement Commissioner cannot hold office into a new cycle. In the new circumstances this may strengthen the notion of answerability to the Parliament since new appointments will have to be reconfirmed. The Treaty also introduces a new element which is to bring the replacement of the President into line with the new procedures. The provisions for proposals for retirement of Commissioners by the Court, which has only happened once when a sick member fell into a coma, are unchanged.

Articles 162 and 163, the last two in Section 3, which are upgraded versions of clauses inherited from the Merger Treaty, provide the only real guidance on how the Commission actually works. They make clear that while the Commission can decide how it acts, it must cooperate with the Council. There is no qualified or weighted majority, which requires an uneven number of members, as there is no provision for a Presidential casting vote.

In reality, of course, the Commission requires much more to help it operate. Three things in particular deserve to be noted here: the Commissioners' *cabinets*; the General Secretariat of the Commission; and the Commission's administrative services and staff. None of these are really set out in the Treaties. Nonetheless, they deserve attention.

To help them in their work the Commissioners have adopted the French practice of personal *cabinets*. These consist of a number of personally appointed political and administrative advisers. By 1989 there were some 300 of these. The tasks of the *cabinets* are essentially threefold. First they are advisory bodies, responsible for briefing their Commissioners. Secondly, they are representative bodies, speaking for their Commissioners in meetings of officials and helping coordinate their administrative responsibilities, which can often overlap a number of Directorates. This is especially true in the case of the President's *cabinet*. Thirdly, the *cabinets* provide liaison between the Commissioners and both other

Community institutions and his or her home state. In all three cases they act as a support and a buffer, allowing Commissioners to work more effectively.

The Secretariat General serves the Commission as a whole, although it is directly responsible to the President and emerges from the Commission's own rules of procedure and not from the Treaty as such. Its head, presently David Williamson, a former Cabinet Office official, sits in on Commission meetings. He is assisted by a large staff divided into eight directorates and a separate Legal Service. The latter employs some 80 lawyers who advise the Commission on legal matters, over which they have a virtual veto; represents the Commission before the ECJ; and run the legal information services.

The Secretariat as such services the Commission, a task which includes drawing up Commission agendas in conjunction with the *chefs de cabinet*. It also provides liaison with other Community institutions, provides planning services, and acts as a spokesman for the Community. Finally it coordinates the administrative services of the Commission influencing its working methods and priorities. These roles make it a politically important body.

The Commission employs over 17,000 staff, some 750 of whom are temporary appointments. This includes about 4,000 research staff in a number of centres throughout the Community and a large number of translators, although the working languages tend to be English and French. Some civil servants are detached from national governments, others are *stagiaires* learning about the Community by working for it, and some are paid consultants. The vast majority gain employment through the Community's normal processes of entry by examination. There are also quotas to ensure that the Community's civil service represents all member states, notably at the two upper grades. Grade A, which requires a university degree and equates with the Administrative class of the UK civil service, also has a number of outside political appointments at the level of Director General. Grade B officials, like the UK Executive Class, require school-leaving qualifications. The lower clerical and manual grades tend to be locally recruited.

The Commission is divided into some 23 Directorates-General (DGs), which are subdivided into Directorates and Divisions, as the diagram shows. Figure 10 shows their present structure and the Commissioners to whom they are responsible. The DGs provide the detailed research, processing and implementation needed by the Community. Though often denounced as being a huge bureaucracy, the Commission actually employs no more staff than a city like Edinburgh or a small national ministry. And staff numbers, as a percentage of Community population, have remained more or less stable over the years. Although they are well paid, Community civil servants have much expected of them. They have to be innovative, effective legislators and managers, skilled negotiators and, above all, highly diplomatic.

All this shows that the Commission in its weekly sessions, its other meetings and its many visits, is supported by a huge range of other meetings and administrative activities. It is also surrounded by a range of advisory, managerial and control committees on which member states and social interests are

Figure 10. The third
Delors Commission,
1993–1994

Jacques Delors (Fr) *President*
 Secretariat General; Forward Studies Unit; Inspectorate General; Legal Service; Monetary Matters;
 Spokesman's Service; Interpretation & Conference Service; Security Office

Henning Christophersen (DK) VP
 DG I: Economic and Financial Affairs
 DG XVIII: Credit and Investments
 Statistical Office

Manuel Marin (Sp) VP
 DG I: External Relations — Economic Cooperation with Mediterranean, Middle & Near East,
 Latin America & Asia
 DG VIII: Development with Lomé Convention
 EC Humanitarian Aid Office

Martin Bangemann (Ger) VP
 DG III: Industrial Affairs
 DG XIII: Information & Telecommunications Technology

Leon Brittan (UK) VP
 DG I: External Economic Affairs — America, Japan, CIS and Europe; Commercial Policy

Abel Matutes (Sp)
 DG XVII: Energy & Euratom Supply Agency
 DG VII: Transport

Peter Schmidhuber (Ger)
 DG XIX: Budgets; DG XX: Financial Control with Fraud Prevention
 DG XXII: Coordination of Structural Instruments including management of Cohesion Funds

Christiane Scrivener (Fr)
 DG XXI: Customs Union and Indirect Taxation and Direct Taxation and Consumer Affairs

Bruce Millan (UK)
 DG XVI: Regional Policy including relations with the Committee of the Regions

Karel Van Miert (Bel)
 DG IV: Competititon
 DG IX: Personnel and Administration including translation and information technology

Hans Van de Broek (NL)
 DG I: External Relations — External Political Relations, Common Foreign and Security Policy,
 and Enlargement Negotiations Task Force

João de Deus Pinheiro (P)
 Relations with the European Parliament
 DG X: Information with Internal Relations with the member states relating to openness,
 communication and information;
 Culture and Audiovisual matters;
 OOPEC

Padraig Flynn (Irl)
 DG V: Employment and Social Affairs with relations with EcoSoc and questions related to
 cooperation on justice and home affairs, including immigration

Antonio Ruberti (It)
 DG XII: Science, Research and Development with Joint Resources Centre and **DG V
 Education**, including human resources, training and youth

René Steichen (Lux)
 DG VI: Agriculture and rural development

Ioannis Paleokrassas (Greece)
 DG XI: Environment & Nuclear Safety with civil protection
 DG XIV: Fisheries

Raniero Vanni d'Archirafi (It)
 DG III: Internal-Market
 DG XV: Financial Institutions
 DG XXIII: Small and Medium-Sized Enterprises Task Force with enterprise policy, trade
 and crafts; plus Institutional questions

represented.[26] All this makes it a relatively open form of governance. Indeed, policies are often floated through the European Parliament and there is more cooperation with the Council than sometimes is imagined.

The Commission then is what the French call the *cheville ouvrière* or the workhorse of the Community. It is a body with more powers than member states sometimes like.[27] As well as acting as the collective conscience of the Community it is also the mechanic with the oil can which keeps the machine on the road. And it is keen on preserving this role, even though the workload is very large and likely to increase with enlargement. There is a case for looking at the extent of its responsibilities and the effectiveness of its working procedures.

However, its influence is limited and its role as a proposer tends to make it seem more potent than it actually is. Hence it needs a better image and more legitimacy. Whether the new procedures of double investiture will give it this kind of accountability and legitimacy is open to question. Its role is thus likely to be central to future debates about the organization of the Union.

Section 3 The Commission

ARTICLE 155

In order to ensure the proper functioning and development of the common market, the Commission shall;
— ensure that the provisions of this Treaty and the measures taken by the institutions pursuant thereto are applied;
— formulate recommendations or deliver opinions on matters dealt with in this Treaty, if it expressly so provides or if the Commission considers it necessary;
— have its own power of decision and participate in the shaping of measures taken by the Council and by the European Parliament in the manner provided for in this Treaty;
— exercise the powers conferred on it by the Council for the implementation of the rules laid down by the latter.

ARTICLE 156

The Commission shall publish annually, not later than one month before the opening of the session of the European Parliament, a general report on the activities of the Community.

ARTICLE 157

1. The Commission shall consist of seventeen members, who shall be chosen on the grounds of their general competence and whose independence is beyond doubt.

The number of members of the Commission may be altered by the Council, acting unanimously.

---

26. These includes expert committees of technical specialists drawn from the member states who look at draft legislation in their field and its political implications; consultative committees drawn from specialist interest groups in agriculture and other fields which advise on policy development; management committees, which bring together member state representatives and others to oversee the management of the Commission's agricultural and other responsibilities, notably where price levels are concerned; and regulatory committees, again composed of member state officials, and dealing with harmonization.

27. The ECJ dismissed a suit by Britain and other member states which sought to show that the Commission had no general legislative powers, only duties of surveillance and implementation. Interestingly, as has already been made clear above, the Council has continued to delegate powers to the Commission. It is also possible that the Commission, by acting as an aunt Sally, serves to lessen national conflicts inside the Community.

Only nationals of Member States may be members of the Commission.

The Commission must include at least one national of each of the Member States, but may not include more than two members having the nationality of the same State.

2. The members of the Commission shall, in the general interest of the Community, be completely independent in the performance of their duties.

In the performance of these duties, they shall neither seek nor take instructions from any government or from any other body. They shall refrain from any action incompatible with their duties. Each Member State undertakes to respect this principle and not to seek to influence the members of the Commission in the performance of their tasks.

*The members of the Commission may not, during their term of office, engage in any other occupation, whether gainful or not. When entering upon their duties they shall give a solemn undertaking that, both during and after their term of office, they will respect the obligations arising therefrom and in particular their duty to behave with integrity and discretion as regards the acceptance, after they have ceased to hold office, of certain appointments or benefits. In the events of any breach of these obligations, the Court of Justice may, on application by the Council or the Commission, rule that the member concerned be, according to the circumstances, either compulsorily retired in accordance with Article **160** or deprived of his rights to a pension or benefits in its stead.*

ARTICLE 158

1. *The members of the Commission shall be appointed,* **in accordance with the procedure referred to in paragraph 2, for a period of five years, subject, if need be, to Article 144.**

Their term of office shall be renewable.

2. *The governments of the Member States shall nominate by common accord,* **after consulting the European Parliament, the person they intend to appoint as President of the Commission.**

The governments of the Member States shall, in consultation with the nominee for President, nominate the other persons whom they intend to appoint as members of the Commission.

The President and the other members of the Commission thus nominated shall be subject as a body to a vote of approval by the European Parliament. After approval by the European Parliament, the President and the other members of the Commission shall be appointed by common accord of the governments of the Member States.

3. Paragraphs 1 and 2 shall be applied for the first time to the President and the other members of the Commission whose term of office begins on 7 January 1995.

The President and the other members of the Commission whose term of office begins on 7 January 1993 shall be appointed by common accord of the governments of the Member States. Their term of office shall expire on 6 January 1995.

ARTICLE 159

Apart from normal replacement, or death, the duties of a member of the Commission shall end when he resigns or is compulsorily retired.

The vacancy thus caused shall be filled for the remainder of the member's term of office **by a new member appointed by common accord of the governments of the Member States.** *The Council may, acting unanimously, decide that such a vacancy need not be filled.*

In the event of resignation, compulsory retirement or death, the President

shall be replaced for the remainder of his term of office. The procedure laid down in Article 158(2) shall be applicable for the replacement of the President.

*Save in the case of compulsory retirement under Article **160**, members of the Commission shall remain in office until they have been replaced.*

ARTICLE 160

If any member of the Commission no longer fulfils the conditions required for the performance of his duties or if he has been guilty of serious misconduct, the Court of Justice may, on application by the Council or the Commission, compulsorily retire him.

ARTICLE 161

The Commission may appoint a Vice-President or two Vice-Presidents from among its members.

ARTICLE 162

1. The Council and the Commission shall consult each other and shall settle by common accord their methods of cooperation.

2. The Commission shall adopt its rules of procedure so as to ensure that both it and its departments operate in accordance with the provisions of **this Treaty**. *It shall ensure that these rules are published.*

ARTICLE 163

*The Commission shall act by a majority of the number of members provided for in Article **157**.*

A meeting of the Commission shall be valid only if the number of members laid down in its rules of procedure is present.

FURTHER READING

Butt Philip, A., *Pressure Groups in the EC*, UACES, London, 1985.

EC, *The European Commission and the Administration of the Community*, OOPEC, Luxembourg, 1989.

Ehlermann, C.-D., 'Commission lacks power in the 1992 process', *European Affairs*, 1990/1, pp. 65–73.

Garrett, G., 'International cooperation and institutional choices: the European Community's Internal Market', *International Organization*, vol. 46, no. 2, 1992, pp. 533–60.

Hailsham, Lord and Vaughan, D. (eds.), *The Law of the European Communities*, Butterworth, London, 1986.

Lasok, D. and Bridge, J., *Introduction to the Law and Institutions of the European Communities*, 3rd edn, Butterworth, London, 1986.

Lodge, J., 'EC policymaking: institutional dynamics', in Lodge, J. (ed.), *The European Community and the Challenge of the Future*, 2nd edn, Pinter, London, 1993, pp. 1–36.

Ludlow, P., 'The Commission' in Keohane, R. and Hoffman, S. (eds.), *The New European Community: Decisionmaking and Institutional Change*, Westview, Boulder, 1991, pp. 85–132.

Mazey, S. and Richardson, J., *Lobbying in the European Community*, Nuffield European Studies, Oxford University Press, Oxford, 1993.

Noël, E., *Working Together: The institutions of the EC*, OOPEC, Luxembourg, 1988.

Padoa-Schioppa, T., 'Sur les institutions politiques de l'Europe nouvelle', *Commentaire*, vol. 15, no. 58, 1992, pp. 283–92.

Peters, B.G., 'Bureaucratic politics and the institutions of the European Community', in Sbragia, A.M. (ed.), *Euro-Politics: Institutions and Policymaking in the 'New' European Community*, Brookings Institution, Washington, 1992, pp. 75–122.

Phinnemore, D., *Sources on the European Community: A handbook for students*, University of Kent, Canterbury, 1992.

Spencer, D. and Edwards, G., *The European Commission*, Longman, London, 1993.

Vahl, Remco E., 'The European Commission on the road to European Union: the consequences of the Treaty on European Union for the Commission's power base', *Acta Politica*, vol. 27, no. 3, 1992, pp. 297–322.

(d) The European Court of Justice and Community Law

The European Court of Justice (ECJ) represents the fourth legitimacy of the Community: its dependence on the rule of law. This would be important in any

Western European democratic structure. It is particularly important in the context of such an unusual political body as the Community, as it was in the ECSC from which the ECJ ultimately derives. With an even more influential High Executive under the ECSC judicial control was especially necessary.

Even today, because the Community has no police or army to enforce its acts, because, for a long while, it lacked effective and representative parliamentary scrutiny, and because the Treaties were produced by politicians, thereby leaving gaps, inconsistencies and uncertainties, the ECJ was the only body available to give final rulings on Treaty meanings and obligations. Indeed, it has been said that without the Court and the legally enforceable framework, integration within the Community could have broken up.

As well as thus symbolizing the 'Law' in general, and the emerging corpus of EC law, the Court has come to play an even more important role. Responding to the deficiencies of the texts, to its own corporate interests (and those of the European legal community) and to the prompting of the other institutions, it has become an activist body with an influence on policy. It also gained authority from the Single European Act which created a subordinate Court of First Instance (CFI).

q.v. EC law pp. 289–92.

All this has made the ECJ somewhat controversial and often unpopular with nationally-minded politicians. On the other hand, all Community institutions and many member states are willing to use it for their own ends. Thus the UK government appeals to it as the embodiment of law; the body which ensures a fair economic playing field; and the means of blocking unacceptable Commission initiatives. It should also be noted that the Court is not wholly exempt from politically imposed rules.

The TEU made some seven changes to the standing of the two Courts. To begin with, some parts of the common activities of the Twelve have, for the second time, been placed outside its jurisdiction. The Court has been largely excluded from dealing with the Common Provisions and the two Pillars.[28] On the other hand, the scope of the ECJ's activities has been expanded by Articles 173 and L. At the same time, the European Parliament has seen its ability to bring suits before the Court increased by Article 175. Fourth, the Treaty texts have been tidied up to take account of the new institutions and processes introduced elsewhere in the TEU. More significantly, the amended third paragraph of Article 165 enables the ECJ to work more effectively. Equally the role of the CFI has been extended by the new Article 168a. Finally, the ECJ's powers of enforcement against recalcitrant member states have been considerably increased by the new provisions of Articles 171(2), 176 and 180.

The text of Section 4 of Chapter 1 now begins by stating the Court's duty to ensure that the Treaties are observed. Since this extends to interpretation and application, the ECJ has both a judicial and an enforcement role, deciding on meaning and overseeing the way national courts actually apply the rules. Yet Article 164 also means that it can only act within the powers allowed it by the

---

28. The role of the Court is, in law, restricted to Articles G, H, I, K.3(2)(c) and L–S of the TEU as such. It also has oversight over most of the Protocols, although some may tie its hands. Its influence over the Declarations, which enjoy a lesser status and are often expressions of hope rather than precise commitments, is even less certain. Prior to the TEU, under the SEA, the ECJ had no jurisdiction over European Political Cooperation.

Treaty of Rome. Hence, while it is the Community's supreme judicial authority, it does not have the kind of general powers enjoyed by the International Court of Justice in the Hague.

The Treaty then moves on to four Articles dealing with the form, membership and services of the body to undertake this role. The heart of the Court are the thirteen Judges who make the ultimate decisions. Rather than stating how they are selected Article 165 only hints at it, leaving it to Article 167 to expand on the subject. Article 165 states that they can meet either all together or in smaller sessions known as 'Chambers', of between three and six Judges, thus enabling the Court to handle more business. Previously the ECJ had, by a Council decision of November 1974 incorporated into the old Article 165, to meet in plenary session whenever member states or other institutions brought cases before it. It now only has to do so if asked, again facilitating its proceedings.

Alongside the Judges, Article 166 adds six Advocates-General. This office is not found in United Kingdom law although it resembles the Public Prosecutor or Government Commissioner found in continental legal systems. The Advocates-General are members of the Court with similar privileges to the Judges, but they fulfil a different role. Rather than being referees they are more consultants. They offer a preliminary look at cases, relating them to national law, examining the relevant EC law, proposing solutions, and suggesting how these solutions might affect future cases.

To some extent their 'reasoned submissions' make up for the facts that there are neither dissenting opinions in ECJ judgements nor the lower 'federal' courts found in the American judicial system. Their ideas are not binding but are made public and are usually followed by the Judges. Hence they have been described as the 'embodied conscience of the ECJ'. Many go on to be Judges themselves. Normally each of the large states, including Spain, nominates one, leaving the smaller states to appoint the sixth in rotation.

The amended Article 167 provides that Judges and Advocates-General should have appropriate legal qualifications.[29] However, although their appointment is supposed to be by 'common consent', the Council usually acquiesces in national nominations. Only in the case of the thirteenth Judge, presently necessary to ensure that there is always a majority in case the Court is split, is the appointee really chosen without regard to nationality. Perhaps because of this the European Parliament has often pressed for a share in nominating the Judges. This might encourage the existing tendency of member states to nominate Judges with 'European' sympathies and lead to the kind of arguments about the political leanings of candidates found in the US Supreme Court.

Article 167 also seeks to ensure that there is a regular turnover in the personnel of the Court. This is to ensure its representativeness and effectiveness. The Council can also increase the numbers involved if it so chooses. As well as

---

29. Judges are required to reside in Luxembourg. They cannot hold any other position while in office as judges. Nor can they take part in cases in which they have an interest. They enjoy certain legal and fiscal immunities. It is worth noting also that the first woman Advocate-General was appointed in 1981 ahead of the first female Commissioner. The Article was amended after Iberian accession.

a President of the ECJ as a whole, there are Presidents of the various Chambers. The President chairs the Court and appoints Judges to specific cases. Each Advocate-General in turn functions as First Advocate-General in a similar fashion.[30]

The Courts as a whole are then, thanks to Article 168, served by an administration of some 650 staff, headed by a Registrar appointed for a six-year term. The Registrar is assisted by an Assistant and a Director of Administration. The Registry, which is divided into four sections, is primarily responsible for authenticating, recording and publishing the Courts' acts. It is also responsible for translation, for legal information and for financial and general administration.

The Court of First Instance emerged in the late 1980s to cope with the growing backlog of cases facing the Community, notably those dealing with disputes between the Community's staff and its institutions. Hence it tends to meet in Chambers and does not have Advocates-General. However, one of the twelve Judges is usually invited to act in a similar fashion. Terms of appointment and rules of procedure are similar to those of the ECJ.

The TEU reinforces the status and influence of the CFI. Previously the Treaties simply allowed the Community to create such a court. Article 168a now states its existence although it does provide for appeal to the ECJ where the CFI might be thought not to have jurisdiction or where it might have misconstrued precedents. The TEU also responded to pressure from the Courts by generally increasing the range of cases which can be referred to the CFI, providing that this does not extend to hearing preliminary rulings under Article 177. These are matters of sensitive legal interpretation which have to be heard by the ECJ itself. This suggests that, in the long run, the lower Court may become the body which normally hears direct cases, leaving the ECJ to become an appeal court. Equally, Declaration 33 gives it jurisdiction over staff cases emanating from the ECB.

q.v.
Declaration
33 p. 441.

The majority of the TEU's judicial provisions, however, are concerned with who should bring cases before the Courts; the kind of cases to be heard by the Court; and with the way they should be heard. Article 169 makes the Commission responsible both for monitoring member states' implementation of Community rules and for delivering a preliminary warning. Where the state does not heed this the Commission can bring proceedings before the Court. Member states are also allowed to sue each other for non-compliance providing the Commission's early warning procedure has been invoked first. In practice states have been reluctant to do this although their right to do so is reasserted by the TEU in Article 170, the next Article. A further provision of this kind appears in Article 184.

One of the innovations of the TEU is in Article 171(2). This allows the Commission to return to the ECJ when a member state ignores a Court ruling. This has been a consistent problem, notably where Italy is concerned, and such a measure was strongly supported by the UK government. The Commission is now allowed to suggest a fine which the ECJ can then impose. The Parliament

---

30. Although the Treaty does not specify this, each Judge and Advocate-General is assisted by one or more Legal Secretaries or Referendaires. These are personal legal advisers. Such posts can also serve as a springboard for a higher position in the ECJ.

is also, under the revised Article 172, to be associated with the Council in drawing up rules on the extent of such fines.

Article 173 also extends the rights of the Court to review decisions of other institutions, by adding the Parliament and the ECB to the list. It leaves unchanged the right of individuals and corporate bodies to bring actions against institutions and member states, which actually form the largest body of cases heard by the ECJ. Article 175 also gives the Court authority to act where states and institutions simply fail to do something expected of them, rather than actually doing something abusively or incorrectly. The modalities of the Court's decisions in such cases are laid down in Article 174 and the amended Article 176.

The Treaties have never allowed individuals to appeal to the ECJ against decision by national courts. However, Article 177 does require national courts, faced with uncertainty on matters of EC law arising from cases before them, to seek advice from Luxembourg. Thanks to the TEU the ECJ no longer has to act *en bloc* to give such rulings, but can refer them to chambers. The Article specifies three possible sets of uncertainties: the content, scope and meaning of the Treaty itself; the validity of acts of Community institutions and the ECB; and the interpretation of the procedural ground rules of some bodies where the former have been endorsed by the Council.

This Article has been of considerable political importance since it has encouraged some landmark Court decisions which have become part of the constitutional *acquis*. It has also helped to involve national legal systems in EC decisions. The references in Articles 178 and 183, which imply a respect for national legal systems, may also have helped in this context. Of course the Court cannot, in virtue of Articles 173 and 177, strike down rulings by national courts.

The Treaties also provide for six other forms of Community jurisdiction. These are for damages arising out of the general liability of the Community at contract (Article 178);[31] for disputes involving the Community's own staff (Article 179); in cases deriving from member states' obligations to the European Investment Bank and now the ECB (Articles 180a and 180d); against measures taken by Governors and Directors of the former (Articles 180b and 180c); for cases where arbitration clauses require it (Article 181); and where member states are in dispute about the Treaty (Article 182). Perhaps the new rules regarding the ECB are the most significant here as they allow sanctions against member states' financial and economic policies. The Court can also issue Opinions notably on the legal appropriateness of foreign agreements concluded by the Community under Article 228.

Lawyers characterize these jurisdictions as involving direct and indirect actions. The former are for non-fulfilment (Articles 169−172); for annulment on grounds of infringement by misuse (Articles 173−174); for infringement by failure to act (Articles 175−176); and for damages (Article 178). The latter include preliminary rulings (Article 177); staff cases (Article 179); arbitration (Article 181); contentious jurisdiction; and opinions. The largest body of cases so far concerns

---

31. The formulation allows the ECJ to limit the potentially vast liabilities deriving from application of Article 215 to the CAP.

staff cases, the CAP, the Customs Union and freedom of movement. Individuals and firms are more prone to bring lawsuits than are institutions and member states.

The final elements of Section 4 deal with the way the Court operates. Article 183 and 184, as already noted, make extra provisions about jurisdiction. The next one, Article 185, allows policies which have been queried to continue in force while the ECJ deliberates unless there are special circumstances or the Court decides to make interim arrangements (Article 186). Court decisions are then (Article 187) declared enforceable according to normal national rules, as is provided in Article 192.

Finally, Article 188 provides a framework for the way the Courts actually work. It draws attention to the ECJ's more detailed 46-Article set of Standing Orders or Statute, which appears as a Protocol to the Treaty of Rome and which, save as indicated by Article 168a, applies to the CFI. The Council is able to change Title III of the Statute which relates to the organization of the Court. However, it can only say yea or nay to the Courts' procedural rules.

q.v. Statute of ECJ pp. 558–64.

The Court actually works mainly by written proceedings, because this is linguistically easier. In oral proceedings the plaintiff can usually decide the language adopted. All proceedings must take place in Luxembourg. The Court begins by appointing a Judge Rapporteur and an Advocate-General to a case. The Court then assembles documentation and evidence. A public hearing can then be held in which lawyers, whether from member states, Community legal services, or the private sector make submissions. Cross-questioning is uncommon and judgment is always reserved at this stage. However, the Court has been willing to allow TV cameras into sessions which are of interest to particular countries.

The Advocate-General then draws up his report and the Judge Rapporteur makes recommendations to the Court, whether Chamber or Plenary. The latter then processes the case without either Advocates-General or legal secretaries being present. It comes to its judgment by secret majority vote, and without publishing any dissenting views. This gives the Judges protection against pressure from member states. The decision sets out the facts and the issues, the reasoning applied to the case and the decisions reached, both on the legal point and the costs. It is then signed by the President and published in the Official Journal. In coming to its decisions the Court uses a variety of means of interpretation: the words used, their context, the apparent intention of the authors of the text in question, the wider legal implications, and the linguistic dimensions. It is not bound by precedent. However, this *modus operandi* can make the Court rather slow and expensive for many of those who use it.

Because of this way of proceeding, the ECJ has been attacked for disregarding the actual texts and seeking to constitutionalize the Treaties in a 'federalist' way. Hence it has upheld the sovereignty of the Community and its institutions. Yet, it has done this with the apparent approval of most national legal systems because of its skilful tactics. Nonetheless, some authorities think that the TEU marks a counter-attack by member states. Through the Protocols on pension equality, the Social Chapter opt-out, and the Irish abortion provisions the legal *acquis* has been overridden. Moreover, the structure of the Union, notably in Article L, may prevent the Court from redressing the position in the way it has done in the past.

q.v. Irish abortion provisions pp. 469–70.

So, the future role both of the Courts and the all-important system of law which they symbolize (see above p. 280) remains uncertain.

q.v. EC Law pp. 289–92.

Section 4   The Court of Justice

ARTICLE 164

The Court of Justice shall ensure that in the interpretation and application of this Treaty the law is observed.

ARTICLE 165

The Court of Justice shall consist of thirteen Judges.

The Court of Justice shall sit in plenary session. It may, however, form chambers each consisting of three or five Judges, either to undertake certain preparatory inquiries or to adjudicate on particular categories of cases in accordance with rules laid down for these purposes.

The Court of Justice shall sit in plenary session when a Member State or a Community institution that is a party to the proceedings so requests.

Should the Court of Justice so request, the Council may, acting unanimously, increase the number of Judges and make necessary adjustments to the second and third paragraphs of this Article and to the second of Article 167.

ARTICLE 166

The Court of Justice shall be assisted by six Advocates-General.

It shall be the duty of the Advocate-General, acting with complete impartiality and independence, to make, in open court, reasoned submissions on cases brought before the Court of Justice, in order to assist the Court in the performance of the task assigned to it in Article 164.

Should the Court of Justice so request, the Council may, acting unanimously, increase the number of Advocates-General and make the necessary adjustments to the third paragraph of Article 167.

ARTICLE 167

The Judges and Advocates-General shall be chosen from persons whose independence is beyond doubt and who possess the qualifications required for appointment to the highest judicial offices in their respective countries or who are jurisconsults of recognized competence; they shall be appointed by common accord of the Governments of the Member States for a term of six years.

Every three years there shall be a partial replacement of the Judges. Seven and six Judges shall be replaced alternately.

Every three years there shall be a partial replacement of the Advocates-General. Three Advocates-General shall be replaced on each occasion.

Retiring Judges and Advocates-General shall be eligible for re-appointment.

The Judges shall elect the President of the Court of Justice from among their number for a term of three years. He may be re-elected.

ARTICLE 168

The Court of Justice shall appoint its Registrar and lay down the rules governing his service.

ARTICLE 168a

1. **A Court of First Instance shall be attached to the Court of Justice** with jurisdiction to hear and determine at first instance, subject to a right of appeal to the Court of Justice on points of law only and in accordance with the conditions laid down by Statute, certain classes of action or proceeding defined **in accordance with the conditions laid down in paragraph 2. The Court of First Instance** shall not be competent to hear and determine questions referred for a preliminary ruling under Article 177.

2. **At the request of the Court of Justice and after consulting the European Parliament and the Commission, the Council, acting unanimously,** shall determine **the classes of action or proceeding referred to in paragraph 1 and the** *composition of* **the Court of First Instance** and shall adopt the necessary adjustments and additional provisions to the Statute of the Court of Justice. Unless the Council decides otherwise, the provisions of this Treaty relating to the Court of Justice, in particular the provisions of the Protocol on the Statute of the Court of Justice, shall apply to the **Court of First Instance.**

3. The members of **the Court of First Instance** shall be chosen from persons whose independence is beyond doubt and who possess the ability required for appointment to judicial office; they shall be appointed by common accord of the governments of the Member States for a term of six years. The membership shall be partially renewed every three years. Retiring members shall be eligible for re-appointment.

4. **The Court of First Instance** shall establish its rules of procedure in agreement with the Court of Justice. Those rules shall require the unanimous approval of the Council.

ARTICLE 169

If the Commission considers that a Member State has failed to fulfil an obligation under this Treaty, it shall deliver a reasoned opinion on the matter after giving the State concerned the opportunity to submit its observations.

If the State concerned does not comply with the opinion within the period laid down by the Commission the latter may bring the matter before the Court of Justice.

ARTICLE 170

A Member State which considers that another Member State has failed to fulfil an obligation under this Treaty may bring the matter before the Court of Justice.

Before a Member State brings an action against another Member State for an alleged infringement of an obligation under this Treaty, it shall bring the matter before the Commission.

The Commission shall deliver a reasoned opinion after each of the States concerned has been given the opportunity to submit its own case and its observations on the other party's case both orally and in writing.

If the Commission has not delivered an opinion within three months of the date on which the matter was brought before it, the absence of such opinion shall not prevent the matter from being brought before the Court of Justice.

ARTICLE 171

1. If the Court of Justice finds that a Member State has failed to fulfil an obligation under this Treaty, the State shall be required to take the necessary measures to comply with the judgment of the Court of Justice.

2. **If the Commission considers that the Member State concerned has not taken such measures it shall, after giving that State the opportunity to submit its observations, issue a reasoned opinion specifying the points on which the Member State concerned has not complied with the judgment of the Court of Justice.**

If the Member State concerned fails to take the necessary measures to comply with the Court's judgment within the time-limit laid down by the Commission, the latter may bring the case before the Court of Justice. In so doing it shall specify the amount of lump sum or penalty payment to be paid by the Member State concerned which it considers appropriate in the circumstances.

If the Court of Justice finds that the Member State concerned has not

complied with its judgment it may impose a lump sum or penalty payment on it.

This procedure shall be without prejudice to Article 170.

ARTICLE 172

Regulations **adopted jointly by the European Parliament and the Council, and** by the Council, pursuant to the provisions of this Treaty, may give the Court of Justice unlimited jurisdiction **with** regard to the penalties provided for in such regulations.

ARTICLE 173

The Court of Justice shall review the legality **of acts adopted jointly by the European Parliament and the Council,** of acts of the Council, of the Commission **and of the ECB,** other than recommendations **and** opinions, **and of acts of the European Parliament intended to produce legal effects vis-à-vis third parties.**

It shall for this purpose have jurisdiction in actions brought by a Member State, the Council or the Commission on grounds of lack of competence, infringement of an essential procedural requirement, infringement of this Treaty or of any rule of law relating to its application, or misuse of powers.

The Court shall have jurisdiction under the same conditions, in actions brought by the European Parliament and by the ECB for the purpose of protecting their prerogatives.

Any natural or legal person may, under the same conditions, institute proceedings against a decision addressed to that person or against a decision which, although in the form of a regulation or a decision addressed to another person, is of direct and individual concern to the former.

The proceedings provided for in this Article shall be instituted within two months of the publication of the measure, or of its notification to the plaintiff, or, in the absence thereof, of the day on which it came to the knowledge of the latter, as the case may be.

ARTICLE 174

If the action is well founded, the Court of Justice shall declare the act concerned to be void.

In the case of a regulation, however, the Court of Justice shall, if it considers this necessary, state which of the effects of the regulation which it has declared void shall be considered as definitive.

ARTICLE 175

Should the **European Parliament,** the Council or the Commission, in infringement of this Treaty, fail to act, the Member States and the other institutions of the Community may bring an action before the Court of Justice to have the infringement established.

The action shall be admissible only if the institution concerned has first been called upon to act. If, within two months of being so called upon, the institution concerned has not defined its position, the action may be brought within a further period of two months.

Any natural or legal person may, under the conditions laid down in the preceding paragraphs, complain to the Court of Justice that an institution of the Community has failed to address to that person any act other than a recommendation or an opinion.

The Court of Justice shall have jurisdiction, under the same conditions, in actions or proceedings brought by the ECB in the areas falling within the latter's field of competence and in actions or proceedings brought against the latter.

ARTICLE 176

The institution **or institutions** whose act has been declared void or whose failure to act has been declared contrary to this Treaty shall be required to take the necessary measures to comply with the judgment of the Court of Justice.

This obligation shall not affect any obligation which may result from the application of the second paragraph of Article 215.

This Article shall also apply to the ECB.

ARTICLE 177

The Court of Justice shall have jurisdiction to give preliminary rulings concerning:

(a) the interpretation of the Treaty;
(b) the validity and interpretation of acts of the institutions of the Community **and of the ECB**;
(c) the interpretation of the statutes of bodies established by an act of the Council, where those statutes so provide.

Where such a question is raised before any court or tribunal of a Member State, that Court or tribunal may, if it considers that a decision on the question is necessary to enable it to give judgment, request the Court of Justice to give a ruling thereon.

Where any such question is raised in a case pending before a court or tribunal of a Member State against whose decisions there is no judicial remedy under national law, the court or tribunal shall bring the matter before the Court of Justice.

ARTICLE 178

The Court of Justice shall have jurisdiction in disputes relating to the compensation for damage provided for in the second paragraph of Article 215.

ARTICLE 179

The Court of Justice shall have jurisdiction in any dispute between the Community and its servants within the limits and under the conditions laid down in the Staff Regulations or the Conditions of Employment.

ARTICLE 180

The Court of Justice shall, within the limits hereinafter laid down, have jurisdiction in disputes concerning:
(a) the fulfilment by Member States of obligations under the Statute of the European Investment Bank. In this connection, the Board of Directors of the Bank shall enjoy the powers conferred upon the Commission by Article 169;
(b) measures adopted by the Board of Governors of the *European Investment Bank*. In this connection, any Member State, the Commission or the Board of Directors of the Bank may institute proceedings under the conditions laid down in Article 173;
(c) measures adopted by the Board of Directors of the *European Investment Bank*. Proceedings against such measures may be instituted only by Member States or by the Commission, under the conditions laid down in Article 173, and solely on the grounds of non-compliance with the procedure provided for in Article 21(2), (5), (6) and (7) of the Statute of the Bank;
(d) the fulfilment by the national central banks of obligations under this Treaty and the Statute of the ESCB. In this connection the powers of the Council of the ECB in respect of national central banks shall be the same as those conferred upon the commission in respect of Member States by Article 169. If the Court of Justice finds that a national central bank has failed to fulfil an obligation under this Treaty, that bank shall be required to take the necessary measures to comply with the judgment of the Court of Justice.

ARTICLE 181

The Court of Justice shall have jurisdiction to give judgment pursuant to any arbitration clause contained in a contract concluded by or on behalf of the Community, whether that contract be governed by public or private law.

ARTICLE 182   The Court of Justice shall have jurisdiction in any dispute between Member States which relates to the subject matter of this Treaty if the dispute is submitted to it under a special agreement between the parties.

ARTICLE 183   Save where jurisdiction is conferred on the Court by this Treaty, disputes to which the Community is a party shall not on that ground be excluded from the jurisdiction of the courts or tribunals of the Member States.

ARTICLE 184   Notwithstanding the expiry of the period laid down in the **fifth** paragraph of Article 173, any party may, in proceedings in which **a regulation adopted jointly by the European Parliament and the Council, or** a regulation of the Council, of the Commission, **or of the ECB** is at issue, plead the grounds specified in the **second** paragraph of Article 173 in order to invoke before the Court of Justice the inapplicability of that regulation.

ARTICLE 185   Actions brought before the Court of Justice shall not have suspensory effect. The Court of Justice may, however, if it considers that circumstances so require, order that application of the contested act be suspended.

ARTICLE 186   The Court of Justice may in any cases before it prescribe any necessary interim measures.

ARTICLE 187   The judgments of the Court of Justice shall be enforceable under the conditions laid down in Article 192.

ARTICLE 188   The Statute of the Court of Justice is laid down in a separate Protocol.

The Council may, acting unanimously at the request of the Court of Justice and after consulting the Commission and the European Parliament, amend the provisions of Title III of the Statute.

The Court of Justice shall adopt its rules of procedure. These shall require the unanimous approval of the Council.

Community law

Although this *Handbook* has looked at the Treaties in a political and policy-orientated way, stressing their constitutional dimension, readers need to be aware of the extent to which this overlaps with the legal aspects of the Union, and of the significance, state, scope and nature of European Community (EC) law. This is something which goes far beyond the Court of Justice and its operation. It also takes us into areas where most ordinary Britons prefer not to go. This is because they regard the law as an arcane and perhaps irrational matter, penetrable only by the mastery of innumerable cases. Yet EC law has become far more important and influential than many are aware.

Law is also immensely important to the Union. There are several reasons for this. To begin with, the Community was created by law and is based on the rule of law. It is a corporate body which can sue and be sued. And the existence of EC law differentiates the Community from other international organizations. Equally, the Community forms a new legal order. That is to say that its rules override national law and require obedience. And, as is discussed in subdivision VII, law can function as a channel to be used by individuals in their dealings with the Community.

The Community is thus a source of law. Law itself also serves as a powerful means of integration thanks to the way it harmonizes or replaces national laws. EC law, furthermore, also has economic purposes and effects, as well as providing means for citizens and others to utilize the Treaties to defend their own interests. Given the fact that neither the Community, nor the Union, are orthodox states providing full rights of participation, EC law is a very important channel of access for individuals. Finally, the Courts and their legal precedents are a major source of interpretation of the Treaties, seeking both to produce homogeneity through Article 177 and to turn vague phrases into clear, precise and unconditional rules which are not dependent on further action. Law, in other words, gives life and substance to the Community even though it is nowhere fully defined in the Treaty. It can draw on the support of the legal community throughout Europe, who have helped to develop its status, overcoming the initial resistance of national courts.

Not surprisingly the status and influence of EC law is considerable. It is directly applicable, takes precedence over national law and must be fully applied. It is often of direct effect in a way that international law is not. Hence, the *Van Gend en Loos* case established that regulations do not require national implementation to make them effective. Moreover, EC law shapes national practice through preliminary rulings. States are thus no longer legally self-contained.

q.v. regulations pp. 301–2.

As has been said there has been 'an irreversible transfer' although the European Parliament in 1984 felt the situation was insufficiently clear. It therefore wanted to spell out the principle of direct applicability the precedence enjoyed by Community over national law. Some UK opinion and rulings have, for instance, treated EC law as enjoying primacy in virtue of the phrasing of the 1972 European Communities Act. The EP also wanted organic laws to prescribe the way it should be implemented. There is an echo of this in Declaration 16 on the proper transposition of Community into national law. States are urged to implement it as fully as their own and the Commission is to ensure that such obligations are met.

The primary sources of EC law are in the Treaties and related Community statutes which set out the objectives, frameworks and powers of the EC. These are filled out by a series of secondary sources, essentially the various enactments of the Community institutions. EC law also draws on customary, general and international law to fill out the primary sources. Thus Article 178 makes specific appeal to the general law of the member states as clearly Community law cannot diverge too far from this. The final secondary source is to be found in judicial rulings. For, while much continental law does not make a great use of cases, Box 15 shows that EC law has been marked by a series of landmark rulings such as *Cassis de Dijon*, which have done much to reinforce and fill out the provisions of the Treaty.

q.v. Community institutions pp. 250–2.

q.v. Cassis de Dijon pp. 126–7.

On the other hand there is a different legal style from that common in England. It emanates from Roman civil law. Thus it tends to adopt an inquisitorial approach and a wider style of interpretation, looking, as already noted, at intention and not just at the detailed text. It can be less detailed than that in the United Kingdom. It also assumes different patterns of recruitment to the judiciary and attitudes to political rulings. Not surprisingly UK Courts had some difficulty at first in adjusting to the new order.

Box 15.
Key cases

> ***Van Gend en Loos* v. *Nederlandse Administratie der Belastingen* 26/62, [1963] CMLR 105** — established that EC law was a new legal order, directly effective in member states and requiring individuals to be aware of this
>
> ***Costa* v. *ENEL* 6/64, [1964] CMLR 425** — established the primacy of EC law, and prevents it being overruled
>
> ***Rewe-Zentral AG* v. *Bundesmonopolverwaltung für Branntwein* (Cassis de Dijon) 120/78, [1989] 3 CMLR 494** — Established the principle of mutual recognition by laying down that where a product had been duly certified in one state it could not be excluded by other Community states
>
> ***Simmenthal SpA* v. *Commission* 92/78, [1980] 1 CMLR 25** — provides that national governments must apply Community law in full, striking down opposing rules, and allowing individuals to appeal to the ECJ where this is not done, thereby creating new rights for individuals
>
> ***R* v. *Secretary of State for Transport, Ex parte Factortane Ltd*, [1990] 3 CMLR 375** — suspended national legislation in conflict with EC law
>
> ***Francovich et* v. *Italy* in State Cases C-6 and 9/91, [1992] IRLR 84** — allowed individuals to sue governments which fail in their duty to implement EC directives
>
> ***Internationale Handelsgesellschaft mbH* 11/70, [1972] CMLR 255; and *Nold* v. *Commission* 4/73, [1974] 2 CMLR 338** — created a human rights jurisprudence in the EC

The scope of EC law goes far beyond what is often thought of as 'the law'. It prescribes rules for society, and rules which are supported by sanctions. If its main endeavours have been in business it goes far beyond this. Its rulings and principles have already made a major impact on ordinary life beyond the constitutional effects of the Treaties.[32] Hence it deserves to be remembered along with the policy and political aspects of the Union.

FURTHER READING

Bengoetxea, J., *The Legal Reasoning of the European Court of Justice*, Clarendon Press, Oxford, 1993.

Boulouis, J., 'Les avis de la Cour de justice des Communautés sur la compatibilité avec le Traité CEE du project d'accord créant l'Espace économique européen (EEE)', *Revue trimestrielle de droit européen*, vol. 28, no. 3, 1992, pp. 457–63.

Burley, A.-M. and Mattli, W., 'Europe before the court: a political theory of legal integration', *International Organization*, vol. 47, no. 1, 1993, pp. 41–76.

Bzdera, A., 'L'enjeu politique de la réforme institutionelle de la Cour de justice de la Communauté européenne', *Revue du Marché commun et de l'Union européenne*, no. 356, 1992, pp. 240–9.

Cullen, P.J., *The UK and the Ratification of the Maastricht Treaty*, Europa Institute, Edinburgh, 1993.

Curtin, D., 'The constitutional structure of the Union: a Europe of bits and pieces', *Common Market Law Review*, vol. 30, no. 1, 1993, pp. 17–69.

EC Commission, *ABC of Community Law*, OOPEC, Luxembourg, 1991.

---

32. Its principles are, *pace* EC Commission, *The ABC of Community Law*, OOPEC, Luxembourg, 1991, conformity with the treaties, liability, legality, proportionality, legal certainty, the protection of legitimate private expectations, equality of treatment, entitlement to a fair legal hearing, the maintenance of fundamental human rights, and protection of the individual.

EC Commission, *The Court of Justice of the European Community*, OOPEC, Luxembourg, 1986.

EC Commission, *The European Community's Legal System*, OOPEC, Luxembourg, 1984.

Fennel, P., 'The Court of First Instance', *European Access* 1990/1 pp. 11–12.

Grossfeld, B., 'The Internal Dynamic of the European Community Law', *International Lawyer*, vol. 26, no. 1, 1992, pp. 125–44.

Hailsham, Lord and Vaughan, D. (eds.), *The Law of the European Communities*, Butterworth, London, 1986.

Lasok, D. and Bridge, J., *Introduction to the Law and Institutions of the European Communities*, 3rd edn, Butterworth, London, 1986.

Lodge, J. (ed.) *The European Community and the Challenge of the Future*, 2nd edn, Pinter, London, 1993.

Louis, J.-V., *The Community Legal Order*, OOPEC, Luxembourg, 1991.

Mathijsen, P.S.R.F., *A Guide to European Community Law*, 5th edn, Sweet and Maxwell, London, 1990.

Mengozzi, P., *European Community Law*, Kluwer, Dordrecht, 1992.

Olmi, G., *Thirty Years of Community Law*, OOPEC, Luxembourg, 1983.

Schermers, H.G., The European Court of First Instance, *Common Market Law Review*, vol. 25, no. 3, 1988, pp. 541–58.

Schermers, H.G., 'The scales in the balance — National Constitutional Court vs Court of Justice', *Common Market Law Review*, vol. 27, no. 1, 1990, pp. 97–106.

Scott, J., *EC Law and the UK*, PNL, London, 1992.

Shapiro, M., 'The European Court of Justice', in Sbragia, A.M. (ed.), *Euro-Politics: Institutions and policymaking in the 'New' European Community*, Brookings Institution, Washington, 1992, pp. 123–56.

Shaw, J., *European Community Law*, Macmillan, London, 1993.

Steyger, E., 'European Community Law and the self-regulatory capacity of society', *Journal of Common Market Studies*, vol. 31, no. 2, 1993, pp. 171–90.

Usher, J., *EC Law and National Law: The irreversible transfer*, Allen and Unwin/UACES, London, 1981.

Vesterdorf, B., 'The Court of First Instance of the European Communities after two full years of operation', *Common Market Law Review*, vol. 29, no. 5, 1992, pp. 897–915.

Wallace R., *International Law*, Sweet and Maxwell, London, 1986.

Weatherill S. and Beaumont, P., *EC Law*, Penguin, Harmondsworth, 1993.

Weiler, J., 'Problems of legitimacy in post 1992 Europe', *Aussenwirtschaft*, vol. 46, Nos. 3–4, 1991, pp. 179–206.

Wyatt, D. and Dashwood, A., *European Community Law*, 3rd edn, Sweet and Maxwell, London, 1993.

Zolynski, B., 'The European Court of Justice and the European Court of First Instance — Bibliographic review', *European Access*, 1992/3, pp. 33–41.

(e) *The Court of Auditors*

The last of the five Community Institutions cited in Article 4 to be discussed is the Court of Auditors. This began life as two audit boards for the EC and Euratom. These were then merged in 1966 and upgraded to the status of a Court — the term used in France for a similar body — in 1977. The elevation reflected the widening range of Community expenditure to things like Lomé and the CAP. The TEU has continued its progress by giving it the status of a Community institution, with the implications of legal activity, decision-making and precedence that this entails. The reference to the limits on its powers found in the old Article 4 of the Treaty of Rome have been struck out. Moreover, the clauses detailing its functions have been moved from their previous position as the last part of the financial provisions of the Rome Treaty to their new position as a separate Section of Chapter I of this Title. The actual powers, which have already helped to improve Community financial procedures, have only been marginally changed.

q.v. Article 4 pp. 63–6.

q.v. CAP pp. 95–105.

The reason for this further promotion seems to lie in the negotiators' desire to give an explicit and enhanced prominence to sound financial management. This reflects suggestions in the 1984 draft Union Treaty and also the fact that, while the Court worked energetically, it has not had the resources or authority to require changes where it found mismanagement. Not merely are such things deliberately referred to in Articles 201a, 205 and, especially, 209a but, Declaration 18 stresses their importance. The subject also reoccurs in the Financial Provisions, as discussed below.

q.v.
Declaration
18 p. 435.

Article 209a is an invitation to a new financial probity and rigour, as the discussion, on pp. 313–16 shows. Equally, Declaration 18 urges all the Community institutions to give their minds to how they can help to make the Court more effective and thus control costs, avert fraud and get better value from Community expenditure. The UK government sees the reinforced Court as helping Council and Parliament to ensure the budget is properly implemented. It will do this by providing them with assurances about the reliability of the Community's accounts and financial transactions. Such functions interact with the enhanced budgetary powers of the Parliament, as will be seen in Article 206.[33] Equally, the Court's consultative role in drawing up new financial regulations remains in the amended Article 209.

As with the ECJ the Treaty starts with a broad statement of the obligations of the Court of Auditors. The nature of the audit is not defined but, by implication, it involves ensuring that revenue and expenditure have been properly accounted for, that management is sound, and that there are no irregularities to prevent the Commission being given a discharge for its budgetary responsibilities. It involves looking at the implementation of the budget, producing a statement of assets and liabilities, and drawing up an analysis of the financial year.

Article 188b, formerly numbered 206(2) and inserted by the Treaty on Certain Financial Provisions, deals with the number, qualifications, tenure, replacement and rights of the members of the Court. By implication each member state appoints a qualified and independent member, though formally the Council appoints them after consulting the Parliament. The latter has been able to force member states to change their nominees. Like other bodies the members of the Court jointly appoint their own President. They also enjoy both similar privileges and rules on replacement.

The final Article 188c, the only one on the Court to be significantly amended by the TEU, deals with the Court's operation. Maastricht imposed two new requirements on the Court. These are to provide assurances that the budget is legal and honest and also to draw up special reports on relevant financial questions. It also requires new bodies to provide it with information.

For the rest the first paragraph of the Article specifies that the Court should examine the accounts of all Community bodies and report to the Parliament and the Council. The second paragraph lays down the criteria to be applied and the third specifies how the Court should proceed. Essentially it works from Commission documents, especially from records of internal financial assessments, but can also quiz the Commission which has often responded defensively to such probings.

The fourth and last paragraph designates the forms in which the Court expresses its views. The most important of these is an annual report, published

---

33. However, the 1993 EP constitutional draft does not go as far as others in building up the Court. Others would allow it, with Parliamentary support, to suspend budgetary 'lines' where there are adverse findings.

with annexes in the Official Journal, submitted to the other institutions. On the basis of this, which has to be submitted by the end of November, the Parliament has to decide by 30 April whether to endorse the Commission's handling of the budget. The other views include observations, opinions, and special reports. These can cover aspects of the audit process, ideas on proposed legislation, and the need for further financial regulations. It produces about three of each every year. Special Reports were emphasized at Maastricht in order to help the fight against fraudulent or slovenly financial control. The Court also has a general duty of assistance to Council and Parliament.

Although the Treaty does not make this clear the Court has its own administration in Luxembourg. This employs some 250 staff. The Court is divided into four sections dealing with the Agricultural Guidance Fund, the Regional Funds, Development Funds and Training and related matters. Such services are necessary if the Court's reports, which can often reveal a shameful waste of money, are to be taken seriously and if there is to be more effective action against fraud. The outgoing UK member expressed his concern both about the lack of agreement inside the Court on the need for detailed spot audits and about the ability of institutions and member states to control Community finances. However, an interinstitutional agreement on budgetary discipline, to reinforce financial honesty and austerity, is under discussion.

Even if this does happen, it is not certain that there will be a new, and healthy, legitimacy of financial probity to the Union. This depends on other bodies and factors than the Court alone. It also remains to be seen whether the Court will become the equal of the other institutions of the post-Maastricht era. There is a suspicion that its elevation has not been fully thought through. Certainly there was no idea of making some reference to it in the new decision-making procedures, spelled out in the next Chapter of the Treaty, although this might have been a further way of demonstrating that it really had the full range of powers normally enjoyed by Community institutions.

Section 5   The Court of Auditors

ARTICLE 188a   *The Court of Auditors shall carry out the audit.*

ARTICLE 188b   *1. The Court of Auditors shall consist of twelve members.*

2. The members of the Court of Auditors shall be chosen from among persons who belong or have belonged in their respective countries to external audit bodies or who are especially qualified for this office. Their independence must be beyond doubt.

3. The members of the Court of Auditors shall be appointed for a term of six years by the Council, acting unanimously after consulting the European Parliament. However, when the first appointments are made, four members of the Court of Auditors, chosen by lot, shall be appointed for a term of office of four years only.

The members of the Court of Auditors shall be eligible for reappointment.

They shall elect the President of the Court of Auditors from among their number for a term of three years. The President may be re-elected.

4. The members of the Court of Auditors shall, in the general interest of the Community, be completely independent in the performance of their duties.

In the performance of these duties, they shall neither seek nor take instructions from any government or from any other body. They shall refrain from any action incompatible with their duties.

5. The members of the Court of Auditors may not, during their term of office, engage in any other occupation, whether gainful or not. When entering upon their duties they shall give a solemn undertaking that, both during and after their term of office, they will respect the obligations arising therefrom and in particular their duty to behave with integrity and discretion as regards the acceptance, after they have ceased to hold office, of certain appointments or benefits.

6. Apart from normal replacement, or death, the duties of a member of the Court of Auditors shall end when he resigns, or is compulsorily retired by a ruling of the Court of Justice pursuant to paragraph 7.

The vacancy thus caused shall be filled for the remainder of the member's term of office.

Save in the case of compulsory retirement, members of the Court of Auditors shall remain in office until they have been replaced.

7. A member of the Court of Auditors may be deprived of his office or of his right to a pension or other benefits in its stead only if the Court of Justice, at the request of the Court of Auditors, finds that he no longer fulfils the requisite conditions or meets the obligations arising from his office.

8. The Council, acting by a qualified majority, shall determine the conditions of employment of the President and the members of the Court of Auditors and in particular their salaries, allowances and pensions. It shall also, by the same majority, determine any payment to be made instead of remuneration.

9. The provisions of the Protocol on the Privileges and Immunities of the European Communities applicable to the Judges of the Court of Justice shall also apply to the members of the Court of Auditors.

ARTICLE 188c

1. The Court of Auditors shall examine the accounts of all revenue and expenditure of the Community. It shall also examine the accounts of all revenue and expenditure of all bodies set up by the Community in so far as the relevant constituent instrument does not preclude such examination.

The Court of Auditors shall provide the European Parliament and the Council with a statement of assurance as to the reliability of the accounts and the legality and regularity of the underlying transactions.

2. The Court of Auditors shall examine whether all revenue has been received and all expenditure incurred in a lawful and regular manner and whether the financial arrangement has been sound.

The audit of revenue shall be carried out on the basis both of the amounts established as due and the amounts actually paid to the Community.

The audit of expenditure shall be carried out on the basis both of commitments undertaken and payments made.

These audits may be carried out before the closure of accounts for the financial year in question.

3. The audit shall be based on records and, if necessary, performed on the spot in other institutions of the Community and Member States. In the Member States the audit shall be carried out in liaison with the national audit bodies or, if these do not have the necessary powers, with the competent national departments. These

bodies or departments shall inform the Court of Auditors whether they intend to take part in the audit.

*The **other** institutions of the Community and the national audit bodies or, if these do not have the necessary powers, the competent national departments, shall forward to the Court of Auditors, at its request, any document or information necessary to carry out its task.*

4. The Court of Auditors shall draw up an annual report after the close of each financial year. It shall be forwarded to the other institutions of the Community and shall be published, together with the replies of these institutions to the observations of the Court of Auditors, in the Official Journal of the European Communities.

*The Court of Auditors may also, at any time, submit observations, **particularly in the form of special reports,** on specific questions and deliver opinions at the request of one of the other institutions of the Community.*

*It shall adopt its annual reports, **special reports** or opinions by a majority of its members.*

It shall assist the European Parliament and the Council in exercising their powers of control over the implementation of the budget.

FURTHER READING

Annual Report [of the Court of Auditors] Concerning the Financial Year 1990, OJL 24, Brussels, 29 January 1991.

EC, *The Court of Auditors*, OOPEC, Luxembourg, 1986.

EC Commission, *Annual Report from the Commission on the Fight against Fraud*, COM(93)141 final, Brussels, 20 April 1993.

Kok, C., 'The Court of Auditors of the European Communities: the other European Court in Luxembourg', *Common Market Law Review*, vol. 26, no. 3, 1989, pp. 345–68.

Levy, R., 'The obscure object of desire: budgetary control in the EC', *Public Administration*, vol. 68, no. 2, 1990, pp. 191–206.

Nicoll, W. and Salmon, T., *Understanding the New European Communities*, 2nd edn, Harvester Wheatsheaf, Hemel Hempstead, 1993.

Zangl, P., 'The inter-institutional agreement on budgetary discipline', *Common Market Law Review*, vol. 26, no. 4, 1989, pp. 675–86.

ii. Provisions common to several institutions

Chapter 2 of Title I on Institutional Provisions is more significant than its title suggests. Common provisions suggests something of a miscellany. In reality the Chapter provides what has been called a 'legislative code'. It shows what the institutions are intended to produce in the way of legislative output, what their working mechanisms for legislating are, and how they should interrelate. The fact that such a Chapter is necessary reminds us that the Community institutions do not have the full autonomy enjoyed by similar national institutions. They have to work within the rules and do only what the Treaty drafters let them do. The rules, in other words, are essentially political both in their origins and their effects. Moreover, other parts of the Treaty which are not specified in this Chapter have implications for the legislative process.

The TEU has continued the development of the Community's legislative process to the benefit of the European Parliament. The Treaty of Rome provided that the Assembly, as it then was, should be consulted on a number of issues and give its assent to one or two more. The Single European Act extended the number of issues dealt with in these ways. Thus the assent procedure was applied to Article 238 so that some accords could not be concluded without a parliamentary majority in support. This also applied, under Article 237, to membership applications. It also added a new form of decision-making. This was the cooperation procedure in which the Parliament was able to make the Council think again about legislation and ensured that it could only override parliamentary amendments if it was unanimous. However, this left the essentials of Council power unchanged.

q.v. Article 238 pp. 337–40.

As a result of Maastricht three further changes of significance were made to these Treaty provisions. Firstly, there was some consequential drafting and reordering. The latter, which involves moving the old Article 149 on the cooperation procedure to Chapter 2, is part of a second change. This is the enhancing of the legislative status of the Parliament, partly by making cooperation a general matter and not something specific to the Parliament, and partly by giving the Parliament a new standing in Articles 175, 189 and 191.

Thirdly, but most importantly, Article 189b introduces a new procedure which gives the Parliament a more equal share in decision-making than was possible with cooperation. However, it does this in a somewhat embarrassed way. Rather than calling this the conciliation procedure, let alone 'codecision', the Treaties talk obliquely of the 'procedure referred to in Article 189b'. So, although the body of the Treaty has several references to this, as it does to the extension of the cooperation procedure, there is still an impression of reluctance to accept real parliamentary authority. On the other hand, although it is not referred to in the Chapter, the application of the assent and consultation procedures have both been extended. Equally, a new right of information has been introduced.

The text of the Chapter now starts with the laying out, in Article 189, of the authority under which the Community acts and the forms which those acts should take. This gives shape and substance to the specific powers already laid down at earlier points in the Treaty. The limiting reference to the necessity for conformity to the Treaty is new, as is the acceptance that Community acts can now be made jointly by Council and Parliament.

At present the Community's legislative output can, as Box 16 shows, take five forms, all of which are defined here. Taken together they make the majority of the secondary sources of EC law. Of these, the Regulation is, unhappily for UK usage, the most numerous, important and binding, being immediately and directly applicable. However, since some Directives are more detailed than the text suggests, the distinction has become a little blurred. The European Parliament has often pressed for an upgrading and clarification of Community acts, seeking to give them the name and status of laws, whether constitutional, organic or ordinary, in line with conventional practice in continental democracies. The negotiators stopped short of accepting this move towards making the Community more of a state but they did, in Declaration 16, commit themselves to future consideration of the hierarchy of Community acts.

q.v. Declaration 16 p. 435.

Article 189a, which used to be part of Article 149 as amended by the SEA, begins the discussion of the mechanisms of legislation. It requires that the Council should vote by unanimity when legislating by amending a Commission proposal,

Box 16.
Types of EC legislation

> **Regulation** — Binding in its entirety and directly applicable on all states and parties, in all their detail. Thus automatically part of national law without any implementing legislation
> **Directive** — Binding as to result on named states, who choose the form of compliance. Thus requires implementation at national level
> **Decisions** — More specific acts, often administrative in nature, binding in their entirety but only on those parties, including states, to whom they are addressed
> **Recommendations** — Non-binding and cannot have direct effect but expressing detailed EC preferences
> **Opinions** — Non-binding and cannot have direct effect

save where the conciliation procedure provides otherwise. This suggests that member state decision making is still seen as the norm. The effect of paragraph 2, however, is to give the Commission greater flexibility than it had enjoyed in the past. Previously it could only change its proposals in the cooperation procedure.

The new provisions of Article 189b, despite the coy way in which they are described, mark significant changes in Community procedures.[34] This is true both of mechanisms and institutional interrelations. The provisions offer the Commission both a role in bringing the two sides together and even, in paragraph 3, a voice in deciding how the Council must vote. However, the essence of these complex and lengthy procedures is to allow the European Parliament two new powers. One is that it will have up to five chances to consider proposed legislation, as is shown by Figure 11. Clearly this maximizes its chances of influencing legislation. The duration of the process may also allow other parties to have a say.

Moreover, the Parliament also now has a power of veto. Indeed, the UK government prefers to talk of the 'negative assent' process. If the Parliament either rejects the outcome of the optional meeting of the Conciliation Committee or finds a majority to reject either the agreed proposals which follow on the obligatory meeting of the Conciliation Committee or the earlier or amended bill, which can be forwarded by the Council when the Conciliation Committee fails to agree, the act cannot be passed. It is also possible, although the text does not make this clear, that the Council can acquiesce in parliamentary rejection of the bill.

Effectively, therefore there is joint decision and conciliation, if not straightforward codecision. How the procedure works will depend on whether the Parliament or the Council finds it easier to obtain majorities. The provisions for voting in the Conciliation Committee seem particularly problematical. The

---

34. The procedure is highly complicated and only its main points are set out in the text. Although it is best followed through the diagram it is worth spelling its five potential phases out a little more. The first phase involves the Commission presenting its proposal to both Council and Parliament. The latter then presents its normal Opinion on which Council then comments. Thereafter if, at second reading, the Parliament rejects the common position, there can be an optional reference to the new Conciliation Committee. This can lead to rejection, approval or further amendment. Amendments to the Common Position can either be approved or trigger a fourth phase centring on an obligatory reference to the Conciliation Committee. This has two possibilities of the act falling, one of it passing and one of a fifth parliamentary consideration.

Figure 11. The EP
conciliation procedure

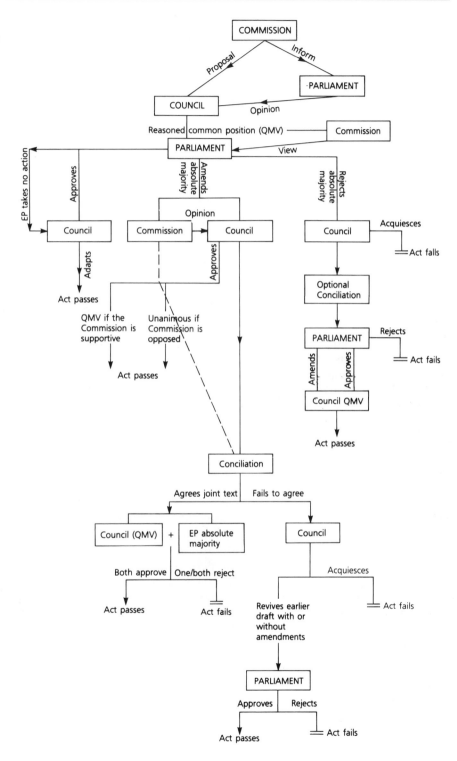

Box 17.
Application of
decision-making
procedures

Application of conciliation procedure under Article 189b
Articles: 49, 54(2), 56(2), 57(1), 57(2), 100a, 100b, 126(4), 128(5)*, 129(4), 129a(2), 129d 130i(1)*, and 130s(3)
    * = with the Council acting unanimously

Application of cooperation procedure under Article 189c
Articles: 6, 75(1), 103(5), 104a(2), 104b(2), 105a(2), 118a(2), 125, 127(4), 129d, 130e, 130o, 130s(1+3),* 130w(1) and Article 2(2) of the Social Chapter
    * = save where 130s(2) requires

Commission's role as both player and fixer may also be important.

These procedures only apply to those Articles of the Treaty which make specific reference to their use. These are more numerous than Foreign Ministers apparently wanted, thanks to decisions by Heads of Government. As Box 17 shows they cover free movement, the Internal Market, research frameworks, environmental strategies, consumer protection, trans-European infrastructure networks, and cooperation in education, culture and public health.[35] Many of these are both relatively general and emerge from the nominally new policy responsibilities introduced by the TEU. There is also provision for extending the application after 1996 on a proposition from the Commission.

The cooperation procedure, which was previously described as such, is given a new Title and position by the TEU in Article 189c. The new Article amends the introductory sentence and leaves out a phrase in (a). The procedure involves two readings by the Parliament as appears in Figure 12. In the first the Parliament simply offers its Opinion on the draft act. Where the Council does not accept this it has to submit a reasoned common position. This becomes law unless the Parliament proposes amendments, on which the Commission can also comment. The Council can only override these amendments if it is unanimous.

The procedure is extended to cohesion, to discrimination on the grounds of nationality, to the Regional Development Fund, and to transport. Although the Parliament did not like this procedure, on grounds of its lack of democratic accountability, it was active in using it after 1988. It proved relatively successful in persuading the Council to adopt its amendments. This is likely to continue since the process encourages consensus and celerity.

Although it is not specified here, the TEU makes other changes in the pattern of decision-making. To begin with, the long established consultation procedure which simply allows the Parliament to express its views, without any sanction other than the blockage caused by any withholding of its Opinion, is extended to a range of social subjects.[36] Equally, the range of the assent procedure is expanded from external matters to a uniform electoral procedure for the Parliament, to the Structural and Cohesion Funds and to new powers for the

---

35. The relevant Articles include 56, 57, 100a, 126, 128 and 130i, while the cooperation procedure is found in Articles 6, 75, 125 and 130e etc. The old Articles 7, 54, 56, 57, 130e and 130q actually used the term cooperation procedure though this was excised at Maastricht.

36. Articles where this applies include 43, 56, 63, 87, 94, 99, 100, 104c/14, 106, 109, 109b, 109f, 130, 130b, 138(3), 201, 228(3) and 235. The Assent procedure is used, *inter alia*, in Articles 105, 106, 130d, 228, 237, and O.

Figure 12. The
interinstitutional
cooperation procedure

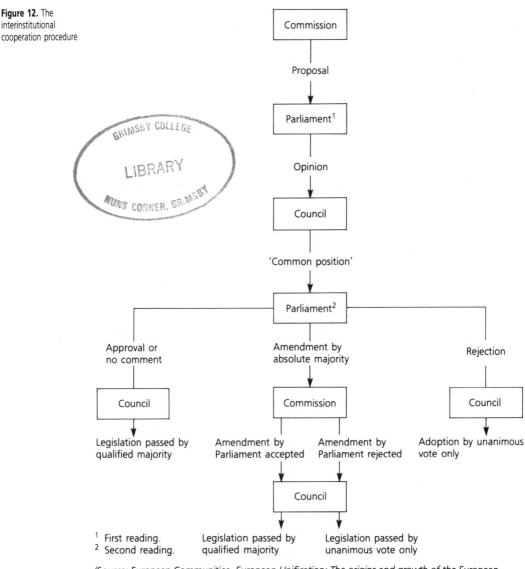

(Source: European Communities, *European Unification: The origins and growth of the European
Community*, 3rd edition, OOPEC, Luxembourg, 1990, p. 32)

Parliament. At the same time the TEU builds on the existing requirement to report
to the Parliament with a new right of information. This applies mainly to EMU
and capital arrangements. It can involve the President of the Council appearing
before the relevant parliamentary committee.[37] This ties in with the specific
budgetary decisions made by the Parliament which are discussed below. So, in

37. Provision for report can be found in Articles 122, 130p, 143 and 203a. Information has to be provided
in virtue of 73c, 73g (see pp. 121–2), 193, 103a, 104c, and 109c(3).

theory, the revised patterns of interinstitutional relations works to the benefit of the Parliament.

The amended Articles 190 and 191(1) return to the mechanisms and forms of legislation. They establish the manner in which Community acts have to be published. The first requires all acts to be accompanied by a statement of reasons. This helps to explain why they are prefaced by a long list of parliamentary resolutions which set out the thinking behind the act and not just the intention as is the case with UK Acts of Parliament. The second both allows the President of Parliament to authenticate some Community legislation and implicitly requires reference in the act to the procedure used to adopt it.

Finally, Articles 191 and 192 deal with publishing and enforcing Community acts. Publication in the Official Journal for generally applicable acts or by direct notification is thus required. Whereas other provisions cover enforcement of acts which are binding on member states, Article 192 deals with acts which apply to individuals or corporate bodies, and brings their enforcement into line with national and EC law.

If the last few Articles are relatively straightforward, the same cannot be said of the decision-making provisions. Their number may strengthen the role of the Parliament, but they do not make for simplicity, speed and transparency. Thus Article 113 provides for different procedures in different clauses. The time needed for the new conciliation procedure to work could also be quite long. All this will make it hard for ordinary people to follow what is going on. Moreover, there are several political imponderables about the way the procedures may work.

q.v. Article 113 pp. 182–3.

Chapter 2   Provisions common to several institutions

ARTICLE 189

In order to carry out their task **and in accordance with the provisions of the Treaty, the European Parliament acting jointly with the Council,** the Council and the Commission shall make regulations and issue directives, take decisions, make recommendations or deliver opinions.

A regulation shall have general application. It shall be binding in its entirety and directly applicable in all Member States.

A directive shall be binding, as to the result to be achieved, upon each Member State to which it is addressed, but shall leave to the national authorities the choice of form and methods.

A decision shall be binding in its entirety upon those to whom it is addressed.

Recommendations and opinions shall have no binding force.

ARTICLE 189a

1. *Where, in pursuance of the Treaty, the Council acts on a proposal from the Commission, unanimity shall be required for an act constituting an amendment to that proposal,* **subject to Article 189b(4) and (5).**

2. *As long as the Council has not acted, the Commission may alter its proposal at any time during the procedures* **leading to the adoption of a Community act.**

ARTICLE 189b

1. **Where reference is made in the Treaty to this Article for the adoption of an act, the following procedures shall apply.**

2. **The Commission shall submit a proposal to the European Parliament and the Council.**

The Council, acting by a qualified majority after obtaining the opinion of the European Parliament, shall adopt a common position. The common position shall be communicated to the European Parliament. The Council shall inform the European Parliament fully of the reasons which led it to adopt its common position. The Commission shall inform the European Parliament fully of its position.

If, within three months of such communication, the European Parliament:
(a) approves the common position, the Council shall definitively adopt the act in question in accordance with that common position;
(b) has not taken a decision, the Council shall adopt the act in question in accordance with its common position;
(c) indicates, by an absolute majority of its component members, that it intends to reject the common position, it shall immediately inform the Council. The Council may convene a meeting of the Conciliation Committee referred to in paragraph 4 to explain further its position. The European Parliament shall thereafter either confirm, by an absolute majority of its component members, its rejection of the common position, in which event the proposed act shall be deemed not to have been adopted, or propose amendments in accordance with subparagraph (d) of this paragraph;
(d) proposes amendments to the common position by an absolute majority of its component members, the amended text shall be forwarded to the Council and to the Commission which shall deliver an opinion on those amendments.

3. If, within three months of the matter being referred to it, the Council action by a qualified majority, approves all the amendments of the European Parliament, it shall amend its common position accordingly and adopt the act in question; however, the Council shall act unanimously on the amendments on which the Commission has delivered a negative opinion. If the Council does not approve the act in question, the President of the Council, in agreement with the President of the European Parliament, shall forthwith convene a meeting of the Conciliation Committee.

4. The Conciliation Committee, which shall be composed of the members of the Council or their representatives and an equal number of representative of the European Parliament, shall have the task of reaching agreement on a joint text, by a qualified majority of the members of the Council or their representatives and by a majority of the representatives of the European Parliament. The Commission shall take part in the Conciliation Committee's proceedings and shall take all the necessary initiatives with a view to reconciling the positions of the European Parliament and the Council.

5. If within six weeks of its being convened, the Conciliation Committee approves a joint text, the European Parliament, acting by an absolute majority of the votes cast, and the Council, acting by a qualified majority, shall have a period of six weeks from that approval in which to adopt the act in question in accordance with the joint text. If one of the two institutions fails to approve the proposed act, it shall be deemed not to have been adopted.

6. Where the Conciliation Committee does not approve a joint text, the proposed act shall be deemed not to have been adopted unless the Council, acting by a qualified majority within six weeks of expiry of the period granted to the Conciliation Committee, confirms the common position to which it agreed before the conciliation procedure was initiated, possibly with the amendments proposed by the European Parliament. In this case, the act in question shall be finally adopted unless the European Parliament, within

six weeks of the date of confirmation by the Council, rejects the text by an absolute majority of its component members, in which case the proposed act shall be deemed not to have been adopted.

7. The periods of three months and six weeks referred to in this Article may be extended by a maximum of one month and two weeks respectively by common accord of the European Parliament and the Council. The period of three months referred to in paragraph 2 shall be automatically extended by two months where paragraph 2(c) applies.

8. The scope of the procedure under this Article may be widened, in accordance with the procedure provided for in Article N(2) of the Treaty on European Union, on the basis of a report to be submitted to the Council by the Commission by 1996 at the latest.

ARTICLE 189c

Where reference is made in this Treaty to this Article for the adoption of an act, the following procedure shall apply:

(a) *The Council, acting by a qualified majority on a proposal from the Commission and after obtaining the opinion of the European Parliament, shall adopt a common position.*

(b) *The Council's common position shall be communicated to the European Parliament. The Council and the Commission shall inform the European Parliament fully of the reasons which led the Council to adopt its common position and also of the Commission's position.*

   If, within three months of such communication, the European Parliament approves this common position or has not taken a decision within that period, the Council shall definitively adopt the act in question in accordance with the common position.

(c) *The European Parliament may, within the period of three months referred to in point (b), by an absolute majority of its component members, propose amendments to the Council's common position. The European Parliament may also, by the same majority, reject the Council's common position. The result of the proceedings shall be transmitted to the Council and the Commission.*

   If the European Parliament has rejected the Council's common position, unanimity shall be required for the Council to act on a second reading.

(d) *The Commission shall, within a period of one month, re-examine the proposal on the basis of which the Council adopted its common position, by taking into account the amendments proposed by the European Parliament.*

   The Commission shall forward to the Council, at the same time as its re-examined proposal, the amendments of the European Parliament which it has not accepted, and shall express its opinion on them. The Council may adopt these amendments unanimously.

(e) *The Council, acting by a qualified majority, shall adopt the proposal as re-examined by the Commission. Unanimity shall be required for the Council to amend the proposal as re-examined by the Commission.*

(f) *In the cases referred to in points (c), (d) and (e), the Council shall be required to act within a period of three months. If no decision is taken within this period, the Commission proposal shall be deemed not to have been adopted.*

(g) *The periods referred to in points (b) and (f) may be extended by a maximum of one month by common accord between the Council and the European Parliament.*

ARTICLE 190

Regulations, directives and decisions **adopted jointly by the European Parliament and the Council, and such acts adopted by** the Council or the Commission, shall state the reasons on which they are based and shall refer to any proposals or opinions which were required to be obtained pursuant to this Treaty.

ARTICLE 191

1. Regulations, directives and decisions adopted in accordance with the procedures referred to in Article 189b shall be signed by the President of the European Parliament and by the President of the Council and published in the Official Journal of the Community. They shall enter into force on the date specified in them or, in the absence thereof, on the twentieth day following that of their publication.

2. Regulations of the Council and of the Commission, as well as directives of those institutions which are addressed to all Member States, shall be published in the Official Journal of the Community. They shall enter into force on the date specified in them or, in the absence thereof, on the twentieth day following that of theii publication.

3. Other directives, and decisions, shall be notified to those whom they address and shall take effect upon such notification.

ARTICLE 192

Decisions of the Council or of the Commission which impose a pecuniary obligation on persons other than States shall be enforceable.

Enforcement shall be governed by the rules of civil procedure in force in the State in the territory of which it is carried out. The order for its enforcement shall be appended to the decision, without other formality than verification of the authenticity of the decision, by the national authority which the Government of each Member State shall designate for this purpose and shall make known to the Commission and to the Court of Justice.

When these formalities have been completed on application by the party concerned, the latter may proceed to enforcement in accordance with the national law, by bringing the matter directly before the competent authority.

Enforcement may be suspended only by a decision of the Court of Justice. However, the courts of the country concerned shall have jurisdiction over complaints that enforcement is being carried out in an irregular manner.

FURTHER READING

Fitzmaurice, J., 'An analysis of the European Community's co-operation procedure', *Journal of Common Market Studies*, vol. 26, no. 4, 1988, pp. 389–400.

Lodge, J. 'Maastricht and political union', *European Access*, 1992/1, pp. 7–10.

Kangis, P., 'Decision making and dissolution of the EP', *European Access*, 1990/3 pp. 12–13.

Kirchner, E., *Decision-making in the European Community: The Council Presidency and European integration*, Manchester University Press, Manchester, 1992.

Lodge, J., 'EC policymaking: institutional dynamics', in Lodge, J. (ed.), *The European Community and the Challenge of the Future*, 2nd edn, Pinter, London, 1993, pp. 1–36.

Padoa-Schioppa, T., 'Sur les institutions politiques de l'Europe nouvelle', *Commentaire*, vol. 15, no. 58, 1992, pp. 283–92.

Phinnemore, D., *Sources on the European Community: A handbook for students*, University of Kent, Canterbury, 1992.

iii. Economic and Social Committee

Having dealt with the main Community institutions and their functioning, the revised Treaty of Rome signals the existence of three other organs. Two of these are long established, the Economic and Social Committee (EcoSoc) dating back to the ECSC, and the European Investment Bank (EIB) to Italian promptings at the time the Treaty of Rome was being negotiated. The Committee of the Regions (CoR) is an upgrading of an official body which emerged in the late 1980s. This is one of three changes made by the TEU to the organs. The other two concern numbering and a reinforcing of the position of EcoSoc.

Both the Committees are advisory bodies although EcoSoc can only advise Council and Commission. They are due, under Protocol 16, to share a single Secretariat although their relationship is slightly ambiguous. They represent civil society's participation in the Community process, which makes their relative lack of status quite significant. And there must be question marks over the likelihood that they can gain promotion in the way the Parliament has done.

q.v.
Protocol 16
p. 427.

The TEU makes a number of changes to the standing of the Economic and Social Committee, stressing the independence of its members and its ability both to meet and to issue opinions of its own volition. However, this really only brings the Treaty into line with previous practice. Own initiative opinions had been encouraged by the 1972 Paris Summit and subsequently incorporated into the Committee's standing orders. And the TEU, while it accepts salaries and budget, subjects these to financial control by the Council.

Article 193 begins by stating the consultative nature of the Committee. However, this is qualified elsewhere in the Treaty, notably in Article 198, where consultation is made mandatory.[38] The Article then goes on to specify the kind of socio-economic and other interests EcoSoc is supposed to represent. In fact tradition rather than law has it that they should represent employers, workers, and other economic actors, including agriculture and the professions. It thus has a quasi-corporatist nature and echoes similar provisions in the constitutions of Benelux, France, Italy and, since 1973, Ireland.

The next two Articles go further into membership by specifying national quotas, all of which are divisible by three so as to allow equal representation of the triad of socio-economic categories already identified, as implied in Article 195. In practice half the employers come from industry and most of the workers' representatives from trade unions. Members are part time but can now be paid, which was not previously the case. They are usually nominated by national governments after domestic soundings have been taken, although the Treaty of Rome does provide for views to be sought from the Commission and European-wide interest groups in order to help make a selection from the original list of nominations. The TEU also takes out references to serving in a personal capacity but adds a new emphasis on members being independent and free of mandating or other pressures, presumably from the lobbies they typify.

Articles 196 and 197 set out the internal organization of the Committee. This involves, to begin with, elective officers. These actually include a thirty-strong Bureau or Steering Committee. Thanks to the TEU EcoSoc can now decide how it meets, works and pays its officials. The right to meet without being instructed

---

38. Consultation is required by Articles such as 49, 54, 63, 75(3), 79, 99, 118, 118a, 121, 125, 126b, 127, 129, 129a, 129d, 130, 130b, 130d, 130e, 130i, 130o and 130s.

to do so by someone else is particularly important. Declaration 22 also gives it the same rights in this as the Court of Auditors. However, it is still bound by the requirement to have an Agricultural and a Transport section.[39] In fact, it is divided into nine sections whose task, despite inherent political divisions, is to process draft opinions for consideration by the Committee of the Whole.

q.v. Declaration 22 p. 436.

The drafts are prepared by Rapporteurs and subcommittees. There are some 300 subcommittee and study group meetings each year, as many miscellaneous gatherings; 70 to 80 section meetings; and up to a dozen plenaries. These are serviced by a 500-strong administration, divided into a Secretariat and four Directorates.

Finally, Article 198 specifies the importance of its consultative opinions, and the form in which they are to be submitted. The right to produce own-initiative Opinions is recognized here, as already noted. In practice it produces between 150 and 180 documents each year, whether mandatory or optional. It also provides information, liaises with other bodies, promotes sectional understanding, and publicizes the views of the interests it represents.

Despite all this, and despite support from the Parliament for it to be given greater autonomy, it has not become a really influential actor. Thus its earlier influence has been eclipsed by that of the now directly elected Parliament. Hence the Commission only really follows its views on technical matters. It has not gained full institutional status and may find the Regional Committee something of a rival. Indeed some would prefer to see it merged or replaced with the new-comer which is more in line with the political dynamics of the 1990s.

Chapter 3   The Economic and Social Committee

ARTICLE 193

An Economic and Social Committee is hereby established. It shall have advisory status.

The Committee shall consist of representatives of the various categories of economic and social activity, in particular, representatives of producers, farmers, carriers, workers, dealers, craftsmen, professional occupations and representatives of the general public.

ARTICLE 194

The number of members of the **Economic and Social** Committee shall be as follows:

Belgium	12
Denmark	9
Germany	24
Greece	12
Spain	21
France	24
Ireland	9
Italy	24
Luxembourg	6

39. There are references to direct consultation of these sections in Articles 47 and 83. The other sections are Energy and Nuclear, Economy and Finance, Industry and Commerce, Social Questions, External Relations, Regional Development, and Environment with Health and Consumer Affairs.

Netherlands   12
Portugal   12
United Kingdom   24

The members of the Committee shall be appointed by the Council, acting unanimously, for four years. Their appointments shall be renewable.

The members of the Committee may not be bound by any mandatory instructions.

They shall be completely independent in the performance of their duties, in the general interest of the Community.

The Council, acting by a qualified majority, shall determine the allowances of members of the Committee.

ARTICLE 195

1. For the appointment of the members of the Committee, each Member State shall provide the Council with a list containing twice as many candidates as there are seats allotted to its nationals.

The composition of the Committee shall take account of the need to ensure adequate representation of the various categories of economic and social activity.

2. The Council shall consult the Commission. It may obtain the opinion of European bodies which are representative of the various economic and social sectors to which the activities of the Community are of concern.

ARTICLE 196

The Committee shall elect its chairman and officers from among its members for a term of two years.

It shall adopt its rules of procedure.

The Committee shall be convened by its chairman at the request of the Council or of the Commission. **It may also meet on its own initiative.**

ARTICLE 197

The Committee shall include specialized sections for the principal fields covered by this Treaty.

In particular, it shall contain an agricultural section and a transport section, which are the subject of special provisions in the Titles relating to agriculture and transport.

These specialized sections shall operate within the general terms of reference of the Committee. They may not be consulted independently of the Committee. Sub-committees may also be established within the Committee to prepare, on specific questions or in specific fields, draft opinions to be submitted to the Committee for its consideration.

The rules of procedure shall lay down the methods of composition and the terms of reference of the specialized sections and of the sub-committees.

ARTICLE 198

The Committee must be consulted by the Council of the Commission where this Treaty so provides. The Committee may be consulted by these institutions in all cases in which they consider it appropriate. **It may issue an opinion on its own initiative in cases in which it considers such action appropriate.**

The Council or the Commission shall, if it considers it necessary, set the Committee, for the submission of its opinion, a time limit which may not be less than **one month** from the date on which the chairman receives notification to this effect. Upon expiry of the time limit, the absence of an opinion shall not prevent further action.

The opinion of the Committee and that of the specialized section, together with a record of the proceedings, shall be forwarded to the Council and to the Commission.

FURTHER READING see p. 313.

iv. The Committee of the Regions

The promotion of the Committee from unofficial status to that of an official advisory organ reflects both the growing political weight of the regions in European politics and the Community's need to develop its links with the grass roots. Many regions have already established liaison offices in Brussels, and have been pushing for more recognition from the Community. Not surprisingly it has been welcomed by regional groups. Indeed, some people feel that the new body could become very significant because of the new importance of the Cohesion and Structural Funds, and because of the salience of environmental questions which are, by definition, local ones.

Moreover, it gives the regions a political voice at the heart of Europe. This might lead to it reviewing all policy relating to regions, perhaps even helping to reshape the identity of Community Europe as the 'Europe of the Regions' implicit in Figure 13. Declarations 25 and 26 already stress the special needs of highly peripheral parts of the Community and its dependencies. On the other hand, if it fails, it could discredit the regional idea. The Community sees it as both a means of opening up its political process to the general public and as a way of influencing member states.

Article 198a formally establishes the Committee and gives it a name and status.[40] It then lays down the number of members coming from each member state. This is exactly the same as for EcoSoc, save that there is no selection from a list submitted by the national government. It has now emerged, partly because of the UK government's defeat on the issue on 8 March 1993, that only elected representatives of local and regional bodies will be eligible. This removes any need for members to be paid during their four-year terms. However, there is provision for alternates, to take account of the fact that local politicians may have timetable clashes or other obligations.

The procedural rules and structures for the new Committee are virtually the same as those for EcoSoc. However the Council of Ministers has to approve its standing orders. Nor is there any provision for sections and subcommittees. And, while Protocol 16 establishes that the new body will have a joint administration with EcoSoc, the Chapter is silent on both its existence and its costs. Having a budget would probably be necessary if the Committee is to become a really significant player in the Union's affairs.

q.v.
Protocol 16
p. 427.

The final Article, 198c, requires that Council and Commission must consult the Committee where the Treaty directs, as well as when they feel it appropriate.[41] It can also issue an Opinion when it feels there are regional issues

---

40. It is important to realize that the new body is quite separate from the Community's advisory committee on regional policy and the Council of Europe's Standing Conference of Local Authorities. It has already become apparent that 'Region' will be interpreted quite loosely since not all member states have fully fledged regional governments. Hence local and municipal authorities will be covered by it.

41. The Treaty provides for the Committee to be consulted under Articles 126, 129, 129d, 130b, 130d and 130e.

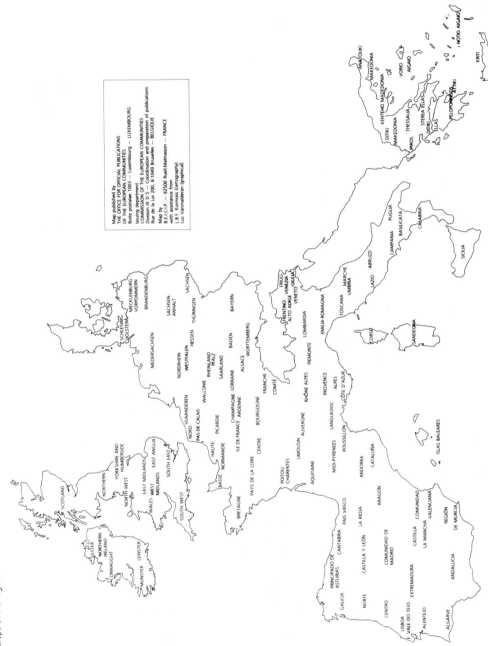

Figure 13. The
Europe of the Regions

involved in matters referred to EcoSoc. While this goes wider than the remit of EcoSoc it does not specifically extend to advising the Parliament and other Community bodies. However, the Committee of the Regions has a right to be informed of such references. It also starts life with the power to make 'own initiative' Opinions. Its Opinions are forwarded to Council and Commission in just the same way as those of EcoSoc. It remains to be seen, however, whether the former make more use of them than they have done in the past.

Chapter 4 The Committee of the Regions

ARTICLE 198a A Committee consisting of representatives of regional and local bodies, hereinafter referred to as 'the Committee of the Regions', is hereby established with advisory status.

The number of members of the Committee of the Regions shall be as follows:

Belgium	12
Denmark	9
Germany	24
Greece	12
Spain	21
France	24
Ireland	9
Italy	24
Luxembourg	6
Netherlands	12
Portugal	12
United Kingdom	24

The members of the Committee and an equal number of alternate members shall be appointed for four years by the Council acting unanimously on proposals from the respective Member States. Their term of office shall be renewable.

The members of the Committee may not be bound by any mandatory instructions. They shall be completely independent in the performance of their duties, in the general interest of the Community.

ARTICLE 198b The Committee of the Regions shall elect its chairman and officers from among its members for a term of two years.

It shall adopt its rules of procedure and shall submit them for approval to the Council, acting unanimously.

The Committee shall be convened by its chairman at the request of the Council or of the Commission. It may also meet on its own initiative.

ARTICLE 198c The Committee of the Regions shall be consulted by the Council or by the Commission where this Treaty so provides and in all other cases in which one of these two institutions considers it appropriate.

The Council or the Commission shall, if it considers it necessary, set the Committee, for the submission of its opinion, a time-limit which may not be less than one month from the date on which the chairman receives notification to this effect. Upon expiry of the time-limit the absence of an opinion shall not prevent further action.

Where the Economic and Social Committee is consulted pursuant to Article

> **198, the Committee of the Regions shall be informed by the Council or the Commission of the request for an opinion. Where it considers that specific regional interests are involved, the Committee of the Regions may issue an opinion on the matter.**
>
> **It may issue an opinion on its own initiative in cases in which it considers such action appropriate.**
>
> **The opinion of the Committee, together with a record of the proceedings, shall be forwarded to the Council and to the Commission.**

FURTHER READING see p. 313.

v. The European Investment Bank

This is a very different kind of body. Prior to Maastricht it was the subject of Articles 129 and 130 of the Rome Treaty. The move to Part Five, Title I, probably does not affect its status for, while it is picked out as a body in its own right, it is separated from the other monetary organs of the Community. Nor has it been given a closer relationship to mainstream decision-making processes. It thus remains an autonomous and free-standing body.

Article 198d leaves out the reference to 'is hereby established' as this is redundant after nearly forty years of existence. It gives way to a statement which reflects the fact that the European Investment Bank (EIB) is an active body able both to sue and be sued at law. The EIB's internal organization is laid down in a separate Statute attached to the original Rome Treaty. It has a Board of Governors drawn from national Finance Ministers, which lays down broad targets and guidelines for lending, a Board of nationally nominated part-time Directors who make individual decisions on lending, and a supervisory Management Committee which handles day to day matters. The latter consists of a President and six Vice-Presidents appointed by the Governors. Its offices are in Luxembourg.

q.v. Statute on EIB pp. 544–53.

The EIB, according to Article 198e, has three specific aims, of assisting less developed regions (which was its original dynamic); of helping to modernize the Community economy; and of supporting projects which are of interest to more than one country. It is partly under this heading that it has helped finance the Channel Tunnel. Such aims are seen as a contribution, through capital investment, to the harmonious economic development of the Community as a whole. Over the course of time it has also sought to aid associated countries. The TEU has added in a new subclause which requires it to cooperate with other relevant Community funds and policies.

Its funds come partly from support from the member states and partly from monies raised on the open capital market.[42] It then provides fixed rate loans to appropriate projects plus occasional guarantees for loans and credits to

---

42. Of its base funding France, Germany, Italy and Britain all provide 19.1%, Spain 7%, the Netherlands and Belgium 5.3% each, Denmark 2.7%, Greece 1.4%, Portugal 0.9%, Ireland 0.7% and Luxembourg 0.1%. It is able to lend up to 250% of its capital although its capital and ceilings are changed from time to time.

intermediary bodies. It only lends on large-scale projects costing over ECU 10 million. Applicants have to justify the projects for which they are seeking capital in terms of their congruence with EIB objectives. Its other criteria are that the projects involved are secure and economically viable. Because its funds come in part from the money markets it has to respect normal banking standards. It never lends more than 50 per cent of total costs and the interest rates it charges are competitive. So far it has been successful and enjoys a high reputation.

Chapter 5 European Investment Bank

ARTICLE 198d   The European Investment Bank shall have legal personality.

The members of the European Investment Bank shall be the Member States.

The Statute of the European Investment Bank is laid down in a Protocol annexed to this Treaty.

ARTICLE 198e   *The task of the European Investment Bank shall be to contribute, by having recourse to the capital market and utilizing its own resources, to the balanced and steady development of the common market in the interest of the Community. For this purpose the Bank shall, operating on a non-profit-making basis, grant loans and give guarantees which facilitate the financing of the following projects in all sectors of the economy:*

(a) projects for developing less-developed regions;

(b) projects for modernizing or converting undertakings or for developing fresh activities called for by the progressive establishment of the common market, where these projects are of such a size or nature that they cannot be entirely financed by the various means available in the individual Member States;

(c) projects of common interest to several Member States which are of such a size or nature that they cannot be entirely financed by the various means available in the individual Member States.

In carrying out its task, the Bank shall facilitate the financing of investment programmes in conjunction with assistance from the structural Funds and other Community financial instruments.

FURTHER READING

Bourin, P., *The European Investment Bank*, Athlone Press, London, 1993.

Gallacher, J., 'Subsidiarity and political union. An opportunity for local government', *European Information Service*, no. 134, November 1992, pp. 3–5.

George, S., *Politics and Policy in the European Community*, Oxford University Press, Oxford, 1992.

Jones, J., 'The Value of the Economic and Social Committee', *European Access*, 1989/4, pp. 12–13.

Lodge, J., *The Institutions and Policies of the EC*, Pinter, London, 1983.

Kirchner, E., *Trade Unions as a Pressure Group in The EC*, Saxon House, Farnborough, 1977.

vi. Financial provisions

Institutions, like policies, need money to help them operate. Hence the Treaty of Rome has always had a financial element which enjoys the status of a separate

Title. However, the Treaty does not tell us everything we need to know about Community financing, which is why a discussion of the budget is included below. What the Treaty offers are definitions of the budget, the procedures by which it is to be agreed, and the forms of accountability which it requires. The last emerged somewhat strengthened from the Intergovernmental Conferences of 1990−1 so that it is more of a code of good practice than it had been. However, because it involves money, the excesses of the CAP and the balance of power between institutions and member states, finance has always been controversial and is likely to remain so.

The TEU made five main changes to the Financial Provisions of the Rome Treaty. To begin with it does a certain amount of tidying up and updating to bring them into line with actual practices. Secondly, it extends the budget to cover the administrative costs of the other pillars of the Union. Thirdly, as just noted, it reinforces the Community's commitment to good financial management, as in Articles 201, 205, 209, and 209a. This is linked to a formal obligation to deal with fraud. Finally, and partly in relation to these concerns, the role of the European Parliament in financial control is strengthened.

The first six or so Articles deal with the definition of the budget. Article 199 begins by defining the scope of the budget which is to include all Community revenue and expenditure. This excludes both ECSC finances and capital provision for the EIB and the Lomé countries. However, the European Parliament believes that the budget should be all inclusive. The old Articles would have excluded expenditure on the Common Foreign and Security Policy and Cooperation on Justice and Home Affairs pillars as these are not within the Community. This is the rationale for the inserted paragraph which allows the budget to pay salaries and such operational costs as may be agreed under J.11(2) and K.8(2).

q.v. Article J.11(2) p. 381.

The Article also requires the budget to be balanced. And so far there has, formally, been no deficit financing. However, the budget has been topped up by member states on occasions or massaged by creative accounting. In any case the Community budget is not a full budget in the classic sense. Thus it has no fiscal policy, no economic management and no borrowing. In fact, it is more an agreed statement that monies will be made available to meet the expenditure necessary to achieve the Community's ends. This shows how far the Community is from being an autonomous state.

q.v. Article K.8(2) p. 386.

After repealing outdated provisions relating to national donations to the Community, the revised Article 201 recognizes the fact that the Community now has its own sources of revenue, known as 'own resources'. These come from a proportion of VAT, the customs duties charged by the Community under the CET; the product of levies on imported agricultural produce; and a charge related to member states' share of Community GDP. Of these VAT accounts for more than half of all revenues. The reference to other revenues is to take account of the fact that the Community does receive miscellaneous payments over and above those actually agreed and maintains the principle that there must be 'own resources' to cover all agreed expenditure.

q.v. CET pp. 86−7.

The new Article 201a further requires the Commission to ensure that there is room in the budget for any altered or new proposals. It provides reasons, processes and conditions for doing this. Equally, Declaration 18 notes the Commission's acceptance that it should assess the impact of its proposals on the public finances of the member states. All this ties in with the new concern for sound financial management.

q.v. Declaration 18 p. 435.

Article 202 continues to regulate the expenditure side of the budget, limiting long-term commitments but allowing the Community to carry forward any unspent balances. The Article also outlines the heads of expenditure, which are in part determined by the institutions which incur them as well as by function. Here the upgrading of the Economic and Social Committee is significant although there is no mention of the crucial distinction between compulsory and non-compulsory expenditure. Nonetheless, the implication is that there must be a legal basis for all expenditure, normally in the form of a policy decision under Title II of the Rome Treaty. The question of whether the Community can move monies allocated for one purpose to another, known as the right of *virement*, is dealt with in Article 205.

The final element of the first, definitional, stage of the Title in Articles 202 and 203(1) stresses the annual nature of the budget. In other words, monies are to be balanced and controlled every year. In practice the Community now works on a longer time scale. Hence the Delors II package, agreed at Edinburgh, lays down detailed ceilings for the period from 1993 to 1999. However, there still has to be a specific budget for each year. It should also be noted that money can be committed in one year but actually spent in another.

The next two Articles establish the procedure for agreeing the budget as already defined. The very long Article 203 provides 'an approximate and rather formal guide' to the budgetary process. The Commission usually starts work in the early part of one year and submits its proposed draft budget to the Budget Council in May or June. The latter, after consulting the Parliament, usually produces a revised (and usually slimmed down) draft in July. This is then submitted to the Parliament's Budget Committee and thence to a plenary meeting in October. The Parliament has authority over non-compulsory expenditure, but not over compulsory expenditure such as that on the CAP.

The Council then has to reconsider the amended budget and requires a qualified majority to rule on parliamentary amendments. The resulting draft then returns to the Parliament for final approval. It can, as has happened in the past, reject the budget with a two-thirds majority. If this happens, Article 204 allows business to continue by the payment of twelfths of the previous year's budget, provided this is not above a twelfth of the draft budget under discussion. This prevents any escape from budgetary cuts.

Since 1988 budgetary disputes have been less acute than they were but, since the Parliament, like the poorer states, has very different views from the northern member states, the potential for conflict is still there. The provisions for accountability which end the Title do not really do away with this. The Commission is responsible for implementing, rather than managing the budget, and the TEU has added a new caveat in Article 205 about doing this in a spirit of sound financial management. It is allowed to vire monies from one heading to another, reflecting the fact that the Community does not always spend up to its limits. The Commission also has to present a full Financial Report to the other institutions. This has to include notes on what the Community actually holds or owes.

The Parliament then decides whether to accept the accounts and decide whether the Commission has managed the finances properly. It does this not just on the basis of the accounts, which it and the Council scrutinize, but on the basis of special reports from the Court of Auditors, and further evidence from the Commission (Article 206). This was one of the innovations of Maastricht as was paragraph 3 which requires the Commission not just to carry out parliamentary requirements but also to report on the way it does this. This goes only part way to meet Parliament's desire for greater powers of control and makes it harder for it to avoid taking remedial actions. However, the text does not specify what happens if the Parliament refuses to grant a discharge.

Articles 207 and 208 lay down rules for the way in which monies are actually paid to the Community, given that there are no Ecu notes. The former still carries a reference to now defunct Treaty Articles and forms of payment. The Articles also specify what the Commission may do with the monies received since investments, etc., can generate surplus revenues. Article 208 makes it hard for the Commission to bypass national treasuries in such dealings.

Finally, Article 209 provides the basis for more detailed financial regulations which have been invoked on several occasions in the Title. The TEU modernizes paragraph b and extends paragraph c to include all financial controllers. This is further testimony of the negotiators' concern for sound financial management. And to underline this a new Article rounds off the Title by urging member states to treat fraud against the Community as seriously as they would fraud against themselves, indicating how this might be done (Article 209a). This is in line with the new stress on financial probity which has already been noted.

An Annex to the Edinburgh Summit conclusions contains further provisions on budgetary discipline while an interinstitutional agreement on the subject is also likely. The Parliament's new involvement with decision-making, which has clear financial implications, may change the way it treats financial matters, forcing it to take costs much more into consideration than it has in the past. Previously it has used the budget as a political weapon although this is not immediately apparent from the text of the Treaty.

Title II Financial provisions

ARTICLE 199   All items of revenue and expenditure of the Community, including those relating to the European Social Fund, shall be included in estimates to be drawn up for each financial year and shall be shown in the budget.

Administrative expenditure occasioned for the institutions by the provisions of the Treaty on European Union relating to common foreign and security policy and to cooperation in the fields of justice and home affairs shall be charged to the budget. The operational expenditure occasioned by the implementation of the said provisions may, under the conditions referred to therein, be charged to the budget.

The revenue and expenditure shown in the budget shall be in balance.

Article 200 is repealed.[43]

ARTICLE 201

Without prejudice to other revenue, the budget shall be financed wholly from own resources.

The Council, acting unanimously **on a proposal from the Commission and** *after consulting the European Parliament,* **shall** *lay down provisions* **relating to the system of own resources of the Community,** *which it shall recommend to the Member States for adoption in accordance with their respective constitutional requirements.*

ARTICLE 201a

With a view to maintaining budgetary discipline, the Commission shall not make any proposal for a Community act, or alter its proposals, or adopt any implementing measure which is likely to have appreciable implications for the budget without providing the assurance that the proposal or that measure is capable of being financed within the limit of the Community's own resources arising under provisions laid down by the Council pursuant to Article 201.

ARTICLE 202

The expenditure shown in the budget shall be authorized for one financial year, unless the regulations made pursuant to Article 209 provide otherwise.

In accordance with conditions to be laid down pursuant to Article 209, any appropriations, other than those relating to staff expenditure, that are unexpended at the end of the financial year may be carried forward to the next financial year only.

Appropriations shall be classified under different chapters grouping items of expenditure according to their nature or purpose and subdivided, as far as may be necessary, in accordance with the regulations made pursuant to Article 209.

The expenditure of the European Parliament, the Council, the Commission and the Court of Justice shall be set out in separate parts of the budget, without prejudice to special arrangements for certain common items of expenditure.

ARTICLE 203

1. The financial year shall run from 1 January to 31 December.

2. Each institution of the Community shall, before 1 July, draw up estimates of its expenditure. The Commission shall consolidate these estimates in a preliminary draft budget. It shall attach thereto an opinion which may contain different estimates.

The preliminary draft budget shall contain an estimate of revenue and an estimate of expenditure.

3. The Commission shall place the preliminary draft budget before the Council not later than 1 September of the year preceding that in which the budget is to be implemented.

The Council shall consult the Commission and, where appropriate, the other institutions concerned whenever it intends to depart from the preliminary draft budget.

The Council, acting by a qualified majority, shall establish the draft budget and forward it to the European Parliament.

---

43. The old Articles listed the payments made by the original six member states when the Community was financed by the donations they made to it and the European Social Fund. The reference to it, which still exists in Article 207, must have escaped the attention of the negotiators and drafters.

4. The draft budget shall be placed before the European Parliament not later than 5 October of the year preceding that in which the budget is to be implemented.

The European Parliament shall have the right to amend the draft budget, acting by a majority of its members, and to propose to the Council, acting by an absolute majority of the votes cast, modifications to the draft budget relating to expenditure necessarily resulting from this Treaty or from acts adopted in accordance therewith.

If, within forty-five days of the draft budget being placed before it, the European Parliament has given its approval, the budget shall stand as finally adopted. If within this period the European Parliament has not amended the draft budget nor proposed any modifications thereto, the budget shall be deemed to be finally adopted.

If within this period the European Parliament has adopted amendments or proposed modifications, the draft budget together with the amendments or proposed modifications shall be forwarded to the Council.

5. After discussing the draft budget with the Commission and, where appropriate, with the other institutions concerned, the Council shall act under the following conditions:

(a) The Council may, acting by a qualified majority, modify any of the amendments adopted by the European Parliament;

(b) With regard to the proposed modifications:

— where a modification proposed by the European Parliament does not have the effect of increasing the total amount of the expenditure of an institution, owing in particular to the fact that the increase in expenditure which it would involve would be expressly compensated by one or more proposed modifications correspondingly reducing expenditure, the Council may, acting by a qualified majority, reject the proposed modification. In the absence of a decision to reject it, the proposed modification shall stand as accepted;

— where a modification proposed by the European Parliament has the effect of increasing the total amount of the expenditure of an institution, the Council may, acting by a qualified majority, accept this proposed modification. In the absence of a decision to accept it, the proposed modification shall stand as rejected; where in pursuance of one of the two preceding subparagraphs, the Council has rejected a proposed modification, it may, acting by a qualified majority, either retain the amount shown in the draft budget or fix another amount.

The draft budget shall be modified on the basis of the proposed modifications accepted by the Council.

If, within fifteen days of the draft budget being placed before it, the Council has not modified any of the amendments adopted by the European Parliament and if the modifications proposed by the latter have been accepted, the budget shall be deemed to be finally adopted. The Council shall inform the European Parliament that it has not modified any of the amendments and that the proposed modifications have been accepted.

If, within this period the Council has modified one or more of the amendments adopted by the European Parliament or if the modifications proposed by the latter have been rejected or modified, the modified draft budget shall again be forwarded to the European Parliament. The Council shall inform the European Parliament of the results of its deliberations.

6. Within fifteen days of the draft budget being placed before it, the European Parliament, which shall have been notified of the action taken on its proposed

modifications, may, acting by a majority of its members and three-fifths of the votes cast, amend or reject the modifications to its amendments made by the Council and shall adopt the budget accordingly. If, within this period the European Parliament has not acted, the budget shall be deemed to be finally adopted.

7. When the procedure provided for in this Article has been completed, the President of the European Parliament shall declare that the budget has been finally adopted.

8. However, the European Parliament, acting by a majority of its members and two-thirds of the votes cast, may if there are important reasons reject the draft budget and ask for a new draft to be submitted to it.

9. A maximum rate of increase in relation to the expenditure of the same type to be incurred during the current year shall be fixed annually for the total expenditure other than that necessarily resulting from this Treaty or from acts adopted in accordance therewith.

The Commission shall, after consulting the Economic Policy Committee, declare what this maximum rate is as it results from:
— the trend, in terms of volume, of the gross national products within the Community;
— the average variation in the budgets of the Member States; and
— the trend of the cost of living during the preceding financial year.

The maximum rate shall be communicated, before 1 May, to all the institutions of the Community. The latter shall be required to conform to this during the budgetary procedure, subject to the provisions of the fourth and fifth subparagraphs of this paragraph.

If, in respect of expenditure other than that necessarily resulting from this Treaty or from acts adopted in accordance therewith, the actual rate of increase in the draft budget established by the Council is over half the maximum rate, the European Parliament may, exercising its right of amendment, further increase the total amount of that expenditure to a limit not exceeding half the maximum rate.

Where the European Parliament, the Council or the Commission consider that the activities of the Communities require that the rate determined according to the procedure laid down in this paragraph should be exceeded, another rate may be fixed by agreement between the Council, acting by a qualified majority, and the European Parliament, acting by a majority of its members and three-fifths of the votes cast.

10. Each institution shall exercise the powers conferred upon it by this Article, with due regard for the provisions of the Treaty and for acts adopted in accordance therewith, in particular those relating to the Communities' own resources and to the balance between revenue and expenditure.

ARTICLE 204

If, at the beginning of a financial year, the budget has not yet been voted, a sum equivalent to not more than one-twelfth of the budget appropriations for the preceding financial year may be spent each month in respect of any chapter or other subdivision of the budget in accordance with the provisions of the regulations made pursuant to Article 209; this arrangement shall not, however, have the effect of placing at the disposal of the Commission appropriations in excess of one-twelfth of those provided for in the draft budget in course of preparation.

The Council may, acting by a qualified majority, provided that the other conditions laid down in the first subparagraph are observed, authorize expenditure in excess of one-twelfth.

If the decision relates to expenditure which does not necessarily result from this Treaty or from acts adopted in accordance therewith, the Council shall forward it immediately to the European Parliament; within thirty days the European Parliament, acting by a majority of its members and three-fifths of the votes cast, may adopt a different decision on the expenditure in excess of the one-twelfth referred to in the first subparagraph. This part of the decision of the Council shall be suspended until the European Parliament has taken its decision. If within the period the European Parliament has not taken a decision which differs from the decision of the Council, the latter shall be deemed to be finally adopted.

The decisions referred to in the second and third subparagraphs shall lay down the necessary measures relating to resources to ensure application of this Article.

ARTICLE 205

The Commission shall implement the budget, in accordance with the provisions of the regulations made pursuant to Article 209, on its own responsibility and within the limits of the appropriations, **having regard to the principles of sound financial management.**

The regulations shall lay down detailed rules for each institution concerning its part in effecting its own expenditure.

Within the budget, the Commission may, subject to the limits and conditions laid down in the regulations made pursuant to Article 209, transfer appropriations from one chapter to another or from one subdivision to another.

ARTICLE 205a

The Commission shall submit annually to the Council and to the European Parliament the accounts of the preceding financial year relating to the implementation of the budget. The Commission shall also forward to them a financial statement of the assets and liabilities of the Community.

ARTICLE 206

1. The European Parliament, acting on a recommendation from the Council which shall act by qualified majority, shall give a discharge to the Commission in respect of the implementation of the budget. To this end, the Council and the European Parliament in turn shall examine the accounts and the financial statement referred to in Article 205a, the annual report by the Court of Auditors together with the replies of the institutions under audit to the observations of the Court of Auditors **and any relevant special reports by the Court of auditors.**

2. Before giving a discharge to the Commission, or for any other purpose in connection with the exercise of its power over the implementation of the budget, the European Parliament may ask to hear the Commission give evidence with regard to the execution of expenditure or the operation of financial control systems. The Commission shall submit any necessary information to the European Parliament at the latter's request.

3. The Commission shall take all appropriate steps to act on the observations in the decisions giving discharge and on other observations by the European Parliament relating to the execution of expenditure, as well as on comments accompanying the recommendations on discharge adopted by the Council.

At the request of the European Parliament or the Council, the Commission shall report on the measures taken in the light of these observations and comments and in particular on the instructions given to the departments which are responsible for the implementation of the budget. These reports shall also be forwarded to the Court of Auditors.

Articles 206a and 206b are repealed.[44]

---

44. Although the official view is that these two clauses were repealed the reality is that Article 206a has actually

ARTICLE 207   The budget shall be drawn up in the unit of account determined in accordance with the provisions of the regulations made pursuant to Article 209.

The financial contributions provided for in Article 200(1) shall be placed at the disposal of the Community by the Member States in their national currencies.

The available balances of these contributions shall be deposited with the Treasuries of Member States or with bodies designated by them. While on deposit, such funds shall retain the value corresponding to the parity, at the date of deposit, in relation to the unit of account referred to in the first paragraph.

The balances may be invested on terms to be agreed between the Commission and the Member State concerned.

The regulations made pursuant to Article 209 shall lay down the technical conditions under which financial operations relating to the European Social Fund shall be carried out.

ARTICLE 208   The Commission may, provided it notifies the competent authorities of the Member States concerned, transfer into the currency of one of the Member States its holdings in the currency of another Member State, to the extent necessary to enable them to be used for purposes which come within the scope of this Treaty.

The Commission shall as far as possible avoid making such transfers if it possesses cash or liquid assets in the currencies which it needs.

The Commission shall deal with each Member State through the authority designated by the State concerned. In carrying out financial operations the Commission shall employ the services of the bank of issue of the Member State concerned or of any other financial institution approved by that State.

ARTICLE 209   The Council, acting unanimously on a proposal from the Commission and after consulting the European Parliament and obtaining the opinion of the Court of Auditors, shall:
(a) make Financial Regulations specifying in particular the procedure to be adopted for establishing and implementing the budget and for presenting and auditing accounts;
(b) determine the methods and procedure whereby the budget revenue provided under the arrangements relating to the *Community's* own resources shall be made available to the Commission, and determine the measures to be applied, if need be, to meet cash requirements;
(c) lay down rules concerning the responsibility of **financial controllers,** authorizing officers and accounting officers, and concerning appropriate arrangements for inspection.

ARTICLE 209a   **Member States shall take the same measures to counter fraud affecting the financial interests of the Community as they take to counter fraud affecting their own financial interests.**

Without prejudice to the other provisions of the Treaty, Member States shall coordinate their action aimed at protecting the financial interests of the Community against fraud. To this end they shall organize, with the help of the Commission, close and regular cooperation between the competent departments of their administrations.

---

been transferred to the newly created Article 188b, along with the old Article 206. And Article 206b, which had been added by the Treaty amending Certain Financial Provisions, now becomes clause 1 of the new Article 206, albeit with modifications and additions. The move came right at the end of the IGC and does not appear in early drafts of the TEU.

vi. a) The budget and its significance

Examination of the Financial Provisions has shown that they are largely procedural and exhortatory. They do not say much about the politics of Community financing whether past or present. These are omnipresent because money is often seen as a part of sovereignty. Nor do they provide a real insight into either the actual size of the budget nor about the real shape of income and expenditure. Equally, they do not mention other financial programmes which deserved to be noted because they qualify the Treaty provisions. These include the so-called Delors II financial package which has been drawn up to help finance the decisions made at Maastricht up till the end of this decade.

At present the budget is financed almost entirely from the Community's own resources. This was not always so. The ECSC had been financed by a somewhat problematical levy on coal and steel production. So, at first, the EEC was financed by donations from its member states which reflected their GDP, although the Treaty of Rome looked forward to an eventual system of 'own resources'. The donation system was seen as restricting the autonomy of the Community and so, in 1970, the decision was taken to change this in line with Article 201. The new system was phased in over the first half of that decade but was only fully operational by 1980.

By then the revenues agreed were proving insufficient to meet the Community's growing, depression-related, needs. Partly because of this, the directly elected Parliament began to use its powers to criticize and block budgetary proposals, notably in 1979–80. Finding a solution was complicated by the UK budgetary problem since the United Kingdom felt that any simple increase in 'own resources' would simply cost them more. A solution was found at Fontainbleau in 1984, which included increasing the share of VAT to 1.4 per cent as well as agreeing a special rebate for the United Kingdom.

However, this increase also proved insufficient and further changes were made in 1988. These took account of the changes made by the SEA, and involved the addition of both a fourth resource and new controls on the monies the Community could raise and spend over the next four years. These included a ceiling on agricultural expenditure, so as to permit other types of expenditure, notably on structural funds. The new system, known as Delors I and involving more specific administrative procedures laid down in an interinstitutional agreement, worked well enough. However, it did not solve all the political difficulties inherent in the budget. Maastricht also reinforced the need for a new spending plan to take effect from 1993, thus compounding the problems.

The budget, because it deals with monies which ultimately come from or are spent in the member states, is the cause of several conflicts. To begin with there are conflicts about the nature and sources of Community revenues. Not all states like the use of a resource related to GNP as this affects their payments. Equally, supporters of further integration want to see Brussels enjoying greater control over its own revenues. They also want to see a considerable increase in the Community budget so as to allow its institutions greater authority, its policies greater effectiveness, and its ability to act as a means of redistribution greater weight. Hence there is a major conflict between the member states and institutions like the Parliament and the Commission.

Equally, there is a major divide between those countries who are net contributors to the budget and those who are net beneficiaries, the so-called 'cohesion group', mainly Greece, Ireland, Portugal and Spain.[45] The former, aware of both overspending and unmet needs at home, are very loath to pay more into the Community. In 1991 Germany paid some 27 per cent of the budget, France 19 per cent, Italy 17 per cent, the United Kingdom 8.5 per cent and Spain 8 per cent. Given qualified majority voting, the United Kingdom and Germany are able to block expenditure, since they only need the support of one smaller state for a qualified majority. Similarly, the poorer countries, some of whom have accepted painful sacrifices in order to meet the challenges of Community membership and the Single Market, believe that they have a right to assistance in order to help them catch up. This was very clear in the campaign leading up to the Irish referendum on ratifying the TEU. Such states can often threaten to use their veto if their demands are not met, as have the Spaniards on both the EEA and Maastricht.

There are other conflicts over Community expenditures. To begin with there is the battle between compulsory, mainly agricultural, and non-compulsory expenditure. Some member states, like the United Kingdom, together with the Parliament and even some Ministers of Finance in states with strong agricultural lobbies believe that far too much of the budget goes on the CAP. The strait-jacket this imposes either costs contributor states too much or crowds out more worthwhile spending. However, only the R&D Council can set its own targets. For the rest the Budgetary Council has the last word. So, even after the 1988 capping, there can still be deep divisions about the share of the budget enjoyed by farmers. There are also other arguments about the destination of expenditure such as those amongst various Directorates-General of the Commission who all lobby DG XIX, the Directorate responsible for budget, to ensure that their projects are protected.

There are also parliamentary resistances to the emergence of what has, since 1988, been called 'privileged' non-compulsory expenditure. This refers to spending on longer-term programmes. The Parliament no doubt feels that this classification further reduces its control over the budget. The Parliament also wants to see that the monies allocated are actually spent. Although this is not always realized, the Community does not always spend up to the ceilings which have been agreed. In 1992 several billion ECU went unspent according to some

---

45. The Community is slightly chary of providing figures for net gains and losses since they are very difficult to estimate. In any case it feels that this is not the way to look at a communal venture. However, the 1991 *Annual Report Concerning the Financial Year 1992*, produced by the Court of Auditors on 16 November 1993 and which is printed in the *Official Journal of the EC* 91/C 324/01, suggests, at pp. 15 and 39–40, that Belgium contributed 4.0% of own resources and received 4.1% from the EC; Denmark 1.8% and 2.2%; France 18.7% and 15.5%; Germany 30.2% and 12.5%; Greece 1.3% and 7.4%; Ireland 0.8% and 4.4%; Italy 14.7% and 13.3%; Luxembourg 0.2% and 0.5%; the Netherlands 6.3% and 4.6%; Portugal 1.5% and 4.1%; Spain 8.6% and 12.9%; and the United Kingdom 11.9% and 7.4%. The 1992 expenditure figures include 10.1% of expenditure not allocated to any particular state. France has only been a net contributor since 1989 and Italy has sometimes been so while the UK deficit fell slightly in the late 1980s.

sources. Utilization rates, in fact, vary between 93 per cent and 97 per cent of sums allowed.

Given that the Parliament has more influence over the budget than over most other policies it has sought to use this fact to the full. It does this not just in order to achieve its financial aims but to redress the democratic deficit in the Community. This would have the, for it happy, effect of reducing the powers of the member states assembled in Council. Equally, the member states have sought to exercise increasing control over the destination of expenditure so as to exclude the Parliament.

This links up with the final conflict. This, as the discussion of the Court of Auditors has suggested, is the emerging confrontation over financial management in the Community. This springs from the inadequacies of the CAP and, to a lesser extent, from the growing importance of structural and cohesion funds which have been increased by both the SEA and the TEU. The EEA will also increase them whenever it comes into effect. All this reflects the inherent dynamism of Community expenditure since 1987. This has to be seen against a background of possibly declining GDP. In order to prevent waste and fraud in this situation, there are pressures from the net contributors and, to be fair, from the Parliament, to ensure much better financial control. The Commission has set up its own anti-fraud services and has engaged in much more inspection and tighter policy controls. However, all this can conflict with ideas of increased Community spending and autonomy. So the budget has implications for the interinstitutional balance as well as for the balance between member states.

q.v. Court of Auditors pp. 292–6.

The budget which occasions so much controversy is, in comparative terms, relatively small. The EC's outgoings presently amount to some ECU 60 billion or £45 billion per year. This compares with the £250 billion of the UK budget.[46] EC spending is, moreover, only about 4.5 per cent of the total spending of the governments of the Twelve. Another way of looking at it is that, in the early 1990s, it accounted for not much more than 1.25 per cent of Community GDP, although its target was then 1.4 per cent. Today the figure is about 1.7 per cent. This compares with the 2 per cent to 7 per cent estimated to be necessary if the Community is to play a meaningful role of financial equalization as other federal-type bodies do.

Some member states spend the equivalent of half or more of their GDP and more. They also borrow a great deal more than the Community. In 1991 the EC borrowed something under £7 billion compared to the United Kingdom's £50 billion. In per capita terms the EC spends about ECU 173 per year for each European, or about £130. This compares with the £4,550 or so which the United Kingdom state spends on behalf of each of its citizens. Member states also control far more by way of assets than the Community, with its restricted range of properties, the debts it is owed and its share of food stores. Nonetheless, the sums

---

46. Figures for recent spending come, in the main, from the Communities' own *Financial Report* for 1991 (OOPEC, Luxembourg, 1992). The details of the Delors II package come from *Agence Presse Europe*, Special edition, no. 5878, 13 December 1992.

involved are large in real terms and eclipse the spending of some of the smaller member states.

In 1991 the Community received 53.8 per cent of its revenue of ECU 56.25 billion from VAT own resources, 20.4 per cent from customs duties, 13.2 per cent from the 'fourth resource', 4.4 per cent from agricultural and sugar levies, and 8.2 per cent from miscellaneous income, including surpluses from 1989 and 1990. The share from VAT has proved by far and away the most buoyant over the years. In 1991 the revenue received was about ECU 164 million more than had been forecast. However, on other occasions the budget has had to be bailed out. It can also be affected by currency fluctuations and harvest conditions.

In expenditure terms the Community had commitments of some ECU 60 billion in 1991, although not all of this was actually spent that year. Items were brought forward from previous years and carried forward to later ones where both payments and commitments were concerned. Of its commitments 54.7 per cent went on agricultural price support. Four products of the ten listed accounted for over half the ECU 31 billion spent. These were oils and fats, milk and milk products, cereals and beef and veal. The next largest share was that of the Structural Funds. These accounted for 26.9 per cent and were spent on the Regional Fund, the Social Fund, agricultural restructuring and the former East German *Länder* in that order.

All the other items in the budget received very small amounts. Thus only 6 per cent went to cooperation payments, mainly to the newly emerging democracies of Central and Eastern Europe. Aid to Lomé countries is not included here, for reasons already noted. Research and development attracted 3.0 per cent; repayments to member states (mainly for butter stores) 2.2 per cent; Peoples' Europe costs (including environmental and training costs) 1.0 per cent; and energy and fisheries 0.8 per cent each. Finally administration costs accounted for 4.6 per cent. Two-thirds of this went on salaries and one-third on other running expenses. This brings out the fact that the budget does not distinguish between recurrent and capital expenditure, partly because the EC has so little of the latter. Many of its buildings in Brussels do not actually belong to it for instance.

The figures indicated here are likely to change in the near future. This is because, throughout 1992, a new financial package was negotiated to meet the extra costs of the TEU, and in particular the Cohesion Fund promised to the poorer countries. The Commission tabled its Delors II proposals in February with the aims of providing adequate resources, apply budgetary discipline, reflecting the ability of member states to pay and acting on commitments made at Maastricht and Lisbon. Eventually the UK Presidency put forward revised figures and a final compromise was reached at the Edinburgh Summit.

q.v. Cohesion Fund p. 223.

This involved an extremely detailed seven-year framework of expenditure, in which commitments would rise from ECU 69 billion in 1993 to 84 billion (at 1992 prices) in 1999. Further details are given in Box 18. Within this framework, agricultural expenditure is due to rise from only ECU 35 to 38 billion over the seven years. This represents a fall from nearly 52 per cent to 46 per cent of total budgetary expenditure. In other words the ceiling is, theoretically, pressing down on agricultural spending.

Box 18. EC Budget (1993–1999) as agreed at the Edinburgh Summit, December 1992

	1993	1994	1995	1996	1997	1998	1999
Agricultural guideline	35 230	35 095	35 722	36 364	37 023	37 697	38 389
Structural actions	21 277	21 885	23 480	24 990	26 526	28 240	30 000
Cohesion Fund	*1 500*	*1 750*	*2 000*	*2 250*	*2 500*	*2 550*	*2 600*
Structural Funds and other operations	*19 777*	*20 135*	*21 480*	*22 740*	*24 026*	*25 690*	*27 400*
Internal policies	3 940	4 084	4 323	4 520	4 710	4 910	5 100
External activities	3 950	4 000	4 280	4 560	4 830	5 180	5 600
Administrative expenditure	3 280	3 580	3 580	3 690	3 800	3 850	3 900
Reserves	1 500	1 500	1 100	1 100	1 100	1 100	1 100
Monetary reserves	*1 000*	*1 000*	*500*	*500*	*500*	*500*	*500*
Emergency aid	*200*	*200*	*300*	*300*	*300*	*300*	*300*
Loan guarantees	*300*	*300*	*300*	*300*	*300*	*300*	*300*
Total appropriations for commitments	69 177	69 944	72 485	75 224	77 989	80 977	84 089
Appropriations for payments required	65 908	67 036	69 150	71 290	74 491	77 249	80 114
Appropriations for payments (% GNP)	1.20	1.19	1.20	1.21	1.23	1.25	1.26
Margin for unforeseen expenditure (% GNP)	0.00	0.01	0.01	0.01	0.01	0.01	0.01
Own resources ceiling (% GNP)	1.20	1.20	1.21	1.22	1.24	1.26	1.27

At the same time, the Structural Funds are due to rise from nearly ECU 20 billion to over 27 billion, representing a rise from 29 per cent to 32 per cent. They will, however, be subject to stricter controls. The new Cohesion Fund will start at ECU 1.5 billion and then rise to 2.6 billion. For the rest modest rises are allowed for internal policies and external actions. Industrial policy is not funded. Administrative costs are virtually frozen and reserves are due to decline.

No more than 0.01 per cent is allowed as a margin of error. Nor has provision yet been made for the extra building costs that leaving the EP at Strasbourg, another recent decision, will involve. All this testifies to the desire of member states both to curtail and control expenditure, sometimes to the detriment of the Community interest.

The new spending commitments are to be financed by an increase in own resources from 1.20 per cent of GNP to 1.27 per cent, with a switch from VAT to the fourth resource, the ceiling on VAT being reduced. However, the latter is to be levied, from 1995, on only 50 per cent of GNP and not 55 per cent, thereby aiding poorer states. These ceilings are to be strictly enforced. Little interest was shown in a fifth, as yet undefined, resource sought by some enthusiasts. Nevertheless, the matter will be reconsidered in 1995 along with a uniform rate of VAT. The UK rebate is to continue, though it was much criticized, and further attention will be given to budgetary discipline.

Whether this will be effective remains to be seen as does the question of whether these new limits will be met. However, the figures do reinforce the view taken above, that the Community budget is a limited and imposed financial instrument. Neither its size not its structure allow it to act as a real motor for change, whether in economic management, monetary policy, or for equalizing regional disparities. It is a statement of financing conceded by the member states, together with their reluctant agreement to make available sufficient funds to finance the confirmed aims of the Community, after a 10 per cent collection fee.

However, its symbolic importance remains and the budget is large enough to make the Community financially attractive and influential. This attraction is likely to continue because of the economic depression in Europe. However, such economic conditions also make it harder for better-off states to provide more resources for the budget, as the poorer states wish. As a result conflict is likely to continue.

FURTHER READING

Archer, C. and Butler, F., *The European Community: Structure and Process*, Pinter, London, 1992.

Ardy, B., 'The national incidence of the Community budget', *Journal of Common Market Studies*, vol. 26, no. 4, 1988, pp. 401–30.

Baziadoly, S., 'Le refus de la décharge par le Parlement européen', *Revue du Marché commun et de l'Union européenne*, no. 357, 1992, pp. 287–92.

EC, *Financial Report 1991*, OOPEC, Luxembourg, 1992.

EC Commission, *The EC Budget*, OOPEC, Luxembourg, 1986.

El-Agraa, A.M., *The Economics of the European Community*, 4th edn, Harvester Wheatsheaf, Hemel Hempstead, 1994.

Franklin, M., *The EC Budget: Realism, redistribution and radical reform*, RIIA, London, 1992.

George, S., *Politics and Policy in the European Community*, Oxford University Press, Oxford, 1992.

Nicoll, W., 'The Long March of the EC's 1988 Budget', *Journal of Common Market Studies*, vol. 27, no. 2, 1988, pp. 161–70.

Nicoll W. and Salmon T., *Understanding the New European Communities*, 2nd edn, Harvester Wheatsheaf, Hemel Hempstead, 1993.

Scott, A., 'Financing the Community: The Delors II package', in Lodge, J. (ed.), *The European Community and the Challenge of the Future*, 2nd edn, Pinter, London, 1993, pp. 69–88.

Shackleton, M., 'The EC's budget in the move to a single market', *Governance*, vol. 4, no. 1, 1991, pp. 94–114.

Shackleton, M., *Financing the European Community*, Pinter/RIIA, London, 1990.

Shackleton, M., 'The budget of the EC: structure and process', in Lodge, J. (ed.), *The European Community and the Challenge of the Future*, 2nd edn, Pinter, London, 1993, pp. 89–111.

Swann, D., *The Economics of the Common Market*, 7th edn, Penguin, Harmondsworth, 1992.

Thomson, I., 'The budget: a bibliographical snapshot' *European Access*, 1993/1, pp. 44–8.

Wallace, H., *Budgetary Politics: The finances of the European Community*, Allen and Unwin, London, 1980.

vii. General and Final Provisions A: legal principles and obligations

The sixth and final Part of the Treaty of Rome contains both those Articles which do not fall into the precise categories already considered and formalities about the document itself. Some of these Articles are more significant than this general description might suggest and the Part should not be confused with the Final Act. For the sake of convenience and comprehension the *Handbook* subdivides the Part into three: legalities and procedures (Articles 210–227); external aspects (Articles 227–238); and transitional and final formalities (Articles 239–248). However, the actual order of the Articles is not always as logical as this suggests.

q.v. Final Act pp. 427–9.

Nevertheless, the legal and procedural Articles can themselves be considered under four further headings: the legal status of the EC and its servants (Articles 210–218), obligations and rights (Articles 213–223), basic procedures (Articles 216–217), and arrangements for times of crisis (Articles 223–226). While the abortive Dutch draft would have inserted a new Article 220a requiring the cooperation on judicial and home affairs now found in K.1 and K.4, the TEU as ratified made only one change to all of these. This was to add a reference to the ECB in Article 215. Moreover, the drafters did not take the opportunity to upgrade the status of the inheritances from the Merger Treaty in Articles 212 and 218 as they had when dealing with institutional questions in Part Five.

The first element of Part Six thus still begins with the question of the legal status of the Community. This occupies Articles 210–212, 215 and 218. The key provision is that in Article 210. This states that the Community has a 'legal personality'. By this is meant that the Community as a body, like the ECSC before it, can act in law like an ordinary individual or firm. It thus has the autonomy and authority to bear rights and duties. These include owning property, entering into legally binding agreements, suing and being sued. Its legal personality is distinct from that of the member states.

However, whereas the member states have this as an inherent right, the Community's legal personality is bestowed by the Treaty and by law. It must therefore be exercised within the limits of the Treaty. Nonetheless, this allows the Community and its institutions, which normally act for it, to carry out its functions and objectives in a legally binding way. This is important in such matters as contracts, employment and external relations.[47] And it should be noted that the Union as such does not enjoy legal personality. Indeed, one of the Lords' amendments to the UK's EC Amendment Act would have written this denial into the legislation.

Article 211 defines the nature and extent of the Community's freedom to take legally enforceable actions. It has as full powers as national laws provide for any other corporate body. Article 212 then begins the definition of the status of the employees of the Communities. They are to form one administration and be subject to Staff Regulations. The latter are justiciable in the Court of First Instance. They are also subject to the rules on confidentiality laid down in Article 214, which is the nearest the EC gets to an Official Secrets Act.

One of the essential elements of having legal personality is the ability to enter into contracts with third parties. Article 215 therefore establishes the Community's liability to normal national laws of contract. Thus a contract concluded with a Danish furniture company for desks would be governed by Danish law as well as by EC law. The Article also establishes the Community's general liability in cases where no special relations exist between the Community and a third party. It thus provides that third parties can sue the Community if actions by its

---

47. The Community institutions as such do not enjoy legal personality in their own right. They can only act as agents of the Community. This point is made specifically in the last sentence of Article 211. And, as already noted, the Legal Service would itself act for the Commission. The contractual liability of the Community is seen as both a private and a public law matter, reflecting French dualist traditions of law, rather than the unified approach found in Britain.

institutions or servants — this being the somewhat pejorative legal term for employees, and now extended to those of the ECB (and the EMI *ad interim*) — cause them damage.

Finally, Article 218 slightly qualifies this by establishing the member states' willingness to concede quasi-diplomatic status to Community servants. The precise status, which is particularly relevant in matters of external relations, is defined in a Protocol on the Privileges and Immunities of the European Communities, deriving from the Rome Treaty's Final Act. The Protocol was actually attached to the Merger Treaty of 1965. This was amended to cover the institutions of EMU by Protocol 17 of the TEU. The amended Protocol also continues to provide for the inviolability of Community premises, papers and messengers. Envoys accredited to the Community also have quasi-diplomatic status.

q.v.
Protocol 17
p. 427.

The second subset of Articles deals with the more political obligations imposed by the Treaty. Thus Article 213 empowers the Commission to collect such information and undertake such monitoring as the Treaty requires. The next Article follows logically by providing some guarantee that such information will be treated responsibly. Equally, Article 219 provides a guarantee of good behaviour by the member states who agree to use only the Treaty in settling disputes. The next Articles (Articles 220 and 221) extend and clarify this undertaking by providing guidelines on the legal treatment to be accorded foreign individuals, businesses and courts within the Community context. Article 222 then balances this by giving assurances to member states about their rules on property ownership, an assurance extended to Denmark by Protocol 1 attached to the TEU.[48]

q.v.
Protocol 1
p. 394.

Finally, Article 223(1) makes it plain that disclosure of information, presumably under 213, does not extend to national security of the member states, any more than it does to times of crisis. This, as will be seen, is covered by Articles 224–226. The principle of applicability to the member states, as well as its geographical extent, is restated by Article 227 in the next section. By this the Treaties are freed of subjection to national law.

The remainder of the third subset specifies the location of the Community institutions and the languages used in their operation. Article 216 unfortunately, presupposes an accord which does not exist. For many years the allocation of Community institutions was provisional. However, this meant that the EP in particular was divided between Strasbourg, Luxembourg and increasingly Brussels. This, as already noted, causes a vast amount of expensive commuting for people, papers and other facilities. In the early 1980s the Parliament tried to pre-empt the issue and its draft Treaty threatened to take away the decision if the other institutions failed to resolve it within two years.

However, places like Strasbourg and Luxembourg City have a great deal of money and pride invested in acting as headquarters cities. They have tried to

---

48. This provision, which, as already noted, allows the Danes to limit foreigners' — essentially Germans' — rights to buy holiday houses on the Danish coast, is seen by some authorities as a major infringement both of the integrity of European law and of the four freedoms of the Single Market. It is claimed that the new provisions, which allow the Danes to maintain existing legislation on second homes notwithstanding the rest of the TEU, conflicts with Articles 30 and 36.

outbid Brussels with new facilities. And their governments have gone to court to try and prevent rationalization in Brussels. The Edinburgh Summit, however, more or less codified the present shambles, although allowing the Parliament to have more meetings in Brussels where a new building is being prepared for it. Whether this decision will hold remains very uncertain.

Article 217 ostensibly allows the Council to decide the languages used by Community institutions. In practice institutions often decide for themselves. Almost all published documents are translated into the nine official languages, as the Official Journal has to be, and no one version has precedence. Not all working documents are translated and the working languages of the Community tend to be English and French. However, there is pressure for German to be given equal status. Enlargement, especially to the East, will make language an increasingly sensitive question since it will bring efficiency into conflict with national pride. Declaration 29 of the TEU provides that language in the CFSP should follow EC and EPC rules, although all papers presented to the Commission and the Council must be translated. Similar considerations apply to the Treaty itself as the discussion of Article 248 shows.

q.v.
Declaration
29 pp.
437–8.

Finally, Articles 223–226 provide for emergency action and national interests. They start by allowing national security and especially arms provision to enjoy a special status. The states can choose their own procedures and do not have to consult the EP. However, a list regulates the extent of this exemption. There is also special provision for crises in the capital and monetary fields in Article 73g while the CFSP also has a clause of this kind. Then Article 224 organizes cooperation in emergencies when domestic violence, wars or other kinds of international difficulties force special measures on member states. These are subject to appeal to the ECJ. Special arrangements are next made in Article 225 for dealing with distortions caused by the application of the two previous Articles.

Finally, Article 226 allows member states, and the Commission, to take protective measures in case of severe sectoral dislocation. These clauses have been seen by some EFTA neutrals as allowing them to preserve their neutrality in cases where the Community would have imposed economic sanctions. This view is contested and the Articles have not been seen as a major source of intergovernmentalism inside the Community. However the question, like some others discussed here, does have implications for the Community's dealings with outsiders.

Part Six   General and final provisions

ARTICLE 210   The Community shall have legal personality.

ARTICLE 211   In each of the Member States, the Community shall enjoy the most extensive legal capacity accorded to legal persons under their laws; it may, in particular, acquire or dispose of movable and immovable property and may be a party to legal proceedings. To this end, the Community shall be represented by the Commission.

ARTICLE 212

[was repealed by the Merger Treaty. Article 24 of the latter is therefore now in force. This reads as follows:]

1. The officials and other servants of the European Coal and Steel Community, the European Economic Community and the European Atomic Energy Community shall, at the date of entry into force of this Treaty, become officials and other servants of the European Communities and form part of the single administration of those Communities.

The Council shall, acting by a qualified majority on a proposal from the Commission and after consulting the other institutions concerned lay down the Staff Regulations of officials of the European Communities and the Conditions of Employment of other servants of those Communities.

ARTICLE 213

The Commission may, within the limits and under the conditions laid down by the Council in accordance with the provisions of this Treaty, collect any information and carry out any checks required for the performance of the tasks entrusted to it.

ARTICLE 214

The members of the institutions of the Community, the members of committees and the officials and other servants of the Community shall be required, even after their duties have ceased, not to disclose information of the kind covered by the obligation of professional secrecy, in particular information about undertakings, their business relations or their cost components.

ARTICLE 215

The contractual liability of the Community shall be governed by the law applicable to the contract in question.

In the case of non-contractual liability, the Community shall, in accordance with the general principles common to the law of the Member States, make good any damage caused by its institutions or by its servants in the performance of their duties.

The preceding paragraph shall apply under the same conditions to damage caused by the ECB or by its servants in the performance of their duties.

The personal liability of its servants towards the Community shall be governed by the provisions laid down in their Staff Regulations or in the Conditions of Employment applicable to them.

ARTICLE 216

The seat of the institutions of the Community shall be determined by common accord of the Governments of the Member States.

ARTICLE 217

The rules governing the languages of the institutions of the Community shall, without prejudice to the provisions contained in the rules of procedure of the Court of Justice, be determined by the Council, acting unanimously.

ARTICLE 218

[was repealed by the Merger Treaty. The first paragraph of Article 28 of the Merger Treaty is therefore now in force. This reads as follows:]

The European Communities shall enjoy in the territories of the Member States such privileges and immunities as are necessary for the performance of their tasks, under the conditions laid down in the Protocol annexed to this Treaty. The same shall apply to the European Investment Bank.

ARTICLE 219

Member States undertake not to submit a dispute concerning the interpretation or application of this Treaty to any method of settlement other than those provided for therein.

ARTICLE 220   Member States shall, so far as is necessary, enter into negotiations with each other with a view to securing for the benefit of their nationals:

— the protection of persons and the enjoyment and protection of rights under the same conditions as those accorded by each State to its own nationals;
— the abolition of double taxation within the Community;
— the mutual recognition of companies or firms within the meaning of the second paragraph of Article 58, the retention of legal personality in the event of transfer of their seat from one country to another, and the possibility of mergers between companies or firms governed by the laws of different countries;
— the simplification of formalities governing the reciprocal recognition and enforcement of judgments of courts or tribunals and of arbitration awards.

ARTICLE 221   Within three years of the entry into force of this Treaty, Member States shall accord nationals of the other Member States the same treatment as their own nationals as regards participation in the capital of companies or firms within the meaning of Article 58, without prejudice to the application of the other provisions of this Treaty.

ARTICLE 222   This Treaty shall in no way prejudice the rules in Member States governing the system of property ownership.

ARTICLE 223   1. The provisions of this Treaty shall not preclude the application of the following rules:
(a) No Member State shall be obliged to supply information the disclosure of which it considers contrary to the essential interests of its security;
(b) Any Member State may take such measures as it considers necessary for the protection of the essential interests of its security which are connected with the production of or trade in arms, munitions and war material; such measures shall not, however, adversely affect the conditions of competition in the common market regarding products which are not intended for specifically military purposes.

2. During the first year after the entry into force of this Treaty, the Council shall, acting unanimously, draw up a list of products to which the provisions of paragraph 1 (b) shall apply.

3. The Council may, acting unanimously on a proposal from the Commission, make changes in this list.

ARTICLE 224   Member States shall consult each other with a view to taking together the steps needed to prevent the functioning of the common market being affected by measures which a Member State may be called upon to take in the event of serious internal disturbance affecting the maintenance of law and order, in the event of war or serious international tension constituting a threat of war, or in order to carry out obligations it has accepted for the purpose of maintaining peace and international security.

ARTICLE 225   If measures taken in the circumstances referred to in Articles 223 and 224 have the effect of distorting the conditions of competition in the common market, the Commission shall, together with the State concerned examine how these measures can be adjusted to the rules laid down in this Treaty.

By way of derogation from the procedure laid down in Articles 169 and 170, the Commission or any Member State may bring the matter directly before the Court of Justice if it considers that another Member State is making improper use of the powers provided for in Articles 223 and 224. The Court of Justice shall give its ruling in camera.

ARTICLE 226

1. If, during the transitional period, difficulties arise which are serious and liable to persist in any sector of the economy or which could bring about serious deterioration in the economic situation of a given area, a Member State may apply for authorisation to take protective measures in order to rectify the situation and adjust the sector concerned to the economy of the common market.

2. On application by the State concerned, the Commission shall, by emergency procedure, determine without delay the protective measures which it considers necessary, specifying the circumstances and the manner in which they are to be put into effect.

3. The measures authorised under paragraph 2 may involve derogations from the rules of this Treaty, to such an extent and for such periods as are strictly necessary in order to attain the objectives referred to in paragraph 1. Priority shall be given to such measures as will least disturb the functioning of the common market.

FURTHER READING

Hailsham, Lord and Vaughan, D. (eds.), *The Law of the European Communities*, Butterworth, London, 1986.

Lasok, D. and Bridge, J., *Introduction to the Institution and Laws of the EC*, Butterworth, London, 1991.

Lysen, J., 'Three questions on the non-contractual liability of the EC', *Legal Issues of European Integration*, 1985/2, pp. 86–120.

Weatherill, S. and Beaumont, P., *EC Law*, Penguin, Harmondsworth, 1993.

viii. General and Final Provisions B: external applicability

Up till now the Treaty of Rome has very largely been concerned with matters affecting its own members. However, the very nature of its activities and the scope of its membership means that it has implications for the world outside. So, while the Treaty does not here set out principles of foreign policy, it does indicate the extent and manner in which the Treaty is applicable outside Europe and the kinds of formal agreements the Community can conclude with other international actors. However, it was left to the SEA and the TEU to provide the rudiments of a real foreign policy in Treaty form, albeit one run more by the member states than the Community as such.

These Articles had to be included at this point in the Treaty, because they are both legally a Community matter and an outgrowth of specific EC Treaty powers. This was confirmed by the ECJ's 1971 ERTA judgment which established that the Community had external jurisdiction wherever it had internal powers. Not all the Treaty Articles with an external dimension actually appear in Part Six.[49] The specific Articles here are also so placed because they are the logical extension of the idea of legal personality established in Article 210. All this ruled out any question or possibility of the Articles moving to the CFSP pillar.

q.v. CFSP pp. 373–81.

---

49. Thus Articles 3, 111 to 116, and 131 are among those which confer such powers. Articles 43, 75 and 101 of the Euratom give specific rights in relation to fisheries, transport and nuclear energy. Moreover the ECJ has interpreted Article 210 as allowing the Community to enter into contracts with foreign organizations, etc. The Court also ensures that all agreements are in conformity with the Treaties, thus re-enforcing this point.

In other words, although the Treaty does not address this point directly, the Community enjoys the right and capacity to act outside the territories of the member states. International personality is an accumulation of attributes which show that the entity concerned is a subject of international law and has the legal right, and the capability, to pursue its international rights and duties by bringing legal claims, etc. These include the abilities to send and receive envoys and, especially here, to enter into binding foreign treaty agreements in its own right. Indeed, the EC does not act in virtue of the powers of the member states, the normal actors in international law.

The Community also does this in a way recognized by international law. Although the old USSR refused to acknowledge the EC as an autonomous international actor until the 1980s, the conventional wisdom in international law accepts that the EC is such a player on the world scene. However, there are some doubts about both the extent of recognition and of the precise nature of its status. The latter is because the EC often acts more as an international organization than as a purely supranational body. The introduction of the CFSP does not really resolve these points.

This part of the Final Provisions contains five elements. These deal with the applicability of the Treaty, procedures for foreign relations, specific relations, obligations, and association agreements. The Articles also spill over into questions of a broader application which ought not to be overlooked, like those in Article 235. However, there is little in the way of general principles of policy. The Community's nature as a limited and civilian body, with a set of disparate rights to conclude treaties rather than the full panoply of state powers, stands out very clearly.

The TEU did not make any major changes in this part of the Treaty.[50] What it did do was, firstly, to tidy up items like Articles 227 and 231 to bring them into line with geopolitical realities. Secondly, it changed the procedural mechanisms of Articles 228 and 238 to reflect both the post-Maastricht institutional balance and the desire of some states to restrict the Commission's freedom of action. Thirdly, it built in necessary references to the Union's CFSP in Articles 228 and 229a. Fourth, it transferred the question of new membership, which is to some extent an external matter, to the TEU's Final Provisions. Fifth, it changed the definition of the subjects of association agreements in Article 238. There was also the not insignificant transfer out of the amendment procedure.

The first external element is that the fact that, while the Treaty under Article 227 applies throughout the territories of the member states as such, it can have a slightly different application in their dependencies. Metropolitan territory is to be understood as including air space, continental shelf, plus planes and vessels under member state control. Paragraph 2 deletes reference to Algeria, which had long since ceased to be French, and is partly updated in other ways. Paragraph

---

50. The abortive Dutch draft of 3 October 1991 would have added a Part Four entitled 'External Relations' to the Rome Treaty, before the institutional Articles. This would have contained four titles: CFSP; Commercial policies; Development cooperation and the Representation of the Community. Parliament would also have been given the right to assent to new powers undertaken in virtue of Article 235.

5(a) is then stripped of detail on the procedures previously laid down to decide how much should apply to the Faroes. Generally the Article recognizes that circumstances in colonial and non-independent territories are different from those in Europe proper and that the extent to which the Treaties apply needs to be specified.[51]

Elsewhere special arrangements were also made for relations with the former GDR. However, European microstates like Andorra and Monaco, which are linked to member states, were not considered. On the other hand, Declaration 6 of Maastricht now makes provision for taking their needs into account when a single currency is introduced. Declaration 5 does the same for other non-member states, notably those in Europe.

q.v. Declaration 6 pp. 432–3.

Assuming that the Treaty of Rome has already established the principle of the Community concluding external agreements, Article 228 then supplies the more basic second element, the internal mechanisms for conducting them. Essentially this much enlarged Article now allows the Council to oversee the negotiation of agreements. Previously the Commission's role as negotiator was stated without qualification even if it usually worked with Council observers present, as under Article 113. Now it has formally to ask the Council to proceed, work within the mandate laid down, and work conjointly with Council representatives and guidelines. The idea of the mandate is also drawn from the procedure for commercial policy accords laid down in Article 113.

q.v. Declaration 5 p. 432.

q.v. Article 113 pp. 182–3.

The Council's right to conclude agreements is also emphasized by the new paragraph 2. In some cases like associations it can only do this by unanimous decision. All this suggests that Douglas Hurd's view, that the rights of the Commission have been reduced, is justified. Moreover, some authorities believe that subsidiarity could still apply here, taking the reduction further. The Commission retains its responsibilities for Euratom external relations and paragraph 4 allows the Council to give it extra responsibilities. But the phraseology implies that the Commission will be kept on a short leash.

The European Parliament is also given more standing here, notably through the extra assent procedures indicated in the latter part of paragraph 3. However, it is often only consulted even where conciliation or cooperation normally applies to the field in which the agreement is being negotiated. Commercial agreements under Article 113(3) are still excluded and the Parliament, unlike the other institutions, cannot refer accords to the ECJ. Where agreements involve Treaty changes the Parliament will have to be consulted, and references to Article N are included to this effect.

The next five Articles are shorter but, in some ways, more specific. They cover different aspects of external relations. Article 228a is a wholly new reference to imposing economic sanctions under the CFSP, for which the Treaty of Rome makes no real provision. It provides a procedure for such urgent decisions to be taken.

---

51. The extent and nature of EC relations with the French overseas departments, European autonomous regions and independent microstates within the EC's boundaries are conveniently summarized in a Background Report from the Community's London Office of 10 December 1992 (ISEC/B33/92). Mention should also be made of Association under Part Four (see pp. 246–8) in this context.

Article 229 gives the Commission as such authority to maintain relations with the United Nations (UN), the General Agreement on Tariffs and Trade (GATT) and other international bodies. In fact the Community is an observer at the UN and has a variety of relations with its agencies. Thus it exchanges information with the International Labour Organization, accepts UN Educational, Scientific and Cultural Organization obligations on intellectual copyright, and is observer on the UN's Economic Commission for Europe. It has also signed a number of sectoral conventions. It is not recognized as such in GATT but is able to exercise the powers of a participant. The Commission presently leads the negotiations in the Uruguay Round.

The next two Articles give the Community responsibility for relations with two other international bodies, probably because they were European (see below pp. 488–90). In fact Maastricht updates the reference to the OEEC to make it the Organization for Economic Cooperation and Development (OECD), as it has been since 1961. The Community has a particularly favourable status where the OECD is concerned, thanks to Article 13 of its Convention and a special Protocol. The next Treaty of Rome Article, Article 232, notes that other relations can be carried out in virtue of the other founding Treaties.

The third element deals with the obligations deriving from external relations. This reflects the fact that agreements impinge on national sovereignty, even though these are not self-executing. Article 233 thus establishes that there is no problem with the Benelux Union, even though many of its aims are now pursued by the Community. Then Article 234 establishes the general principle behind this, which is that previous accords concluded by member states, are not rendered void by Community membership. Indeed, the EC is actually bound by some of these. The EC cannot, in other words, make unilateral changes to existing Acts of nation states. However, the text does urge adjustment of incompatible accords and the advantages of the Community method. The ECJ has also ruled that member states are only constrained by Community Treaties in so far as this is necessary to safeguard EC policies. There is no general infringement of their sovereignty.

At this point the old Treaty diverged a little from external concerns, although only Article 235 now remains here. This is a catch-all clause which allows the Community to do things not otherwise specified in the Treaty. This has been increasingly used for external affairs though it is of general effect. It has thus been used for educational and public health purposes. The Union has a similar provision in Article F. This is surprising given UK dislike of what it sees as 'creeping competence'. However, some authorities think that Article 235 could be circumscribed by the first sentence of Article 3b, in which case the intergovernmental elements of the Treaty would have been strengthened.[52]

q.v.
creeping
competence
p. 46.

Maastricht also transferred two Articles, those dealing with Treaty amendment

---

52. On the other hand, some critics of the TEU have claimed that Article 3a is likely to be circumscribed by Article 235. The Luxembourg draft treaty did in fact limit the acquisition of new powers to the fields covered by Article 3a. It also provided both for the Parliament to have the right of assent to Council proposals and for the principle of subsidiarity to be taken into account. The Dutch draft dropped all but the reference to assent. Both drafts allowed for the Council to decide which, if any, new powers could be exercised through majority voting. Allowing the old article to stand unchanged thus appears a doubly contradictory decision.

and Community enlargement, to the new Articles N and O. This is not just a drafting amendment since it carries the implication that the Treaty of Rome cannot be substantially changed except through the procedures of the Union, thus limiting the status and autonomy of the Community. Equally there can be no further membership of the EC as such. The Treaty of Rome does, of course, allow for relatively simple minor amendments in such things as the number of Advocates-General.

q.v. Articles N and O pp. 353–6.

Finally, the TEU changes the Article on association. This had originally been used as the framework for a whole range of relationships. Over time, this has gradually changed and now the reference to third states and unions of states has gone, leaving only states and international organizations. The TEU has also deleted both the addition to Article 238 made by the SEA, which allowed the Council to conclude association agreements, subject to parliamentary assent, and the provision that any Treaty amendments consequent on association has be dealt with in the normal way.

This is a logical consequence of the rewriting of Article 228 which allows the Council to conclude association accords by unanimity, while treating assent to association as a derogation from the norm in the second paragraph of 228(3). This does not demean the Parliament because this now needs only to find a simple majority. However, the new precision about the nature of association it also implies, is perhaps understandable in view of the increasing pressures for membership and the way the Community's foreign agenda has moved on. And it is typical of the somewhat messy and imprecise handling of external relations in the revised Treaty of Rome. All this means that the realities of the Community's external relations need further examination.

ARTICLE 227

1. This Treaty shall apply to the Kingdom of Belgium, the Kingdom of Denmark, the Federal Republic of Germany, the Hellenic Republic, the Kingdom of Spain, the French Republic, Ireland, the Italian Republic, the Grand Duchy of Luxembourg, the Kingdom of the Netherlands, the Portuguese Republic and the United Kingdom of Great Britain and Northern Ireland.

2. *With regard to the French overseas departments, the general and particular provisions of this Treaty relating to*:
— the free movement of goods;
— agriculture, save for Article 40(4);
— the liberalization of services
— the rules on competition;
— the protective measures provided for in Articles **109h, 109i** and 226;
— the institutions,
shall apply as soon as this Treaty enters into force.

The conditions under which the other provisions of this Treaty are to apply shall be determined, within two years of entry into force of this Treaty, by decisions of the Council, acting unanimously on a proposal from the Commission.

The institutions of the Community will, within the framework of the procedures provided for in this Treaty, in particular Article 226, take care that the economic and social developments of these areas is made possible.

3. The special arrangements for association set out in Part Four of this Treaty shall apply to the overseas countries and territories listed in Annex IV to this Treaty.

This Treaty shall not apply to those overseas countries and territories having special relations with the United Kingdom of Great Britain and Northern Ireland which are not included in the aforementioned list.

4. The provisions of this Treaty shall apply to the European territories for whose external relations a Member State is responsible.

5. (a) *This Treaty shall not apply to the Faroe Islands.*
   (b) This Treaty shall not apply to the Sovereign Base Areas of the United Kingdom of Great Britain and Northern Ireland in Cyprus.
   (c) This Treaty shall apply to the Channel Islands and the Isle of Man only to the extent necessary to ensure the implementation of the arrangements for those islands set out in the Treaty concerning the accession of new Member States to the European Economic Community and to the European Atomic Energy Community signed on 22 January 1972.

ARTICLE 228

1. Where this Treaty provides for the conclusion of agreements between the Community and one or more States or international organizations, **the Commission shall make recommendations to the Council, which shall authorize the Commission to open the necessary negotiations. The Commission shall conduct these negotiations in consultation with special committees appointed by the Council to assist it in this task and within the framework of such directives as the Council may issue to it.**

In exercising the powers conferred upon it by this paragraph, the Council shall act by a qualified majority, except in the cases provided for in the second sentence of paragraph 2, for which it shall act unanimously.

2. *Subject to the powers vested in the Commission in this field, the agreements shall be concluded by the Council,* **acting by a qualified majority** *on a proposal from the Commission.* **The Council shall act unanimously when the agreement covers a field for which unanimity is required for the adoption of internal rules, and for the agreements referred to in Article 238.**

3. **The Council shall conclude agreements after consulting the European Parliament, except for the agreements referred to in Article 113(3), including cases where the agreement covers a field for which the procedure referred to in Article 189b or that referred to in Article 189c is required for the adoption of internal rules. The European Parliament shall deliver its opinion within a time-limit which the Council may lay down according to the urgency of the matter. In the absence of an opinion within that time-limit, the Council may act.**

By way of derogation from the previous subparagraph, agreements referred to in Article 238, other agreements establishing a specific institutional framework by organizing cooperation procedures, agreements having important budgetary implications for the Community and agreements entailing amendment of an act adopted under the procedure referred to in Article 189b shall be concluded after the assent of the European Parliament has been obtained.

The Council and the European Parliament may, in an urgent situation, agree upon a time limit for the assent.

4. **When concluding an agreement, the Council may, by way of derogation from paragraph 2, authorize the Commission to approve modifications on behalf of the Community where the agreement provides for them to be adopted by a simplified procedure or by a body set up by the agreement; it may attach specific conditions to such authorization.**

5. When the Council envisages concluding an agreement which calls for amendments to the Treaty, the amendments must first be adopted in accordance with the procedure laid down in Article N of the Treaty on European Union.

6. The Council, the Commission or a Member State may obtain the opinion of the Court of Justice as to whether an agreement envisaged is compatible with the provisions of this Treaty. Where the opinion of the Court of Justice is adverse, the agreement may enter into force only in accordance with Article **N of the Treaty on European Union**.

7. Agreements concluded under the conditions set out in this Article shall be binding on the institutions of the Community and on Member States.

ARTICLE 228a

Where it is provided, in a common position or in a joint action adopted according to the provisions of the Treaty on European Union relating to the common foreign and security policy, for an action by the Community to interrupt or to reduce, in part or completely, economic relations with one or more third countries, the Council shall take the necessary urgent measures. The Council shall act by a qualified majority on a proposal from the Commission.

ARTICLE 229

It shall be for the Commission to ensure the maintenance of all appropriate relations with the organs of the United Nations, of its specialized agencies and of the General Agreement on Tariffs and Trade.

The Commission shall also maintain such relations as are appropriate with all international organizations.

ARTICLE 230

The Community shall establish all appropriate forms of cooperation with the Council of Europe.

ARTICLE 231

The Community shall establish close cooperation with the *Organization for Economic Cooperation and Development,* the details of which shall be determined by common accord.

ARTICLE 232

1. The provisions of this Treaty shall not affect the provisions of the Treaty establishing the European Coal and Steel Community, in particular as regards the rights and obligations of Member States, the powers of the institutions of that Community and the rules laid down by that Treaty for the functioning of the common market in coal and steel.

2. The provisions of this Treaty shall not derogate from those of the Treaty establishing the European Atomic Energy Community.

ARTICLE 233

The provisions of this Treaty shall not preclude the existence or completion of regional unions between Belgium and Luxembourg, or between Belgium, Luxembourg and the Netherlands, to the extent that the objectives of these regional unions are not attained by application of this Treaty.

ARTICLE 234

The rights and obligations arising from agreements concluded before the entry into force of this Treaty between one or more Member States on the one hand, and one or more third countries on the other, shall not be affected by the provisions of this Treaty.

To the extent that such agreements are not compatible with this Treaty, the Member State or States concerned shall take all appropriate steps to eliminate the incompatibilities established. Member States shall, where necessary, assist each other to this end and shall, where appropriate, adopt a common attitude.

In applying the agreements referred to in the first paragraph, Member States shall take into account the fact that the advantages accorded under this Treaty by each Member State form an integral part of the establishment of the Community and are thereby inseparably linked with the creation of common institutions, the conferring of powers upon them and the granting of the same advantages by all the other Member States.

ARTICLE 235   If action by the Community should prove necessary to attain, in the course of the operation of the common market, one of the objectives of the Community and this Treaty has not provided the necessary powers, the Council shall, acting unanimously on a proposal from the Commission and after consulting the European Parliament, take the appropriate measures.

Article 236 and 237 are repealed.[53]

ARTICLE 238   *The Community may conclude with one or more states or international organizations agreements establishing an association involving reciprocal rights and obligations, common action and special procedures.*[54]

ix. Community external relations

The Treaty of Rome is probably at its least revealing when it deals with external relations. We would hardly imagine from its few, tangential Articles on the subject, that the Community has been immensely active and influential outside its borders, establishing what has been called a 'presence' on both the European and world scenes. Nor is it immediately apparent that the policies which derive from this weak constitutional base have been seen as very successful, both by commentators and by the many states which have sought relations with the Community. This is despite the old jibe that the Community is an economic giant but a political pygmy. Public opinion polls also often suggest that the Community's external activities are relatively popular with voters, despite the débâcle in Yugoslavia and the fact that the Heads of Government felt it necessary to invent a specific structure for a common foreign and security policy.

This suggests examining five specific questions. These are: what exactly are the Community's external relations? How are they organized, both generally and through European Political Cooperation (EPC)? To what regions do they apply? What are the current problems? And how should they be assessed over all?

Although critics of the Community resent it having a foreign policy because this is the mark of a state, the Community is nothing like a normal state. Thus it does not have its own population, central government or territories. Nor can it defend its borders, acquire colonies, or raise troops. Equally it does not have

---

53. Again, as in other instances where the TEU speaks of repealing articles of the EC Treaty, this is a half truth. It may not use the numbers but the substance of Articles 236 (which dealt with amending the Treaty) and 237 (on applications to join the Community) has actually been transferred to articles N and O of the TEU. See below pp. 336–7.

54. In the official versions of the Treaty of Rome, Articles 239 and 240 appear here, with the Setting up of the Institutions following as a separate element of the Treaty. However, for the sake of logic and clarity, they are included here in the next element of this sub-subdivision of the *Handbook* where some people might have said Article 235 really belonged.

the power of war and peace. The Community is essentially a civilian power which has certain specified treaty-making powers (emerging from its internal rights); an international influence because of its economic and policy weight; and a set of member states with wide general political interests.

Because of this the Community's external relations have, until recently, been essentially dualist. It does not have a single clear vision of foreign policy or sense of 'national interest'. On the one hand there are the economic and policy actions, deriving directly from the Treaties and dating back to the late 1950s. Many of these have a political dimension. On the other, there are the more general political stances created by EPC. This is an intergovernmental system of coordination which emerged in the early 1970s. However, in recent years the distinction between economic and political relations has faded somewhat.

Together the two things have meant that the Community now has relations with about 150 countries, most of them accredited to Brussels as well as to member states. In turn the Community maintains about 80 delegations abroad. These are quasi-embassies headed by a representative who ranks between an ambassador and a consul. In addition the Community is involved in a whole range of bilateral deals, in over thirty multilateral accords and in a number of sectoral activities and international organizations. Over and beyond this is a good deal of informal diplomacy. An indication of the resulting structure is given in Figure 14. All this makes the Community a real force in world affairs which overlaps with that of its member states.

How are the Community's economically-based relations organized? While decisions are taken by the Council this is usually on the basis of Commission proposals. The Commission is the Community's main negotiator. Hence the Commission's first Directorate-General is devoted to external relations. This is divided into eleven Directorates most of which deal with specific regions or organizations.[55] There is also provision for protocol and relations with delegations. At present the DG answers to three commissioners, Sir Leon Brittan for economic questions such as GATT, Hans van den Broek for political questions and enlargement and Miguel Marin for development aid.

Commissioners often make a lot of foreign visits, thereby acting as roving ambassadors. This is in addition to the work of the Delegates. They are appointed by the Commission after consultation with member states. Other Directorates also have a voice in external policies when there are questions arising relating to the sector for which they are responsible. And member state representatives abroad often liaise closely with Commission officials on external policy matters.

The Community has a whole range of instruments available to give shape to its external relations. Thus it has a variety of agreements of different applicability, significance and status. Third parties can be very aware of distinctions of status. The agreements can be simple ones signed by the Community as such, or mixed agreements which are signed by the EC and its

---

55. These are for GATT and OECD; North America and Australasia etc.; General Economic Policies; Sectoral Economic Policies; Newly Independent States; China and Japan; Central and Eastern Europe; Mediterranean and Middle East; North–South relations; Latin America; and Asia.

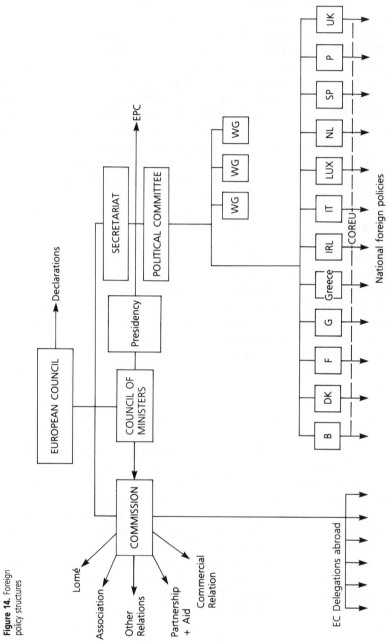

Figure 14. Foreign policy structures

member states. This is, for example, the case with the EEA Agreement and the Europe Agreements. These require ratification by all member states, which can usually be a slow process.

Some of the agreements are bilateral, that is with single states. Thus the Swiss have over 140 separate agreements with the Community, usually in technical and trade fields. The Common Commercial Policy gives rise to large numbers of trade agreements and interventions, controlling access to the Single Market, establishing trade relations, dealing with dumping or unfair subsidies, and providing credits. These can refer to the EC market, to partners and to third markets where Community firms compete with others from competitor states. In all these the Commission negotiates for the Community instead of the member states, albeit within a mandate laid down by the Council.

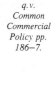

q.v.
Common
Commercial
Policy pp.
186–7.

Many of these negotiations are multilateral whether general, such as the Lomé agreements, or specific to individual sectors. Thus the Community is the only non-state to sign the Montreal Convention on protecting the ozone layer. The Community also takes part in the OECD consensus on credit. It is also much involved with environmental, health and human rights programmes. At the same time the Community is an observer or participant in a number of other international organizations. These include GATT, OECD, the UN, UNESCO, UNECE (United Nations Economic Committee for Europe), and UNCTAD.

The Community also has instruments which are specific to itself. These include the traditional form of association, now extended to the EEA, which lays down a framework for political, financial and trade relations with specific countries. These can hold out the hope of membership as is the case with the so-called Europe Agreements with the Visegrad countries. Countries without this hope are usually given cooperation agreements, built round trade and aid. A new style of partnership agreement is also being developed with Russia and other major eastern states. This will supplement the technical assistance provided under the new TACIS (Trade and Cooperation with the Commonwealth of Independent States) programme.

The Community also places a good deal of stress on what is called political dialog which involves regular meetings between ministers and others to exchange views. A lot of information is also provided by the Community. Finally the Community also develops relations through what might be called policy measures. In Western Europe many of its programmes, such as ERASMUS, have been opened to non-member countries, thereby bringing them into the network. At the same time the Community has developed integrated programmes of aid and development for countries fringing Western Europe.

The more political elements of Community external relations are rather different from this. The growth of the Community in the 1960s made the Six feel that they needed to coordinate their policies to maximize their influence and eliminate dangerous divergences. When this was suggested by the Fouchet Plan in 1961–2 it failed to gain acceptance, just as the European Defence Community and the related European Political Community before it. However, after de Gaulle resigned, the Hague Summit commissioned Vicomte Davignon to suggest a structure for foreign policy coordination. His report was accepted at the Paris and Copenhagen Summits in the early 1970s and set up a new form of policy coordination separate from that of the Community, although involving some of its institutions.

These got EPC rolling. Although it experienced some difficulties during the oil crisis when states went their own way and the Arabs insisted on linking political and economic issues, the British helped to keep it moving.[56] It was revised by the London Report of 1980. Further encouragement came from the success of some political pronouncements in the early 1980s and, in particular, from the Stuttgart Solemn Declaration in 1983. Finally, following the urgings of the Dooge Committee, EPC was additionally codified in 1986 and given more status through its inclusion in the Single European Act as an addition to Community activity. This represented the minimalist solution. It did not mean the creation of a real EC foreign policy.

EPC, as now constituted, symbolizes the Twelve acting as a unity in traditional foreign policy fields but it is still a relatively slim structure. It is essentially aimed at coordination and producing 'common positions' which leave the member states complete freedom. It presently consists of twelve elements. These are (i) a commitment to coordinate policies and to consult before setting national priorities; (ii) one meeting of European Council per Presidency to offer guidelines; (iii) an active and relatively high profile role for the Presidency which is held by the EC Presidency state to steer the system, sometimes with the Troika of past and future Presidencies; (iv) two ministerial meetings per Presidency; (v) provision for rapid emergency ministerial meetings in case of crisis; (vi) a small Secretariat which works with the Presidency; (vii) a special COREU telex network to provide continuous correspondence and information; (viii) a Political Committee of senior officials from the political sections of Foreign Ministries to act as a clearing house; (ix) various technical working groups; (x) colloquia to discuss policy options; (xi) collaboration in the CSCE and the UN, where EPC is regularly represented; and (xii) some cooperation between embassies in third countries. Consultations are confidential and decisions made by consensus. However, regular reports are made to the European Parliament. EPC only has two working languages: English and French.

Although some people expected nothing to come of the system, it has had some achievements to its credit. It has proved flexible and pragmatic in a quiet way, facilitating European solidarity within the old CSCE, thus exercising useful pressure on human rights, non-proliferation and the development of dialog. During the Falklands crisis it facilitated a rapid and largely supportive stance against Argentinean aggression. As with South Africa and Iraq in 1990 it provided a framework for sanctions. It also assisted in the making of clear policy statements on critical areas like Poland, Libya and Afghanistan at various times in the 1970s and 1980s. This was the case, for instance on South Africa in 1976–7 and again

---

56. On the other hand the Danes had considerable reservations and, in November 1973, insisted on the Foreign Ministers of the Nine flying from Copenhagen to Brussels to resume their meeting, so as to make the point that EPC and the EC were quite distinct.

in 1985. Equally the Venice Declaration on the Middle East in 1980 was one of a number of initiatives in that region during the decade.

At the same time EPC facilitates very close contact amongst the foreign policy establishments. Hence these become very knowledgeable about the policies of their eleven partners. People have become used to consulting before deciding on their own action. However, it is less certain as to whether it has either promoted a real understanding of the position of others or produced effective action. A kind of plateau of tolerance has been reached but this can fall short of a real political will to act together, as the failure to react to the shooting down of the South Korean Boeing 747 jet in 1983 showed. This has been made even more apparent over the former Yugoslavia. Because EPC has not determined national policies it has not really maximized Community influence.

It has also become more interchangeable with economic diplomacy with the passage of time. This is partly because of external circumstances and the needs of fora such as the CSCE which blur distinctions between the economic and the political. It is also due to the fact that some of the actors with whom the Community deals wish to link the two, as did the Arab states in the mid-1970s. Nor do they always appreciate the theological distinctions between what is done in EPC and what is done via 'the Community method' of largely trade-based relations conducted by the Commission.

Hence the EC's relations with various parts of the world have been affected by rather differing combinations of the two approaches. Inside Western Europe, for instance, the Community first developed free trade agreements with the EFTA countries and then more complex forms of economic and technical cooperation, through both bilateral arrangements and the post-1984 Luxembourg process. The weaknesses of this helped to trigger the negotiations leading to the extension of the Single Market to EFTA via the EEA. Then, in turn, the shortcomings of the EEA helped to trigger the rush of EFTA applications for Community membership in 1989–92.

q.v. EFTA states pp. 482–5.

In the south of Europe much the same has been true. As well as providing association agreements with Greece, Turkey, Malta and Cyprus, the EC has entered into larger policy programmes such as that with the Maghreb states in 1976. Since then Greece has entered the Community and Turkey has made an application to do the same. This was turned down but the Community is trying both to encourage Turkey to complete a Customs Union with it and to devise new and more political relationships. These are felt necessary because of Turkey's new bridge role between the West and the emerging Islamic world of Central Asia.

q.v. Maghreb p. 496.

The Community is also considering membership applications from Cyprus and Malta. It is now using the former as a means of trying to press Ankara and the Turks of Northern Cyprus to resolve the long-running partition problem. At the same time it is hoping to devise new aid programmes which will foster development along the North African coast and thus relieve migratory pressures on southern Europe. These are part of its Global Mediterranean Policy approach. At present only Libya does not have some kind of relationship with the Community.

Relationships with the East were, for a long time, blocked by the Communist refusal to recognize the EC as a genuine international actor. With *perestroika* and economic decline in the East this began to fade, leading to mutual recognition in 1988. This proved a convenient springboard for a large number of trade and cooperation deals with the emerging democracies. In the case of Poland, Hungary and what was Czechoslovakia this led to more developed Association agreements and to the acceptance of the idea of membership. Much later Bulgaria and Romania were granted Associate status.

At the same time the EC was active in providing aid, even to countries like Albania, within the framework of the G-24 PHARE (Assistance for the Economic Reconstruction of Central and Eastern Europe) programme. The Community has also been much involved in aid to Russia, notably after the coup of August 1991. On the political side there has also been much concern about the withdrawal of Russian troops from areas such as the Baltics. The instability on its eastern fringes is of growing concern to the Community, especially as the latter faces the possibility of enlargement to the North and the East.

Because of its dependence on Middle Eastern oil and the tendency of the Palestinian problem to create trouble in the West, the Community has been much concerned with the Middle East. It has tried to act as peace-maker, has provided aid through the Mashreq accord of 1977 with most of the Levant countries, and has supported, with varying degrees of enthusiasm, the measures against Saddam Hussein. However, it has often made itself unpopular in Jerusalem because of its critical view of recent Israeli actions. A cooperation agreement was signed with the Gulf Cooperation Council in 1988.

Policy towards Africa and Asia has differed somewhat. The majority of African countries have been included in the Lomé programmes, along with Caribbean and Pacific states. This is the world's largest aid programme now into its fifth phase. It provides dialog, aid, market access, price stabilization and without requiring reciprocity. In addition there have been the special programmes for those countries on the Mediterranean coast of Africa, together with EC involvement in humanitarian action in East Africa and critical policies on South Africa. However, there was considerable division on the latter in the 1980s.

q.v. Lomé pp. 242–4.

In Asia many counties in the Indian sub-continent have had cooperation and sectoral trade access agreements with the Community since the 1970s. In 1980 the EC also signed a framework agreement with the ASEAN (Association of South East Asian Nations) countries of South-East Asia. This looks to developing investment and political dialog as well as trade. Asian countries also enjoy generalized tariff preferences and food aid. Trade thus plays a larger role than aid but there is an emerging concern for human rights and democracy. Relations with China, where such problems are quite acute, seem somewhat underdeveloped so far.

On the other hand, there has been a great deal of concern with Japan and, albeit to a lesser extent, other highly competitive economies like Singapore and South Korea. Given the growing trade imbalances between Japan and Europe, the EC has sought to do three things. To begin with there has been much pressure on the Japanese to open their markets to European products. In order to encourage this the Commission has monitored Japanese exports for unfair practices, while seeking voluntary restraints as in 1983, or canvassing the imposition of barriers against Japanese products. Thirdly, the Community has sought to benefit from Japanese strength by encouraging direct investment and cooperation in high technology fields.

There is a similar element of conflict in attitudes to the United States. For although, historically, the United States has been a strong supporter of closer European integration, it has often seen the EC as a major economic competitor. Hence, while the United States once even considered association with the Community, there have often been difficulties in the relationship. More recently there has been friction over trade, notably over steel imports into the United States and the whole question of agricultural support both within and without the Uruguay Round. On the other hand, Europe both fears American competition and looks, uneasily, to it for strategic leadership.

This unease reflects considerable political differences among the member states. This is despite much contact and frequent protestations of the closeness of the relationship. So it is not clear that the Washington Declaration of November 1990 which institutionalized a new US—EC dialogue at Presidential, Foreign Ministry, Cabinet and other levels, will overcome these ambivalences. Canada has had its own cooperation agreement since 1976 and this has now been upgraded in line with relations with the United States. And the Community is watching the North American Free Trade Agreement with interest.

Latin America has enjoyed a similar relationship with the Community to parts of Africa and Asia, with generalized tariff preferences and bilateral deals with countries like Mexico. With the prospect of Iberian enlargement the profile of Latin America rose in the 1980s. This showed itself in framework agreements with the Andean Pact in 1983 and the Central American states in 1985. At the same time there was increasing close dialogue with the Contadora group of states to the North of the continent. In 1987 the enlarged EC publicly committed itself to closer links with Latin America and, in 1990, entered into structured relationships with the eleven countries of the Rio group. The Caribbean states also play a large part in Lomé while some of the islands have a special status because they are part of France.

Finally, there are some problems with Australia, New Zealand and other countries in the Cairns group. They have been much affected by the CAP and have played an active role in the Uruguay Round. This is a key element in the EC's worldwide economic diplomacy in GATT and other world fora. Thus virtually every part of the globe has some relations with the Community, over and above those it has with the EC's member states as such. This can be, as is normally the case, because of its economic importance and policies, or because of its political concerns.

This might suggest that all is well with Community external relations. However, there are at least five problems. To begin with the policies are patchy and difficult to manage, partly because of the divide between EPC and Community policies. Secondly, the persistence of national interests can make the Community unfortunately protectionist, as in its recent relationships with Eastern Europe. Indeed, there are fears that the Single Market might make Europe into an inwardly-looking fortress. Thirdly, there are considerable ideological differences amongst the political parties governing the member states. This makes agreement hard.

Again, the Community's domestic policies can often affect its external relations in unfortunate ways. Thus its stress on price stability and EMU has not been helpful to the Nordic countries and their currencies. Equally, the CAP has played a major part in souring relations with both advanced and Third World countries. Some authorities believe that the Community has actually gone backwards in its relationships with the latter.

Finally, the Community has never developed policies which can hope to shape the world in which it operates. With its dependence on energy and other natural resources it is exposed to changes in the outside environment, no less so than in the 1970s. Today the world depression is impacting on domestic policies and politics, making it harder for the Community either to agree or to develop policies of long-term self-interest. The impact of a Europe without frontiers remains uncertain as a result. Equally, the Yugoslav crisis caught the Community unprepared and it has proved unable to develop the kind of authority and activity which might have halted the crisis in its early stages. The failure to act has not been helpful to the general standing and development of the Community.

Overall, the Community's external relations have greatly evolved. However, they have not yet matured into a coherent and uniform foreign policy. External relations are a complex and intermeshed network of attitudes and deals, typical of a body which is not a single state. It is more a group of states pursuing similar aims than a single entity with the full range of diplomatic instruments needed to fulfil its aims. The dual structure of EC external relations means that it is easier for the Community to take positions and to provide economic deals than it is to achieve other policy impacts.

Nonetheless, the EC has emerged as a major international actor economically and, to a lesser extent, politically. It is present, one way or another, throughout the world as a result particularly of the CCP. All this can be a strength but it can also promote inconsistency and confusion. Further enlargement could increase this problem, especially with more neutral states involved. Hence the case for a common foreign and security policy is easily made. Unfortunately, this encourages just those forces which have resisted more effective Community action in the past. Equally, it does not overcome the structural problems already noted. So the new external policy of the Union could simply be more of the same, CFSP or no CFSP.

q.v. CCP
pp. 183–7.

q.v. CFSP
pp.
373–81.

FURTHER READING

Bridges, B., *EC–Japanese Relations: In search of a partnership*, RIIA, London, 1993.

Brückner, P., 'The European Community and the United Nations', *European Journal of International Law*, vol. 1, nos. 1–2, 1990, pp. 174–92.

Edwards, G. and Regelsberger, E. (eds.), *Europe's Global Links: The European Community and inter-regional cooperation*, Pinter, London, 1990.

Fielding, L., *Europe as a Global partner*, UACES, London, 1992.

Freudenstein, R., 'Japan and the New Europe', *The World Today*, vol. 47, no. 1, 1991, pp. 11–16.

Garrett, G., 'International cooperation and institutional choices: the European Community's internal market', *International Organization*, vol. 46, no. 2, 1992, pp. 533–60.

Ginsborg, R.H., *Foreign Policy Actions of the European Community*, Rienner, Boulder, 1989.

Holland, M., 'The EC and South Africa', *International Affairs*, vol. 64, no. 3, 1988, pp. 95–115.

Holland, M. (ed.), *The Future of European Political Cooperation: Essays on theory and practice*, Macmillan, London, 1991.

Ifestos, P., *European Political Cooperation: Towards a framework of supranational diplomacy?*, Gower, Aldershot, 1987.

Journal of Common Market Studies, Special number on 'The EC and the Developing Countries', vol. 29, no. 2, 1990.

Kramer, H., 'The European Community's response to the "New Eastern Europe"', *Journal of Common Market Studies*, vol. 31, no. 2, 1993, pp. 213–44.

Krenzler H. and Kaiser, W., 'The Transatlantic declaration', *Aussenpolitik*, vol. 42, no. 2, 1991, pp. 363–72.

Lak, M., 'Interaction between EPC and the EC (external) etc.', *Common Market Law Review*, vol. 26, no. 2, 1989, pp. 281–300.

McDonald, F., 'The European Community and the USA and Japan', in McDonald, F. and Dearden, S. (eds.), *European Economic Integration*, Longman,

London, 1992, pp. 199–213.

McDonald, F. and Penketh, K., 'The European Community and the rest of Europe', in McDonald, F. and Dearden, S. (eds.), *European Economic Integration*, Longman, London, 1992, pp. 75–198.

Pelkmans, J. and Murphy, A., 'Catapulted into leadership: the Community's trade and aid policies vis-à-vis Eastern Europe', *Journal of European Integration*, vol. 14, nos. 2–3, 1991, pp. 125–51.

Pinder, J., *The European Community and Eastern Europe*, Pinter/RIIA, London, 1991.

Redmond, J. (ed.), *The External Relations of the European Community: The international response to 1992*, Macmillan, London, 1992.

Salmon, T.C., 'Testing times for European Political Cooperation: The Gulf and Yugoslavia', *International Affairs*, vol. 68, no. 2, 1992, pp. 233–55.

Smith, M.E., 'Clinton and the EC: how much of a new agenda', *The World Today*, vol. 49, no. 4, 1993, pp. 70–3.

Smith, M.E., 'The External Relations of the EC' in *The European Communities Encyclopedia and Directory*, Europa, London, 1991, pp. 119–28.

Zielonka, J., 'Europe's security', *International Affairs*, vol. 67, no. 1, 1991, pp. 127–38.

x. General and Final Provisions C: transitional and other arrangements

The last Articles of Part Six may seem both ritualistic and often redundant. Yet they are necessary. Thus they help to define the Treaty and make it operative. Moreover, two of them raise politically sensitive issues. They fall into three groups: those dealing with the nature of the Treaty (Articles 239–240); those setting up the institutions specified in the Treaty (Articles 241–246): and those confirming the status of the Treaty document, described in the Treaty as the Final Provisions (Articles 247–248). Of these the first and last are the most important. None of them, however, was altered at Maastricht.

Article 239 thus asserts that the Protocols attached to the Rome Treaty are an integral part of the Treaty, essentially because they are agreed by all parties to the Treaty. This helps to resolve the problems raised in the first and last subdivisions of the *Handbook*. The rule applies, by extension, to the new Protocols attached to the Maastricht document. This has led some authorities to see the clause as a means of changing the *acquis* since the Protocols contain provisions, like the decisions on Danish property ownership, female pensions and the various opt-outs, which undermine the integrity of European law and decision-making.[57] Interestingly the 1984 European Parliament draft Treaty

---

57. This is the view of Curtin, in 'The constitutional structure of the Union: A Europe of Bits and Pieces', *Common Market Law Review*, vol. 30, no. 1, 1993, esp. pp. 44–60.

would have done away with them probably because they can indicate reservations, often of a nationalist kind, which are out of place in the constitution of a supranational Union. Equally the new draft makes no reference to them.

At first sight the statement that the Treaty is concluded for an unlimited period might appear relatively harmless. It is identical with that in the Euratom Treaty although the ECSC Treaty was concluded for a set period of 50 years. However, the aim of the Article is to make the EC irreversible and thereby committed to continuing constitutional development, thus emphasizing the significance of the steps taken in Rome. Many UK critics seem unaware of this, and of the fact that, not surprisingly, there is no mention of suspension of membership, let alone of secession.

There is a partial precedent for this happening with Greenland which was allowed to leave the EC in 1984−5. However, this is such an unusual territory both geographically and politically that it is anything but a safe test case. While neither the Article nor anything else in the Treaty precludes secession, they do not encourage it either. All the Accession Treaties make it clear that the Treaties can only be changed by the procedure laid down in the founding Treaties. One possibility might therefore be a revision of the Treaty, under Article O, to exclude all reference to the state which wishes to leave. However, this would have to be approved by all the existing members. This could not be relied on. And, although the Community has no means of preventing a state leaving, the practicalities are very much against this. Enoch Powell's argument that an amendment to the 1972 Act would do it leaves out most of the changes which would be necessary.[58]

q.v. Article O pp. 354−6.

The Transitional Arrangements were introduced in the 1950s to provide guidelines to those setting up the institutions. These envisaged the Council meeting and then setting EcoSoc on its way, while the Assembly (as it then was) and the Commission looked after themselves. However, standing orders for such bodies were required first. There are also provisional financial arrangements. None of this seems relevant to the early 1990s and it is a source of some surprise that the drafters did not tidy the Articles away. Leaving them in place could be seen as stressing the very recent roots of the Community and implying that the Treaties are essentially intergovernmental. This does not sit well with the idea of creating a broader Union. The abortive Dutch draft had suggested just this and it may have been because of a reaction against the single trunk approach found in the document that the drafters decided not to touch the Articles.

The Final Provisions as such consist of two Articles. The first, Article 247, demands that all parties to the Treaty must ratify it for it to become operative. There is a clear implication here that the member states are prior to the Community and have autonomy in deciding their own constitutional arrangements. The requirement for unanimous ratification gives dissenting states a kind of veto. Much was made of this during the Maastricht ratification debate so that this Article too is politically very significant.

---

58. J. Enoch Powell, quoted in 'A prophet in his own country', *The Times*, 3 August 1993.

The instrument of ratification, such as that which was handed over by the UK Ambassador in Rome on 2 August 1993 once Lord Rees-Mogg had decided not to appeal against the rejection of his application for a judicial review, is a sealed vellum document to which the official Seal is affixed detailing the ratification procedures, the treaties ratified and the authority to ratify. The Italian Ministry of Foreign Affairs holds all the documents because it was in Rome that the original Treaty was signed. This confers no powers on Italy.

Lastly, Article 248 provides that variants of the Treaty in the languages of the signatory states are equally valid. This is redundant in detail though not in principle. The Accession Treaties give equal standing to versions in the languages of the new signatory states. This is both wise and democratic, but it can cause problems of interpretation of the Treaty as it can with Community legislation and law. There then follow two formal sentences stressing the validity of the document, where it was done, and the sovereign right of the signatories to sign it on behalf of their states. Thus the Treaty of Rome ends as a Treaty rather than as a constitution.

ARTICLE 239   The Protocols annexed to this Treaty by common accord of the Member States shall form an integral part thereof.[59]

ARTICLE 240   This Treaty is concluded for an unlimited period.

Setting up of the Institutions

ARTICLE 241   The Council shall meet within one month of the entry into force of this Treaty.

ARTICLE 242   The Council shall, within three months of its first meeting, take all appropriate measures to constitute the Economic and Social Committee.

ARTICLE 243   The Assembly[60] shall meet within two months of the first meeting of the Council, having been convened by the President of the Council, in order to elect its officers and draw up its rules of procedure. Pending the election of its officers, the oldest member shall take the chair.

ARTICLE 244   The Court of Justice shall take up its duties as soon as its members have been appointed. Its first President shall be appointed for three years in the same manner as its members.

The Court of Justice shall adopt its rules of procedure within three months of taking up its duties.

No matter may be brought before the Court of Justice until its rules of procedure have been published. The time within which an action must be brought shall run only from the date of this publication.

---

59. The TEU also makes consequential changes in the Annexes at this point inserting a new Title in Annex III i.e. 'List of invisible transactions referred to in Article 73h of this treaty' and amending references to Articles 129 and 130 in the EIB Statute Protocol to refer to Articles 198d and 198e.

60. This term has not been changed to 'European Parliament' as required by Article 3 of the SEA because to do so is historically inaccurate. The EP was only an Assembly at the time to which these transitional Articles refer.

Upon his appointment, the President of the Court of Justice shall exercise the powers conferred upon him by this Treaty.

ARTICLE 245

The Commission shall take up its duties and assume the responsibilities conferred upon it by this Treaty as soon as its members have been appointed.

Upon taking up its duties, the Commission shall undertake the studies and arrange the contacts needed for making an overall survey of the economic situation of the Community.

ARTICLE 246

1. The first financial year shall run from the date on which this Treaty enters into force until 31 December following. Should this Treaty, however, enter into force during the second half of the year, the first financial year shall run until 31 December of the following year.

2. Until the budget for the first financial year has been established, Member States shall make the Community interest-free advances which shall be deducted from their financial contributions to the implementation of the budget.

3. Until the Staff Regulations of officials and the Conditions of Employment of other servants of the Community provided for in Article 212 have been laid down, each institution shall recruit the staff it needs and to this end conclude contracts of limited duration.

Each institution shall examine together with the Council any question concerning the number, remuneration and distribution of posts.

Final provisions

ARTICLE 247

This Treaty shall be ratified by the High Contracting Parties in accordance with their respective constitutional requirements. The instruments of ratification shall be deposited with the Government of the Italian Republic.

This Treaty shall enter into force on the first day of the month following the deposit of the instrument of ratification by the last signatory State to take this step. If, however, such deposit is made less than fifteen days before the beginning of the following month, this Treaty shall not enter into force until the first day of the second month after the date of such deposit.[61]

ARTICLE 248

This Treaty, drawn up in a single original in the Dutch, French, German and Italian languages, all four texts being equally authentic, shall be deposited in the archives of the Government of the Italian Republic, which shall transmit a certified copy to each of the Governments of the other signatory States.

In witness whereof, the undersigned Plenipotentiaries have signed this Treaty.

Done at Rome this twenty-fifth day of March in the year one thousand nine hundred and fifty-seven.[62]

---

61. The Treaty actually entered into force on 1 January 1958.

62. Here follow the signatures of two representatives of the original six member states, usually prime ministers and foreign ministers. The signatures of representatives of states who joined later are to be found on the respective accession treaties. The Treaty of Rome also has a Final Act which was signed in Rome on 25 March 1957. It adopted the EEC Treaty (together with its Annexes), its Protocols, the Euratom Treaty, and the Convention on Certain Institutions common to the European Communities. It also agreed six joint Declarations and noted 3 other unilateral national declarations. Finally it agreed to draft and attach Protocols on the Statutes and Privileges of the ECJ and the EEC etc. For further details see pp. 553–63 below.

xi. The Union Treaty Final Provisions

This last element of the present subdivision leaves the Treaty of Rome to cover Title VII of the TEU. In theory the Articles here, from Article L to S, should round things off, pull the Union together, and provide for the TEU and the Union to come into effect. In fact, while the TEU does the last, it rather fails on the first two. This reflects the political sensitivity of some of its components which meant that the Title had a rather chequered history. As a result it raises a number of new uncertainties about the standing and future of the Union.

The shape of these Final Provisions underwent several changes. The initial Luxembourg draft included both General and Final Provisions, the former largely relating to the CFSP and the latter taking the questions of amendment and enlargement out of the Rome Treaty. The abortive Dutch draft, because of its single trunk approach, had no need for such a section and left Articles 236 and 237 where they were. However, it did have a conference declaration on a further IGC in 1996 and specified that it would change decision-making procedures, the hierarchy of norms, and the powers of the Parliament. The revised Dutch draft of 20 October 1991 produced a five Article section, including what had been Articles 236 and 237, but with a different set of letters. The version of the TEU circulated to the heads of government at Maastricht kept the letters but added three new Articles. In the course of the Summit the leaders struck out a reference to the purpose of the IGC being to strengthen 'the federal character of the Union'.

q.v. Article D pp. 56–7.

q.v. Articles A to F pp. 56–8.

Article L was one of the late additions. It confirms the provisions of Article D by largely excluding the ECJ from the two new intergovernmental pillars and from the Common Provisions of the Union in Articles A to F. This means the Court can neither rule on the institutional arrangements of the Union nor directly on the rights of nations and individuals laid down in F. However, the Court is allowed to adjudicate on Title VII, because this deals with amendments, enlargement and the status of the Rome Treaty. To have refused the Court access to these questions would have denied it the powers otherwise reinforced by the Article. Either way, it could have implications for amending the Treaty. All this reflects the ambiguities of the Union, especially those caused by maintaining the EC within the Union but without the potential of amendment.

This implicit stress on the EC is manifest in Article M which very clearly upholds the integrity of the founding Treaties. Their validity remains save as specified elsewhere whereas parts of the Merger Treaty and the Single European Act are formally repealed in Article P. The Articles of the former, relating to the Council and Commission, which had appeared as *de facto* Treaty of Rome provisions in official versions of the EEC Treaty, had already been revised by Article G of Maastricht. Perhaps the drafters thought they were like Dracula and could only be permanently silenced by a further stake. Much the same is true of the changes made to the SEA which replace the reference to the European Council and wind up EPC.

Article N figures logically here as any sensible Treaty or constitution must make allowances for revision before it concludes. The present text is largely transferred from Article 236 of the Treaty of Rome. However, it makes three significant changes. The first allows for revision of all the founding Treaties, including the TEU. So, as noted above, amendment of the EC is only possible as part of a change to the Union. Secondly, the ECB is given a consultative voice on changes in EMU. This could prove to be a somewhat uncomfortable procedural obstacle.[63]

The third change is the insertion of a reference to the calling of a new IGC in 1996 to oversee the revision of those parts of the Treaty where this is called for. This includes the size of the Commission and Parliament, the extension of the conciliation process, and security questions under J.4(6) and J.10. It is more than likely that it would, in any case, range more widely than this, given the present circumstances. This conference is made more mandatory than IGCs in general, presumably to prevent a few member states blocking it as the United Kingdom would have liked to do before the SEA, and perhaps at Maastricht. Certainly, there are now pressures on John Major to ensure that there are no further reforms in the EC and Union. This sounds a little like Canute's courtiers speaking.

The cumbersome process inherited from the Rome Treaty is to safeguard the constitutional nature of the Treaties by preventing substantial amendments being made too easily. This is in line with normal constitutional practice. Constitutions, as noted much earlier, serve as a touchstone for judging new legislation and as structure for major revisions. The Parliament only has a consultative role and not the rights of initiation and decision-making suggested in the EP's 1993 draft constitution.

However, the 1996 IGC is no longer required to strengthen the federal character of the Union as the Dutch wished, but it is bound to comply with the objectives of building an ever-closer union in which decisions are taken as closely as possible to the citizen. The reference to Article A also seems to exclude the Conference from doing away with the EC as such in any revisions. While this, like the invocation of subsidiarity, may satisfy Eurosceptics the provisions of Article B for the maintenance both of the *acquis* and of Union citizenship point in a different direction. And, while the phraseology may be read as demanding consideration but not necessarily decision, the needs of enlargement and the pressures from enthusiasts for further, and rapid, institutional change will work against this.

q.v. Article A pp. 55–6.

q.v. Article B pp. 56–7.

Article O transposes Article 237 of the Treaty of Rome, as amended by the SEA, which added the requirement for parliamentary assent. So enlargement needs the support of 260 MEPs. However, unanimity and member state ratification are

---

63. If the events of August 1993 do derail the whole EMU process, as many people think they will, then the 1996 IGC conference may not be able to comply with Article N(1), especially should it conclude its deliberations before 1998. The ECB is only really due to come into existence then and may, in fact be delayed for a long time. And Article 109f(9) does not include Article N amongst the Articles where the EMI can take its place in the interim. The fact that Article L expressly gives the ECJ jurisdiction over Title VII could open the way to a challenge to any amendments which do not result from consulting the ECB on monetary changes. One possibility is that the EMI or the Committee of Governors (see pp. 154–6) could be consulted. This, along with the question of the mode of reform of the Treaty of Rome, may also have implications for those who would wish to restore the EC to what they see as its pristine status of a 'mere common market'. There could also be implications for those who wish to strengthen the Parliament's role under Article 189b(8), and perhaps even for enlargement. As Ollie would have said to Stan 'This is another fine mess you've got us into!'.

still required. And, by moving the Article here and changing Community to Union, Maastricht rules out the possibility of new states joining the EC alone.[64] They also have to accept the pillar structure. By extension this presumably rules out present member states transferring back from the Union to the EC.

As already noted Article P underlines the supercession of specific elements of earlier treaties previously used as part of the Treaty of Rome. Thus Articles 2−6 of the Merger Treaty had provided details on the Presidency, the meetings and procedures of the Council of Ministers, COREPER, and voting on ECJ salaries. Articles 10−18 dealt with the composition, nomination, resignation, officers and procedures of the Commission. The last two articles in each sequence repealed previous rules on these subjects. Where the SEA is concerned the TEU repeals its provisions both on the European Council and on EPC, especially the detailed Title III. In both cases the TEU had already upgraded their status. One of the effects of Article P, however, is to re-inforce the complexity of the Union and its relation to previous treaties.

All the last three Articles, Q, R and S, replicate provisions in the Treaty of Rome. The first makes the Union a body of equally unlimited duration, even if some of its arrangements are legally and practically transitory. Article R largely replicates Article 247 of the Treaty of Rome and does not respond to Parliament's desire, expressed in the 1993 draft constitution, to share in ratification and remove the reference to member states own 'constitutional requirements'. It does, on the other hand, provide a starting date because the Union is a new body.

The delay after the deposit of the last act of ratification, which should be that of Germany, is to give a breathing space to get the new arrangements organized. However, in practice much preparation will already have been done and some of the TEU's provisions have already been anticipated. Finally, Article S lays down the standard provisions for authenticating and confirming ratification. All this anticipated a much smoother passage than was actually to be the case, because of the way that Maastricht politicized European integration, as the next subdivision of the *Handbook* will make clear.

Title VII   Final provisions

ARTICLE L

The provisions of the Treaty establishing the European Community, the Treaty establishing the European Coal and Steel Community and the Treaty establishing the European Atomic Energy Community concerning the powers of the Court of Justice of the European Communities and the exercise of those powers shall apply only to the following provisions of this Treaty:

(a) provisions amending the Treaty establishing the European Economic Community, the Treaty establishing the European Coal and Steel Community and the Treaty establishing the European Atomic Energy Community;

(b) the third subparagraph of Article K.3(2)(c);

(c) articles L to S.

---

64. Of course, it has never been possible just to join the EEC alone. New applicants also had to sign up to the ECSC and Euratom at the same time. This will remain true as long as it is decided not to consolidate the three Treaties into one.

ARTICLE M   Subject to the provisions amending the Treaty establishing the European Economic Community with a view to establishing the European Community, the Treaty establishing the European Coal and Steel Community and the Treaty establishing the European Atomic Energy Community, and to these final provisions, nothing in this Treaty shall affect the Treaties establishing the European Communities or the subsequent Treaties and Acts modifying or supplementing them.

ARTICLE N   *1. The government of any Member State or the Commission may submit to the Council proposals for the amendment* of the Treaties on which the Union is founded.

If the Council, after consulting the European Parliament and, where appropriate, the Commission, delivers an opinion in favour of calling a conference of representatives of the governments of the Member States, the conference shall be convened by the President of the Council for the purpose of determining by common accord the amendments to be made to those Treaties. The European Central Bank shall also be consulted in the case of institutional changes in the monetary area.

The amendments shall enter into force after being ratified by all the Member States in accordance with their respective constitutional requirements.

2. A conference of representatives of the governments of the Member States shall be convened in 1996 to examine those provisions of this Treaty for which revision is provided, in accordance with the objectives set out in Articles A and B.

ARTICLE O   *Any European State may apply to become a Member of the* Union. *It shall address its application to the Council, which shall act unanimously after consulting the Commission and after receiving the assent of the European Parliament, which shall act by an absolute majority of its component members.*

The conditions of admission and the adjustments to the Treaties on which the Union is founded which such admission entails shall be the subject of an agreement between the Member States and the applicant State. This agreement shall be submitted for ratification by all the contracting States in accordance with their respective constitutional requirements.

ARTICLE P   1. Articles 2 to 7 and 10 to 19 of the Treaty establishing a Single Council and a Single Commission of the European Communities, signed in Brussels on 8 April 1965, are hereby repealed.

2. Article 2, Article 3(2) and Title III of the Single European Act signed in Luxembourg on 17 February 1986 and in the Hague on February 1986 are hereby repealed.

ARTICLE Q   This Treaty is concluded for an unlimited period.

ARTICLE R   1. This Treaty shall be ratified by the High Contracting Parties in accordance with their respective constitutional requirements. The instruments of ratification shall be deposited with the government of the Italian Republic.

2. This Treaty shall enter into force on 1 January 1993, provided that all the instruments of ratification have been deposited, or, failing that, on the first day of the month following the deposit of the instrument of ratification by the last signatory State to take this step.

ARTICLE S   This Treaty, drawn up in a single original in the Danish, Dutch, English, French, German, Greek, Irish, Italian, Portuguese and Spanish languages, the texts in each of these languages being equally authentic, shall be deposited in the archives of the government of the Italian Republic, which will transmit a certified copy to each of the governments of the other signatory States.

IN WITNESS WHEREOF, the undersigned Plenipotentiaries have signed this Treaty.

Done at Maastricht on the seventh day of February one thousand nine hundred and ninety two.[65]

FURTHER READING

Bradshaw, J., 'Institutional reform in the EC beyond Maastricht', *European Trends*, 1991/4, pp. 82–93.

Brittan, L., 'The institutional development of the EC', Henry Street Memorial Lecture, University of Manchester, 16 October 1992.

Burgess, M. and Gagnon, A., *Comparative Federalism and Federation, Competing Traditions and Future Challenges*, Harvester Wheatsheaf, Hemel Hempstead, 1993.

Cafruny, A.W. and Rosenthal, G.G., *The State of the European Community: Maastricht and beyond*, Longman, London, 1993.

Coombes, D., *Understanding European Union*, Longman, London, 1994.

Cullen, P.J., *The UK and the Ratification of the Maastricht Treaty*, Europa Institute, Edinburgh, 1993.

Curtin, D., 'The constitutional structure of the Union: a Europe of bits and pieces', *Common Market Law Review*, vol. 30, no. 1, 1993, pp. 17–69.

Hailsham, Lord and Vaughan, D. (eds.), *The Law of the European Communities*, Butterworth, London, 1986.

Lodge, J., 'Maastricht and political union', *European Access* 1992/1 pp. 7–11.

Phinnemore, D., *Sources on the European Community: A handbook for students*, University of Kent, Canterbury, 1992.

Schmitter, P., *Interests, Powers and Functions*, Stanford University Working Paper, April 1992.

Schwok, R., *Switzerland and the European Common Market*, Praeger, New York, 1991.

Weatherill, S. and Beaumont, P., *EC Law*, Penguin, Harmondsworth, 1993.

Wincott, D., 'A troublesome legacy? Some "legal" implications of the political development of the European Community', *PSA Annual Conference Paper*, April 1993.

Wincott, D., *The Treaty of Maastricht: An adequate constitution for the European Union?*, European Public Policy Institute Occasional Paper 93/6, University of Warwick, 1993.

---

65. The two sentences stating that the signatures testify to approval and that the final document was signed on 7 February 1992, appear ten times, once for each of the recognized official languages of the member states. Neither these, nor the signatures of those who signed the Treaty on behalf of their head of state, are reproduced in the *Handbook*. They can be found in official editions of the Treaties.

VI. The Union Treaty E:
Other Treaties, Pillars and Protocols

The TEU has been widely criticized due to its size and inaccessibility. This stems in the main from the fact that the length of the document exceeds 60,000 words and contains for the most part turgid legalistic language. However, the complex nature of the Treaty, as indicated in the previous four subdivisions of the *Handbook*, also has its roots in the numerous Titles contained within it, the Protocols attached to it, and the Declarations relating to it. This is reflected in the content of this subdivision of the *Handbook*. For, although almost half of the TEU is taken up with introducing amendments to the Treaty of Rome, the Treaty also contains amendments to other Treaties and provisions fundamental to the so-called 'pillar' structure of the envisaged European Union.

Whereas the two IGCs which began work in December 1990 had as their task the amendment of the Treaty of Rome to allow for the creation of a political and an economic and monetary union, following the Maastricht Summit in December 1991 two further IGCs were convened to amend the Treaty establishing the European Coal and Steel Community (ECSC) and the Treaty establishing the European Atomic Energy Community (Euratom) in the light of the agreed amendments to the Treaty of Rome. These IGCs were called since Article C of the TEU, as agreed on at Maastricht, requires the Union to be served by a single institutional framework. Consequently, the amended provisions of the Treaty of Rome concerning the composition of the various EC institutions had to be incorporated into the ECSC and Euratom Treaties as well. The two conferences met in the following February and completed their work within a few days allowing the final version of the TEU to be signed on 8 February 1992. The amendments the two IGCs introduced to the ECSC and Euratom Treaties are contained in Titles III and IV of the TEU respectively.

q.v. Article C pp. 57–8.

Titles V and VI of the TEU create the second and third pillars of the European Union. The first of these two pillars is the Union's Common Foreign and Security Policy (CFSP), the second, Cooperation in the Fields of Justice and Home Affairs (JHA). They are termed 'pillars' since, although fundamental to the structure of the Union, they remain separate from the Union's central building block, the European Community. Such a structure, while apparently novel, is not new.

Essentially, the post-SEA Community was formed of two pillars: the EC *per se* and EPC.

q.v. EPC
pp. 340–4.

The main effect of the pillar structure is that the provisions governing the CFSP and JHA are not subject to the normal decision-making processes of the EC. This, as Wincott infers, makes a mockery of the idea that the Union is to be served by a 'single institutional structure'.[1] Moreover, neither of the pillars is subject to the scrutiny of the European Court of Justice. Rather, all decisions are taken on an intergovernmental basis. While this clearly disappointed protagonists of a more singular structure to the Union, the contents of the two Titles, as indicated in this subdivision, none the less represent a step forward in the direction of closer European cooperation on several fronts.

In addition to examining the four Titles mentioned above, this subdivision also concerns itself with the various Protocols and Declarations which appear in copies of the TEU, as well as the Treaty's Final Act. The 17 Protocols, most of which have already been referred to, since all but one relate directly to provisions in the amended Treaty of Rome, are an integral part of the TEU and as such are legally binding on the signatories. The 33 Declarations, meanwhile, stand outside the Treaty appearing annexed to the Final Act. For the most part they offer guidance in interpreting certain provisions contained in the TEU, and express the intentions of the signatories in implementing miscellaneous aspects of the Treaty. However, as will be seen, they have no legal force.

i. Changes to the European Coal and Steel Community Treaty

Title III of the TEU introduces amendments to the Treaty establishing the European Coal and Steel Community (ECSC) signed in Paris on 18 April 1951.[2] All of the amendments relate to the institutions of the Community or to the Community budget. Furthermore, the majority mirror corresponding amendments to the Treaty of Rome as agreed at Maastricht in December 1991. Consequently, they consolidate many of the amendments introduced by the Merger Treaty by inserting Merger Treaty provisions either in their original form (Articles 17 and 29), in a slightly amended form (Articles 9 and 13), or in a significantly modified or amended form (Articles 10, 11, 12, 16, 18, 27 and 30). However, Title III does introduce seven new Articles (Articles 12a, 20a, 20b, 20c, 20d, 27a and 78i), although these are not specific to the ECSC Treaty. Instead, they are often exact replicas of corresponding provisions in the amended Treaty of Rome. These are indicated in Box 19 which lists all the provisions of the ECSC Treaty amended by the TEU, and provides a brief summary of what the Articles relate to.

1. Wincott, D., *The Treaty of Maastricht: An adequate 'constitution' for the European Union?*, European Public Policy Institute Occasional Paper 93/6, University of Warwick, 1993, pp. 14–16.

2. The text of the Treaty establishing the European Coal and Steel Community, as amended by the SEA, but not the TEU, can be found in *Treaties Establishing the European Communities*, Abridged edn, OOPEC, Luxembourg, 1987, pp. 15–114. Table 3 in Annex 4 provides details of where the ECSC Treaty has been amended since it was signed in 1951 (see p. 529).

Box 19. Changes to the ECSC Treaty introduced by the TEU and the corresponding Article in the amended Treaty of Rome

ECSC Treaty	Treaty of Rome	Subject area/Comments
7	4	Institutions of the Community. The ECSC Treaty differs from the Treaty of Rome in the titles of the five institutions. Also, under the ECSC Treaty, the Commission is assisted by a Consultative Committee, rather than the EcoSoc and the Committee of the Regions
9	157	Composition of the Commission
10	158	Commission's term of office
11	161	Commission Vice-Presidents
12	159	Vacancies in Commission
12a	160	(New Art.) Compulsory retirement of Commissioners
13	163	Voting procedure in Commission
16 1st and 2nd paras.	None	Commission to make own administrative arrangements and set up study committees, including an economic study committee
16 3rd and 4th paras.	162	Commission rules of procedure and methods of cooperation with Council
17	156	Publication annually by the Commission of General Report on the Community's activities
18 new subpara.	None	Council to determine payments, instead of remuneration to members of the ECSC's Consultative Committee
20a–d	138b(2nd para.)–e	(New Art.) Role of the EP: Committee of Enquiry, Ombudsman. Right of citizens to petition EP
21(3)	138(3)	Proposals for direct elections to EP on the basis of a uniform procedure
24	143 and 144	EP to discuss General Report. Right to censure whole Commission. Period of office of new post-censure Commission
27	146	Composition of Council and rotation of presidency
27a	147	(New Art.) Convening the Council
29	154	Council to determine pay of Community officials
30	151	Role of COREPER and Council's General Secretariat
32	165	Composition and sitting of the Court of Justice
32d	168a	Composition and role of the Court of First Instance
33		Role of Court of Justice
45a, b, c(1–4)	188a–c	Composition, term of office and duties of the Court of Auditors
45c(5)	None	Court of Auditors' report
78c	205	Implementation of the budget by the Commission
78e–78f	Repealed	See Arts. 45a–45c
78g	206	EP observation of the implementation of the budget
78h	209	Council's role in determining the budget

78i	209a	(New Art.) Anti-fraud measures
79(a)	227(5a)	Treaty not applicable to the Faroe Islands
96	Repealed	Procedure for amending the ECSC Treaty. See TEU, Art. N
98	Repealed	Accession to the ECSC. See TEU Art. O

Following the introduction of these amendments, the post-TEU ECSC Treaty consists of a Preamble and four Titles. In all these contain 118 Articles. The first of these Titles, entitled the European Coal and Steel Community, and reproduced below, lays down the general aims and principles of the Community (Articles 1—6). Essentially, these are the establishment of a common market for coal and steel among the member states and the creation of a set of common institutions to administer the common market. Title II of the Treaty, which covers Articles 7—45c, contains provisions relating to the Community's institutions. Individual Chapters within the Title are dedicated to the High Authority, otherwise referred to as the Commission; the European Parliament; the Council; the Court; and, since the TEU, the Court of Auditors. Title III (Articles 46—75) contains ten Chapters covering the economic and social provisions of the Treaty. The Chapters relate to general provisions; financial provisions; investment and financial aid; production; prices; agreements and concentrations; interference with conditions of competition; wages and movement of workers; transport; and commercial policy. The final Title (Articles 76—100) contains general provisions including those relating to the ECSC's budget.

While the format of the ECSC Treaty is in principle broadly similar to that of the Treaty of Rome and the Euratom Treaty, it differs significantly in that it is not concluded for an unlimited period of time. Article 97 states that the Treaty is only concluded for a period of fifty years from the date of its entry into force. Consequently the Treaty becomes defunct on 31 March 2002. While there is no apparent desire among the member states of the Community to see the ECSC's activities cease after this date, the question of the latter's future has not yet been resolved. The most likely scenario is the gradual incorporation of the provisions of the ECSC into the Treaty of Rome prior to 2002.[3]

Reproduced below are the key Articles defining the tasks, principles and status of the ECSC:

ARTICLE 1

By this Treaty, the HIGH CONTRACTING PARTIES establish among themselves a EUROPEAN COAL AND STEEL COMMUNITY, founded upon a common market, common objectives and common institutions.

ARTICLE 2

The European Coal and Steel Community shall have as its task to contribute, in harmony with the general economy of the Member States and through the establishment of a common market as provided in Article 4, to economic

---

3. This approach gained the broad support of the Council in April 1991 and was subsequently endorsed by the ECSC Consultative Committee. See also EC Commission, 'Is There a Future for the ECSC Treaty?', Background Report ISEC/B14/91, London, 20 May 1991.

expansion, growth of employment and a rising standard of living in the Member States.

The Community shall progressively bring about conditions which will of themselves ensure the most rational distribution of production at the highest possible level of productivity, while safeguarding continuity of employment and taking care not to provoke fundamental and persistent disturbances in the economies of Member States.

ARTICLE 3

The institutions of the Community shall, within the limits of their respective powers, in the common interest:

(a) ensure an orderly supply to the common market, taking into account the needs of third countries;

(b) ensure that all comparably placed consumers in the common market have equal access to the sources of production;

(c) ensure the establishment of the lowest prices under such conditions that these prices do not result in higher prices charged by the same undertakings in other transactions or in a higher general price level at another time, while allowing necessary amortization and normal return on invested capital;

(d) ensure the maintenance of conditions which will encourage undertakings to expand and improve their production potential and to promote a policy of using natural resources rationally and avoiding their unconsidered exhaustion;

(e) promote improved working conditions and an improved standard of living for the workers in each of the industries for which it is responsible, so as to make possible their harmonization while the improvement is being maintained;

(f) promote the growth of international trade and ensure that equitable limits are observed in export pricing;

(g) promote the orderly expansion and modernization of production, and the improvement of quality, with no protection against competing industries that is not justified by improper action on their part or in their favour.

ARTICLE 4

The following are recognized as incompatible with the common market for coal and steel and shall accordingly be abolished and prohibited within the Community, as provided in this Treaty:

(a) import and export duties, or charges having equivalent effect, and quantitative restrictions on the movement of products;

(b) measures or practices which discriminate between producers, between purchasers or between consumers, especially in prices and delivery terms or transport rates and conditions, and measures or practices which interfere with the purchaser's free choice of supplier;

(c) subsidies or aids granted by States, or special charges imposed by States, in any form whatsoever;

(d) restrictive practices which tend towards the sharing or exploiting of markets.

ARTICLE 5

The Community shall carry out its task in accordance with this Treaty, with a limited measure of intervention.

To this end the Community shall:

— provide guidance and assistance for the parties concerned, by obtaining information, organizing consultations and laying down general objectives;

— place financial resources at the disposal of undertakings for their investment and bear part of the cost of readaptation;

— ensure the establishment, maintenance and observance of normal competitive conditions and exert direct influence upon production or upon the market

only when circumstances so require;
— publish the reasons for its actions and take the necessary measures to ensure the observance of the rules laid down in this Treaty.

The institutions of the Community shall carry out these activities with a minimum of administrative machinery and in close co-operation with the parties concerned.

ARTICLE 6   The Community shall have legal personality.

In international relations, the Community shall enjoy the legal capacity it requires to perform its functions and attain its objectives.

In each of the Member States, the Community shall enjoy the most extensive legal capacity accorded to legal persons constituted in that State; it may, in particular, acquire or dispose of movable and immovable property and may be a party to legal proceedings.

The community shall be represented by its institutions, each within the limits of its powers.

Coal and steel policy

When the ECSC Treaty was signed in 1951, the choice of coal and steel as the basis for a European community reflected the strategic importance of these two products for the reconstruction and expansion of the European economy in the early 1950s. As a result the aim of the ECSC was to contribute to ensuring and maintaining supplies of coal and steel to European industry. However, since the 1960s the fortunes of the European coal and steel industries have declined. As a result, by the early 1990s overcapacity had become widespread, and pressure for a wholesale restructuring of both industries had become intense.

In the first half of the 1960s the current twelve members of the Community collectively produced in excess of 400 million tonnes of coal annually. However, as a result of traditional coal users switching to cheaper energy sources, such as oil and gas, by 1991 production was only slightly over half of this level at 208 million tonnes. Production of crude steel meanwhile, although fluctuating for most of the 1970s and 1980s, had stabilized in the early 1990s at around 136 million tonnes per annum, slightly lower than the levels of two decades earlier. However, with demand for steel either stable or declining, increased productivity rates had the effect of promoting overcapacity. As a result of the subsequent need to reduce capacity many plants throughout Europe were forced to shed workers and in several cases close down entirely. Consequently, whereas in its formative years the emphasis of the ECSC's work was on ensuring that demand for coal and steel was met, by the late 1970s this had shifted to overseeing and cushioning the decline of the Community's coal and steel industries. Nevertheless, the ECSC still fulfils many of the functions entrusted to it when it was first established. For the most part these fall into four categories.

Firstly, the ECSC regulates the common market for coal and steel and ensures that producers comply with the rules governing it as laid down in the Treaty. However, the reluctance of many member state governments to see their coal and steel industries decline beyond the levels to which they had been reduced following the depression in both industries in the 1970s, means that state subsidies and price distortion remain commonplace. As a result competition within the Community is severely distorted. Indeed, at the beginning of 1992 over 2,287 cases relating to ECSC rules on competition were pending decisions. Of these, the vast majority (1,732) concerned companies seeking exemptions. Others involved applications from member states for authorization to grant financial aid to their coal industries. Prominent among the applicants here has been Germany which, it is estimated, currently subsidizes its coal industry to the tune of ECU 33,000 per miner.[4]

Secondly, the Community attempts to protect domestic producers from outside competition by restricting imports of foreign coal and steel either through tariffs or quotas. The rules governing steel imports have effectively remained unchanged since they were formulated in 1978. Now, as then, the rules ensure that the level of permitted imports is sufficiently low as to prevent any significant disruption to the Community market. However, the ECSC has come under increasing pressure to relax restrictions on imports of coal and steel, especially from the countries of Central and Eastern Europe, since steel production particularly is one of the few areas where these countries have a competitive advantage over Community producers.

Thirdly, the Community is heavily involved in granting aid to regions affected by the closure of coal mines or of steel plants. In the period 1975–91 such involvement saw the ECSC invest ECU 6723 million in creating over 435,000 jobs in affected areas throughout the Community through the RESIDER (steel) and RECHAR (coal) initiatives. The United Kingdom was the largest recipient of this aid, receiving over ECU 2466 million. The number of jobs created in the United Kingdom as a result is estimated to have been over 142,000.[5]

Finally, the ECSC is a major source of funds for research and development into projects centring on steel production, health and safety in mines, and pollution control around steelworks. In 1991, 142 projects related to the steel industry were approved, while ECU 18 million was allocated to 82 projects on health and safety and pollution control.

Reconciling the establishment of a common market for coal and steel with the persistent decline in fortunes of the two industries has proved almost impossible for the Community. While the 1980s saw the philosophy of the free market take hold throughout Western Europe, few substantial proposals were made to extend this philosophy to coal and, more particularly, to steel. In 1990 the Commission did propose that the Community adopt a medium-term policy for steel aimed at liberalizing economic policies; securing greater compliance with competition rules; and supporting corporate initiatives to solve the problems affecting the industry. However, by 1991 measures were being put forward which would grant the steel industry ECU 900 million for the period 1993–5. Moreover, the Community was becoming increasingly willing to impose anti-dumping duties on imports of steel from Central and Eastern Europe in an attempt to protect domestic producers further.

---

4. 'UK could lead the fields', *The European*, 21–24 January 1993.
5. EC Commission, *XXV General Report of the Activities of the European Communities*, 1991, p. 162.

The accusations of protectionism which ensued coincided with a widespread recognition that a further restructuring of the Community's steel industry was long overdue. By 1992, overproduction and overcapacity had returned, and prices had fallen by 30 per cent. Thus it was widely agreed that capacity would have to be reduced to 80 to 85 per cent of its current level if the industry were to survive. Needless to say, while the idea of cuts in production was accepted, disagreement existed on where exactly the cuts should be implemented. Consequently, by mid-1993 no firm decisions had been made on the future of the steel industry within the Community.[6] Nor had any agreement been reached on opening up the EC market to imports from Central and Eastern Europe, despite a political commitment to do so.

Furthermore, overcapacity, alongside enormous price distortion, was also evident in the coal industry in the early 1990s. The latter was most apparent in the fact that the cost of coal within the Community varied significantly between member states. While the unsubsidized UK coal industry was producing coal at ECU 69 per tonne in 1992, Spanish and German producers, often heavily subsidised by their national governments, were charging respectively ECU 127 and ECU 143 per tonne. Yet, despite pressure for subsidies to be reduced and for state aid to be directed at restructuring national coal industries thus reducing costs, little evidence existed to suggest that capacity would be reduced and the Community market for coal liberalized. Nevertheless, with pressure increasing for a switch away from coal to more environmentally friendly and renewable energy sources, the need to restructure the industry is becoming greater.

With the future of the Community's coal and steel industries in a state of uncertainty, the expiry of the ECSC Treaty in 2002 may provide the Community with an opportunity to reduce the existing protectionist philosophy and apply the free market principles which have been central to the creation of the Single Market. However, as yet it is not entirely clear whether the likely incorporation of the Community's competences under the ECSC Treaty into the Treaty of Rome will actually involve a significant shift in the market philosophy surrounding coal and steel. Indeed, as recessionary forces continue to dominate the European economy as a whole, few governments are likely to accept the political fallout of job losses and possible regional decline which will result from the necessary further restructuring of the two industries. What remains certain, however, is that recent trends in Community involvement in coal and steel towards granting regional aid and for promoting environmental considerations throughout industry will continue. Hence, whereas coal and steel may have provided the foundation on which the European Community was originally built, their future relevance to the development of European integration will undoubtedly be limited.

---

6. 'EC steel strategy faces "chaos"', *Financial Times*, 8 July 1993.

FURTHER READING[7]

EC Commission, *Challenge for Europe's Steel Industry*, Background Report ISEC/B19/93, London, 22 June 1993.

EC Commission, *Commission Report on the Application of the Community Rules for State Aid to the Coal Industry in 1991*, COM(93)116 final, Brussels, 29 March 1993.

EC Commission, *Commission Report on the Availability of Coal with a Low Sulphur Content*, COM(92)563 final, Brussels, 18 December 1992.

EC Commission, *Information Note Concerning the Implementation of the Social Measures for the Restructuring of the Steel Industry (1993–1995)*, COM(93)178 final, Brussels, 28 April 1993.

EC Commission, *Is There a Future for the ECSC Treaty?*, Background Report ISEC/B14/91, London, 20 May 1991.

ECSC Consultative Committee, *Resolution (93/C 14/03) of the European Coal and Steel Community (ECSC) Consultative Committee on the Restructuring of the Community Steel Industry*, OJC 14, 20 January 1993.

ECSC Consultative Committee, *Resolution (93/C 14/02) of the European Coal and Steel Community (ECSC) Consultative Committee Towards a Coal Policy in the Internal Market*, OJC 14, 20 January 1993.

European Parliament, *The Situation of the Coal Mining Industry in the European Community*, Directorate-General for Research, Energy and Research Series, no. 7, 1993.

ii. Changes to the European Atomic Energy Community Treaty

Title IV of the TEU introduces amendments to the Treaty establishing the European Atomic Energy Community (Euratom) signed in March 1957 on the same day as the Treaty of Rome.[8] As with the amendments to the ECSC Treaty introduced by the TEU, those relating to the Euratom Treaty are restricted to provisions relating to the institutions and to the budget, and mirror those introduced to the Treaty of Rome. In the case of the Euratom Treaty all but two of the amended Articles (Articles 3 and 206) are identical to the amended Articles in the Treaty of Rome (see Box 20). Several amendments formally insert provisions originally found in the Merger Treaty (Articles 117, 123, 126 and 129), while others insert amended Merger Treaty provisions (Articles 116, 121, 126, 127, 128, 130, 131 and 132).

Following the amendments introduced by the TEU, the Euratom Treaty consists of 215 Articles. These are contained in six Titles and a set of Final Provisions, and preceded by the statutory Preamble. The first Title, reproduced below, contains three Articles (Articles 1–3) and sets out the tasks of the Community. These are the promotion of research; the establishment of uniform safety standards; the guaranteeing of supplies; the creation of a common market for specialized materials; and the promotion of cooperation with third countries and international organizations. Title II then contains provisions for the encouragement of progress in the field of nuclear energy (Articles 4–106). These include the promotion of research; the dissemination of information; health and

---

7. See also Further reading list below, pp. 372–3.

8. The text of the Treaty establishing the European Coal and Steel Community, as amended by the SEA, but not the TEU, can be found in *Treaties establishing the European Communities*, abridged edn, OOPEC, Luxembourg, 1987, pp. 385–52. Table 4 in Annex 4 provides details of where the Euratom Treaty has been amended since it was signed in 1957. See p. 530.

Box 20. Changes to the Euratom Treaty introduced by the TEU and the corresponding Articles in the amended Treaty of Rome

Euratom Treaty	Treaty of Rome	Subject area/Comments
3	4	Institutions of the Community. Under the Euratom Treaty, the Commission is only assisted in its work by the EcoSoc, and not by the Committee of Regions
107a–107d	138b(2nd para.)–138d	(New Arts.) Role of the EP: Committee of Enquiry, Ombudsman. Right of citizens to petition EP
108(3)	138(3)	Proposals for direct elections to EP on the basis of a uniform procedure
114 2nd subpara.	144 2nd subpara.	Period of office of a new post-censure Commission
116	146	Composition of Council and rotation of Presidency
117	147	Convening the Council
121	151	Role of COREPER and Council's General Secretariat
123	154	Council to determine pay of Community officials
125	156	Publication annually by the Commission of General Report on the Community's activities
126	157	Composition of the Commission
127	158	Commission's term of office
128	159	Vacancies in Commission
129	160	Compulsory retirement of Commissioners
130	161	Commission Vice-Presidents
131	162	Commission rules of procedure and methods of Cooperation with Council
132	163	Voting procedure in Commission
133	Repealed	Member state liaison with the Commission. Originally repealed by Art. 19 of Merger Treaty
137	165	Composition and sitting of the Court of Justice
140a	168a	Composition and role of the Court of First Instance
143	171	Fining of member states for non-compliance with Treaty obligations
146	173	Role and jurisdiction of the Court of Justice
160a–160c	188a–188c	Composition, term of office and duties of Court of Auditors
166	194	Composition of EcoSoc
168	196	EcoSoc's rules of procedure
170	198	EcoSoc opinions
172 paras. 1–3	Repealed	Budget revenue
173	201	Own resources in budget
173a	201a	(New Art.) Budgetary discipline
179	205	Implementation of the budget by the Commission

180–180a	Repealed	See Arts. 160a–160c
180b	206	EP observation of the implementation of the budget
183	209	Council's role in determining budget
183a	209a	(New Art.) Anti-fraud measures
198(a)	227(5a)	Treaty not applicable to the Faroe Islands
201	231	Cooperation with the OECD
204	Repealed	Procedure for amending Euratom Treaty. See TEU Art. N
205	Repealed	Accession to Euratom. See TEU Art. O
206	238	Association agreements. Such agreements with Euratom are concluded in accordance with the pre-TEU procedure and not that laid down in Art. 228 of the amended Treaty of Rome

safety; investment; joint undertakings; supplies; safeguards; property ownership; the nuclear common market; and the Community's external relations. Provisions governing the institutions are contained in Title III (Articles 107–170). These are divided into the provisions relating to the European Parliament, the Council, the Commission, the Court of Justice, and since the TEU, the Court of Auditors (Articles 107–106c); those common to several institutions (Articles 161–164); and those concerning the Economic and Social Committee (Articles 165–170). Titles IV (Articles 171–183a) and V (Articles 184–208) contain financial and general provisions respectively. There then follows a Title dedicated to provisions relating to the initial period of Euratom's existence (Articles 209–223) and two Articles containing the final provisions (Articles 224–225). In contrast to the ECSC Treaty, the Euratom Treaty is, according to Article 208, concluded for an unlimited period.

ARTICLE 1

By this Treaty the HIGH CONTRACTING PARTIES establish among themselves a EUROPEAN ATOMIC ENERGY COMMUNITY (EURATOM).

It shall be the task of the Community to contribute to the raising of the standard of living in the Member States and to contribute to the development of relations with other countries by creating the conditions necessary for the speedy establishment and growth of nuclear industries.

ARTICLE 2

In order to perform its task, the Community shall, as provided for in this Treaty:

(a) promote research and ensure the dissemination of technical information;
(b) establish uniform safety standards to protect the health of workers and of the general public and ensure that they are applied;
(c) facilitate investment and ensure, particularly by encouraging ventures on the part of undertakings, the establishment of basic installations necessary for the development of nuclear energy in the Community;
(d) ensure that all users in the Community receive a regular and equitable supply of ores and nuclear fuels;
(e) make certain, by appropriate supervision, that nuclear materials are not diverted to purposes other than those for which they are intended;
(f) exercise the right of ownership conferred upon it with respect to fissile materials;

(g) ensure wide commercial outlets and access to the best technical facilities by the creation of a common market in specialized materials and equipment, by the free movement of capital for investment in the field of nuclear energy and by freedom of employment for specialists within the Community;

(h) establish with other countries and international organizations as will foster progress in the peaceful uses of nuclear energy.

ARTICLE 3

1. The tasks entrusted to the Community shall be carried out by the following institutions:

— a EUROPEAN PARLIAMENT,
— a COUNCIL,
— a COMMISSION.
— a COURT OF JUSTICE.
— **a COURT OF AUDITORS.**

Each institution shall act within the limits of the powers conferred upon it by this Treaty.

2. The Council and the Commission shall be assisted by an *Economic and Social Committee*[9] acting in an advisory capacity.[10]

Atomic energy policy

When the *rélance* of the process of European integration was initiated in the mid-1950s, many saw the creation of an atomic energy community as the most appropriate vehicle, given the enthusiasm at the time for atomic energy, to promote the organization of Europe along supranational lines. Indeed, when the European Atomic Energy Community (Euratom) was set up in 1958 it was anticipated that it would be more successful than the EEC. However, while atomic energy was hailed as the energy source of the future in the 1950s and 1960s, Euratom failed to create a single European atomic energy industry. Indeed, its envisaged success failed to materialize and Euratom soon found itself considerably overshadowed by the development of its *confrére*, the EEC.

Nevertheless, Euratom did pursue important activities in a variety of areas, three of which remain central to its continued existence today. Firstly, Euratom has ensured the continued production of atomic energy by guaranteeing supplies of natural uranium for which Community producers are 70 per cent reliant on imports. This it has achieved through the conclusion of long-term supply contracts with the world's main producers. More recently, proposals have been put forward to create a single market in nuclear power plant components.

Secondly, Euratom has sought to maintain and improve safety within the atomic energy industry and all sectors related to it. Every year Euratom officials check over 800 installations throughout the Community, with the safeguards directorate annually checking over 203 tonnes of plutonium and 200,000 tonnes

---

9. The use of italic on the words 'Economic and Social Committee' does not indicate an amendment brought about by the TEU. Italic is used here in the version of the Euratom Treaty reproduced in *Treaties establishing the European Communities*, abridged edn, OOPEC, Luxembourg, 1987.

10. There was formerly a third paragraph added under Article 19 of the Treaty amending Certain Financial Provisions (1977) relating to the Court of Auditors.

of low enriched natural uranium. Such checks have also been extended to plants in Central and Eastern Europe where the safety of nuclear installations has become a major environmental concern particularly since the Chernobyl disaster of 1985. Since 1989 these checks have been accompanied by intense cooperation on nuclear safety with the new governments in the region. On a more global level, Euratom has worked closely with the International Atomic Energy Agency in promoting nuclear safety.

Finally, Euratom has been instrumental in developing research into the non-military applications of atomic energy, primarily through the European Fusion Programme. Such research, which in the period 1988–92 received ECU 735 million in funding from the Community, has also spurred the wider development of R&D within the EC. Four research centres in the Community have been set up and several extensive projects launched, most noticeably the JET (Joint European Torus) programme into thermonuclear fusion which Euratom participates in along with Sweden and Switzerland. In addition, Euratom has linked up with the United States and Japan in plans for the creation of an international thermonuclear reactor (ITER).

The extent to which Euratom has failed to develop as originally envisaged in the 1950s has meant that it is often overlooked in analyses of the EC's activities. Nonetheless, it has played and continues to play an important role within the world of R&D and nuclear safety. However, its importance *vis-à-vis* the wider process of European integration and the establishment of the European Union remains limited.

Non-nuclear energy policy

While coal and nuclear energy have a relatively high profile within the Community due to their prominence in the ECSC and Euratom Treaties, the Treaty of Rome, until the TEU, made no mention of energy as an area of explicit EC competence. Indeed, although Article 3(t) of the amended Treaty of Rome empowers the EC to adopt measures in the sphere of energy, and Article 129b calls for the development of trans-European energy infrastructures, no Title specifically dedicated to energy was inserted into the Treaty despite the original intention of the drafters of the TEU to do so. Instead, it was agreed that the possibility of introducing a Title on energy into the Treaty of Rome would be examined in the intergovernmental conference to be set up by the end of 1996 in accordance with Article N of the TEU.[11] All the same, since the violent rises in oil prices in the mid-1970s, EC minds have been increasingly focused on access to energy and energy use within the Community. Consequently, as the EC entered the 1990s, an EC energy policy was beginning to emerge.

The three main planks of the EC's emerging energy policy are the proposed

q.v. Article 3(t) pp. 64–5.

q.v. Article 129b p. 213.

q.v. Article N p. 356.

11. See Declaration 1, pp. 431–2.

single energy market; the more global European Energy Charter; and the recently proposed EC carbon/energy tax. The first of these, the single energy market, is evidently an extension of the Single Market covering the free movement of goods, services, capital and persons. As such, its essential aim is the liberalization of European gas and electricity markets by 2000 thus breaking up the dominant positions currently held by state monopolies. Initial steps in this direction have already been taken, with the issuing of directives on price transparency and the promotion of energy transit within the EC, as well as efforts to liberalize energy production, promote third-party access to energy networks, and finally develop European energy infrastructures.[12] However, progress in implementing Commission proposals in many of these areas has been slow. Plans to open up the electricity market have been watered down significantly, and Commissions proposals to challenge national governments over energy monopolies postponed.[13]

q.v. Single Market pp. 122–30.

As indicated above, the second plank of the Community's energy policy, the EC-inspired European Energy Charter,[14] is not confined to the Community alone. Instead, the Charter, which was originally signed in The Hague in December 1991 by 38 countries, currently has over 50 signatories from throughout Europe and the former USSR, as well as the United States, Canada and Japan. From the point of view of the EC, the Charter is an attempt by the Community to find a solution to two problems. Firstly, as over the last decade EC industry has become increasingly dependent on imported energy supplies, the need to secure such supplies has become a prime concern of governments. However, while the future development and indeed survival of European industry depends on these supplies, ensuring any guarantee of supply is anything but straightforward given the often tenuous links the EC and its member states have with the major oil- and gas-producing states in the Middle East and North Africa. Yet, with the collapse of the Soviet Union and the end of the Cold War, the opportunity has emerged for the EC to help develop the rich oil and gas reserves of the USSR's successor states as a stable source of energy. Hence the European Energy Charter was proposed. Secondly, the Charter provides the Western world with an opportunity to assist Central and Eastern Europe and the countries of the former USSR in the transition to the market economy by providing assistance in developing an industry whose product, energy, has a valuable open and growing export market. Similarly, by promoting modernization of the energy industries in these countries, the EC and the West in general would be helping to promote economic and political stability in the region.

Alongside the awareness of the increasing industrial demand for energy within the EC, there has been a growing awareness of the impact of energy use on the

---

12. See *Proposal for a Council Directive concerning common rules for the internal market in electricity; Proposal for a Council Directive concerning common rules for the internal market in natural gas*, COM(91)548 final, Brussels, 21 February 1992.

13. 'Compromise and persuasion', *Financial Times*, 22 June 1993; 'Brussels postpones action on energy monopoly', *Financial Times*, 16 July 1993.

14. The original Commission proposals were contained in *European Energy Charter*, COM(91)36 final, Brussels, 14 February 1991. The Charter, as signed in The Hague, is reproduced in OJC 13, 20 January 1992.

environment. Consequently, the development of an EC energy policy is closely linked with the Community's environmental policy. This is most evident in the third plank of the EC's energy policy: the commitment, agreed as part of the 1992 Rio Climate Change Convention, to stabilize carbon dioxide emissions at 1990 levels by the year 2000.[15] While this commitment is widely accepted among the member states, the means to achieve the end result remain contentious. Most significant here is the Commission's proposal to promote efficient energy use through the introduction of a carbon/energy tax.[16] This would involve a tax being levied on oil produced within the Community as well as on the fuel and carbon content of all non-renewable fuel. While the proposals have received support from Germany, the Benelux countries, Denmark and Italy, energy-intensive industries as well as the poorer member states have all raised objections based on the proposed distribution of the tax. Similarly, concerns have been raised about the tax's impact on the competitiveness of European industry if the United States and Japan do not levy similar taxes on their energy users. Opposition to the proposal has also come from the United Kingdom, although this revolves more around the principle of an EC-wide tax. However, despite the opposition to the proposed tax, it is generally accepted that some measure similar to the tax is necessary if the EC is to fulfil its Rio commitments. A boost to the proposals came in early 1993 when it was revealed that the new Clinton administration in the United States proposed introducing a tax along the lines proposed by the EC.

The growing energy requirements of European industry and the EC's commitment to the environment and to the stabilizing, if not reduction, of carbon dioxide emissions, has ensured that energy will remain a concern of the Community beyond the completion of a single energy market. Indeed, with energy likely to become a fully recognized area of Community competence after 1996, its place on the EC's policy agenda is almost secured. However, as with many areas of EC activity, the full Treaty base energy is likely to acquire, should not be hailed as new addition to the Treaty of Rome, but rather as recognition of existing Community action.

q.v. environ-mental policy pp. 235–9.

FURTHER READING

Cardosa E. Cunha, A. 'Energy policy for the Internal Market', *European Access*, 1992/4, pp. 12–15.

Cook, M., 'Do we need a common energy policy', *European Research*, vol. 2, no. 2, 1991, pp. 9–13.

EC Commission, *A Community strategy to limit Carbon Dioxide emissions and improve energy efficiency*, COM(92)246 final, Brussels, 1 June 1992.

EC Commission, *Amended proposal for a Council Decision for a monitoring mechanism of Community CO_2 and other greenhouse emissions*, COM(93)125 final, Brussels, 22 March 1993.

---

15. *United Nations Framework Convention on Climate Change*, reproduced in *Proposal for a Council Decision concerning the conclusion of the Framework Convention on Climate Change*, COM(92)508 final, Brussels, 14 December 1992.

16. *A Community strategy to limit Carbon Dioxide emissions and improve energy efficiency*, COM(92)246 final, Brussels, 1 June 1992; *Proposal for a Council Directive introducing a tax on carbon dioxide emissions and energy*, COM(92)226 final, Brussels, 30 June 1992; *Amended proposal for a Council Decision for a monitoring mechanism of Community CO2 and other greenhouse emissions*, COM(93)125 final, Brussels, 22 March 1993.

EC Commission, *Energy in Europe*, half yearly.

EC Commission, *European Energy Charter*, COM(91)36 final, Brussels, 14 February 1991.

EC Commission, *Proposal for a Council Directive concerning common rules for the internal market in electricity; Proposal for a Council Directive concerning common rules for the internal market in natural gas*, COM(92)548 final, Brussels, 21 February 1992.

EC Commission, *Proposal for a Council Decision concerning the conclusion of the framework Convention on Climate Change*, COM(92)508 final, Brussels, 14 December 1992.

EC Commission, *Proposal for a Council Directive introducing a tax on carbon dioxide emissions and energy*, COM(92)226 final, Brussels, 30 June 1992.

EC Commission, *Second Progress Report on the Internal Energy Market*, COM(93)261 final, Brussels, 2 July 1993.

EC Commission, *Specific action for greater penetration of renewable energy resources: Altener*, COM(92)180 final, Brussels, 29 June 1992.

Hancher, L., 'Energy and the environment: striking a balance', *Common Market Law Review*, vol. 26, no. 3, 1989, pp. 475–512.

House of Lords, *Carbon Energy Tax*, Select Committee on the European Communities, 8th Report, 1991–2, HL-52, 10 March 1992.

House of Lords, *Structure of the Single Market for Energy*, Select Committee on the European Communities, 17th Report, 1992–3, HL-56, 9 February 1993.

Official Journal of the European Communities, *European Energy Charter*, OJC 13, 20 January 1992.

Padgett, S., 'The single energy market: the politics of realization', *Journal of Common Market Studies*, vol. 30, no. 1, 1992, pp. 53–75.

iii Provisions on a Common Foreign and Security Policy

q.v.
Common
Commercial
Policy pp.
183–7.

As already noted, the Union created by the TEU comprises three pillars. Having examined the first of these, that encompassing the three European Communities, the Handbook now turns to the second pillar, that comprising the Common Foreign and Security Policy (CFSP). However, it should be made clear that the provisions for a CFSP contained in Title V are not the only bases on which the Union may conduct its external relations. As noted earlier in the brief discussion of the EC's Common Commercial Policy, the association of overseas countries and territories and the provisions contained in Articles 228–231, 234 and 237–238, the Union has, through the EC, a host of mechanisms for conducting not only trade relations with third countries, but also political relations. Given the enormous array of agreements and relationships these have resulted in, a discussion of the Union's and the EC's overall external relations is provided in subdivisions V and VII of the *Handbook*.

q.v.
association
of overseas
countries
and
territories
pp. 346–8.

q.v.
General
and Final
Provisions
B –
External
applicability
pp. 333–9.

When the IGC on political union opened in December 1990 one of its primary aims, and one accepted by all the member states, was to heighten the international profile of the European Community and increase foreign policy cooperation between the member states beyond that already being developed within the framework of European Political Cooperation (EPC), an intergovernmental forum for foreign policy coordination set up in the early 1970s and formalized in Title III of the Single European Act. More specifically, the IGC was charged with facilitating collective action by the member states in dealing with the challenges and opportunities posed by the events of 1989 and 1990 in Central and Eastern Europe and by the perceived dawning of a new world order now that the Soviet empire was in terminal decline. Moreover, it was argued that the Community should also be developing a political role on the international scene commensurate with its economic standing.

However, while all the member states agreed on the basic need to increase foreign policy cooperation, significant differences existed over the extent to which the Union should establish common policies and whether these should embrace security and defence as well as simply foreign policy issues. While some, such as the British, preferred to envisage only closer coordination of foreign policies, others, such as the French, were willing to consider the creation of common foreign, security and defence policies. Similarly, divisions existed among the member states as to whether such policies should be integrated into the Treaty of Rome, involve majority voting and be subject to review by the European Court of Justice, or whether they should remain the subject of intergovernmental cooperation and thus outside the decision-making structure of the EC. Such differences of opinion are reflected in the essentially minimalist CFSP provisions which were actually agreed at Maastricht.

For supporters and opponents of a more integrated Europe, the point most often emphasized about the CFSP is that it is not an integral part of the EC. Rather, it is to be found in its own pillar separate from that containing the amended Treaties of the European communities. Like EPC before it,[17] the CFSP is not incorporated into the Treaty of Rome, but is subject to its own decision-making and implementation procedures and not those which govern the formulation and execution of EC policies. Equally, the CFSP is not subject to judicial review by the ECJ (Article L). Hence, it remains an essentially intergovernmental procedure, and is recognized by some as only a mild improvement on the original EPC structures.[18]

q.v. Article L p. 355.

For those who see closer European integration as synonymous with the loss of national sovereignty and independence, such a structure based firmly on intergovernmentalism is acceptable since the policies in question remain firmly in the hands of member states and not the European institutions. Conversely, critics of such an approach voice concern that the CFSP will remain the hostage of national interests and prove impossible to implement, thus preventing the Union from reacting with sufficient speed to the rapidly changing political and security environment in which it finds itself.

The actual aim of the Union with regard to foreign affairs is laid down in Article B of the TEU's Common Provisions. Thus the Union seeks to assert its identity on the international scene through the implementation of a common foreign and security policy and the eventual framing of a common defence policy, possibly leading to common defence. Consequently, the provisions laid down in the twelve articles (Articles J—J.11) which make up Title V and the aims of the Union expressed therein not only relate to foreign and security policy but also to defence.

q.v. Article B p. 57.

17. Article P(2) of the TEU repeals the provisions for European Political Cooperation as laid down in Title III of the Single European Act (1986). See p. 356.

18. Müller-Graff, P-C., 'Europäische Politische Zusammenarbeit und Gemeinsame Außen- und Sicherheitspolitik: Kohärenzgebot aus rechtlicher Sicht', *Integration*, vol. 16, no. 3, 1993, pp. 147–57; Regelsberger, E., 'Die gemeinsame Außen- und Sicherheitspolitik nach Maastricht — Minimalreformen in neuer Entwicklungsperspektiven', *Integration*, vol. 15, no. 2, 1992, pp. 83–93. Wincott, D., *The Treaty of Maastricht: An Adequate 'Constitution' for the European Union?*, European Public Policy Institute Occasional Paper 93/6, University of Warwick, 1993, pp. 14–15.

The essential objectives of the Union's CFSP, unlike the principles according to which the policy is to be implemented, are clearly defined by the TEU. They involve safeguarding the Union's common values, interests and security; preserving peace and strengthening international security; promoting international cooperation; and developing democracy, the rule of law and respect for human rights (Article J.1).[19] However, it is left to the European Council to define the principles and guidelines according to which the Union is to implement the CFSP (Article J.8). Meanwhile, the actual scope of the Union activity is effectively limitless since the Treaty requires member states to define and implement the CFSP 'covering all areas of foreign and security policy' (Article J.1).

The Union has at its disposal two mechanisms it may use to pursue these objectives. First, the TEU requires the member states to establish between themselves 'systemic cooperation' through a process of information, consultation, and policy coordination. Where necessary, this is to involve the Council defining a common position which all member states must adhere to and uphold in international fora (Article J.2). In effect, this process mirrors that employed under EPC, with one exception. Under the TEU, it is no longer the 'High Contracting Parties' which are responsible for taking decisions relating to foreign policy matters, as was the case under EPC, but the 'Member States' and the 'Council'. This shift of responsibility for decision-making on foreign policy towards Community institutions is reinforced by the fact that the Commission as well as member states may refer questions and make proposals to the Council on matters relating to the CFSP (Article J.8(3)), a function also assigned to the Political Committee of Political Directors which was set up by the TEU to monitor the international scene on behalf of the Council (Article J.8(5)).[20] However, it is the second mechanism of the CFSP which represents a more significant step in the direction of a fully-fledged common foreign and security policy.

This second mechanism introduces the concept of 'joint action' being taken by members of the Union in dealing with CFSP matters. Such matters are to be defined by the Council on the basis of unanimity in line with guidelines handed down by the European Council. However, while this clearly emphasizes the intergovernmental nature of the CFSP and maintains the right of each member state to veto any proposal, provision is made for the Council to define areas where it may act by a qualified majority vote. Where a joint action is agreed, this commits member states to adopt it in the conduct of their foreign policy (Article J.3).[21] While such a procedure clearly obliges member states to adhere to decisions agreed

---

19. The reference here to the respect for the rule of law and respect for human rights is further evidenced by the EC's insistence that all future agreements with non-member states include such a reference.

20. According to the Declaration 28, the division of work between the Political Committee and COREPER, the merging of the EPC and Council Secretariats, and cooperation between the latter and the Commission is to be examined at some point in the future (see p. 437). The rules regarding the use of languages in the CFSP are laid down in the Declaration 27 (see pp. 437–8).

21. Furthermore, in a Declaration attached to the TEU's Final Act, it was agreed that on matters relating to the CFSP which require a unanimous vote, member states would avoid preventing a unanimous decision where a qualified majority exists. See Declaration 27, p. 437. However, the Declaration is not legally binding and cannot override existing Treaty provisions — a point seized upon by the UK government in agreeing to accept the Declaration.

upon, the absence of any form of judicial review covering the CFSP means that member states are not under any legal obligation to comply with the provisions of the joint action. Indeed, where a member state believes that the nature of a situation covered by CFSP has changed such as to require new measures and the Council fails to take any action, the member state is free to take whatever unilateral action it deems appropriate provided this does not run counter to the objectives of the joint action or reduce its effectiveness (Articles J.1(4) and J.3(6)).

Responsibility for implementing the CFSP and representing the Union in matters relating to the policy lies with the Council Presidency and the Political Committee, not the Commission as is the norm within the EC. Where required the Presidency is to be assisted by the previous and next member states to hold the post (Article J.5). Nevertheless, the Commission, as it was under EPC, is to be fully associated with the work carried out with regard to the CFSP (Article J.9). In addition Commission delegations in third countries are to work alongside the diplomatic and consular missions of the member states in ensuring that common positions and common measures are complied with and implemented (Article J.6). No mention is made, however, as to whether these bodies are to carry out a similar function with regard to joint actions.

The remaining tasks of the Presidency relate to the European Parliament. Under the TEU, the Presidency is to consult the EP on the 'main aspects and the basic choices' of the CFSP and to ensure that any views expressed by the latter are duly taken into consideration. Beyond this, the Presidency along with the Commission is required to keep the EP informed of how the CFSP is developing. For its part, the EP is allowed to question and make recommendations to the Council on the CFSP and is obliged to hold an annual debate on the progress made in implementing the CFSP (Article J.7). Essentially, therefore the EP's role is no greater than under EPC.

As Article J points out, the aim of the Union is to establish a common foreign and security policy. However, Article J.4 states that the Union also has as its goal the 'eventual framing of a common defence policy, which might in time lead to a common defence'. The omission of the word 'defence' from the title of Title V underlines the sensitivity shared by several national governments, particularly that of neutral Ireland, which surrounds the idea of defence competences being transferred to the Union. Equally, however, it highlights the reluctance of several member states to see a European alternative to NATO emerge. Indeed, several references are made to the obligations member states have as members of the organization. Nonetheless, the TEU openly promotes the idea of a defence policy being established. However, for the time being, defence matters are to be handled by the Western European Union (WEU), although a tentative provision is made in Article J.4 for the integration of the WEU into the Union when its founding treaty, the Brussels Treaty, expires in 1998 (Article J.4).[22]

---

22. The response of the WEU to the proposals contained within Title V is included in two Declarations from the organization which are contained in a single Declaration attached to the Final Act of the TEU (see Declaration 30, pp. 438–40). The Declarations welcome the Union's desire to pursue a common defence policy and express the willingness of the WEU to elaborate and implement decisions and actions taken by the Union which have defence implications. They then set out measures which the WEU will take to develop a close working relationship with

While the provisions for a CFSP may not have met the aspirations of the more federalist-minded participants in the IGCs and may yet prove to be inadequate in dealing with the security problems which currently face the Union, they nevertheless represent a qualitative, albeit minimal, step forward towards a common European Union policy on foreign, security and defence matters. They extend the scope of policy coordination; improve the decision-making procedures formally used in EPC; and introduce a new policy mechanism in 'joint actions'. However, whether these new elements will be sufficient for the attainment of the Union's objectives remains to be seen. Success will depend very much on the political will of the member states to use the provisions of Title V effectively.

q.v. The Wider Europe pp. 479–87.

FURTHER READING

Allen, D. and Smith, M., 'Western Europe's presence in the contemporary international arena', *Review of International Studies*, 1990/1, pp. 19–38.

Bomsdorf, F. *et al. Confronting Insecurity in Eastern Europe: Challenges for the European Community*, RIIA, London, 1992.

Buchan, D., *Europe: The strange superpower*, Dartmouth, Aldershot, 1993.

Collet, A., 'Le Traité de Maastricht et la défense', *Revue trimestrielle de droit européen*, vol. 29, no. 2, 1993, pp. 225–33.

Dinan, D., 'European political cooperation', in: Hurwitz, L. and Lequesne, C. (eds.), *The State of the European Community: Policies, institutions and debates in the transition years*, Longman, London, 1991, pp. 403–21.

De Gucht, K. and Keukeleire, S., 'The European security architecture. The role of the European Community in shaping a new European geopolitical landscape', *Studia Diplomatica*, vol. 44, no. 6, 1991, pp. 29–90.

European Security: Towards 2000, Manchester University Press, Manchester, 1991.

Holland, M. (ed.) *The Future of European Political Cooperation: Essays on theory and practice*, Macmillan, London, 1991.

Lodge, J., *A Common Foreign and Security Policy: Beyond the rhetoric*, European Community Research Unit, University of Hull, 1991.

Lodge, J., 'From civilian power to speaking with a common voice: the transition to a CFSP', in Lodge, J. (ed.), *The European Community and the Challenge of the Future*, 2nd edn, Pinter, London, 1993. pp. 227–51.

Müller-Graff, P.-C., 'Europäische Politische Zusammenarbeit und Gemeinsame Außen- und Sicherheitspolitik: Kohärenzgebot aus rechtlicher Sicht', *Integration*, vol. 16, no. 3, 1993, pp. 147–57.

Nuttal, S. J., *European Political Cooperation*, Clarendon, Oxford, 1992.

Pöttering, H.-G., 'The EC on the Way towards a Common Security Policy', *Aussenpolitik*, vol. 42, no. 2, 1991, pp. 147–51.

Regelsberger, E., 'Die gemeinsame Außen- und Sicherheitspolitik nach Maastricht — Minimal-reformen in neuer Entwicklungsperspektiven', *Integration*, vol. 15, no. 2, 1992, pp. 83–93.

Regelsberger, E., 'European political cooperation', in Story, J. (ed.), *The New Europe: Politics, government and economy since 1945*, Blackwell, Oxford, 1993, pp. 270–91.

Remacle, É. 'Les dispositions du Traité de Maastricht: politique étrangère et sécurité de l'Union européenne', *Études internationales*, vol. 23, no. 2, 1992, pp. 377–94.

Rummel, R., 'Integration, disintegration, and security in Europe: preparing the Community for a multi-institutional response', *International Journal*, vol. 47, no. 1, 1992, pp. 64–92.

Salmon, T. C., 'The Union, the CFSP and the European security debate', in Lodge, J. (ed.), *The European Community and the Challenge of the Future*, 2nd edn, Pinter, London, 1993. pp. 252–70.

Seeler, H.-J. 'Neue Wege einer europäischen Sicherheits- und Verteidigungspolitik', *Europa Archiv*, vol. 48, no. 1, 1993, pp. 12–18.

the Union, including the transfer of its headquarters to Brussels, and invite other members of the Union to accede to or become observers at the WEU. An invitation is also extended to European members of NATO to become associate members of the organization. Agreements making Greece a full member, and Turkey, Norway and Iceland associate members of the WEU were signed in November 1992. As yet, Denmark and Ireland have decided to adopt only observer status.

Title V Provisions on a common foreign and security policy[23]

ARTICLE J

A common foreign and security policy is hereby established which shall be governed by the following provisions.

ARTICLE J.1

1. The Union and its Member States shall define and implement a common foreign and security policy, governed by the provisions of this Title and covering all areas of foreign and security policy.

2. These objectives of the common foreign and security policy shall be:
— to safeguard the common values, fundamental interests and independence of the Union;
— to strengthen the security of the Union and its Member States in all ways;
— to preserve peace and strengthen international security, in accordance with the principles of the United Nations Charter as well as the principles of the Helsinki Final Act and the objectives of the Paris Charter;
— to promote international cooperation;
— to develop and consolidate democracy and the rule of law, and respect for human rights and fundamental freedoms.

3. The Union shall pursue these objectives;
— by establishing systematic cooperation between Member States in the conduct of policy, in accordance with Article J.2;
— by gradually implementing, in accordance with Article J.3, joint action in the areas in which the Member States have important interests in common.

4. The Member States shall support the Union's external and security policy actively and unreservedly in a spirit of loyalty and mutual solidarity. They shall refrain from *any action* which is contrary to the interests of the Union or likely to impair its *effectiveness as a cohesive force in international relations.* The Council shall ensure that these principles are complied with.

ARTICLE J.2

1. Member States shall *inform and consult one another* within the Council *on any matter of foreign* and security *policy of general interest in order to ensure that their combined influence is* exerted *as effectively as possible by means of* concerted and convergent *action.*
2. Whenever it deems it necessary, the Council shall define a common position.

Member States shall ensure that their national policies conform on the common positions.

3. Member States shall coordinate their action *in international organizations and at international conferences.* They shall uphold the common positions in such fora.

In international organizations and at international conferences where not all the Member States *participate, those which do take part shall* uphold the common positions.

ARTICLE J.3

The procedure for adopting joint action in matters covered by foreign and security policy shall be the following:

1. The Council shall decide, on the basis of general guidelines from the European Council, that a matter should be the subject of joint action.

---

23. The words and phrases which appear in italics have either been copied directly from or are reworded versions of provisions governing EPC as contained in Title III of the SEA.

Whenever the Council decides on the principle of joint action, it shall lay down the specific scope, the Union's general and specific objectives in carrying out such action, if necessary its duration, and the means, procedures and conditions for its implementation.

2. The Council shall, when adopting the joint action and at any stage during its development, define those matters on which decisions are to be taken by a qualified majority.

Where the Council is required to act by a qualified majority pursuant to the preceding subparagraph, the votes of its members shall be weighted in accordance with Article 148(2) of the Treaty establishing the European Community, and for their adoption, acts of the Council shall require at least fifty-four votes in favour, cast by at least eight members.

3. If there is a change in circumstances having a substantial effect on a question subject to joint action, the Council shall review the principles and objectives of that action and take the necessary decisions. As long as the Council has not acted, the joint action shall stand.

4. Joint actions shall commit the Member States in the positions they adopt and in the conduct of their activity.

5. Whenever there is any plan to adopt a national position or take national action pursuant to a joint action, information shall be provided in time to allow, if necessary, for prior consultations within the Council. The obligation to provide prior information shall not apply to measures which are merely a national transposition of Council decisions.

6. In cases of imperative need arising from changes in the situation and failing a Council decision, Member States may take the necessary measures as a matter of urgency having regard to the general objectives of the joint action. The Member State concerned shall inform the Council immediately of any such measures.

7. Should there be any major difficulties in implementing a joint action, a Member State shall refer them to the Council which shall discuss them and seek appropriate solutions. Such solutions shall not run counter to the objectives of the joint action or impair its effectiveness.

ARTICLE J.4

1. The common foreign and security policy shall include all questions related to the security of the Union, including the eventual framing of a common defence policy, which might in time lead to a common defence.

2. The Union requests the Western European Union (WEU), which is an integral part of the development of the Union, to elaborate and implement decisions and actions of the Union which have defence implications. The Council shall, in agreement with the institutions of the WEU, adopt the necessary practical arrangements.

3. Issues having defence implications dealt with under this Article shall not be subject to the procedures set out in Article J.3.

4. The policy of the Union in accordance with this Article shall not prejudice the specific character of the security and defence policy of certain Member States and shall respect the obligations of certain Member States under the North Atlantic Treaty and be compatible with the common security and defence policy established within that framework.

5. *The provisions of this* **Article** *shall not prevent the development of closer cooperation between two or more Member States on a bilateral level, in the framework of the WEU and the Atlantic Alliance*, **provided such cooperation does not run counter to or impede that provided for in this Title.**

6. With a view to furthering the objective of this Treaty, and having in view the date of 1998 in the context of Article XII of the Brussels Treaty, the provisions of this Article may be revised as provided for in Article N(2) on the basis of a report to be presented in 1996 by the Council to the European Council, which shall include an evaluation of the progress made and the experience gained until then.

ARTICLE J.5

1. *The Presidency shall represent* the Union in matters coming within the common foreign and security policy.

2. *The Presidency shall be responsible* for the implementation of common measures; in that capacity it shall in principle express the position of the Union in international organizations and international conferences.

3. In the tasks referred to in paragraphs 1 and 2, the Presidency shall be assisted if needs be by the previous and next Member States to hold the Presidency. The Commission shall be fully associated in these tasks.

4. Without prejudice to Article J.2(3) and Article J.3(4), Member States represented in international organizations or international conferences where not all the Member States participate shall keep the latter informed of any matter of common interest.

Member States which are also members of the United Nations Security Council will concert and keep the other Member States fully informed. Member States which are permanent members of the Security Council will, in the execution of their functions, ensure the defence of the positions and the interests of the Union, without prejudice to their responsibilities under the provisions of the United Nations Charter.

ARTICLE J.6

The diplomatic and consular missions of the Member States and the Commission Delegations in third countries and international conferences, and their representations to international organizations, shall cooperate in ensuring that the common positions and common measures adopted by the Council are complied with and implemented.

They shall step up cooperation by exchanging information, carrying out joint assessments and contributing to the implementation of the provisions referred to in Article 8c of the Treaty establishing the European Community.

ARTICLE J.7

The Presidency shall consult the European Parliament on the main aspects and the basic choices of the common foreign and security policy and *shall ensure that the views of the European Parliament are duly taken into consideration. The European Parliament shall be kept regularly informed by the Presidency* and the Commission of the development of the Union's foreign and security policy.

The European Parliament may ask questions of the Council or make recommendations to it. It shall hold an annual debate on progress in implementing the common foreign and security policy.

ARTICLE J.8

1. The European Council shall define the principles of and general guidelines for the common foreign and security policy.

2. The Council shall take the decisions necessary for defining and implementing the common foreign and security policy on the basis of the general guidelines adopted by the European Council. It shall ensure the unity, consistency and effectiveness of action by the Union.

The Council shall act unanimously, except for procedural questions and in the case referred to in Article J.3(2).

3. Any Member State or the Commission may refer to the Council any question relating to the common foreign and security policy and may submit proposals to the Council.

4. In cases requiring a rapid decision, the Presidency, of its own motion, or at the request of the Commission or a Member State, shall convene an extraordinary Council meeting within forty-eight hours or, in an emergency, within a shorter period.

5. Without prejudice to Article 151 of the Treaty establishing the European Community, a Political Committee consisting of Political Directors shall monitor the international situation in the areas covered by common foreign and security policy and contribute to the definition of policies by delivering opinions to the Council at the request of the Council or on its own initiative. It shall also monitor the implementation of agreed policies, without prejudice to the responsibility of the Presidency and the Commission.

ARTICLE J.9

The Commission shall be fully associated with the work carried out in the common foreign and security policy field.

ARTICLE J.10

On the occasion of any review of the security provisions under Article J.4, the Conference which is convened to that effect shall also examine whether any other amendments need to be made to provisions relating to the common foreign and security policy.

ARTICLE J.11

1. The provisions referred to in Articles 137, 138, 139 to 142, 146, 147, 150 to 153, 157 to 163 and 217 of the Treaty establishing the European Community shall apply to the provisions relating to the areas referred to in this Title.

2. Administrative expenditure which the provisions relating to the areas referred to in this Title entail for the institutions shall be charged to the budget of the European Communities.

The Council may also:

— either decide unanimously that operational expenditure to which the implementation of those provisions gives rise is to be charged to the budget of the European Communities; in that event, the budgetary procedure laid down in the Treaty establishing the European Community shall be applicable;

— or determine that such expenditure shall be charged to the Member States, where appropriate in accordance with a scale to be decided.

iv. Provisions on cooperation in the fields of justice and home affairs

The third pillar of the European Union consists of intergovernmental cooperation between the member states on justice and home affairs. The provisions relating to this pillar are found in Title VI of the TEU which contains ten Articles (Articles K–K.9). Given the pillar structure of the Union, the areas covered by such cooperation are, therefore, like the CFSP, not dealt with by the Community institutions in the same way as policy areas laid down in the Treaty of Rome. Instead cooperation is based on agreements reached on an intergovernmental basis and as such is not automatically subject to judicial review by the Court of Justice

(Article L,). Although critics of the Treaty's pillar structure may regret the fact that the provisions relating to cooperation in the fields of justice and home affairs are not included as part of the amended Treaty of Rome, their inclusion in the TEU does represent a significant step forward in the development of a European home affairs and justice policy. Whereas previously the EC member states had cooperated on matters related to justice and home affairs within the informal framework of TREVI, the TEU places such cooperation on a formal footing and brings it closer to becoming a primary source of Community legislation. In fact, certain elements of such cooperation, such as visa policy were actually incorporated into the amended Treaty of Rome.

q.v. Article L p. 355.

q.v. Articles 100c and 100d pp. 149–50.

The impetus for the inclusion of provisions relating to justice and home affairs in the TEU did not come from the original Commission proposals on political union, although the principles of the Single Market, especially the free movement of people, by rights demand cooperation on matters such as police cooperation. Instead the perceived need for such provisions as an integral component of the proposed union gradually emerged during the Luxembourg Presidency. This culminated in Chancellor Kohl's call, at the Luxembourg Summit of June 1991, for provisions relating to rights of asylum, immigration and the establishment of a European Police Office to be included in the treaty then under negotiation. In effect, what emerged in the final document actually exceeded these demands.

Article K.1 lists ten areas of common interest to the member states of the Union and provides for the creation of a European Police Office (Europol).[24] These areas of common interest range from asylum and immigration policy to cooperation in combating drug trafficking, fraud and terrorism, and from customs and judicial cooperation in civil and criminal matters to combating drug addiction. However, while this list of areas for cooperation may appear quite extensive, no provision is made in the Title for additional areas of common interest to be added to the list at a later date. While Article K.3 effectively confirms existing intergovernmental practice of coordinating action on matters related to justice and home affairs, the provisions included within Title VI do represent a qualitative step forward towards more substantial and effective cooperation between the members of the Union.

First, as in the second pillar of the Union, whereas existing cooperation on justice and home affairs was carried out between the member states in almost total isolation from the Community institutions, under Title VI roles are assigned to each of the main institutions. Consequently, it can be argued that, although the third pillar is separate from the Community, the policy areas dealt with in it have moved closer towards becoming competences of the EC.

Second, Article K.3 allows for the Council, on the initiative of either a member state or the Commission, to move beyond the traditional coordination of action to adopt joint positions or joint action or to draw up conventions in any of the areas referred to in Articles K.1.[25] Joint positions, although not legally binding

---

24. For further details, see Declaration 32, p. 441.

25. It should be noted that the Commission may only put forward proposals in areas referred to in Articles K.1(1)–(6). Hence, the Commission has no right of initiative over judicial cooperation in criminal matters, customs cooperation, or police cooperation.

on member states, are nevertheless to be defended by the member states within international fora (Article K.5). While the non-binding nature of decisions taken under Title VI may appear to reinforce the intergovernmental nature of the Union, provision is made for the Council to place the interpretation of the provisions contained in any conventions it may draw up under the jurisdiction of the Court of Justice (Article K.3(2)). However, although this clearly increases the potential supranational character of the Union's third pillar, granting the ECJ jurisdiction requires unanimity within the Council and may only be granted with respect to conventions, and not joint action or joint positions adopted.

Third, although all measures covered by Title VI are to be adopted on the basis of unanimity, the Council may decide that measures to implement joint action be adopted on the basis of a qualified majority. Similarly, procedural matters are to be adopted by a qualified majority in the Council and measures implementing a convention by a two-thirds majority (Article K.3(2) and K.4(3)). However, while this may facilitate a more effective implementation of decisions, each member state retains the right to veto any initiative put before the Council.

Fourth, as far as the main Community institutions are concerned, the Commission, as under the provisions relating to the CFSP, is to be fully associated with work in the areas referred to in Title VI (Article K.4(2)). More significantly, as already mentioned, the Commission also has a right to put forward proposals to the Council. However, such a right is not conferred upon the EP. The Parliament's role within the third pillar is purely consultative, and then only on the principal aspects, rather than the substance of the activities undertaken. While the EP has the right to be kept regularly informed of discussions within the Council by the Presidency and by the Commission, and is required to hold an annual debate on the progress made in implementing joint actions, the Council is only required to take 'into consideration' any recommendations the Parliament may make to it (Article K.6). However, provision is made in Article K.9 to use the decision-making process laid down in Article 100c of the amended Treaty of Rome for areas covered by Article K.1.(1–6) where agreed by a unanimous vote in the Council. While this clearly opens up the possibility of the EP becoming involved in determining more than just visa policy, at present the significance of this option being made available to the Council remains purely symbolic since each member state still has the right to veto any proposal which would transfer legislative authority to the Community institutions.[26] Nevertheless, the provision does recognize that the Community may in the future be competent in any, if not all, of the areas covered by Title VI.[27]

q.v. Article 100c pp. 149–50.

Fifth, Article K.4(1) entrusts ensuring the coordination of any action agreed upon by the member states to a Coordinating Committee of senior officials. The Committee is also to provide the Council with opinions and contribute, along with COREPER, to the preparation of the Council's discussions (Article K.4(1)).

---

26. According to the Declaration 31 (see p. 441), areas of asylum policy may be transferred to the EC via Art. K.9 by the end of 1993.

27. Nanz, K.P., 'Der "3 Pfeiler der Europäischen Union" Zusammenarbeit in der Innen- und Justizpolitik', *Integration*, vol. 15, no. 3, 1992, at p. 130.

It therefore fulfils a role similar to that of the Political Committee established under Title V.

Finally, Article K.2 requires that the cooperation entered into by the member states complies with the Council of Europe's European Convention for the Protection of Human Rights and Fundamental Freedoms (1950) and the Convention relating to the Status of Refugees (1951). However, while this enhances the status of the two conventions, the TEU fails to incorporate either convention in the text of the Treaty, despite calls to do so from the Council of Europe. One reason behind this was the reluctance of several member states to see Conventions, which they had not adopted as a primary source of law, effectively enter their legal systems through the back door.

Title VI Provisions on cooperation in the fields of justice and home affairs

ARTICLE K

Cooperation in the fields of justice and home affairs shall be governed by the following provisions.

ARTICLE K.1

For the purposes of achieving the objectives of the Union, in particular the free movement of persons, and without prejudice to the powers of the European Community, Member States shall regard the following areas as matters of common interest:

1. asylum policy;

2. rules governing the crossing by persons of the external borders of the Member States and the exercise of controls thereon;

3. immigration policy and policy regarding nationals of third countries;

(a) conditions of entry and movement by nationals of third countries on the territory of Member States;

(b) conditions of residence by nationals of third countries on the territory of Member States, including family reunion and access to employment;

(c) combating unauthorized immigration, residence and work by nationals of third countries on the territory of Member States;

4. combating drug addiction in so far as this is not covered by 7 to 9;

5. combating fraud on an international scale in so far as this is not covered by 7 to 9;

6. judicial cooperation in civil matters;

7. judicial cooperation in criminal matters;

8. customs cooperation;

9. police cooperation for the purposes of preventing and combating terrorism, unlawful drug trafficking and other serious forms of international crime, including if necessary certain aspects of customs cooperation, in connection with the organization of a Union-wide system for exchanging information within a European Police Office (Europol).

ARTICLE K.2

1. The matters referred to in Article K.1 shall be dealt with in compliance with the European Convention for the Protection of Human Rights and Fundamental Freedoms of 4 November 1950 and the Convention relating to the Status of Refugees of 28 July 1951 and having regard to the protection afforded by Member States to persons persecuted on political grounds.

2. This Title shall not affect the exercise of the responsibilities incumbent upon Member States with regard to the maintenance of law and order and the safeguarding of internal security.

ARTICLE K.3

1. In the areas referred to in Article K.1, Member States shall inform and consult one another within the Council with a view to coordinating their action. To that end, they shall establish collaboration between the relevant departments of their administrations.

2. The Council may:

— on the initiative of any Member State or of the Commission, in the areas referred to in Article K.1(1) to (6);
— on the initiative of any Member State, in the areas referred to Article K1(7) to (9):

    (a) adopt joint positions and promote, using the appropriate form and procedures, any cooperation contributing to the pursuit of the objectives of the Union;
    (b) adopt joint action in so far as the objectives of the Union can be attained better by joint action than by the Member States acting individually on account of the scale or effects of the action envisaged; it may decide that measures implementing joint action are to be adopted by a qualified majority;
    (c) without prejudice to Article 220 of the Treaty establishing the European Community, draw up conventions which it shall recommend to the Member States for adoption in accordance with their respective constitutional requirements.

Unless otherwise provided by such conventions, measures implementing them shall be adopted within the Council by a majority of two-thirds of the High Contracting Parties.

Such conventions may stipulate that the Court of Justice shall have jurisdiction to interpret their provisions and to rule on any disputes regarding their application, in accordance with such arrangements as they may lay down.

ARTICLE K.4

1. A Coordinating Committee shall be set up consisting of senior officials. In additions to its coordinating role, it shall be the task of the Committee to:

— give opinions for the attention of the Council, either at the Council's request or on its own initiative;
— contribute, without prejudice to Article 151 of the Treaty establishing the European Community, to the preparation of the Council's discussions in the areas referred to in Article K.1 and, in accordance with the conditions laid down in Article 100d of the Treaty establishing the European Community, in the areas referred to in Article 100c of that Treaty.

2. The Commission shall be fully associated with the work in the areas referred to in this Title.

3. The Council shall act unanimously, except on matters of procedure and in cases where Article K.3 expressly provides for other voting rules.

Where the Council is required to act by a qualified majority, the votes of its members shall be weighted as laid down in Article 148(2) of the Treaty establishing the European Community, and for their adoption, acts of the Council shall require at least fifty-four votes in favour, cast by at least eight members.

ARTICLE K.5   Within international organizations and at international conferences in which they take part, Member States shall defend the common positions adopted under the provisions of this Title.

ARTICLE K.6   The Presidency and the Commission shall regularly inform the European Parliament of discussions in the areas covered by this Title.

The Presidency shall consult the European Parliament on the principal aspects of activities in the areas referred to in this Title and shall ensure that the views of the European Parliament are duly taken into consideration.

The European Parliament may ask questions of the Council or make recommendations to it. Each year, it shall hold a debate on the progress made in implementation of the areas referred to in this Title.

ARTICLE K.7   The provisions of this Title shall not prevent the establishment or development of closer cooperation between two or more Member States in so far as such cooperation does not conflict with, or impede, that provided for in this Title.

ARTICLE K.8   1. The provisions referred to in Article 137, 138, 139 to 142, 146, 147, 150 to 153, 157 to 163 and 217 of the Treaty establishing the European Community shall apply to the provisions relating to the areas referred to in this Title.

2. Administrative expenditure which the provisions relating to the areas referred to in this Title entail for the institutions shall be charged to the budget of European Communities.

The Council may also:

— either decide unanimously that operational expenditure to which the implementation of those provisions gives rise is to be charged to the budget of the European Communities; in that event, the budgetary procedure laid down in the Treaty establishing the European Community shall be applicable;
— or determine that such expenditure shall be charged to the Member States, where appropriate in accordance with a scale to be decided.

ARTICLE K.9   The Council, acting unanimously on the initiative of the Commission or a Member State, may decide to apply Article 100c of the Treaty establishing the European Community to action in areas referred to in Article K.1(1) to (6), and at the same time determine the relevant voting conditions relating to it. It shall recommend the Member States to adopt that decision in accordance with their respective constitutional requirements.

Justice and home affairs policy

While the inclusion of cooperation in the fields of justice and home affairs as the third pillar of the Union may suggest that the Twelve are about to enter into new areas of cooperation, as has been seen elsewhere in the *Handbook*, the provisions contained in the TEU to a large extent simply give formal recognition to existing practice. This is certainly the case with regard to Title VI. Indeed, although the Treaty of Rome did not provide the Community with any real scope for action in the areas of justice and home affairs, since the mid-1970s EC member states have, on an intergovernmental basis, been pursuing various degrees of cooperation in matters ranging from immigration and asylum policy to police cooperation in combating international crime. Such cooperation was developed further following the launch of the Single Market programme. This, with the aim of removing all barriers to the free movement of goods, services, capital and more significantly persons, required the member states to take qualitative steps in intensifying and extending their cooperation.

The first initiative relating to justice and home affairs launched by the member states of the EC was TREVI (Terrorisme, Radicalisme, Extrémisme, Violence Internationale). This was set up in 1975–6 and today remains the main forum for intergovernmental cooperation on matters relating to internal security within the EC. Meeting twice a year and always in secret, justice and home affairs ministers aim to promote cooperation in fighting organized crime, terrorism and drug trafficking, and to coordinate asylum and immigration policies. However, while much of TREVI's work in the 1970s and 1980s was determined by an *ad hoc* agenda, once the Commission's White Paper on the completion of the Internal Market had identified the need for close coordination of national asylum and immigration policies, and a Declaration by the national governments in the SEA committed the member states to cooperate in combating terrorism, crime, illicit trading and drug trafficking,[28] a more structured approach began to emerge. Consequently, several specialized subgroups of TREVI have since been established.

The foremost among these is the Ad Hoc Group on Immigration set up in October 1986. This has been responsible for promoting the tightening of controls on external Community borders; coordinating national visa policies; promoting information exchanges on immigrants; and bringing national provisions on the rights of asylum closer into line. While initially informal cooperation appeared to suffice in dealing with the problems posed by the prospect of the free movement of people within the EC from 31 December 1992, the increase in immigration from Central and Eastern Europe and the former USSR from the late 1980s onwards as well as increased migration from traditional sources, such as North Africa, led several member states to demand more formal arrangements regarding immigration and asylum to be established. Prominent among these was Germany, which given its traditionally liberal asylum laws, its geographical location in the centre of Europe, and its economic attraction to migrants, was keen for its EC partners to share the burden of an increase in the number of people seeking asylum from 169,000 in 1988 to 327,000 in 1990. As a result, in June 1990 the Dublin Convention on Asylum was signed by all the EC member states, with the exception of Denmark.[29]

Under the terms of the Convention once an individual has been refused asylum in one member state and this has been rejected, the individual in question may not seek asylum in any of the other signatory states. However, as immigration

---

28. The *Political Declaration by the Governments of the Member States on the free movement of persons* is reproduced in *Treaties Establishing the European Communities*, abridged edn, OOPEC, Luxembourg, 1987, p. 595.

29. The Dublin Convention, on Asylum of 15 June 1990 is reproduced in Cm 1623, HMSO, London, September 1991. Denmark became a signatory to the Convention in June 1991. However, by June 1993 only six signatories had actually ratified the Convention.

into the Community increased with the collapse of the Soviet Union and the outbreak of war in the former Yugoslavia, further action in the direction of a common immigration and asylum policy was deemed necessary. Consequently, in June 1991 the twelve EC member states agreed to set up a Quick Reaction Consultation Centre to deal with large-scale and sudden migratory flows into the Community. Furthermore, the Commission, which was now being involved in the discussions held within the framework of TREVI, was asked to prepare reports on immigration and asylum as well as a set of proposals for a Community response to the current situation in Europe.

However, while EC ministers acknowledged the need, as laid down in the Commission's reports,[30] for a common approach to the problems posed by the increase in immigration into the Community and the rising number of applications for asylum, they were reluctant to see immigration and asylum policy transferred to the supranational EC level. Consequently, both areas appear in the third pillar of the European Union created by the TEU, and it is only visa policy which has been made a competence of the EC. However, in providing for the transfer of areas covered in Title VI of the TEU on cooperation in the fields of justice and home affairs to within the competences of the Community (Article K.9), it can be argued that the Twelve at Maastricht did not wish to rule out the development of single or common EC immigration and asylum policies in the foreseeable future. Indeed, the inclusion of Article K.9, in addition to the TEU's review clause (Article N), implies that the Twelve are intent on transferring some areas covered by Articles K.1(1−6) into the Treaty of Rome at some point before the Intergovernmental Conference, to be convened for 1996, has finished its work. If this is not the case, the purpose of Article K.9 appears to be undermined.[31]

q.v. Articles 100c and 100d pp. 149–50.

q.v. Article N p. 356.

While external pressures were requiring the Twelve to develop more coordinated immigration and asylum policies, the perceived consequences for internal security of completing the Internal Market were forcing governments to consider intensifying cooperation in other traditional areas of TREVI-based activity. As a result, following the European Council in Rhodes in December 1990, Coordination Group — Free Movement was established to ensure that preparations for the abolition of internal border controls by 31 December 1992 would proceed smoothly, and that the necessary information-exchange process would be operable. This was followed in December 1989 by the creation of a Coordination Group on Drugs (CELAD). Its objectives, which in many respects build on those which have been pursued within the Council of Europe's Pompidou Group set up in 1971, are to promote cooperation, both among the Twelve and with third states and international organizations, on all drug-related matters. These include combating drug trafficking, preventing money laundering, and monitoring drugs which have the potential of being misused. The importance attached to controlling illegal drug-related activities was reinforced in 1991 with the proposal to set up a European Drugs Unit and the subsequent moves in 1993 to establish a European

---

30. *Communication on Immigration*, SEC(91)1855, Brussels, 23 October 1991; *Communication on Asylum*, SEC(91)1857, Brussels, 11 October 1991.

31. This is borne out by Declaration 31 which outlines the aim of the member states to apply Article K.9 to certain aspects of their asylum policies by the end of 1993 (see p. 441).

anti-drug squad as part of the embryonic Europol. Finally, the member states have set up two groups to promote customs cooperation. These are GAM '92 which encourages cooperation in combating illegal trade, particularly in strategic goods, armaments and pornography, and SCENT, which acts as a forum in which the Twelve can adopt measures to fight fraud.

However, while the activities of the TREVI groups have involved all member states, closer cooperation in matters covered by Title VI has been pursued by certain member states within the framework of the Schengen Agreement. This was set up by the original six EC member states in 1985 in an attempt to remove all controls on the movement of persons between their countries in advance of the envisaged completion of the Internal Market on 31 December 1992. Hence, it was originally proposed that controls would be removed by 1 January 1990. However, despite the initial enthusiasm for the proposal the date has been altered on a number of occasions, thus casting a shadow over the efforts of the signatories to remove all internal border controls. Nevertheless, the impetus the Schengen countries gave to the development of cooperation between EC member states on matters relating to justice and home affairs should not be underestimated.

*q.v.
Schengen
Agreement
pp. 125–6.*

Indeed, much of the pressure for closer cooperation which led to the establishment of the various TREVI sub-groups noted above and more significantly the inclusion of the pillar on cooperation in justice and home affairs in the TEU, was a direct consequence of efforts pursued by the Schengen countries to harmonize their policies *vis-à-vis* external borders, visas, asylum, immigration, and police and judicial cooperation. Provided the Single Market becomes a reality such pressure will undoubtedly increase. Indeed, the establishment of Europol in mid-1993 to help coordinate police activities more effectively is an indication of how important many of the member states view cooperation in justice and home affairs. Furthermore, pressure for developing such cooperation and implementing the provisions of Title VI is increasing as the number of asylum seekers grows and immigration reaches levels three times those of the mid-1980s. Hence, it would appear appropriate for the member states to act. However, resistance from some quarters to common policies means that future action may be limited. Nevertheless, with a firm legal basis for cooperation now established by the TEU and the Commission eager to see this utilized, few member states will be able to ignore the need and opportunities for joint action.

FURTHER READING

Blanc, H., 'Schengen: le chemin de la libre circulation en Europe', *Revue du Marché commun et de l'Union européen*, no. 351, 1991, pp. 722–6.

Callovi, G., 'Regulation of immigration in 1993: pieces of the European Community jig-saw puzzle', *International Migration Review*, vol. 26, no. 2, 1992, pp. 353–72.

Carlier, J. -Y., 'Harmonisation des politiques d'asile des pays d'Europe: les enjeux juridiques', *Revue de droit des étrangers*, no. 69, 1992, pp. 153–9.

Hailbronner, K., 'Perspectives of a harmonization of the law of asylum after the Maastricht Summit', *Common Market Law Review*, vol. 29, no. 5, 1992, pp. 917–39.

Joly, D. *et al. Refugees — Asylum in Europe?*, Westview, Oxford, 1993.

Lary, H. de, 'Les problèmes de l'immigration dans l'Europe de demain', *Revue française des affaires sociales*, vol. 46, Décembre 1992, pp. 197–217.

Lejeune, P., *La Coopération Policière en Europe contre le terrorisme*, Etablissements Emile Bruylant S. A., Brussels, 1992.

Lodge, J. 'Internal security and judicial cooperation', in Lodge, J. (ed.), *The European Community and the Challenge of the Future*, 2nd edn, Pinter, London, 1993. pp. 315–39.

Mortimer, E., 'Behind closed doors', *Financial Times*, 28 October 1992.

Nanz, K. P., 'Der "3 Pfeiler der Europäischen Union" Zusammenarbeit in der Innen- und Justizpolitik', *Integration*, vol. 15, no. 3, 1992, pp. 126–40.

O'Keefe, D., 'The free movement of persons in the Single Market', *European Law Review*, vol. 17, no. 1, 1991, pp. 3–19.

Politische Studien, 'Das Inkrafttreten des Schengener Abkommen — Eine Herausforderung für die innere Sicherheit Europas', vol. 43, no. 326, 1992.

Rupprecht, R. and Hellenthal, M. (eds.), *Innere Sicherheit im Europäischen Binnenmarkt, Strategien und Optionen für die Zukunft Europas — Grundlagen, vol. 10*, Bertelsmann Stiftung, Gütersloh, 1992.

Schutte, J. J. E., 'Schengen: its meaning for the free movement of persons in Europe', *Common Market Law Review*, vol. 28, no. 3, 1991, pp. 549–70.

'The European Community after 1992: the freedom of movement of people and its limitations', *Vanderbilt Journal of Transnational Law*, vol. 25, no. 4, 1992, pp. 643–80.

Tomuschat, C., 'A right to asylum in Europe', *Human Rights Law Journal*, vol. 13, no. 7–8, 1992, pp. 257–65.

Vaeren, C. van der 'Le Comité Européen de Lutte Anti-Drogue (CELAD) — Essai d'analyse institutionelle', *Revue du Marché commun et de l'Union européen*, no. 366, 1993, pp. 207–21.

Weber, Al., 'Einwanderungs- und Asylpolitik nach Maastricht', *Zeitschrift für Ausländerrecht und Ausländerpolitik*, 1993/1, pp. 11–18.

v. Protocols

As mentioned earlier the TEU consists of seven Titles supplemented by 17 Protocols. These Protocols appear within the actual Treaty immediately before the Final Act. Consequently, they are an integral part of the TEU. They are then listed and numbered in the Final Act along with the Declarations. Sixteen of the Protocols contain provisions relating to the EC in its post-TEU form and are thus annexed to the amended Treaty of Rome, although one Protocol, that on privileges and immunities (Protocol 7),[32] does relate to all three European Communities and not to the EC alone.[33] The final Protocol, that relating to Ireland's anti-abortion legislation, is actually annexed to the TEU and the Treaties establishing the European Communities (Protocol 17).[34]

q.v. Final Act pp. 427–9.

Like the seven Titles which precede them, the Protocols have been agreed

32. The numbering used to denote the Protocols is that found in the list contained in the Final Act, see pp. 428–9.

33. These Protocols join the thirteen Protocols already attached to the Treaty of Rome. These include eleven which were attached to the Treaty when it was signed on 25 March 1957 (Protocol on the Statute of the European Investment Bank (see pp. 544–53); Protocol on German Internal Trade and Connected Problems; Protocol on certain provisions relating to France; Protocol on Italy; Protocol on the Grand Duchy of Luxembourg; Protocol on Goods originating in and coming from Certain Countries and enjoying Special Treatment when imported into a Member State; Protocol on the Treatment to be applied to Products within the Province of the European Coal and Steel Community in respect of Algeria and the Overseas Departments of the French Republic; Protocol on Mineral Oils and Certain of their Derivatives; Protocol on the Application of the Treaty establishing the European Economic Community to the non-European Parts of the Kingdom of the Netherlands; Protocol on the Tariff Quota for Imports of Bananas; and the Protocol on the Tariff Quota for Imports of Raw Coffee). These are reproduced in *Treaties establishing the European Communities*, OOPEC, Luxembourg, 1973, pp. 407–61. The two remaining Protocols are the Protocol on the Statute of the Court of Justice of the European Economic Community, attached to the Treaty of Rome on 17 April 1957; and the Protocol on Special Arrangements for Greenland (13 March 1984). The first of these is reproduced below in Annex 6, while the Protocol relating to Greenland can be found in the *Treaty amending, with regard to Greenland, the Treaties establishing the European Communities*, OJL 29, 1 February 1985. A further Protocol, the Protocol on Privileges and Immunities is attached to the Merger Treaty. This is also reproduced below in Annex 6. No Protocols were attached to the Treaty of Rome by the SEA.

34. A Declaration relating to this Protocol was adopted by the signatories to the TEU on 1 May 1992 (see p. 536).

by the so-called 'HIGH CONTRACTING PARTIES'. Furthermore, it is clearly stated in Article 239 of the Treaty of Rome that protocols 'form an integral part' of the Treaty. Consequently, as Curtin has pointed out, the Protocols 'must be considered as if belonging to the Treaty itself with all the consequences that entails in terms of judicial protection and legal effect'.[35] Thus, unlike the Declarations which are found attached to the Final Act of the TEU, the provisions contained within the Protocols are legally binding on the member states of the Union and must be applied in conjunction with the Treaty provisions to which they relate.[36]

q.v. Article 239 p. 351.

The function of the Protocols is essentially to elucidate certain provisions of the Treaties to which they relate. Hence, they often contain lengthy and detailed provisions which, if contained in the Treaty proper, would make it even more cumbersome to read. Indeed, of the sixteen Protocols annexed to the Treaty of Rome by the TEU, three clarify the provisions of specific Treaty Articles or provisions. A further six relate to exemptions from Treaty provisions granted to individual member states; four relate to rules governing institutions created by Treaty provisions; two contain political declarations by the signatories; and one relates to additional commitments entered into by 11 of the member states. However, whereas the need to avoid excessive 'clutter' within the Treaty of Rome is welcome, particularly with respect to the Protocols relating to the institutions of EMU, concerns have been voiced over the nature of the Protocols adopted at Maastricht compared with that of those originally attached to the Treaty.

Whereas the majority of the Protocols agreed in the 1950s and 1960s were essentially transitional in nature and seen to contain only temporary derogations, those agreed upon within the context of the TEU appear to either restate existing exemptions (Protocol 1 on second homes in Denmark,) or provide permanent derogations from new areas of Community integration (Protocol 11 on the United Kingdom's opt-out from Stage III of EMU,). This runs counter to the express objective of the Union, laid down in Article B of the TEU, of maintaining in full the *acquis communautaire* and of building on it. As a result, commentators have accused the TEU of 'hijacking' the *acquis* and of undermining the general application of EC law.[37] Moreover, doubts have been raised as to the Community's and indeed Union's ability to maintain clear and coherent legal structures in the light of the Protocols. These can be highlighted by looking at the Protocol on Social Policy.

q.v. Article B p. 57.

Referred to in Britain as the United Kingdom's second opt-out, and more widely as the 'Social Chapter', the existence of the Protocol on Social Policy (Protocol 14,) was instrumental in securing the United Kingdom's agreement to

---

35. Curtin, D., 'The constitutional status of the Union: a Europe of bits and pieces', *Common Market Law Review*, vol. 30, no. 1, 1993, pp. 17–69. Article 208 of the Euratom Treaty contains an identical provision relating to the Protocols attached to the treaty.

36. The legally binding status of treaty Protocols within Community law was defined during the formative years of the European Coal and Steel Community. See Cases 7 and 9/54, *Industries Sidérurigiques Luxembourgeoises v. HA* [1956] 175 at p. 194.

37. Curtin, 'The Constitutional Status of the Union', pp. 44–61; Wincott, D., *The Treaty of Maastricht: An Adequate 'Constitution' for the European Union?*, European Public Policy Institute Occasional Papers 93/6, University of Warwick, 1993, pp. 12–13.

the TEU at Maastricht in December 1991. This is because it effectively exempts the United Kingdom from any future social policy legislation other than that adopted on the basis of existing provisions in the Treaty of Rome. The other eleven member states may, as a result of an agreement attached to the Protocol, adopt legislation aimed at fulfilling the objectives laid down in the Social Charter adopted by them in 1989. Such legislation is to be adopted using the Community's institutions and decision-making procedures, albeit without the participation of the United Kingdom, and subject to the jurisdiction of the ECJ. While this may have been an acceptable political solution to UK objections concerning the extension of Community competences in the social field, as Curtin points out, it appears to institutionalize the possibility of the differentiated application of EC law, contrary to the provisions of Article 227. Thus it undermines the concept of developing the *acquis*. Moreover, it sets a precedent for future IGCs, in effect sanctioning permanent exemptions from new areas of Community competence.

q.v. Social Charter p. 197.

q.v. Article 227 p. 337.

Turning to the remaining Protocols, of the three which clarify specific provisions contained within the amended Treaty of Rome, two relate to the criteria which member states must meet if they are to proceed to Stage III of EMU. The first defines various values to be used in assessing whether a member state has an excessive government deficit as referred to in Article 104c of the amended Treaty of Rome (Protocol 5), while the second clarifies the provisions regarding the convergence criteria laid down in Article 109j (Protocol 6). Whereas, these two Protocols raise few, if any, legal or political questions, the same cannot be said for the third Protocol in this category. Protocol 2, the so-called 'Barber' Protocol, restricts the definition of remuneration under Article 119 of the Treaty of Rome. While seemingly straightforward, the Protocol effectively undermines the ECJ's ability to clarify its own judgments by inserting into EC law a politically acceptable and financially convenient interpretation of a given Treaty provision.[38]

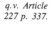
q.v. Article 104c pp. 162–4.

q.v. Article 119 p. 192.

As significant for the United Kingdom, and indeed the EC, as the Protocol on Social Policy, is the Protocol containing the so-called UK 'opt-out' exempting the United Kingdom from moving to Stage III of EMU without a decision to do so from the UK Parliament and the government (Protocol 11). While necessary for gaining UK acceptance of the TEU, the Protocol does institutionalize the idea of what has been widely described as a 'two-speed Europe'. However, it should be noted that the Protocol does not commit the United Kingdom to proceed to Stage III of EMU at any point in the future, specified or unspecified. Hence, introducing the concept of 'speeds' here may be seen as misleading. Rather, the Protocol should be regarded as providing the United Kingdom with a permanent opt-out from full EMU, should it wish to avail itself of it.

In addition to the United Kingdom's Protocol on EMU five other Protocols provide individual member states with exemptions from provisions laid down in the amended Treaty of Rome. Of these, three relate to Denmark and include Denmark's right to maintain — in direct contrast to the provisions of Article 59 of the Treaty of Rome — existing legislation on the acquisition of second homes

---

38. For further details, see Curtin, 'The Constitutional Status of the Union', pp. 50–52.

(Protocol 1);[39] the Bank of Denmark's right to carry out its existing responsibilities with regard to Greenland and the Faroe Islands (Protocol 8); and Denmark's right not to participate in Stage III of EMU (Protocol 12). The two other Protocols relate to the interest-free credit facility Portugal provides the Azores and Madeira (Protocol 9), and France's right to maintain its monetary control over French overseas territories (Protocol 13). A seventh Protocol (Protocol 17), and one which applies to the provisions of the TEU and the Treaties establishing the European Communities, grants the anti-abortion provisions in the Irish Constitution special status. Thus, nothing in any of the above Treaties may affect the application in Ireland of Article 40.3.3 of the Constitution. Once again, the implication for the future of the Union of this Protocol is that it sets a precedent for the application of specific national constitutional provisions to be exempt from the law of the Community. Given the concerns voiced during the ratification debate over constitutional guarantees being undermined by the TEU, notably in Germany, it is possible that the precedent Protocol 17 sets could prove highly damaging to the integrative efforts of the EC and of the Union, and to the uniform application of EC law.[40]

The longest of the seventeen Protocols are the two which relate to the European System of Central Banks and the European Central Bank, and the European Monetary Institute. These both contain the statutes of the relevant institutions, and thus fulfil an identical function to earlier protocols on the European Investment Bank and the Court of Auditors. The first of the two Protocols contains the statute of the ESCB and the ECB and consists of 53 Articles divided into nine Chapters (Protocol 3). These cover the constitution of the ESCB; the objectives and task of the bank; its organization; its monetary functions and operations; prudential supervision; the bank's financial provisions; general provisions; the procedure for amending the Statute; and various transitional and other provisions. Several of the Articles are also contained within the second of the Protocols concerning the Statute of the European Monetary Institute (Protocol 4). This Protocol is nevertheless shorter, containing only 23 Articles. The Statute and functions of all three institutions have been discussed earlier in the *Handbook*. The two remaining Protocols which relate to institutions state that the Committee of Regions and the Economic and Social Committee are to have a common organizational structure (Protocol 16), and add a new Article to the existing Protocol attached to the Treaty of Rome concerning the privileges and immunities of the European Communities (Protocol 7).

Of the two Protocols which contain political declarations by the twelve, the first declares the irreversible character of the Community's movement to Stage III of EMU and requires all member states to respect the will of the Community to proceed towards this goal (Protocol 10). The second declaratory Protocol, included in the Treaty to reaffirm the Community's aim to compensate its poorer members for the possible economic impact of EMU on their economies, concerns strengthening economic and social cohesion among member states (Protocol 15).

q.v. European Investment Bank pp. 312–13.

q.v. Court of Auditors pp. 292–96.

q.v. EMU pp. 155–8.

---

39. Greece sought an identical Protocol, but the request was rejected on the basis that it was made too late.
40. For a fuller discussion of the debate surrounding Protocol 17, see Curtin, 'The Constitutional Status of the Union', pp. 47–49.

Protocol on the acquisition of property in Denmark

THE HIGH CONTRACTING PARTIES,
DESIRING to settle certain particular problems relating to Denmark,
HAVE AGREED UPON the following provision, which shall be annexed
to the Treaty establishing the European Community:

Notwithstanding the provisions of this Treaty, Denmark may maintain the
existing legislation on the acquisition of second homes.

Protocol concerning Article 119 of the Treaty establishing the European Community

THE HIGH CONTRACTING PARTIES,
HAVE AGREED UPON the following provision, which shall be annexed
to the Treaty establishing the European Community:

For the purposes of Article 119 of this Treaty, benefits under occupational
social security schemes shall not be considered as remuneration if and in
so far as they are attributable to periods of employment prior to 17 May
1990, except in the case of workers or those claiming under them who have
before that date initiated legal proceedings or introduced an equivalent claim
under the applicable national law.

Protocol on the Statute of the European System of Central Banks and of the European Central Bank

THE HIGH CONTRACTING PARTIES,
DESIRING to lay down the Statute of the European System of Central Banks
and of the European Central Bank provided for in Article 4a of the Treaty
establishing the European Community,
HAVE AGREED upon the following provisions, which shall be annexed to
the treaty establishing the European Community:

Chapter I Constitution of the ESCB

ARTICLE 1
The European System of Central Banks

1.1. The European System of Central Banks (ESCB) and the European
Central Bank (ECB) shall be established in accordance with Article 4a of
this Treaty; they shall perform their tasks and carry on their activities in
accordance with the provisions of this Treaty and of this Statute.

1.2. In accordance with Article 106(1) of this Treaty, the ESCB shall be
composed of the ECB and the central banks of the Member States ('national
central banks'). The Insitut monétaire luxembourgeois will be the central
bank of Luxembourg.

Chapter II Objectives and tasks of the ESCB

ARTICLE 2

Objectives

In accordance with Article 105(1) of this Treaty, the primary objective of the ESCB shall be to maintain price stability. Without prejudice to the objective of price stability, it shall support the general economic policies in the Community with a view to contributing to the achievement of the objectives of the Community as laid down in Article 2 of this Treaty. The ESCB shall act in accordance with the principle of an open market economy with free competition, favouring an efficient allocation of resources, and in compliance with the principles set out in Article 3a of this Treaty.

ARTICLE 3

Tasks

3.1. In accordance with Article 105(2) of this Treaty, the basic tasks to be carried out through the ESCB shall be:

— to define and implement the monetary policy of the Community;
— to conduct foreign exchange operations consistent with the provisions of Article 109 of this Treaty;
— to hold and manage the official foreign reserves of the Member States;
— to promote the smooth operation of payment systems.

3.2. In accordance with Article 105(3) of this Treaty, the third indent of Article 3.1 shall be without prejudice to the holding and management by the governments of Member States of foreign exchange working balances.

3.3. In accordance with Article 105(5) of this Treaty, the ESCB shall contribute to the smooth conduct of policies pursued by the competent authorities relating to the prudential supervision of credit institutions and the stability of the financial system.

ARTICLE 4

Advisory functions

In accordance with Article 105(4) of this Treaty:

(a) the ECB shall be consulted:

— on any proposed Community act in its fields of competence;
— by national authorities regarding any draft legislative provision in its fields of competence, but within the limits and under the conditions set out by the Council in accordance with the procedure laid down in Article 42;

(b) the ECB may submit opinions to the appropriate Community institutions or bodies or to national authorities on matters in its fields of competence.

ARTICLE 5

Collection of statistical information

5.1. In order to undertake the tasks of the ESCB, the ECB, assisted by the national central banks, shall collect the necessary statistical information either from the competent national authorities or directly from economic agents. For these purposes it shall cooperate with the Community institutions or bodies and with the competent authorities of the Member States or third countries and with international organizations.

5.2. The national central banks shall carry out, to the extent possible, the tasks described in Article 5.1.

5.3. The ECB shall contribute to the harmonization, where necessary, of the rules and practices governing the collection, compilation and distribution of statistics in the areas within its fields of competence.

5.4. The Council, in accordance with the procedure laid down in Article 42, shall define the natural and legal persons subject to reporting requirements, the confidentiality regime and the appropriate provisions for enforcement.

ARTICLE 6

International cooperation

6.1. In the field of international cooperation involving the tasks entrusted to the ESCB, the ECB shall decide how the ESCB shall be represented.

6.2. The ECB and, subject to its approval, the national central banks may participate in international monetary institutions.

6.3. Articles 6.1 and 6.2 shall be without prejudice to Article 109(4) of this Treaty.

Chapter III Organization of the ESCB

ARTICLE 7

Independence

In accordance with Article 107 of this Treaty, when exercising the powers and carrying out the tasks and duties conferred upon them by this Treaty and this Statute, neither the ECB, nor a national central bank, nor any member of their decision-making bodies shall seek or take instructions from Community institutions or bodies, from any government of a Member State or from any other body. The Community institutions and bodies and the governments of the Member States undertake to respect this principle and not to seek to influence the members of the decision-making bodies of the ECB or of the national central banks in the performance of their tasks.

ARTICLE 8

General principle

The ESCB shall be governed by the decision-making bodies of the ECB.

ARTICLE 9

The European Central Bank

9.1. The ECB which, in accordance with Article 106(2) of this Treaty, shall have legal personality, shall enjoy in each of the Member States the most extensive legal capacity accorded to legal persons under its law; it may, in particular, acquire or dispose of movable and immovable property and may be a party to legal proceedings.

9.2. The ECB shall ensure that the tasks conferred upon the ESCB under Article 105(2), (3) and (5) of this Treaty are implemented either by its own activities pursuant to this Statute or through the national central bank pursuant to Articles 12.1 and 14.

9.3 In accordance with Article 106(3) of this Treaty, the decision-making bodies of the ECB shall be the Governing Council and the Executive Board.

ARTICLE 10

The Governing Council

10.1. In accordance with Article 109a(1) of this Treaty, the Governing Council shall comprise the members of the Executive Board of the ECB and the Governors of the national central banks.

10.2. Subject to Article 10.3, only members of the Governing Council present in person shall have the right to vote. By way of derogation from this rule, the Rules of Procedure referred to in Article 12.3 may lay down that members of the Governing Council may cast their vote by means of teleconferencing.

These rules shall also provide that a member of the Governing Council who is prevented from voting for a prolonged period may appoint an alternate as a member of the Governing Council.

Subject to Articles 10.3 and 11.3, each member of the Governing Council shall have one vote. Save as otherwise provided for in this Statute, the Governing Council shall act by a simple majority. In the event of a tie the President shall have the casting vote.

In order for the Governing Council to vote, there shall be a quorum of two-thirds of the members. If the quorum is not met, the President may convene an extraordinary meeting at which decisions may be taken without regard to the quorum.

10.3. For any decisions to be taken under Articles 28, 29, 30, 32, 33 and 51, the votes in the Governing Council shall be weighted according to the national central banks' shares in the subscribed capital of the ECB. The weights of the votes of the members of the Executive Board shall be zero. A decision requiring a qualified majority shall be adopted if the votes cast in favour represent at least two-thirds of the subscribed capital of the ECB and represent at least half of the shareholders. If a Governor in unable to be present, he may nominate an alternate to cast his weighted vote.

10.4. The proceedings of the meetings shall be confidential. The Governing Council may decide to make the outcome of its deliberations public.

10.5. The Governing Council shall meet at least ten times a year.

ARTICLE 11

The Executive Board

11.1. In accordance with Article 109a(2)(a) of this Treaty, the Executive Board shall comprise the President, the Vice-President and four other members.
The members shall perform their duties on a full-time basis. No member shall engage in any occupation, whether gainful or not, unless exemption is exceptionally granted by the Governing Council.

11.2. In accordance with Article 109a(2)(b) of this Treaty, the President, the Vice-President and the other Members of the Executive Board shall be appointed from among persons of recognized standing and professional experience in monetary or banking matters by common accord of the governments of the Member States at the level of the Heads of State or of Government, on a recommendation from the Council after it has consulted the European Parliament and the Governing Council.

Their term of office shall be 8 years and shall not be renewable. Only nationals of Member States may be members of the Executive Board.

11.3. The terms and conditions of employment of the members of the Executive Board, in particular their salaries, pensions and other social security benefits shall be the subject of contracts with the ECB and shall be fixed by the Governing Council on a proposal from a Committee comprising three members appointed by the Governing Council and three members appointed by the Council. The members of the Executive Board shall not have the right to vote on matters referred to in this paragraph.

11.4. If a member of the Executive Board no longer fulfils the conditions required for the performance of his duties or if he has been guilty of serious misconduct, the Court of Justice may, on application by the Governing Council or the Executive Board, compulsorily retire him.

11.5. Each member of the Executive Board present in person shall have the right to vote and shall have, for that purpose, one vote. Save as otherwise provided, the Executive Board shall act by a simple majority of the votes cast. In the event of a tie, the President shall have the casting vote. The voting arrangements shall be specified in the Rules of Procedure referred to in Article 12.3.

11.6. The Executive Board shall be responsible for the current business of the ECB.

11.7. Any vacancy on the Executive Board shall be filled by the appointment of a new member in accordance with Article 11.2.

ARTICLE 12

Responsibilities of the decision-making bodies

12.1. The Governing Council shall adopt the guidelines and take the decisions necessary to ensure the performance of the tasks entrusted to the ESCB under this Treaty and this Statute. The Governing Council shall formulate the monetary policy of the Community including, as appropriate, decisions relating to intermediate monetary objectives, key interest rates and the supply of reserves in the ESCB and shall establish the necessary guidelines for their implementation.

The Executive Board shall implement monetary policy in accordance with the guidelines and decisions laid down by the Governing Council. In doing so the Executive Board shall give the necessary instructions to national central banks. In addition the Executive Board may have certain powers delegated to it where the Governing Council so decides.

To the extent deemed possible and appropriate and without prejudice to the provisions of this Article, the ECB shall have recourse to the national central banks to carry out operations which form part of the tasks of the ESCB.

12.2. The Executive Board shall have responsibility for the preparation of meetings of the Governing Council.

12.3. The Governing Council shall adopt Rules of Procedure which determine the internal organization of the ECB and its decision-making bodies.

12.4. The Governing Council shall exercise the advisory functions referred to Article 4.

12.5. The Governing Council shall take the decisions referred to Article 6.

ARTICLE 13

The President

13.1. The President or, in his absence, the Vice-President shall chair the governing Council and the Executive Board of the ECB.

13.2. Without prejudice to Article 39, the President or his nominee shall represent the ECB externally.

ARTICLE 14

National central banks

14.1. In accordance with Article 108 of this Treaty, each Member State shall ensure, at the latest at the date of the establishment of the ESCB, that its national legislation, including the statutes of its national central bank, is compatible with this Treaty and this Statute.

14.2. The statutes of national central banks shall, in particular, provide that the term of office of a Governor of a national central bank shall be no less than 5 years.

A Governor may be relieved from office only if he no longer fulfils the conditions required for the performance of his duties or if he has been guilty of serious misconduct. A decision to this effect may be referred to the Court of Justice by the Governor concerned or the Governing Council on grounds of infringement of this Treaty or of any rule of law relating to its application. Such proceedings shall be instituted within two months of the publication of the decision or of its notification to the plaintiff or, in the absence thereof, of the day on which it came to the knowledge of the latter, as the case may be.

14.3. The national central banks are an integral part of the ESCB and shall act in accordance with the guidelines and instructions of ECB. The Governing Council shall take the necessary steps to ensure compliance with the guidelines and instructions of the ECB, and shall require that any necessary information be given to it.

14.4 National central banks may perform functions other than those specified in this Statute unless the Governing Council finds, by a majority of two thirds of the votes cast, that these interfere with the objectives and tasks of the ESCB. Such functions shall be performed on the responsibility and liability of national central banks and shall not be regarded as being part of the functions of the ESCB.

ARTICLE 15

Reporting commitments

15.1. The ECB shall draw up and publish reports on the activities of the ESCB at least quarterly.

15.2. A consolidated financial statement of the ESCB shall be published each week.

15.3. In accordance with Article 109b(3) of this Treaty, the ECB shall address an annual report on the activities of the ESCB and on the monetary policy of both the previous and the current year to the European Parliament, the Council and the Commission, and also the European Council.

15.4. The reports and statements referred to in this Article shall be made available to interested parties free of charge.

ARTICLE 16

Bank notes

In accordance with Article 105a(1) of this Treaty, the Governing Council shall have the exclusive right to authorize the issue of bank notes within the Community. The ECB and the national central banks may issue such notes.

The bank notes issued by the ECB and the national central banks shall be the only such notes to have the status of legal tender within the Community.

The ECB shall respect as far as possible existing practices regarding the issue and design of bank notes.

Chapter IV Monetary functions and operations of the ESCB

ARTICLE 17

Accounts with the ECB and the national central banks

In order to conduct their operations, the ECB and the national central banks may open accounts for credit institutions, public entities and other market participants and accept assets, including book-entry securities, as collateral.

ARTICLE 18

Open market and credit operations

18.1. In order to achieve the objectives of the ESCB and to carry out its tasks, the ECB and the national central banks may:

— operate in the financial markets by buying and selling outright (spot and forward) or under repurchase agreement and by lending or borrowing

claims and marketable instruments, whether in Community or in non-Community currencies, as well as precious metals;
— conduct credit operations with credit institutions and other market participants, with lending being based on adequate collateral.

18.2. The ECB shall establish general principles for open market and credit operations carried out by itself or the national central banks, including for the announcement of conditions under which they stand ready to enter into such transactions.

ARTICLE 19   Minimum reserves

19.1. Subject to Article 2, the ECB may require credit institutions established in Member States to hold minimum reserves on accounts with the ECB and national central banks in pursuance of monetary policy objectives. Regulations concerning the calculation and determination of the required minimum reserves may be established by the Governing Council. In cases of non-compliance the ECB shall be entitled to levy penalty interest and to impose other sanctions with comparable effect.

19.2. For the application of this Article, the Council shall, in accordance with the procedure laid down in Article 42, define the basis for minimum reserves and the maximum permissible ratios between those reserves and their basis, as well as the appropriate sanctions in cases of non-compliance.

ARTICLE 20   Other instruments of monetary control

The Governing Council may, by a majority of two-thirds of the votes cast, decide upon the use of such other operational methods of monetary control as it sees fit, respecting Article 2.

The Council shall, in accordance with the procedure laid down in Article 42, define the scope of such methods if they impose obligations on third parties.

ARTICLE 21   Operations with public entities

21.1. In accordance with Article 104 of the Treaty, overdrafts or any other type of credit facility with the ECB or with the national central banks in favour of Community institutions or bodies, central governments, regional, local or other public authorities, other bodies governed by public law, or public undertakings of Member States shall be prohibited, as shall the purchase directly from them by the ECB or national central banks of debt instruments.

21.2. The ECB and national central banks may act as fiscal agents for the entities referred to in 21.1.

21.3. The provisions of this Article shall not apply to publicly-owned credit institutions which, in the context of the supply of reserves by central banks, shall be given the same treatment by national central banks and the ECB as private credit institutions.

ARTICLE 22   Clearing and payment systems
The ECB and national central banks may provide facilities, and the ECB may make regulations, to ensure efficient and sound clearing and payment systems within the Community and with other countries.

ARTICLE 23   External operations
The ECB and national central banks may:

— establish relations with central banks and financial institutions in other countries and, where appropriate, with international organizations;

— acquire and sell spot and forward all types of foreign exchange assets and precious metals; the term 'foreign exchange asset' shall include securities and all other assets in the currency of any country or units of account in whatever form held;

— hold and manage the assets referred to in this Article;

— conduct all types of banking transactions in relations with third countries and international organizations, including borrowing and lending operations.

ARTICLE 24   Other operations

In addition to operations arising from their tasks, the ECB and national central banks may enter into operations for their administrative purposes or for their staff.

Chapter V Prudential supervision

ARTICLE 25   Prudential supervision

25.1. The ECB may offer advice to and be consulted by the Council, the Commission and the competent authorities of the Member States on the scope and implementation of Community legislation relating to the prudential supervision of credit institutions and to the stability of the financial system.

25.2. In accordance with any decision of the Council under Article 105(6) of this Treaty, the ECB may perform specific tasks concerning policies relating to the prudential supervision of credit institutions and other financial institutions with the exception of insurance undertakings.

Chapter VI Financial provisions of the ESCB

ARTICLE 26   Financial accounts

26.1. The financial year of the ECB and national central banks shall begin on the first day of January and end on the last day of December.

26.2. The annual accounts of the ECB shall be drawn up the Executive Board, in accordance with the principles established by the Governing Council. The accounts shall be approved by the Governing Council and shall thereafter be published.

26.3. For analytical and operational purposes, the Executive Board shall draw up a consolidated balance sheet of the ESCB, comprising those assets and liabilities of the national central banks that fall within the ESCB.

26.4. For the application of this Article, the Governing Council shall establish the necessary rules for standardizing the accounting and reporting of operations undertaken by the national central banks.

ARTICLE 27   Auditing

27.1. The account of the ECB and national central banks shall be audited by independent external auditors recommended by the Governing Council and approved by the Council. The auditors shall have full power to examine all books and accounts of the ECB and national central banks and obtain full information about their transactions.

27.2. The provisions of Article 188c of this Treaty shall only apply to an examination of the operational efficiency of the management of the ECB.

ARTICLE 28

Capital of the ECB

28.1. The capital of the ECB, which shall become operational upon its establishment, shall be ECU 5 000 million. The capital may be increased by such amounts as may be decided by the Governing Council acting by the qualified majority provided for in Article 10.3, within the limits and under the conditions set by the Council under the procedure laid down in Article 42.

28.2. The national central banks shall be the sole subscribers to and holders of the capital of the ECB. The subscription of capital shall be according to the key established in accordance with Article 29.

28.3. The Governing Council, acting by the qualified majority provided for in Article 10.3, shall determine the extent to which and the form in which the capital shall be paid up.

28.4. Subject to Article 28.5, the shares of the national central banks in the subscribed capital of the ECB may not be transferred, pledged or attached.

28.5. If the key referred to in Article 29 is adjusted, the national central banks shall transfer among themselves capital shares to the extent necessary to ensure that the distribution of capital shares corresponds to the adjusted key. The Governing Council shall determine the terms and conditions of such transfers.

ARTICLE 29

Key for capital subscription

29.1. When in accordance with the procedure referred to in Article 109l(1) of this Treaty the ESCB and the ECB have been established, the key for subscription of the ECB's capital shall be established. Each national central bank shall be assigned a weighting in this key which shall be equal to the sum of:

— 50% of the share of its respective Member State in the population of the Community in the penultimate year preceding the establishment of the ESCB;
— 50% of the share of its respective Member State in the gross domestic product at market prices of the Community as recorded in the last five years preceding the penultimate year before the establishment of the ESCB;

The percentages shall be rounded up to the nearest multiple of 0.05 percentage points.

29.2 The statistical data to be used for the application of this Article shall be provided by the Commission in accordance with the rules adopted by the Council under the procedure provided for in Article 42.

29.3. The weightings assigned to the national central banks shall be adjusted every five years after the establishment of the ESCB by analogy with the provisions laid down in Article 29.1. The adjusted key shall apply with effect from the first day of the following year.

29.4. The Governing Council shall take all other measures necessary for the application of this Article.

ARTICLE 30

Transfer of foreign reserve assets to the ECB

30.1. Without prejudice to Article 28, the ECB shall be provided by the national central banks with foreign reserve assets, other than Member States' currencies, ECUs, IMF reserve positions and SDRs, up to an amount equivalent to ECU 50 000 million. The Governing Council shall decide upon the proportion to be called up by the ECB following its establishment and the amounts called up at later dates. The ECB shall have the full right to hold and manage the foreign reserves that are transferred to it and to use them for the purposes set out in this Statute.

30.2. The contributions of each national central bank shall be fixed in proportion to its share in the subscribed capital of the ECB.

30.3. Each national central bank shall be credited by the ECB with a claim equivalent to its contribution. The Governing Council shall determine the denomination and remuneration of such claims.

30.4. Further calls of foreign reserve assets beyond the limit set in Article 30.1. may be effected by the ECB, in accordance with Article 30.2, within the limits and under the conditions set by the Council in accordance with the procedure laid down in Article 42.

30.5. The ECB may hold and manage IMF reserve positions and SDRs and provide for the pooling of such assets.

30.6. The Governing Council shall take all other measures necessary for the application of this Article.

ARTICLE 31

Foreign reserve assets held by national central banks

31.1. The national central banks shall be allowed to perform transactions in fulfilment of their obligations towards international organizations in accordance with Article 23.

31.2. All other operations in foreign reserve assets remaining with the national central banks after the transfers referred to in Article 30, and Member States' transactions with their foreign exchange working balances shall, above a certain limit to be established within the framework of Article 31.3, be subject to approval by the ECB in order to ensure consistency with the exchange rate and monetary policies of the Community.

31.3. The Governing Council shall issue guidelines with a view to facilitating such operations.

ARTICLE 32

Allocation of monetary income of national central banks

32.1. The income accruing to the national central banks in the performance of the ESCB's monetary policy function (hereinafter referred to as 'monetary income') shall be allocated at the end of each financial year in accordance with the provisions of this Article.

32.2. Subject to Article 32.3, the amount of each national central bank's monetary income shall be equal to its annual income derived from its assets held against notes in circulation and deposit liabilities to credit institutions. These assets shall be earmarked by national central banks in accordance with guidelines to be established by the Governing Council.

32.3. If, after the start of the third stage, the balance sheet structures of the national central banks do not, in the judgment of the Governing Council, permit the application of Article 32.2, the Governing Council, acting by a qualified majority, may decide that, by way of derogation form Article 32.2, monetary income shall be measured according to an alternative method for a period of not more than five years.

32.4. The amount of each national central bank's monetary income shall be reduced by an amount equivalent to any interest paid by that central bank on its deposit liabilities to credit institutions in accordance with Article 19.

The Governing Council may decide that national central banks shall be indemnified against costs incurred in connection with the issue of bank notes or in exceptional circumstances for specific losses arising from monetary policy operations undertaken for the ESCB. Indemnification shall be in a form deemed appropriate in the judgment of the Governing Council; these amounts may be offset against the national central banks' monetary income.

32.5. The sum of the national central banks' monetary income shall be allocated to the national central banks in proportion to their paid-up shares in the capital of the ECB, subject to any decision taken by the Governing Council pursuant to Article 33.2.

32.6. The clearing and settlement of the balances arising from the allocation of monetary income shall be carried out by the ECB in accordance with guidelines established by the Governing Council.

32.7. The Governing Council shall take all other measures necessary for the application of this Article.

ARTICLE 33

Allocation of net profits and losses of the ECB

33.1. The net profit of the ECB shall be transferred in the following order:

(a) an amount to be determined by the Governing Council, which may not exceed 20 per cent of the net profit, shall be transferred to the general reserve fund subject to a limit equal to 100% of the capital;

(b) the remaining net profit shall be distributed to the shareholders of the ECB in proportion to their paid-up shares.

33.2. In the event of a loss incurred by the ECB, the shortfall may be offset against the general reserve fund of the ECB and, if necessary, following a decision by the Governing Council, against the monetary income of the relevant financial year in proportion and up to the amounts allocated to the national central banks in accordance with Article 32.5.

Chapter VII General provisions

ARTICLE 34

Legal acts

34.1. In accordance with Article 108a of this Treaty, the ECB shall:

— make regulations to the extent necessary to implement the tasks defined in Article 3.1, first indent, Articles 19.1, 22 or 25.2 and in cases which shall be laid down in the acts of the Council referred to in Article 42;
— take decisions necessary for carrying out the tasks entrusted to the ESCB under this Treaty and this Statute;
— make recommendations and deliver opinions.

34.2. A regulation shall have general application. It shall be binding in its entirety and directly applicable in all Member States.

Recommendations and opinions shall have no binding force.

A decision shall be binding in its entirety upon those to whom it is addressed.

Articles 190 to 192 of this Treaty shall apply to regulations and decisions adopted by the ECB.

The ECB may decide to publish its decisions, recommendations and opinions.

34.3. Within the limits and under the conditions adopted by the Council under the procedure laid down in Article 42, the ECB shall be entitled to impose fines or periodic penalty payments on undertakings for failure to comply with obligations under its regulations and decisions.

ARTICLE 35

Judicial control and related matters

35.1. The acts or omissions of the ECB shall be open to review or interpretation by the Court of Justice in the cases and under the conditions laid down in this Treaty. The ECB may institute proceedings in the cases and under the conditions laid down in this Treaty.

35.2. Disputes between the ECB, on the one hand, and its creditors, debtors or any other person, on the other, shall be decided by the competent national courts, save where jurisdiction has been conferred upon the Court of Justice.

35.3. The ECB shall be subject to the liability regime provided for in Article 215 of this Treaty. The national central banks shall be liable according to their respective national laws.

35.4. The Court of Justice shall have jurisdiction to give judgment pursuant to any arbitration clause contained in a contract concluded by or on behalf of the ECB, whether that contract be governed by public or private law.

35.5. A decision of the ECB to bring an action before the Court of Justice shall be taken by the Governing Council.

35.6. The Court of Justice shall have jurisdiction in disputes concerning the fulfilment by a national central bank of obligations under this Statute. If the ECB considers that a national central bank has failed to fulfil an obligation under this Statute, it shall deliver a reasoned opinion on the matter after giving the national central bank concerned the opportunity to submit its observations. If the national central bank concerned does not comply with the opinion within the period laid down by the ECB, the latter may bring the matter before the Court of Justice.

ARTICLE 36

Staff

36.1. The Governing Council, on a proposal from the Executive Board, shall lay down the conditions of employment of the staff of the ECB.

36.2. The Court of Justice shall have jurisdiction in any dispute between the ECB and its servants within the limits and under the conditions laid down in the conditions of employment.

ARTICLE 37

Seat

Before the end of 1992, the decision as to where the seat of the ECB will be established shall be taken by common accord of the governments of the Member States at the level of Heads of State or of Government.

ARTICLE 38

Professional secrecy

38.1. Members of the governing bodies and the staff of the ECB and the national central banks shall be required, even after their duties have ceased, not to disclose information of the kind covered by the obligation of professional secrecy.

38.2. Persons having access to data covered by Community legislation imposing an obligation of secrecy shall be subject to such legislation.

ARTICLE 39

Signatories

The ECB shall be legally committed to third parties by the President or by two members of the Executive Board or by the signatures of two members of the staff of the ECB who have been duly authorized by the President to sign on behalf of the ECB.

ARTICLE 40   Privileges and immunities

The ECB shall enjoy in the territories of the Member States such privileges and immunities as are necessary for the performance of its tasks, under the conditions laid down in the Protocol on the Privileges and Immunities of the European Communities annexed to the Treaty establishing a Single Council and a Single Commission of the European Communities.

Chapter VIII Amendment of the Statute and complementary legislation

ARTICLE 41   Simplified amendment procedure

41.1. In accordance with Article 106(5) of this Treaty, Articles 5.1, 5.2, 5.3, 17, 18, 19.1, 22, 23, 24, 26, 32.3, 32.4, 32.2, 32.6, 33.1(a) and 36 of this Statute may be amended by the Council, acting either by a qualified majority on a recommendation from the ECB and after consulting the Commission, or unanimously on a proposal from the Commission and after consulting the ECB. In either case the assent of the European Parliament shall be required.

41.2. A recommendation made by the ECB under this Article shall require a unanimous decision by the Governing Council.

ARTICLE 42   Complementary legislation

In accordance with Article 106(6) of this Treaty, immediately after the decision on the date for the beginning of the third stage, the Council, acting by a qualified majority either on a proposal from the Commission and after consulting the European Parliament and the ECB or on a recommendation from the ECB and after consulting the European Parliament and the Commission, shall adopt the provisions referred to in Articles 4, 5.4, 19.2, 20, 28.1, 29.2, 30.4, and 34.3. of this Statute.

Chapter IX Transitional and other provisions for the ESCB

ARTICLE 43   General Provisions

43.1. A derogation as referred to in Article 109k(1) of this Treaty shall entail that the following Articles of this Statute shall not confer any rights or impose any obligations on the Member State concerned: 3, 6, 9.2, 12.1, 14.3, 16, 18, 19, 20, 22, 23, 26.2, 27, 30, 31, 32, 33, 34, 50 and 52.

43.2. The central banks of Member States with derogation as specified in Article 109k(1) of this Treaty shall retain their powers in the field of monetary policy according to national law.

43.3. In accordance with Article 109k(4) of this Treaty, 'Member States' shall be read as 'Member States without a derogation' in the following Articles of this Statute: 3, 11.2, 19, 34.2 and 50.

43.4 'National central banks' shall be read as 'central banks of Member States without a derogation' in the following Articles of this Statute: 9.2, 10.1, 10.3, 12.1, 16, 17, 18, 22, 23, 27, 30, 31, 32, 33.2 and 52.

43.5. 'Shareholders' shall be read as 'central banks of Member States without a derogation' in Articles 10.3 and 33.1.

43.6. 'Subscribed capital of the ECB' shall be read as 'capital of the ECB subscribed by the central banks of Member States without a derogation' in Articles 10.3 and 30.2.

ARTICLE 44

Transitional tasks of the ECB

The ECB shall take over those tasks of the EMI which, because of the derogations of one or more Member States, still have to be performed in the third stage.

The ECB shall give advice in the preparations for the abrogation of the derogations specified in Article 109k of this Treaty.

ARTICLE 45

The General Council of the ECB

45.1. Without prejudice to Article 106(3) of this Treaty, the General Council shall be constituted as a third decision-making body of the ECB.

45.2. The General Council shall comprise the President and Vice-President of the ECB and the Governors of the national central banks. The other members of the Executive Board may participate, without having the right to vote, in meetings of the General Council.

45.3. The responsibilities of the General Council are listed in full in Article 47 of this Statute.

ARTICLE 46

Rules of procedure of the General Council

46.1. The President or, in his absence, the Vice-President of the ECB shall chair the General Council of the ECB.

46.2. The President of the Council and a member of the Commission may participate, without having the right to vote, meetings of the General Council.

46.3. The President shall prepare the meetings of the General Council.

46.4. By way of derogation from Article 12.3, the General Council shall adopt its Rules of Procedure.

46.5. The Secretariat of the General Council shall be provided by the ECB.

ARTICLE 47

Responsibilities of the General Council

47.1. The General Council shall:
— perform the tasks referred to in Article 44;
— contribute to the advisory functions referred to in Articles 4 and 25.1.

47.2. The General Council shall contribute to:
— the collection of statistical information as referred to in Article 5;
— the reporting activities of the ECB as referred to in Article 15;
— the establishment of the necessary rules for the application of Article 26 as referred to in Article 26.4;
— the taking of all other measures necessary for the application of Article 29 as referred to in Article 29.4;
— the laying down of the conditions of employment of the staff of the ECB as referred to in Article 36.

47.3. The General Council shall contribute to the necessary preparations for irrevocably fixing the exchange rates of the currencies of Member States with a derogation against the currencies, or the single currency, of the Member States without a derogation, as referred to in Article 109l(5) of this Treaty.

47.4. The General Council shall be informed by the President of the ECB of decisions of the Governing Council.

ARTICLE 48

Transitional provisions for the capital of the ECB

In accordance with Article 29.1 each national central bank shall be assigned a weighting in the key for subscription of the ECB's capital. By way of derogation from Article 28.3, central banks of Member States with a derogation shall not pay up their subscribed capital unless the General Council, acting by as majority representing at least two-thirds of the subscribed capital of the ECB and at least half of the shareholders, decides that a minimal percentage has to be paid up as a contribution to the operational costs of the ECB.

ARTICLE 49

Deferred payment of capital, reserves and provisions of the ECB

49.1. The central bank of a Member State whose derogation has been abrogated shall pay up its subscribed share of the capital of the ECB to the same extent as the central banks of other Member States without a derogation, and shall transfer to the ECB foreign reserve assets in accordance with Article 30.1. The sum to be transferred shall be determined by multiplying the ECU value at current exchange rates of the foreign reserve assets which have already been transferred to the ECB in accordance with Article 30.1, by the ratio between the number of shares subscribed by the national central bank concerned and the number of shares already paid up by the other national central banks.

49.2. In addition to the payment to be made in accordance with Article 49.1, the central bank concerned shall contribute to the reserve of the ECB, to those provisions equivalent to reserves, and to the amount still to be appropriated to the reserves and provisions corresponding to the balance of the profit and loss account as at 31 December of the year prior to the abrogation of the derogation. The sum to be contributed shall be determined by multiplying the amount of the reserves, as defined above and as stated in the approved balance sheet of the ECB, by the ratio between the number of shares subscribed by the central bank concerned and the number of shares already paid up the other central banks.

ARTICLE 50

Initial appointment of the members of the Executive Board

When the Executive Board of the ECB is being established, the President, the Vice-President and the other members of the Executive Board shall be appointed by common accord of the governments of the Member States at the level of Heads of State or of Government, on a recommendation from the Council and after consulting the European Parliament and the Council of the EMI. The President of the Executive Board shall be appointed for 8 years. By way of derogation from Article 11.2, the Vice-President shall be appointed for 4 years and the other members of the Executive Board for terms of office of between 5 and 8 years. No term of office shall be renewable. The number of members of the Executive Board may be smaller than provided for in Article 11.1, but in no circumstance shall it be less than four.

ARTICLE 51

Derogation from Article 32

51.1. If, after the start of the third stage, the Governing Council decides that the application of Article 32 results in significant changes in national central banks' relative income positions, the amount of income to be allocated pursuant to Article 32 shall be reduced by a uniform percentage which shall not exceed 60% in the first financial year after the start of the third stage and which shall decrease by at least 12 percentage points in each subsequent financial year.

51.2 Article 51.1. shall be applicable for not more than five financial years after the start of the third stage.

ARTICLE 52

Exchange of bank notes in Community currencies

Following the irrevocable fixing of exchange rates, the Governing Council shall take the necessary measures to ensure that bank notes denominated in currencies with irrevocably fixed exchange rates are exchanged by the national central banks at their respective par values.

ARTICLE 53

Applicability of the transitional provisions

If and as long as there are Member States with a derogation Articles 43 to 48 shall be applicable.

Protocol on the Statute of the European Monetary Institute

THE HIGH CONTRACTING PARTIES,
DESIRING to lay down the Statute of the European Monetary Institute,
HAVE AGREED upon the following provision, which shall be annexed to the Treaty establishing the European Community;

ARTICLE 1

Constitution and name

1.1. The European Monetary Institute (EMI) shall be established in accordance with Article 109f of this Treaty; it shall perform its functions and carry out its activities in accordance with the provisions of this Treaty and of this Statute.

1.2. The members of the EMI shall be the central banks of the Member States ('national central banks'). For the purposes of this Statute, the Institut monétaire luxembourgeois shall be regarded as the central bank of Luxembourg.

1.3. Pursuant to Article 109f of this Treaty, both the Committee of Governors and the European Monetary Cooperation Fund (EMCF) shall be dissolved. All assets and liabilities of the EMCF shall pass automatically to the EMI.

ARTICLE 2

Objectives

The EMI shall contribute to the realization of the conditions necessary for the transition to the third stage of Economic and Monetary Union, in particular by:

— strengthening the coordination of monetary policies with a view to ensuring price stability;
— making the preparations required for the establishment of the European System of Central Banks (ESCB), and for the conduct of a single monetary policy and the creation of a single currency in the third stage;
— overseeing the development of the ECU.

ARTICLE 3

General principles

3.1. The EMI shall carry out the tasks and functions conferred upon it by this Treaty and this Statute without prejudice to the responsibility of the competent authorities for the conduct of the monetary policy within the respective Member States.

3.2. The EMI shall act in accordance with the objectives and principles stated in Article 2 of the Statute of the ESCB.

ARTICLE 4

Primary tasks

4.1. In accordance with Article 109f(2) of this Treaty, the EMI shall:

— strengthen cooperation between the national central banks;
— strengthen the coordination of the monetary policies of the Member States with the aim of ensuring price stability;
— monitor the functioning of the European Monetary System (EMS);
— hold consultations concerning issues falling within the competence of the national central banks and affecting the stability of financial institutions and markets;
— take over the tasks of the EMCF; in particular it shall perform the functions referred to in Articles 6.1, 6.2 and 6.3;
— facilitate the use of the ECU and oversee its development, including the smooth functioning of the ECU clearing system.

The EMI shall also:

— hold regular consultations concerning the course of monetary policies and the use of monetary policy instruments;
— normally be consulted by the national monetary authorities before they take decisions on the course of monetary policy in the context of the common framework for ex ante coordination.

4.2. At the latest by 31 December 1996, the EMI shall specify the regulatory, organizational and logistical framework necessary for the ESCB to perform its tasks in the third stage, in accordance with the principle of an open market economy with free competition. This framework shall be submitted by the Council of the EMI for decision to the ECB at the date of its establishment. In accordance with Article 109f(3) of this Treaty, the EMI shall in particular:

— prepare the instruments and the procedures necessary for carrying out a single monetary policy in the third stage;
— promote the harmonization, where necessary, of the rules and practices governing the collection, compilation and distribution of statistics in the areas within its field of competence;
— prepare the rules for operations to be undertaken by the national central banks in the framework of the ESCB;
— promote the efficiency of cross-border payments;
— supervise the technical preparation of ECU bank notes.

ARTICLE 5

Advisory functions

5.1. In accordance with Article 109f(4) of this Treaty, the Council of the EMI may formulate opinions or recommendations on the overall orientation of monetary policy and exchange rate policy as well as on related measures introduced in each Member State. The EMI may submit opinions or recommendations to governments and to the Council on policies which might affect the internal or external monetary situation in the Community and, in particular, the functioning of the EMS.

5.2. The Council of the EMI may also make recommendations to the monetary authorities of the Member States concerning the conduct of their monetary policy.

5.3. In accordance with Article 109f(6) of this Treaty, the EMI shall be consulted by the Council regarding any proposed Community act within its field of competence.

Within the limits and under the conditions set out by the Council acting by a qualified majority on a proposal from the Commission and after consulting the European Parliament and the EMI, the EMI shall be consulted by the authorities of the Member States on any draft legislative provision within its field of competence, in particular with regard to Article 4.2.

5.4. In accordance with Article 109f(5) of this Treaty, the EMI may decide to publish its opinions and its recommendations.

ARTICLE 6

Operational and technical functions

6.1. The EMI shall;

— provide for the multilateralization of positions resulting from interventions by the national central banks in Community currencies and the multilateralization of intra-Community settlements;
— administer the very short-term financing mechanism provided for by the Agreement of 13 March 1979 between the central banks of the Member States of the European Economic Community laying down the operating procedures for the European Monetary System (hereinafter referred to as 'EMS Agreement') and the short-term monetary support mechanism provided for in the Agreement between the central banks of the Member States of the European Economic Community of 9 February 1970, as amended;
— perform the functions referred to in Article 11 of Council Regulation (EEC) No 1969/88 of 24 June 1988 establishing a single facility providing medium-term financial assistance for Member States' balances of payments.

6.2. The EMI may receive monetary reserves from the national central banks and issue ECUs against such assets for the purpose of implementing the EMS Agreement. These ECUs may be used by the EMI and the national central banks as a means of settlement and for transactions between them and the EMI. The EMI shall take the necessary administrative measures for the implementation of this paragraph.

6.3. The EMI may grant to the monetary authorities of third countries and to international monetary institutions the status of 'Other Holders' of ECUs and fix the terms and conditions under which such ECUs may be acquired, held or used by Other Holders.

6.4. The EMI shall be entitled to hold and manage foreign exchange reserves as an agent for and at the request of national central banks. Profits and losses regarding these reserves shall be for the account of the national central bank depositing the reserves. The EMI shall perform this function on the basis of bilateral contracts in accordance with rules laid down in a decision of the EMI. These rules shall ensure that transactions with these reserves shall not interfere with the monetary policy and exchange rate policy of the competent monetary authority of any Member State and shall be consistent with the objectives of the EMI and the proper functioning of the Exchange Rate Mechanism of the EMS.

ARTICLE 7

Other tasks

7.1. Once a year the EMI shall address a report to the Council on the state of the preparations for the third stage. These reports shall include an assessment of the progress towards convergence in the Community, and cover in particular the adaptation of monetary policy instruments and the preparation of the procedures necessary for carrying out a single monetary policy in the third stage, as well as the statutory requirements to be fulfilled for national central banks to become an integral part of the ESCB.

7.2. In accordance with the Council decisions referred to in Article 109f(7) of this Treaty, the EMI may perform other tasks for the preparation of the third stage.

ARTICLE 8   Independence

The members of the Council of the EMI who are the representatives of their institutions shall, with respect to their activities, act according to their own responsibilities. In exercising the powers and performing the tasks and duties conferred upon them by this Treaty and this Statute, the Council of the EMI may not seek or take any instructions from Community institutions or bodies or governments of Member States. The Community institutions and bodies as well as the governments of the Member States undertake to respect this principle and not seek to influence the Council of the EMI in the performance of its tasks.

ARTICLE 9   Administration

9.1. In accordance with Article 109f(1) of this Treaty, the EMI shall be directed and managed by the Council of the EMI.

9.2. The Council of the EMI shall consist of a President and the Governors of the national central banks, one of whom shall be Vice-President. If a Governor is prevented from attending a meeting, he may nominate another representative of his institution.

9.3. The President shall be appointed by common accord of the governments of the Member States at the level of Heads of State or of Government, on a recommendation from, as the case may be, the Committee of Governors or the Council of the EMI, and after consulting the European Parliament and the Council. The President shall be selected from among persons of recognized standing and professional experience in monetary or banking matters. Only nationals of Member States may be President of the EMI. The Council of the EMI shall appoint the Vice-President. The President and Vice-President shall be appointed for a period of three years.

9.4. The President shall perform his duties on a full-time basis. He shall not engage in any occupation, whether gainful or not, unless exemption is exceptionally granted by the Council of the EMI.

9.5. The President shall

— prepare and chair meetings of the Council of the EMI;
— without prejudice to Article 22, present the views of the EMI externally;
— be responsible for the day-to-day management of the EMI.

In the absence of the President, his duties shall be performed by the Vice-President.

9.6. The terms and conditions of employment of the President, in particular his salary, pension and other social security benefits, shall be the subject of a contract with the EMI and shall be fixed by the Council of the EMI on a proposal from a Committee comprising three members appointed by the Committee of Governors or the Council of the EMI, as the case may be, and three members appointed by the Council. The President shall not have the right to vote on matters referred to in this paragraph.

9.7. If the President no longer fulfils the conditions required for the performance of his duties or if he has been guilty of serious misconduct, the Court of Justice may, on application by the Council of the EMI, compulsorily retire him.

9.8. The Rules of Procedure of the EMI shall be adopted by the Council of the EMI.

ARTICLE 10 Meetings of the Council of the EMI and voting procedures

10.1 The Council of the EMI shall meet at least ten times a year. The proceedings of Council meetings shall be confidential. The Council of the EMI may, acting unanimously, decide to make the outcome of its deliberations public.

10.2. Each member of the Council of the EMI or his nominee shall have one vote.

10.3. Save as otherwise provided for in this Statute, the Council of the EMI shall act by a simple majority of its members.

10.4. Decisions to be taken in the context of Articles 4.2, 5.4, 6.2, and 6.3 shall require unanimity of the members of the Council of the EMI.

The adoption of opinions and recommendations under Articles 5.1 and 5.2, the adoption of decisions under Articles 6.4, 16 and 23.6 and the adoption of guidelines under Article 15.3 shall require a qualified majority of two thirds of the members of the Council of the EMI.

ARTICLE 11 Interinstitutional cooperation and reporting requirements

11.1 The President of the Council and a member of the Commission may participate, without having the right to vote, in meetings of the Council of the EMI.

11.2. The President of the EMI shall be invited to participate in Council meetings when the Council is discussing matters relating to the objectives and tasks of the EMI.

11.3. At a date to be established in the Rules of Procedure, the EMI shall prepare an annual report on its activities and on monetary and financial conditions in the Community. The annual report, together with the annual accounts of the EMI, shall be addressed to the European Parliament, the Council and the Commission and also to the European Council.

The President of the EMI may, at the request of the European Parliament or on his own initiative, be heard by the competent Committees of the European Parliament.

11.4. Reports published by the EMI shall be made available to interested parties free of charge.

ARTICLE 12 Currency denomination

The operations of the EMI shall be expressed in ECUs.

ARTICLE 13 Seat

Before the end of 1992, the decision as to where the seat of the EMI will be established shall be taken by common accord of the governments of the Member States at the level of Heads of State or of Government.

ARTICLE 14 Legal capacity

The EMI, which in accordance with Article 109f(1) of this Treaty shall have legal personality, shall enjoy in each of the Member States the most extensive legal capacity accorded to legal persons under their law; it may, in particular, acquire or dispose of movable or immovable property and may be a party to legal proceedings.

ARTICLE 15 Legal acts

15.1. In the performance of its tasks, and under the conditions laid down in this Statute, the EMI shall:

— deliver opinions;

— make recommendations;

— adopt guidelines, and take decisions, which shall be addressed to the national central banks.

15.2. Opinions and recommendations of the EMI shall have no binding force.

15.3. The Council of the EMI may adopt guidelines laying down the methods for the implementation of the conditions necessary for the ESCB to perform its functions in the third stage. EMI guidelines shall have no binding force; they shall be submitted for decision to the ECB.

15.4. Without prejudice to Article 3.1, a decision of the EMI shall be binding in its entirety upon those to whom it is addressed. Articles 190 and 191 of this Treaty shall apply to these decisions.

ARTICLE 16

Financial resources

16.1. The EMI shall be endowed with its own resources. The size of the resources of the EMI shall be determined by the Council of the EMI with a view to ensuring the income deemed necessary to cover the administrative expenditure incurred in the performance of the tasks and functions of the EMI.

16.2. The resources of the EMI determined in accordance with Article 16.1 shall be provided out of contributions by the national central banks in accordance with the key referred to in Article 29.1 of the Statute of the ESCB and be paid up at the establishment of the EMI. For this purpose, the statistical data to be used for the determination of the key shall be provided by the Commission, in accordance with the rules adopted by the Council, acting by a qualified majority on a proposal from the Commission and after consulting the European Parliament, the Committee of Governors and the Committee referred to in Article 109c of this Treaty.

16.3. The Council of the EMI shall determine the form in which contributions shall be paid up.

ARTICLE 17

Annual accounts and auditing

17.1. The financial year of the EMI shall begin on the first day of January and end on the last day of December.

17.2. The Council of the EMI shall adopt an annual budget before the beginning of each financial year.

17.3. The annual accounts shall be drawn up in accordance with the principles established by the Council of the EMI. The annual accounts shall be approved by the Council of the EMI and shall thereafter be published.

17.4. The annual accounts shall be audited by independent external auditors approved by the Council of the EMI. The auditors shall have full power to examine all books and accounts of the EMI and to obtain full information about its transactions.

The provisions of Article 188c of this Treaty shall only apply to an examination of the operational efficiency of the management of the EMI.

17.5. Any surplus of the EMI shall be transferred in the following order

(a) an amount to be determined by the Council of the EMI shall be transferred to the general reserve fund of the EMI.

(b) any remaining surplus shall be distributed to the national central banks in accordance with the key referred to in Article 16.2.

17.6. In the event of a loss incurred by the EMI, the shortfall shall be offset against the general reserve fund of the EMI. Any remaining shortfall shall be made good by contributions from the national central banks, in accordance with the key as referred to in Article 16.2.

ARTICLE 18   Staff

18.1. The Council of the EMI shall lay down the conditions of employment of the staff of the EMI.

18.2. The Court of Justice shall have jurisdiction in any dispute between the EMI and its servants within the limits and under the conditions laid down in the conditions of employment.

ARTICLE 19   Judicial control and related matters

19.1. The acts or omissions of the EMI shall be open to review or interpretation by the Court of Justice in the cases and under the conditions laid down in this Treaty. The EMI may institute proceedings in the cases and under the conditions laid down in this Treaty.

19.2. Disputes between the EMI, on the one hand, and its creditors, debtors or any other person, on the other, shall fall within the jurisdiction of the competent national courts, save where jurisdiction has been conferred upon the Court of Justice.

19.3. The EMI shall be subject to the liability regime provided for in Article 215 of this Treaty.

19.4. The Court of Justice shall have jurisdiction to give judgment pursuant to any arbitration clause contained in a contract concluded by or on behalf of the EMI, whether that contract be governed by public or private law.

19.5. A decision of the EMI to bring an action before the Court of Justice shall be taken by the Council of the EMI.

ARTICLE 20   Professional secrecy

20.1. Members of the Council of the EMI and the staff of the EMI shall be required, even after their duties have ceased, not to disclose information of the kind covered by the obligation of professional secrecy.

20.2. Persons having access to data covered by Community legislation imposing an obligation of secrecy shall be subject to such legislation.

ARTICLE 21   Privileges and immunities

The EMI shall enjoy in the territories of the Member States such privileges and immunities as are necessary for the performance of its tasks, under the conditions laid down in the Protocol on the Privileges and Immunities of the European Communities annexed to the Treaty establishing a Single Council and a Single Commission of the European Communities.

ARTICLE 22   Signatories

The EMI shall be legally committed to third parties by the President or the Vice-President or by the signatures of two members of the staff of the EMI who have been duly authorized by the President to sign on behalf of the EMI.

ARTICLE 23   Liquidation of the EMI

23.1. In accordance with Article 109l of this Treaty, the EMI shall go into liquidation on the establishment of the ECB. All assets and liabilities of the

EMI shall then pass automatically to the ECB. The latter shall liquidate the EMI according to the provisions of this Article. The liquidation shall be completed by the beginning of the third stage.

23.2. The mechanism for the creation of ECUs against gold and US dollars as provided for by Article 17 of the EMS agreement shall be unwound by the first day of the third stage in accordance with Article 20 of the said Agreement.

23.3. All claims and liabilities arising from the very short-term financing mechanism and the short-term monetary support mechanism, under the Agreements referred to in Article 6.1, shall be settled by the first day of the third stage.

23.4. All remaining assets of the EMI shall be disposed of and all remaining liabilities of the EMI shall be settled.

23.5. The proceeds of the liquidation described in Article 23.4. shall be distributed to the national central banks in accordance with the key referred to in Article 16.2

23.6. The Council of the EMI may take the measures necessary for the application of Articles 23.4. and 23.5.

23.7. Upon the establishment of the ECB, the President of the EMI shall relinquish his office.

Protocol on the excessive deficit procedure[41]

THE HIGH CONTRACTING PARTIES,
DESIRING to lay down the details of the excessive deficit procedure referred to in Article 104c of the Treaty establishing the European Community,
HAVE AGREED upon the following provisions, which shall be annexed to the Treaty establishing the European Community:

ARTICLE 1

The reference values referred to in Article 104c(2) of this Treaty are:

— 3% for the ratio of the planned or actual government deficit to gross domestic product at market prices;
— 60% for the ratio of government debt to gross domestic product at market prices.

ARTICLE 2

In Article 104c of this Treaty and in this Protocol:

— government means general government, that is central government, regional or local government and social security funds, to the exclusion of commercial operations, as defined in the European System of Integrated Economic Accounts;
— deficit means net borrowing as defined in the European System of Integrated Economic Accounts;
— investment means gross fixed capital formation as defined in the European System of Integrated Economic Accounts;
— debt means total gross debt at nominal value outstanding at the end of the year and consolidated between and within the sectors of general government as defined in the first indent.

41. This Protocol is to be replaced at a future date in accordance with the provisions of Article 104c(14), see p. 164.

ARTICLE 3   In order to ensure the effectiveness of the excessive deficit procedure, the governments of the Member States shall be responsible under this procedure for the deficits of general government as defined in the first indent of Article 2. The Member States shall ensure that national procedures in the budgetary area enable them to meet their obligations in this area deriving from this Treaty. The Member States shall report their planned and actual deficits and the levels of their debt promptly and regularly to the Commission.

ARTICLE 4   The statistical data to be used for the application of this Protocol shall be provided by the Commission.

Protocol on the convergence criteria referred to in Article 109j of the Treaty establishing the European Community

THE HIGH CONTRACTING PARTIES,
DESIRING to lay down the details of the convergence criteria which shall guide the Community in taking decisions on the passage to the third stage of economic and monetary union, referred to in Article 109j(1) of this Treaty, HAVE AGREED upon the following provisions, which shall be annexed to the Treaty establishing the European Community:

ARTICLE 1   The criterion on stability referred to in the first indent of Article 109j(1) of this Treaty shall mean that a Member State has a price performance that is sustainable and an average rate of inflation, observed over a period of one year before the examination, that does not exceed by more than $1\frac{1}{2}$ percentage points that of, at most, the three best performing Member States in terms of price stability. Inflation shall be measured by means of the consumer price index on a comparable basis, taking into account differences in national definitions.

ARTICLE 2   The criterion on the government budgetary position referred to in the second indent of Article 109j(1) of this Treaty shall mean that at the time of the examination the Member State is not the subject of a Council decision under Article 104c(6) of this Treaty that an excessive deficit exists.

ARTICLE 3   The criterion on participation in the Exchange Rate Mechanism of the European Monetary System referred to in the third indent of Article 109j(1) of this Treaty shall mean that a Member State has respected the normal fluctuation margins provided for by the Exchange Rate Mechanism of the European Monetary System without severe tensions for at least the last two years before the examination. In particular, the Member State shall not have devalued its currency's bilateral central rate against any other Member State's currency on its own initiative for the same period.

ARTICLE 4   The criterion on the convergence of interest rates referred to in the fourth indent of Article 109j(1) of this Treaty shall mean that, observed over a period of one year before the examination, a Member State has had an average nominal long-term interest rate that does not exceed by more than 2 percentage points that of, at most, the three best performing Member States in terms of price stability. Interest rates shall be measured on the basis of long term government bonds or comparable securities, taking into account differences in national definitions.

ARTICLE 5 The statistical data to be used for the application of this Protocol shall be provided by the Commission.

ARTICLE 6 The Council shall, acting unanimously on a proposal from the Commission and after consulting the European Parliament, the EMI or the ECB as the case may be, and the Committee referred to in Article 109c, adopt appropriate provisions to lay down the details of the convergence criteria referred to Article 109j of this Treaty, which shall then replace this Protocol.

Protocol amending the Protocol on the privileges and immunities of the European Communities[42]

THE HIGH CONTRACTING PARTIES,
CONSIDERING that, in accordance with Article 40 of the Statute of the European Central Bank and Article 21 of the Statute of the European Monetary Institute, the European Central Bank and the European Monetary Institute shall enjoy in the territories of the Member States such privileges and immunities as are necessary for the performance of their tasks,
HAVE AGREED upon the following provisions, which shall be annexed to the Treaty establishing the European Community:

Sole Article The Protocol on the Privileges and Immunities of the European Communities, annexed to the Treaty establishing a Single Council and a Single Commission of the European Communities, shall be supplemented by the following provisions:

'Article 23
This Protocol shall also apply to the European Central Bank, to the members of its organs and to its staff, without prejudice to the provisions of the Protocol on the Statute of the European System of Central Banks and the European Central Bank.

The European Central Bank shall, in addition, be exempt from any form of taxation or imposition of a like nature on the occasion of any increase in its capital and from the various formalities which may be connected therewith in the State where the bank has its seat. The activities of the Bank and of its organs carried on in accordance with the Statute of the European System of Central Banks and of the European Central Bank shall not be subject to any turnover tax.

The above provisions shall also apply to the European Monetary Institute. Its dissolution or liquidation shall not give rise to any imposition.'

Protocol on Denmark

THE HIGH CONTRACTING PARTIES,
DESIRING to settle certain particular problems relating to Denmark,
HAVE AGREED upon the following provisions, which shall be annexed to the Treaty establishing the European Community:

The provisions of Article 14 of the Protocol on the Statute of the European System of Central Banks and of the European Central Banks and of the

---

42. For the full text of this Protocol, see pp. 554–8.

European Central Bank shall not affect the right of the National Bank of Denmark to carry out its existing tasks concerning those parts of the Kingdom of Denmark which are not part of the Community.

Protocol on Portugal

THE HIGH CONTRACTING PARTIES,
DESIRING to settle certain particular problems relating to Portugal,
HAVE AGREED upon the following provisions, which shall be annexed to the Treaty establishing the European Community:

1. Portugal is hereby authorized to maintain the facility afforded to the Autonomous Regions of Azores and Madeira to benefit from an interest-free credit facility with the Banco de Portugal under the terms established by existing Portuguese law.

2. Portugal commits itself to pursue its best endeavours in order to put an end to the abovementioned facility as soon as possible.

Protocol on the transition to the third stage of Economic and Monetary Union

THE HIGH CONTRACTING PARTIES,
DECLARE the irreversible character of the Community's movement to the third stage of Economic and Monetary Union by signing the new Treaty provisions on Economic and Monetary Union.

Therefore all Member States shall, whether they fulfil the necessary conditions for the adoption of a single currency or not, respect the will for the Community to enter swiftly into the third stage, and therefore no Member State shall prevent the entering into the third stage.

If by the end of 1997 the date of the beginning of the third stage has not been set, the Member States concerned, the Community institutions and other bodies involved shall expedite all preparatory work during 1998, in order to enable the Community to enter the third stage irrevocably on 1 January 1999 and to enable the ECB and ESCB to start their full functioning from this date.

This Protocol shall be annexed to the Treaty establishing the European Community.

Protocol on certain provisions relating to the United Kingdom of Great Britain and Northern Ireland

THE HIGH CONTRACTING PARTIES,
RECOGNIZING that the United Kingdom shall not be obliged or committed to move to the third stage of Economic and Monetary Union without a separate decision to do so by its government and Parliament,
NOTING the practice of the government of the United Kingdom to fund its borrowing requirement by the sale of debt to the private sector,
HAVE AGREED the following provisions, which shall be annexed to the Treaty establishing the European Community:

1. The United Kingdom shall notify the Council whether it intends to move to the third stage before the Council makes its assessment under Article 109j(2) of this Treaty.

Unless the United Kingdom notifies the Council that it intends to move to the third stage, it shall be under no obligation to do so.

If no date is set for the beginning of the third stage under Article 109j(3) of this Treaty, the United Kingdom may notify its intention to move to the third stage before 1 January 1998.

2. Paragraphs 3 to 9 shall have effect if the United Kingdom notifies the Council that it does not intend to move to the third stage.

3. The United Kingdom shall not be included among the majority of Member States which fulfil the necessary conditions referred to in the second indent of Article 109j(2) and the first indent of Article 109j(3) of this Treaty.

4. The United Kingdom shall retain its powers in the field of monetary policy according to national law.

5. Articles 3a(2), 104c(1), (9) and (11), 105(1) to (5), 105a, 107, 108, 108a, 109, 109a(1) and (2)(b) and 109l(4) and (5) of this Treaty shall not apply to the United Kingdom. In these provisions references to the Community or the Member States shall not include the United Kingdom and references to national central banks shall not include the Bank of England.

6. Articles 109e(4) and 109h and i of this Treaty shall continue to apply to the United Kingdom. Articles 109c(4) and 109m shall apply to the United Kingdom as if it had a derogation.

7. The voting rights of the United Kingdom shall be suspended in respect of acts of the Council referred to in Articles listed in paragraph 5. For this purpose the weighted votes of the United Kingdom shall be excluded from any calculation of a qualified majority under Article 109k(5) of this Treaty.

The United Kingdom shall also have no right to participate in the appointment of the President, the Vice-President and the other members of the Executive Board of the ECB under Articles 109a(2)(b) and 109l(1) of this Treaty.

8. Articles 3, 4, 6, 7, 9.2, 10.1, 10.3, 11.2, 12.1, 14, 16, 18 to 20, 22, 23, 26, 27, 30 to 34, 50 and 52 of the Protocol on the Statute of the European System of Central Banks and of the European Central Bank ('the Statute') shall not apply to the United Kingdom.

In those Articles, references to the Community or the Member States shall not include the United Kingdom and references to national central banks or shareholders shall not include the Bank of England.

References in Articles 10.3 and 30.2. of the Statute to 'subscribed capital of the ECB' shall not include capital subscribed by the Bank of England.

9. Article 109l(3) of this Treaty and Articles 44 to 48 of the Statute shall have effect, whether or not there is any Member State with a derogation, subject to the following amendments:

(a) References in Article 44 to the tasks of the ECB and the EMI shall include those tasks that still need to be performed in the third stage owing to any decision of the United Kingdom not to move to that stage.

(b) In addition to the tasks referred to in Article 47 the ECB shall also give advice in relation to and contribute to the preparation of any decision of the Council with regard to the United Kingdom taken in accordance with paragraphs 10(a) and 10(c).

(c) The Bank of England shall pay up its subscription to the capital of the

ECB as a contribution to its operational costs on the same basis as national central banks of Member States with a derogation.

10. If the United Kingdom does not move to the third stage, it may change its notification at any time after the beginning of that stage. In that event:

(a) The United Kingdom shall have the right to move to the third stage provided only that it satisfies the necessary conditions. The Council, acting at the request of the United Kingdom and under the conditions and in accordance with the procedure laid down in Article 109k(2) of this Treaty, shall decide whether it fulfils the necessary conditions.

(b) The Bank of England shall pay up its subscribed capital, transfer to the ECB foreign reserve assets and contribute to its reserves on the same basis as the national central bank of a Member State whose derogation has been abrogated.

(c) The Council, acting under the conditions and in accordance with the procedure laid down in Article 1091(5) of this Treaty, shall take all other necessary decisions to enable the United Kingdom to move to the third stage.

If the United Kingdom moves to the third stage pursuant to the provisions of this Protocol, paragraphs 3 to 9 shall cease to have effect.

11. Notwithstanding Articles 104 and 109e(3) of this Treaty and Article 21.1 of the Statute, the government of the United Kingdom may maintain its Ways and Means facility with the Bank of England if and so long as the United Kingdom does not move to the third stage.

Protocol on certain provisions relating to Denmark

THE HIGH CONTRACTING PARTIES,
DESIRING to settle, in accordance with the general objectives of the Treaty establishing the European Community, certain particular problems existing at the present time,
TAKING INTO ACCOUNT that the Danish Constitution contains provisions which may imply a referendum in Denmark prior to Danish participation in the third stage of Economic and Monetary Union,
HAVE AGREED on the following provisions, which shall be annexed to the Treaty establishing the European Community:

1. The Danish Government shall notify[43] the Council of its position concerning participation in the third stage before the Council makes its assessment under Article 109j(2) of this Treaty.

2. In the event of a notification that Denmark will not participate in the third stage, Denmark shall have an exemption. The effect of the exemption shall be that all Articles and provisions of this Treaty and the Statute of the ESCB referring to a derogation shall be applicable to Denmark.

3. In such case, Denmark shall not be included among the majority of Member States which fulfil the necessary conditions referred to in the second indent of Article 109j(2) and the first indent of Article 109j(3) of this Treaty.

4. As for the abrogation of the exemption, the procedure referred to in Article 109k(2) shall only be initiated at the request of Denmark.

---

43. Denmark notified the Council in December 1992 of its wish not to participate in Stage III, see p. 553.

5. In the event of abrogation of the exemption status, the provisions of this Protocol shall cease to apply.

Protocol on France

THE HIGH CONTRACTING PARTIES,

DESIRING to take into account a particular point relating to France,

HAVE AGREED upon the following provisions, which shall be annexed to the Treaty establishing the European Community.

France will keep the privilege of monetary emission in its overseas territories under the terms established by its national laws, and will be solely entitled to determine the parity of the CFP franc.

Protocol on social policy

THE HIGH CONTRACTING PARTIES,

NOTING that eleven Member States, that is to say the Kingdom of Belgium, the Kingdom of Denmark, and the Federal Republic of Germany, the Hellenic Republic, the Kingdom of Spain, the French Republic, Ireland, the Italian Republic, the Grand Duchy of Luxembourg, the Kingdom of the Netherlands and the Portuguese Republic, wish to continue along the path laid down in the 1989 Social Charter; that they have adopted among themselves an Agreement to this end; that this Agreement is annexed to this Protocol; that this Protocol and the said Agreement are without prejudice to the provisions of this Treaty, particularly those relating to social policy which constitute an integral part of the 'acquis communautaire':

1. Agree to authorize those eleven Member States to have recourse to the institutions, procedures and mechanisms of the Treaty for the purposes of taking among themselves and applying as far as they are concerned the acts and decisions required for giving effect to the abovementioned Agreement.

2. The United Kingdom of Great Britain and Northern Ireland shall not take part in the deliberations and the adoption by the Council of Commission proposals made on the basis of the Protocol and the abovementioned Agreement.

By way of derogation from Article 148(2) of the Treaty, acts of the Council which are made pursuant to this Protocol and which must be adopted by a qualified majority shall be deemed to be so adopted if they have received at least forty-four votes in favour. The unanimity of the members of the Council, with the exception of the United Kingdom of Great Britain and Northern Ireland, shall be necessary for acts of the Council which must be adopted unanimously and for those amending the Commission proposal.

Acts adopted by the Council and any financial consequences other than administrative costs entailed for the institutions shall not be applicable to the United Kingdom of Great Britain and Northern Ireland.

3. This Protocol shall be annexed to the Treaty establishing the European Community.

Agreement on social policy concluded between the Member States of the European Community with the exception of the United Kingdom of Great Britain and Northern Ireland

The undersigned eleven HIGH CONTRACTING PARTIES, that is to say, the Kingdom of Belgium, the Kingdom of Denmark, the Federal Republic of Germany, the Hellenic Republic, the Kingdom of Spain, the French Republic, Ireland, the Italian Republic, the Grand Duchy of Luxembourg, the Kingdom of the Netherlands and the Portuguese Republic (hereinafter referred to as 'the Member States'),

WISHING to implement to the 1989 Social Charter on the basis of the 'acquis communautaire',

CONSIDERING the Protocol on social policy,

HAVE AGREED as follows:

ARTICLE 1

The Community and the Member States shall have as their objectives the promotion of employment, improved living and working conditions, proper social protection, dialogue between management and labour, the development of human resources with a view to lasting high employment and the combating of exclusion. To this end the Community and the Member States shall implement measures which take account of the diverse forms of national practices, in particular in the field of contractual relations, and the need to maintain the competitiveness of the Community economy.

ARTICLE 2

1. With a view to achieving the objectives of Article 1, the Community shall support and complement the activities of the Member States in the following fields:

— improvement in particular of the working environment to protect workers' health and safety;
— working conditions;
— the information and consultation of workers;
— equality between men and women with regard to labour market opportunities and treatment at work;
— the integration of persons excluded from the labour market, without prejudice to Article 127 of the Treaty establishing the European Community (hereinafter referred to as 'the Treaty').

2. To this end, the Council may adopt, by means of directives, minimum requirements for gradual implementation, having regard to the conditions and technical rules obtaining in each of the Member States. Such directives shall avoid imposing administrative, financial and legal constraints in a way which would hold back the creation and development of small and medium-sized undertakings.

The Council shall act in accordance with the procedure referred to in Article 189c of the Treaty after consulting the Economic and Social Committee.

3. However, the Council shall act unanimously on a proposal from the Commission, after consulting the European Parliament and the Economic and Social Committee, in the following areas:

— social security and social protection of workers;
— protection of workers where their employment contract is terminated;
— representation and collective defence of the interests of workers and employers, including co-determination, subject to paragraph 6;
— conditions of employment for third-country nationals legally residing in Community territory;

— financial contributions for promotion of employment and job-creation, without prejudice to the provisions relating to the Social Fund.

4. A Member State may entrust management and labour, at their joint request, with the implementation of directives adopted pursuant to paragraphs 2 and 3.

In this case, it shall ensure that, no later than the date on which a directive must be transposed in accordance with Article 189, management and labour have introduced the necessary measures by agreement, the Member State concerned being required to take any necessary measure enabling it at any time to be in a position to guarantee the results imposed by that directive.

5. The provisions adopted pursuant to this Article shall not prevent any Member State from maintaining or introducing more stringent protective measures compatible with the Treaty.

6. The provisions of this Article shall not apply to pay, the right of association, the right to strike or the right to impose lock-outs.

ARTICLE 3

1. The Commission shall have the task of promoting the consultation of management and labour at Community level and shall take any relevant measure to facilitate their dialogue by ensuring balanced support for the parties.

2. To this end, before submitting proposals in the social policy field, the Commission shall consult management and labour on the possible direction of Community action.

3. If, after such consultation, the Commission considers Community action advisable, it shall consult management and labour on the content of the envisaged proposal. Management and labour shall forward to the Commission an opinion or, where appropriate, a recommendation.

4. On the occasion of such consultation, management and labour may inform the Commission of their wish to initiate the process provided for in Article 4. The duration of the procedure shall not exceed nine months, unless the management and labour concerned and the Commission decide jointly to extend it.

ARTICLE 4

1. Should management and labour so desire, the dialogue between them at Community level may lead to contractual relations, including agreements.

2. Agreements concluded at Community level shall be implemented either in accordance with the procedures and practices specific to management and labour and the Member States or, in matters covered by Article 2, at the joint request of the signatory parties, by a Council decision on a proposal from the Commission.

The Council shall act by qualified majority, except where the agreement in question contains one or more provisions relating to one of the areas referred to in Article 2(3), in which case it shall act unanimously.

ARTICLE 5

With a view to achieving the objectives of Article 1 and without prejudice to the other provisions of the Treaty, the Commission shall encourage cooperation between the Member States and facilitate the coordination of their action in all social policy fields under this Agreement.

ARTICLE 6

1. Each Member State shall ensure that the principle of equal pay for male and female workers for equal work is applied.

2. For the purpose of this Article, 'pay' means the ordinary basic or minimum wage or salary and any other consideration, whether in cash or in kind, which the worker receives directly or indirectly, in respect of his employment, from his employer.

Equal pay without discrimination based on sex means:

(a) that pay for the same work at piece rates shall be calculated on the basis of the same unit of measurement.

(b) that pay for work at time rates shall be the same for the same job.

3. This Article shall not prevent any Member State from maintaining or adopting measures providing for specific advantages in order to make it easier for women to pursue a vocational activity or to prevent or compensate for disadvantages in their professional careers.

ARTICLE 7

The Commission shall draw up a report each year on progress in achieving the objectives of Article 1, including the demographic situation in the Community. It shall forward the report to the European Parliament, the Council and the Economic and Social Committee.

The European Parliament may invite the Commission to draw up reports on particular problems concerning the social situation.

Declarations

1. Declaration on Article 2(2)
The eleven High Contracting Parties note that in the discussions on Article 2(2) of the Agreement it was agreed that the Community does not intend, in laying down minimum requirements for the protection of the safety and health of employees, to discriminate in a manner unjustified by the circumstances against employees in small and medium-sized undertakings.

2. Declaration on Article 4(2)
The eleven High Contracting Parties declare that the first of the arrangements for application of the agreements between management and labour at Community level — referred to in Article 4(2) — will consist in developing, by collective bargaining according to the rules of each Member State, the content of the agreements, and that consequently this arrangement implies no obligation on the Member States to apply the agreements directly or to work out rules for their transposition, or any obligation to amend national legislation in force to facilitate their implementation.

Protocol on economic and social cohesion

THE HIGH CONTRACTING PARTIES,
RECALLING that the Union has set itself the objective of promoting economic and social progress, inter alia, through the strengthening of economic and social cohesion;
RECALLING that Article 2 of the Treaty establishing the European Community includes the task of promoting economic and social cohesion and solidarity between Member States and that the strengthening of economic and social cohesion figures among the activities of the Community listed in Article 3;
RECALLING that the provisions of Part Three, Title XIV, on economic

and social cohesion as a whole provide the legal basis for consolidating and further developing the Community's action in the field of economic and social cohesion, including the creation of a new fund;

RECALLING that the provisions of Part Three, Title XII on trans- European networks and Title XVI on environment envisage a Cohesion Fund to be set up before 31 December 1993;

STATING their belief that progress towards Economic and Monetary Union will contribute to the economic growth of all Member States;

NOTING that the Community's Structural Funds are being doubled in real terms between 1987 and 1993, implying large transfers, especially as a proportion of GDP of the less prosperous Member States;

NOTING that the European Investment Bank is lending large and increasing amounts for the benefit of the poorer regions;

NOTING the desire for greater flexibility in the arrangements for allocations from the Structural Funds;

NOTING the desire for modulation of the levels of Community participation in programmes and projects in certain countries;

NOTING the proposal to take greater account of the relative prosperity of Member States in the system of own resources,

REAFFIRM that the promotion of economic and social cohesion is vital to the full development and enduring success of the Community, and underline the importance of the inclusion of economic and social cohesion in Articles 2 and 3 of this Treaty;

REAFFIRM their conviction that the Structural Funds should continue to play a considerable part in the achievement of Community objectives in the field of cohesion;

REAFFIRM their conviction that the European Investment Bank should continue to devote the majority of its resources to the promotion of economic and social cohesion, and declare their willingness to review the capital needs of the European Investment Bank as soon as this is necessary for that purpose;

REAFFIRM the need for a thorough evaluation of the operation and effectiveness of the Structural Funds in 1992, and the need to review, on that occasion, the appropriate size of these Funds in the light of the tasks of the Community in the area of economic and social cohesion;

AGREE that the Cohesion Fund to be set up before 31 December 1993 will provide Community financial contributions to projects in the fields of environment and trans-European networks in Member States with a per capita GNP of less than 90% of the Community average which have a programme leading to the fulfilment of the conditions of economic convergence as set out in Article 104c;

DECLARE their intention of allowing a greater margin of flexibility in allocating financing from the Structural Funds to specific needs not covered under the present Structural Funds regulations;

DECLARE their willingness to modulate the levels of Community participation in the context of programmes and projects of the Structural Funds, with a view to avoiding excessive increases in budgetary expenditure in the less prosperous Member States;

RECOGNIZE the need to monitor regularly the progress made towards achieving economic and social cohesion and state their willingness to study all necessary measures in this respect;

DECLARE their intention of taking greater account of the contributive capacity of individual Member States in the system of own resources, and of examining means of correcting, for the less prosperous Member States, regressive elements existing in the present own resources system;

AGREE to annex this Protocol to the Treaty establishing the European Community.

Protocol on the Economic and Social Committee and the Committee of the Regions

> THE HIGH CONTRACTING PARTIES
> HAVE AGREED upon the following provision, which shall be annexed to this Treaty establishing the European Community:
>
> The Economic and Social Committee and the Committee of the Regions shall have a common organizational structure.

Protocol annexed to the Treaty on Eurpean Union and to the Treaties establishing the European Communities[44]

> THE HIGH CONTRACTING PARTIES,
> HAVE AGREED upon the following provision, which shall be annexed to the Treaty on European Union and to the Treaties establishing the European Communities:
>
> Nothing in the Treaty on European Union, or in the Treaties establishing the European Communities, or in the Treaties or Acts modifying or supplementing those Treaties, shall affect the application in Ireland of Article 40.3.3.3 of the Constitution of Ireland.

vi. Final Act

The Final Act, which appears immediately after the Protocols, is not part of the TEU. Rather, as its title suggests, it is the final act of the intergovernmental conferences which drew up the TEU. Its primary function, therefore, is to summarize exactly which texts the IGCs agreed to adopt. These are listed as the Treaty on European Union, the 19 Protocols referred to above, and a series of 33 Declarations. While not expanding on the content of the TEU, the Final Act does include formal lists of all the Protocols and of all the Declarations. It states clearly which Protocols the IGCs in their deliberations agreed to annex to which Treaties, and establishes that the Declarations are to be annexed to the Final Act itself and not the TEU. As such, therefore, the Final Act concludes the work of the IGCs and acts as a summary of what was agreed. It is interesting to note that the two IGCs that were convened in December 1990 were not the only ones involved in drafting the TEU. Two were convened on 3 February 1992, four days before the TEU was finally signed, to amend certain institutional provisions contained in the ECSC and Euratom Treaties following amendments to the Treaty of Rome.

q.v. ECSC Treaty pp. 359–61 and Euratom Treaty pp. 366–8.

---

44. According to Declaration 34 (see p. 536), the contents of this Protocol may be amended in line with amendments to the Irish Constitution.

Final Act

1. The Conferences of the Representatives of the Governments of the Member States convened in Rome on 15 December 1990 to adopt by common accord the amendments to be made to the Treaty establishing the European Economic Community with a view to the achievement of political union and with a view to the final stages of economic and monetary union, and those convened in Brussels on 3 February 1992 with a view to amending the Treaties establishing respectively the European Coal and Steel Community and the European Atomic Energy Community as a result of the amendments envisaged for the Treaty establishing the European Economic Community have adopted the following texts:

I   The Treaty on European Union

II   Protocols

1. Protocol on the acquisition of property in Denmark
2. Protocol concerning Article 119 of the Treaty establishing the European Community
3. Protocol on the Statute of the European System of Central Banks and of the European Central Bank
4. Protocol on the Statute of the European Monetary Institute
5. Protocol on the excessive deficit procedure
6. Protocol on the convergence criteria referred to in Article 109j of the Treaty establishing the European Community
7. Protocol amending the Protocol on the privileges and immunities of the European Communities
8. Protocol on Denmark
9. Protocol on Portugal
10. Protocol on the transition to the third stage of economic and monetary union
11. Protocol on certain provisions relating to the United Kingdom of Great Britain and Northern Ireland
12. Protocol on certain provisions relating to Denmark
13. Protocol on France
14. Protocol on social policy, to which is annexed an agreement concluded between the Member States of the European Community with the exception of the United Kingdom of Great Britain and Northern Ireland, to which two declarations are attached
15. Protocol on economic and social cohesion
16. Protocol on the Economic and Social Committee and the Committee of the Regions
17. Protocol annexed to the Treaty on European Union and to the Treaties establishing the European Communities

The Conferences agreed that the Protocols referred to in 1 to 16 above will be annexed to the Treaty establishing the European Community and that the Protocol referred to in 17 above will be annexed to the Treaty of European Union and to the Treaties establishing the European Communities.

2. At the time of signature of these texts, the Conferences adopted the declarations listed below and annexed to this Final Act:

III   Declarations

1. Declaration on civil protection, energy and tourism
2. Declaration on nationality of a Member State

3. Declaration on Part Three, Titles III and VI, of the Treaty establishing the European Community
4. Declaration on Part Three, Title VI, of the Treaty establishing the European Community
5. Declaration on monetary cooperation with non-Community countries
6. Declaration on monetary relations with the Republic of San Marino, the Vatican City and the Principality of Monaco
7. Declaration on Article 73d of the Treaty establishing the European Community
8. Declaration on Article 109 of the Treaty establishing the European Community
9. Declaration on Part Three, Title XVI, of the Treaty establishing the European Community
10. Declaration on Articles 109, 130r and 130y of the Treaty establishing the European Community
11. Declaration on the Directive of 24 November 1988 (Emissions)
12. Declaration of the European Development Fund
13. Declaration on the role of national parliaments in the European Union
14. Declaration on the Conference of the Parliaments
15. Declaration on the number of members of the Commission and of the European Parliament
16. Declaration on the hierarchy of Community Acts
17. Declaration on the right of access to information
18. Declaration on estimated costs under Commission proposals
19. Declaration on the implementation of Community law
20. Declaration on assessment of the environmental impact of Community measures
21. Declaration on the Court of Auditors
22. Declaration on the Economic and Social Committee
23. Declaration on cooperation with charitable associations
24. Declaration on the protection of animals
25. Declaration on the representation of the interests of the overseas countries and territories referred to in Article 227(3) and (5)(a) and (b) of the Treaty establishing the European Community
26. Declaration on the outermost regions of the Community
27. Declaration on voting in the field of the common foreign and security policy
28. Declaration on practical arrangements in the field of the common foreign and security policy
29. Declaration on the use of languages in the field of the common foreign and security policy
30. Declaration on Western European Union
31. Declaration on asylum
32. Declaration on police cooperation
33. Declaration on disputes between the ECB and the EMI and their servants

Done at Maastricht this seventh day of February in the year one thousand nine hundred and ninety-two.

vii. Declarations

As has been the case with the Final Acts of the Treaty of Rome and the SEA, the Final Act of the TEU has listed and numbered in it, and annexed to it a series of 34 Declarations.[45] These differ from the Protocols annexed to the amended Treaty of Rome and to the TEU in two respects. Firstly, they are not the result of agreements reached by the so-called High Contracting Parties, but the result of agreements reached by the intergovernmental conferences that drew up the TEU.[46] Hence, they are not ratified by the signatories to the TEU in line with the provisions of Article 236, and as such do not enter into force. Consequently, they do not have the same legal status as legally binding Protocols. Instead, they are often simply expressions of interpretation or declarations of intent, or means by which an IGC confirms existing Community practice or clarifies the meaning of certain Treaty provisions. As such, they are neither legally binding, nor are they subject to the jurisdiction of the ECJ, nor do they place any obligations on any of the member states or Community institutions.[47]

q.v. Article 236 p. 340.

This status is reinforced by the second difference in that Declarations do not constitute part of the TEU itself. Rather, they are annexed to the Final Act of the IGCs that stands separate from the TEU. Nevertheless, the 34 Declarations do provide guidance for any individual, institution or member state in interpreting the provisions of the TEU and of the amended Community Treaties. However, it should be stressed that in line with Article L of the TEU, the jurisdiction of the ECJ does not extend to either the Final Act of the TEU or the Declarations attached thereto. Consequently, the ECJ is neither obliged, nor more importantly, as Toth has argued in relation to the Declarations attached to the SEA, permitted to take the Declarations into consideration in interpreting the provisions of Community Treaties.[48] However, it should be noted that while this line of argument may be applicable to Declarations concerning areas of EC activity within the jurisdiction of the ECJ, it remains to be seen whether it also applies to those

q.v. Article L p. 355.

45. When the TEU was signed, 33 Declaratons were annexed to the Final Act. However, a 34th Declaration, the *Declaration of the High Contracting Parties to the Treaty on European Union*, relating to Ireland's abortion law, was added to the Final Act on 1 May 1992. It is reproduced in the Annex on p. 536 and is also discussed below and pp. 446–7. The Final Act of the Treaty of Rome has a total of nine Declarations annexed to it. Six of these were adopted by the IGC which drafted the Treaty, and three were simply taken note of. The Final Act of the SEA, meanwhile, has annexed to it eleven Declarations adopted by the IGC and nine which it merely took note of. In the cases of both Treaties the Declarations the IGC only took note of are unilateral Declarations by member states or Community institutions. The Declarations annexed to the Final Act of the Treaty of Rome are reproduced in *Treaties establishing the European Communities*, OOPEC, Luxembourg, 1973, pp. 497–505, and those annexed to the Final Act of the SEA in *Treaties establishing the European Communities*, abridged edn, OOPEC, Luxembourg, 1987, pp. 583–602.

46. It is interesting to note that in contrast to the Declarations attached to the Final Acts of the Treaty of Rome and the SEA, not one of the Declarations attached to the Final Act of the TEU is a Declaration by a single member state or institution. All Declarations are made by the IGCs and thus by all the member states. The absence of unilateral declarations may suggest greater uniformity of opinion among the member states. However, it should be noted that several of the Protocols attached to the Treaty of Rome by the TEU refer to single member states.

47. For a discussion of the legal status of Declarations see Toth, A.G., 'The Legal Status of the Declarations annexed to the Single European Act', *Common Market Law Review*, vol. 23, no. 4, 1986, pp. 803–812.

48. Toth (1986, ibid., note 46), p. 810. The legal status of Declarations and the position the ECJ may take in relation to them is of particular interest to the United Kingdom with regard to the abolition of border controls as part of the Internal Market programme. According to the General Declaration on Articles 13 to 19 of the Single European Act attached to the Final Act of the SEA 'Nothing in [the provisions of the SEA] shall affect the right of Member States to take such measures as they consider necessary for the purpose of controlling immigration from third countries, and to combat terrorism, crime, the traffic in drugs and illicit trading in works of art and antiques.' This has been quoted by the UK government in defence of its refusal to remove all border controls on persons entering the United Kingdom from elsewhere in the EC by 31 December 1992. If, as was rumoured in early 1993, the Commission were to take the UK government to the ECJ, it is unlikely that the Court would be able to take the Declaration into account in its deliberations. Hence, so the argument goes, the UK government would lose. See Howe, M., *Europe and the Constitution after Maastricht*, Nelson and Pollard, Oxford, 1993, pp. 26–28.

Declarations concerning the CFSP and JHA pillars of the Union (Declarations 27–32[49]). These Declarations concern intergovernmental arrangements which in turn are not subject to the judicial review of any apparent independent authority.

Like the Protocols discussed above, the Declarations attached to the Final Act relate to a variety of areas dealt with in the TEU. Consequently, there are Declarations relating to specific policies of the Union, to individual EC institutions, and to EC law. In addition, there are Declarations relating to the rights of individuals and of member states; to the future development of the Union; and several miscellaneous ones. Yet, as stated earlier, none of the Declarations is legally binding.

For the most part, the Declarations consist of between one and three paragraphs. The most significant exception to this general rule is the Declaration on Western European Union. This is over two pages long and itself contains two Declarations by those member states of the Union which are also members of the WEU (Declaration 30).

Of those Declarations relating to specific Union policies, six relate to EMU (Declarations 3–8); three to the environment (Declarations 9, 11, and 20); one to the regions (Declaration 26); one to the European Development Fund (Declaration 12); four to the common foreign and security policy of the Union (Declarations 27–30); and two to cooperation in the fields of justice and home affairs (Declarations 31–32). References to these have been made earlier in the *Handbook*. In addition, one Declaration provides for the question of introducing Titles relating to civil protection, energy and tourism into the Treaty of Rome to be discussed at the IGC which is to take place in 1996 (Declaration 1). References have also been made earlier in the *Handbook* to the seven Declarations which concern the institutions of the Community (Declarations 13–15, 18, 21–22, and 33), and to the three which relate to Community law (Declarations 10, 16, and 19). Those Declarations which refer to the rights of individuals (Declaration 17), and to member states (Declaration 2) were dealt with in the second subdivision of the *Handbook*. The remaining three Declarations relate to cooperation with charitable associations, the protection of animals in developing the CAP, and the interests of certain overseas countries and territories (Declarations 23–25).

Declaration on civil protection, energy and tourism

> The Conference declares that the question of introducing into the Treaty establishing the European Community Titles relating to the spheres referred to in Article 3(t) of that Treaty will be examined, in accordance with the procedure laid down in Article N(2) of the Treaty on European Union, on the basis of a report which the Commission will submit to the Council by 1996 at the latest.

---

49. The numbering used to denote the Declarations is that contained in the list in the Final Act, see pp. 428–9.

The Commission declares that Community action in those spheres will be pursued on the basis of the present provisions of the Treaties establishing the European Communities.

Declaration on nationality of a Member State

The Conference declares that, wherever in the Treaty establishing the European Community reference is made to nationals of the Member States, the question whether an individual possesses the nationality of a Member State shall be settled solely by reference to the national law of the Member State concerned. Member States may declare, for information, who are to be considered their nationals for Community purposes by way of a declaration lodged with the Presidency and may amend any such declaration when necessary.

Declaration on Part Three, Titles III and VI, of the Treaty establishing the European Community

The Conference affirms that, for the purposes of applying the provisions set out in Part Three, Title III, Chapter 4 on capital and payments, and Title VI on economic and monetary policy, of this Treaty, the usual practice, according to which the Council meets in the composition of Economic and Finance Ministers, shall be continued, without prejudice to Article 109j(2) to (4) and Article 109k(2).

Declaration on Part Three, Title VI, of the Treaty establishing the European Community

The Conference affirms that the President of the European Council shall invite the Economic and Finance Ministers to participate in European Council meetings when the European Council is discussing matters relating to economic and monetary union.

Declaration on monetary cooperation with non-Community countries

The Conference affirms that the Community shall aim to contribute to stable international monetary relations. To this end the Community shall be prepared to cooperate with other European countries and with those non-European countries with which the Community has close economic ties.

Declaration on monetary relations with the Republic of San Marino, the Vatican City and the Principality of Monaco

The Conference agrees that the existing monetary relations between Italy and San Marino and the Vatican City and between France and Monaco remain unaffected by the Treaty establishing the European Community until the introduction of the ECU as the single currency of the Community.

The Community undertakes to facilitate such renegotiations of existing arrangements as might become necessary as a result of the introduction of the ECU as a single currency.

Declaration on Article 73d of the Treaty establishing the European Community

The Conference affirms that the right of Member States to apply the relevant provisions of their tax law as referred to in Article 73d(1)(a) of this Treaty will apply only with respect to the relevant provisions which exist at the end of 1993. However, this Declaration shall apply only to capital movements between Member States and to payments effected between Member States.

Declaration on Article 109 of the Treaty establishing the European Community

The Conference emphasizes that use of the term 'formal agreements' in Article 109(1) is not intended to create a new category of international agreement within the meaning of Community law.

Declaration on Part Three, Title XVI, of the Treaty establishing the European Community

The Conference considers that, in view of the increasing importance of nature conservation at national, Community and international level, the Community should, in exercising its powers under the provisions of Part Three, Title XVI, take account of the specific requirements of this area.

Declaration on Articles 109, 130r and 130y of the Treaty establishing the European Community

The Conference considers that the provisions of Article 109(5),[50] Article 130r(4), second subparagraph, and Article 130y do not affect the principles resulting from the judgment handed down by the Court of Justice in the AETR case.[51]

Declaration on the Directive of 24 November 1988 (Emissions)

The Conference declares that changes in Community legislation cannot undermine the derogations granted to Spain and Portugal until 31 December 1999 under the Council Directive of 24 November 1988 on the limitation of emissions of certain pollutants into the air from large combustion plants.

---

50. The reference to Article 109(5) was inserted into the Declaration after the Maastricht Summit in December 1991 before the TEU was formally signed in February 1992.

51. In the case *Commission* v. *Council* (AETR) 22/70, [1971] CMLR 335, the ECJ ruled that where the Community has an explicit internal competence it has a parallel external competence. In such areas, member states may not therefore act independently of the Community. Furthermore where a member state does enter into an obligation under an international agreement which conflicts with Community law, the latter overrides any such an obligation.

Declaration on the European Development Fund

The Conference agrees that the European Development Fund will continue to be financed by national contributions in accordance with the current provisions.

Declaration on the role of national Parliaments in the European Union

The Conference considers that it is important to encourage greater involvement of national parliaments in the activities of the European Union.

To this end, the exchange of information between the national Parliaments and the European Parliament should be stepped up. In this context, the governments of the Member States will ensure, *inter alia*, that national parliaments receive Commission proposals for legislation in good time for information or possible examination.

Similarly, the Conference considers that it is important for contacts between the national parliaments and the European Parliament to be stepped up, in particular through the granting of appropriate reciprocal facilities and regular meetings between members of Parliament interested in the same issues.

Declaration on the Conference of the Parliaments

The Conference invites the European Parliament and the national parliaments to meet as necessary as a Conference of the Parliaments (or 'Assises').

The Conference of the Parliaments will be consulted on the main features of the European Union, without prejudice to the powers of the European Parliament and the rights of the national parliaments. The President of the European Council and the President of the Commission will report to each session of the Conference of the Parliaments on the state of the Union.

Declaration on the number of members of the Commission and of the European Parliament

The Conference agrees that the Member States will examine the questions relating to the number of members of the Commission and the number of members of the European Parliament no later than at the end of 1992,[52] with a view to reaching an agreement which will permit the establishment of the necessary legal basis for fixing the number of members of the European Parliament in good time for the 1994 elections. The decisions will be taken in the light, *inter alia*, of the need to establish the overall size of the European Parliament in an enlarged Community.

---

52. There appears to be a slight anomaly here in that the member states are required to implement a Declaration annexed to the Final Act of a Treaty before the actual Treaty is due to enter into force!

Declaration on the hierarchy of Community acts

The Conference agrees that the Intergovernmental Conference to be convened in 1996 will examine to what extent it might be possible to review the classification of Community acts with a view to establishing an appropriate hierarchy between the different categories of act.

Declaration on the right of access to information

The Conference considers that transparency of the decision-making process strengthens the democratic nature of the institutions and the public's confidence in the administration. The Conference accordingly recommends that the Commission submit to the Council no later than 1993 a report on measures designed to improve public access to the information available to the institutions.

Declaration on estimated costs under Commission proposals

The Conference notes that the Commission undertakes, by basing itself where appropriate on any consultations it considers necessary and by strengthening its system for evaluating Community legislation, to take account in its legislative proposals of costs and benefits to the Member States' public authorities and all the parties concerned.

Declaration on the implementation of Community law

1. The Conference stresses that it is central to the coherence and unity of the process of European construction that each Member State should fully and accurately transpose into national law the Community Directives addressed to it within the deadlines laid down therein.

Moreover, the Conference, while recognizing that it must be for each Member State to determine how the provisions of Community law can best be enforced in the light of its own particular institutions, legal system and other circumstances, but in any event in compliance with Article 189 of the Treaty establishing the European Community, considers it essential for the proper functioning of the Community that the measures taken by the different Member States should result in Community law being applied with the same effectiveness and rigour as in the application of their national law.

2. The Conference calls on the Commission to ensure, in exercising its powers under Article 155 of this Treaty, that Member States fulfil their obligations. It asks the Commission to publish periodically a full report for the Member States and the European Parliament.

Declaration on assessment of the environmental impact of Community measures

The Conference notes that the Commission undertakes in its proposals, and that the Member States undertake in implementing those proposals, to take full account of their environmental impact and of the principle of sustainable growth.

Declaration on the Court of Auditors

The Conference emphasizes the special importance it attaches to the task assigned to the Court of Auditors by Articles 188a, 188b, 188c and 206 of the Treaty establishing the European Community.

It requests the other Community institutions to consider, together with the Court of Auditors, all appropriate ways of enhancing the effectiveness of its work.

Declaration on the Economic and Social Committee

The Conference agrees that the Economic and Social Committee will enjoy the same independence with regard to its budget and staff management as the Court Auditors has enjoyed hitherto.

Declaration on cooperation with charitable associations

The Conference stresses the importance, in pursuing the objectives of Article 117 on the Treaty establishing the European Community, of cooperation between the latter and charitable associations and foundations as institutions responsible for social welfare establishments and services.

Declaration on the protection of animals[53]

The Conference calls upon the European Parliament, the Council and the Commission, as well as the Member States, when drafting and implementing Community legislation on the common agricultural policy, transport, the internal market and research, to pay full regard to the welfare requirements of animals.

Declaration on the representation of the interests of the overseas countries and territories referred to in Article 227(3) and (5)(a) and (b) of the Treaty establishing the European Community

The Conference, noting that in exceptional circumstances divergences may arise between the interests of the Union and those of the overseas countries and territories referred to in Article 227(3) and (5)(a) and (b), agrees that the Council will seek to reach a solution which accords with the position of the Union. However, in the event that this proves impossible, the Conference agrees that the Member State concerned may act separately in

---

53. See EC Commission, *Communication on the Protection of Animals*, COM(93)384 final, Brussels, 22 July 1993.

the interests of the said overseas countries and territories, without this affecting the Community's interests. The Member State concerned will give notice to the Council and the Commission where such a divergence of interests is likely to occur and, when separate action proves unavoidable, make it clear that it is acting in the interests of overseas territory mentioned above.

This declaration also applies to Macao and East Timor.

Declaration on the outermost regions of the Community

The Conference acknowledges that the outermost regions of the Community (the French overseas departments, Azores and Madeira and Canary Islands) suffer from major structural backwardness compounded by several phenomena (remoteness, island status, small size, difficult topography and climate, economic dependence on a few products), the permanence and combination of which severely restrain their economic and social development.

It considers that, while the provisions of the Treaty establishing the European Community and secondary legislation apply automatically to the outermost regions, it is none the less possible to adopt specific measures to assist them inasmuch and as long as there is an objective need to take such measures with a view to the economic and social development of those regions. Such measures should have as their aim both the completion of the internal market and a recognition of the regional reality to enable the outermost regions to achieve the average economic and social level of the Community.

Declaration on voting in the field of the Common Foreign and Security Policy

The Conference agrees that, with regard to Council decisions requiring unanimity, Member States will, to the extent possible, avoid preventing a unanimous decision where a qualified majority exists in favour of that decision.

Declaration on practical arrangements in the field of the Common Foreign and Security Policy

The Conference agrees that the division of work between the Political Committee and the Committee of Permanent Representatives will be examined at a later stage, as will the practical arrangements for merging the Political Cooperation Secretariat with the General Secretariat of the Council and for cooperation between the latter and the Commission.

Declaration on the use of languages in the field of the Common Foreign and Security Policy

The Conference agrees that the use of languages shall be in accordance with the rules of the European Communities.

For COREU communications, the current practice of European political cooperation will serve as a guide for the time being.

All common foreign and security policy texts which are submitted to or adopted at meeting of the European Council and of the Council as well as all texts which are to be published are immediately and simultaneously translated into all the official Community languages.

Declaration on Western European Union

The Conference notes the following declarations:

I Declaration

by Belgium, Germany, Spain, France, Italy, Luxembourg, the Netherlands, Portugal and the United Kingdom of Great Britain and Northern Ireland, which are members of the Western European Union and also members of the European Union on
THE ROLE OF THE WESTERN EUROPEAN UNION AND ITS RELATIONS WITH THE EUROPEAN UNION AND WITH THE ATLANTIC ALLIANCE

Introduction

1. WEU Member States agree on the need to develop a genuine European security and defence identity and a greater European responsibility on defence matters. This identity will be pursued through a gradual process involving successive phases. WEU will form an integral part of the process of the development of the European Union and will enhance its contribution to solidarity within the Atlantic Alliance. WEU Member States agree to strengthen the role of WEU, in the longer term perspective of a common defence policy within the European Union which might in time lead to a common defence, compatible with that of the Atlantic Alliance.

2. WEU will be developed as the defence component of the European Union and as a means to strengthen the European pillar of the Atlantic Alliance. To this end, it will formulate common European defence policy and carry forward its concrete implementation through the further development of its own operational role.

WEU Member States take note of Article J.4 relating to the common foreign and security policy of the Treaty on European Union which reads as follows: [the text is reproduced above on pp. 379–80]

A. WEU's relations with the European Union

3. The objective is to build up WEU in stages as the defence component of the European Union. To this end, WEU is prepared, at the request of the European Union, to elaborate and implement decisions and actions of the Union which have defence implications.

To this end, WEU will take the following measures to develop a close working relationship with the Union:

— as appropriate, synchronization of the dates and venues of meetings and harmonization of working methods;

— establishment of close cooperation between the Council and Secretariat-General of WEU on the one hand, and the Council of the Union and General Secretariat of the Council on the other;

— consideration of the harmonization of the sequence and duration of the respective Presidencies;

— arranging for appropriate modalities so as to ensure that the Commission of the European Communities is regularly informed and, as appropriate, consulted on WEU activities in accordance with the role of the Commission in the common foreign and security policy as defined in the Treaty on European Union;

— encouragement of closer cooperation between the Parliamentary Assembly of WEU and the European Parliament.

The WEU Council shall, in agreement with the competent bodies of the European Union, adopt the necessary practical arrangements.

B.   WEU's relations with the Atlantic Alliance

4. The objective is to develop WEU as a means to strengthen the European pillar of the Atlantic Alliance. Accordingly WEU is prepared to develop further the close working links between WEU and the Alliance and to strengthen the role, responsibilities and contributions of WEU Member States in the Alliance. This will be undertaken on the basis of the necessary transparency and complementarity between the emerging European security and defence identity and the Alliance. WEU will act in conformity with the positions adopted in the Atlantic Alliance.

— WEU Member States will intensify their coordination on Alliance issues which represent an important common interest with the aim of introducing joint positions agreed in WEU into the process of consultation in the Alliance which will remain the essential forum for consultation among its members and the venue for agreement on policies bearing on the security and defence commitments of Allies under the North Atlantic Treaty.

— Where necessary, dates and venues of meetings will be synchronized and working methods harmonized.

— Close cooperation will be established between the Secretariats-General of WEU and NATO.

C.   Operational role of WEU

5. WEU's operational role will be strengthened by examining and defining appropriate missions, structures and means, covering in particular:

— WEU planning cell;

— closer military cooperation complementary to the Alliance in particular in the fields of logistics, transport, training and strategic surveillance;

— meetings of WEU Chiefs of Defence Staff;

— military units answerable to WEU.

Other proposals will be examined further including:

— enhanced cooperation in the field of armaments with the aim of creating a European armaments agency;

— development of the WEU Institute into a European Security and Defence Academy.

Arrangements aimed at giving WEU a stronger operational role will be fully compatible with the military dispositions necessary to ensure the collective defence of all Allies.

D. Other measures

6. As a consequence of the measures set out above, and in order to facilitate the strengthening of WEU's role, the seat of the WEU Council and Secretariat will be transferred to Brussels.

7. Representation of the WEU Council must be such that the Council is able to exercise its functions continuously in accordance with Article VIII of the modified Brussels Treaty. Member States may draw on a double-hatting formula, to be worked out, consisting of their representatives to the Alliance and to the European Union.

8. WEU notes that, in accordance with the provisions of Article J.4(6) concerning the common foreign and security policy of the Treaty on European Union, the Union will decide to review the provisions of this Article with a view to furthering the objective to be set by it in accordance with the procedure defined. The WEU will re-examine the present provisions in 1996. This re-examination will take account of the progress and experience acquired and will extend to relations between WEU and the Atlantic Alliance.

II Declaration

by Belgium, Germany, Spain, France, Italy, Luxembourg, the Netherlands, Portugal and the United Kingdom of Great Britain and Northern Ireland which are members of the Western European Union.

'The Member States of WEU welcome the development of the European security and defence identity. They are determined, taking into account the role of WEU as the defence component of the European Union and as the means to strengthen the European pillar of the Atlantic Alliance, to put the relationship between WEU and the other European States on a new basis for the sake of stability and security in Europe. In this spirit, they propose the following:

States which are members of the European Union are invited to accede to WEU on conditions to be agreed in accordance with Article XI of the modified Brussels Treaty, or to become observers if they so wish. Simultaneously, other European Member States of NATO are invited to become associate members of WEU in a way which will give them the possibility of participating fully in the activities of WEU.

The Member States of WEU assume that treaties and agreements corresponding with the above proposals will be concluded before 31 December 1992.'[54]

---

54. The Council/Commission version of the TEU (ISBN 92-824-0959-7) has this section in italics. Other versions do not (OJC 191, 29 July 1992; OJC 224, 31 August 1992; *The Unseen Treaty*, David Pollard Publishing, Oxford, 1992; Cm 1934, HMSO, London, 1992; *Journaux officiels*, Paris, 1992; *Presse- und Informationsamt der Bundesregierung*, Bonn, 1992; *Presse- und Informationsamt der Bundesregierung*, Bonn, 1993).

Declaration on asylum

1. The Conference agrees that, in the context of the proceedings provided for in Articles K.1 and K.3 of the provisions on cooperation in the fields of justice and home affairs, the Council will consider as a matter of priority questions concerning Member States' asylum policies, with the aim of adoption by the beginning of 1993, common action to harmonize aspects of them, in the light of the work programme and timetable contained in the report on asylum drawn up at the request of the European Council meeting in Luxembourg on 28 and 29 June 1991.

2. In this connection, the Council will also consider, by the end of 1993, on the basis of a report, the possibility of applying Article K.9 to such matters.

Declaration on police cooperation

The Conference confirms the agreement of the Member States on the objectives underlying the German delegation's proposals at the European Council meeting in Luxembourg on 28 and 29 June 1991.

For the present, the Member States agree to examine as a matter of priority the drafts submitted to them, on the basis of the work programme and timetable agreed upon in the report drawn up at the request of the Luxembourg European Council, and they are willing to envisage the adoption of practical measures in areas such as those suggested by the German delegation, relating to the following functions in the exchange of information and experience:

— support for national criminal investigation and security authorities, in particular in the coordination of investigations and search operations;
— creation of data bases;
— central analysis and assessment of information in order to take stock of the situation and identify investigative approaches;
— collection and analysis of national prevention programmes for forwarding to Member States and for drawing up Europe-wide prevention strategies;
— measures relating to further training, research, forensic matters and criminal records departments.

Member States agree to consider on the basis of a report, during 1994 at the latest, whether the scope of such cooperation should be extended.

Declaration on disputes between the ECB and the EMI and their servants[55]

The Conference considers it proper that the Court of First Instance should hear this class of action in accordance with Article 168a of the Treaty establishing the European Community. The Conference therefore invites the institutions to adapt the relevant rules accordingly.

---

55. This Declaration was inserted into the Final Act after the Maastricht Summit in December 1991 before the TEU was formally signed in February 1992.

VII. The Union in Context

The preceding analysis and exposition shows that, as well as being complex and capable of several interpretations, the Union, and the Treaties which constitute it, have manifold ramifications. However, they have yet to become the dominant element in European developments. Indeed, in the course of 1992−3, the Treaties underwent a baptism of fire in Community Europe, its member states and its economic and financial markets. At the same time the development of the Union was closely linked to developments elsewhere in Europe, to the processes leading to enlargement of the Community, to the workings of other European institutions, and to the increasingly unstable and violent situation in Yugoslavia and other peripheries of the continent.

These contexts have already had a significant effect on the way the Treaties are likely to be 'read'. Equally, they also have their own importance and ought not to be overlooked in a *Handbook* such as this. Moreover, they may well have a significant effect on the development of the Treaties and of the Union, a development which now seems much more uncertain than in the euphoric days of 1989−91.

So, in order to complete our understanding of the Treaties, it is important to set the Union in its wider European context. This final subdivision of the *Handbook* therefore looks at this setting by, in the first instance, considering six topics: the general relationship between the Union and Europe during 1992−3; the dual patterns of political and economic change inside the Community during the process of ratification; the parallel fluctuations in member states and their attitudes to the Union; the interactions between this, the combined European Economic Area (EEA) and enlargement process, and the other states involved in them; the evolving relationship between the post-Maastricht Union and other international organizations in Europe; and the interrelations between the Maastricht process and events in the southern and eastern peripheries of Europe.

Having done this, it becomes possible to make some estimates of where the Union now stands, what the future might hold for it, and how its progress might be followed by interested readers. What is important to remember here, is that even though the continent became an increasingly unhappy place in 1992–3, the questions which Maastricht was trying to answer about European relations remained real ones. What was at issue was the validity of the answers being offered: whether they were appropriate for all member states; whether they were acceptable to European citizens in general; whether they embodied the correct legitimacy for the new Europe; whether they were based on the right mode of integration; and whether they had been posed sufficiently openly and in the right quarters. The answer seems to be that, irrespective of its many faults, the TEU remained 'the only deal on the table'. Hence, many doubters came to accept that ratifying it was a necessary step towards any better developments in Europe since, without it, the situation might have become even more uncertain.

i. Europe and the Union

One thing which became clear in 1992 was that the Union is not just a matter for the Community and its decision-makers alone, whether those in Brussels or in the national capitals of the Twelve. It has implications for the whole of Europe. This is true whether one defines Europe in political, economic or geographical terms. Thus politically, the decisions made at Maastricht were called into question by a sizeable body of public opinion within the Community. The unhappiness of much grassroots opinion in the Twelve about the way they were being governed and where they were being led became increasingly apparent. So the euphoria of early 1992 gave way to an apparent explosion of public unease about political elites — described by one observer as the 'Holy Alliance of the Self Important'; their style of governance; and their Maastricht deal. Partly as a result of this, the ratification process was infinitely more fraught politically than had been anticipated, both at Community level and in domestic politics.

These problems, already visible at the time the Treaty was being negotiated, proved to be more influential than the problems of post-Cold War Europe which the creation of a Union was intended to solve. Maastricht became a problem because of this and also because it focuses attention on the sensitive issues of national identity and political tradition. Hence the ratification process changed from a formality into an apparently never-ending series of uncertainties. Ratification interacted with political anger and instability inside the member states where public opinion was increasingly unhappy about economic conditions.

At the same time, the behaviour of the international currency markets several times threatened the foundations of both the ERM and EMU. This was a reflection of the increasingly acute economic depression in Europe which demanded other solutions than those foreseen by the convergence conditions of the TEU and the high interest rates needed by ERM states to maintain their position in the mechanism, where the German mark was artificially buoyed up by the tight monetary policies pursued by the Bundesbank in order to cope with the costly aftermath of unification. All this rather overshadowed the nominal completion of the Single Market. Again, such factors interacted with the developing political malaise inside the member states of the Community. All this made it very plain that the Europe of the Union was a much deeper, more diverse and less disciplined community than assumed at Maastricht.

The fact that Europe was also much wider geographically than the Community also became painfully apparent in 1992–3. To begin with, many of the smaller states of Western Europe, who were seeking both to negotiate admission to the Single Market through the European Economic Area (EEA) and to gain entry to the Community, suffered similar political and economic difficulties. The turmoil inside the Community and its member states encouraged similar feelings about Europe in some of the EFTA countries, highlighted by the Swiss people's rejection of the EEA Agreement.

Further east, the Visegrad states also suffered the spillover effects from the Community's own problems. While seeking their own forms of relationship with the Union, progress in ratifying the agreements already reached with the EC was very slow. EFTA states found themselves in a similar position with regard to the ratification of the EEA within the Community. The EC's own role in other European institutions and in the increasingly violent and unhappy situation in former Yugoslavia was also affected by its problems over Maastricht.

q.v.
Visegrad
pp. 485–7.

Equally, developments in other parts of Europe have had, and will continue to have, implications for the Union. Non-Community Europe was itself caught up in the deeper political and economic processes which underlay the crises of ratification. Moreover, unease in other countries sometimes fed back into the Community's own difficulties.

All this reflects the multiple nature of the Union. As an economic entity the development of the Union symbolizes not just the now notionally completed Single Market, but also the development of a single currency and central banking system. No state in Europe could expect to manage without access to the Single Market whether for sales or for supplies. This means that the health of the Union economy, and the standards applied there, will have a determining effect on affairs elsewhere. It is also likely that the emergence of a monetary union would have a direct impact on most non-member states and their currencies.

Equally the new social norms implied in the TEU, even though rejected by the United Kingdom, will also have an impact on the policies devised by other states outside the Union. This is probably likely to be true of a wide range of Community policies with which many states will have to come to terms if they are not to be marginalized and discriminated against. No other European institution offers such a range of policy standards on which outside states can model their legislation. Already the Visegrad countries are adopting elements of EC law. This is particularly so with competition policy, the adherence to which is a requirement of their Europe Agreements with the EC. European firms, groups and institutions will also be keen to enter, or remain in, the many Community programmes covering education and science.

Politically, the Union is the body which many European states now seek to enter. This is not just because of its economic role but because it provides influence and security. Being inside the Union offers outside states political reassurance and a share in decision-making. And many countries see the Community as the only body likely to provide real security in an uncertain world, especially should the Union come to develop common foreign, security and even defence policies. This has implications for a whole range of other international institutions in Europe.

While governments find themselves drawn towards the Union, their citizens may well be less keen. Although the Union consolidates new opportunities, the way the Community already impinges on the life and work of large numbers of people, inside and outside its borders, leads them to query many of its activities. So, the Union is a factor in the internal political dynamics of a number of European countries. It has already affected the climate of public opinion, especially where relations with the Community have implications for national political institutions and practices. It can even influence government formation.

At the same time political changes in other countries can, as already suggested, affect the Union, just as do those in its member states. On the one hand, events in what were the USSR and, especially, Yugoslavia influence the emergence of a security dimension in the Union. More generally, developments in the East threaten the Union with new pressures for aid, for trade openings and from migration. The latter can be very poorly received in the Union and its member states, encouraging the trend towards xenophobia.

Economic circumstances in other parts of Europe will also have large implications for the Union. Continuing depression will block market openings and discourage the provision of aid. In the long run all this could increase external European pressures on the Union. Hence the Union's relations with the rest of the continent, and with many of its own citizens, are immensely complicated and uncertain. Such pressures from the peripheries were, however, largely obscured in 1992–3 by the turmoil inside the Community and its member states over ratification.

Yet, even so, such developments inside the Community do not mean that the latter is yet coextensive with Europe. Other actors, other developments and other institutions have long been playing their parts in the evolution of the continent. They continue to provide not just a context but also an important influence on the Community and the identity of Europe. So, the wider Europe is likely to play a significant part in the progress of the Union. In other words, it could have an impact on the way the TEU is likely to be understood, applied and developed.

FURTHER READING

Ashford, S. and Timms, N., *What Europe Thinks: A study of Western values*, Dartmouth, Aldershot, 1992.

Baldassarri, M. and Mundell, R., *Building the New Europe*, Macmillan, London, 1993.

Cafruny, A.W. and Rosenthal, G.G., *The State of the European Community: Maastricht and beyond*, Longman, London, 1993.

Collinson, S., Miall, H. and Michalski, A., *A Wider European Union? Integration and Cooperation in the New Europe*, RIIA, London, 1993.

Dawson, A., *A Geography of European Integration*, Belhaven Press, London, 1993.

Garcia, S., *European Identity and the Search for Legitimacy*, Pinter, London, 1993.

Lankowski, C., *Europe's Emerging Identity: Regional integration vs. opposition movements in the European Community* Adamantine Press, London, 1992.

Nötzold J. and Rummel, R., 'On the way to a New European Order', *Aussenpolitik*, vol. 41, no. 3,

1990 pp. 212–24.

Padoa-Schioppa, T., 'Sur les institutions politiques de l'Europe nouvelle', *Commentaire*, vol. 15, no. 58, 1992, pp. 283–92.

Story, J., 'Opinions publiques et intégration européenne', *Politique étrangére*, vol. 57, no. 4, 1992, pp.

893–913.

Wilson, T.M. and Estellie Smith, M., *Cultural Change and the New Europe: Perspectives on the European Community*, Westview, Boulder, 1992.

ii. The road from Maastricht

The post-Maastricht period has not, as already suggested, been a happy one for the Community. Indeed, after a few honeymoon months following agreement on, and the final signing of the TEU in February 1992, the settlement, and indeed the Community as a whole, was buffeted by two, interrelated, winds of crisis: the political and the monetary. Politically, while Europe has faced debilitating external challenges, notably in what was Yugoslavia, the ratification process revealed deep-seated public unease about the TEU, suggesting that the permissive consensus, on which the integration process has traditionally relied, no longer exists. At the same time, the European economies nose-dived into depression, thus unsettling the currency markets. These then began to challenge both the ERM and the prospects for monetary union, even though ratification became increasingly likely as 1993 wore on. The fiscal and economic crisis also forced the Community to adopt a new, and enhanced role in coordinating the fight for recovery.

The economic downturn and the political malaise were clearly interrelated, and would have been unsettling enough for the Community in any event. In fact, they were complicated by events inside member states and beyond. This turned the crises into a deep-seated challenge to European integration, creating a new stridency and instability inside and outside the Community. In turn, this encouraged a re-thinking of the way the Treaty is likely to be 'read' and implemented once ratification is concluded.

Political responses to Maastricht

At the outset, Maastricht seemed likely to enjoy a relatively unproblematic future. While the Community completed the signing of the finalized Treaty and began to plan for its financial and general implementation, the European Parliament approved the deal and the Twelve were confident enough to agree a change to the text. This involved a further Declaration to resolve the Irish abortion problem.

Protocol 17 of the TEU states that the new arrangements did not threaten the Irish constitutional ban on abortion. However, when a ruling by the Irish Attorney General confirmed that the Constitution could be used to prohibit Irish citizens from going to the United Kingdom for abortions, the Protocol appeared to be in breach of Irish rights of free movement. The right of access to information freely available elsewhere was also at risk. (See pp. 469–70 below.) Since all this threatened to make the pro-choice lobby in Ireland vote against the Treaty,

q.v.
Protocol 17
p. 427.

because it restricted such rights and enshrined a private concession to anti-abortion forces, the Community agreed in April to clarify the situation.

Thus the Declaration provided an authoritative, although not legally binding interpretation of the Protocol. This was that the latter was not intended to prohibit freedom of travel or information. However, it does not explicitly permit the provision of abortion services in Ireland. The Twelve also undertook to amend the original Protocol to bring it into line with any revised constitutional articles on abortion.

q.v.
Declaration
34 p. 536.

Apart from this, there was little sign of popular opposition to Maastricht. Hence, if there was considerable debate in Denmark, the Folketing approved the Treaty easily enough, voting by 130 to 25 in favour in the spring of 1992. The French ratification process also started unproblematically. Moreover, all the main parties in the United Kingdom's April 1992 general election campaigned in support of the Treaty, which was given a Second Reading in the House of Commons by 336 to 92 on 21 May.

Things were to change dramatically, however, in late May and June. The reason for the change was the sudden eruption of public opinion on the scene. Prior to Maastricht populations had been content to let governments decide European policy on their own. In the run-up to the Danish referendum, however, the virtues and failings of Maastricht began to be widely debated. Then, when the referendum narrowly went against the Treaty, the situation was changed again. The Community was forced to change its initial assumption that, should a single country fail to ratify the TEU, the other eleven would simply proceed on their own. The Danish decision thus proved a catalyst for underlying doubts not only about the essential legitimacy of the Treaty but also about both the whole process of integration and the whole style of West European governance.

The referendum in Denmark (details of which are provided in Box 21 along with those of other ratification votes), was lost for a variety of reasons. These included the complacency and unpopularity of the government. This had circulated the Treaty widely but without a commentary, making it hard to resist arguments that the country was giving up not just its sovereignty but also its young men to a foreign bureaucracy intent on conscripting them into a European army. Gaffes from one of Delors' aides and Chancellor Kohl about the limited role that small states were likely to face in the future Union encouraged such beliefs. There were also fears for Denmark's currency and social welfare system standards at the hands of a free market inclined Union. The vigour of the opposition, and its skill in arguing that the country could say 'No' without incurring any costs, was also important.

For many in Europe, the whole Maastricht process seemed to have lost its legitimacy that June because the TEU could only become operative if it was ratified in all twelve member states. The Danish 'No' meant that this could not happen, as opponents elsewhere were quick to point out. The defeat threw a harsh new light on the Treaty and its meaning. Responding to internal opposition, including calls for a referendum, the UK government delayed the ratification process pending clarification of the Danish position. This was despite the clear majority for ratification achieved at the TEU's second reading in the House of Commons.

Box 21. Ratification of the TEU

Country	Referenda				Parliamentary ratification					
	Date	Yes %	No[1] %	Turnout %	Date	Chamber	For	Against	Abstain	Absent
Belgium	—	—	—	—	19.07.1992	Lower	146	33	3	30
					04.11.1992	Upper	115	26	1	42
Denmark	02.06.1992	49.3	50.7	84.6	12.05.1992	Unicameral	130	25	1	19
	18.05.1993	56.8	43.2	86.2	28.04.1993	Unicameral[2]	154	16	0	5
France[3]	20.09.1992	51.05	48.95	70.0	—	—	—	—	—	—
Germany	—	—	—	—	02.12.1992	Lower	543	17	8	95
					18.12.1992	Upper	69	0	0	0
Greece	—	—	—	—	31.07.1992	Unicameral	286	8	1	6
Ireland[4]	18.06.1992	68.7	31.3	57.0	—	—	—	—	—	—
Italy	—	—	—	—	29.10.1992	Lower	403	46	18	163
					17.09.1992	Upper	176	16	1	157
Luxembourg	—	—	—	—	02.07.1992	Unicameral	51	6	0	0
Netherlands	—	—	—	—	12.11.1992	Lower	137	12	0	1
					19.12.1992	Upper	67	8	0	0
Portugal	—	—	—	—	10.12.1992	Unicameral	200	21	9	0
Spain	—	—	—	—	29.10.1992	Lower	314	3	8	25
					25.11.1992	Upper	222	0	3	29
United Kingdom	—	—	—	—	20.05.1993	Lower	292	112	245[5]	762
					20.07.1993	Upper	141	29	271	
European Parliament[6]	—	—	—	—	07.04.1992	Unicameral	226	62	31	199

Source: The information contained in the table hass been compiled from information contained in: Rideau, Joël, 'Les procédures de ratification du traité sur l'Union européenne', *Revue française du droit constitutionnel*, 1992/12, pp. 611–24; Schmuck, Otto, 'Heterogene Diskussionslandschaft zu Maastricht: Die Ratifizierungsdebatten zum Vertrag über die Europäische Union', *Integration*, Vol. 15, No. 4, 1992, pp. 206–15; and communications from national parliaments and embassies.

1 Spoiled ballot papers have been included in the figures for no votes.

2 A final parliamentary vote ratifying the TEU and the Edinburgh Decision relating to Denmark (see pp. 532–5) was held on 9 June 1993 after the second referendum. Of the MPs which took part, 153 voted in favour of ratification and 16 against.

3 Ratification of the TEU in France was determined by the outcome of the referendum alone. No formal vote was required in either the *Assemblée nationale* nor the *Sénat*.

4 Ratification of the TEU in Ireland was determined by the outcome of the referendum alone. No formal vote was required in either the *Dáil* or the *Seanad*.

5 This figure represents the number of MPs who did not vote in the debate. The breakdown between actual abstainers and those absent from the vote is not available

6 The positive vote in the European Parliament was not a formal requirement of the ratification process, hence the low turnout. It is nevertless included here for information purposes.

The decision caused much annoyance amongst the UK's partners.

Their reaction symbolized the fact that some interests still wanted to press ahead with the Treaty and not renegotiate. This added a new element to the debate by convincing many that critics of Brussels' ambitions were quite right. Community governments, including that of Denmark, were intent on proceeding with the plans laid down in the TEU to create a European Union. Danish reservations about economic and monetary union, a common defence policy and Union citizenship were not deemed sufficient to halt the progress of European integration. Community elites were aware that renegotiation would simply intensify divisions and could prevent the limited progress made possible by the delicate compromises of Maastricht. Thus, on 3 June 1992, President Mitterrand called for a referendum in France, assuming that this would win an easy endorsement for the TEU, thereby overshadowing the Danish rejection.

With all options, save renegotiation, left open, the Danes were left to consider how the rejection might best be overcome. While commitments were made to try and bring the Community closer to its citizens, the pressures for continuing with ratification were reinforced by the bad-tempered Lisbon Summit in late June. This decided to press on, not only with Maastricht, but also with its financing. However, the Summit made less progress on enlargement and completing the Single Market.

Despite the first parliamentary ratifications, in Belgium and Luxembourg, and the successful referendum in Ireland (where economic arguments largely carried the day), opposition did not wane. Ratification, indeed, seemed to be another example of politicians ignoring both the rules and the wishes of the electorate. This helped to mobilize large-scale opposition to the Treaty while also inducing a change of heart in many of its supporters. This was notably the case in the United Kingdom where the crisis played into the hands of elements — including those inside established parties — traditionally sceptical about integration, but normally marginalized by the overcentralized UK political system. They were joined by Lady Thatcher and some of her former lieutenants who began to campaign vigorously for a referendum in the United Kingdom.

Motives in other countries were usually more varied and pragmatic than those in the United Kingdom. Nonetheless, opinion polls in many countries showed significant majorities against the Treaty and in favour of a referendum, as was the case in both the Netherlands and Germany. In June the *Rassemblement pour la République* (RPR) abstained on the constitutional amendments needed to make Maastricht legal in France and the next month two of its leaders, Charles Pasqua and Philippe Seguin, launched the highly successful opposition movement: the 'Rally for a "No" Vote'. Jean-Pierre Chevènement, a left-wing Socialist who resigned as a minister, also launched his own anti-TEU movement. Public support for ratification, as reported in polls, fell from 65 per cent in mid-June to 49 per cent in late August.

Public opinion in Germany, meanwhile, was also restive, partly because of fears of increased immigration, and especially because of the threat posed to the DM by proposals for a single currency under EMU. The DM was, for many Germans, the symbol of both their prosperity and their determination not to repeat the inflationary and anti-democratic mistakes of the interwar years. By the summer, only 25 per cent were reported to be in favour of a single currency. The possible erosion of the rights of the *Länder*, as a result of the TEU, was also a significant factor in reducing support for the Maastricht settlement.

Faced with all this, some of those who had been lukewarm about the Treaty felt they had to rally to its defence. This was one of a number of ways in which understandings of what had been done at Maastricht began to change. At the same time Delors began to put more stress both on subsidiarity and on openness in Commission operations. This led to a lot of background work on proposals on subsidiarity. It was hoped that this might help to make the Treaty more acceptable to the Danes, thereby encouraging them to reverse their decision. The Delors II financial package was held up, although some limited progress was made on enlargement. And, in Germany, Kohl began to promise greater influence to the *Länder*, remarking in the autumn that 'account will have to be taken of the wishes and fears of the populations and, if we reach the conclusion that Brussels is regulating things too much . . . this will have to be stopped and reversed'. This eventually led to the Bundestag being unilaterally promised the right to decide on German adoption of a single currency.

Such moves helped the government campaign in France to win back some of its support in the weeks before the referendum. Yet, in the event the margin was slim and there was clear evidence of public disdain both for the Socialist government and for the Treaty's inroads on French sovereignty. The majority of French regions actually voted against the Treaty. Coming on top, as will be seen, of the upheavals in the currency markets that month, this evidence of French lukewarmness on the Treaty dealt a further blow to its credibility, ratification in Greece and the Italian Senate notwithstanding. At the same time, the narrow referendum result gave increased impetus to opponents in the United Kingdom and elsewhere. Even in France polls later suggested that more than half the French wished they had voted against ratification.

Such feelings made life hard for the increasingly embattled and partial UK Presidency. This was already under increasing attack, both at home for conceding too much, and abroad for being belligerent and un-*communautaire*. At home opposition meant that hopes of ratifying the Treaty after the French vote were dashed. Indeed, the government only won the so called 'paving debate' in early November by three votes. This owed much both to the support of the Liberal Democrats and to last-minute promises to Tory rebels that they would not ratify until the Danish people had voted a second time.

Abroad, the Presidency's subsidiarity proposals and its public style were found unacceptable by many other states, whose parliaments made considerable progress with ratification in October and November. Hence ominous warnings about the future of the UK budget rebate were heard. Earlier, the European Council Summit in Birmingham was able to do no more than paper over the cracks. This was partly because it was side-tracked by the UK row over the closure of the coal mines.

Nonetheless, the Summit welcomed Danish proposals. The Danish government had set about identifying those areas of the Treaty which lay behind the referendum defeat. By October 1992 it had produced the so-called White Book analysing Denmark's position *vis-à-vis* the TEU and putting forward possible options. On the basis of this, the majority of Danish parties, including some of those which had been most critical of the original Treaty agreed a set of proposals, known as the 'National Compromise'. These were for a legally binding agreement between Denmark and the other eleven member states. This, it was hoped, would allay the fears of the Danish people thereby allowing their government to put the issue to a second referendum, at some time during the first half of 1993, with the possibility of a successful outcome.

Acceptance of the deal was poised on the proverbial knife edge in the run up to Edinburgh, especially as German progress with ratification was balanced by the Swiss vote against the EEA. In the end Major was able to steer through a deal and partly restore the reputation of the Presidency. Edinburgh offered the Danes two things: a new form of legal instrument, a Declaration by the Heads of State and Government who had signed up for Maastricht; and an underwriting of unilateral Danish declarations which would be attached to the Treaty. Taken together they provided interpretations of some of the areas which caused the Danes difficulties: citizenship, EMU, and defence policy, social-security standards and parliamentary control over justice and home affairs activities.

q.v. EEA pp. 479–82.

Although the statements hardly seem to differ from what was already in the Treaty, they served an important psychological function. They offered a double reassurance to Danish electors that the 'reading' of the Treaty would be the one they wanted. As an interpretation it was fully consonant with the Treaty and did not legally modify it, a point on which both Euroenthusiasts and Eurosceptics agreed, albeit for different reasons. Politically of course it did modify the Treaty by changing the way it would be understood and interpreted. Thus Edinburgh reinforced the effects of earlier criticisms. For this reason the document is reprinted on pp. 532–5. The settlement it embodies will have to be reviewed in 1996.

q.v. subsidiarity pp. 68–75.

All this has, rather like the TEU itself, to be regarded as a symbolic fudge. Nonetheless, whatever its nature, it was reinforced by new commitments to subsidiarity and transparency in the way the Community operated. These were clearly made with opponents of the Treaty in mind. Edinburgh also achieved progress in other fields including the related financial package, the commencement of enlargement negotiations, and policies to encourage economic growth. Here too the decisions taken are important for understandings of the Treaty.

It was hoped that the Edinburgh settlement would ensure that the ratification process could be speeded up, perhaps even opening the way for further integration, now that a new Commission was in place. The desire to do this was symbolized by the publication in February 1993 of the European Parliament's second draft constitution. Yet this was not to be so, despite final parliamentary ratification in Germany and the Netherlands. The failure to press on was partly due to the way the sudden change of government in Denmark held up the referendum process there. It was also due to the fact that over twenty legal challenges to ratification were presented to the German Constitutional Court in Karlsruhe.

Even more important was the slow progress being made in the UK House of Commons. The Committee stage began in December 1992 and, with the two-page bill amending the 1972 European Communities Act attracting 370 amendments, government business managers found the going very hard. Tory Europhobes were adept in tabling amendments which they hoped would wreck the Treaty or, at least, force a referendum. They inflicted a number of moral and actual victories on the government which had to resort to some questionable interpretational and political devices to make progress.

Progress was also threatened by the Labour opposition. This objected to the UK opt-out from the Protocol on the Social Chapter and pushed its opposition to almost un-European extremes. In the end it was able to force a parliamentary debate on the issue after ratification as well as win an amendment vote on the Social Protocol. This, which the government had to accept, deleted the latter from the list of Protocols which the United Kingdom would ratify. The government now claimed that the Protocol had no legal effect and need not impede ratification. Others were less certain given that some ministers had earlier seen it as inimical to ratification.

q.v. Social Chapter pp. 423–5.

Other signs of continuing unease came in France, where the election, in late March 1993, saw unparalleled gains for the Right and notably the doubters of the RPR. Known anti-Maastricht figures like Pasqua and Seguin gained high office. Currency uncertainties also continued. And, in Denmark, opinion polls appeared to suggest that the 'No' vote was growing, even amongst supporters of the governing Social Democratic Party.

In the event, by late April, the Commons' committee stage of the Bill was finished. Then, on 18 May, the Danish people, by a surprisingly large margin of 56.8 per cent to 43.2 per cent, voted to approve the TEU as, apparently, reinterpreted by the Edinburgh Declaration. This helped to blunt some of the enthusiasm of the opposition allowing the Commons in late May to give a Third Reading to the Bill by 292 to 112. Forty-one Tory MPs voted against while 5 labour members supported ratification. This still left the Treaty to run the gauntlet of Margaret Thatcher and her supporters in the House of Lords where they continued to press for rejection or referendum. However, this raised the possibility of a constitutional crisis and, after a very educated debate, the Lords gave the Treaty an even larger majority.

q.v. Edinburgh Declaration pp. 532–5.

This was not the end of the matter because, such was the strength of opposition in the Commons, that the government could not get the resolution of the House on the Social Chapter which it needed to complete ratification. Late in July it was defeated by an alliance of Labour and its own rebels. However, the latter upheld the government in a vote of confidence in the government's position on social policy. This made ratification possible.

Even then, further trouble ensued. The day after Royal Assent to the Bill had been given, Lord Rees-Mogg launched a legal challenge to ratification. This threatened to delay the process into the autumn. However, the crushing nature of the judicial rejection of the challenge, combined with the fact that people were losing interest, especially as the markets suggested that the TEU's financial clauses might never be implemented, persuaded him not to appeal. Hence the UK government duly ratified the Treaty on 3 August 1993. This still left the TEU facing a further legal challenge in Germany, not to mention the renewed buffeting it received from the markets in the late summer. As well as its economic foundations being shaken, the prospects for its common foreign and security policy were also called into question by continuing divisions over Bosnia, where European policy remained controversial and ineffective.

Although at the time of writing, at the very end of August 1993, the odds are in favour of the Constitutional Court in Karlsruhe ruling in favour of ratification, it is clear that the Treaty continues to be politically contentious. Exactly how divisive the question actually was is unclear since both sides tend to overstress their support. Nor has any real research has been done. However, a Eurobarometer poll across the Twelve reported in late May 1993 that, while 41 per cent were in favour of the TEU, 24 per cent were against and 35 per cent were still undecided.

Another problem is that opposition to Maastricht is so bound up with other considerations that it is not clear exactly how real a challenge there was to the precise details of the TEU. This was because hostility to Maastricht was not only a nationalist reaction to its proposals. Certainly these were seen as threatening to deprive members states of their sovereignty and identity to the benefit of unelected bankers and Community officials. People were also aware of how far the Community had developed, and how it was increasingly involved in the whole range of national policies, including very sensitive ones. As has been said, after Maastricht 'public opinion bulldozed its way into the arena'.

At the same time, the Treaty provided an outlet for expression of the wider discontents with individual governments and political systems which have already been noted. The increasing professionalization and personalization of political parties have helped to cut them off from ordinary electors, who have become increasingly sceptical of their honesty and efficacy. Maastricht was often seen as the political elites playing yet more games for their own benefit. Interestingly, well over half those ministers who signed the Treaty in February 1993 had left office within eighteen months of doing so.

So, hostility to Maastricht was a twofold phenomenon. Both aspects were intimately related to the deteriorating economic circumstances. Indeed, events in the early 1990s mirrored those of the early 1970s. However, the turbulence of the currency markets was a new and highly destabilizing factor.

The economic standing of Maastricht

Since the TEU rests on economic as well as on political aspirations, its activation requires not just ratification but also supportive economic conditions. In 1992, however, these too began to work against the Maastricht settlement, as previously suggested. They did this in three ways. Firstly, the ERM experienced stormy conditions in the world money markets. Secondly, and at the same time, the way Europe as a whole plunged into recession created new economic pressures on the Community. These two factors also conspired to produce the third factor, the way the financial assumptions of Maastricht were upset, threatening not merely the attaining of both economic convergence and EMU, but also the continuing existence of the ERM itself.

Some authorities think that the markets delivered a worse blow to the idea of Union than did disaffection among electors. By querying both the ERM and the likelihood of EMU being achieved, the markets threatened the dynamo of the whole Maastricht settlement. This has major implications for understandings of the Treaty. In economic terms this not merely overshadowed the fact that the Single Market, in theory, came into effect at the start of 1993, but also put the issue of economic recovery firmly on the Community agenda.

The Danish rejection of Maastricht, which was not uninfluenced by the impact of convergence conditions on property and labour markets, triggered off a wave of uncertainty in the foreign exchange markets in the second half of 1992. The 'No' vote suggested to many that, despite ringing public endorsements by politicians and businessmen, EMU might not come about. This threatened the ERM, leaving some of its weaker currencies rather exposed. The root problem lay in the dominance of Germany and the DM in the EMS and the fact that the ERM, especially as then interpreted, forced other countries to pay the price of Germany's domestic difficulties. Unification had proved to be far more expensive than anyone had expected, or had been willing to admit. The German government was therefore forced to borrow to meet the costs, having promised there would be no tax increases. The resultant fiscal expansion caused the ever cautious Bundesbank to raise interest rates so as to prevent inflation. The bank may also have thought this would persuade employers to attack the high social costs accepted by German industry. These higher interest rates had to be matched in other countries to stop money seeping into Germany at a time when bank lending was, in any case, drying up and American interest rates were falling. The economic costs of artificially high interest rates imposed on other European countries in the form of bankruptcies and unemployment were very high and undermined the standing of their currencies.

Scandinavian currencies thus came under pressure that summer and in the early autumn of 1992 so did many Community currencies. Firms, and to a lesser extent speculators, began to fear devaluations and sought to move their holdings out of threatened monies so as to protect their assets. In theory the ERM, as a flexible instrument, could have adjusted to this by revaluations. However, as already noted in the third subdivision of the *Handbook*, the system became much more rigid at the turn of the decade. This reflected the way the ERM had come to serve as the foundation of EMU rather than just a means of managing currency fluctuations. So much political capital and pride was tied up in it, that elites were very reluctant to change things. To do so would be to admit that the economic pain inflicted on their countries had been unnecessary. Unpopular governments were particularly unwilling to lose face in this way. So they tried to hold the line.

Unfortunately the liberalization of capital markets, brought about by the Single Market, made this increasingly hard to do. With something like $900 billion moving through foreign exchange markets every day, national reserves were quite insufficient to support market rates. Fears in the United Kingdom and France prevented a realignment in early September, leaving the rates very vulnerable.

With contradictory signals coming from the Bundesbank about future interest-rate policies, the winds of currency change increased to gale force. On 16 September 1992, despite lunatically large increases in interest rates and massive national bank intervention in the markets, sterling and the Italian lira suspended their membership. Shortly afterwards the peseta and other currencies had to be devalued within the ERM.

While this enabled the pound to find a much lower level, allowing interest rates to fall, it did not end the problems. Pressure was then directed to the French franc. This was seen off during the autumn of 1993, thanks to support from the Bundesbank, which was accused of doing more to help the Elysée than it had Downing Street. So the crisis induced a good deal of bitterness amongst states. Some of this faded as the Bundesbank began to cut interest rates gradually over the winter. However, this did not prevent an attack on the Irish punt which also had to be devalued in January 1993.

Thereafter there was a brief pause before the problems reasserted themselves. The pause allowed the Community to try and tackle its increasingly bleak economic situation. This, of course, had hardly been helped by the currency crisis. The problem was a triple one. First there was a worldwide recession. Economic prospects were already deteriorating in 1991–2, even in Japan. Secondly, the interdependence of the West European economies meant that problems in one meant problems for all, as UK manufacturers found when their new, lower, prices failed to win increased sales because their continental customers were not buying because their economies were sliding further into depression.

Thirdly, recovery was hamstrung by the demands of the ERM. Adherence to ERM norms had helped to bring inflation down, but at a severe cost in jobs and investment. European growth, notably in manufacturing, slumped in 1992–3, even in Germany which experienced its first trade deficit in years. High interest rates, high wages and welfare costs, and weak competitiveness all had an effect. The steel industry was particularly badly hit. Growth was estimated to be likely to go down from 1.2 per cent in 1992 to 0.75 per cent in 1993. Inflation was also inching upwards.

The coming of the Single Market seemed to offer no real relief. And the debts left over from the boom of the 1980s made consumers increasingly unwilling to buy. Unemployment began to rise remorselessly once again, threatening to reach 8.6 per cent in OECD countries in 1993.

The scale of the depression, which took many by surprise, led to pressure for something to be done at the Community level. Although protectionist urges were emerging, the Edinburgh Summit did manage to agree the principle of trying to stimulate economic activity. This led in April to the launching of a package of loosely coordinated measures across the EC and EFTA to try and revive both the economy and the labour market through better training, help to small businesses and infrastructural investment. This mainly involved action by member states, although the EC's structural funds and a proposed European Investment Fund for transnational infrastructural projects could play a part.

It was hoped that the package would add 0.6 per cent to GDP growth in 1993–4, as well as creating 450,000 jobs. These were carried further at the

Copenhagen Summit. The financing package for Maastricht, known as Delors II, was also agreed over the winter with less difficulty than had been imagined. However, whether these new measures will actually reverse the economic cycle and restore confidence in the Maastricht settlement remains to be seen. Some change will have to come from increased flexibility in the way the economy operates. Such alterations are often resisted in times of economic decline.

In any case, before the package could begin to work, the pause in currency instability not merely brought to an end the perceived success, but virtually destroyed the EMS. To begin with the peseta and the escudo had to devalue for a second time in May 1993, in order to lessen pressure on fast-dwindling reserves and economies. Then, in late July and early August the core currencies of the ERM found themselves at the eye of a new typhoon. This seems to have had its roots in late June and early July when the French began to cut interest rates to aid their hard-pressed economy, and to talk of the franc replacing the DM as the anchor currency of the EMS because the German economy was declining even more precipitately. This left the franc exposed because the Bundesbank showed little inclination to cut its rates. Warnings that trouble lay ahead were heard in mid-July. The currency markets felt that there would be a revaluation because the weaker economies could not sustain the cripplingly high rates of interest and subsequent economic collapse deriving from the politically inspired link to the DM. Hence holding French or Belgian francs became too risky. Share prices began to rise in anticipation of the higher profits which cuts in interest rates would bring.

When, at the end of the month, the Bundesbank refused to cut interest rates, the storm broke. The Bank felt it had to continue its fight against inflation and rigidities inside German industry. So there was a barrage of selling, leading to 'Black Thursday' on 29 July. Despite national banks spending anything up to $80 billion from reserves to support the parities, the franc was pinned to the bottom of its range in the ERM. The Danes and others again pushed their interest rates up to try and defend their parities, also without success. The Commission was left very much on the fringes of the crisis.

So, although Prime Minister Balladur claimed the ERM was working well, the Spaniards were already calling for change and the Banque de France had recognized the inevitability of a realignment. Balladur refused to allow this at first, hoping that Chancellor Kohl might pressurize the Bundesbank into cutting interest rates. This would have aided the franc and punished the markets.

However, it did not happen and the 22-hour-long meeting of the EMS Monetary Committee on 1−2 August was bitter and fraught. The Germans, with French support, offered to take the DM out of the EMS but the other member states refused to accept this. They wished to stay within the DM zone as the franc did not offer enough protection. So the initial German idea of widening the bands was eventually accepted, only a margin of manoeuvre of 15 per cent on each side was agreed for all but the Dutch florin. This meant that, nominally, the ERM was preserved though in reality it became so fluid as to lose most practical significance. This was a convenient fix but it left many questions unanswered about the future of EMS and EMU.

Ironically 'Black Thursday' did not lead to immediate interest-rate cuts save in Portugal. This was partly because some governments felt that this could destroy the Single Market by encouraging competitive devaluations. It was also a sign of the continuing addiction to the political role of the EMS as a stepping stone to EMU. Moreover the French, having used up most of their currency reserves, needed higher rates to protect the franc against continuing pressure. These derived from rising share prices, as investors anticipated rate cuts, and Germany. There, in the second half of August, the Bundesbank refused to consider the DM losing its anchor role, let alone to cut interest rates at its 26 August meeting. All this involved a good deal of bitterness both between Euroenthusiasts, who saw the market turbulence as evidence of a deliberate 'Anglo-Saxon' onslaught on European integration in general and the Franco-German axis in particular; and between the French and Germans themselves. While there may have been some desire to test the ERM, many of the currency movements can be explained by the natural instinct for self-preservation among banks, firms and financial institutions faced with currency uncertainties.

The future of the Maastricht monetary settlement was further undermined by the new crisis. This was because the fragility of Community currencies and the deteriorating economic cycle also affected government finances, reducing revenues and increasing welfare expenditures. States were thus forced into deficit and large-scale borrowings. As a result new fiscal obstacles to achieving EMU convergence conditions by 1999, let alone 1997, emerged. This increased doubts about whether EMU was viable or desirable.

Towards the end of 1992 many countries had seemed on track for doing this, but by August 1993 many had been driven badly off course. Thus, while the United Kingdom effectively refused to entertain any efforts aimed at meeting the convergence criteria by 1997, despite the fact that in 1992 it met most of the requirements, the majority of European governments introduced budgets aimed specifically at this goal. Indeed, several governments could comfortably argue that economically they were in a position to move to the final stage of EMU. Towards the end of 1992 countries such as Denmark, France, Ireland, Luxembourg and the Netherlands, as well as membership candidates such as Austria, all found themselves meeting most if not all of the convergence criteria. In addition, each country was still experiencing economic growth, albeit at levels lower than in the late 1980s.

In the case of Denmark, inflation stood at slightly above 2 per cent, while the budget deficit was a modest 4.4 per cent of GDP. In Luxembourg, inflation was well below the Community average, as was the budget deficit. The Netherlands, meanwhile, met four of the convergence criteria, although the country's budgetary deficit remained slightly above the permitted level for EMU. Ireland was in a similar position, although here it was the level of public debt, standing at around 100 per cent of GDP, which prevented the government from claiming membership of the select band which was in a position to proceed to Stage III. France, on the other hand, was in a position to meet all the criteria: inflation stood at 2.6 per cent while interest rates were just under 10 per cent, well within the EMU requirements. Similarly, the level of the country's public debt and budget deficit met the criteria.

The one remaining member of the ERM's narrow band, Belgium, was not in a position to meet two of the criteria. However, although the government was faced with a public debt of 130 per cent of GDP and a budget deficit of 6 per cent of GDP, it reinforced its repeatedly declared intention of being ready to proceed to Stage III in 1997. For the Mediterranean members of the Community, such an ambition appeared to be a mere dream. Only Spain in 1992 was in a position to fill any of the criteria for EMU. Following its departure from the ERM, Italy, with a public debt in excess of 100 per cent of the country's GDP, a budgetary deficit accounting for almost 10 per cent of GDP and an inflation rate well above the Community average, failed to meet any of the requirements.

Similarly, Portugal was not in a position to meet any of the criteria agreed upon at Maastricht. However, in 1992 both the Italian and the Portuguese governments announced public expenditure cuts in an attempt to move closer to the EMU requirements. Meanwhile, Greece, the only member of the EC not to have joined the ERM, remained the country least likely to move to EMU. Inflation remained at four times the Community average while the country's budget deficit stood at over 16 per cent of GDP.

Despite these facts, the majority of governments in Europe still hoped to proceed to EMU, convinced that the present crisis made it more necessary than ever. However, even more countries were falling short of the criteria so that, by midsummer of 1993 only Luxembourg and one aspirant member state, Austria, seemed to meet them. The extent to which the events of late July and August magnified the shortfalls has not yet become fully apparent. Underlying problems thus continue, despite the optimistic talk of pressing ahead with EMU.

In the face of depression it is unlikely that governments will be able to maintain the price-stability rules inherent in Maastricht, thereby feeding Bundesbank fears of possible laxity under EMU. With the German economy, the cornerstone of any economic or monetary union, slipping further into recession, the future for EMU may be more complicated than the Treaty suggests. Hence, while the Commission denied that the timetable was being relaxed, the Belgians were pleading for a softening of the rules in order to allow them to take part. At the same time, the Community was still trying to develop its programme to promote economic recovery.

All this means that the road from Maastricht has been, and is likely to continue to be exceptionally bumpy, economically as well as politically. The changing economic conditions also helped to weaken the permissive consensus on which political elites had counted in their push for ever closer union. This was visible not just at the European level but also inside individual member states.

FURTHER READING

Allen, D. and Smith, M., 'The European Community in the new Europe: bearing the burden of change', *International Journal*, vol. 47, no. 1, 1992, pp. 1–28.

Barnes, I., 'Economic and Monetary Union After Maastricht', *European Access*, 1992/1, pp, 11–13.

Barrell, R., *Macroeconomic Policy Coordination in Europe: The ERM and monetary union*, Sage, London, 1992.

Coombes, D., *Understanding European Union*, Longman, London, 1994.

Crawford, M., *One Money for Europe? The Economies*

and Politics of Maastricht, Macmillan, London, 1993.

Dahrendorf, R., 'The New Europe', *Journal of European Social Policy*, vol. 2, no. 2, 1992, pp. 79–85.

Danish Embassy, *Denmark in Europe*, Press Release, London, 30 October 1992.

Danish Foreign Ministry, *Press Release*, no. 101/92, Udenrigsministeriet, Copenhagen, 1992.

EC Commission, *European Council in Edinburgh — 11 and 12 December 1992 — Conclusions of the Presidency*, London, December 1992.

EC Commission, *Legislative Programme of the Commission for 1993*, COM(93)43 final, Brussels, 3 February 1993.

EC Commission, *Promoting Economic Recovery in Europe (The Edinburgh Growth Initiative)*, COM(93)164 final, Brussels, 22 April 1993.

Foreign and Commonwealth Office, *Developments in the European Community*, HMSO, London, twice Yearly.

Gnesotto, N., 'European Union after Minsk and Maastricht', *International Affairs*, vol. 68, no. 2, 1992, pp. 223–32.

Hartley, A., 'Maastricht's problematic future', *The World Today*, vol. 48, no. 10, 1992, pp. 179–82.

Hoffman, S., 'Goodbye to a United Europe', *New York Review of Books*, 27 May 93, pp. 27–31.

Hogan, M.J., *The End of the Cold War: Its meaning and implications*, Cambridge University Press, Cambridge, 1992.

Jacquemin A. and Wright, D. (eds.), *European Challenges Post-1992: Shaping factors, shaping actors*, Edward Elgar, Aldershot, 1993.

Jochimsen, R., 'European Economic and Monetary Union: the do's and the dont's', *The World Today*, vol. 49, no. 6, 1993, pp. 115–21.

Kaltetsky, A., 'What really happened the day the ERM collapsed', *The Times*, 12 August 1993, p. 27.

Langguth, G., 'Interdependence between economic and political integration', *Aussenpolitik*, vol. 44, no. 2, 1993, pp. 173–80.

Laughland, J., 'The Court turned the EC upside down',

The Wall Street Journal, 14 October 1993.

Leonardi, R. (ed.), *European Community Policy and Politics: A review*, Pinter, London, 1994.

Milward, A. S., Lynch, M.B., Romero, F., and Sorensen, V., *The Frontier of National Sovereignty: History and theory, 1945–1992*, Routledge, London, 1993.

Mortimer, E., 'Same deal as before', *Financial Times*, 27 January 1993.

Nugent, N., 'European integration After Maastricht', *European Access*, 1992/3, pp. 8–11.

Nugent, N., *The European Community 1992: Annual review of activities*, Blackwell, Oxford, 1993.

Pigott, J. and Cook, M., *International Business Economics: A European perspective*, Longman, London, 1993.

Price, L., Shrimpton, M. and Howe, M., *European Council of 12th December 1992 — Denmark and the Maastricht Treaty: A legal assessment*, Great College Street Paper no. 1, 21 December 1992.

Rideau, J., 'Les procédures de ratification du traité sur l'Union européenne', *Revue française du droit constitutionnel*, 1992/12, pp. 611–24.

Schmuck, O., 'Heterogene Diskussionslandschaft zu Maastricht: Die Ratifizierungsdebatten zum Vertrag über die Europäische Union', *Integration*, vol. 15, no. 4, 1992, pp. 206–15.

Scott, A., 'Financing the Community: the Delors II package', in Lodge, J. (ed.), *The European Community and the Challenge of the Future*, 2nd edn, Pinter, London, 1993, pp. 69–88.

Story, J. (ed.), *The New Europe: Politics, Government and Economy since 1945*, Blackwell, Oxford, 1993.

Thomson, I., 'The European Community in 1992 — bibliographic snapshot', *European Access*, 1992/6, pp. 38–41.

Tsoukalis, L., *The New European Economy*, Oxford University Press, Oxford, 1993.

Weiler, J.H.H., 'Problems of Legitimacy in Post-1992 Europe', *Aussenwirtschaft*, vol. 46, nos. 3–4, 1991, pp. 179–206.

iii. The Community member states

Although many Eurosceptics and other concerned citizens feel that the TEU is crowding out and undermining the member nation states, the evidence suggests that the latter remain a, if not the, dominant factor in deciding the way the Community develops. Not merely did they, as already seen, play a large part in influencing the pre-Maastricht negotiations, but they have continued to demonstrate their individuality throughout the ratification process. This has led to changes in alignments within the EC. However, this does not mean that they always take up intergovernmentalist positions in Community affairs. Hence developments in the Community and its policies are greatly affected by their domestic conditions and the often different, and changing, attitudes which, as a result, governments and peoples have adopted to the questions raised at Maastricht. As all this seems likely to remain true of the Union, a brief survey of prevailing conditions in each of the Twelve may be helpful.

Belgium

Traditionally, Belgium has been a stalwart of the Community and ideas of further integration have caused little debate there. As part of the conventional wisdom, 'Europe' has rarely been questioned. The main response to the Single European Act was regret that things had not gone further. Hence, the Belgian government has been active in pushing for institutional development both before and after Maastricht, as in its March 1990 and October 1992 memoranda on remedying the democratic deficit. And, after Maastricht, Belgium moved rapidly to ratification.

Yet at the same time, the Maastricht process poses considerable problems for Belgian finances. The growing move to decentralization on linguistic grounds has, along with a generous system of social security, added greatly to public-sector costs. Despite the progress made since constitutional reform started in the early 1970s, the language divide has also helped to make domestic politics unruly and unstable, perhaps even ungovernable.

In 1988 it was agreed in principle to take further steps towards making Belgium a real federation. Implementation proved difficult and it was thrown into doubt by the fall of the Maertens cabinet in the autumn of 1991 because of Flemish resentment over the lack of progress on devolution and, especially, of the licensing of arms sales desired by firms in French-speaking Wallonia. However, a majority for constitutional reform was achieved.

This necessitated a general election in November 1991, in which the government parties lost ground, somewhat to the benefit of xenophobic and Green parties. It then took a hundred days to reconstitute a Socialist and Christian Socialist cabinet under Jean-Luc Dehaene. Between late September 1992 and November this was able to agree on concrete proposals for full federalization. These involved turning the national government into a supervisory federal executive and upgrading regional administrations into 'governments' for Flanders, the French-speaking community and the Walloon region. These are to enjoy increased powers including some rights in external affairs. Legal and parliamentary structures will also be changed, thereby paralleling the subsidiarity of the TEU.

Unfortunately the government then found itself faced with considerable financial problems since meeting the Maastricht convergence conditions is extremely hard, given the excessive levels of Belgian public expenditure. Proposals, in the budget for 1993, to cut the debt, which presently stands at 130 per cent of GDP and use savings from abolishing wage indexation to prop up the depleted social security fund, were rejected by the French Socialists (representing the declining heavy industries of Wallonia). This prompted another crisis for the cabinet in early 1993, after only a year in office. The crisis held up the constitutional proposals, threatened preparations for the Belgian Presidency of the EC which began in July 1993, and aroused fears of an actual break-up of the nation.

However, King Baudoin refused to accept Dehaene's resignation and an agreement to carry on with devolution was cobbled together, although the financial problems were not resolved. At the same time, the Belgian economy began to suffer from its ERM links, raising the question of whether the country would be able to meet the convergence criteria by which its politicians place such store. The sudden death of the king in August 1993 added to Belgian difficulties. Hence the majority for constitutional reforms remains uncertain and Belgian political cohesion is still at risk.

Nonetheless, the commitment of Belgium to further European integration has yet to become a real issue. For, while academic voices are now raised in favour of abandoning the link and rebuilding the economy, the government has yet to heed them. Its commitment to EMU has remained untarnished as it seeks, as President, to get EMU back on the road. For the moment then, there is a happy coincidence between what the government sees as Belgian interests and the implementation of the TEU.

Denmark

By the early 1990s the Danes seemed to have broken with their past as the 'footdraggers' of Europe. However, events were to show that, if the elite had changed its view, a majority of the people had not. Entry in 1972 had not been without its difficulties and, once inside, the Danes stuck to a minimalist interpretation of the Treaties and subjected government and Brussels initiatives to punitive supervision. Even so, anti-EC movements won European Parliament seats after 1979. And, when the Danish opposition to new IGCs was overruled and the SEA negotiated, the Folketing refused to accept the new Treaty. The government immediately appealed over Parliament's head to the people by calling a consultative referendum, as the constitution allowed. It then won a clear majority in 1987.

Thereafter the Danes seemed to come to terms with the Community. Not only were they less obstructive, even on EMU, but they went on to urge the other Nordic states to enter the Community. Public opinion polls began to show increasing support for the EC, especially after German unification. The snap election in December 1990 also saw a decline in the votes for anti-EC parties. And, even though some of the coalition partners lost ground to the Social Democrats, Prime Minister Schlouter was able to reform his minority government and to establish cross-party agreement on the budget for the first time in many years. This consensus largely held during the IGCs and the ratification debate. As a result, only the far left Socialist Peoples' Party and the anti-tax, anti-immigrant Progress Party voted in the Folketing against ratification of the TEU. However, this was enough to prevent the size of majority which would have dispensed with a referendum.

Although, or indeed because, the majority of parties supported the Treaty, the Danish people narrowly voted against ratification on 2 June 1992. This was essentially due to public disillusion with the parties, and particularly with the Schlouter government and its long-standing, but unpopular, foreign minister Uffe Elleman-Jensen. This may have been related to the economic difficulties experienced at the time. These partly reflected the deflationary pressures of ERM membership, although the Danish economy has generally been performing relatively well. The 'No' vote also reflected the fact that, while the opposition campaign was very vigorous, that of the government campaign was flawed. The elitist 'Yes' campaign was complacent, short, and not fully supported either by industry or the Social Democrats. The Social Democrats had appointed a new leader after their years out of power in order to try and exploit any difficulties over Maastricht — a stance which appealed to the large Eurosceptic minority in the party.

The 'No' campaigners skilfully argued that a 'No' vote was neither anti-European nor likely to damage Denmark. The opposition was helped, as already seen, both by Community gaffes and by the wide circulation of the Treaty text. It was also able to play on fears about the country's social and military future. All this helped to mobilize many women, public-sector white-collar workers and people from the radical 1968 generation against the arrogance, bureaucracy and citizenship aspirations of Brussels.

The Schlouter government rather lost the initiative as a result of the referendum, allowing the reinvigorated Socialist People's Party (SPP) and others to make the running. The Social Democrats felt it safer to go along with the SPP so as to strengthen their position. This, and the intensive discussions on Europe, led to the emergence of the White Paper in October 1992 spelling out the possibilities for Denmark. Some of the parties had erroneous and inflated ideas both of what was in Maastricht and of what kind of a deal they could extract from the Community. In the end, come mid-November, seven of the eight leading parties agreed a 'National Compromise' stressing the need for greater transparency and for a legally binding deal. In all this the aim was more to win votes at home than to produce a convincing and logical statement.

The Compromise and the ensuing Agreement reached at the Edinburgh Summit were supported by the SPP and the Social Democrats as well as the government parties. This became doubly significant when, in early January 1993, the Schlouter government was forced to resign because of the 'Tamilgate' scandal, involving ministers misleading Parliament about the implementation of policy on immigrants. This brought the SDP, now in alliance with three small parties, back into power just as the Danish Presidency of the Council of Ministers started. Social Democratic support helped to push the opinion polls up to a point at which it seemed that a 'Yes' vote became possible. However, the party was not always able to hold on to its supporters.

So, although on 18 May 1993 the Danes, as already noted, voted to ratify the Maastricht and Edinburgh agreements, this dissidence, coupled with the underlying popular suspicion of political parties, suggests that the Danes will remain reserved about further integration. The currency troubles of the summer of 1993 also bore down on the krone, although the economy is in a fairly healthy state. Hence, scepticism about EMU may have been enhanced.

France

France has always been at the other end of the scale from Denmark, committed at both political and popular levels to developing integration. After initial hesitation President Mitterrand, after 1983, committed his government to accepting the disciplines of the ERM and developing further European integration. This was accentuated after the fall of the Berlin Wall to the extent that the whole Maastricht process was seen not merely as 'a French project', but as one which was designed to increase the profile of the Presidency. Mitterrand showed his confidence in French support for Europe and government policy when he boldly called a referendum in France after the Danish 'No'.

However, as in Denmark, the events of 1992–3 have shown that things are changing and that the European consensus in France is under pressure. This was partly because of the way in which French public opinion turned against the Socialist Party. Accusations of corruption (over contaminated blood, party funding and share dealing), divisions in the party and the deteriorating economic situation, itself partly caused by way that the French economy was tied to the exchange and interest rates dictated by the ERM, all bore down on the Socialist government. The Rocard government had faced rising social unrest, and this continued when Mitterrand abruptly replaced him with Edith Cresson in May 1991, in an attempt to give the government a new dynamism by winning back the party's left-wing supporters. This failed and, with Cresson proving the most unpopular premier, ever despite a flirtation with anti-immigrant policies, the party was routed in the 1992 local elections. However, the right also lost ground to the xenophobic *Front National* and, especially, to the ecologists.

This forced yet another change of Premier with former finance minister, Pierre Bérégovoy, being appointed to try and restore both the economy and party fortunes. This again proved an impossible task. For, although there was some economic improvement, unemployment and social problems continued. And though in June, Parliament approved constitutional changes necessary to implement the TEU — with the Gaullist RPR abstaining — the government experienced new problems over Europe. It was faced with an anti-Maastricht secession by its most senior left-winger Jean-Pierre Chevènement. Other allied forces also refused it support.

The referendum campaign also revealed that there was a growing body of Euroscepticism in France, led by Philippe Seguin and Charles Pasqua of the RPR. Unease about the EC in the RPR had become visible as early as 1988, while public support for Europe peaked in 1989–90. Thereafter there were increasing complaints of Brussels bureaucracy and threats to French identity and sovereignty. The *Front National* and the Communist Party (PCF) were also hostile to the Community. With the government's unpopularity also rubbing off on Maastricht, such opposition helped to mobilize latent French reservations about Europe in general and citizenship, EMU and supranationality in particular. In the end only big city votes carried the day despite an almost wholly hostile countryside. Indeed more than half the *départements* voted against.

The Socialist government then found itself in further difficulty. The franc came under heavy pressure in the autumn and was only rescued by the intervention of the Bundesbank. This hit already straitened state finances, despite some moves towards privatization. Unemployment was rising to almost 3 million or 10.5 per cent. There was also great pressure from farmers over a pre-GATT deal with the United States which was being pushed by Germany and other Community states. Their protests were part of continuing social unrest which spread to the fishing industry in 1993. Public opinion was not comforted by progress with an anti-corruption law.

Unease over Europe played some part in the total electoral humiliation inflicted on the Socialists at the end of March 1993. Their numbers were cut by 80 per cent leaving Edouard Balladur of the RPR at the head of a huge right-wing majority. Yet the latter's victory was mitigated because so many people simply refused to vote, spoiled their ballot papers or supported the extremists of the *Front National*. The new government was not merely faced with massive problems of economic reconstruction but with internal divisions on Europe. The fact that the RPR did better than the more pro-European *Union pour la démocratie française* (UDF) is significant in this respect. In appointing the new government, Mitterrand made it very plain that he intended to ensure that there would be continuity in European and security policy.

So far the new government has made it clear that it intends to continue the main thrust of French policy on Europe: the links with Germany, the search for more political and military cohesion (whether at Ten, Eleven or Twelve) and reinforcing the EMS. Hence it will defend the franc and give the Banque Nationale its independence despite having to cope with an escalating deficit. Equally it has threatened to block enlargement if Maastricht is not ratified. Balladur has also advanced a new plan for a European Security treaty which has only latterly been described as part of the common foreign and security policy.

Yet, at the same time, it proposes to give its Parliament more of a say on European legislation. More significantly it slowed down implementation of the Schengen Agreement, queried the GATT deal, and called for Brussels to have a legislative holiday to allow states to catch up and maintain their independence. Then, as already seen, it tried to pressurize Germany into cutting interest rates further so as to ease the economic crisis. This proved doubly self-defeating, especially for President Mitterrand. On the one hand it exposed the franc to the onslaughts of the markets. On the other, it soured the close relationship with Germany which had been the basis of France's European policy and the motor of the Maastricht process.

Although the divisions have been papered over, there are major differences about Bosnia, implementation of the ERM and the GATT talks. The French feel both resentful that they did not get the support they expected from Bonn during the currency crisis and alarmed that Germany is now threatening to go its own way, rather then working with Paris. This is especially worrying given the belief that the 'Anglo Saxons' deliberately engineered the crisis to smash the Maastricht blueprint. So far Balladur has proved a resolute supporter of the *franc fort* policy and the idea that the markets can be controlled politically in support of France's geopolitical aims. In this he has the support of the PS, while many in his own party oppose him, possibly including Jacques Chirac. The Constitutional Council has also strengthened the hands of anti-Europeans like Pasqua in a recent ruling on entry to France after Schengen. This may need constitutional amendments, delaying the Schengen process further.

With this and the divisions over the Presidential election due in 1995, likely to affect both the Right — with its feuding old-guard candidates — and the still very fractious and shell-shocked Socialists, the French commitment to Europe seems rather less certain and consistent than previously. Public opinion has been less concerned by the currency crises than might have been expected but continuing economic problems could change this. The outcome of the GATT talks could also prove very unsettling.

Germany

Along with France, Germany was one of the major supporters of the Maastricht process. This reflected the long-standing constitutional and political commitment to Europe which has anchored the country's post-Nazi identity. To a large measure this has remained the case. However, even here ratification began to raise question marks about the extent of German commitment to closer integration. And the country has also suffered from its own economic and political difficulties.

The first all-German elections had seen the Christian Democratic (CDU)-led government of Helmut Kohl gain a clear victory over the Social Democrats (SPD), albeit on a low turn-out. Their standing in the polls was undone by their Cassandra-like attitude to unification. At the same time, the Greens were also excluded from the Bundestag. At the same time the CDU share of the vote fell to its lowest since 1949, a fact which reinforced its determination not to raise taxes to pay for unification. The government also went forward with its ideas of developing the Union in order to reinforce its bona fides. It also clung to ideas of military collaboration with France although this, like the way it bounced the Community into recognizing Croatia for essentially domestic reasons, caused some difficulties with other member states.

Moreover, the unforeseen costs, demands and duration of the rebuilding process were both to force policy changes and to undermine the position of the coalition. In the end taxes had to be raised, and a new solidarity pact negotiated in January 1993 to provide a further DM 18 billion for the East in order to overcome the widening gap between the two halves of the country. This failed to stop rising social discontent and alienation, symbolized by a major strike in the Eastern steel industry over the failure to equalize wages with the West. Equally, the costs of unification forced the Bundesbank to maintain high interest rates to contain inflationary pressures. It did this at a time when the economy, which at one stage seemed to have avoided depression, was moving into sharp recession with unemployment likely to rise to 3.5 million and GDP to fall by 2 per cent in 1993.

This also had implications for Germany's partners in the ERM, notably in September 1992 when the Bundesbank was accused of helping to undermine rather than defend the pound. Kohl was later to accuse opponents of European integration of deliberately speculating on the currency markets. This was in line with his continuing commitment to closer union, even though the possibility of seeing the DM replaced by the ECU was badly received in Germany. Public anger led to submissions to the Constitutional Court seeking to declare the proposed transfer of monetary sovereignty to the ECB incompatible with the *Grundgesetz*. This was to delay ratification even though the government, unilaterally, promised the Bundestag a veto on the final move to EMU. Parliament ratified the Treaty with a huge majority and the country remained committed to moving ahead with France and others should the general move to integration not materialize.

The government also found itself under pressure over the possible diminution of the rights of the *Länder*, just as it had over the Single European Act. Having lost control of the Bundesrat because of regional electoral defeats by the SPD it was forced to concede new rights of consultation notably over any further European moves to change the status of the *Länder*. This reflected the way some 61 per cent of the population had come round to think that the Twelve had divergent rather than convergent interests. And, while Kohl remained supportive of John Major, he was also willing to consider being part of a core economic union should all Twelve states not ratify the Treaty.

However, the government was weakened politically by Kohl's lacklustre leadership, by disagreement with the Free Democrats (FDP) over Europe and asylum policy, and by a string of scandals. These affected both the CDU and its coalition partner. A number of ministers had to be replaced as a result. Despite leadership problems of its own, SPD strength in both the Bundestag and Bundesrat, also made it very hard for the CDU-led government to get agreement on changing the constitution to allow German forces to serve outside the NATO area and to remove generous rights of asylum.

These were increasingly resented as, in 1992, the country received 438,191 immigrants, together with 231,00 ethnic Germans returning from the east. This helped to trigger a 50 per cent increase in racial attacks, to 2,285, notably in places like Rostock in Eastern Germany. Equally in 1992, both the SPD and CDU lost ground to the far-right Republicans in Berlin and Baden-Württemberg and to the German People's Union (DVU) in Bremen and Schleswig-Holstein. This ultimately led to new measures against right-wing violence, although events at Solingen in 1993 were to show that these were ineffective. All this suggested that, while the government's commitment to Union remained, Germany was neither as united nor as powerful as some had feared. Its need for derogations from EC law to help develop the eastern *Länder* may militate against it exercising a dominating role in the Union.

Although few currency dealers speculated against the DM in the summer of 1993, Germany was still affected by the crisis. Its leaders felt they were pushed too far by France at a time when their own economic difficulties were daily increasing. Even Mercedes had to lay off about a third of its workforce in face of a massive drop in sales. The government also realized that with a whole cycle of elections ahead of it, beginning in Hamburg in September 1993 and ending with general elections in late 1994, its lack of popularity did not allow it to give way on the DM.

Hence Kohl has spoken of an inevitable delay in the implementation of EMU. Hints have also been dropped that Germany will only accept EMU if Frankfurt gets the ECB, along with new assurances about consultation with the *Länder* prior to moving to Stage III have been given. And if Germany is standing firm over this and GATT where France is concerned, German opinion is also critical of the United Kingdom over Bosnia. So the German position in the evolution of Maastricht is likely to change further.

Greece

Greece has continued to be a paradoxical problem for the Community in the early 1990s, causing economic and political problems while at the same time demanding further integration. The conservative New Democracy government which finally replaced Andreas Papandreous' socialist PASOK party in April 1990 has found it very hard to cope with the economic problems it inherited. Under pressure from Brussels it has sought to redress both structural weaknesses and unhealthy public finances. Greece suffers from a continuing trade deficit and has seen its GDP fall over recent years. It also has a debt equal to some 140 per cent of GDP, the servicing of which takes up a quarter of all state revenues. In 1991 a stabilization plan was introduced to help prepare the country for ERM membership and this had helped to cut inflation from over 20 per cent to some 14 per cent by early 1993. However, privatization has been very limited and the civil service, which is one of the major causes of the debt, has continued to expand. As economic stagnation continued so attempts to reduce public-sector salaries were greeted by large-scale strikes in the autumn of 1992. This has helped strengthen the PASOK challenge now that Papandreous has been cleared of corruption charges. However, there could be changes in the party system after resignations from New Democracy.

The government's ability to deal with the country's problems was also undermined by general dissatisfaction with all political parties, by claims of nepotism and corruption, and especially by foreign policy problems. Greece has always been very sensitive about Community policy on Cyprus and Turkey, but the developing crisis in the Balkans has added a whole new dimension of touchiness. First there were difficulties with Albania over the Greek population there. Then the January 1992 demand for international recognition of the former Yugoslavian Republic of Macedonia triggered a wave of patriotic fervour amongst Greeks. It was felt that the very name of the would-be state constituted a threat to Greece's territorial integrity. Greek forces on the borders were placed on a state of high alert.

Although the Eleven were not happy about the Greek obsessions, especially given complaints about the country's human-rights record, three European Councils agreed not to recognize Macedonia. This was, in part, to support the government of Constantine Mitsotakis and keep PASOK out. However, non-recognition encouraged the Greek fortress mentality, in which a torrent of public criticism made the government seek a vote of confidence in October 1992 against accusations that it was pandering to the Community and not defending national interests. This was followed by a reshuffle in December. Nevertheless, a massive demonstration about the 'Macedonian threat' in Athens just before the Edinburgh Summit still went ahead.

Community support in not recognizing Macedonia was one reason why the Greek Parliament, the Vouli, voted by 286 to 8 to ratify the TEU. Ratification also reflected the desperate Greek need for Community financial aid. This need makes it imperative for Greece to fit in with Maastricht, almost irrespective of the costs. This attitude also showed itself in the stress placed on the Cohesion Fund and the Delors II package. For some Greeks this was also *sine qua non* for allowing enlargement. So although the opposition (and some members of New Democracy) worried about convergence conditions, declining financial autonomy, and the threat of punishment for non-implementation of EC rules — a chronic problem in Greece — it voted for the TEU. As in Italy, the government was also glad of the extra discipline the Treaty would provide.

Equally it welcomed the additional influence offered by membership in the WEU from November. With new elections threatening, all this suggests that the ambivalent Greek relation with the Union is likely to continue. This is especially so given that the currency crisis may have made it even more unlikely that the drachma could join the ERM. The increasingly frenetic political atmosphere, as shown by the reaction to a holiday visit by ex-King Constantine, does not bode well for the future either.

Ireland

Echoes of this kind of ambivalence were also partly visible in Ireland which has been described as being 'conditionally integrationist'. While the Community has been consistently supported, because of the economic and financial assistance it brings, its political constraints have sometimes created difficulties for a political system very much under strain. Ireland has been unhappy about reform of the CAP, about Schengen and about the threats to its neutrality implicit in the TEU. The Irish opposition to abortion has constituted a special problem.

The 1990s started in Ireland with the unexpected triumph of the independent candidate for President, Mary Robinson, who defeated an old *Fianna Fáil* warhorse in Brian Lenihan. He lost because of allegations that he had lied about his role in forcing a previous President to concede a dissolution. This symbolized a series of personal and other scandals which afflicted the coalition government under Charles Haughey, then gradually moving to economic convergence with Europe.

When Haughey was challenged over irregular property and financial deals, he dismissed his finance minister, Albert Reynolds. This, along with charges from his Progressive Democrat (PD) partners that his fiscal policy was insufficiently rigorous, terminally weakened his government. Further scandals finally forced his resignation in 1992. He was succeeded by Albert Reynolds who purged Haughey's supporters from the cabinet but was then confronted by a major crisis over abortion linked to Maastricht.

After the Irish Attorney-General refused, in February 1992, to allow a raped 14-year-old to travel to England for an abortion, the Supreme Court then ruled that she should be allowed to do so. This suggested that, contrary to the general understanding of the Constitution, abortion was legal in Ireland. As the Haughey government had inserted a Protocol in the TEU upholding the relevant clause, many Irish people felt that Maastricht was making abortion legal in Ireland. Others felt that Ireland was restricting free movement and free circulation of goods. However, although EC aid was the determining issue, all this complicated the ratification debate, and forced further constitutional clarifications.

q.v.
Protocol 17
p. 427.

Reynolds then unnecessarily quarrelled with the Progressive Democrats, accusing their leader of lying under oath. The PDs withdrew their support, bringing the government down and precipitating an early election late in 1992. The PDs gained four seats but the real victors were the Labour Party with seventeen new seats. Labour decided that it could not form a government with its previous coalition partners, notably the listless *Fine Gael* party. Instead, after a seven week crisis, they joined with *Fianna Fáil*, which had lost heavily, to form a new government. Action on unemployment and new initiatives on Northern Ireland were key elements in their programme.

This meant not only that Ireland had the first majority government since 1971 but that the government had the largest majority in Irish history. This was very necessary since recession was hitting Ireland badly. The situation was complicated by speculation against the punt which finally forced a devaluation early in 1993. This meant that the country was spared the worst of the later currency crisis. However, while growth was expected to be faster than elsewhere in the Community, there was also continuing unease over IRA terrorism, the debate on abortion and problems over how to fund social services when taxation was already very high. So the political situation remains somewhat strained.

Italy

However, such trials are as nothing to the travails suffered by the Italian political system in recent years. Here the developing public dissatisfaction with the domination of the political parties, or *partitocrazia*, has finally exploded. Whether this will result in a stable and accepted new republic remains to be seen. What is certain, however, is that the current situation complicates the country's strong support for further integration.

Italy has been a maximalist in terms of rhetorical commitment to European Union, but a minimalist in implementing actual Community legislation. Thus, the Italians sought to go further than the SEA and justly claimed that the establishment of the IGC on political union was their doing. On the other hand, there have been more Commission charges and ECJ judgments against Italy than against any other member state. And, because few have been acted upon, the *Francovich* judgment has allowed individuals to sue the Italian government for its failure to apply EC rules. At the same time there has been much unease about Italy's ability to meet the convergence conditions for Stage III of EMU because of the calamitous

q.v.
Francovich
judgment p.
291.

state of public finances. Despite Community aid, now running at some ECU 900 million annually, the current account deficit is now 10 per cent of GDP, government expenditure 53 per cent and public debt 100 per cent. Not merely have Community loans become very important to the Italians but it was partly to invoke European economic and political influence to discipline the economic and political system that led Italy to support the Maastricht settlement.

The inability or unwillingness of the parties to deal with the financial crisis and the problems of the dual economy, let alone the continuing Mafia violence, have long annoyed many ordinary Italians, especially in the North. They felt that a change in the electoral system was needed and some 450 MPs, led by a former Christian Democrat Mario Segni, committed themselves to abandoning proportional representation (PR) in 1991. In June 1991 the electorate ignored the advice of the parties and accepted a referendum proposal to curtail preference voting. At the same time regionalist leagues began to make major electoral gains at the expense of the old increasingly discredited parties.

The first accusations of corruption in the Socialist Party (PSI) in Milan then began to surface. The refusal of former Prime Minister Craxi to resign helped to precipitate an early general election in April 1992. This proved to be the most bitterly contested in years, and produced a clear swing against the main parties including Christian Democrats (DC), PSI and the now divided Communists. Local elections later in the year confirmed that the real beneficiaries of the growing popular discontent were the northern *Leghe* whose share of the vote went up from 8.7 per cent in the general elections to 37 per cent in places like Brescia. Shortly after the local elections President Cossiga, who had become a trenchant critic of the system, resigned.

He was replaced by Oscar Scalfaro who helped to cobble together another coalition of DC, PSI, Social Democrats and Liberals under the Socialist Amato. This was then faced with both a series of brutal Mafia murders, including that of a Sicilian MEP rumoured to be the DC's link with the Mafia, and a currency crisis. As a result of the latter, the lira was forced out of the ERM despite the deployment of most of the country's foreign exchange reserves. The country also faced difficult foreign policy problems because of Albanian refugees and the Community's inability to cope with the Yugoslav crisis.

Faced with all this the Amato government, which had a majority of only 16 seats, not surprisingly proved quite unable to resist the tidal wave of judicial investigations into corruption which developed in 1992–3. Some 3,000 MPs, business leaders and officials were charged with paying or accepting backhanders or *tangenti* which developed in 1992–1993. The search for 'clean hands' reached right up not merely into the cabinet, but also to former prime ministers Goria, Craxi and, especially, Andreotti. With the electorate voting massively in April 1993 to do away with both PR for Senate elections and public subsidies for political parties, a reshuffle proved ineffective and Amato was forced to step down.

He was replaced by a technocrat caretaker prime minister, Carlo Azeglio Ciampi from the Bank of Italy. But with Parliament refusing to lift Craxi's immunity, some parties refused to take part in the Ciampi cabinet. The new government finally gained investiture and lived up to its commitment to pushing ahead both with electoral reform for the *Camera* and with a tough budget, which will raise taxes and cut public spending. Both houses of Parliament finally accepted a new electoral law during the summer of 1993, paving the way for new elections, the outcome of which are very uncertain especially with the Ciampi cabinet experiencing tribulations of its own and with the *Leghe* continuing to gain strength locally in the North. Whether the Christian Democrat's change of name and leadership will help it remains to be seen.

However, the economic situation remains difficult. And trade unions are still very strongly opposed to cuts. However, the new, wider, bands could help the lira to return to the ERM. Much of this, then will curb Italy's role in the Community, though both reformers and the *Leghe*'s wish to remain in the European mainstream so as to help redress internal weaknesses.

Luxembourg

Luxembourg has been a stable and ultra-reliable pillar of European integration. The left/right coalition of the Christian Social Party and Socialists has lasted for almost ten years. This is despite challenges from both the far Right and from such surge parties as the Greens and the pensioners. Unease over giving voting rights to the very large foreign population has not produced a significant xenophobic movement.

Economic management has been remarkably successful despite the slow down after 1990−1. This has caused difficulties for the steel industry. Not merely has Luxembourg maintained high growth rates and low unemployment, but its tax reforms have helped maintain fiscal discipline. By 1993, therefore, the Grand Duchy was the country best able to meet the EMU convergence conditions. However, harmonizing its tax regime and state aids policies with the Single Market may cause some problems. The BCCI affair also suggested there were still weaknesses in the regulation of its massive banking sector.

Despite its size and the problems of the Gulf War and Yugoslavia, the Luxembourg Presidency during the first half of 1991 went well. With the Grand Duchy hoping to provide the seat for the European Central Bank, it was not surprising that the TEU was massively approved in July 1992. There has, however, been a vigorous campaign against threats to move the Parliament's services to Brussels. The difficulties of the Belgian franc in the summer 1993 obviously had implications for the Grand Duchy. This apart, Luxembourg is likely to continue as a consistent, if often overlooked, supporter of further integration.

The Netherlands

The Netherlands has been another stable and consistent supporter of further integration, being convinced that a federal Union is the best protection for small states. It has long been afraid of the largest states going their own way, particularly where the Bundesbank is concerned. At the same time the Dutch are strong supporters of NATO and are not greatly enamoured of rival European security schemes. The Dutch made a notable contribution to the allied war effort in the Gulf. Equally, they have been more in favour of deregulation, notably in air transport, than some other smaller member states.

Since late 1989 the Netherlands has had its own right/left coalition between the Christian Democratic Appeal (CDA) of Prime Minister Ruud Lubbers and the Labour Party. The former chose to work with Labour rather than the CDA's previous rather unpopular right-wing partners in the Liberal Party (VVD). At first the coalition was able to survive differences over foreign policy, notably in the Gulf crisis, and over reactions to the recession. With a public-sector deficit of 10 per cent of GDP and unusual inflationary pressures, the government has sought both to benefit from the peace dividend and to curb the escalating costs of social security. Hence conscription is being phased out and cuts are being made in health and housing.

While the Labour Party has gone along with this at first and, indeed, accepted a wage freeze, things began to change. Thus trade union opposition showed itself in strikes, despite relatively high levels of unemployment. Equally, the Labour Party began to lose votes because of its support for austerity policies. The coalition also had severe tensions in 1991 over social security cuts. And, by the summer of 1993, there was a looming cabinet crisis which threatened the continuing existence of the coalition. This sprang from difficulties inside the Labour Party, two of whose ministers have resigned, and attacks on the CDA Minister of Transport for withholding information from his colleagues.

However, there was consensus on the strongly federalist line in European affairs visible in the June 1990 memorandum and in the controversial Presidency in the second half of 1991, which saw the rejection of the Dutch proposals for a more unitary Union structure. Since then the Netherlands has been a firm supporter of Schengen, although the tolerant drug policies practised there do not endear themselves to France. There has also been unease about the Bundesbank's strategy. The public has also acted angrily to signs of anti-immigrant feeling. Yet, while there have also been conflicts with the Community over environmental and transport policy, it is unlikely that forthcoming elections there, and in Luxembourg, will change the country's line on Europe. Significantly the florin was the one currency to remain in a narrow band with the DM after the events of Black Thursday.

Portugal

Although one of the poorest countries in Europe, with a third of its population having less than half the average EC income, Portugal has moved courageously towards economic convergence. Since 1991 this has involved a programme of encouraging greater competitiveness through privatization, and by cutting public sector costs, limiting wages and improving tax collection. The escudo also entered the ERM. French and Spanish firms have begun to buy their way into the

Portuguese economy.

Such policies have been possible in part because of Community aid. This now accounts for 11 per cent of all inward investment and 2 per cent of GDP. It also pays for half the infrastructural investment in the country. All this has had a dynamic effect on the Portuguese economy, encouraging restructuring and retraining. It has also helped to raise living standards although illiteracy and infant mortality remain high.

This successful policy adaptation also owes much to the country's new found political maturity. With a clearly elected Socialist President in Mario Soares and a charismatic Premier in Cavaçao da Silva, whose Social Democrats again won an absolute majority in the October 1991 general election, the country has turned its back on post-revolutionary instability. The party even won seats in the Communist Party's former fiefs. There has been a good deal of consensus especially as the government has sought to balance integration and modernization with social protection.

However, Portugal's progress towards Europeanization has not been untroubled. At home there were disagreements between President and Prime Minister, including over whether to hold a referendum on Maastricht. This was, in the event, ratified without difficulty. There have also been strikes against the partial privatization of health care and changes in education and the civil service. In 1992−3 currency pressures three times forced devaluation on a reluctant government first in late November 1992, then in mid-May 1993 and, finally, after the general relaxing of ERM in August. This enabled the Portuguese to start cutting interest rates.

Externally Portugal has not been happy with the budgetary constraints imposed by Maastricht and has been concerned about solidarity and cohesion funds. This has made it somewhat reserved on ratifying the Europe Agreements and opening the Community up to competition from producers in Central and Eastern Europe. On the other hand, the Portuguese desperately wish to avoid a two-tier Europe. Hence, the Portuguese tend to push for further integration because this facilitates continuing transfers of funds.

q.v. Europe Agreements pp. 485–6.

Spain

The Spanish situation has been very similar to that in Portugal. However, the position of the government has been much weaker partly because of the rapid onset of recession in the 1990s. Not surprisingly the stress on Community solidarity in European policy is even more marked than in Portugal. The 1993 election and the strong regional dimension to Spanish politics are complicating factors.

For the last few years the country has been governed by Felipe Gonzalez' Socialist Party (PSOE). However, by the early 1990s its dominant position was coming under considerable strain. To begin with it was internally divided between the Prime Minister and his technocratic policies, and the Left and the unions who have found the policy of austerity hard to stomach. This led to waves of strikes in May 1991 and April 1992. At the same time, the party has been compromised by accusations of corruption over the financing of the last election, patronage and bribes for public works contracts. This coincided with the renewal of the Spanish Right. All this showed itself in the PSOE's further loss of seats in the early general election in June 1993, which forced it into reliance on minority nationalist parties.

The Spanish economy did enjoy boom conditions in the late 1980s, symbolized by the peseta's entry into the ERM. However, this came to a rapid end in the early 1990s because of overheating, excessive spending on the civil service and projects like Seville '92 and the 1992 Olympics, and tight monetary policies. The crisis was worsened by the sudden withdrawal of the Kuwaiti Investment Office stake in Spain. Thus an economy which still only enjoyed 70 per cent of EC per capita GDP found itself facing stubbornly high unemployment rates of well over 20 per cent, a huge public-sector deficit and a massive imbalance in its trade.

This left the country very exposed to currency speculation, which forced two devaluations in 1992 and, despite exchange controls, a third in May 1993. The PSOE government tried to meet the crisis by introducing an austerity budget for 1993 which involved raising taxes, capping civil service pay, and the privatization both of state-owned firms and the benefits system. This was followed by an emergency public-works package in February 1993 but, because Gonzalez was caught between the need for votes and a lack of fiscal resources, reflation was only limited.

The economic situation has called into question Spain's support not just for Maastricht but for its desire to go even further and reduce its deficit to no more than 1 per cent of GDP. Meeting tighter convergence targets in such unhelpful conditions will be difficult if not impossible. Not surprisingly, Spain has been placing increasing stress on the need for more cohesion funds, not just from the Community but also from EFTA. Hence it has held up ratification of the revised EEA agreement. It has also been uneasy about trade concessions to the countries of Central and Eastern Europe and there are now signs of xenophobia inside Spain. Open access for Spanish agricultural products and fishermen is also a major concern.

The fourth socialist electoral victory, due in part to continuing fears of the Popular Alliance's Francoist past, suggests that there is unlikely to be great change. The PSOE remained the largest party but was forced to seek a coalition partner for the first time, and this was to prove difficult. So the delay in giving the Bank of Spain more autonomy continued for longer than many had expected. Any government would, moreover, find it hard to resist domestic pressures for more aid, whether from Madrid or Brussels. Regional forces, on whom the new minority PSOE government may come to depend, would also push in this direction. However, the arrest by the French of the Basque Separatist leader in late February 1993 suggests that the decline of terrorism may continue. Nevertheless, the Spanish commitment to Schengen is likely to carry on, though the price of meeting the Maastricht conditions may be very high.

The peseta also suffered more than most during the currency crises of 1993.

At the time of the August crisis the government had to introduce drastic cuts in public spending, increases in petrol tax and curbs on both public-sector pay and unemployment benefits. The last came at a time when unemployment was rising to over 22 per cent. Whether all this will lead the Spanish to reconsider their support for further integration must remain an open question.

United Kingdom

The United Kingdom's position in European politics continued to prove very problematic in the early 1990s. When, in the autumn of 1990, Mrs Thatcher was forced to step down because her personality and policies, notably on Europe and the poll tax, were seen as damaging Conservative prospects, it seemed that a sea change was under way. Yet, despite having a more emollient Prime Minister and a Labour Party which completed its policy modernization by accepting a firm European commitment, UK political divisions have become more complex, more bitter and their outcome even more uncertain.

The Major government at first enjoyed something of a honeymoon. At home this owed something to the success of the Gulf War and the retreat from the poll tax. In Europe, Major established reasonable working relations with fellow leaders and, though his idea of a hard ECU was dropped and a number of bruising political battles were fought, it proved possible to win some concessions at Maastricht. And this was, at first, relatively well received.

Hence, despite evidence from local government and by-elections of continuing unpopularity, the Conservatives were able to turn the tables on Labour and win a fourth victory in the April 1992 general election. Labour increased its share of seats but was held back by fears over its likely economic and fiscal stance. Neil Kinnock thereupon stood down, to be replaced by John Smith. The Liberal Democrats more or less held their own.

Despite this, 1992–3 proved to be an *annus horribilis* for the government as well as for the royal family. Domestically, the former developed a reputation for arrogance and a lack of understanding, notably over its claims that economic recovery was starting. Equally, it lost too many ministers because of press complaints over their behaviour while Tory Party funding became a major source of embarrassment. A number of its key policies also backfired: the closure of the coal mines, educational testing, health reforms, imposition of VAT on domestic energy, railway privatization, sentencing policy, social security philosophy and university admissions. Externally, its handling of the Bosnian crisis was also much criticized at home and abroad, as was its scaling down of the armed services and its apparent connivance in arms sales to Iraq.

However, it was over Europe that the government experienced its worst moments. An anti-Maastricht coalition built up in the United Kingdom more rapidly and effectively than anywhere else, drawing on long-standing scepticism about integration. This was aided by the way that the general election and the late publication of the TEU delayed the start of ratification. This could, conceivably, have been achieved, without too much difficulty, in the spring of 1992.

Since much of the opposition came from inside the Tory Party, the government chose to delay the ratification process. It was only a further concession of this kind which enabled it to avoid defeat on the November 1992 paving motion. Even so, the Committee stage of the Ratification Bill produced a long and humiliating series of tactical evasions and retreats. All this alienated other Community states, especially when the problems at home made for a Presidency which, despite Edinburgh, was manifestly less than successful, even in the policy areas of most interest to the United Kingdom.

Things were made even worse by the currency crisis which forced the government to use up its foreign exchange reserves in a vain attempt to maintain the pound's value in the ERM. Although hailed by some as the beginning of a new economic miracle, sterling's departure from the ERM in September 1992 did little to reverse the longest and deepest recession since the Second World War. With industrial shut-downs continuing, unemployment rising and a damaging crisis in the housing market, business confidence plunged and labour relations began to deteriorate. The depth of the recession forced the government into massive borrowing and an unpopular review of public spending to cope with a £50 billion deficit. Even though things improved in 1993, such gains as there were, were partly offset by the way that European markets dried up.

The government was also badly damaged by Conservative splits over Europe. Although united by opposition to the Social Chapter Protocol the party was divided over Maastricht. Its hesitations were exploited by Lady Thatcher and the Tory Euro-sceptics who used every device to try and derail the Treaty. Consequently both the economic policy and the leadership of the Chancellor and Prime Minister were regularly questioned. Eventually, the former had to be sacrificed because of his lack of credibility.

However, this did not redound as much to the benefit of Labour as might have been expected. This reflected the lacklustre leadership of John Smith and the party's willingness to pursue tactical advantage over principle. So, in May 1993 it was the Liberal Democrats, the most consistently pro-European party, who virtually destroyed Tory control of county councils. And it was Liberal Democratic votes which helped the government to win both the Third Reading votes and the defeat of Labour's Social Chapter amendment. They also won the Newbury and Christchurch by-elections, inflicting humiliating defeats on both anti-federalist candidates and the Tories. Whether this meant that the UK electorate had been converted to Europe, rather than losing interest in Maastricht, is doubtful.

Despite this, the Major government had a very torrid time during the later summer. Despite the unexpectedly smooth passage of the Ratification Bill through the Lords (where the government had carried the Third Reading by 141 to 29), both the completion of ratification and the future balance of power remained in doubt for a long while. Ratification, as already noted, depended on the Commons passing a resolution on the Social Chapter. On 22 July 1993 the government fought off a Labour amendment to ratify with the Social Chapter by two votes (319–317), one of which was a casting vote by the Speaker made necessary by a mistake on the part of the Tellers. Amidst total uproar the government then saw its own motion defeated by 324 to 316 votes, despite support from the Ulster Unionists, who found the possibility of a Labour government a greater threat than the TEU. Fifteen Tories voted with Labour and twenty-three against their own government.

This left the government in an impasse. But it took its opponents by surprise by immediately tabling a vote of confidence. This was debated on 23 July, amidst high excitement, and saw a Labour amendment defeated by 339 to 301 and the government motion carried by 339 to 299. The difference derived from the fact that two Ulster Unionists abstained rather than voting against the government on the second motion. The hard core of rebels, with one exception, returned tamely to the fold for reasons which many people felt to be hypocritical and self-serving. There was, however, some suggestion that the government would give the Euro-sceptics a say in future policy-making on Europe. It was symbolic of a debate which had been more concerned with power in the United Kingdom than about the details of Maastricht. The impact that the punch-up mentality of both sides might have on UK attempts to defend its policies in Europe never crossed the collective parliamentary mind.

Thereafter Lord Rees-Mogg, on behalf of a group of Eurosceptics, took the government to court on the grounds that the ratification procedure was technically flawed. This was because it was claimed to contravene an Act of 1978 on the powers of the European Parliament, because ratification of the Social Protocol altered the TEU without parliamentary approval, and because the acceptance of the CFSP was outside the executive's powers. The government agreed to postpone ratification pending the law suit, although the Speaker and others warned the Courts against interfering with parliamentary rights.

The case was heard in late July and resulted in the proceedings being quashed on the grounds that they were both technically misconceived and profoundly exaggerated. With the ERM collapsing, the Eurosceptics gave up the fight, allowing ratification to go ahead the next week. This left the Major government very bruised, especially after suffering the largest ever post-war swing which cost it the Christchurch seat. Thereafter the currency crisis allowed the government to reassert the wisdom of its policies, even to the extent of reviving the hard ECU plan. However, its future remains unsure especially with the emergence of new divisions over budgetary policy.

All this was merely the worst example of the ambiguities, divisions and uncertainties which affected the Twelve in the aftermath of Maastricht. These had interacted with the process of ratification and economic consolidation. Such troubles were also to spill over into the Community's external actions and relations. So all this had implications for other states and institutions in Europe, notably those with the closest links with the Community. Although it seems unlikely that democracy is at risk, it does bear out Jean Monnet's warning that 'the nearer we get to European Union the greater the opposition will become'. So there may be further surprises in store before the Treaty is finally ratified and then implemented. And the legacy of the difficulties on the road will certainly affect the way in which the TEU is actually put into practice.

FURTHER READING

Baker, D., Gamble, A. and Ludlam, S., 'Whips or scorpions? The Maastricht Vote and Conservative MPs', *Parliamentary Affairs*, vol. 46, no. 2, 1993, pp. 151–66.

Bidwell, C., *Maastricht and the UK*, PACE, Oxford, 1993.

Bregnsbo, H. and Sidenius, N.C., 'Adapting Danish interests to European integration', *Scandinavian Political Studies*, vol. 16, no. 1, 1993, pp. 73–91.

Carlsen Norup, H., *When No means Yes: Danish visions of a different Europe*, Adamantine Press, London, 1993.

Cosgrove, K., 'The odd man out: The United Kingdom's semi-detached relationship with Community Europe', *International Relations*, vol. 11, no. 3, 1992, pp. 269–84.

Criddle, B., 'The French referendum on the Maastricht Treaty, September 1992', *Parliamentary Affairs*, vol. 46, no. 2, 1993, pp. 228–38.

Cullen, P., *The UK and the Ratification of the Maastricht Treaty: The constitutional position*, Europa Institute, Edinburgh, 1993.

Danish Embassy, *Denmark in Europe*, Press Release, London, 30 October 1992.

Danish Foreign Ministry, *Press Release*, Nr. 101/92, Udenrigsministeriet, Copenhagen, 1992.

Foreign and Commonwealth Office, *Developments in the European Community*, HMSO, London, twice yearly.

Hendricks, G.E., 'West Germany's role in the EC', *European Access* 1990/2 pp. 10–12.

Hine, D., *Governing Italy: The politics of bargained pluralism*, Oxford University Press, Oxford, 1993.

Howe, M., *Europe and the Constitution After Maastricht*, Nelson and Pollard, Oxford, 1992.

Petersen. K.S., 'Denmark and 1992: Why the Danes drag their feet', *European Access*, 1990/2, pp. 15–16.

Siune, K., 'The Danes said No to the Maastricht Treaty — The Danish referendum of June 1992', *Scandinavian Political Studies*, vol. 16, no. 1, 1993, pp. 93–103.

Smith, G.W., 'Germany and Maastricht', *Politics and Society in Germany, Austria and Switzerland*, vol. 5, 1993, pp. 61–9.

Sutton, M., 'France and the Maastricht design', *The World Today*, vol. 49, no. 1, 1993, pp. 4–8.

Taylor, R., 'British sovereignty and the EC', *Millenium*, 20 January 1991.

The Economist, 'A rude awakening — a survey of the European Community', 3 July 1993.

Wieczorek-Zeul, H., 'Der Vertrag von Maastricht im Deutschen Bundestag', *Europa-Archiv*, vol. 48, no. 13–14, 1993, pp. 405–12.

Worre, T., 'Denmark at the crossroads: the Danish referendum of 28 February 1986', *Journal of Common Market Studies*, vol. 26, no. 4, 1988, pp. 361–88.

Yannopoulos, G., *Greece and the European Economic Community: Integration and Convergence*, Macmillan, London 1986.

iv. Towards a wider Western Europe

The TEU itself, like the political and economic roller coaster of 1992–3, had an effect on closely related states in Europe and on other European organizations. Conversely, events there were not without effect on what was happening in the Community. This was the case with the EEA, with ideas of EC enlargement to include other Western European states, and with developments inside EFTA countries such as Switzerland. The Community's problems also interacted on the progress of the Europe Agreements with the Visegrad states and with relations with some of the southern associates of the Community. These two groups of states, pictured in Figure 15, therefore moved closer to becoming part of an institutionalized Western Europe, in a way which was not true of more peripheral zones of Europe.

The EEA and enlargement

The Maastricht Summit came very shortly after agreement had been reached between the Community and the EFTA states on the creation of a European

Figure 15. The EEA and the Associated States

Economic Area (EEA). This started as an attempt to create a structured relationship with some of the Community's closest trading partners in Western Europe. The idea had been launched by Delors in January 1989 but proved extremely difficult to negotiate. It ultimately developed into a complicated deal to allow the EFTA states to share in the Single Market.

The EEA, as it was agreed at the end of October 1991, involved acceptance by EFTA of much of the *acquis* dealing with the four freedoms and some of its flanking policies, together with special agreements on fish and transit. Access to Community programmes was also increased. At the same time the EFTA states undertook to provide financial aid to the poorer Community member states. All this is to be policed by a new institutional structure of Ministerial Council, Joint Committee of Officials and dual enforcement procedures.

The final arrangements were therefore very far from what most EFTA governments really wanted. The institutional arrangements provided them with only limited influence on policy-making, while making them both speak as one in the EEA Council and set up their own Surveillance Agency to parallel the Commission. Moreover, almost at the time of Maastricht, the ECJ was querying the EEA's judicial arrangements. The Court's opposition forced the abandonment of a single, separate, EEA court. Eventually a revised agreement, with twin judicial authorities, was signed at Porto on 2 May 1992.

The contrast between these difficulties and the Maastricht Agreement played a part in deciding some of the EFTA countries to apply for Community membership in 1991–2. However, the ending of the Maastricht honeymoon had its effects on the EEA. Thus, although ratification began at once in the EFTA countries and was largely completed by October, progress was much slower in Community countries where it took second place to Maastricht. Then, on 6 December 1992, the Swiss population voted by 50.3 per cent to 49.7 per cent not to ratify the Agreement. Although this was primarily a vote of no confidence in the Swiss establishment, it also reflected the poor image of the Community, as well as the prevalent suspicion of its negotiating style and treatment of small nations. It also revealed that many Swiss feared the social and economic consequences of the Single Market. Not surprisingly the vote was welcomed by UK Europhobes.

Even though the effects of the Swiss decision were partly offset by the fact that, a week later, Liechtenstein voted 56 per cent to 44 per cent for ratification, the vote set the EEA back on its heels. The Swiss surrendered their Presidency of EFTA and saw some EFTA offices, existing and projected, transferred to Brussels. More negotiations were then required to produce a Protocol which altered the reading of the Agreement to remove references to Switzerland in its working and institutions. This was signed on 17 March 1993.

However, the new accord also needed ratification, at a time when some Community states notably Spain, had yet to ratify the original agreement. This was partly because the Swiss withdrawal threatened both the cohesion fund and concessions on agricultural products and labour on which the Spaniards had been counting. The Spanish have, on some occasions, threatened to make the EEA conditional on ratification of Maastricht because of this. So it seems unlikely that the revised agreement will come into effect much before the end of 1993.

None of this was calculated to change the minds of those EFTA governments which had decided that Community entry was a better deal than the EEA. It also helped to clarify Community thinking. However, it did have an adverse effect on public opinion in their countries, as did the travails of the post-Maastricht Community. As a result doubts within the EC about enlargement were not wholly silenced.

Nonetheless, the new dynamism of the Community, the ending of the Cold War and the need for full political and economic participation in the all-important Single Market had already led most of the EFTA countries to apply for membership.

Austria was the first to do so in the summer 1989. The economic crises of 1990 then drove the Swedes to follow suit in the summer of 1991. Finland did the same in the spring of 1992 and the Swiss later that May. By then it was clear that the Norwegians would do the same, although it was only after the Labour Party Congress that autumn that the application was actually tabled. This was done in November 1992. Clearly the Maastricht Agreement did interrupt this process. Most of the EFTA states believed they could live with it and some positively welcomed it.

The Commission *avis* on the early applicants were very favourable and, bruised by the road from Maastricht, the Community came round to accepting that the EFTA states could be accepted without further institutional change. However, much stress was laid on the need for the 'EFTAns' both to accept that they would be entering the Union and to commit themselves to the totality of the aims of Maastricht. This raised some difficulties over neutrality. The Lisbon European Council was hesitant about enlargement and the UK Presidency did not give it as much emphasis as had been expected.

In the end, the Edinburgh Summit did resolve the budgetary question, which had been a precondition for enlargement laid down at Maastricht, and authorized the opening of negotiations. Those with Austria, Finland and Sweden in February duly began in early February 1993. They took place in an atmosphere of openness derived from the Edinburgh agreement. Those with Norway followed a few weeks later. The Swiss application was frozen because of the December vote against the EEA which deprived the policy of its credibility.

Progress was to be slow but steady, while calls for further institutional change to cope with enlargement were still heard from inside the Community. In the candidate countries meanwhile, public opinion, which had initially been supportive of Community entry, began to veer off course in much the same way as it had in EC member states. Public opinion polls therefore showed a declining level of support for entry in most EFTA countries. Nevertheless, the EFTA governments pressed on and the general expectation by the end of the summer of 1993 was that the accession talks would be concluded successfully over the coming winter. Allowing a year for ratification, the new members could hope to take up their places in early 1995 or, at worst, 1996. The real question was whether public opinion in the applicant states would accept the deals negotiated on their behalf.

The EFTA states

The difficulties of finalizing and ratifying the EEA, combined with the economic and political crisis experienced by the Community, began to pose new difficulties for the EFTA states. Thus Community entry has become more of an issue than it had been, and opinion polls have begun to suggest that entry could be rejected. At the same time, economic conditions could pose very severe challenges to governments. Hence, as in the Community, the progress of integration has become inextricably linked to domestic political change.

In **Austria** the ruling left/right coalition, which had originally sought membership for economic reasons, became increasingly keen on entry because of the security problems posed for it by the Yugoslav crisis. Its own military capacity was quite insufficient to cope with any spillover from the South or from the other ethnic problems in surrounding countries. However, there was worrying opposition to both the idea of EC entry and to foreigners from Jörg Haider and the Austrian Freedom Party (FPÖ). This inflicted a number of defeats on the coalition parties until Haider's own excesses caused a secession from the FPÖ which then underwent a change of heart on Europe.

Nonetheless, public opinion became increasingly worried about the threat to neutrality and some 40 per cent were reported to be hostile to entry as a result. With economic growth slowing down, the outcome of the 1994 elections looks uncertain. However, Austria remains economically capable of meeting the TEU's convergence conditions. Events in both Bosnia and the money markets have reinforced the conviction of the main parties that Austria has to join the Union.

For **Finland** the early 1990s have been a period of economic and general trauma. The collapse of the USSR thus destroyed its whole security strategy while at the same time costing it around 6 per cent of its GDP. This has forced the centre-right coalition led by Esko Aho of the Centre Party to turn rapidly towards Europe. Neutrality was reconsidered, the markka tied to the ECU and an application for Community entry made. However, the policy switch was not enough either to save the country from successive devaluations in 1991 and 1992, or to overcome internal unease over the government's austerity policies.

In fact, relations between the government and the unions have rapidly deteriorated. And, with competition for the first direct popular presidential elections in 1994 distracting the cabinet, its survival is not assured. The elections may also provide an opening for anti-Community feelings although these are less marked than in other EFTA countries. Finland's position on the exposed Russian periphery of Europe and the extent of its economic problems convince most Finns that they must become a full part of Europe, and this means entering the Union.

In **Iceland** the Social Democratic-Independence party coalition under David Oddsson has experienced similar problems. Despite privatization, devaluation was forced on the krona in November 1992 and government spending has run into deficit. With the all-important fishing industry contracting, a good deal of opposition had to be overcome before the EEA was ratified. No parties presently support Community entry.

The tiny principality of **Liechtenstein** is a very recent entrant to EFTA. It decided that this was the best way of preserving its standard of living, while its ratification of the EEA underlined its intention of playing a political role independent of Switzerland. It was also a way of ensuring its continuing prosperity. However, disentangling its 1923 Customs Union with the latter is proving tricky and it is possible that a second referendum may be needed before it can take a full part in the EEA.

The present Labour government in **Norway** came to power in the autumn of 1990 after its Conservative predecessor was brought down by the Centre Party's opposition to making initial concessions on the EEA. Although memories of the divisive 1972 referendum led the government to prefer the EEA, its weaknesses, plus the possibility of being marginalized inside Scandinavia and NATO, led the Labour Party towards membership. It moved very slowly, hoping to exorcize ghosts by so doing, but failed in its attempt. For although the Storting easily endorsed the application, popular opposition was fanned by the Danish experience, and the Labour Party's standing in the polls plummeted for a while. This raised the possibility of a bitterly contested election in September 1993, and perhaps even a change of government and policy.

The fact that North Sea oil did not prevent economic decline and that the Community has publicly opposed the unilateral Norwegian resumption of whaling threaten to add to the antagonisms. These showed themselves in electoral attacks on the UK Environment Minister. Because the local elite are sometimes seen as the heirs of previous Danish overlords, ordinary Norwegians are extremely suspicious of them. So public opinion in Norway is less warm to the EC than that in any other EFTA country and its participation in the Union must therefore be regarded as equally less certain.

Sweden suffered even more from the depression of the 1990s. Indeed it found itself forced to apply for membership in order to reassure the markets, tying the krona to the ECU in the summer of 1991. After the September 1991 election the move towards Europe was speeded up by Carl Bildt's minority centre-right government as part of a broader strategy of reversing the corporatism, neutrality and stagnation of the so-called 'Swedish Way'. The latter was coming under increasing pressure from changing economic conditions.

However, economic pressures did not relent and, despite resorting to astronomical interest rates, the krona had to be devalued three times, notably on 24 August 1992. Bildt was then forced to work with the Social Democrats to get a new Finance Bill through in 1992–3. The government was also threatened on the right by the rise of the populist and mildly xenophobic New Democracy movement and on the left by Greens and others who began to query the move towards Europe. Public opinion also became somewhat cooler.

Finally, in **Switzerland** the European issue has proved doubly divisive. The country's long history of reticence towards political links with Europe was reversed in 1991–2 when the establishment sought to realign its diplomacy, neutrality and security policy around Europe. it canvassed not just Community membership but also participation in a future European security order. For a while this seemed to enjoy popular approval but, from the spring of 1992 onward, opposition began to develop. After a very vigorous campaign the latter was able to carry the day on 6 December, profiting from the government's own divisions and hesitations. Hence, as seen, the country narrowly rejected the EEA.

The depth and bitterness of the division over Europe, which also ran along the language frontier between French and German speakers, shocked the Swiss. Meanwhile the depression was beginning to make unwanted inroads in the Swiss economy. So, while opinions on Europe began to change, the country remained polarized between pro and anti factions. The government was unable to do much more than wait for something to turn up. It still felt that entry was the best policy but realized that this was politically impossible. Hence it was not happy when sufficient signatures were collected in July 1993 to force a second vote on the EEA. This was because a new referendum would renew divisions, as would an anti-European initiative which will also have to be voted upon. A second defeat would be politically damaging, while a victory might force the country to enter a dying institution, thereby further reducing chances of EC entry. Whether the country will be able to escape from its political paralysis is very unclear. This has implications for the EEA and for EFTA, assuming that the other candidate countries succeed in entering the Union. The EEA would be too cumbersome for Iceland, Liechtenstein and Switzerland, but the future of EFTA would also be somewhat problematic. One side effect of this would be that EFTA's agreements with the Visegrad states would also lapse.

The associated states

This combination of domestic unease and doubt about the nature, process and structures of European integration has also affected the Community's associated states, especially the Visegrad countries — the most advanced and pluralist of the ex-Soviet satellites. Poland, Hungary and the then Czechoslovakia had, in December 1991, finally negotiated terms with the Community for association agreements under Article 238. Such agreements create a framework for close relations between the Community and states for whom immediate membership is not appropriate. In this case the agreements, known as Europe Agreements, provide for asymmetrical free trade, political dialogue, financial support and technical cooperation.

q.v. Article 238 pp. 337–40.

However, while the agreements have been ratified in Hungary and Poland, two Community countries have yet to do so. The Czechoslovak accord was also overtaken by the division of the country into separate republics on 1 January 1993. New talks had then to be held to produce two separate agreements, a task largely finished by June 1993. As a result only interim agreements, covering the trade elements of the deals, are presently in operation.

The Community's slowness to act shows that the Maastricht malaise has exacerbated underlying divisions about relations with Central and Eastern Europe. Two problems in particular have emerged. On the one hand, there have been fears about the impact the Europe Agreements might have on sensitive economic sectors in the West, such as agriculture and steel. These showed themselves in the very difficult negotiations and have recently surfaced both in the so-called 'Cattle War', in which fears of foot and mouth disease were used to justify bans on eastern livestock exports, and in resistance to Commission plans to widen market access for the would-be associates. The Twelve have, in fact, imposed anti-dumping measures on steel.

On the other hand, there are related, but more political fears, about the long-term implications of Community relations with its Central European neighbours. Countries like France are not convinced that the former satellites are ready for entry, especially if the Community does not deepen first. Hence, since the Europe Agreements were eventually agreed, progress in implementing them and developing closer relations has been slow, forcing the Visegrad states to issue joint statements in the autumn of 1992 and the summer of 1993 calling on the Community to be more encouraging and open. Nonetheless, the Commission's May 1993 proposals for going further at first encountered resistance.

The Commission wanted open acceptance that the Visegrad states would eventually enter the Union, together with measures to help them prepare for membership including market access, targeted economic assistance and close political contact. The aim is to use the idea of developing the agreements as a means of preventing the reform processes in those countries from going off the rails. Despite previous reticence, this was largely endorsed by the Copenhagen European Council. And, a few days later, association agreements with the Czechs and Slovaks were initialled. The Community has subsequently moved to implement the new trade concessions agreed at Copenhagen. However, as noted above, ratification of the Europe Agreements has yet to be completed.

Essentially, the problem facing the EC is one of balancing short-term losses, which are keenly felt in a period of depression, against the long-term gains of improved human rights and preventing Central Europe from falling back into chaos. At the moment, the situation in the Visegrad countries is not promising. Economic depression hit hard after the early gains made in privatization in Poland and elsewhere. Social conditions have deteriorated, with both unemployment and crime rates rising. Despite signs of upturn in Poland, and the slowing down of decline elsewhere, countries with a highly fragmented political system, have found it hard to attain stable government.

In May 1993 the Polish *Sejm* thus brought down the Suchoka government because it would not concede inflationary wage rises or slow down privatization. New elections are due to be held in September. With Western trade falling off, and a third devaluation of the zloty necessary in August 1993, consolidating the reform process is thus at risk. The Hungarian scene has been more stable and reform more restrained than the Polish 'big bang'. However, the Antall government has come under attack both from the Liberal opposition and from nationalists in its own ranks. The latter went on to secede in June 1993 and form their own party. The country also has major problems with refugees and geopolitical instability, encouraging it to turn to a reluctant NATO for help. Both countries are also experiencing steep falls in GDP and the ability to export more to the West would be a great help in reversing this.

In what was Czechoslovakia, the velvet revolution ultimately led to a split over economic policy. With the more vulnerable Slovaks couching their resistance to liberalization in terms of more autonomy, the elections of summer 1992 thus led to a separation between the two halves of the country. However, it is not certain that this is what the people, including some Slovak leaders, really wanted. As a result the Meciar government soon found itself in trouble in 1993, unpopular, internally divided, forced to privatize in order to attract outside investment, and facing massive unemployment. Some of the other Visegrad states also looked somewhat askance at a regime which was still run by ex-Communists.

The Czech Republic has developed much closer relations with Germany and the West, partly because its voucher privatization scheme is much more in line with Western thinking. So far it has been more stable politically and less troubled by security problems than Slovakia. It is also less economically depressed although conditions are still hard. All this makes it clear than closer links to the Community are essential, both in the short and longer term. The slowness and uncertainty of renegotiation and ratification of the Europe Agreements has not helped to provide this.

The hopes of Cyprus and Malta, the two small Mediterranean associates, of entering the Community have also not been helped by the post-Maastricht malaise. Despite its tax reform and currency links with the ERM, the former still has immense legal problems. This is because the division of the island after the Turkish invasion of 1974 has yet to be resolved. For a long time the Community has believed that it could not really accept a state which does not control two-thirds of its nominal territory. However, with the publication of the *avis* in the summer of 1993 things have changed somewhat. The Community has warned that if negotiations with the Turks of Northern Cyprus do not lead to a solution, then it will consider negotiating separately with the Greek Cypriot government. This has a new and more open-minded President in George Clerides.

Malta has confirmed its Western orientation with a second victory for the conservative National Party in February 1992. Like the other associates it has come to terms with the Community's influence, power and policies, so closer links would be very helpful. But it too has been affected by the currency turmoil which forced devaluation in November 1992. It was kept waiting by the Community, despite wanting the support of Union membership, until the summer of 1993 for its *avis*. This too was relatively welcoming, though it remains to be seen whether the Twelve have the political will to tackle further enlargement in the near future. Failure to resolve the question has been destabilizing as, indeed, it has in wider European relations. Nonetheless, the main policy guidelines both of reform and of allowing such countries into the Community circle have so far survived the crisis.

FURTHER READING

Arnold, H., 'Austria and the EC', in *Aussenpolitik*, vol. 40, no. 4, 1989, pp. 385–96.

Arter, D., *The Politics of European Integration in the Twentieth Century*, Dartmouth, Aldershot, 1993.

Baldassarri, M and Mundell, R., *Building the New Europe*, Macmillan, London, 1993.

G. Blazyca and Rapacki, R., *Poland into the 1990s*, Pinter, London, 1991.

Bozoki, A. and Horosenyi, A., *Post Communist Transition: Emerging pluralism in Hungary*, Pinter, London, 1992.

Church C.H., *Switzerland and Europe: Problem or pattern?*, European Policy Forum, London, 1993.

Church, C.H., 'Switzerland: the spectres at the feast', *The World Today*, vol. 49, no. 2, 1993, pp. 23–5.

Church, C.H. (ed.), *Widening the Community Circle*, UACES, London, 1990.

Coombes, D., *Understanding European Union*, Longman, London, 1994.

Dudley, J., *1993 and Beyond*, Kogan Page, London, 1993.

House of Lords, *Enlargement of the Community*, Select Committee on the European Communities, 1st Report, 1992–3, HC-5, 9 June 1992.

Jacquemin A. and Wright, D., *European Challenges Post-1992: Shaping factors, shaping actors*, Edward Elgar, Aldershot, 1993.

Journal of Common Market Studies, Special issue on 'The EC, EFTA and the New Europe', vol. 28, no. 4, 1990.

Kannuzzi, G., 'Le prospettive dell'Unione dopo Maastricht', *Rivista di Studi politici internazionali*, vol. 59, no. 1, 1992.

Kramer, H., 'The European Community's response to the

"New Eastern Europe"', *Journal of Common Market Studies*, vol. 31, no. 2, 1993, pp. 213–44.

Lansing, P. and Bye, P.J., 'New membership and the future of the European Community', *World Competition*, vol. 15, no. 3, 1992, pp. 59–73.

Laursen, F., 'The EC and its European neighbours: special partnerships or widened membership?', *International Journal*, vol. 47, no. 1, 1992, pp. 29–63.

Laursen, F., 'The Maastricht Treaty: Implications for the Nordic Countries', *Cooperation and Conflict*, vol. 28, no. 2, 1993, pp. 115–42.

Lysen, G., 'Some views on neutrality and membership of the EC: the case of Sweden', *Common Market Law Review*, vol. 29, no. 2, 1992, pp. 229–56.

McDonald, F. and Penketh, K., 'The European Community and the rest of Europe', in McDonald, F. and Dearden, S. (eds.), *European Economic Integration*, Longman, London, 1992, pp. 175–98.

Maillet, P. *et al.* 'La demande d'adhésion de la Suède', *Revue du Marché commun et de l'Union européenne*, special issue, no. 346, 1992.

Michalski, A. and Wallace, H., *The European Community and the Challenge of Enlargement*, 2nd edn, RIIA, London, 1992.

Mauritzen, H., 'The "Musterknaben" and the naughty boy: Sweden, Finland and Denmark in the process of Eurpean integration', *Cooperation and Conflict*, vol. 28, no. 4, 1993, pp. 373–402.

Palenki, T., *The EC and Central Europe: The Hungarian case*, Westview, Boulder, 1991.

Palmasdottir, B., *Independence and Interdependence: Iceland and the EC*, Reading Papers in Politics, Reading University, 1991.

Ross, G., 'After Maastricht: hard choices for Europe',

World Policy Journal, vol. 9, no. 3, 1992, pp. 487–513.

Schultz, D., 'Austria in the international arena', *West European Politics*, vol. 16, no. 1, 1992, pp. 173–200.

Svåsand, L. and Lindström, L., 'Norway: sliding towards membership', *Government and Opposition*, vol. 27, no. 3, 1992, pp. 330–344.

Sword, K., *The Times Guide to Eastern Europe*, 2nd edn, Times Books, London, 1991.

Thompson, K., *Poland in a World of Change*, University Press of America, Lanham, 1992.

Tovias, A., 'EC Eastern Europe: a case study of Hungary', *Journal of Common Market Studies*, vol. 29, no. 3, 1991, pp. 291–315.

Ungerer, W., 'Institutional consequences of broadening and deepening the Community — the consequences for the decision-making process', *Common Market Law Review*, vol. 30, no. 1, 1993, pp. 71–83.

Van Ham, P., *The EC and Central Europe*, Pinter, London, 1993.

Wessels, W., 'Deepening and/or widening — debate on the shape of EC-Europe in the nineties', *Aussenwirtschaft*, vol. 46, no. 2, 1991, pp. 157–69.

Wessels, W., 'Erweiterung, Vertiefung, Verkleinerung — Vitale Fragen für die Europäische Union', *Europa-Archiv*, vol. 48, no. 10, 1993, pp. 308–16.

Willgerodt, H., 'Armut als Integrationshindernis? Zum Konflikt zwischen Vertiefung und Erweiterung der Europäischen Gemeinschaft', *Zeitschrift für Wirtschaftspolitik*, vol. 41, no. 2, 1992, pp. 95–123.

Wolchik, S., *Czechoslovakia*, Pinter, London, 1991.

v. The Union and other European institutions

As well as impacting on associate and would-be member states, the nature and effectiveness of the Union is likely to be a key factor in the evolution of an institutional architecture for the 'New Europe'. This is partly because the Treaties provide such an important structure for the conduct of intergovernmental relations. It is also partly because the Community is active in three of the main fields of European cooperation: the political, the economic and the security. Even in regional relationships it is not without its effects. However, because of its multidimensional impact, the Union may have a problematic relationship with other European organizations. Figure 16 gives some ides of their inter-relationships.

On the political front the main European organization, apart from the Community, is the *Council of Europe*. Originally intended as the basis for a European state, this has developed into a loose intergovernmental organization specializing in, on the one hand, human rights and democracy and, on the other, in social, educational and cultural affairs. The Council works through a Council

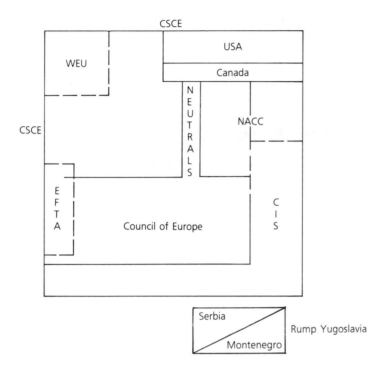

Figure 16. Other European institutions

of Ministers, loosely coordinated by a Presidency state, and a 177-strong advisory Parliamentary Assembly of nominated members from national parliaments.

The Council tends to work through the development of conventions. These are then signed by those states who wish to do so, and then come into effect once they have been ratified by a minimum number of states. Hence they do not always exert immediate and binding influence. However, they can provide basic standards and guide states' behaviour. The most notable of these is the 1949 Convention on Human Rights (ECHR), referred to in Article F of the TEU. This is the nearest that the Community has yet got to underwriting the Convention. The procedures provide individuals with access, through a screening Commission which decides if there is a prima facie case to be answered, to a Court in Strasbourg which can issue rulings against member states. The Council also has charters on local government autonomy, on minority languages and social affairs. Its Social Charter, dating from 1961, should not be confused with that of the Community being much broader than the latter.

This points to an area of overlap and sometimes of conflict between the two bodies. The Council likes to think of itself as a kind of European umbrella organization and hears reports on the work of other bodies such as EFTA and the OECD. However, the Community has never done this and has increasingly moved into areas, such as education and culture, which the Council liked to think were its preserve. It has also developed its own ideas on human rights. Attempts at delimitation did not always work. A Summit meeting has been planned for Vienna in October 1993 to consider the Council's future role now that it has

q.v. Article F pp. 56–8.

recognized that the European Union will be the core of European integration once the TEU is ratified.

More recently the Council has played a major role in introducing central and eastern European states into the circle of democratic nations. It has encouraged the discussion and development of democracy, including monitoring elections in the former satellites. As a result, membership — now enjoyed by some thirty states — is a *sine qua non* for Community membership. Hence it may still have a role, alongside the Union, for some time to come.

The economic management of Europe involves three other bodies besides the Community. One of these is, as has already been seen, the *European Free Trade Association* (EFTA). Set up as a rival to the EC, this has evolved into a useful means of managing the relations of smaller states with the Community. Acting by consensus through a Council of Ministers, assisted by a small Secretariat based in Geneva, it has proved unable to sustain the economic needs of its members. Hence, it has expanded and developed as a pillar of the EEA. Given the referendum result of December 1992, the Swiss now occupy an ambivalent observer status in EFTA's dealings with the EEA.

Although there has been some rather loose talk of EFTA serving as a staging ground for central and east European states, the reality is, as has been made clear, that its medium- to long-term future now looks uncertain. Moreover, there is even greater disparity between the EFTA states and the former satellites than with those of the Community. And EFTA offers little politically. Its agreements with southern and eastern states would clearly expire, once the majority of its states joined the Union, unless they were subsumed in those negotiated by the Community.

The other two economic institutions are the *United Nations Economic Committee for Europe* (UNECE) and the *Organization for Economic Cooperation and Development* (OECD). The former was set up in 1947 and has advised states on economic and, increasingly, environmental problems. The latter, which is based in Paris, emerged as a means of coordinating Marshall Aid in Europe but has since developed, like the UNECE, into a combination of Western monitoring agency and think tank. Its assessments of economic performance and prospects are highly esteemed, and the Commission participates in its activities. Hence they are likely to continue no matter how the Union develops.

Mention should also be made of the *European Bank for Reconstruction and Development* (EBRD), sometimes known as the BERD, because of its French title. This is not an umbrella body but a more technical institution aimed at helping the economic development of Eastern Europe. Stimulated by the EC in 1989–90, it is based in London, and financed by western and eastern states. Its initial activities have proved somewhat disappointing and controversial.

The *Conference on Security and Cooperation in Europe* (CSCE) has often been seen as the best means of establishing security in the New Europe. Originally set up in the early 1970s as a means of consolidating the *de facto* recognition of post-1945 borders, by acting as a bridge between East and West, it played a significant part in undermining the Soviet order through the pressure it exerted in the field of human rights. For its part, the Community played a role in coordinating Western participation. Hence, in 1990, the Paris Charter tried to provide an institutionalized forum for solving conflicts in Europe. It did this partly by welcoming all the former states of the USSR and its satellites, so that it now has over 50 members.

The Paris Charter thus laid down both a code of conduct and provided for regular ministerial and official meetings, together with small agencies for elections, conflicts and a secretariat. The CSCE has also tried to set up a Parliamentary Assembly, which has caused some friction with the Council of Europe, and economic and security fora. There has also been a new interest in minority matters, in the peaceful solution of disputes and observing such crises as Ngorno-Karabakh. Yet even here the UN is now becoming more active.

The CSCE is also seeking to develop an economic role. However, the CSCE is hamstrung by its large size, its lack of resources, its dependence on consensus, the non-binding nature of its declarations and its lack of economic and political muscle. All this has made many people somewhat sceptical about the contribution it can make to a world in which internal problems are just as explosive as conflicts between states. Its role in the former Yugoslavia seems to highlight such problems.

This scepticism has reinforced the potential importance of the Union. It has also placed a new stress on the *North Atlantic Treaty Organization* (NATO) and the *Western European Union* (WEU). And the latter is, in turn developing a new relationship with the Union because of Maastricht. NATO has begun to move towards cooperation with the CSCE and the UN in areas which were not its original concern during the Cold War. It has also refocused its strategy to allow it the possibility of more rapid intervention in crisis situations.

However, NATO has not moved very far in providing the new democracies of central Europe with real military guarantees. Given their uneasy situation on the unstable eastern fringe of Europe they desperately want reassurances that they can call on outside help in case of invasion or crisis. The Yugoslav crisis suggests that only NATO is really able to provide this. Rather than giving such assurances, however, NATO has set up the North Atlantic Cooperation Council. This gives representatives of the states, who were previously members of the rival Warsaw Pact, the chance to discuss matters of common interest with the members of NATO.

The latter has, since December 1990, sought to strengthen cooperation with the EC. The Community, in turn, has moved towards the defence and security dimension even before the TEU is ratified. Its tool for this has been the Western European Union, an often moribund body deriving from the Brussels Treaty of 1948 and the failure of the European Defence Community project in 1954. In the last few years the scope of the WEU has been considerably expanded, both through new members and through observer status for countries such as Denmark, Ireland, Norway and Turkey. Because the TEU identifies it as part of the security pillar of the Union, it has moved its headquarters to Brussels, created a planning cell and entered into new contacts with the Central and East European and Mediterranean countries. Nine of these now take part in its Consultation Forum.

So far it has only played a minor naval role in the Yugoslav crisis. However, this activity conceals a continuing debate as to whether the WEU is to be an independent European defence agency, as the French would like, or simply the

European pillar of NATO, as the United Kingdom and others would prefer. Maastricht left this question unresolved, at least until discussions begin on the expiry of the Treaties establishing the WEU in 1998. In the meantime the French and Germans have set up a joint brigade in which other states are interested and may well join.

As a result, there are still major questions to be answered about how Community Europe is to define its security aims and organize its defence. The Yugoslav crisis has made this all too apparent as will be seen. So, while the Union is heavily involved in all this, it is not yet clear that it will be able to play the role which many wish for it. Moreover, what Laffan calls the 'rich tapestry of organizations' presently at work in Europe may constitute a further barrier to coordinated European action not just in the security fields but others as well.

In addition, it has to be remembered that Europe also now includes a number of other regional organizations. As well as the Benelux Union there are others which bring together Community states and other European actors. Thus there are the Nordic Council, the Baltic Sea Cooperation Council, the Alp-Adria group, and the Pentagonale. And, at a lower level, there are a host of transfrontier activities which play an often overlooked role in developing European integration. Good examples of these are the Basel-Gebiet and the Trans-Manche frontier Region, involving Kent, the French region of Nord-Pas-de-Calais and some of the Belgian provinces.

For these too the evolution of the Union and, especially the Single Market, is a matter of considerable importance. It makes it clear that the Union is already the core of European integration and cooperation, a position it is likely to retain, given the scepticism and limitations of some of the other bodies involved. Therefore its own problems will be of continuing significance for others. Nowhere is this more likely to be true than on the peripheries of Europe.

FURTHER READING

Allen, D. and Smith, M., 'The European Community in the new Europe: bearing the burden of change', *International Journal*, vol. 47, no. 1, 1992, pp. 1–28.

Buchan, D., *Europe: The strange superpower*, Dartmouth, Aldershot, 1993.

Brückner, P., 'The European Community and the United Nations', *European Journal of International Law*, vol. 1, no. 1/2, 1990, pp. 174–92.

Collinson, S., Miall, H. and Michalski, A., *A Wider European Union? Integration and Cooperation in the New Europe*, RIIA Discussion Papers 48, RIIA, London, 1993.

Crouch C. and Marquand, D., *Towards a Greater Europe*, Blackwell, Oxford, 1992.

Hoffman, S., 'Goodbye to a United Europe', *New York Review of Books*, 27 May 93 pp. 27–31.

Holtermann, H. (ed.), *CSCE: From idea to institution*, DJOF Publishing, Copenhagen, 1993.

Kloten, N., 'Europäische Perspektiven nach Maastricht',

Europa-Archiv, vol. 48, no. 13–14, 1993, pp. 397–404.

Laffan, B., *Integration and Co-operation in Europe*, Routledge, London, 1992.

Lodge, J. (ed.), *The European Community and the Challenge of the Future*, 2nd edn, Pinter, London, 1993.

Nugent, N., 'European integration after Maastricht', *European Access*, 1992/3, pp. 8–11.

Ropers, N. and Schlotter, P., 'Vor den Herausforderungen des Nationalismus: Die KSZE in den neunziger Jahren', *Aus Politik und Zeitgeschichte*, B-15-16/93, 9 April 1993, pp. 20–7.

Story, J. (ed.), *The New Europe: Politics, Government and Economy*, Blackwell, Oxford, 1993.

Van Meerhaeghe, J., *International Economic Institutions*, Kluwer, Dordrecht, 1992.

Wallace, W., *The Transformation of Western Europe*, Pinter, London, 1990.

vi. The Union and the peripheries of Europe

Interaction between the Union and Europe does not stop with Western Europe and its institutions. Indeed, it is probably on the southern and eastern peripheries of Europe, as defined in Figure 17, that the Union faces its greatest challenges. The inherent explosiveness of ethnic patterns there has raised new and paradoxical questions about the Union. Both challenges and questions are symbolized by the crises in former Yugoslavia, and most notably in Bosnia-Herzegovina. However, they go beyond this to the rest of the Balkans, to Turkey and the Mediterranean, and to what was the USSR, both the powder keg of the Caucasus and its western fringes. Not merely does the Union have a moral responsibility to stabilize its peripheries but it is in its own long-term interest to do so. Failure to act now means that, in the long run, the Union may have to pay a higher price in escalating economic collapse, westwards migration and widespread war.

Yet, if exercising its responsibility may be in the Union's best interests, doing so demands far greater commitment and consistency than the Community has yet been able to muster. Nor is it certain that the TEU and the new CFSP pillar will actually remedy the problem. Indeed, the impact of the new readings of the TEU which have emerged on the road from Maastricht threaten to increase friction and nationally motivated divergences within the Union. It is more than ironic, therefore, that the very people who are loudest in their condemnations of the 'overweening ambitions' of Brussels are often the same as those who attack the Community for its impotence in what was Yugoslavia. The problems that have dogged the TEU therefore, have also been visible in Yugoslavia and other peripheral areas. Community involvement in Yugoslavia started out very promisingly with the expression of great concern over Serbian treatment of the Albanians of Kosovo. Indeed, when the war started in Slovenia in 1991, the Twelve were given a mandate to mediate by the CSCE. Threats of withholding financial aid helped to freeze moves to independence and then allowed the EC to broker a cease-fire that September, freeing Slovenia of Yugoslav troops. However, while EC pressures helped to make some progress, including setting up an international conference on Yugoslavia and putting pressure on the Serbian economy, the situation on the ground deteriorated rapidly. By the time the fourteenth cease-fire finally held in January 1992, and UN negotiation and policing of a definitive peace was agreed, the Serbs had established their control over a good part of Croatia even though the latter, like Slovenia, had gained independence.

By then Bosnia was also under threat. The extension of the conflict to the latter has been blamed on the Community's precipitate offer of recognition to former regional states of Yugoslavia in early 1992. This was due to heavy German pressure, motivated by genuine concern for the sufferings of Croatia and Slovenia and guilt about German intervention there in the last war. This consolidated the independence of the two northern states, though Greek susceptibilities and intransigence held up recognition of Macedonia. Serbia and Montenegro rejected the offer and moved to declare their own new Yugoslav state which, by the early autumn of 1993 had still to be recognized.

Figure 17. Ex-Yugoslavia and the wider Europe (Source: Story, J. (ed.), *The New Europe*, Blackwell, Oxford, 1993)

All this encouraged first a Bosnian referendum on independence, and then an onslaught by the Serbs on Bosnia, before their territorial ambitions there could be thwarted. With Community mediation failing, and UN aid and military operations slow to get under way, an appalling war in Bosnia broke out in April 1992. With Croats, Muslims and, especially, Serbs all playing their part in ethnic cleansing and other atrocities, the war assumed horrifying proportions. This was despite both sanctions and the humanitarian efforts of the UK, French, Spanish and other UN troops. And it was events on the ground rather than the tortuous EC–UN peace negotiations which really decided things. Hence, by the time the Vance–Owen plan for cantonalization was agreed in the winter of 1992–3, things had gone beyond this.

So, in 1993, the EC and the rest of the international community oscillated uncertainly between threats and acceptance of the emerging *de facto* partition of Bosnia. By the summer limited military defence of safe havens was the best that could be arranged, but this was not really effective. It also shifted attention to individual states rather than the Community. Indeed, the French and the United Kingdom did not even bother to notify the Commission of agreements on containment. It was then left to NATO to arrange military support for the UN. Neither the international community at large, nor the EC, were able to agree on new arrangements, there being disagreements about whether to end the arms embargo on the Muslims and about whether there should be air-strikes. Opinion in the various countries became increasingly critical of the behaviour of other nations involved in the crisis. This did little for the internal harmony of the Community.

By the end of the summer, the international community came round to accepting a tripartite ethnic division of Bosnia, within a fig-leaf confederal structure. The problem then became how to persuade the Bosnian government to accept the partition. This was hard because the proposed settlement not merely gave the Bosnians less territory than they wanted, but seemed both to reward violent ethnic cleansing and to destroy the idea of a multiethnic Bosnian state. Whether this will solve the immediate crisis remains to be seen. Previous precedents are not encouraging. In any case, the violence, hatreds and destruction are bound to haunt not just the Union but Europe as a whole.

At the same time, concentration on the Serb—Croat—Bosnian crisis did not help the Community to devise policies in the rest of the Balkans. Here, while Slovenia has moved towards Europe, there are both new trouble spots and areas of underdevelopment. Slovenia has made some progress towards democratization and privatization but its belief that its economic superiority to the rest of what was Yugoslavia qualifies it for Europe has been called into question by the 21 per cent fall in GDP in 1992. The Croatian economy, of course, is in an even worse situation. It has lost 30 per cent of its territory, is being forced to bear the brunt of the refugee problem, and is facing sanctions for its general lack of human rights and its support of recent onslaughts against the Moslems of Mostar.

What is now described as the former Yugoslav Republic of Macedonia still faces the threat of possible dissolution because of its ethnic fragmentation and lack of international recognition, despite the preventative deployment of peace monitors. Its economic position is also parlous. Equally Albania faces something like 50 per cent unemployment and a 60 per cent fall in its already low GDP. With starvation still looming and its parties weak and divided, the possibility of further mass exoduses remains. Moreover, there are still fears of Albanian military involvement in the Serbian province of Kosovo if there is further conflict between the Albanian majority and Serb forces.

Bulgaria and Romania pose slightly different problems. While there are ethnic problems in both, involving Turks in Bulgaria and Magyars in Romania, not to mention the latter's complications with Moldova, the major problem is the lack of decommunization. The fact that, especially in Romania, the old regime and its security forces still seem to remain well entrenched in power means that there have been corrosive confrontations between loose opposition movements and the new governments. At the same time economic conditions have deteriorated rapidly with falls of about 20 per cent in GDP, while inflation has yet to be controlled. Community and IMF aid is therefore vital.

As a result of all this, progress towards Europe Agreements has been very slow, and has been accompanied by minatory warnings about human rights. The agreements have been finalized, and were intended to be largely operative by the end of 1993. However, the progress of economic and political transition remains more uncertain there than in other parts of Eastern Europe. And it is not clear that the Community has really developed a coherent overall approach either to the Balkans in general or to states like Romania and Bulgaria.

There are also pressures from the rest of the Mediterranean area. On the one hand, there is considerable concern, especially in southern Community states, about security in the Mediterranean. With a large number of Islamic states facing a combination of limited economic development with massive population growth and rising Islamic fundamentalism, there are fears about terrorism, political instability and, especially, northwards migration. The EC's Integrated Mediterranean Programmes of aid to most of the states involved are unlikely to avert the problem. So there is talk of both more aid and of a regional version of the CSCE. However, although Morocco did once enquire about membership this seems an unlikely prospect.

Turkey poses a rather different problem. For, while it shares some of these problems, such as its Islamic nature and its population growth, it also has two special characteristics of its own. To begin with, it has had an association agreement with the Community since 1963 and put in a membership application in 1987. This was more or less rejected on grounds of human rights abuses, of the instability of democracy in Turkey, and economic problems, especially labour mobility and agricultural competition, not to mention Greek objections. However, since 1992 efforts have been made to develop relations with Turkey through political dialogue and other means.

This reflects the second facet of Turkey's relations with the Community: its size and strategic importance. With a population of 60 million, Turkey is an important state, especially given the size of its armed forces. With Greece inside the Community and long-standing differences existing between the two, the Turkish dimension is unlikely to be overlooked. And, while its Cold War role has faded, the opening up of what was Soviet Central Asia, (whose peoples are often Turkic as well as Islamic), the North Cyprus question, Kurdish violence in Western Europe, and the Islamic interest in Bosnia and Macedonia have made it again important. The Community has an interest both in encouraging its democratic stability and in using it as a bridge to another unsettled region. However, Turkish responses to the Kurdish problem do not, despite the appointment of a new President and a new female Prime Minister, encourage the West to overlook its human rights problems.

This points to the fact that the break-up of the USSR and the relative failure of the Confederation of Independent States (CIS) to act as a stabilizing force has created another powder keg in the Caucasus and beyond. While such countries are a long way away from the Europe of the Union they still pose problems. The development of conflict, especially that between Armenia and Azerbaijan over Ngorno-Karabakh, does have implications for the West. The instability of the states of what was Soviet Central Asia also touches on broader concerns about Islamic fundamentalism and, in the case of Kazakhstan, of nuclear disarmament. Moreover, beyond all this are the questions of whether the CIS will play any real international role and, even more worryingly, whether the Russian Federation itself will survive, or whether it too, will fragment into quarrelsome and unstable ethnic states. If it does it will change the whole strategic situation of the Union.

Finally, there are also related problems a little closer to home. The western fringes of the former Soviet Union pose other challenges for the Union: in the Baltic coast, in the south-west, and in Russia itself. Where the Baltic states are concerned, the Community was initially only partly supportive of their search for independence, because it did not wish to destabilize Gorbachev. After the coup in August 1991 things changed and the Baltics, often with much Nordic support, have returned to the international arena. They are now seeking association agreements with the Community.

However, economic collapse, the electoral successes of national-Communist political forces, and the rancid disputes with Russia have made this a problem area. The disputes involve compensation for the damage inflicted by occupation, the withdrawal of Russian troops, and the rights of the Russian minorities who have settled there since the 1930s. With the area playing a key role in Russian military defence and economic outlets to the West, feelings run very high on both sides. If the possibility of military conflict remains slim, it cannot be wholly excluded. Hence the Baltic states' desire to move to association and beyond may be somewhat embarrassing to Brussels. There are also problems between Lithuania and Poland. The heavily militarized Russian exclave of Kaliningrad, formerly East Prussia, is a further complication.

To the south-east of the Baltic lie three other new states which also add to the uncertainties on the Union's peripheries. Thus the Ukraine is an ethnically divided state, which has failed to develop a post-communist regime or economy or resolve its differences over territory and the Black Sea fleet with Russia. It also tends to use its share of the Soviet nuclear arsenal as a bargaining counter with both Moscow and Washington. At the same time it has vague, and very optimistic, ideas of Community membership.

At first Belarus sought to carve out a neutral role for itself. However, this seems to have given way to a new alliance with Russia. If this is unlikely to prove destabilizing, the position of Moldova certainly already is. Although largely Romanian-speaking it has a number of minorities. These fear not just the possible reunion with Romania, but the loss of their own rights in the new state. Hence there has been a low-level civil war between the Russian immigrants in the Trans-Dniester strip and the Moldavian authorities. With the rise of nationalist feeling in Russia proper, symbolized by the parliamentary opposition to Boris Yeltsin and his constitutional projects, there is the potential for a wider conflict.

All this means, on the one hand, that the eastern periphery of the Union remains very uncertain, especially if the latter enlarges to take in the Nordic and

Visegrad states. On the other hand, the problems there demand a great deal in the way of economic aid, political support, and innovative diplomacy. The EC is now providing a large-scale Technical Assistance programme to the area, known as TACIS. This involves at least ECU 850 billion and is aimed at assisting the transition to market economies.

Notwithstanding such initiatives, the impression remains that the Union will need to overcome its internal divisions and constitutional hesitations if it is to have any chance of coping with conditions on its peripheries. Internal unity in the Union is necessary in order to take action to defuse critical situations. Such problems could otherwise overwhelm those states who presently wish to deny the Union consistency. At the same time, the state of the Union is likely to affect the way those same peripheries develop.

FURTHER READING

Batt, J., *Eastern Central Europe From Reform to Transformation*, Pinter, London, 1991.

Bonvicini, G. *et al. The European Community and the Emerging New Democracies*, RIIA, London, 1991.

Collinson, S., Miall, H. and Michalski, A., *A Wider European Union? Integration and Cooperation in the New Europe*, RIIA, London, 1993.

Fertila, B., *The Economics and Politics of the Socialist Debacle: Yugoslavia*, University Press of America, Lanham, 1991.

Glenny, M., *The Fall of Yugoslavia*, Penguin, Harmondsworth, 1992.

Gnesotto, N., 'European Union after Minsk and Maastricht', *International Affairs*, vol. 68, no. 2, 1992, pp. 223–32.

Goldstein, W., Europe after Maastricht, *Foreign Affairs*, vol. 72, no. 5, 1992, pp. 117–32.

Jackson, R. (ed.), *Europe in Transition: The management of security after the Cold War*, Adamantine, London, 1992.

John, I.G., *EEC Policy Towards Eastern Europe*, Saxon House, Farnborough, 1976.

Kramer, H., 'The EC and the stabilization of Eastern Europe', *Aussenpolitik*, vol. 43, no. 1, 1992, pp. 12–21.

Kramer, H., 'The European Community's response to the "New Eastern Europe"', *Journal of Common Market Studies*, vol. 31, no. 2, 1993, pp. 213–44.

Longet, R., Quoted in *Le Nouveau Quotidien*, 30 June 1993, p. 24.

McDonald, F. and Penketh, K., 'The European Community and the rest of Europe', in McDonald, F. and Dearden, S. (eds), *European Economic Integration*, Longman, London, 1992, pp. 175–98.

Magas, B., *The Widening Gyre: The strange death of Yugoslav Communism*, Blackwell, Oxford, 1993.

Marescu, M., 'The EC, Eastern Europe and the USSR' in Redmond J. (ed.), *The External Relations of the EC*, Macmillan/St Martins, London, 1992, pp. 93–119.

Pelkmans, J. and Murphy, A., 'Catapulted into leadership: the Community's trade and aid policies vis-à-vis Eastern Europe', *Journal of European Integration*, vol. 14, nos. 2–3, 1991, pp. 125–51.

Pinder, J., *The European Community and Eastern Europe*, Pinter/RIIA, London, 1991.

Ratesh, N., *Romania, The Entangled Revolution*, Praeger, New York, 1992.

Smart, V., 'Black hole of Bosnia is EC's shame' *The European*, 3 June 1993, p. 7.

Soros, G., Quoted in *The Times*, 9 June 1993, p. 27.

Sword, K., *The Times Guide to Eastern Europe*, 2nd edn, Times Books, London, 1991.

Szajkowski, B., 'Will Russia disintegrate into Bantustans?', *The World Today*, vol. 49, nos. 8–9, 1993, pp. 172–5.

Taylor, T., 'What kind of security for Europe?' *The World Today*, vol. 47, nos. 8–9, 1991, 138–41.

Ullman, R., *Securing Europe*, Adamantine, London, 1992.

Van Ham, P., *The EC and Central Europe*, Pinter, London, 1993.

vii. Prospects for the Union

Conditions in the broader European context will be one factor likely to influence the development of the Union. And both that context and that development will have moved on by the time that the *Handbook* appears in print. This fact raises three final questions. These are 'Where are we now?'; 'How might things develop?'; and 'What does this all say about Maastricht and the TEU?' Related to this is a more prosaic concern for readers: 'How can we get, and stay, up to date?'

The present and the future of the Union

After traversing the long and hard road from Maastricht, the present state of play is that ratification now seems almost certain. Hence, the Union is likely to come into existence by 1994. However, the actual components of the Union, especially in the economic field, remain uncertain. And the way the political elements in the Treaty are applied is likely to be less centralizing than might otherwise have been the case thanks to the way the Maastricht settlement and the process of ratification of the TEU have made Community affairs much more salient.

A harsher light now shines on European affairs. So it is now much harder for European elites to push European integration forward without anyone noticing or protesting. Union by stealth, in other words, has become much more difficult, if not impossible. This is also true of automatic integration. Public awareness and involvement means that one aim of the settlement has been achieved, even though this unprecedented popular participation has actually proved very uncomfortable for those who signed the Treaty.

At the same time the road from Maastricht has not dispelled the political unease and uncertainty about the legitimacy, nature and processes of integration. The journey has changed things inside member states and beyond, so doubts remain. These are complicated further by altered 'readings' of the TEU. So understandings of Maastricht may have been as much muddied as clarified by the recent debate. Hence a Eurobarometer poll in May 1993 showed that only 41 per cent were in favour of the TEU and 35 per cent did not know. If no more than 24 per cent were against, there was still considerable resistance in Iberia and around the shores of the North Sea.

Nor has the ratification process removed any of the failings of the Treaties. Jochimsen has described Maastricht as *lex imperfecta* and *lex incompleta* because it is, on the one hand written in what Schmitter calls 'turgid Euro-speak'. It still remains an opaque and complex fudge, embracing both statism and supranationality, precisely because it was designed to paper over profound differences amongst the states who signed it. There is no single right way of reading it because it was intended as, or has become, a Treaty which attempts to be all things to all people. Indeed, developments since December 1991 may have made the settlement even more complicated and uncertain. On the other hand, it is incomplete because there are now so many things left to decide about how it will be read and implemented in the light of changing attitudes and circumstances.

However, despite all the debate, no real and widely acceptable alternatives to the TEU have emerged. This is partly because it does embrace so many conflicting views and partly because some of its initial critics have realized that they have no choice other than to defend it. So it has remained the only deal on the table. As Roy Jenkins said in the House of Lords:

> The ratification of Maastricht will not, in itself, pull everyone out of the mud and put them on their feet again. It will not in itself solve the problem of disarray. But it is a necessary condition for beginning to do so ... If Maastricht ... is not God's gift to man, its ratification is now essential if Europe is to conduct a reappraisal of its future in an atmosphere of common purpose rather than one of mutual suspicion. (Hansard, Lords, 7 June 1993, cols 555–8)

In other words, not to ratify might encourage the gathering forces of destructive balkanization in European politics.

So the answer to the second question of where we might go in the future begins by starting with the TEU. However, the precise answer to the question will depend on at least seven, interrelated factors. These include the depth and length of the current depression; the behaviour of the markets; the way in which member states handle subsidiarity and convergence; the changing political balance inside member and other states; the way in which relationships between member states such as France and Germany evolve; the way 'European' decision-making elites choose to behave; the extent to which the Union remains salient to the public at large; and the external situation of the 'New Europe', notably in places like Bosnia. In other words the reading of the Treaties and the development of the Union will continue to be greatly affected by the wider context.

Given all this, it is clearly impossible to predict exactly how these things will actually come together. It is also unwise, and not in line with the approach generally taken in the *Handbook*, to favour any particular outcome. However, with the pressures for further reconsideration, change is inevitable. As Box 22 indicates, five possible scenarios suggest themselves.

To begin with, there is the full steam ahead possibility. That is to say that the elites will seek to implement the whole of the Treaty as soon as possible, although perhaps on the basis of a few core countries. If there is economic recovery and if ethnic conflicts do not get out of hand (or, indeed, if their severity forces further collective action), then it is possible that there could be further progress towards monetary and political integration without undue public opposition. Thus there could be a new revised constitutional settlement, which enjoys general support, by the end of the decade. In this case Maastricht would be the beginning of a more united and harmonious Europe. However, if the markets remain actively sceptical and there are economic and diplomatic difficulties then this could produce damaging acrimony. For, if the Eurosceptics'

Box 22. Scenarios	1. Full steam ahead to further integration 2. Combining verbal commitment to integration with a pause 3. Limiting damage arising from malaise of 1992–1993 4. Europeanizing the EC 5. Dismantling the EC

claim that implementation will destroy the Community is exaggerated, it is likely that an attempt to ignore the lessons of the last couple of years would create continuing divisions amongst states, elites and the public at large. And there could be a further, economically destabilizing, re-nationalization of European politics. So it is a high-risk strategy which could end in implementation with tears.

A second possibility is that there could be a fudge. That is to say that, as with the recent changes to the EMS, the claim would be made that things were proceeding as planned. However, the way they worked could be very much altered, thus allowing the Union to adjust to its new situation. For example the Union could decide to implement EMU at a distant date in the next century. However, this could cause the Union to lose credibility and might mean crucial issues festering until 1996 and beyond, even if things would not be as acute as in the first scenario.

Equally, the difficulties of implementing monetary union and the pull of internal problems might encourage paper commitments to the ends of Maastricht but without fully or faithfully meeting them. This might avoid some of the problems but would leave many questions unanswered. It would be unlikely to produce real harmony. In such cases the TEU would turn into a continuing aspiration, but one postponed for a long time, possibly well beyond 1996.

A third possibility is what might be called damage limitation. Here a start would be made on implementing the Treaty but, as Kohl has suggested, things could get pushed back and amended. In other words, if the Union decides that the lessons of ratification have to be learned then there could be pragmatic adaptation. The way in which the reading of Maastricht has changed already points in this direction. This might produce a multispeed and variable geometry implementation of the Union, especially on the monetary front, perhaps using the EMI for a longer period than envisaged. This might satisfy opponents and the public, but not the Euroenthusiasts. Nor would it rule out further change, as envisaged for 1996, but this is likely to be evolutionary and remedial rather than a wholly new start.

One other rather unlikely scenario is what might be called the re-Europeanization option. Here the Union could be revamped now, ahead of 1996, on much more democratic and open lines, involving the people more fully. However, this would demand further sacrifices of the peoples of Europe, at the expense of their national institutions. And nation is likely to prove stronger than democracy, especially with economic difficulties and troubles in the Balkans. This is the 'catch 22' of coping with the problems of Maastricht.

Equally unlikely is the Euro-sceptic ideal of dismantling the EC whether completely or by abolishing convergence conditions, enshrining subsidiarity and intergovernmentalism, and cutting the Commission and the ECJ down to size. But, just as much as going full steam ahead, this is likely to encounter fierce political opposition which could use the Union's mechanisms to block any such change. And while public opinion has been sceptical of the TEU, the lessons of the UK referendum on EC membership in 1975 suggest that, were the question of doing away with the Union actually to be put, people would vote to keep it.

All these scenarios are, of course, mere guesses. They will also no doubt be out of date by the time they are published. However, it seems clear that, whatever happens, developing European unity will remain a much debated and very uncertain process. Every solution is likely to offend one of the interests involved. Hence neat, schematic and all-embracing solutions are much less likely than continuing fudging and muddling through in the face of difficulty, disagreement and diversity. This will be disappointing to those with strong convictions for and against a single European state but it may be all that real Europeans, imperfect as they are, can manage.

In this process ironically, the TEU may prove less of a fossil than Norman Lamont and others have recently suggested. Significantly, all the scenarios actually draw on Maastricht and the TEU. So, to answer the third question, if it is true that, according to de Gaulle, treaties are like girls and roses, because they each have their day, the day of Maastricht may not yet be over. Thus, to begin with, the deadlines built into the TEU, whether for EMU or for common action in judicial and home affairs, ensure that this will happen.

It is also likely that the TEU will have to be an essential starting point for any improved constitutional deal for the nations of the Union, whether in 1996 or at some other time. So the ratification process and the events which accompanied it, constitute not just the consolidation of what had been happening, but the beginnings of a further debate. Indeed, that debate has already started. And in almost all cases, thinking tends to start by looking at what is actually in the TEU.

The European Parliament has already been considering both adaptations to help the Union cope with new member states and a new constitutional deal. Equally, think tanks have begun to consider the constitutional way ahead, aware that only by starting serious public discussion now can a repeat of the post-Maastricht gulf between elites and public be avoided when the 1996 IGC meets. Other voices have also been heard calling for a new summit or conference once ratification is complete so as to give a new impetus and direction to the debate. The contents of Maastricht are likely to remain significant, therefore, for some time to come, whatever the final outcome may be. However, questions of consistency, efficacy and legitimacy will all have to be solved.

That final outcome may, in practice, turn out to owe rather more to Maastricht even than this. The TEU's strength, as well as its weakness, is that, in its answers to these questions, it reflects the conflicting beliefs and aspirations of the Twelve, differences which testify to the absence of the preconditions for a real European state, something which the Union was never intended to be. We shall have to live with these fundamental disagreements for a long while yet. So, even if people go back to the drawing board, these differences will still be there and a kind of Maastricht-like deal would be the most likely outcome, 'measured, pragmatic and hard headed' as Douglas Hurd rather generously called it.

Philippe Schmitter has gone yet further than this and argued that, because of its very failure to create a polity with all the marks of a normal state, the Maastricht settlement may actually have hit upon a blueprint for a quite unique condominium style of polity, which will be the only kind of solution which will work in the present circumstances. For, rather than being a classical state, the

Union in his view is a polity without a single locus of unchallengeable supreme authority; without an established, central hierarchy of public office; without a predefined and distinctive sphere of competence within which decisions binding on all can be taken; without a fixed and contiguous territory; without exclusive international recognition; without an overarching identity and presence; without a monopoly of coercion; without a unique capacity for direct implementation of its decisions; and without exclusive control of internal movement within its border. Yet it does have the capacity to take decisions, resolve conflicts, produce public goods, coordinate public behaviour, respond to interests and allocate expenditures. As such it offers an alternative to the conventional view of what the state should be. This condominium might, nonetheless, prove not just an answer to present difficulties, but also a way ahead for the future.

If this is so, and were to be recognized to be so, it would mean that Maastricht would be neither the end of one phase of European integration nor the beginning of a new and more rational phase, but the continuation of a unique yet uncertain development. Despite the initial altercations, Maastricht could lead to something less controversial, perhaps the juridic and institutional identity imagined by Jacques Santer, rather than the culturally-based European superstate some both desire and fear. And, as long as the gains of the peaceful Europe arising out of the process of integration are not lost, then there will be some realistic hope for the continent.

FURTHER READING

Arter, D., *The Politics of European Integration in the Twentieth Century*, Dartmouth, Aldershot, 1993.

Bonvincini, G., 'The future of EC institutions', *International Spectator*, vol. 27, no. 1, 1992, pp. 3–16.

Eichengreen, B., *Should the Maastricht Treaty be Saved?*, Princeton University Studies in International Finance 74, Princeton, 1992.

European Constitutional Group, *European Constitutional Settlement: Draft report*. European Policy Forum, London, 1993.

Hoffman, S., 'Goodbye to a United Europe', *New York Review of Books*, 27 May 1993, pp. 27–31.

House of Commons Foreign Affairs Committee, *Europe After Maastricht: Interim report*, HMSO, HC-205, 1992.

Hurd, D., 'A good deal of British sense', *The Times*, 6 August 1993, p. 16.

Jochimsen, R., 'European Economic and Monetary Union: the do's and the dont's', *The World Today*, vol. 49, no. 6, June 1993, pp. 115–21.

Lodge J. (ed.), *The European Community and the Challenge of the Future*, 2nd edn, Pinter, London, 1993.

Mancini, G., 'The making of a constitution for Europe', *Common Market Law Review*, vol. 26, no. 4, 1899, pp. 505–614.

Santer, J., 'L'Europe après Maastricht', *The College in 1992*, College of Europe, Bruges, 1993.

Schmitter, P., *Interests, Powers and Functions; Emergent properties and unintended consequences in the European Polity*, Centre for Advanced Study in the Behavioral Sciences, Working Paper, Stanford University, April 1992.

Schmitter, P., 'Representation and the future Euro-Polity', *Staatswissenschaften und Praxis*, 1992/3, pp. 379–405.

Sidjanksi, D., *L'avenir fédéraliste de l'Europe: La Communauté européene, des origines au Traité de Maastricht*, Presse Universitaire de France, Paris, 1992.

Weidenfeld, W., *The Shaping of a European Constitution*, Bertelsmann Foundation, Gütersloh, 1990.

Taking things further

If this is so, then there will be a continuing need to think about the Union, its present and its future. This brings us to the last question of how to find out about its ongoing evolution. Here there are at least five answers.

To begin with there is the press. Daily newspapers and weekly magazines are obvious sources of information. English newspapers such as the *Financial Times*, *The Guardian*, *The Independent* and *The Times* provide some coverage of events in Brussels and throughout the Community as do, often more fully, such foreign quality newspapers as *Die Zeit*, the *Frankfurter Allgemeine Zeitung*, the *Süddeutsche Zeitung*, *Le Monde*, and *La Repubblica*. Similarly weekly magazines like *The Economist*, and its continental equivalents can provide reports on Community affairs.

Second, the Community itself provides a series of introductions to its own activities as well as more detailed sources of information. These range from the Commission's own annual *General Report on the Activities of the European Communities* through the pamphlets of the European File and European Documentation series, to the single-page information memoranda of the Commission in Brussels. *European Economy Supplements* provide survey results and details of recent economic trends. *Eurobarometer*, which appears every six months, publishes the results of various surveys conducted among the general public of the EC and beyond.

More comprehensive official information is provided in the monthly *Bulletin of the European Communities*, which is published (along with important *Supplements*) by the Commission, and in the *Official Journal of the European Communities* (OJ) which covers all Community institutions. Preliminary versions of Commission proposals and draft legislation appear as COM.docs. Many of the other Community institutions also have their own publications. Details can be found in the bibliographical Annex II and in any European Documentation Centre of which there are many in the United Kingdom and beyond. The Commission's London office also publishes *The Week in Europe*, a brief weekly information sheet providing details of the more important events in the Community, as well as *Background Reports*. Extracts from major periodical articles on EC matters are reproduced in the Commission Library's Biblio series.

A third set of sources can be found in the increasing number of publications by 'Brussels' watchers who offer more encapsulated accounts of what is going on. These include the *Annual Report on the Activities of the European Community*, published each year in the second Yearbook number of the *Journal of Common Market Studies*. Others include *European Access*, the *Bulletin of the Centre for European Policy Research*, *European Information*, the Economist Intelligence Unit's *European Trends*, the *Annual Review of European Community Affairs* produced by the Centre for European Policy Studies in Brussels, the *Jahrbuch der Europäischen Integration* produced by the Institut für Europäische Politik in Bonn, and the Council of Europe's *European Yearbook*. However, the Brussels-based daily report *Agence Europe* provides the most extensive regular coverage of the Community and its doings.

Fourthly, a number of academic periodicals provide regular analytical articles on various aspects of the European Community. These include many of the titles already referred to in the *Handbook* such as *Economic Policy*, *Integration*, the *Journal of Common Market Studies*, the *Journal of European Integration* and the *Revue du marché commun et de l'Union européen*. On the legal side *The Common Market Law Review* and *Legal Issues of European Integration* are also valuable sources. However, virtually all UK and continental academic journals, in economics, politics, and law now cover Community affairs. As already noted the Biblio series abstracts many relevant articles from such journals.

Finally, it is hoped that this *Handbook* will be regularly updated so that it remains abreast of changes in the Treaties, and also of developments in the Union and its context. The authors hope that by approaching the Treaties neither as Holy Writ nor as the work of the Devil, but as a messy, changeable but still workable fact of European life, they will facilitate a better understanding of what the Union is and may become. Whether this is so can only be judged by readers. So, the authors will be happy to receive any suggestions for improving the Handbook. For, as the ratification process of the Treaties themselves has shown, justification depends on public acceptance and involvement.

Annex 1: Glossary

Acquis Term denoting basic EC law, whether the Treaties or substantive legislation, passed to date and also symbolizing the EC's general achievements. Sometimes translated into English as the 'Community patrimony'.

Antici Informal grouping of assistants to the Member States' Permanent Representatives in Brussels with which the Presidency often discusses work programmes and procedures.

Approximation Process of eliminating unwarranted differences between national legislation which has a bearing on the Single Market. Proposals for doing this emanate from the Commission and are approved by the Council.

Article Basic clause or unit of a Community Treaty. Can be subdivided into paragraphs.

Assizes Term used to describe consultative gatherings of representatives of national parliaments called to help develop understanding of and support for the integration process.

Association Form of relationship with the Community offered either to colonial territories under Part Four of the Treaty of Rome or to states seeking reciprocal relations with, and possibly membership of, the Community under Article 238.

Avis Commission statement on the acceptability of an application for membership of the Community and Union.

Benelux name given to the post-war Economic Union of Belgium, the Netherlands and Luxembourg. The first and the last also have a currency union.

Brussels Term of convenience used to indicate either the Community in general or, less admiringly, the Community bureaucracy and decision-makers.

Budget System of agreed expenditure with guaranteed funds used to support Community institutions and activities.

Cabinet In the Community system a group of personal advisors and aides attached to each Commissioner to help him or her with political and policy advice and liaison.

Chapter A subdivision of a Title in a Community Treaty. It can, in turn, be subdivided into Sections.

Citizenship Legally defined membership of a political community, usually a nation state, with rights (such as sharing in electoral decision-making) and obligations. Linked to the concepts of civil and human rights.

Codecision Term often used to denote what is described in the *Handbook* as the conciliation procedure.

Cohesion Process of reducing socio-economic disparities between the regions of the Community through financial redistribution. The term was introduced by the SEA and was developed by the EEA and the TEU. The process relies on the use of the Structural Funds.

Comitology Process of Commission policy-making within committees consisting of national civil servants, technical experts and representatives of lobbies.

Common market Technically a more developed form of economic integration in which there is free movement of goods and services, etc., within a single customs frontier. Politically the term can be used to denote what critics of Brussels think the Community was, or should be, rather than what it actually is.

Community An organic social or political group united by shared characteristics and activities, identity or status, as opposed to a loose association by contract. In the EC context the term implies a sense of belonging to a common enterprise with a life of its own and not one dependent on the member states.

Community Method Integration or policy making using the institutions of the EC as opposed to intergovernmental mechanisms.

Competence Term used to describe the Community's authority to undertake specific activities, usually deriving from a Treaty article.

Competition Economic process in which economic efficiency and consumer advantage comes from having more than one producer in a market. Much of the Community's legislation and activity is designed to enforce fair competition.

Conciliation New process of decision-making which allows the EP to block legislation if, after discussion with the Council in a Conciliation Committee, it is not satisfied with the outcome. Sometimes called codecision.

Convergence Process of encouraging the economies of the Twelve to work in the same direction and achieve better performance in inflation, deficits and interest rates. Achieving this will facilitate movement towards EMU.

Cooperation Term given to process of achieving harmony and uniform means of intergovernmental action without the creation of special structures. Often opposed to integration or the Community method.

Cooperation procedure Decision-making process initiated by the SEA which requires the Council to rethink its proposals and pass them by unanimity when the Parliament is not satisfied with the proposals.

Culture Concept which can mean either the fine arts and literature or, as in the Community context, those wider practices and patterns which help to define national identity.

Customs Union An economic area in which there is a single external tariff, applied by all member states, and no internal duties so that goods can move freely.

Decision Third-level Community legislative act

which is binding on the state, firm or individual to whom it is directed.

Declaration Either a proclamation by the Community or other conference, of limited judicial enforceability, or a subordinate part of a Treaty, attached to the Final Act and expressing the intentions of those intending to implement the Treaty. Of lesser status than Protocols.

Democratic deficit The belief that the Community is lacking in proper parliamentary authority to which its executive and administrative bodies can be accountable, thereby breaking the normal link between authority and electors.

Depression Downturn in economic activity, greater than a recession but less than a slump.

Deregulation Policy of sweeping away unnecessary rules governing the working of the economy to reduce government interference and increase competitive efficiency. Can also be described as liberalization.

Derogation Permission given to a state not to apply certain Community rules because application would damage the national economy. Usually only granted for a given period of time.

Directive EC legislative act which is binding in principle but not in its application, thereby allowing member states some flexibility in meeting EC aims.

Directorate-General Specialized subdivision into which the administrative services of bodies such as the Commission, the Council and the Parliament are divided. In the case of the first these can very roughly be equated with a Ministry in a member state.

ECU European Currency Unit, the equivalent of a money, based on a basket of member-state currencies and used to facilitate Community financial transfers, budgeting, and exchange rate relations.

Enlargement Process of allowing new states to join the Community or Union. It began with the admission of Britain in 1973 and is likely to extend to the EFTA and Visegrad states in the future.

Europeanization Process of alignment of political and other processes on Western European, and usually Community, norms.

European Movement Political lobby in Britain and elsewhere which supports further Community-led integration.

Euro-sceptics Mainly British opponents of Maastricht and further integration who prefer inter-governmental and free trade cooperation to centralized integration. They are also sometimes described as 'Euro-phobes' because they can seem to reject all forms of European Construction.

Federal Political science term used to denote states with different levels of coordinate authority as opposed to unitary states with a single locus of power. In the EC context it can be used to mean both decentralizing and centralizing processes, depending on the political views of those using the term. Thus Eurosceptics see the Commission as trying to build a federal Europe based on Brussels whereas others see federalism as a means to prevent such concentration of power.

Federalist Term somewhat inaccurately used by Euro-sceptics to attack those persons and policies wishing to increase centralized integration. Such persons are better described as Federationists or institutionalists etc.

Free trade area Group of states who agree to impose no tariffs on goods moving between them but who all maintain their own customs barriers against goods from third party states.

Harmonization A more constraining version of approximation which involves realigning member state legislation, usually in the Single Market, on Community norms.

Institution An agency of the Community or Union which enjoys enhanced status and powers, as compared to an organ.

Institutions The central decision-making bodies of the Community which enjoy a special status in the treaties and Community practice. Not all Community organizations are 'institutions' in this sense.

Integration The process of bringing together individuals, groups and especially states into a more cohesive and united state, i.e. to make many one. When using the Community's institution-based method, integration is often contrasted with cooperation.

Intergovernmental Integration or activity undertaken by states which decide, of their own volition, to cooperate, usually carried on by delegates of the states involved and without use of autonomous institutional structures. Often contrasted with supranational.

Investiture Process of conferring authority on the Commission to act as the Community's quasi-government. Under the TEU known as double investiture because the Commission is approved both by Council and Parliament.

Justiciable A matter which can, under the Treaty, be submitted for decision to the Community judiciary, as constituted by the ECJ and the CFI, in case of dispute.

Legal Personality The condition which enables a body to take autonomous actions in international law rather than requiring governments or others to act on its behalf.

Legislation Decisions on policy etc., passed by an authorized body such as the Council or, in the national context, a parliament.

Liberalization Process of opening up the economy by abolishing unnecessary obstacles and restraints. Slightly wider than deregulation with which it is closely associated.

Lomé Capital of Togo where EC agreements with the ACP countries have been signed. Term thus used to describe the Community's aid and development policy.

Maastricht Conventionally used to describe the process which led to the signing of the TEU at Maastricht in December 1991 and the political bargains and Treaty changes arrived at there.

Merger This can mean either the amalgamation of two firms, which can be subject to EC rules if it affects competition, or the creation of one Commission to service the three original Communities, as per the 1965 Treaty.

Neo-functionalism Economic and political theory which explains the process of integration by successful cooperation in carrying out specific tasks, and the support these generate, rather than as the result of great political ambitions such as federalism.

Opinion Non-binding advice issued by a Community institution, including the ECJ.

Opt-out Term deriving from Maastricht and describing a statutory right given to a state not to take part in a Community or Union activity.

Organ Lower-level, usually advisory, Community body without the powers of Institutions.

Paragraph A subdivision of a Treaty Article. Usually numbered.

Part The main subdivision of the Treaties. Can itself be subdivided into Titles.

Pillar Term colloquially given to the three elements of the Union: the Community, the CSFP, and the JHA.

Policy Strategy and series of legislative enactments designed to achieve Community aims in specific fields such as agriculture or transport.

Preamble The opening sentences of a Treaty which set out the aims of those signing it and the main themes contained in it. Can be drawn on by the ECJ in defining Community law.

Protocol Auxiliary element of a Treaty which enjoys equal status with the Treaty proper but contains material that is either too bulky for inclusion or is simply required to provide detailed implementation of general provisos in the actual Treaty.

Provisions General term used to describe the aims and contents of a Treaty. Interchangeable with provisos.

Qualified majority voting Means used to reflect the different size of Community states when decisions are taken. Large states are awarded ten votes and others less. Quotas are then fixed to ensure that the large states cannot dictate affairs.

Quantitative restrictions Quotas imposed on imports into the Community. Many have been abolished as a result of agreements with non-member states. However, some still exist in areas such as agriculture and textiles, and for some manufactured goods.

Ratification Process of approval of Treaty changes by signatory states, according to their own constitutional rules, as required by the Treaty of Rome. Can involve either parliamentary votes or a referendum.

Recommendations Advisory statement by a Community institution or the equivalent of a regulation within the context of the ECSC.

Region Geographical term used either to describe a subdivison of the world, i.e. the European region or, in the Community context, subdivisions of nations. These need not have their own political identity.

Regulation The highest form of Community legislation, being generally binding and is immediately and fully applicable within member states.

Schengen Agreement amongst certain Community countries to ensure total abolition of border controls, going beyond that provided for in the Treaties.

Section A subdivision of a Chapter and, as such the lowest level of Treaty subdivision above the individual Article.

Single/Internal Market Programme emerging in the 1980s to realize the Treaty of Rome's aim of creating a completely free economic area in which all goods, services, capital and persons can move freely, thereby obtaining maximum economic benefit. Nominally complete as of 31 December 1992.

Social Chapter/Charter Protocol of the TEU which provides a mechanism for eleven member states to implement the 1989 Social Charter on living and working conditions. Seen by many as merely a necessary codification of existing practice which would help to mitigate the effects of the Single Market, the UK government sees it as a recipe for destroying competitiveness. The Council of Europe also has a Social Charter to which the United Kingdom is a signatory.

Spillover Process of developing integration by transference of activity and loyalty to the EC level seen as essential to integration by neo-functionalists.

Stabilizers Fixed ceilings on agricultural production introduced to help control CAP prices.

Stagiaire Short term, supernumerary appointees who are attached to Commission offices as a form of apprenticeship and who provide additional administrative help.

Structural Having to do with the structures of the economy or the Union as opposed to processes of change. The term is also used to describe funds such as the ESF, the ERDF and EAGGF whose aim is to develop the structures of poorer areas so that they are able to compete with better provided regions.

Subsidiarity Controversial political principle to be used under the TEU to guide the way that Union powers are exercized. Sometimes used in British usage as a synonym for national sovereignty but, historically and practically, it has wider implications.

Summit Meeting of Heads of Government and, in the French case, of State, which has become institutionalized as the European Council. The terms are often used interchangeably.

Supranational Quality of a law or institution which is superior to, and to some extent, independent of states. Contrasted with intergovernmental, the term is used to describe the Community's institutions.

Sustainable A form of economic growth which can be maintained without exhausting natural resources.

Title Subdivision of the Treaty below a Part. It can itself be divided into Chapters.

Transparency Vogue term implying greater public openness and access in the working of the Union.

Trevi Gathering of Ministers of the Interior established to improve cooperation in matters of crime, terrorism and public order. Out of it has grown the JHA pillar of the TEU.

Troika The immediate past, present and prospective Presidencies, of EPC or the Community, working together to give extra weight to the political aims of the Twelve.

Union Both the long-standing aim of the founding Treaties and the new umbrella institution created at Maastricht. Its precise definition remains unclear.

Visegrád Town in Hungary where Ministers from Hungary, Poland and what was Czechoslovakia meet to discuss matters of common interest.

Voluntary export restraints A bilateral agreement with a non-member state whereby the latter agrees to restrict exports to the EC.

Annex 2: Bibliography

THE TREATY ON EUROPEAN UNION:
TEXTS

The following is a list of publications which contain the text of the TEU. It should be noted, however, that none of them is an official legal text. An official version of the Treaty was due to be pubilshed in the Official Journal (OJ) once the ratification process had been completed. However, as far as consolidated versions of the Treaty are concerned, a finalized text was only produced at the very end of 1993 (ISBN 92-824-1109-5).

Agence Presse Europe, 'Treaty on European Union', *Europe Documents*, no. 1759/60, 7 February 1992 (and no. 1759/60 bis, 26 February 1992).

Belmont European Policy Centre, *The New Treaty on European Union I*, Belmont European Policy Centre, Brussels, 1992.

British Data Management Foundation, *The Maastricht Treaty in Perspective: Consolidated treaty of European Union*, British Data Management Foundation, Stroud, 1992.

CCH Europe, 'Union Treaty', *Common Market Law Report*, Insert no. 706, 14 June 1992.

La Documentation Française, *L'Union Européenne: Les Traités de Rome et de Maastricht*, La Documentation Française, Paris, 1992.

Duffy, P. and Yves de Cara, J., *European Union: The lawyers' guide*, Longman, London, 1992.

EC Council and EC Commission, *Treaty on European Union*, Council of the European Communities, Commission of the European Communities, OOPEC, Luxembourg, 1992.

Europa Union, *Europäische Gemeinschaft — Europäische Union: Die Vertragstexte von Maastricht*, Presse- und Informationsamt der Bundesregierung/Europa Union, Bonn, 1992.

Europa Union, *Der Vertrag: Europäische Gemeinschaft — Europäische Union: Die Vertragstexte von Maastricht mit den Deutschen Begleitgesetzen*, Presse- und Informationsamt der Bundesregierung/Europa Union, Bonn, 1993.

European Information Service, 'Treaty on European Union', *European Report*, no. 1746, 22 February 1992.

Groeben, H. von der *et al. Vertrag über die Europäische Union von Maastricht mit Schlußfolgerungen des Europäischen Rates von Lissabon*, Nomos Verlagsgesellschaft, Baden-Baden, 1992.

Hummings, N.M. and MacDonald-Hill, J., 'The Treaty on European Union', *Common Market Law Report*, vol. 63, no. 11, 1992, pp. 573–792.

Journaux officiels, *Traité sur l'Union européenne*, Imprimerie Nationale, Paris, 1992.

Nelson, S. and Pollard, D., *The Unseen Treaty: Treaty on European Union Maastricht 1992*, Nelson and Pollard, Oxford, 1992.

Nelson, S. and Pollard, D., *The Unseen Treaty: Treaty on European Union Maastricht 1992*, 2nd edn, Nelson and Pollard, Oxford, 1992.

Official Journal of the European Communities, *Treaty on European Union, Together with the Complete Text of the Treaty Establishing the European Community*, OJC 224, 31 August 1992.

Official Journal of the European Communities, *Treaty on European Union*, OJC 191, 29 July 1992.

Pollard, D. (ed.), *The Convoluted Treaties I: Maastricht convoluted with Rome etc.*, Nelson and Pollard, Oxford, forthcoming.

Presse- und Informationsamt der Bundesregierung, 'Vertrag über die Europäische Union', *Bulletin*, Nr. 16, Bonn, 1992.

Real, M.D. *et al.*, *Union Europea y Communidad Europea*, Editorial Tecnos, Madrid, 1993.

The Sunday Times 'The Treaty on European Union: the full text and a step-by-step guide', 11 October 1992.

THE TREATY ON EUROPEAN UNION:
COMMENTARIES

Arnold, H., '"Maastricht" — the beginning or end of a development?', *Aussenpolitik*, vol. 44, no. 3, 1993, pp. 271–80.

Belmont European Policy Centre, *The New Treaty on European Union*, Belmont European Policy Centre, Brussels, 1992.

Bidwell, C., *Maastricht and the UK*, Public Affairs Consultants Europe, Oxford, 1993.

Cloos, J. et al., *Le Traité de Maastricht: Genèse, analyse, commentaire*, Organisation Internationales et Relations Internationales, Brussels, 1993.

Collas, P., 'La traité de Maastricht et la souveraineté nationale', *Revue politique et parlementaire*, no. 960, 1992, pp. 7–18.

Corbett, R., *The Treaty of Maastricht*, Longman, London, 1993.

Curtin, D., 'The constitutional structure of the Union: a Europe of bits and pieces', *Common Market Law Review*, vol. 30, no. 1, 1993, pp. 17–69.

Doutriaux, Y., *Le Traité sur l'Union européenne*, Editions Armand-Colin, Paris, 1993.

Duffy, P. and Yves de Cara, J., *European Union: The lawyers' guide*, Longman, London, 1992.

European Parliament, *Maastricht — The Treaty on European Union: The position of the European Parliament*, OOPEC, Luxembourg, 1992.

Everling, U., 'Reflections on the structure of the European Union', *Common Market Law Review*, vol. 29, no. 5, 1992, pp. 1053–77.

Hahn, H. J., *Der Vertrag von Maastricht als völkerrechtliche Übereinkunft und Verfassung*, Nomos Verlagsgesellschaft, Baden-Baden, 1992.

Hartley, T.C., 'Constitutional and institutional aspects of the Maastricht Agreement', *International and Comparative Law Quarterly*, vol. 42, no. 2, 1993, pp. 213–37.

Holden, N., *The Single European act And Maastricht*, Thornhill Press, Cheltenham, 1992.

International Currency Review, 'Annotated Maastricht Treaty text', vol. 21, no. 3, 1991–2, pp. 171–219.

Louis, J.V., 'Les accords de Maastricht — un premier bilan', *Revue du Marché Unique européen*, 1991/4.

Luff, P., *The Simple Guide to Maastricht*, European Movement, London, 1992.

Maillet, P., 'Le double visage de Maastricht: achèvement et nouveau départ', *Revue du marché commun et de l'Union européenne*, no. 356, 1992, pp. 209–19.

Martin, D., *Maastricht in a Minute*, David Martin, Edinburgh, 1992.

Melchior, F., 'Le Traité de Maastricht sur l'union européene (essai de présentation synthétique)', *Actualités du droit*, 1992/4, pp. 1209–54.

Mosconi, F., 'Il trattato di Maastricht: una costituzione per l'Europa', *Il Politico*, vol. 57, no. 3, 1992, pp. 421–38.

Noël, E., 'Reflections on the Maastricht Treaty', *Government and Opposition*, vol. 27, no. 2, 1992, pp. 148–57.

O'Keeffe, D. and Twomey, P.M., (eds.), *Legal Issues of the Maastricht Treaty*, Chancery Law/John Wiley, Chichester, 1994.

Reich, C., 'Le traité sur l'Union européenne et le Parlement européen', *Revue du marché commun et de l'Union européenne*, no. 357, 1992, pp. 287–92.

Schmuck, O., 'Der Maastrichter Vertrag zur Europäischen Union: Fortschritt und Ausdifferenzierung der Europäischen Einigung', *Europa Archiv*, vol. 47, no. 4, 1992, pp. 97–106.

Schoutheete, P. de, 'Réflexions sur le Traité de Maastricht', *Annales de droit de Louvain*, 1/1993, pp. 73–90.

Seidel, M., 'Zur Verfassung der Europäischen Gemeinschaft nach Maastricht', *Europarecht*, vol. 27, no. 2, 1992, pp. 125–44.

Spicer, M., *A Treaty Too Far: A new policy for Europe*, Fourth Estate, London, 1992.

The European, 'Maastricht made simple', *The European*, London, 1992.

The European, 'Maastricht made simple: the essential guide to the treaty that will shape Europe' (video), Screenpro, London, 1993.

The Independent on Sunday, 'The Treaty of Maastricht — what it says and what it means', 11 October 1992.

The Independent on Sunday, 'The Treaty of Maastricht — what it says and what it means', (cassette), John Newton, 1992.

Themaat, P. ver Loren Van, 'Les défis de Maastricht: une nouvelle étape importante, mais vers quels horizons?', *Revue du marché commun et de l'Union européenne*, no. 356, 1992, pp. 203–08.

Treaty on European Union: Synopsis of provisions on Economic and Monetary Union, Europa Institute, Edinburgh, 1992.

Treaty on European Union: Synopsis of section on European Political Union, Europa Institute, Edinburgh, 1992.

Wincott, D., *The Treaty of Maastricht: An adequate 'Constitution' for the European Union?*, European Public Policy Institute Occasional Paper 93/6, University of Warwick, 1993.

Zylberstein, J. and Barenboim, A. (eds.), *Traité de Maastricht: mode d'emploi*, 10/18, Paris, 1992.

THE EUROPEAN UNION: GENERAL BIBLIOGRAPHY

The bibliography which follows contains a selection of general texts relevant to the European Union. The majority deal with the European Community, while others are concerned with the wider process of European integration. Readers wishing for specialized texts on aspects of the Union should consult the relevant Further Reading lists which follow the individual analyses in the *Handbook*.

Almarcha, A. (ed.), *Spain and EC Membership Evaluated*, Pinter, London, 1993.

Archer, C. and Butler, F., *The European Community: Structure and process*, Pinter, London, 1992.

Arter, D., *The Politics of European Integration in the Twentieth Century*, Dartmouth, Aldershot, 1993.

Ashford, S. and Timms, N., *What Europe Thinks: A study of Western values*, Dartmouth, Aldershot, 1992.

Attina, F., *Il Sistema politico della Comunità europea*, Giuffré Editore, Milano, 1992.

Baldassarri, M. and Mundell, R., *Building the New Europe*, Macmillan, London, 1993.

Barrell, R., *Macroeconomic Policy Coordination in Europe: The ERM and Monetary Union*, Sage, London, 1992.

Bogdandy, A. von (ed.), *Die europäische Option*, Nomos Verlagsgesellschaft, Baden-Baden, 1993.

Bonvicini, G. *et al. The Community and the Emerging European Democracies*, RIIA, London, 1991.

Buchan, D., *Europe: The strange superpower*, Dartmouth, Aldershot, 1993.

Budd, S.A. and Jones, A., *The European Community: A guide to the maze*, 4th edn, Kogan Page, London, 1991.

Bulmer, S., George, S. and Scott, A. (eds.), *The United Kingdom and EC Membership Evaluated*, Pinter, London, 1992.

Burgenmeir B. and Muchhielli, J., *Multinationals and Europe 1992*, Routledge, London, 1991.

Burgess, M. and Gagnon, A., *Comparative Federalism and Federation, Competing Traditions and Future Challenges*, Harvester Wheatsheaf, Hemel Hempstead, 1993.

Burthscher, W., *Das Abkommen über den Europäischen Wirtschaftsraum (EWR): Entstehung, Kurzdarstellung, Textauswahl*, WUV Universitätsverlag, Wien, 1992.

Cafruny, A.W. and Rosenthal, G.G., *The State of the European Community: Maastricht and beyond*, Longman, London, 1993.

Carlsen Norup, H., *When No means Yes: Danish visions of a different Europe*, Adamantine Press, London, 1993.

Casses, A., Clapham, A. and Weiler, J. (eds.), *Human Rights and the European Community: European Union — the human rights challenge*, 3 vols., Nomos Velagsgesellschaft, Baden-Baden, 1991.

Church, C.H. and Keogh, D. (eds.), *The Single European Act: A transnational study*, Erasmus Consortium, University College, Cork, 1991.

Clapham, A., *Human Rights and the European Community: A critical overview*, 2 vols., Nomos Velagsgesellschaft, Baden-Baden, 1991.

Cless, A. and Vernon, R. (eds.), *The European Community after 1992: A new role in world politics*, Nomos Velagsgesellschaft, Baden-Baden, 1992.

Coffey, P., *The EC and the United States: The implications of 1992*, Pinter, London, 1992.

Cole, J. and Cole, F., *The Geography of the European Community*, Routledge, London, 1993.

Collinson, S., Miall, H. and Michalski, A., *A Wider European Union? Integration and Cooperation in the New Europe*, RIIA Discussion Papers 48, RIIA, London, 1993.

Coombes, D., *Understanding European Union*, Longman, London, 1994.

Dawe, S., *Maastricht or a Green Europe*, The Green Party, London, 1993.

Dawson, A., *A Geography of European Integration*, Belhaven Press, London, 1993.

Deubillioner, C. (ed.), *Die Europäische Gemeinschaft in einem neuen Europa*, Nomos Verlagsgesellschaft, Baden-Baden, 1991.

Dreyfus, F-G., Morizet, J. and Payrard, M. (eds.), *France and EC Membership Evaluated*, Pinter, London, 1993.

Dudley, J., *1993 and Beyond*, Kogan Page, London, 1993.

Edwards, G. and Regelsberger, E. (eds.), *Europe's Global Links: The European Community and inter-regional cooperation*, Pinter, London, 1990.

El-Agraa, A.M., *The Economics of The European Community*, 4th edn, Harvester Wheatsheaf, Hemel Hempstead, 1994.

Engel, C. and Wessels, W., *From Luxembourg to Maastricht*, Europa Union Verlag, Bonn, 1992.

Engel, C. and Wessels, W., *The European Union in the 1990s*, Europa Union Verlag, Bonn, 1993.

Estellie Smith, M., *Perspectives on the European Community*, Westview, Boulder, 1992.

European Parliament, *Committee on Institutional Affairs: Working documents on the constitution of the European Union*, Strasbourg, 9 and 15 September 1993; PE 203.601/B and PE 203.601/rev.

Francioni, F. (ed.), *Italy and EC Membership Evaluated*, Pinter, London, 1992.

Garcia, S., *European Identity and the Search for Legitimacy*, Pinter, London, 1993.

George, S., *Britain and the European Community*, Oxford University Press, Oxford, 1992.

George, S., *Britain and European Integration since 1945*, Blackwell, Oxford, 1991.

George, S., *Politics and Policy in the European Community*, 2nd edn, Oxford University Press, Oxford, 1992.

Goodman, S.F., *The European Community*, 2nd edn, Macmillan, London, 1993.

Griffiths, A., *European Community Survey: The European Community*, Longman, London, 1992.

Guéguen, D., *A Pratical Guide to the EEC Labyrinth: Structures, powers and procedures*, Cedar Tree House, Loughton, 1992.

Harrop, J., *The Political Economy of Integration in the European Community*, 2nd edn, Edward Elgar, Cheltenham, 1992.

Hitiris, T., *European Community Economics*, 2nd edn, Harvester Wheatsheaf, Hemel Hempstead, 1991.

Hogan, M.J., *The End of the Cold War: Its meaning and implications*, Cambridge University Press, Cambridge, 1992.

Holland, M., *European Community Integration*, Pinter, London, 1992.

Hommel, K., *Spanien und die Europäische Wirtschaftsgemeinschaft*, Nomos Velagsgesellschaft, Baden-Baden, 1992.

Hurwitz, L. and Lequesne, C. (eds.), *The State of the European Community: Policies, institutions and debates in the transition years*, Longman, London, 1991.

Issacs, A., *European Culture: A contemporary companion*, Cassell, London, 1993.

Jacquemin, A. and Wright, D. (eds.), *The European Challenges Post-1992: Shaping factors, shaping actors*, Edward Elgar, Aldershot, 1993.

Jeffery, C. and Sturm, R., 'Federalism, Unification and European Integration', *West European Politics*, Special issue, 1993.

Keatinge, P. (ed.), *Political Union*, Studies in European Union no. 1, Institute of European Affairs, Dublin, 1991.

Keatinge, P. (ed.), *Ireland and EC Membership Evaluated*, Pinter, London, 1991.

Kelstrup, M. (ed.), *European Integration and Denmark's Participation*, Copenhagen Political Studies Press, Copenhagen, 1992.

Keohane, R.E., and Hoffman, S. (eds.), *The New European Community: Decisionmaking and institutional challenge*, Westview, Boulder, 1991.

King, P. and Bosco, A., *A Constitution for Europe: A comparative study of federal constitutions and plans for the United States of Europe*, Lothian Foundation Press, London, 1991.

Laffan, B., *Integration and Co-operation in Europe*, Routledge, London, 1992.

Lankowski, C., *Europe's Emerging Identity: Regional integration vs. opposition movements in the European Community*, Adamantine Press, London, 1992.

Laursen, F. and Vanhoonacker, S. (eds.), *The Intergovernmental Conference on Political Union: Institutional reforms, new policies and international Identity of the European Community*, Martinus Nijhoff, Maastricht, 1992.

Leonardi, R. (ed.), *European Community Policies and Politics*, Pinter, London, 1994.

Lippert. B. and Stevens-Ströhmann, R., *German Unification and EC Integration: German and British perspectives*, Pinter/RIIA, London, 1993.

Lodge, J. (ed.), *The European Community and the Challenge of the Future*, Pinter, London, 1989.

Lodge, J. (ed.), *The European Community and the Challenge of the Future*, 2nd edn, Pinter, London, 1993.

Lyck, L. (ed.), *Denmark and EC Membership Evaluated*, Pinter, London, 1992.

McDonald, F. and Dearden, S. (eds.), *European Economic Integration*, Longman, London, 1992.

McKenzie, G. and Venables, A., *The Economics of the Single European Act*, Macmillan, London, 1991.

Martin, D., *Europe: An ever closer union*, Spokesman, Nottingham, 1991.

Mayes, D.G. (ed.), *External Implications of European Integration*, Harvester Wheatsheaf, Hemel Hempstead, 1993.

Meinhard, H. and Tomuschat, C. (eds.), *EG und Drittstaatbeziehungen nach 1992*, Nomos Velagsgesellschaft, Baden-Baden, 1991.

Michalski, A. and Wallace, H., *The European Community and the challenge of enlargement*, 2nd edn, RIIA, London, 1992.

Milliband, D., *A More Perfect Union? Britain and the New Europe*, Institute for Public Policy Research, London, 1992.

Molle, W., *The Economics of European Integration*, Dartmouth, Aldershot, 1990.

Moussis, N., *Access to Europe*, 3rd edn, Euroconfidentiel, Rixensart, Belgium, 1993.

Nelson, B. *et al. The European Community in the Nineteen Nineties: Economics, politics and defence*, Berg, Oxford, 1992.

Nelson, D. and Pollard, S., *The Convoluted Treaties II: The Treaty of Rome*, Nelson and Pollard, Oxford, 1992.

Nicoll, W. and Salmon, T., *Understanding the New European Communities*, 2nd edn, Harvester Wheatsheaf, Hemel Hempstead, 1993.

Nugent, N., *The European Community 1992: annual review of activities*, Blackwell, Oxford, 1993.

Nugent, N., *The Government and Politics of the European Community*, 2nd edn, Macmillan, London, 1991.

Owen, R. and Dynes, M., *The Times Guide to the European Single Market*, Times Books, London, 1992.

Paterson, W.E. (ed.), *Beyond the Intergovernmental Conferences: European union in the 1990's*, Europa Institute, Edinburgh, 1991.

Paxton, J. (ed.), *European Communities*, vol. 1 of *International Organizations*, Clio, Oxford, 1992.

Petersen, N. and Pedersen, T. (eds.), *The European Community in World Politics*, Pinter, London, 1993.

Pigott, J. and Cook, M., *International Business Economics: A European perspective*, Longman, London, 1993.

Pijpers, A. (ed.), *The European Community at the Crossroads*, Martinus Nijhoff, Dordrecht, 1992.

Pinder, J., *European Community: The building of a nation*, Oxford University Press, 1991.

Pinder, J., *The European Community and Eastern Europe*, Pinter/RIIA, London, 1991.

Ramsay, A., *Eurojargon*, 3rd edn, Capital Planning Information, Stamford, Lincs, 1991.

Rees, G. W., *International Politics in Europe: The new agenda*, Routledge, London, 1993.

Roney, A., *The European Community Fact Book*, 2nd edn, Kogan Page, London, 1991.

Rudden, B. and Wyatt, D. (eds.), *Basic Community Laws*, 3rd edn, Clarendon, Oxford, 1992.

Rummel, R. (ed.), *Toward Political Union*, Nomos Verlagsgesellschaft, Baden-Baden, 1992.

Sbragia, A.M. (ed.), *Euro-politics: Institutions and policymaking in the 'New' European Community*, Brookings Institute, Washington, 1992.

Schauer, H., *Europa der Vernunft — Kritische*

Anmerkungen nach Maastricht, Verlag Bonn Aktuell im Verlag Moderne Industrie, München, 1993.

Schweitzer, C.C. and Karsten, D., *Federal Republic of Germany and EC Membership Evaluated*, Pinter, London, 1990.

Serfaty, S., *Understanding Europe: The politics of unity*, Pinter, London, 1992.

Sidjanski, D., *L'Avenir fédéraliste de l'Europe: La Communauté européenne, des origines au Traité de Maastricht*, Presses Universitaires de France, Paris, 1992.

Silva Lopes, J. de (ed.), *Portugal and EC Membership Evaluated*, Pinter, London, 1993.

Story, J. (ed.), *The New Europe: Politics, government and economy since 1945*, Blackwell, Oxford, 1993.

Swann, D., *The Economics of the Common Market*, 7th edn, Penguin, Harmondsworth, 1992.

Swann, D. (ed.), *The Single European Market and Beyond: A study of the wider implications of the Single European Act*, Routledge, London, 1992.

The European Communities Encyclopedia and Directory 1992, 1st edn, Europa Publications, London, 1991.

Thomson, G. F., *The Economic Emergence of a New Europe*, Edward Elgar, Cheltenham, 1993.

Tsoukalis, L., *The New European Economy: The politics and economics of European integration*, Oxford University Press, Oxford, 1993.

Urwin, D.W., *The Community of Europe*, Longman, London, 1991.

Van Meerhaeghe, M.A.G. (ed.), *Belgium and EC Membership Evaluated*, Pinter, London, 1992.

Vickerman, R., *The Single European Market*, Harvester Wheatsheaf, Oxford, 1992.

Wallace, H., *The Wider Western Europe: Reshaping the EC–EFTA Dialogue*, Pinter/RIIA, London, 1991.

Wallace, W., *The Dynamics of European Integration*, Pinter/RIIA, London, 1991.

Wallace, W., *The Transformation of Western Europe*, Pinter/RIIA, London, 1990.

Wegner, M., *Die Entdeckung Europas: Wirtschaftspolitik der Europäischen Gemeinschaft*, Nomos Velagsgesellschaft, Baden-Baden, 1992.

Weidenfeld, W. (ed.), *Wie Europa verfaßt sein soll — Materialien zur Politischen Union*, Bertelsmann Stiftung, Gütersloh, 1991.

Weidenfeld, W. and Janning, J. (eds.), *Global Responsibilities: Europe in tomorrow's world*, Bertelsmann Foundation, Gütersloh, 1991.

Weidenfeld, W. and Wessels, W. (eds.), *Europa von A–Z: Taschenbuch der europäischen Integration*, 2nd edn, Europa Union Verlag, Bonn, 1992.

Weidenfeld, W. and Wessels, W. (eds.), *Jahrbuch der Europäischen Integration*, Europa Union Verlag, Bonn, Annually.

Weigall, D. and Stirk, P. (eds.), *The Origins and Development of the European Community*, Leicester University Press, Leicester, 1992.

Who's Who — European Communities, 4th edn, Delta/Cedar Tree House, Loughton, 1994.

Who's Who in European Communities and Enterprises, Sutter/Eurospan, London, 1993.

Wieland, B., *Ein Markt — zwölf Regierungen: Zur Organisation der Macht in der europäischen Verfassung*, Nomos Velagsgesellschaft, Baden-Baden, 1992.

Wildenmann, R. (ed.), *Staatswerdung Europas? — Optionen für eine Europäische Union*, Nomos Velagsgesellschaft, Baden-Baden, 1992.

Williams, A., *The European Community: Contradictions of integration*, Blackwell, Oxford, 1991.

Wistrich, E. (ed.), *After 1992: The United States of Europe*, Routledge, London, 1991.

Yearbook of the European Communities and of the other European Organizations, 12th edn, Delta/Cedar Tree House, Loughton.

1993 Directory of EC Information Sources, Euroconfidentiel, Rixensart, Belgium, May 1993.

Annex 3: Amendments to the Treaty of Rome and the Single European Act

In the introduction to the *Handbook* it was pointed out that a significant element of the TEU consisted of amendments to the Treaty of Rome. Indeed, over half of the main body of the TEU text (i.e. excluding Protocols and Declarations) comprises either amendments to existing provisions contained in the Treaty of Rome, or amendments introduced to the Treaty as a result of previous agreements such as the SEA, as well as insertions of entirely new provisions. In addition, several existing provisions are either removed from the Treaty or are renumbered. This can clearly lead to enormous confusion for anybody trying to identify the impact the TEU has had on the provisions contained in the Treaty of Rome and the SEA.

In an attempt to remedy this situation the two tables in this Annex provide an indication of what has happened to each of the Articles contained in the Treaty of Rome and SEA as a result of the amendments introduced by the TEU.

Table 1 lists all the provisions contained within the Treaty of Rome immediately prior to the entry into force of the TEU.[1] These are numbered in the first column and include those Articles (in italics) which have either been added to the Treaty or which have replaced Articles deleted or repealed by treaties amending the Treaty of Rome. The second column then provides a brief description of the content of each Article. Also included here is a description of the relevant Articles of the Merger Treaty which replaced existing Treaty of Rome Articles repealed by the Merger Treaty.[2] In the third column those Treaties and Council decisions which have amended the provisions described in column two are listed. The next four columns then indicate what effect the TEU has had on each Article. The first of these columns (I) states whether the Article has been inserted into the Treaty having originally been contained in another Treaty, as

---

1. The table is based upon the consolidated version of the Treaty of Rome contained in *Treaties establishing the European Communities (ECSC, EEC, EAEC) — Single European Act — Other basic instruments*, abridged edition, OOPEC, Luxembourg, 1987; *Treaty on European Union*, OOPEC, Luxembourg, 1992; and the *Treaty on European Union, together with the complete text of the Treaty establishing the European Community*, OJC 224, 31 August 1992.

2. Article P(1) of the TEU repealed Articles 2–7 and 10–17 of the Merger Treaty (see pp. 356–7).

indicated in the first column. An indication is then given in columns four to six as to whether the Article indicated in the first column was amended (A), renumbered (R), or deleted (D) by the TEU. The final column then provides, where applicable, details of where the original provisions in their post-TEU form may be found, and whether the number of a deleted Article is still in use. Examples of how to read the table are given below.

Table 2, looking at the effect of the TEU on the provisions contained in the SEA, has a similar layout to Table 1. The first column lists all the Articles contained in the SEA. The second column then indicates the function of these Articles, leaving the third column to describe the issue to which they are addressed. The next three columns indicate, as in columns four to six in the first table, the effect the TEU had on the Article. Where appropriate, additional information relating to the changes brought about by the TEU is provided in the final column. For the sake of convenience the more formal title 'EEC Treaty' is used in the table to indicate the Treaty of Rome.

Examples of how to read the tables

1. In Table 1 (EEC Treaty), Article 7, which was amended by the SEA, is renumbered by the TEU, now appearing in the EEC Treaty as Article 6.
2. In the same table (EEC Treaty), Article 157, the original version of which was replaced by Article 10 of the Merger Treaty, and amended by the Act concerning the Conditions of Accession and the Adjustments to the Treaties — Accession to the European Communities of the Kingdom of Spain and the Portuguese Republic, is amended and inserted into the EEC Treaty by the TEU.
3. In Table 1 (EEC Treaty), Article 237, which was amended by the SEA, is deleted by the TEU. A similar provision is now found in Art. O of the TEU.
4. In Table 2 (SEA), Article 20 inserted Article 102a into the EEC Treaty. This insertion, Article 102a, has been amended and renumbered by the TEU, now appearing in Article 109m(1) of the amended EEC Treaty.

Abbreviations used in the tables

CCI	*Convention on Certain Institutions Common to the European Communities,* 25 March 1957
CFP	*Treaty amending Certain Financial Provisions of the Treaty establishing the European Communities and of the Treaty establishing a Single Council and a Single Commission of the European Communities,* OJL 359, 31 December 1977
CD	*Council Decision of 26 November 1974,* OJL 318, 28 November 1974
DK/IRE/UK	*Decision of the Council of the European Communities of 1 January 1973 adjusting the documents concerning the*

	accession of new Member States to the European Communities, OJL 2, 1 January 1973
EP	*Act concerning the election of the representatives of the Assembly by direct universal suffrage*, OJL 278, 8 October 1976
GT	*Treaty amending, with regard to Greenland, the Treaties establishing the European Communities*, OJL 29, 1 February 1985
MT	*Treaty establishing a Single Council and a Single Commission of the European Communities*, OJ 152, 13 July 1967
SEA	*Single European Act*, OJL 169, 29 June 1987
SP/PO	*Act concerning the Conditions of Accession and the Adjustments to the Treaties — Accession to the European Communities of the Kingdom of Spain and the Portuguese Republic*, OJL 302, 15 November 1985

Table 1: The impact of the TEU on the provisions contained in the Treaty of Rome — an overview

Article	Content	Amended by	Effect of TEU I A R D	Notes
1	Establishment of EEC		I*	
2	Tasks of Community		I*	
3	Activities of Community		I*	
4	Institutions	SEA	I*	
5	Obligations of member states			
6	Coordination of economic policy		R*	New Art. 6
7	Discrimination on grounds of nationality	SEA	A*	Now Art. 6
8	Establishment of common market		A*	Now Art. 7
8a (SEA)	Establishment of Internal Market	SEA	A*	Now Art. 7a
8b (SEA)	Ensuring progress on Internal Market	SEA	A*	Now Art. 7b
8c (SEA)	Derogations within Internal Market	SEA	A*	Now Art. 7c
9	Customs union			
10	Free circulation of goods from third countries			
11	Obligations of member states			
12	Customs duties			
13	Customs duties on imports			
14	Timetable for reductions of customs duties			
15	Suspending and reducing customs duties			
16	Customs duties on exports			
17	Customs duties of a fiscal nature			
18	Development of international trade			
19	Common customs tariff			
20	Customs duties on list G products			
21	Technical difficulties arising from Arts. 19 & 20			
22	Customs duties of a fiscal nature and CCT			

Article	Content	Amended by	Effect of TEU I A R D	Notes
23	Introduction of CCT			
24	Individual reductions of customs duties			
25	Tariff quotas at a reduced rate			
26	Postponing reductions of customs duties			
27	Approximation of laws relating to customs matters			
28 (SEA)	Autonomous alterations and suspensions of duties	SEA		
29	Guidelines for Commission in carrying out its tasks			
30	Prohibition of quantitative restrictions on imports			
31	Prohibition of new quantitative restrictions			
32	Abolition of quotas on intra-Community trade			
33	Conversion of national quotas to global quotas			
34	Prohibition of quantitative restrictions on exports			
35	Abolition of quantitative restrictions			
36	Grounds for restrictions			
37	Adjustment of state monopolies			
38	Common market in agricultural goods			
39	Objectives of Common Agricultural Policy			
40	Common organization of agricultural matters			
41	Promotion of agriculture			
42	Aid to agriculture			
43	Procedure for adopting common agricultural policy			
44	Minimum prices			
45	Transitional provisions regarding the common policy			
46	Countervailing charges on agricultural goods			
47	ECOSOC and agriculture			
48	Free movement of workers			
49	Facilitating free movement	SEA	*	
50	Exchange of youth workers			
51	Social security and free movement			
52	Freedom of establishment			
53	Prohibition of new restrictions on right of establishment			
54	Programme to abolish restrictions	SEA	*	
55	Exemptions from provisions of Arts. 52–58			
56	Grounds for restrictions	SEA	*	
57	Mutual recognition of qualifications, coordination of laws	SEA	*	

Article	Content	Amended by	Effect of TEU I A R D	Notes
58	Treatment of companies and firms			
59	Free movement of services	SEA		
60	Definition of 'services'			
61	Transport, banking and insurance			
62	Prohibition of new restrictions on freedom to provide services			
63	Abolition of restrictions on freedom to provide services			
64	Extending liberalization of services			
65	Non-discrimination on grounds of nationality			
66	Applicability of Arts. 55–58 to provisions in Arts. 59–65			
67	Abolition of restrictions on capital movements			
68	Non-discriminatory application of provisions on capital			
69	Implementing abolition of restrictions			
70	Progressive coordination of national exchange policies	SEA		
71	Extending liberalization of capital movements			
72	Informing Commission of capital movements			
73	Protective measures in the field of capital movements			
74	Establishment of a Common Transport Policy			
75	Content of Common Transport Policy		*	
76	Rules on transport prior to adoption of common policy			
77	Compatibility of aid to transport with treaty			
78	Economic situation of carriers and the adoption of measures			
79	Abolishing discrimination within transport sector			
80	State support to and protection of transport			
81	Reducing border crossing charges			
82	Transport policy and the FRG			
83	Establishment of Advisory Committee on Transport			
84	Areas where Arts. 74–83 are applicable	SEA		
85	Rules governing competition			
86	Rules governing competition			
87	Adopting measures to ensure fair competition			
88	Procedure prior to entry into force of Art. 87 measures			
89	Ensuring application of principles in Arts. 85 & 86			

Article	Content	Amended by	Effect of TEU				Notes
			I	A	R	D	
90	Competition rules and public undertakings						
91	Rules governing dumping						
92	State aid compatible with common market		*				
93	Procedure governing the misuse of state aid						
94	Applying Arts. 92 & 93		*				
95	Prohibition of internal taxation on imports within EC						
96	Repayment of internal taxation on exports within EC						
97	Turnover taxes						
98	Charges other than indirect taxation						
99	Harmonization of taxes	SEA	*				
100	Approximation of laws		*				
100a (SEA)	Approximation of laws relating to the Internal Market	SEA					
100b (SEA)	Recognition of laws not harmonized	SEA					
101	Procedure for amending laws which distort competition						
102	Preventing the distortion of competition						
102a (SEA)	Further development in economic and monetary policy	SEA	*	*			See Art. 109m(1)
103	Promotion of conjunctural policy		*				
104	Maintaining balance of payments equilibrium				*		New Art. 104
105	Coordination of economic policies				*		New Art. 105
106	Liberalization of payments		*	*			See Art. 73h
107	Exchange rate policy		*	*	*		New Art. 107, see Art. 109m(2)
108	Procedure in case of balance of payments difficulties		*	*			See Art. 109h
109	Procedure in case of balance of payments crisis		*	*			See Art. 109i
110	Commitment to liberalization of world trade						
111	Commercial policy during the transitional stage			*			
112	Harmonization of export aid systems						
113	Commercial agreements with third countries		*				
114	Concluding agreements under Arts. 111 & 113				*		See Art. 228
115	Common commercial policy and trade deflection		*				
116	Common action in international economic organizations				*		See Title V of TEU
117	Promotion of workers' well being						
118	Areas of cooperation in social field						
118a (SEA)	Improving working conditions	SEA					
118b (SEA)	Development of employer— employee dialog	SEA					

Article	Content	Amended by	Effect of TEU				Notes
			I	A	R	D	
119	Equal pay for men and women						
120	Holiday schemes						
121	Assigning Commission tasks under Arts. 48--51						
123	Establishment of ESF						
124	Administration of ESF						
125	Rules on assistance granted by ESF					*	New Art. 125
126	Development of ESF after the transitional period					*	New Art. 126
127	Implementation of Arts. 124–126					*	New Art. 127
128	Implementation of a common vocational policy					*	See Art. 127
129	Establishment and membership of the EIB		*		*		See Art. 198d
130	Tasks of the EIB		*		*		See Art. 198e
130a (SEA)	Promotion of economic and social cohesion	SEA	*				
130b (SEA)	Attaining economic and social cohesion	SEA	*				
130c (SEA)	Role of ERDF	SEA	*				
130d (SEA)	Reorganizing structure and operation of structural funds	SEA	*				
130e (SEA)	Procedure for implementing ERDF decisions	SEA	*				
130f (SEA)	Strengthening scientific and technological base of industry	SEA	*				
130g (SEA)	Tasks of Community	SEA	*				
130h (SEA)	Coordination of national policies	SEA	*				
130i (SEA)	Adoption of R&D multiannual framework programme	SEA	*				
130k (SEA)	Implementation of multiannual framework programme	SEA	*		*		See Arts. 130i & 130j
130l (SEA)	Supplementary programmes	SEA			*		See Art. 130k
130m (SEA)	Participation in member states' R&D programmes	SEA	*		*		See Art. 130l
130n (SEA)	R&D cooperation with third countries	SEA	*		*		See Art. 130m
130o (SEA)	Creation of joint undertakings to execute R&D programmes	SEA	*		*		See Art. 130n
130p (SEA)	Financing R&D programmes	SEA				*	
130q (SEA)	Adopting proposals relating to R&D programmes	SEA	*		*		See Art. 130o
130r (SEA)	Objectives and principles of action on the environment	SEA	*				
130s (SEA)	Deciding on action	SEA	*				
130t (SEA)	Right of member states to maintain more stringent measures	SEA	*				
131	Association of overseas countries and territories	DK/IRE/UK, GT					
132	Objectives of association						
133	Customs relations with associates						
134	Remedying trade deflection						
135	Freedom of movement within associations						

Article	Content	Amended by	Effect of TEU I A R D	Notes
136	Procedure for establishing association			
136a (GT)	Applicability of Arts. 131–136 to Greenland	G		
137	Role of EP		*	
138	Election of and allocation of MEPs	EP, SP/PO	*	
139	Sittings of the EP	MT, EP		
140	Election of officers, relations with Council and Commission			
141	Voting procedure			
142	Adoption of rules of procedure			
143	Discussion of Commission's Annual General Report			
144	Motions of censure on the Commission		*	
145	Tasks of the Council	SEA		
146(MT)	Composition of Council, rotation of presidency (MT, Art. 2)	MT	* *	
147(MT)	Meetings of the Council (MT, Art. 3)	MT	*	
148	Voting rules	SP/PO		
149	Cooperation procedure	SEA	*	See Art. 189c
150	Proxy votes			
151(MT)	Adoption of rules of procedure (MT, Arts. 4 & 5)	MT	* *	
152	Requesting Commission to carry out studies			
153	Adopting rules governing committees			
154(MT)	Salaries of Community officials (MT, Art. 6)	MT	*	
155	Tasks of the Commission			
156(MT)	Annual report of Communities' activities (MT, Art. 18)	MT	*	
157(MT)	Composition and independence of the Commission (MT, Art. 10)	MT, SP/PO	* *	
158(MT)	Term of office for Commissioners (MT, Art. 11)	MT	* *	
159(MT)	Replacement of Commissioners (MT, Art. 12)	MT	* *	
160(MT)	Compulsory retirement of Commissioners (MT, Art. 13)	MT	*	
161(MT)	Presidents and Vice-Presidents of the Commission (MT, Art. 14)	MT, SP/PO	* *	
162(MT)	Rules of procedure for the Commission (MT, Arts. 15 & 16)	MT	* *	
163(MT)	Voting procedure in the Commission (MT, Art. 17)	MT	* *	
164	Tasks of the ECJ			
165	Composition of the ECJ	CD, SP/PO	*	
166	Role and number of Advocates-General	SP/PO		
167	Appointment of Judges and Advocates-General	SP/PO		
168	Appointment of Registrar to the ECJ		*	

Article	Content	Amended by	Effect of TEU I A R D				Notes
168a (SEA)	Composition and tasks of Court of First Instance	SEA		*			
169	Procedure for Commission to bring matters before the ECJ						
170	Procedure for member states to bring matters before the ECJ						
171	Compliance of member states with ECJ judgments			*			
172	Jurisdiction of ECJ with regard to regulations			*			
173	Judicial review. Right of individuals to institute proceedings			*			
174	Declaring actions void						
175	Procedure governing infringements by EC institutions			*			
176	Compliance with ECJ judgments			*			
177	Jurisdiction of ECJ			*			
178	Jurisdiction of ECJ						
179	Jurisdiction of ECJ						
180	Jurisdiction of ECJ			*			
181	Jurisdiction of ECJ						
182	Jurisdiction of ECJ						
183	Jurisdiction of ECJ						
184	Appeals to the ECJ			*			
185	Suspension of actions brought before ECJ						
186	Interim measures regarding cases brought before ECJ						
187	Enforcement of ECJ judgments						
188	Rules of procedure for ECJ, Statute of ECJ	SEA					
189	Regulatory instruments			*			
190	Content of regulations, directives and decisions			*			
191	Publication of regulations, notification of directives and decisions			*			
192	Enforcement of decisions						
193	Establishment and composition of EcoSoc						
194	Composition of EcoSoc	SP/PO		*			
195	Appointment of EcoSoc members. Consultation of other bodies						
196	Rules of procedure for EcoSoc			*			
197	EcoSoc specialized sections and subcommittees						
198	Consulting EcoSoc		*				
199	Revenue and expenditure		*				
200	Budgetary contributions				*		
201	Own resources		*				
202	Classification of expenditure						
203	Procedure for adopting the budget	CFP					
204	Procedure for extending previous year's budget	CFP					

Article	Content	Amended by	Effect of TEU				Notes
			I	A	R	D	
205	Implementing the budget		*				
205a(CFP)	Presentation of annual accounts	CFP					
206	Establishment, composition and independence of the Court of Auditors	CFP, SP/PO	*	*			See Arts. 188a & 188b
206a(CFP)	Tasks of the Court of Auditors	CFP	*	*			See Art. 188c
206b(CFP)	Monitoring the Community's finances	CFP	*	*			See Art. 206(1)
207	Availability to the Community of financial contributions						
208	Transferring finances into other currencies						
209	Formulating rules relating to the budget	CFP	*				
210	Legal personality of the Community						
211	Legal capacity of the Community						
212	Status of Community officials	MT					
213	Commission's right to information						
214	Official secrecy						
215	Contractual liability of the Community		*				
216	Determining the seat of Community institutions						
217	Determining the rules governing languages used in Community institutions						
218	Privileges and immunities of Communities						
219	·Settlement of disputes						
220	Areas to be covered by intergovernmental cooperation						
221	Equal treatment for Community nationals						
222	Property ownership						
223	Maintenance of national security						
224	Functioning of the common market in the event of war						
225	Reducing distorting effect of Arts. 223 & 224 on competition						
226	Protective measures during the transitional period						
227	Geographic application of the treaty	DK/IRE/UK, SP/PO	*				
228	Negotiating procedure for international agreements		*				
229	Relations with the UN						
230	Cooperation with the Council of Europe						
231	Cooperation with the OEEC		*				
232	Status of treaty *vis-à-vis* ECSC and Euratom Treaties						
233	Regional unions within the Community						
234	Status of international agreements concluded prior to 1958						

Article	Content	Amended by	Effect of TEU I A R D	Notes
235	Attainment of treaty objectives — 'catch-all' article			
236	Amending the Treaty		*	See Art. N of TEU, p. 356
237	Accession to the Community	SEA	*	See Art. O of TEU, p. 356
238	Association with the Community	SEA	*	See also Art. 228
239	Status of protocols annexed to the Treaty			
240	Treaty concluded for an unlimited period			
241	First Council meeting			
242	Setting up the EcoSoc			
243	First meeting of the Assembly (EP)			
244	Assumption of duties by the ECJ			
245	Assumption of duties by the Commission			
246	Provisions relating to the first budget			
247	Ratification of the Treaty and its entry into force			
248	Authenticity of original texts			

Table 2: The impact of the TEU on the provisions contained in the Single European Act — an overview

Article	Function	Content	Effect of TEU A R D	Notes
1	SEA common provisions	Objectives of EC and EPC		
2	SEA common provisions	European Council	*	See Art. D of TEU
3	SEA common provisions	Powers and jurisdiction of EC and EPC institutions	*	TEU only repealed Art. 3(2) of SEA
4	Addition to Art. 32d of ECSC Treaty	Court of First Instance	*	
5	Addition to Art. 45 of ECSC Treaty	Provision to amend Statute of ECSC Court		
6(1)	Introduction of cooperation procedure to Arts. 7, 49, 54(2), 56(2), 57, 100a, 100b, 118a, 130e, 130q(2) of the amended EEC Treaty	Introduction of Cooperation Procedure	* *	TEU amended Arts. 49, 54(2), 56(2), 57, 100a, 130e. It also renumbered Art. 130q 130o of EEC Treaty
6(2–7)	Amendment to Arts. 7, 49, 54(2), 56(2), and 57 of the EEC Treaty	Changes in decision-making procedure	* *	See Table 1 above
7	Insertion of new Art. 149 into EEC Treaty	Cooperation procedure	* *	See Art. 189c of amended EEC Treaty
8	Amendment to Art. 237 of EEC Treaty	Role of EP	*	See Art. O of TEU
9	Amendment to Art. 238 of EEC Treaty	Role of EP	*	See also Art. 228 of amended EEC Treaty
10	Addition to Art. 145 of EEC Treaty	Conferral of powers on the Commission		
11	Insertion of Art. 168a of EEC Treaty	Court of First Instance	*	

Article	Function	Content	Effect of TEU A R D	Notes
12	Addition to Art. 188 of EEC Treaty	Provision to amend Statute of ECJ		
13	Insertion of Art. 8a of EEC Treaty	Single Market	*	Now Art. 7a of EEC Treaty
14	Insertion of Art. 8b of EEC Treaty	Single Market	*	Now Art. 7b of EEC Treaty
15	Insertion of Art. 8c of EEC Treaty	Single Market	*	Now Art. 7c of EEC Treaty
16	Amendments to Arts. 28, 57(2), 59, 70(1), 84(2) and 84 of the EEC Treaty	Changes in voting requirements	*	TEU only amended Art. 57(2) of EEC Treaty
17	Insertion of new Art. 99 into EEC Treaty	Approximation of laws	*	
18	Insertion of Art. 100a into EEC Treaty	Approximation of laws	*	
19	Insertion of Art. 100b into EEC Treaty	Approximation of laws		
20	Insertion of Art. 102a into EEC Treaty	Economic and monetary policy	* *	See Arts. 109m(1) of amended EEC Treaty
21	Insertion of Art. 118a into EEC Treaty	Health and safety	*	
22	Insertion of Art. 118b into EEC Treaty	Employer—employee dialog		
23	Insertion of Arts. 130a—130e into EEC Treaty	Economic and social cohesion	*	
24	Insertion of Arts. 130f—130i and 130k—130q into EEC Treaty	Research and development	* *	See Arts. 130—130p of amended EEC Treaty
25	Insertion of Art. 130r—130t into EEC Treaty	Environment	*	
26	Insertion of Art. 140a into Euratom Treaty	Court of First Instance	*	
27	Addition to Art. 160 of Euratom Treaty	Provision to amend Statute of ECJ		
28	SEA general provisions	SEA and Accession Treaties with Spain and Portugal		
29	SEA general provisions	Amendment to Art. 4(2) of Council Decision 85/257/EEC		
30	New provisions on foreign policy cooperation	European political cooperation	*	See Title V of TEU
31	SEA general and final provisions	Jurisdiction of ECJ		
32	SEA general and final provisions	Effect of SEA on Community Treaties		
33	SEA general and final provisions	Ratification and entry into force of SEA		
34	SEA general and final provisions	Authenticity of original texts		

Annex 4: Amendments to the ECSC and Euratom Treaties

The following two tables provide the reader with an indication of which provisions in the ECSC and Euratom Treaties have been amended since they entered into force in 1952 and 1958 respectively. Each table identifies the major divisions of the respective Treaties and then lists each Article which has been amended or added to the Treaty. These Articles are listed in the first column. Where the Article originally contained in the Treaty when it was signed was replaced in its entirety, or a new article was inserted prior to the TEU, the responsible Treaty or Agreement is listed in parentheses. The key to the abbreviations used here can be found on pp. 518−19. The second column then indicates which Treaty or Agreement has amended the Articles concerned. There then follows an indication as to the effect the TEU has had on each Article. Thus column three states whether the Article has been inserted (I) into the Treaty having originally been contained in another Treaty, as indicated in the first column. Columns four to six then denote whether the TEU has amended (A), renumbered (R), or deleted (D) the Article as listed in the first column. The final column then provides, either directly or through reference to the Boxes on pp. 360−1 and pp. 367−8, a description of the area to which the amendment refers.

Examples of how to read the tables

1. In Table 3 (ECSC Treaty), Article 29, the original version of which was replaced by Article 6 of the Merger Treaty, is simply inserted into the amended ECSC Treaty by the TEU.
2. In the same table (ECSC Treaty), Article 30, the original version of which was replaced by Article 5 of the Merger Treaty, is inserted into the amended ECSC Treaty and also amended by the TEU.
3. In Table 4 (Euratom Treaty), Article 108, which was amended by the Act concerning the election of the representatives of the Assembly by direct universal suffrage, and the Act concerning the Conditions of Accession and the Adjustments to the Treaties — Accession to the European Communities

of the Kingdom of Spain and the Portuguese Republic, is also amended by the TEU.

4. In the same table (Euratom Treaty), Article 180a, which was inserted into the Euratom Treaty by the Treaty amending Certain Financial Provisions of the Treaty establishing the European Communities and of the Treaty establishing a Single Council and a Single Commission of the European Communities, is amended and then renumbered Article 160c by the TEU, with the TEU finally deleting Article 180a from the Euratom Treaty.

Table 3: The impact of the TEU on the provisions of the Treaty establishing the European Coal and Steel Community

Article	Amended by	I	A	R	D	Notes
			Effect of TEU			
Title I The European Coal and Steel Community (Arts. 1–6)						
Title II Institutions (Arts. 7–45)						
7	CFP		*			See Box 19, p. 360–1
9 (MT, Art. 10)	MT, SP/PO	*	*			See Box 19, p. 360–1
10 (MT, Art. 11)	MT	*	*			See Box 19, p. 360–1
11 (MT, Art. 14)	MT, SP/PO	*	*			See Box 19, p. 360–1
12 (MT, Art. 12)	MT	*	*			See Box 19, p. 360–1
13 (MT, Art. 17)	MT	*	*			See Box 19, p. 360–1
16	MT		*			See Box 19, p. 360–1
17 (MT, Art. 18)	MT	*				See Box 19, p. 360–1
18	MT, SP/PO		*			See Box 19, p. 360–1
21	EP, SP/PO, CCI		*			See Box 19, p. 360–1
22	MT, EP					Convening the EP
24	EP		*			See Box 19, p. 360–1
27 (MT, Art. 2)	MT, SP/PO	*	*			See Box 19, p. 360–1
28	SP/PO					Voting procedure in the Council
29 (MT, Art. 6)	MT	*				See Box 19, p. 360–1
30 (MT, Art. 5)	MT	*	*			See Box 19, p. 360–1
32	CCI, CD, SP/PO		*			See Box 19, p. 360–1
32a (CCI, Art. 4(2(a)))	CCI, SP/PO					Advocates-General & ECJ
32b (CCI, Art. 4(2(a)))	CCI, SP/PO					Judges & Advocates-General
32c (CCI, Art. 4(2(a)))	CCI					ECJ Registrar
32d (SEA, Art. 4)	SEA		*			See Box 19, p. 360–1
33			*			See Box 19, p. 360–1
40	MT					Jurisdiction of ECJ
45	SEA					Statute of ECJ, see pp. 558–64
Title III Economic and social provisions (Arts. 46–75)						
56	See Art. 95					Job losses in coal and steel
Title IV General provisions (Arts. 76–100)						
76 (MT, Art. 28)	MT	*				Privileges and immunities
78	CFP					Budgetary procedure
78a	CFP					Budgetary expenditure
78b	CFP					Budgetary system of twelfths
78c	CFP		*			See Box 19, p. 360–1
78d	CFP					Annual financial statement
78e	CFP, SP/PO			*	*	See new Arts. 45a and 45b, Box 19, p. 360–1
78f	CFP			*	*	See new Art. 45c, Box 19, p. 360–1
78g	CFP		*			See Box 19, p. 360–1
78h	CFP		*			See Box 19, p. 360–1
79	DK/IRE/UK, GT		*			See Box 19, p. 360–1
95	SP/PO					Catch-all, cf. Art. 135 EEC Treaty
96					*	See TEU Art. N, see p. 356
98					*	See TEU Art. O, see p. 356

Table 4: The impact of the TEU on the provisions of the Treaty establishing the European Atomic Energy Community

Article	Amended by	I	A	R	D	Notes

Title I   The tasks of the Community (Arts. 1–3)

Article	Amended by	I	A	R	D	Notes
3	CFP	*				See Box 20, pp. 367–8

Title II   Provisions for the encouragement of progress in the field of nuclear energy (Arts. 4–106)
Title III   Provisions governing the institutions (Arts. 107–170)

Article	Amended by	I	A	R	D	Notes
108	EP, SP/PO	*				See Box 20, pp. 367–8
109	MT					Convening the EP
114		*				See Box 20, pp. 367–8
116 (MT, Art. 2)	SP/PO	*	*			See Box 20, pp. 367–8
117 (MT, Art. 3)		*				See Box 20, pp. 367–8
118	SP/PO					Voting procedure in the Council
121 (MT, Arts. 4 & 5)		*	*			See Box 20, pp. 367–8
123 (MT, Art. 6)		*				See Box 20, pp. 367–8
125 (MT, Art. 18)		*	*			See Box 20, pp. 367–8
126 (MT, Art. 19)	SP/PO	*				See Box 20, pp. 367–8
127 (MT, Art. 11)		*	*			See Box 20, pp. 367–8
128 (MT, Art. 12)		*	*			See Box 20, pp. 367–8
129 (MT, Art. 13)		*				See Box 20, pp. 367–8
130 (MT, Art. 14)	SP/PO	*	*			See Box 20, pp. 367–8
131 (MT, Arts. 15 & 16)		*	*			See Box 20, pp. 367–8
132 (MT, Art. 17)		*	*			See Box 20, pp. 367–8
133	MT			*		Repealed by MT, Art. 19
134	SP/PO					Scientific and Technical Committee
137	CD, SP/PO	*				See Box 20, pp. 367–8
138	SP/PO					Advocates General & ECJ
139	SP/PO					Judges and Advocates-General
140a (SEA, Art. 26)		*				See Box 20, pp. 367–8
143		*				See Box 20, pp. 367–8
146		*				See Box 20, pp. 367–8
160	SEA					Statute of ECJ, see pp. 558–64
166	SP/PO	*				See Box 20, pp. 367–8
168		*				See Box 20, pp. 367–8
170		*				See Box 20, pp. 367–8

Title IV   Financial provisions (Arts. 171–183)

Article	Amended by	I	A	R	D	Notes
172		*				See Box 20, pp. 367–8
173				*		New Art. 173, see p. 287
177	CFP					Budgetary procedure
178	CFP					Budgetary expenditure
179		*				See Box 20, pp. 367–8
179a (CFP, Art. 22)						Annual financial statement
180	CFP, SP/PO	*	*		*	See new Arts. 160a & 160b, Box 20, pp. 367–8
180a (CFP, Art. 24)		*	*		*	See new Art. 160c, Box 20, pp. 367–8
180b (CFP, Art. 25)		*				See Box 20, pp. 367–8
183	CFP	*				See Box 20, pp. 367–8

Title V   General provisions (Arts. 184–208)

Article	Amended by	I	A	R	D	Notes
186 (MT, Art. 24(1))	MT	*				Single administration of EC
191 (MT, Art. 28)	MT	*				Privileges and immunities
198	DK/IRE/UK, GT	*				See Box 20, pp. 367–8
201		*				See Box 20, pp. 367–8
204				*		See TEU, Art. N, p. 356
205				*		See TEU, Art. O, p. 356
206		*				See Box 20, pp. 367–8

Title VI   Provisions relating to the initial period (Arts. 209–223)
Final provisions (Arts. 224–225)

Annex 5: Other Supporting Documents

At various points in the text of the Handbook reference has been made to certain other key documents. Although these are not legally part of the TEU, it has been felt that it would be helpful to reproduce them here. This is because they may well affect the reading of the Treaty. They are:

1. The Luxembourg Compromise, 1966
2. Denmark and the Treaty on European Union, Edinburgh, 1992
3. Declaration of the High Contracting Parties on European Union, Guimarães, 1992
4. Birmingham Declaration: A Community Close to its Citizens, Birmingham, 1992
5. Overall Approach to the Application by the Council of the Subsidiarity Principle and Article 3b of the Treaty on European Union, Edinburgh, 1992

It should be noted that the conventions of presentation used elsewhere in the *Handbook* do not apply here. Hence, the fact that all the documents are reproduced in normal print does not imply that they are part of the Treaty of Rome. Nevertheless, the Declaration of the High Contracting Parties to the European Union is reproduced in bold in line with the practice followed with regard to Declarations in subdivision VI of the *Handbook*.

1. The Luxembourg Compromise[1]

> I. Where, in the case of decisions which may be taken by majority vote on a proposal of the Commission, very important interests of one or more partners are at stake, the Members of the Council will endeavour, within a reasonable time, to reach solutions which can be adopted by all the Members of the Council while respecting their mutual interests and those of the Community, in accordance with Art. 2 of the Treaty.
>
> II. With regard to the preceding paragraph, the French delegation considers that

---

1. *Bulletin of the European Economic Community*, no. 3, 1966, pp. 9–10.

where very important interests are at stake the discussion must be continued until unanimous agreement is reached.

III. The six delegations note that there is a divergence of views on what should be done in the event of a failure to reach complete agreement.

IV. The six delegations nevertheless consider that this divergence does not prevent the Community's work being resumed in accordance with the normal procedure.

2. Denmark and the Treaty on European Union

Denmark and the Treaty on European Union[2]

The European Council recalled that the entry into force of the Treaty signed in Maastricht requires ratification by all the twelve Member States in accordance with their respective constitutional requirements, and reaffirmed the importance of concluding the process as soon as possible, without reopening the present text, as foreseen in Article R of the Treaty.

The European Council noted that Denmark has submitted to Member States on 30 October a document entitled 'Denmark in Europe', which sets out the following points as being of particular importance:

— the defence policy dimension,
— the third stage of Economic and Monetary Union,
— citizenship of the Union,
— co-operation in the fields of justice and home affairs,
— openness and transparency in the Community's decision making process,
— the effective application of the principle of subsidiarity,
— promotion of cooperation between the Member States to combat unemployment.

Against this background, the European Council has agreed on the following set of arrangements, which are fully compatible with the Treaty, are designed to meet Danish concerns, and therefore apply exclusively to Denmark and not to other existing or acceding Member States:

(a) Decision concerning certain problems raised by Denmark on the Treaty on European Union (Annex 1). This Decision will take effect on the date of entry into force of the Treaty on European Union;
(b) The declarations in Annex 2.

The European Council has also taken cognizance of the unilateral declarations in Annex 3, which will be associated with the Danish act of ratification of the Treaty on European Union.

Annex 1 Decision of the Heads of State and Government, meeting within the European Council, concerning certain problems raised by Denmark on the Treaty on European Union

The Heads of State and Government, meeting within the European Council, whose Governments are signatories of the Treaty on European Union, which involved

---

2. OJC 348, 31 December 1992.

independent and sovereign States having freely decided, in accordance with the existing Treaties, to exercise in common some of their competences,

desiring to settle, in conformity with the Treaty on European Union, particular problems existing at the present time specifically for Denmark and raised in its Memorandum 'Denmark in Europe' of 30 October 1992,

having regard to the conclusions of the Edinburgh European Council on subsidiarity and transparency,

noting the declarations of the Edinburgh European Council relating to Denmark, taking cognisance of the unilateral declarations of Denmark made on the same occasion which will be associated with its act of ratification,

noting that Denmark does not intend to make use of the following provisions in such a way as to prevent closer cooperation and action among Member States compatible with the Treaty and within the framework of the Union and its objectives,

Have agreed on the following decision:

Section A   Citizenship

The provisions of Part Two of the Treaty establishing the European Community relating to citizenship of the Union give nationals of the Member States additional rights and protection as specified in that Part. They do not in any way take the place of national citizenship. The question whether an individual possesses the nationality of a Member State will be settled solely by reference to the national law of the Member State concerned.

Section B   Economic and Monetary Union

1. The Protocol on certain provisions relating to Denmark attached to the Treaty establishing the European Community gives Denmark the right to notify the Council of the European Communities of its position concerning participation in the third stage of Economic and Monetary Union. Denmark has given notification that it will not participate in the third stage. This notification will take effect upon the coming into effect of this decision.

2. As a consequence, Denmark will not participate in the single currency, will not be bound by the rules concerning economic policy which apply only to the Member States participating in the third stage of Economic and Monetary Union and will retain its existing powers in the field of monetary policy according to its national laws and regulations, including powers of the National Bank of Denmark in the field of monetary policy.

3. Denmark will participate fully in the second stage of Economic and Monetary Union and will continue to participate in exchange-rate cooperation within the EMS.

Section C   Defence policy

The Heads of State and Government note that, in response to the invitation from the Western European Union (WEU), Denmark has become an observer to that organization. They also note that nothing in the Treaty on European Union commits Denmark to become a member of the WEU. Accordingly, Denmark does not participate in the elaboration and the implementation of decisions and actions of the Union which have defence implications, but will not prevent the development of closer cooperation between Member States in this area.

Section D   Justice and Home Affairs

Denmark will participate fully in cooperation on Justice and Home Affairs on the basis of the provisions of Title VI of the Treaty on European Union.

Section E   Final provisions

1. This decision will take effect on the date of entry into force of the Treaty on European Union; its duration shall be governed by Articles Q and N(2) of that Treaty.

2. At any time Denmark may, in accordance with its constitutional requirements, inform other Member States that it no longer wishes to avail itself of all or part of this decision. In that event, Denmark will apply in full all relevant measures then in force taken within the framework of the European Union.

Annex 2   Declarations of the European Council

Declaration on social policy, consumers, environment, distribution of income

1. The Treaty on European Union does not prevent any Member State from maintaining or introducing more stringent protection measures compatible with the EC Treaty:
— in the field of working conditions and in social policy (Article 118a(3) of the EC Treaty and Article 2(5) of the Agreement on social policy concluded between the Member States of the European community with the exception of United Kingdom);
— in order to attain a high level of consumer protection (Article 129a(3) of the EC Treaty).
— in order to pursue the objectives of protection of the environment (Article 130t of the EC Treaty.

2. The provisions introduced by the Treaty on European Union, including the provisions on Economic and Monetary Union, permit each Member State to pursue its own policy with regard to distribution of income and maintain or improve social welfare benefits.

Declaration on defence

The European Council takes note that Denmark will renounce its right to exercise the Presidency of the Union in each case involving the elaboration and the implementation of decisions and actions of the Union which have defence implications. The normal rules for replacing the President, in the case of the President being indisposed, shall apply. These rules will also apply with regard to the representation of the Union in international organizations, international conferences and with third countries.

Annex 3   Unilateral Declarations of Denmark, to be associated to the Danish Act of the Treaty on European Union and of which the eleven other Member States will take cognisance

Declaration on citizenship of the Union

1. Citizenship of the Union is a political and legal concept which is entirely different from the concept of citizenship within the meaning of the Constitution of the Kingdom of Denmark and of the Danish legal system. Nothing in the Treaty on European Union implies or foresees an undertaking to create a citizenship of the Union in the sense of citizenship of a nation-state. The question of Denmark participating in any such development does, therefore, not arise.

2. Citizenship of the Union in no way in itself gives a national of another Member State the right to obtain Danish citizenship or any of the rights, duties, privileges or advantages that are inherent in Danish citizenship by virtue of Denmark's constitutional, legal and administrative rules. Denmark will fully respect all specific rights expressly provided for in the Treaty and applying to nationals of the Member States.

3. Nationals of the other Member States of the European Community enjoy in Denmark the right to vote and to stand as a candidate at municipal elections, foreseen in Article 8b of the European Community Treaty. Denmark intends to introduce legislation granting nationals of the other Member States the right to vote and to stand as a candidate for elections to the European Parliament in good time before the next elections in 1994. Denmark has no intention of accepting that the detailed arrangements foreseen in paragraphs 1 and 2 of this Article could lead to rules detracting from the rights already given in Denmark in that matter.

4. Without prejudice to the other provisions of the Treaty establishing the European Community, Article 8e requires the unanimity of all the Members of the Council of the European Communities, i.e. all Member States, for the adoption of any provision to strengthen or to add to the rights laid down in Part Two of the EC Treaty. Moreover, any unanimous decision of the Council, before coming into force, will have to be adopted in each Member State, in accordance with its constitutional requirements. In Denmark, such adoption will, in the case of a transfer of sovereignty, as defined in the Danish Constitution, require either a majority of 5/6 of Members of the Folketing or both a majority of the Members of the Folketing and a majority of voters in a referendum.

Declaration on cooperation in the fields of Justice and Home Affairs

Article K9 of the Treaty on European Union requires the unanimity of all the Members of the Council of the European Union, i.e. all Members States, to the adoption of any decision to apply Article 100c of the Treaty establishing the European Community to action in areas referred to in Article K1(1) to (6). Moreover, any unanimous decision of the Council, before coming into force, will have to be adopted in each Member State, in accordance with its constitutional requirements. In Denmark, such adoption will, in the case of a transfer of sovereignty, as defined in the Danish Constitution, require either a majority of 5/6 of Members of the Folketing or both a majority of the Members of the Folketing and a majority of voters in a referendum.

3. Declaration of the High Contracting Parties to the Treaty on European Union[3]

On 1 May 1992, in Guimarães (Portugal), the High Contracting Parties to the Treaty on European Union adopted the following Declaration:

Declaration of the High Contracting Parties to the Treaty on European Union

The High Contracting Parties to the Treaty on European Union signed at Maastricht on the seventh day of February 1992,
Having considered the terms of Protocol No 17[4] to the said Treaty on European Union which is annexed to that Treaty and to the Treaties establishing the European Communities,
Hereby give the following legal interpretation:

That it was and is their intention that the Protocol shall not limit freedom to travel between Member States or, in accordance with conditions which may be laid down, in conformity with Community law, by Irish legislation, to obtain or make available in Ireland information relating to services lawfully available in Member States.

At the same time the High Contracting Parties solemnly declare that, in the event of a future constitutional amendment in Ireland which concerns the subject matter of Article 40.3.3 of the Constitution of Ireland and which does not conflict with the intention of the High Contracting Parties hereinbefore expressed, they will, following the entry into force of the Treaty on European Union, be favourably disposed to amending the said Protocol so as to extend its application to such constitutional amendment if Ireland so requests.

4. Birmingham Declaration: a community close to its citizens[5]

1. We reaffirm our commitment to the Maastricht Treaty: We need to ratify it to make progress towards European Union if the Community is to remain an anchor of stability and prosperity in a rapidly changing continent, building on its success over the last quarter of a century.

2. As a community of democracies, we can only move forward with the support of our citizens. We are determined to respond to the concerns raised in the recent public debate. We must:

— demonstrate to our citizens the benefits of the Community and the Maastricht Treaty;
— make the Community more open, to ensure a better informed public debate on its activities;

---

3. For the legal standing of Declarations, see pp. 429–31.
4. Protocol 17 is reproduced on p. 427.
5. *Agence Presse Europe*, special edn, no. 5839 (n.s.), 18 October 1992.

— respect the history, culture and traditions of individual nations, with a clearer understanding of what Member States should do and what needs to be done by the Community;

— make clear that citizenship of the Union brings our citizens additional rights and protection without in any way taking the place of their national citizenship.

3. Foreign Ministers will suggest ways, before the Edinburgh European Council, of opening up the work of the Community's institutions, including the possibility of some open Council discussion — for example on future work programmes. We welcome the Commission's offer to consult more widely before proposing legislation which could include consultation with all the Member States and a more systematic use of consultation documents (Green Papers). We ask the Commission to complete by early next year its work on improving public access to the information available to it and to other Community institutions. We want Community legislation to become simpler and clearer.

4. We stress the European Parliament's important role in the democratic life of the Community and we welcome the growing contacts between national parliaments and the European Parliament. We reaffirm that national parliaments should be more closely involved in the Community's activities. We shall discuss this with our Parliaments. We welcome the Commission's readiness to respond positively to requests from national parliaments for explanations of its proposals. We underline the importance we attach to the Conference of Parliaments and to the Committee of the Regions.

5. We reaffirm that decisions must be taken as closely as possible to the citizen. Greater unity can be achieved without excessive centralization. It is for each Member State to decide how its powers should be exercised domestically. The Community can only act where Member States have given it the power to do so in the treaties. Action at the Community level should happen only when proper and necessary: the Maastricht Treaty provides the right framework and objectives for this. Bringing to life this principle — 'subsidiarity', or 'nearness' — is essential if the Community is to develop with the support of its citizens. We look forward to decisions at Edinburgh on the basis of reports on:

— adapting the Council's procedures and practices — as the Commission for its part has already done — so that the principle becomes an integral part of the Community's decision-making, as the Maastricht Treaty requires;

— guidelines for applying the principle in practice, for instance by using the lightest possible form of legislation, with maximum freedom for Member States on how best to achieve the objective in question. Community legislation must be implemented and enforced effectively, and without interfering unnecessarily in the daily life of our citizens.

We shall also have a look at the first fruits of the Commission's review of past Community legislation with examples.

6. Making the principle of subsidiarity work should be a priority for all the Community institutions, without affecting the balance between them. We will seek an agreement about this with the European Parliament.

7. The Maastricht Treaty will bring direct benefits to individual citizens. All of us — Council, Commission and Parliament — must do more to make this clear.

8. The European Council in conformity with the responsibilities given to it by the Treaty will ensure that the fundamental principles of the European Union will be fully observed.

5. Overall approach to the application by the Council of the subsidiarity principle and Article 3b of the Treaty on European Union

I Basic principles

European Union rests on the principle of subsidiarity, as is made clear in Articles A and B of Title I of the Treaty on European Union. This principle contributes to the respect for the national identities of Member States and safeguards their powers. It aims at decisions within the European Union being taken as closely as possible to the citizen.

1. Article 3b of the EC Treaty[6] covers three main elements:

— a strict limit on Community action (first paragraph);
— a rule (second paragraph) to answer the question 'Should the Community act?'. This applies to areas which do not fall within the Community's exclusive competence;
— a rule (third paragraph) to answer the question: 'What should be the intensity or nature of the Community's action?'. This applies whether or not the action is within the Community's exclusive competence.

2. The three paragraphs cover three distinct legal concepts which have historical antecedents in existing Community Treaties or in the case-law of the Court of Justice:

(i)   The principle that the Community can only act where given the power to do so — implying that national powers are the rule and the Community's the exception — has always been a basic feature of the Community legal order. (The principle of attribution of powers).

(ii) The principle that the Community should only take action where an objective can better be attained at the level of the Community than at the level of the individual Member States is present in embryonic or implicit form in some provisions of the ECSC Treaty and the EEC Treaty; the Single European Act spelled out the principle in the environment field. (The principle of subsidiarity in the strict legal sense).

(iii) The principle that the means to be employed by the Community should be proportional to the objective pursued is the subject of a well-established case-law of the Court of Justice which, however, has been limited in scope and developed with the support of a specific article in the Treaty. (The principle of proportionality or intensity).

3. The Treaty on European Union defines these principles in explicit terms and gives them a new legal significance.

— by setting them out in Article 3b as general principles of Community law;

---

6. Article 3b, as introduced in the EC Treaty by the Treaty on European Union, reads as follows:

The Community shall act within the limits of the powers conferred upon it by this Treaty and of the objectives assigned to it therein.

In areas which do not fall within its exclusive competence, the Community shall take action, in accordance with the principle of subsidiarity, only if and in so far as the objectives of the proposed action cannot be sufficiently achieved by the Member States and can therefore, by reason of the scale or effects of the proposed action, be better achieved by the Community.

Any action by this Community shall not go beyond what is necessary to achieve the objectives of this Treaty.

— by setting out the principle of subsidiarity as a basic principle of the European Union;[7]

— by reflecting the idea of subsidiarity in the drafting of several new Treaty articles.[8]

4. The implementation of Article 3b should respect the following basic principles.

— Making the principle of subsidiarity and Article 3b work is an obligation for all the Community institutions, without affecting the balance between them. (An agreement shall be sought to this effect between the European Parliament, the Council and the Commission, in the framework of the interinstitutional dialogue which is taking place among these institutions.)

— The principle of subsidiarity does not relate to and cannot call into question the powers conferred on the European Community by the Treaty as interpreted by the Court. It provides a guide as to how those powers are to be exercised at the Community level, including in the application of Article 235. The application of the principle shall respect the general provisions of the Maastricht Treaty, including the 'maintaining in full of the acquis communautaire', and it shall not affect the primacy of Community law nor shall it call into question the principle set out in Article F(3) of the Treaty on European Union, according to which the Union shall provide itself with the means necessary to attain its objectives and carry through its policies.

Furthermore, Article K.3(2)b directly incorporates the principle of subsidiarity.

— Subsidiarity is a dynamic concept and should be applied in the light of the objectives set out in the Treaty. It allows Community action to be expanded where circumstances so require, and conversely, to be restricted or discontinued where it is no longer justified.

— Where the application of the subsidiarity test excludes Community action, Member States would still be required in their action to comply with the general rules laid down in Article 5 of the Treaty, by taking all appropriate measures to ensure fulfilment of their obligations under the Treaty and by abstaining from any measure which could jeopardise the attainment of the objectives of the Treaty.

— The principle of subsidiarity cannot be regarded as having direct effect. However, interpretation of this principle, as well as review of compliance with it by the Community institutions are subject to control by the Court of Justice, as far as matters falling within the Treaty establishing the European Community are concerned.

— Paragraphs 2 and 3 of Article 3b apply only to the extent that the Treaty gives to the institution concerned the choice whether to act and/or a choice as to the nature and extent of the action. The more specific the nature of a Treaty requirement, the less scope exists for applying subsidiarity. The Treaty imposes a number of specific obligations upon the Community institutions, for example concerning the implementation and enforcement of Community law, competition policy and the protection of Community funds. These obligations are not affected by Article 3b: in particular the principle of subsidiarity cannot reduce the need for Community measures to contain adequate provision for the Commission and the Member States to ensure that Community law is properly enforced and to fulfil their obligations to safeguard Community expenditures.

---

7. See Articles A and B of the Treaty on European Union.

8. Articles 118a, 126, 127,128, 129, 129a, 130 and 130g of the EC Treaty, Article 2 of the Agreement on social policy.

> — Where the Community acts in an area falling under shared powers the type
> of measures to apply has to be decided on a case by case basis in the light
> of the relevant provisions of the Treaty.[9]

II Guidelines

In compliance with the basic principles set out above, the following guidelines
— specific to each paragraph of Article 3b — should be used in examining whether
a proposal for a Community measure conforms to the provisions of Article 3b.

First paragraph (limit on Community action)

Compliance with the criteria laid down in this paragraph is a condition for any
Community action.

In order to apply this paragraph correctly the institutions need to be satisfied
that the proposed action is within the limits of the powers conferred by the Treaty
and is aimed at meeting one or more of its objectives. The examination of the
draft measure should establish the objective to be achieved and whether it can
be justified in relation to an objective of the Treaty and that the necessary legal
basis for its adoption exists.

Second paragraph (should the Community act?)

(i)   This paragraph does not apply to matters falling within the Community's
exclusive competence.

For Community action to be justified the Council must be satisfied that both
aspects of the subsidiarity criterion are met: the objectives of the proposed action
cannot be sufficiently achieved by Member States' action and they can therefore
be better achieved by action on the part of the Community.

(ii)   The following guidelines should be used in examining whether the abovementioned condition is fulfilled:

— the issue under consideration has transnational aspects which cannot
be satisfactorily regulated by action by Member States; and/or

— actions by Member States alone or lack of Community action would
conflict with the requirements of the Treaty (such as the need to correct
distortion of competition or avoid disguised restrictions on trade or
strengthen economic and social cohesion) or would otherwise
significantly damage Member States' interests; and/or

— the Council must be satisfied that action at Community level would
produce clear benefits by reason of its scale or effects compared with
action at the level of the Member States.

(iii)   The Community should only take action involving harmonization of national

---

9. The new Articles 126 to 129 of the EC Treaty in the area of education, vocational training and youth, culture
and public health will explicitly rule out harmonization of laws and regulations of Member States. It follows that
the use of Article 235 for harmonization measures in pursuit of the specific objectives laid down in Articles 126
to 129 will be ruled out. This does not mean that the pursuit of other Community objectives through Treaty articles
other than 126 to 129 might not produce effects in these areas. Where Articles 126, 128 and 129 refer to 'incentive
measures', the Council considers that this expression refers to Community measures designed to encourage
cooperation between Member States or to support or supplement their action in the areas concerned, including
where appropriate through financial support for Community programmes or national or cooperative measures
designed to achieve the objectives of these articles.

legislation, norms or standards where this is necessary to achieve the objectives of the Treaty.

(iv)   The objective of presenting a single position of the Member States vis-a-vis third countries is not in itself a justification for internal Community action in the area concerned.

(v)   The reasons for concluding that a Community objective cannot be sufficiently achieved by the Member States but can be better achieved by the Community must be substantiated by qualitative, or, wherever possible, quantitative indicators.

Third paragraph (nature and extent of Community action)

(i)   This paragraph applies to all Community action, whether or not within exclusive competence.

(ii)   Any burdens, whether financial or administrative, falling upon the Community, national governments, local authorities, economic operators and citizens, should be minimized and should be proportionate to the objective to be achieved.

(iii) Community measures should leave as much scope for national decision as possible, consistent with securing the aim of the measure and observing the requirements of the Treaty. While respecting Community law, care should be taken to respect well established national arrangements and the organization and working of Member States' legal systems. Where appropriate and subject to the need for proper enforcement, Community measures should provide Member States with alternative ways to achieve the objectives of the measures.

(iv)   Where it is necessary to set standards at Community level, consideration should be given to setting minimum standards, with freedom for Member States to set higher national standards, not only in the areas where the treaty so requires (118a, 130t) but also in other areas where this would not conflict with the objectives of the proposed measure or with the Treaty.

(v)   The form of action should be as simple as possible, consistent with satisfactory achievement of the objective of the measure and the need for effective enforcement. The Community should legislate only to the extent necessary. Other things being equal, directives should be preferred to regulations and framework directives to detailed measures. Non-binding measures such as recommendations should be preferred where appropriate. Consideration should also be given where appropriate to the use of voluntary codes of conduct.

(vi)   Where appropriate under the Treaty, and provided this is sufficient to achieve its objectives, preference in choosing the type of Community action should be given to encouraging co-operation between Member States, co-ordinating national action or to complementing, supplementing or supporting such action.

(vii) Where difficulties are localized and only certain Member States are affected, any necessary Community action should not be extended to other Member States unless this is necessary to achieve an objective of the Treaty.

III Procedures and practices

The Treaty on European Union obliges all institutions to consider, when examining a Community measure, whether the provisions of Article 3b are observed.

For this purpose, the following procedures and practices will be applied in the framework of the basic principles set out under paragraph II and without prejudice to a future interinstitutional agreement.

(a) Commission

The Commission has a crucial role to play in the effective implementation of Article 3b, given its right of initiative under the Treaty, which is not called into question by the application of this article.

The Commission has indicated that it will consult more widely before proposing legislation, which could include consultation with all the Member States and a more systematic use of consultation documents (Green Papers). Consultation could include the subsidiarity aspects of a proposal. The Commission has also made it clear that, from now on and according to the procedure it already established in accordance with the commitment taken at the European Council in Lisbon, it will justify in a recital the relevance of its initiative with regard to the principle of subsidiarity. Whenever necessary, the explanatory memorandum accompanying the proposal will give details on the considerations of the Commission in the context of Article 3b. The overall monitoring by the Commission of the observance of the provisions of Article 3b in all its activities is essential and measures have been taken by the Commission in this respect. The Commission will submit an annual report to the European Council and the European Parliament through the General Affairs Council on the application of the Treaty in this area. This report will be of value in the debate on the annual report which the European Council has to submit to the European Parliament on progress achieved by the Union (see Article D in the Treaty on European Union).

(b) Council

The following procedure will be applied by the Council from the entry into force of the Treaty. In the meantime they will guide the work of the Council.

The examination of the compliance of a measure with the provisions of Article 3b should be undertaken on a regular basis; it should become an integral part of the overall examination of any Commission proposal and be based on the substance of the proposal. The relevant existing Council rules, including those on voting, apply to such examination.[10] This examination includes the Council's own evaluation of whether the Commission proposal is totally or partially in conformity with the provisions of Article 3b (taking as a starting point for the examination the Commission's recital and explanatory memorandum) and whether any change in the proposal envisaged by the Council is in conformity with those provisions. The Council decision on the subsidiarity aspects shall be taken at the same time as the decision on substance and according to the voting requirements set out in the Treaty. Care should be taken not to impede decision-making in the Council and to avoid a system of preliminary or parallel decision-making.

---

10. In the course of this examination, any Member State has the right to require that the examination of a proposal which raises Article 3b issues be inscribed on the provisional agenda of a Council in accordance with Article 2 of the Council's rules or procedure. If such examination, which will include all relevant points of substance covered by the Commission proposal, shows that the majority required for the adoption of the act does not exist, the possible outcomes include amendments of the proposal by the Commission, continued examination by the Council with a view to putting it into conformity with Article 3b or a provisional suspension of discussion of the proposal. This does not prejudice Member States or Commission rights under Article 2 of the Council's rules of procedure nor the Council obligation to consider the opinion of the European Parliament.

The Article 3b examination and debate will take place in the Council responsible for dealing with the matter. The General Affairs Council will have responsibility for general questions relating to the application of Article 3b. In this context the General Affairs Council will accompany the annual report from the Commission (see III(a) above) with any appropriate considerations on the application of this Article by the Council.

Various practical steps to ensure the effectiveness of the Article 3b examination will be put into effect including:

— working group reports and COREPER reports on a given proposal will, where appropriate, describe how Article 3b has been applied,
— in all cases of implementation of the Article 189b and 189c procedure.

The European Parliament will be fully informed of the Council's position concerning the observance of Article 3b, in the explanatory memorandum with the Council will likewise inform the Parliament if it partially or totally rejects a Commission proposal on the ground that it does not comply with the principle of Article 3b.

Annex 6: Supplementary EC Statutes

As noted in subsection VI of the *Handbook*, the Treaty of Rome has annexed to it a series of Protocols. Two of the most widely referred to are those containing the Statutes of the European Investment Bank and the Court of Justice. Indeed, reference has been made to these earlier in the *Handbook* as part of the discussion of the Community's institutions. Both Protocols are reproduced below. Also reproduced is the Protocol on the Privileges and Immunities of the European Communities. This was amended by Protocol 7 attached to the TEU.

*q.v.
institutions
pp.
250–96.*

*q.v.
Protocol 7
p. 418.*

Protocol on the Statute of the European Investment Bank

Of the three Protocols contained in this Annex, that relating to the European Investment Bank (EIB) is the oldest, having been signed on 25 March 1957, the same day as the Treaty of Rome. This reflects the fact the Article 129, now Article 198d, of the Treaty of Rome required that the Statute of the EIB, the Community's development bank, be contained in a Protocol annexed to the Treaty. The Statute sets out in its 29 Articles the composition of the Bank; the value of its resources; and the conditions under which it may borrow and lend money. As for the tasks of the Bank, Article 2 of the Statute refers the reader to the relevant section of the Treaty of Rome. The provisions of the Statute have undergone a series of amendments, primarily as a result of enlargements to the Community.[1] However, these have not led to any fundamental changes in the Statute.

*q.v. EIB
pp.
312–13.*

---

1. It would appear that not all enlargements have brought about an amendment of exactly the same provisions. Hence, the amendments introduced to Articles 5(2), 5(3), 9(3), 11(2), 12(1) and 13(1) by the Accession Treaties with Denmark, Ireland and the United Kingdom remain valid, as does that to Article 7 by the Accession Treaty with Greece. Articles 3, 4(1), 5(1), 10, 11(2), 12(2) and 13(1), however, underwent their most recent amendments with the accession of Spain and Portugal to the Community. Article 4(1) also has valid amendments resulting from a 1981 Decision of the Bank's Board of Governors (OJL 311, 30 October 1981) and from the Treaty amending the Protocol on the Statute of the Bank (OJL 91, 06 April 1977). An amendment to Article 9(3) was also introduced by the 1977 Treaty.

THE HIGH CONTRACTING PARTIES,

DESIRING to lay down the Statute of the European Investment Bank provided for in Article **198d** of this Treaty.[2]

HAVE AGREED upon the following provisions, which shall be annexed to this Treaty:

ARTICLE 1

The European Investment Bank established by Article **198d** of this Treaty (hereinafter called the 'Bank') is hereby constituted; it shall perform its functions and carry on its activities in accordance with the provisions of this Treaty and of this Statute.

The seat of the Bank shall be determined by common accord of the Governments of the Member States.

ARTICLE 2

The task of the Bank shall be that defined in Article **198e** of this Treaty.

ARTICLE 3

In accordance with Article **198d** of this Treaty, the following shall be members of the Bank:
[here follow the names of the member states]

ARTICLE 4

1. The capital of the Bank shall be twenty-eight thousand eight hundred million ECU, subscribed by the Member States as follows:

Germany	5 508 725 000
France	5 508 725 000
Italy	5 508 725 000
United Kingdom	5 508 725 000
Spain	2 024 928 000
Belgium	1 526 980 000
Netherlands	1 526 980 000
Denmark	773 154 000
Greece	414 190 000
Portugal	266 922 000
Ireland	193 288 000
Luxembourg	38 658 000

The unit of account shall be defined as being the ECU used by the European Communities. The Board of Governors, acting unanimously on a proposal from the Board of Directors, may alter the definition of the unit of account.

The Member States shall be liable only up to the amount of their share of the capital subscribed and not paid up.

2. The admission of a new member shall entail an increase in the subscribed capital corresponding to the capital brought in by the new member.

3. The Board of Governors may, acting unanimously, decide to increase the subscribed capital.

4. The share of a member in the subscribed capital may not be transferred, pledged or attached.

ARTICLE 5

1. The subscribed capital shall be paid in by Member States to the extent of 9.01367457% on average of the amounts laid down in Article 4(1).

---

2. The original references in the Statute to Articles 129 and 130 were replaced by references to Articles 198d and 198e respectively by Article G(86) of the TEU. This was in line with a renumbering of the Treaty of Rome provisions relating to the EIB by the TEU.

2. In the event of an increase in the subscribed capital, the Board of Governors, acting unanimously, shall fix the percentage to be paid up and the arrangements for payment.

3. The Board of Directors may require payment of the balance of the subscribed capital, to such extent as may be required for the Bank to meet its obligations towards those who have made loans to it.

Each Member State shall make this payment in proportion to its share of the subscribed capital in the currencies required by the Bank to meet these obligations.

ARTICLE 6

1. The Board of Governors may, acting by a qualified majority on a proposal from the Board of Directors, decide that Member States shall grant the Bank special interest-bearing loans if and to the extent that the Bank requires such loans to finance specific projects and the Board of Directors shows that the Bank is unable to obtain the necessary funds on the capital markets on terms appropriate to the nature and purpose of the projects to be financed.

2. Special loans may not be called for until the beginning of the fourth year after the entry into force of this Treaty. They shall not exceed 400 million units of account in the aggregate or 100 million units of account per annum.

3. The term of special loans shall be related to the term of the loans or guarantees which the Bank proposes to grant by means of the special loans; it shall not exceed twenty years. The Board of Governors may, acting by a qualified majority on a proposal from the Board of Directors, decide upon the prior repayment of special loans.

4. Special loans shall bear interest at 4% per annum, unless the Board of Governors, taking into account the trend and level of interest rates on the capital markets, decides to fix a different rate.

5. Special loans shall be granted by Member States in proportion to their share in the subscribed capital; payment shall be made in national currency within six months of such loans being called for.

6. Should the Bank go into liquidation, special loans granted by Member States shall be repaid only after the other debts of the Bank have been settled.

ARTICLE 7

1. Should the value of the currency of a Member State in relation to the unit of account defined in Article 4 be reduced, that State shall adjust the amount of its capital share paid in its own currency in proportion to the change in value by making a supplementary payment to the Bank.

2. Should the value of currency of a Member State in relation to the unit of account defined in Article 4 be increased, the Bank shall adjust the amount of the capital share paid in by that State in its own currency in proportion to the change in value by making a repayment to that State.

3. For the purpose of this Article, the value of the currency of a Member State in relation to the unit of account, defined in Article 4, shall correspond to the rate for converting the unit of account into this currency and vice versa based on market rates.

4. The Board of Governors, acting unanimously on a proposal from the Board of Directors, may alter the method of converting sums expressed in units of account into national currencies and vice versa.

Furthermore, acting unanimously on a proposal from the Board of Directors, it may define the method for adjusting the capital referred to in paragraphs 1 and 2 of this Articles; adjustment payments must be made at least once a year.

ARTICLE 8

The Bank shall be directed and managed by a Board of Governors, a Board of Directors and a Management Committee.

ARTICLE 9

1. The Board of Governors shall consist of the Ministers designated by the Member States.

2. The Board of Governors shall lay down general directives for the credit policy of the Bank, with particular reference to the objectives to be pursued as progress is made in the attainment of the common market.
The board of Governors shall ensure that these directives are implemented.

3. The Board of Governors shall in addition:
(a) decide whether to increase the subscribed capital in accordance with Article 4 (3) and Article 5 (2);
(b) exercise the powers provided in Article 6 in respect of special loans;
(c) exercise the powers provided in Articles 11 and 13 in respect of the appointment and the compulsory retirement of the members of the Board of Directors and the Management Committee, and those powers provided in the second subparagraph of Article 13 (1);
(d) authorise the derogation provided for in Article 18 (1);
(e) approve the annual report of the Board of Directors;
(f) approve the annual balance sheet and profit and loss account;
(g) exercise the powers and functions provided in Articles 4, 7, 14, 17, 26, and 27;
(h) approve the rules of procedure of the Bank.

4. Within the framework of this Treaty and this Statute, the Board of Governors shall be competent to take, acting unanimously, any decision concerning the suspension of the operations of the Bank and, should the event arise, its liquidation.

ARTICLE 10

Save as otherwise provided in this Statute, decisions of the Board of Governors shall be taken by a majority of its members. This majority must represent at least 45% of the subscribed capital. Voting by the Board of Governors shall be in accordance with the provisions of Article 148 of this Treaty.

ARTICLE 11

1. The Board of Directors shall have sole power to take decisions in respect of granting loans and guarantees and raising loans; it shall fix the interest rates on loans granted and the commission on guarantees; it shall see that the Bank is properly run; it shall ensure that the Bank is managed in accordance with the provisions of this Treaty and of this Statute and with the general directives laid down by the Board of Governors.

At the end of the financial year the Board of Directors shall submit a report to the Board of Governors and shall publish it when approved.

2. The Board of Directors shall consist of 22 directors and 12 alternates. The directors shall be appointed by the Board of Governors for five years as shown below:

— three directors nominated by the Federal Republic of Germany,
— three directors nominated by the French Republic,
— three directors nominated by the Italian Republic,
— three directors nominated by the United Kingdom of Great Britain and Northern Ireland,
— two directors nominated by the Kingdom of Spain,
— one director nominated by the Kingdom of Belgium,

— one director nominated by the Kingdom of Denmark,
— one director nominated by the Hellenic Republic,
— one director nominated by Ireland,
— one director nominated by the Grand Duchy of Luxembourg,
— one director nominated by the Kingdom of the Netherlands,
— one director nominated by the Portuguese Republic,
— one director nominated by the Commission.

The alternates shall be appointed by the Board of Governors for five years as shown below:

— two alternates nominated by the Federal Republic of Germany,
— two alternates nominated by the French Republic,
— two alternates nominated by the Italian Republic,
— two alternates nominated by the United Kingdom of Great Britain and Northern Ireland,
— one alternate nominated by common accord of the Kingdom of Denmark, the Hellenic Republic of Ireland,
— one alternate nominated by common accord of the Benelux countries,
— one alternate nominated by common accord of the Kingdom of Spain and the Portuguese Republic,
— one alternate nominated by the Commission.

The appointments of the directors and the alternates shall be renewable.

Alternates may take part in the meetings of the Board of Directors. Alternates nominated by a State, or by common accord of several States, or by the Commission, may replace directors nominated by that State, by one of those States or by the Commission respectively. Alternates shall have no right of vote except where they replace one director or more than one director or where they have been delegated for this purpose in accordance with Article 12 (1).

The President of the Management Committee or, in his absence, one of the Vice-Presidents, shall preside over meetings of the Board of Directors but shall not vote.

Members of the Board of Directors shall be chosen from persons whose independence and competence are beyond doubt; they shall be responsible only to the Bank.

3. A director may be compulsorily retired by the Board of Governors only if he no longer fulfils the conditions required for the performance of his duties: the Board must act by a qualified majority.

If the annual report is not approved, the Board of Directors shall resign.

4. Any vacancy arising as a result of death, voluntary resignation, compulsory retirement or collective resignation shall be filled in accordance with paragraph 2. A member shall be replaced for the remainder of his term of office, save where the entire Board of Directors is being replaced.

5. The Board of Governors shall determine the remuneration of members of the Board of Directors. The Board of Governors shall, acting unanimously, lay down what activities are incompatible with the duties of a director or an alternate.

ARTICLE 12

1. Each director shall have one vote on the Board of Directors. He may delegate his vote in all cases, according to procedures to be laid down in the rules of procedure of the Bank.

2. Save as otherwise provided in this Statute, decisions of the Board of Directors shall be taken by a simple majority of the members entitled to vote. A qualified majority shall require fifteen votes in favour. The rules of procedure of the Bank shall lay down how many members of the Board of Directors constitute the quorum needed for the adoption of decisions.

ARTICLE 13

1. The Management Committee shall consist of a President and six Vice-Presidents appointed for a period of six years by the Board of Governors on a proposal from the Board of Directors. Their appointments shall be renewable.

The Board of Governors acting unanimously, may vary the number of members on the Management Committee.

2. On a proposal from the Board of Directors adopted by a qualified majority, the Board of Governors may, acting in its turn by a qualified majority, compulsorily retire a member of the Management Committee.

3. The Management Committee shall be responsible for the current business of the Bank, under the authority of the President and the supervision of the Board of Directors.

It shall prepare the decisions of the Board of Directors, in particular decisions on the raising of loans and the granting of loans and guarantees; it shall ensure that these decisions are implemented.

4. The Management Committee shall act by a majority when delivering opinions on proposals for raising loans or granting loans and guarantees.

5. The Board of Governors shall determine the remuneration of members of the Management Committee and shall lay down what activities are incompatible with their duties.

6. The President or, if he is prevented, a Vice-President shall represent the Bank in judicial and other matters.

7. The officials and other employees of the Bank shall be under the authority of the President. They shall be engaged and discharged by him. In the selection of staff, account shall be taken not only of personal ability and qualifications but also of an equitable representation of nationals of Member States.

8. The Management Committee and the staff of the Bank shall be responsible only to the Bank and shall be completely independent in the performance of their duties.

ARTICLE 14

1. A Committee consisting of three members, appointed on the grounds of their competence by the Board of Governors, shall annually verify that the operations of the Bank have been conducted and its books kept in a proper manner.

2. The Committee shall confirm that the balance sheet and profit and loss account are in agreement with the accounts and faithfully reflect the position of the Bank in respect of its assets and liabilities.

ARTICLE 15

The Bank shall deal with each Member State through the authority designated by that State. In the conduct of financial operations the Bank shall have recourse to the bank of issue of the Member State concerned or to other financial institutions approved by that State.

ARTICLE 16

1. The Bank shall cooperate with all international organizations active in fields similar to its own.

2. The Bank shall seek to establish all appropriate contacts in the interests of cooperation with banking and financial institutions in the countries to which its operations extend.

ARTICLE 17

At the request of a Member State or of the Commission, or on its own initiative, the Board of Governors, shall, in accordance with the same provisions as governed their adoption, interpret or supplement the directives laid down by it under Article 9 of this Statute.

ARTICLE 18

1. Within the framework of the task set out in Article **198e** of this Treaty, the Bank shall grant loans to its members or to private or public undertakings for investment projects to be carried out in the European territories of Member States, to the extent that funds are not available from other sources on reasonable terms.

However, by way of derogation authorized by the Board of Governors, acting unanimously on a proposal from the Board of Directors, the Bank may grant loans for investment projects to be carried out, in whole or in part, outside the European territories of Member States.

2. As far as possible, loans shall be granted only on condition that other sources of finance are also used.

3. When granting a loan to an undertaking or to a body other than a Member State, the Bank shall make the loan conditional either on a guarantee from the Member State in whose territory the project will be carried out or on other adequate guarantees.

4. The Bank may guarantee loans contracted by public or private undertakings or other bodies for the purpose of carrying out projects provided for in Article **198e** of this Treaty.

5. The aggregate amount outstanding at any time of loans and guarantees granted by the Bank shall not exceed 250% of its subscribed capital.

6. The Bank shall protect itself against exchange risks by including in contracts for loans and guarantees such clauses as it considers appropriate.

ARTICLE 19

1. Interest rates on loans to be granted by the Bank and commission on guarantees shall be adjusted to conditions prevailing on the capital market and shall be calculated in such a way that the income therefrom shall enable the Bank to meet its obligations, to cover its expenses and to build up a reserve fund as provided for in Article 24.

2. The Bank shall not grant any reduction in interest rates. Where a reduction in the interest rate appears desirable in view of the nature of the project to be financed, the Member State concerned or some other agency may grant aid towards the payment of interest to the extent that this is compatible with Article 92 of this Treaty.

ARTICLE 20

In its loan and guarantee operations, the Bank shall observe the following principles:

1. It shall ensure that its funds are employed as rationally as possible in the interests of the Community.

It may grant loans or guarantees only:
(a) where, in the case of projects carried out by undertakings in the production sector, interest and amortization payments are covered out of operating profits, or, in other cases, either by a commitment entered into by the State in which the project is carried out or by some other means; and
(b) where the execution of the project contributes to an increase in economic productivity in general and promotes the attainment of the common market.

2. It shall neither acquire any interest in an undertaking nor assume any responsibility in its management unless this is required to safeguard the rights of the Bank in ensuring recovery of funds lent.

3. It may dispose of its claims on the capital market and may, to this end, require its debtors to issue bonds or other securities.

4. Neither the Bank nor the Member States shall impose conditions requiring funds lent by the Bank to be spent within a specified Member State.

5. The Bank may make its loans conditional on international invitations to tender being arranged.

6. The Bank shall not finance, in whole or in part, any project opposed by the Member State in whose territory it is to be carried out.

ARTICLE 21

1. Applications for loans or guarantees may be made to the Bank either through the Commission or through the Member State in whose territory the project will be carried out. An undertaking may also apply direct to the Bank for a loan or guarantee.

2. Applications made through the Commission shall be submitted for an opinion to the Member State in whose territory the project will be carried out. Applications made through a Member State shall be submitted to the Commission for an opinion.
Applications made direct by an undertaking shall be submitted to the Member State concerned and to the Commission.

The Member State concerned and the Commission shall deliver their opinions within two months. If no reply is received within this period, the Bank may assume that there is no objection to the project in question.

3. The Board of Directors shall rule on applications for loans or guarantees submitted to it by the Management Committee.

4. The Management Committee shall examine whether applications for loans or guarantees submitted to it comply with the provisions of this Statute, in particular with Article 20. Where the Management Committee is in favour of granting the loan or guarantee, it shall submit the draft contract to the Board of Directors; the Committee may make its favourable opinion subject to such conditions as it considers essential. Where the Management Committee is against granting the loan or guarantee, it shall submit the relevant documents together with its opinion to the Board of Directors.

5. Where the Management Committee delivers an unfavourable opinion, the Board of Directors may not grant the loan or guarantee concerned unless its decision is unanimous.

6. Where the Commission delivers an unfavourable opinion, the Board of Directors may not grant the loan or guarantee concerned unless its decision is unanimous, the director nominated by the Commission abstaining.

7. Where both the Management Committee and the Commission deliver an unfavourable opinion, the Board of Directors may not grant the loan or guarantee.

ARTICLE 22

1. The Bank shall borrow on the international capital markets the funds necessary for the performance of its tasks.

2. The Bank may borrow on the capital market of a Member State either in accordance with the legal provisions applying to the internal issues, or, if there are no such provisions in a Member State, after the Bank and the Member State concerned have conferred together and reached agreement on the proposed loan.

The competent authorities in the Member State concerned may refuse to give their assent only if there is reason to fear serious disturbances on the capital market of that State.

ARTICLE 23

1. The Bank may employ any available funds which it does not immediately require to meet its obligations in the following ways:

(a) it may invest on the money markets;
(b) it may, subject to the provisions of Article 20 (2), buy and sell securities issued by itself or by those who have borrowed from it;

(c) it may carry out any other financial operation linked with its objectives.

2. Without prejudice to the provisions of Article 25, the Bank shall not, in managing its investments, engage in any currency arbitrage not directly required to carry out its lending operations or fulfil commitments arising out of loans raised or guarantees granted by it.

3. The Bank shall, in the fields covered by this Article, act in agreement with the competent authorities or with the bank of issue of the Member State concerned.

ARTICLE 24

1. A reserve fund of up to 10% of the subscribed capital shall be built up progressively. If the state of the liabilities of the Bank should so justify, the Board of Directors may decide to set aside additional reserves. Until such times as the reserve fund has been fully built up, it shall be fed by:

(a) interest received on loans granted by the Bank out of sums to be paid up by the Member States pursuant to Article 5;
(b) interest received on loans granted by the Bank out of funds derived from repayment of the loans referred to in (a);

to the extent that this income is not required to meet the obligations of the Bank or to cover its expenses.

2. The resources of the reserve fund shall be so invested as to be available at any time to meet the purpose of the fund.

ARTICLE 25

1. The Bank shall at all times be entitled to transfer its assets in the currency of one Member State into the currency of another Member State in order to carry out financial operations corresponding to the task set out in Article **198e** of this Treaty, taking into account the provisions of Article 23 of this Statute. The Bank shall, as far as possible, avoid making such transfers if it has cash or liquid assets in the currency required.

2. The Bank may not convert its assets in the currency of a Member State into the currency of a third country without the agreement of the Member State concerned.

3. The Bank may freely dispose of that part of its capital which is paid up in gold or convertible currency and of any currency borrowed on markets outside the Community.

4. The Member States undertake to make available to the debtors of the Bank the currency needed to repay the capital and pay the interest on loans or commissions on guarantees granted by the Bank for projects to be carried out in their territory.

ARTICLE 26

If a Member State fails to meet the obligations of membership arising from this Statute, in particular the obligation to pay its share of the subscribed capital, to grant its special loans or to service its borrowings, the granting of loans or guarantees to that Member State or its nationals may be suspended by a decision of the Board of Governors, acting by a qualified majority.

Such decision shall not release either the State or its nationals from their obligations towards the Bank.

ARTICLE 27

1. If the Board of Governors decides to suspend the operations of the Bank, all its activities shall cease forthwith, except those required to ensure the due realization, protection and preservation of its assets and the settlement of its liabilities.

2. In the event of liquidation, the Board of Governors shall appoint the liquidators and give them instructions for carrying out the liquidation.

ARTICLE 28

1. In each of the Member States, the Bank shall enjoy the most extensive legal capacity accorded to legal persons under their laws; it may, in particular, acquire or dispose of moveable or immoveable property and may be a party to legal proceedings.

The European Communities shall enjoy in the territories of the Member States such privileges and immunities as are necessary for the performance of their tasks, under the conditions laid down in the Protocol annexed to this Treaty. The same shall apply to the European Investment Bank.[3]

2. The property of the Bank shall be exempt from all forms of requisition or expropriation.

ARTICLE 29

Disputes between the Bank on the one hand, and its creditors, debtors or any other person on the other, shall be decided by the competent national courts, save where jurisdiction has been conferred on the Court of Justice.

The Bank shall have an address for service in each Member Sate. It may, however, in any contract, specify a particular address for service or provide for arbitration.

The property and assets of the Bank shall not be liable to attachment or to seizure by way of execution except by decision of a court.

Protocol on privileges and immunities of the European Communities

When the Treaty of Rome was originally signed in the mid-1950s, a provision was included in a decision of the IGC which drew up the Treaty for a Protocol governing the privileges and immunities of the then EEC. This was duly drawn up and attached to the Treaty of Rome. A similar Protocol had already been attached to the ECSC Treaty and one would also be drawn up and attached to the Euratom Treaty. However, when the institutions of the three Communities were combined in the 1960s, Article 28 of the Treaty establishing a Single Council and a Single Commission of the European Communities of 1965, otherwise known as the Merger Treaty, replaced these Protocols with a single Protocol on Privileges and Immunities of the European Communities.[4]

As its title indicates, this Protocol lays down the privileges and immunities of those who are members of or work for the Communities' institutions. Hence, reference is made in the Protocol to MEPs, representatives of the member states taking part in the work of the institutions, officials and servants of the Commission, those involved in the work of the Communities' overseas missions, and those involved in the work of the Court of Justice. Furthermore, the Protocol

---

3. The original second subparagraph was repealed by the second paragraph of Article 28 of the Merger Treaty. The current wording is that found in the first paragraph of Article 28 of the Merger Treaty. The TEU did not, however, formally insert the new provision. It is reproduced here for sake of consistency.

4. Reference to the original Protocol attached to the Treaty of Rome was originally contained in Article 218 of the Treaty of Rome. However, this Article was repealed by the Merger Treaty. Reference, thereafter to the new Protocol, was contained in Article 28 of the Merger Treaty. However, whereas the TEU for the most part inserted relevant provisions of the Merger Treaty into the Treaty of Rome, it did not do so in respect of the Protocol on Privileges and Immunities of the European Communities. Rather, the TEU left Article 218 bereft of provisions. Consequently, consolidated versions of the post-TEU Treaty of Rome, this *Handbook* included, refer readers to the relevant provisions of the Merger Treaty, see p. 331.

sets out the privileges and immunities of the Communities themselves within the territory of the EC and of its member states. An additional Article (Article 23), inserted as a result of the TEU, extends the application of the Protocol to the European Central Bank and the European Monetary Institute.

q.v.
European
Central
Bank pp.
158–60.

q.v.
European
Monetary
Institute p.
156.

THE HIGH CONTRACTING PARTIES,

CONSIDERING that, in accordance, with Article 28 of the Treaty establishing a Single Council and a Single Commission of the European Communities, these Communities and the European Investment Bank shall enjoy in the territories of the Member States such privileges and immunities as are necessary for the performance of their tasks,

HAVE AGREED upon the following provisions, which shall be annexed to this Treaty:

Chapter I Property, funds, assets and operations of the European Communities

ARTICLE 1

The premises and buildings of the Communities shall be inviolable. They shall be exempt from search, requisition, confiscation or expropriation. The property and assets of the Communities shall not be the subject of any administrative or legal measure of constraint without the authorization of the Court of Justice.

ARTICLE 2

The archives of the Communities shall be inviolable.

ARTICLE 3

The Communities, their assets, revenues and other property shall be exempt from all direct taxes.

The Government of the Member State shall, wherever possible, take the appropriate measures to remit or refund the amount of indirect taxes or sales taxes included in the price of moveable or immoveable property, where the Communities make, for their official use, substantial purchases the price of which include taxes of this kind. These provisions shall not be applied, however, so as to have the effect of distorting competition within the Communities.

No exemption shall be granted in respect of taxes and dues which amount merely to charges for public utility services.

ARTICLE 4

The Communities shall be exempt from all customs duties, prohibitions and restrictions on imports and exports in respect of articles intended for their official use; articles so imported shall not be disposed of, whether or not in return for payment, in the territory of the country into which they have been imported, except under conditions approved by the Government of that country.

The Communities shall also be exempt from any customs duties and any prohibitions and restrictions on imports and exports in respect of their publications.

ARTICLE 5

The European Coal and Steel Community may hold currency of any kind and operate accounts in any currency.

Chapter II Communications and laissez-passer

ARTICLE 6

For their official communications and the transmission of all their documents, the institutions of the Communities shall enjoy in the territory of each Member State the treatment accorded by that State to diplomatic missions.

Official correspondence and other official communications of the institutions of the Communities shall not be subject to censorship.

ARTICLE 7

1. *Laissez-passer* in a form to be prescribed by the Council, which shall be recognized as valid travel documents by the authorities of the Members States, may be issued to members and servants of the institutions of the Communities by the Presidents of these institutions. These *laissez-passer* shall be issued to officials and other servants under conditions laid down in the Staff Regulations of officials and the Conditions of Employment of other servants of the Communities.

The Commission may conclude agreements for these *laissez-passer* to be recognized as valid travel documents within the territory of third countries.

2. The provisions of Article 6 of the Protocol on the Privileges and Immunities of the European Coal and Steel Community shall, however, remain applicable to members and servants of the institutions who are at the date of entry into force of this Treaty in possession of the *laissez-passer* provided for in that Article, until the provisions of paragraph 1 of this Article are applied.

Chapter III   Members of the European Parliament

ARTICLE 8

No administrative or other restrictions shall be imposed on the free movement of members of the European Parliament travelling to or from the place of meeting of the European Parliament.

Members of the European Parliament shall, in respect of customs and exchange control, be accorded:

(a) by their own Government, the same facilities as those accorded to senior officials travelling abroad on temporary official missions;
(b) by the Governments of other Member States, the same facilities as those accorded to representatives of foreign Governments on temporary official missions.

ARTICLE 9

Members of the European Parliament shall not be subject to any form of inquiry, detention or legal proceedings in respect of opinions expressed or votes cast by them in the performance of their duties.

ARTICLE 10

During the sessions of the European Parliament, its members shall enjoy:

(a) in the territory of their own State, the immunities accorded to members of their parliament;
(b) in the territory of any other Member State, immunity from any measure of detention and from legal proceedings.

Immunity shall likewise apply to members while they are travelling to and from the place of meeting of the European Parliament.

Immunity cannot be claimed when a member is found in the act of committing an offence and shall not prevent the European Parliament from exercising its right to waive the immunity of one of its members.

Chapter IV   Representatives of Member States taking part in the work of the institutions of the European Communities

ARTICLE 11

Representatives of Member States taking part in the work of the institutions of the Communities, their advisers and technical experts shall, in the performance of their duties and during their travel to and from the place of meeting, enjoy the customary privileges, immunities and facilities.

This Article shall also apply to members of the advisory bodies of the Communities.

Chapter V Officials and other servants of the European Communities

ARTICLE 12

In the territory of each Member State and whatever their nationality, officials and other servants of the Communities shall:

(a) subject to the provisions of the Treaties relating, on the one hand, to the rules on the liability of officials and other servants towards the Communities and, on the other hand, to the jurisdiction of the Court in disputes between the Communities and their officials and other servants, be immune from legal proceedings in respect of acts performed by them in their official capacity, including their words spoken or written. They shall continue to enjoy this immunity after they have ceased to hold office;

(b) together with their spouses and dependent members of their families, not be subject to immigration restrictions or to formalities for registration of aliens;

(c) in respect of currency or exchange regulations, be accorded the same facilities as are customarily accorded to officials of international organizations;

(d) enjoy the right to import free of duty their furniture and effects at the time of first taking up their post in the country concerned, and the right to re-export free of duty their furniture and effects, on termination of their duties in that country, subject in either case to the conditions considered to be necessary by the Government of the country in which this right is exercised;

(e) have the right to import free of duty a motor car for their personal use, acquired either in the country of their last residence or in the country of which they are nationals on the terms ruling in the home market in that country, and to re-export it free of duty, subject in either case to the conditions considered to be necessary by the Government of the country concerned.

ARTICLE 13

Officials and other servants of the Communities shall be liable to a tax for the benefit of the Communities on salaries, and emoluments paid to them by the Communities, in accordance with the conditions and procedure laid down by the Council, acting on a proposal from the Commission.

They shall be exempt from national taxes on salaries, wages and emoluments paid by the Communities.

ARTICLE 14

In the application of income tax, wealth tax and death duties and in the application of conventions on the avoidance of double taxation concluded between Members States of the Communities, officials and other servants of the Communities who, solely by reason of the performance of their duties in the service of the Communities, establish their residence in the territory of a Member State other than their country of domicile for tax purposes at the time of entering the service of the Communities, shall be considered, both in the country of their actual residence and in the country of domicile for tax purposes, as having maintained their domicile in the latter country provided that it is a member of the Communities. This provision shall also apply to a spouse to the extent that the latter is not separately engaged in a gainful occupation, and to children dependent on and in the care of the persons referred to in this Article.

Movable property belonging to persons referred to in the first paragraph and situated in the territory of the country where they are staying shall be exempt from death duties in that country; such property shall, for the assessment of such duty, be considered as being in the country of domicile for tax purposes, subject to the rights of third countries and to the possible application of provisions of international conventions on double taxation.

Any domicile acquired solely by reason of the performance of duties in the service of other international organizations shall not be taken into consideration in applying the provisions of this Article.

ARTICLE 15
The Council shall, acting unanimously on a proposal from the Commission, lay down the scheme of social security benefits for officials and other servants of the Communities.

ARTICLE 16
The Council shall, acting on a proposal from the Commission and after consulting the other institutions concerned, determine the categories of officials and other servants of the Communities to whom the provisions of Article 12, the second paragraph of Article 13, and Article 14 shall apply, in whole or in part.

The names, grades and addresses of officials and other servants included in such categories shall be communicated periodically to the Governments of the Member States.

Chapter VI Privileges and immunities of mission of third countries accredited to the European Communities

ARTICLE 17
The Member State in whose territory the Communities have their seats shall accord the customary diplomatic immunities and privileges to missions of third countries accredited to the Communities.

Chapter VII General provisions

ARTICLE 18
Privileges, immunities and facilities shall be accorded to officials and other servants of the Communities solely in the interests of the Communities.

Each institution of the Communities shall be required to waive the immunity accorded to an official or other servant wherever that institution considers that the waiver of such immunity is not contrary to the interests of the Communities.

ARTICLE 19
The institutions of the Communities shall, for the purpose of applying this Protocol, co-operate with the responsible authorities of the Member States concerned.

ARTICLE 20
Articles 12 to 15 and Article 18 shall apply to members of the Commission.

ARTICLE 21
Articles 12 to 15 and Article 18 shall apply to the Judges, the Advocates-General, the Registrar and the Assistant Rapporteurs of the Court of Justice, without prejudice to the provisions of Article 3 of the Protocols on the Statute of the Court of Justice concerning immunity from legal proceedings of Judges and Advocates-General.

ARTICLE 22
The Protocol shall also apply to the European Investment Bank, to the members of its organs, to its staff and to the representatives of the Member States taking

part in its activities, without prejudice to the provisions of the Protocol on the Statute of the Bank.

The European Investment Bank shall in addition be exempt from any form of taxation or imposition of a like nature on the occasion of any increase in its capital and from the various formalities which may be connected therewith in the State where the Bank has its seat. Similarly, its dissolution or liquidation shall not give rise to any imposition. Finally, the activities of the Bank and of its organs carried on it accordance with its Statute shall not be subject to any turnover tax.

ARTICLE 23[5] **This Protocol shall also apply to the European Central Bank, to the members of its organs and to its staff, without prejudice to the provisions of the Protocol on the Statute of the European System of Central Banks and the European Central Bank.**

The European Central Bank shall, in addition, be exempt from any taxation or imposition of a like nature on the occasion of any increase in its capital and from the various formalities which may be connected therewith in the State where the bank has its seat. The activities of the Bank and of its organs carried on in accordance with the Statute of the European System of Central Banks and the European Central Bank shall not be subject to any turnover tax.

The above provisions shall also apply to the European Monetary Institute. Its dissolution or liquidation shall not give rise to any imposition.

Protocol on the Statute of the Court of Justice of the European Community[6]

The Protocol on the Statute of the Court of Justice of the European Economic Community was drawn up on 17 April 1957 in line with a decision of the IGC which drew up the Treaty of Rome. Indeed, its existence is required by Article 188 of the Treaty of Rome. Following the entry into force of the SEA, the second paragraph of the same Article includes a provision whereby the Council, acting unanimously, may amend Title III of the Statute.

q.v. Article 188 p. 289.

THE HIGH CONTRACTING PARTIES TO THE TREATY ESTABLISHING THE *EUROPEAN COMMUNITY*:
DESIRING to lay down the Statute of the Court provided for in Article 188 of this Treaty,
HAVE DESIGNATED as their plenipotentiaries for this purpose: [here follow the names of signatories][7]
WHO, having exchanged their Full Powers, found in good and due form,
HAVE AGREED upon the following provisions, which shall be annexed to the Treaty establishing the *European Community*:

---

5. Article 23 was inserted into the Protocol by the Protocol amending the Protocol on the privileges and immunities of the European Communities, see p. 418.

6. The title of the Protocol has been amended in line with Article G(1) of the TEU (see p. 41, note 2). Prior to the TEU the Protocol's title was 'Protocol on the Statute of the Court of Justice of the European Economic Community'. Former references in the Protocol to the European Economic Community have been amended accordingly.

7. For the names of the plenipotentiaries, see *Treaties establishing the European Communities*, abridged edn, OOPEC, Luxembourg, 1987, pp. 369–70.

ARTICLE 1 — The Court established by Article 4 of this Treaty shall be constituted and shall function in accordance with the provisions of this Treaty and of this Statute.

Title I   Judges and Advocates-General

ARTICLE 2 — Before taking up his duties each judge shall, in open court, take an oath to perform his duties impartially and conscientiously and to preserve the secrecy of the deliberations of the Court.

ARTICLE 3 — The Judges shall be immune from legal proceedings. After they have ceased to hold office, they shall continue to enjoy immunity in respect of acts performed by them in their official capacity including words spoken or written.

The Court, sitting in plenary session, may waive the immunity.

Where immunity has been waived and criminal proceedings are instituted against a Judge, he shall be tried, in any of the Member States, only by the Court competent to judge the members of the highest national judiciary.

ARTICLE 4 — The Judges may not hold any political or administrative office.

They may not engage in any occupation, whether gainful or not, unless exemption is exceptionally granted by the Council.

When taking up their duties, they shall give a solemn undertaking that, both during and after their term of office, they will respect the obligations arising therefrom, in particular the duty to behave with integrity and discretion as regards the acceptance, after they have ceased to hold office, of certain appointments or benefits.

Any doubt on this point shall be settled by decision of the Court.

ARTICLE 5 — Apart from normal replacement, or death, the duties of a Judge shall end when he resigns.

Where a Judge resigns, his letter of resignation shall be addressed to the President of the Court for transmission to the President of the Council. Upon this notification a vacancy shall arise on the bench.

Save where Article 6 applies, a Judge shall continue to hold office until his successor takes up his duties.

ARTICLE 6 — A Judge may be deprived of his office or of his right to a pension or other benefits in its stead only if, in the unanimous opinion of the Judges and Advocates-General of the Court, he no longer fulfils the requisite conditions or meets the obligations arising from his office. The Judge concerned shall not take part in any such deliberations.

The Registrar of the Court shall communicate the decision of the Court to the President of the European Parliament and to the President of the Commission and shall notify it to the President of the Council.

In the case of a decision depriving a Judge of his office, a vacancy shall arise on the bench upon this latter notification.

ARTICLE 7 — A Judge who is to replace a member of the Court whose term of office has not expired shall be appointed for the remainder of his predecessor's term.

ARTICLE 8 — The provisions of Articles 2 to 7 shall apply to the Advocates-General.

Title II   Organization

ARTICLE 9

The Registrar shall take an oath before the Court to perform his duties impartially and conscientiously and to preserve the secrecy of the deliberations of the Court.

ARTICLE 10

The Court shall arrange for replacement of the Registrar on occasions when he is prevented from attending the Court.

ARTICLE 11

Officials and other servants shall be attached to the Court to enable it to function. They shall be responsible to the Registrar under the authority of the President.

ARTICLE 12

On a proposal from the Court, the Council may, acting unanimously, provide for the appointment of Assistant Rapporteurs and lay down the rules governing the service. The Assistant Rapporteurs may be required, under conditions laid down in the rules of procedure, to participate in preparatory inquiries in cases pending before the Court and to cooperate with the Judge who acts as Rapporteur.

The Assistant Rapporteurs shall be chosen from persons whose independence is beyond doubt and who possess the necessary legal qualifications; they shall be appointed by the Council. They shall take an oath before the Court to perform their duties impartially and conscientiously and to preserve the secrecy of the deliberations of the Court.

ARTICLE 13

The Judges, the Advocates-General and the Registrar shall be required to reside at the place where the Court has its seat.

ARTICLE 14

The Court shall remain permanently in session. The duration of the judicial vacations shall be determined by the Court with due regard to the needs of its business.

ARTICLE 15

Decisions of the Court shall be valid only when an uneven number of its members is sitting in the deliberations. Decisions of the full Court shall be valid if seven members are sitting. Decisions of the Chambers shall be valid only if three Judges are sitting; in the event of one of the Judges of a Chamber being prevented from attending, a Judge of another Chamber may be called upon to sit in accordance with conditions laid down in the rules of procedure.

ARTICLE 16

No Judge or Advocate-General may take part in the disposal of any case in which he had previously taken part as an agent or adviser or has acted for one of the parties, or on which he has been called upon to pronounce as a member of a court or tribunal, of a commission of enquiry or in any other capacity.

If, for some special reason, any Judge or Advocate-General considers that he should not take part in the judgment or examination of a particular case, he shall inform the President. If, for some special reason, the President considers that any Judge or Advocate-General should not sit or make submissions in a particular case, he shall notify him accordingly.

Any difficulty arising as to the application of this Article shall be settled by decision of the Court.

A party may not apply for a change in the composition of the Court or of one of its Chambers on the grounds of either the nationality of the Judge or the absence from the Court or from the Chamber of a Judge of the nationality of that party.

Title III Procedure

ARTICLE 17

The States and the institutions of the Community shall be represented before the Court by an agent appointed for each case; the agent may be assisted by an adviser or by a lawyer entitled to practise before a court of a Member State.

Other parties must be represented by a lawyer entitled to practise before a court of a Member State.

Such agents, advisers and lawyers shall, when they appear before the Court, enjoy the rights and immunities necessary to the independent exercise of their duties, under conditions laid down in the rules of procedure.

As regards such advisers and lawyers who appear before it, the Court shall have the powers normally accorded to courts of law, under conditions laid down in the rules of procedure.

University teachers being nationals of a Member State whose law accords them a right of audience shall have the same rights before the Court as are accorded by this Article to lawyers entitled to practise before a court of a Member state.

ARTICLE 18

The procedure before the Court shall consist of two parts: written and oral.

The written procedure shall consist of the communication to the parties and to the institutions of the Community whose decisions are in dispute of applications, statements of case, defences and observations, and of replies, if any, as well as of all papers and documents in support or of certified copies of them.

Communications shall be made by the Registrar in the order and within the time laid down in the rules of procedure.

The oral procedure shall consist of the reading of the report presented by a Judge acting as Rapporteur, the hearing by the Court of agents, advisers and lawyers entitled to practise before a Member State and of the submissions of the Advocate-General, as well as the hearing, if any, of witnesses and experts.

ARTICLE 19

A case shall be brought before the Court by a written application addressed to the Registrar. The application shall contain the applicant's name and permanent address and the description of the signatory, the name of the party against whom the application is made, the subject matter of the dispute, the submissions and a brief statement of the grounds on which the application is based.

The application shall be accompanied, where appropriate, by the measure the annulment of which is sought or, in the circumstances referred to in Article 175 of this Treaty, by documentary evidence of the date on which an institution was, in accordance with that Article, requested to act. If the documents are not submitted with the application, the Registrar shall ask the party concerned to produce them within a reasonable period, but in that event the rights of the party shall not lapse even if such documents are produced after the time limit for bringing proceedings.

ARTICLE 20

In the cases governed by Article 177 of this Treaty, the decision of the court or tribunal of a Member State which suspends its proceedings and refers a case to the Court shall be notified to the Court by the court or tribunal concerned. The decision shall then be notified by the Registrar of the Court to the parties, to the Member States and to the Commission, and also to the Council if the act the validity or interpretation of which is in dispute originates from the Council.

Within two months of this notification, the parties, the Member State, the Commission and, where appropriate, the Council, shall be entitled to submit statements of case or written observations to the Court.

ARTICLE 21
The Court may require the parties to produce all documents and to supply all information which the Court considers desirable. Formal note shall be taken of any refusal.

The Court may also require the Member States and institutions not being parties to the case to supply all information which the Court considers necessary for the proceedings.

ARTICLE 22
The Court may at any time entrust any individual, body, authority, committee or other organization it chooses with the task of giving an expert opinion.

ARTICLE 23
Witnesses may be heard under conditions laid down in the rules of procedure.

ARTICLE 24
With respect to defaulting witnesses the Court shall have the powers generally granted to courts and tribunals and may impose pecuniary penalties under conditions laid down in the rule of procedure.

ARTICLE 25
Witnesses and experts may be heard on oath taken in the form laid down in the rules of procedure or in the manner laid down by the law of the country of the witness or expert.

ARTICLE 26
The Court may order that a witness or expert be heard by the judicial authority of his place of permanent residence.

The order shall be sent for implementation to the competent judicial authority under conditions laid down in the rules of procedure. The documents drawn up in compliance with the letters rogatory shall be returned to the Court under the same conditions.

The Court shall defray the expenses, without prejudice to the right to charge them, where appropriate, to the parties.

ARTICLE 27
A Member State shall treat any violation of an oath by a witness or expert in the same manner as if the offence had been committed before one of its courts with jurisdiction in civil proceedings. At the instance of the Court, the Member State concerned shall prosecute the offender before its competent court.

ARTICLE 28
The hearing in court shall be public, unless the Court, of its own motion or on application by the parties, decides otherwise for serious reasons.

ARTICLE 29
During the hearings the Court may examine the experts, the witnesses and the parties themselves. The latter, however, may address the Court only through their representatives.

ARTICLE 30
Minutes shall be made of each hearing and be signed by the President and the Registrar.

ARTICLE 31
The case list shall be established by the President.

ARTICLE 32
The deliberations of the Court shall be and shall remain secret.

ARTICLE 33
Judgments shall state the reasons on which they are based. They shall contain the names of the Judges who took part in the deliberations.

ARTICLE 34
Judgments shall be signed by the President and the Registrar. They shall be read in open court.

ARTICLE 35   The Court shall adjudicate upon costs.

ARTICLE 36   The President of the Court may, by way of summary procedure, which may, in so far as necessary, differ from some of the rules contained in this Statute and which shall be laid down in the rules of procedure, adjudicate upon applications to suspend execution, as provided for in Article 185 of this Treaty, or to prescribe interim measures in pursuance of Article 186, or to suspend enforcement in accordance with the last paragraph of Article 192.

Should the President be prevented from attending, his place shall be taken by another Judge under conditions laid down in the rules of procedure.

The ruling of the President or of the Judge replacing him shall be provisional and shall in no way prejudice the decision of the Court on the substance of the case.

ARTICLE 37   Member States and institutions of the Community may intervene in cases before the Court.

The same right shall be open to any other person establishing an interest in the result of any case submitted to the Court, save in cases between Member States, between institutions of the Community or between Member States and institutions of the Community.

Submissions made in an application to intervene shall be limited to supporting the submissions of one of the parties.

ARTICLE 38   Where the defending party, after having been duly summoned, fails to file written submissions in defence, judgment shall be given against that party by default. An objection may be lodged against the judgment within one month of it being notified. The objection shall not have the effect of staying enforcement of the judgment by default unless the Court decides otherwise.

ARTICLE 39   Member States, institutions of the Community and any other natural or legal persons may, in cases and under conditions to be determined by the rules of procedure, institute third-party proceedings to contest a judgment rendered without their being heard, where the judgment is prejudicial to their rights.

ARTICLE 40   If the meaning or scope of a judgment is in doubt, the Court shall construe it on application by any party or any institution of the Community establishing an interest therein.

ARTICLE 41   An application for revision of a judgment may be made to the Court only on discovery of a fact which is of such a nature as to be a decisive factor, and which, when the judgment was given, was unknown to the Court and to the party claiming the revision.

The revision shall be opened by a judgment of the Court expressly recording the existence of a new fact, recognizing that it is of such a character as to lay the case open to revision and declaring the application admissible on this ground.

No application for revision may be made after the lapse of ten years from the date of the judgment.

ARTICLE 42   Periods of grace based on considerations of distance shall be determined by the rules of procedure.

No right shall be prejudiced in consequence of the expiry of a time limit if the party concerned proves the existence of unforeseeable circumstances or of *force majeure*.

ARTICLE 43

Proceedings against the Community in matters arising from non-contractual liability shall be barred after a period of five years from the occurrence of the event giving rise thereto. The period of limitation shall be interrupted if proceedings are instituted before the Court or if prior to such proceedings an application is made by the aggrieved party to the relevant institution of the Community. In the latter event the proceedings must be instituted within the period of two months provided for in Article 173; the provisions of the second paragraph of Article 175 shall apply where appropriate.

ARTICLE 44

The rules of procedure of the Court provided for in Article 188 of this Treaty shall contain, from the provisions contemplated by this Statute, any other provisions necessary for applying and, where required, supplementing it.

ARTICLE 45

The Council may, acting unanimously, make such further adjustments to the provisions of this Statute as may be required by reason of measures taken by the Council in accordance with the last paragraph of Article 165 of this Treaty.

ARTICLE 46

Immediately after the oath has been taken, the President of the Council shall proceed to choose by lot the Judges and Advocates-General whose terms of office are to expire at the end of the first three years in accordance with the second and third paragraphs of Article 167 of this Treaty.

Annex 7: Useful Addresses

Commission of the European Communities
Rue de la Loi 200, 1049 Brussels, Belgium.

Tel: 010 32 2 235 11 11; Telex: 21877; Fax: 010 32 2 235 01 22

Commission of the European Communities (London Office)
8 Storey's Gate, London, SW1P 3AT.

Tel: 071 973 1992; Telex: 23208; Fax: 071 973 1900

Commission of the European Communities (Scottish Office)
7 Alva Street, Edinburgh, EH2 4PH.

Tel: 031 225 2058; Telex: 727420; Fax: 031 226 4105

Commission of the European Communities (Northern Ireland Office)
Windsor House, 9–15 Bedford Street, Belfast, BT2 7EG.

Tel: 0232 240 708; Telex: 74117; Fax: 0232 248241

Commission of the European Communities (Welsh Office)
4 Cathedral Road, Cardiff, CF1 9SG.

Tel: 0222 371 631; Telex: 497727; Fax: 0222 395 489

The European Court of Auditors
12 Rue Alcide de Gasperi, L-1615 Luxembourg.

Tel: 010 352 439 81; Telex: 010 352 3512; Fax: 439 342

The Economic and Social Committee (EcoSoc)
Rue Ravenstein 2, 1000 Brussels, Belgium.

Tel: 010 32 2 519 90 11; Telex: 25983; Fax: 010 32 2 513 2893

European Free Trade Association
74 Rue de Trèves, B-1040 Brussels, Belgium.

Tel: 010 32 3 286 17 11; Fax: 010 32 3 286 17 50

European Parliament (Main Secretariat)
Centre Européen, Plateau du Kirchberg, BP 1901, L-2929 Luxembourg.

Tel: 010 352 430 01; Telex: 2894

European Parliament (Plenary Sessions)
Palais de l'Europe, 67006 Strasbourg Cedex, France.

Tel: 010 33 88 37 40 01; Fax: 010 33 88 17 51 84

European Parliament (UK Information Office)
2 Queen Anne's Gate, London, SW1H 9AA.

Tel: 071 222 0411; Fax: 071 222 2713

Council of Ministers (General Secretariat)
Rue de la Loi 170, 1048 Brussels, Belgium.

Tel: 010 32 2 234 61 11; Telex: 21711

Court of Justice of the European Communities
Palais de la Cour de Justice, L-2925 Luxembourg.

Tel: 010 352 430 31; Telex: 2771; Fax: 010 352 4303 2600

European Investment Bank
100 Boulevard Konrad Adenauer, L-2950 Luxembourg

Tel: 010 352 43791; Telex: 3530; Fax: 437 704

Office for Official Publication of the European Communities
5 Rue Mercies, L-2985 Luxembourg.

Tel: 010 352 499 281; Telex: 1324; Fax: 010 352 495 719

Council of Europe
Palais de l'Europe, 67006 Strasbourg Cedex, France.

Tel: 010 33 88 41 20 33; Fax: 010 33 88 41 27 80/90

See also:

The European Communities Encyclopedia and Directory 1992, 1st edition, Europa
Publications, London 1992.

Index

This Index should be used in cooperation with the Synoptic Table which appears on pp. xii–xviii.

Where page numbers appear in *italics*, this indicates Treaty text.